WALDEN
AND
RESISTANCE TO
CIVIL GOVERNMENT

AUTHORITATIVE TEXTS
THOREAU'S JOURNAL
REVIEWS AND ESSAYS IN CRITICISM

SECOND EDITION

A NORTON CRITICAL EDITION

HENRY D. THOREAU

WALDEN
AND
RESISTANCE TO
CIVIL GOVERNMENT

AUTHORITATIVE TEXTS

THOREAU'S JOURNAL

REVIEWS AND ESSAYS IN CRITICISM

SECOND EDITION

Edited by

WILLIAM ROSSI
UNIVERSITY OF OREGON

First Edition edited by

OWEN THOMAS
LATE OF THE UNIVERSITY OF CALIFORNIA, IRVINE

W · W · NORTON & COMPANY

New York · London

Library of Congress Cataloging in Publication Data
Thoreau, Henry David, 1817–1862.
[Walden]
Walden : and, Resistance to civil government : authoritative
texts, Journal, reviews, and essays in criticism / Henry D. Thoreau :
edited by William Rossi.—2nd ed.
p.   cm.—(A Norton critical edition)
Includes bibliographical references and index.
1. Thoreau, Henry David, 1817–1862. Walden.   2. Thoreau, Henry
David, 1817–1862—Civil disobedience.   3. Civil disobedience.
I. Rossi, William John.   II. Thoreau, Henry
David, 1817–1862. Civil disobedience. 1991.   III. Title: Resistance to civil
government.
PS3048.A   1991b
818'.303—dc20   91-17722
ISBN 0-393-95905-8
W. W. Norton & Company, Inc., 500 Fifth Avenue, New York, N.Y. 10110
W. W. Norton & Company, Ltd., 10 Coptic Street, London WC1A 1PU
1 2 3 4 5 6 7 8 9 0

Contents

Preface

In the twenty-five years since the first edition of this volume appeared, the influence and importance of *Walden* and "Resistance to Civil Government" have continued to grow both within and beyond the academy. While *Walden* especially has sustained diverse critical interest, scholarly and critical understanding of both these works has been enriched by the study of Thoreau's other writings and of his dual career as writer and naturalist. At the same time, these works have become even more timely. They speak to a present condition instilled (occasionally drenched) with a daily awareness of the interdependence of all places and of the global consequences for better and worse of individual actions. In this they confirm anew their author's faith that any universality his statement and actions might possess would arise out of an intimate, local knowledge and a deep commitment to his chosen place.

For this second edition, the volume previously edited by the late Owen Thomas has been updated in every respect. A few changes have been made to the *Walden* text, based on comparisons with prior manuscript versions and with Thoreau's corrected page proofs and additions to his own copy of the book. These and all other emendations of the 1854 text of *Walden* are summarized in a table of textual variants. The original placement of Thoreau's map of Walden Pond and the title of his famous essay have been restored, and annotations for both texts have been added or revised as necessary.

The second edition adds two brief reviews of "Resistance to Civil Government" as well as three important reviews of *Walden* that have come to light since 1966. Emerson's influential eulogy is now represented in an authoritative version, and the Criticism and Selected Bibliography sections of the book have been updated, the former focusing on modern criticism published between 1941 and 1990. My task of choosing from among much excellent commentary available on these two works was eased somewhat by the appearance of *Critical Essays on Thoreau's* Walden, edited by Joel Myerson (Boston: Hall, 1988), a volume that, in addition to reprinting all early reviews known to the editor, collects several noteworthy essays on *Walden*. Except in the case of two essays deemed necessary for the present edition, I have not duplicated essays available in Myerson's collection.

Finally, this second edition features an expanded selection of passages from Thoreau's Journal, composed over the entire nine-year period during which he wrote, rethought, and extensively revised *Walden* and in which the Journal itself became a distinct imaginative work. Most of this material is reprinted from the new edition of Thoreau's Journal being published by Princeton University Press as part of the definitive edition of his writings. About one-third of these selections, however, although eventually to be published in forthcoming volumes of the Princeton Journal, have been edited from manuscript photocopies for the present edition.

It is a pleasure to acknowledge the help of many people in preparing this volume. Work reviewing the texts originally established by Owen Thomas was simplified by his scrupulous and loving attention to detail, and Thomas's edition subsequently was made the more accurate by Joseph McElrath's generosity in sharing the results of his independent collation of that edition against a copy of the first edition of *Walden*. Kay Lauster, special collections assistant at the Abernethy Library, Middlebury College, Middlebury, Vermont, contributed expert assistance in deciphering the positioning of Thoreau's additions to his copy of *Walden*. I am indebted as well to previous annotators of *Walden*, "Resistance to Civil Government," and the Journal, especially to Walter Harding, Hershel Parker, and Robert Sattelmeyer. The annotations benefited additionally from the willingness of Bradley P. Dean, Richard Desroches, and Steven Shankman to share their knowledge with me. Robert Sattelmeyer and Louise Westling took the time to read a draft of "The Journal and *Walden*" and to offer valuable suggestions. Elizabeth Hall Witherell, Editor-in-Chief of the Writings of Henry D. Thoreau, graciously granted me permission to use Thoreau Edition transcripts of the manuscript Journal and, assisted by Jody Patterson and Jason Price, provided photocopies of both transcript and manuscript. A unique feature of this edition would thus have been impossible without their friendly assistance. Finally, Lynne Rossi provided kinds of aid and support as impossible to enumerate as they are ever to fully repay.

WILLIAM ROSSI
Eugene, Oregon

The Texts of

WALDEN

and

RESISTANCE TO

CIVIL GOVERNMENT

The Contents of Walden

Walden

I do not propose to write an ode to dejection, but to brag as lustily as chanticleer in the morning, standing on his roost, if only to wake my neighbors up.

Economy

When I wrote the following pages, or rather the bulk of them, I lived alone, in the woods, a mile from any neighbor, in a house which I had built myself, on the shore of Walden Pond, in Concord, Massachusetts, and earned my living by the labor of my hands only. I lived there two years and two months. At present I am a sojourner in civilized life again.

I should not obtrude my affairs so much on the notice of my readers if very particular inquiries had not been made by my townsmen concerning my mode of life, which some would call impertinent, though they do not appear to me at all impertinent, but, considering the circumstances, very natural and pertinent. Some have asked what I got to eat; if I did not feel lonesome; if I was not afraid; and the like. Others have been curious to learn what portion of my income I devoted to charitable purposes; and some, who have large families, how many poor children I maintained. I will therefore ask those of my readers who feel no particular interest in me to pardon me if I undertake to answer some of these questions in this book. In most books, the I, or first person, is omitted; in this it will be retained; that, in respect to egotism, is the main difference. We commonly do not remember that it is, after all, always the first person that is speaking. I should not talk so much about myself if there were any body else whom I knew as well. Unfortunately, I am confined to this theme by the narrowness of my experience. Moreover, I, on my side, require of every writer, first or last, a simple and sincere account of his own life, and not merely what he has heard of other men's lives; some such account as he would send to his kindred from a distant land; for if he has lived sincerely, it must have been in a distant land to me. Perhaps these pages are more particularly addressed to poor students. As for the rest of my readers, they will accept such portions as apply to them. I trust that none will stretch the seams in

1

putting on the coat, for it may do good service to him whom it fits.

I would fain say something, not so much concerning the Chinese and Sandwich Islanders [1] as you who read these pages, who are said to live in New England; something about your condition, especially your outward condition or circumstances in this world, in this town, what it is, whether it is necessary that it be as bad as it is, whether it cannot be improved as well as not. I have travelled a good deal in Concord; and every where, in shops, and offices, and fields, the inhabitants have appeared to me to be doing penance in a thousand remarkable ways. What I have heard of Bramins [2] sitting exposed to four fires and looking in the face of the sun; or hanging suspended, with their heads downward, over flames; or looking at the heavens over their shoulders "until it becomes impossible for them to resume their natural position, while from the twist of the neck nothing but liquids can pass into the stomach;" or dwelling, chained for life, at the foot of a tree; or measuring with their bodies, like caterpillars, the breadth of vast empires; or standing on one leg on the tops of pillars,—even these forms of conscious penance are hardly more incredible and astonishing than the scenes which I daily witness. The twelve labors of Hercules [3] were trifling in comparison with those which my neighbors have undertaken; for they were only twelve, and had an end; but I could never see that these men slew or captured any monster or finished any labor. They have no friend Iolas [4] to burn with a hot iron the root of the hydra's head, but as soon as one head is crushed, two spring up.

I see young men, my townsmen, whose misfortune it is to have inherited farms, houses, barns, cattle, and farming tools; for these are more easily acquired than got rid of. Better if they had been born in the open pasture and suckled by a wolf, that they might have seen with clearer eyes what field they were called to labor in.[5] Who made them serfs of the soil? Why should they eat their sixty acres, when man is condemned to eat only his peck of dirt? Why should they begin digging their graves as soon as they are born? They have got to live a man's life, pushing all these things before them, and get on as well as they can. How many a poor immortal soul have I met well nigh crushed and smothered under its load, creeping down the road of life, pushing before it a barn

1. Hawaiian islanders.
2. Generally spelled Brahmin or Brahman; a member of the highest caste of Hindus.
3. The son of Zeus, in Greek mythology, known for his great strength and for the performance of twelve seemingly impossible tasks.
4. A servant to Hercules who helped him to

overcome the many-headed monster, Hydra, by singeing with fire the stumps that remained after Hercules chopped off its heads.
5. According to Roman legend, the founders of the Republic, Romulus and Remus, were adopted and suckled by a she-wolf.

seventy-five feet by forty, its Augean stables 6 never cleansed, and one hundred acres of land, tillage, mowing, pasture, and wood-lot! The portionless, who struggle with no such unnecessary inherited encumbrances, find it labor enough to subdue and cultivate a few cubic feet of flesh.

But men labor under a mistake. The better part of the man is soon ploughed into the soil for compost. By a seeming fate, commonly called necessity, they are employed, as it says in an old book, laying up treasures which moth and rust will corrupt and thieves break through and steal.7 It is a fool's life, as they will find when they get to the end of it, if not before. It is said that Deucalion and Pyrrha 8 created men by throwing stones over their heads behind them:—

Inde genus durum sumus, experiensque laborum,
Et documenta damus quâ simus origine nati.

Or, as Raleigh rhymes it in his sonorous way,—

"From thence our kind hard-hearted is, enduring pain and care,
Approving that our bodies of a stony nature are."

So much for a blind obedience to a blundering oracle, throwing the stones over their heads behind them, and not seeing where they fell.

Most men, even in this comparatively free country, through mere ignorance and mistake, are so occupied with the factitious cares and superfluously coarse labors of life that its finer fruits cannot be plucked by them. Their fingers, from excessive toil, are too clumsy and tremble too much for that. Actually, the laboring man has not leisure for a true integrity day by day; he cannot afford to sustain the manliest relations to men; his labor would be depreciated in the market. He has no time to be any thing but a machine. How can he remember well his ignorance—which his growth requires—who has so often to use his knowledge? We should feed and clothe him gratuitously sometimes, and recruit him with our cordials, before we judge of him. The finest qualities of our nature, like the bloom on fruits, can be preserved only by the most delicate handling. Yet we do not treat ourselves nor one another thus tenderly.

Some of you, we all know, are poor, find it hard to live, are

6. The home of thousands of cattle whose stalls had not been cleaned in years. As one of his tasks, Hercules was required to clean the stables in a single day.
7. Matthew 6.19.

8. The only human survivors when Zeus destroyed mankind with a flood. Thoreau quotes from Ovid's *Metamorphoses* 1.414–15; the translation is from Sir Walter Raleigh's *History of the World* (1614).

sometimes, as it were, gasping for breath. I have no doubt that some of you who read this book are unable to pay for all the dinners which you have actually eaten, or for the coats and shoes which are fast wearing or are already worn out, and have come to this page to spend borrowed or stolen time, robbing your creditors of an hour. It is very evident what mean and sneaking lives many of you live, for my sight has been whetted by experience; always on the limits, trying to get into business and trying to get out of debt, a very ancient slough, called by the Latins æs *alienum*,[9] another's brass, for some of their coins were made of brass; still living, and dying, and buried by this other's brass; always promising to pay, promising to pay, to-morrow, and dying to-day, insolvent; seeking to curry favor, to get custom, by how many modes, only not state-prison offences; lying, flattering, voting, contracting yourselves into a nutshell of civility, or dilating into an atmosphere of thin and vaporous generosity, that you may persuade your neighbor to let you make his shoes, or his hat, or his coat, or his carriage, or import his groceries for him; making yourselves sick, that you may lay up something against a sick day, something to be tucked away in an old chest, or in a stocking behind the plastering, or, more safely, in the brick bank; no matter where, no matter how much or how little.

I sometimes wonder that we can be so frivolous, I may almost say, as to attend to the gross but somewhat foreign form of servitude called Negro Slavery, there are so many keen and subtle masters that enslave both north and south. It is hard to have a southern overseer; it is worse to have a northern one; but worst of all when you are the slave-driver of yourself. Talk of a divinity in man! Look at the teamster on the highway, wending to market by day or night; does any divinity stir within him? His highest duty to fodder and water his horses! What is his destiny to him compared with the shipping interests? Does not he drive for Squire Make-a-stir? How godlike, how immortal, is he? See how he cowers and sneaks, how vaguely all the day he fears, not being immortal nor divine, but the slave and prisoner of his own opinion of himself, a fame won by his own deeds. Public opinion is a weak tyrant compared with our own private opinion. What a man thinks of himself, that it is which determines, or rather indicates, his fate. Self-emancipation even in the West Indian provinces of the fancy and imagination,—what Wilberforce[1] is there to bring that about? Think, also, of the ladies of the land weaving toilet cushions against the last day, not to betray too green an interest in their fates! As if you could kill time without injuring eternity.

9. Literally, "another's brass"; metaphorically, "another person's money" or "debt."

1. William Wilberforce (1759–1833), leader of the anti-slavery forces in England.

The mass of men lead lives of quiet desperation. What is called resignation is confirmed desperation. From the desperate city you go into the desperate country, and have to console yourself with the bravery of minks and muskrats. A stereotyped but unconscious despair is concealed even under what are called the games and amusements of mankind. There is no play in them, for this comes after work. But it is a characteristic of wisdom not to do desperate things.

When we consider what, to use the words of the catechism, is the chief end of man,[2] and what are the true necessaries and means of life, it appears as if men had deliberately chosen the common mode of living because they preferred it to any other. Yet they honestly think there is no choice left. But alert and healthy natures remember that the sun rose clear. It is never too late to give up our prejudices. No way of thinking or doing, however ancient, can be trusted without proof. What every body echoes or in silence passes by as true to-day may turn out to be falsehood to-morrow, mere smoke of opinion, which some had trusted for a cloud that would sprinkle fertilizing rain on their fields. What old people say you cannot do you try and find that you can. Old deeds for old people, and new deeds for new. Old people did not know enough once, perchance, to fetch fresh fuel to keep the fire a-going; new people put a little dry wood under a pot, and are whirled round the globe with the speed of birds, in a way to kill old people, as the phrase is. Age is no better, hardly so well, qualified for an instructor as youth, for it has not profited so much as it has lost. One may almost doubt if the wisest man has learned any thing of absolute value by living. Practically, the old have no very important advice to give the young, their own experience has been so partial, and their lives have been such miserable failures, for private reasons, as they must believe; and it may be that they have some faith left which belies that experience, and they are only less young than they were. I have lived some thirty years on this planet, and I have yet to hear the first syllable of valuable or even earnest advice from my seniors. They have told me nothing, and probably cannot tell me any thing, to the purpose. Here is life, an experiment to a great extent untried by me; but it does not avail me that they have tried it. If I have any experience which I think valuable, I am sure to reflect that this my Mentors[3] said nothing about.

One farmer says to me, "You cannot live on vegetable food solely, for it furnishes nothing to make bones with;" and so he

---

2. According to the Shorter Catechism in the *New England Primer*, "the chief end of man" is "to glorify God and to enjoy him forever."

3. The wise protector of Telemachus, the son of Odysseus in Homer's *Odyssey*; metaphorically, any wise teacher.

religiously devotes a part of his day to supplying his system with
the raw material of bones; walking all the while he talks behind
his oxen, which, with vegetable-made bones, jerk him and his
lumbering plough along in spite of every obstacle. Some things are
really necessaries of life in some circles, the most helpless and
diseased, which in others are luxuries merely, and in others still
are entirely unknown.

The whole ground of human life seems to some to have been
gone over by their predecessors, both the heights and the valleys,
and all things to have been cared for. According to Evelyn,
"the wise Solomon prescribed ordinances for the very distances of
trees; and the Roman prætors have decided how often you may
go into your neighbor's land to gather the acorns which fall on it
without trespass, and what share belongs to that neighbor."[4] Hip-
pocrates[5] has even left directions how we should cut our nails;
that is, even with the ends of the fingers, neither shorter nor longer.
Undoubtedly the very tedium and ennui which presume to have
exhausted the variety and the joys of life are as old as Adam. But
man's capacities have never been measured; nor are we to judge of
what he can do by any precedents, so little has been tried. Whatever have been thy failures hitherto, "be not afflicted, my child,
for who shall assign to thee what thou hast left undone?"[6]

We might try our lives by a thousand simple tests; as, for instance, that the same sun which ripens my beans illumines at
once a system of earths like ours. If I had remembered this it
would have prevented some mistakes. This was not the light in
which I hoed them. The stars are the apexes of what wonderful
triangles! What distant and different beings in the various mansions
of the universe are contemplating the same one at the same
moment! Nature and human life are as various as our several
constitutions. Who shall say what prospect life offers to another?
Could a greater miracle take place than for us to look through
each other's eyes for an instant? We should live in all the ages of
the world in an hour; ay, in all the worlds of the ages. History,
Poetry, Mythology!—I know of no reading of another's experience so startling and informing as this would be.

The greater part of what my neighbors call good I believe in
my soul to be bad, and if I repent of any thing, it is very likely to
be my good behavior. What demon possessed me that I behaved so
well? You may say the wisest thing you can old man,—you who
have lived seventy years, not without honor of a kind,—I hear an

4. John Evelyn (1620–1706), English horticulturalist and author; from his *Sylva, or a
Discourse of Forest-Trees* (1679).
5. An ancient Greek physician (fl. 300 B.C.),
frequently called "the father of medicine."
6. From the *Vishnu Purana*, a Hindu
scripture.

irresistible voice which invites me away from all that. One generation abandons the enterprises of another like stranded vessels. I think that we may safely trust a good deal more than we do. We may waive just so much care of ourselves as we honestly bestow elsewhere. Nature is as well adapted to our weakness as to our strength. The incessant anxiety and strain of some is a well nigh incurable form of disease. We are made to exaggerate the importance of what work we do; and yet how much is not done by us! or, what if we had been taken sick? How vigilant we are! determined not to live by faith if we can avoid it; all the day long on the alert, at night we unwillingly say our prayers and commit ourselves to uncertainties. So thoroughly and sincerely are we compelled to live, reverencing our life, and denying the possibility of change. This is the only way, we say; but there are as many ways as there can be drawn radii from one centre. All change is a miracle to contemplate; but it is a miracle which is taking place every instant. Confucius said, "To know that we know what we know, and that we do not know what we do not know, that is true knowledge."[7] When one man has reduced a fact of the imagination to be a fact to his understanding, I foresee that all men will at length establish their lives on that basis.

Let us consider for a moment what most of the trouble and anxiety which I have referred to is about, and how much it is necessary that we be troubled, or, at least, careful. It would be some advantage to live a primitive and frontier life, though in the midst of an outward civilization, if only to learn what are the gross necessaries of life and what methods have been taken to obtain them; or even to look over the old day-books of the merchants, to see what it was that men most commonly bought at the stores, what they stored, that is, what are the grossest groceries. For the improvements of ages have had but little influence on the essential laws of man's existence; as our skeletons, probably, are not to be distinguished from those of our ancestors.

By the words, *necessary of life,* I mean whatever, of all that man obtains by his own exertions, has been from the first, or from long use has become, so important to human life that few, if any, whether from savageness, or poverty, or philosophy, ever attempt to do without it. To many creatures there is in this sense but one necessary of life, Food. To the bison of the prairie it is a few inches of palatable grass, with water to drink; unless he seeks the Shelter of the forest or the mountain's shadow. None of the brute creation requires more than Food and Shelter. The necessaries of life for man in this climate may, accurately enough, be dis-

7. Chinese philosopher and teacher (551?–478? B.C.), from his *Analects* 2.17.

tributed under the several heads of Food, Shelter, Clothing, and Fuel; for not till we have secured these are we prepared to entertain the true problems of life with freedom and a prospect of success. Man has invented, not only houses, but clothes and cooked food; and possibly from the accidental discovery of the warmth of fire, and the consequent use of it, at first a luxury, arose the present necessity to sit by it. We observe cats and dogs acquiring the same second nature. By proper Shelter and Clothing we legitimately retain our own internal heat; but with an excess of these, or of Fuel, that is, with an external heat greater than our own internal, may not cookery properly be said to begin? Darwin, the naturalist, says of the inhabitants of Tierra del Fuego, that while his own party, who were well clothed and sitting close to a fire, were far from too warm, these naked savages, who were farther off, were observed, to his great surprise, "to be streaming with perspiration at undergoing such a roasting." [8] So, we are told, the New Hollander [9] goes naked with impunity, while the European shivers in his clothes. Is it impossible to combine the hardiness of these savages with the intellectualness of the civilized man? According to Liebig,[1] man's body is a stove, and food the fuel which keeps up the internal combustion in the lungs. In cold weather we eat more, in warm less. The animal heat is the result of a slow combustion, and disease and death take place when this is too rapid; or for want of fuel, or from some defect in the draught, the fire goes out. Of course the vital heat is not to be confounded with fire; but so much for analogy. It appears, therefore, from the above list, that the expression, *animal life*, is nearly synonymous with the expression, *animal heat*; for while Food may be regarded as the Fuel which keeps up the fire within us,—and Fuel serves only to prepare that Food or to increase the warmth of our bodies by addition from without,—Shelter and Clothing also serve only to retain the *heat* thus generated and absorbed.

The grand necessity, then, for our bodies, is to keep warm, to keep the vital heat in us. What pains we accordingly take, not only with our Food, and Clothing, and Shelter, but with our beds, which are our night-clothes, robbing the nests and breasts of birds to prepare this shelter within a shelter, as the mole has its bed of grass and leaves at the end of its burrow! The poor man is wont to complain that this is a cold world; and to cold, no less physical than social, we refer directly a great part of our ails. The summer,

8. Charles Darwin (1809–82), English naturalist; from his *Journal of Researches . . . during the Voyage of H.M.S. Beagle* (1839). Tierra del Fuego is an island off the southern tip of South America.

9. Aboriginal Australians.
1. Justus von Liebig (1803–73), German organic chemist; from his *Animal Chemistry* (1842).

in some climates, makes possible to man a sort of Elysian life.[2] Fuel, except to cook his Food, is then unnecessary; the sun is his fire, and many of the fruits are sufficiently cooked by its rays; while Food generally is more various, and more easily obtained, and Clothing and Shelter are wholly or half unnecessary. At the present day, and in this country, as I find by my own experience, a few implements, a knife, an axe, a spade, a wheelbarrow, &c., and for the studious, lamplight, stationery, and access to a few books, rank next to necessaries, and can all be obtained at a trifling cost. Yet some, not wise, go to the other side of the globe, to barbarous and unhealthy regions, and devote themselves to trade for ten or twenty years, in order that they may live,—that is, keep comfortably warm,—and die in New England at last. The luxuriously rich are not simply kept comfortably warm, but unnaturally hot; as I implied before, they are cooked, of course à la mode.[3]

Most of the luxuries, and many of the so called comforts of life, are not only not indispensable, but positive hinderances to the elevation of mankind. With respect to luxuries and comforts, the wisest have ever lived a more simple and meagre life than the poor. The ancient philosophers, Chinese, Hindoo, Persian, and Greek, were a class than which none has been poorer in outward riches, none so rich in inward. We know not much about them. It is remarkable that *we* know so much of them as we do. The same is true of the more modern reformers and benefactors of their race. None can be an impartial or wise observer of human life but from the vantage ground of what *we* should call voluntary poverty. Of a life of luxury the fruit is luxury, whether in agriculture, or commerce, or literature, or art. There are nowadays professors of philosophy, but not philosophers. Yet it is admirable to profess because it was once admirable to live. To be a philosopher is not merely to have subtle thoughts, nor even to found a school, but so to love wisdom as to live according to its dictates, a life of simplicity, independence, magnanimity, and trust. It is to solve some of the problems of life, not only theoretically, but practically. The success of great scholars and thinkers is commonly a courtier-like success, not kingly, not manly. They make shift to live merely by conformity, practically as their fathers did, and are in no sense the progenitors of a nobler race of men. But why do men degenerate ever? What makes families run out? What is the nature of the luxury which enervates and destroys nations? Are we sure that there is none of it in our own lives? The philosopher is in

2. In Greek mythology, Elysium was the home of the blessed dead; also called the "Elysian fields."

3. In a fashionable style.

advance of his age even in the outward form of his life. He is not fed, sheltered, clothed, warmed, like his contemporaries. How can a man be a philosopher and not maintain his vital heat by better methods than other men? When a man is warmed by the several modes which I have described, what does he want next? Surely not more warmth of the same kind, as more and richer food, larger and more splendid houses, finer and more abundant clothing, more numerous incessant and hotter fires, and the like. When he has obtained those things which are necessary to life, there is another alternative than to obtain the superfluities; and that is, to adventure on life now, his vacation from humbler toil having commenced. The soil, it appears, is suited to the seed, for it has sent its radicle downward, and it may now send its shoot upward also with confidence. Why has man rooted himself thus firmly in the earth, but that he may rise in the same proportion into the heavens above?—for the nobler plants are valued for the fruit they bear at last in the air and light, far from the ground, and are not treated like the humbler esculents, which, though they may be biennials, are cultivated only till they have perfected their root, and often cut down at top for this purpose, so that most would not know them in their flowering season.

I do not mean to prescribe rules to strong and valiant natures, who will mind their own affairs whether in heaven or hell, and perchance build more magnificently and spend more lavishly than the richest, without ever impoverishing themselves, not knowing how they live,—if, indeed, there are any such, as has been dreamed; nor to those who find their encouragement and inspiration in precisely the present condition of things, and cherish it with the fondness and enthusiasm of lovers,—and, to some extent, I reckon myself in this number; I do not speak to those who are well employed, in whatever circumstances, and they know whether they are well employed or not;—but mainly to the mass of men who are discontented, and idly complaining of the hardness of their lot or of the times, when they might improve them. There are some who complain most energetically and inconsolably of any, because they are, as they say, doing their duty. I also have in my mind that seemingly wealthy, but most terribly impoverished class of all, who have accumulated dross, but know not how to use it, or get rid of it, and thus have forged their own golden or silver fetters.

If I should attempt to tell how I have desired to spend my life in years past, it would probably surprise those of my readers who are somewhat acquainted with its actual history; it would cer-

tainly astonish those who know nothing about it. I will only hint
at some of the enterprises which I have cherished.

In any weather, at any hour of the day or night, I have been
anxious to improve the nick of time, and notch it on my stick too;
to stand on the meeting of two eternities, the past and future,
which is precisely the present moment; to toe that line. You will
pardon some obscurities, for there are more secrets in my trade
than in most men's, and yet not voluntarily kept, but inseparable
from its very nature. I would gladly tell all that I know about it,
and never paint "No Admittance" on my gate.

I long ago lost a hound, a bay horse, and a turtle-dove,[4] and
am still on their trail. Many are the travellers I have spoken concerning them, describing their tracks and what calls they answered
to. I have met one or two who had heard the hound, and the
tramp of the horse, and even seen the dove disappear behind a
cloud, and they seemed as anxious to recover them as if they had
lost them themselves.

To anticipate, not the sunrise and the dawn merely, but, if
possible, Nature herself! How many mornings, summer and winter, before yet any neighbor was stirring about his business, have I
been about mine! No doubt, many of my townsmen have met me
returning from this enterprise, farmers starting for Boston in the
twilight, or woodchoppers going to their work. It is true, I never
assisted the sun materially in his rising, but, doubt not, it was of
the last importance only to be present at it.

So many autumn, ay, and winter days, spent outside the town,
trying to hear what was in the wind, to hear and carry it express!
I well-nigh sunk all my capital in it, and lost my own breath into
the bargain, running in the face of it. If it had concerned either of
the political parties, depend upon it, it would have appeared in the
Gazette [5] with the earliest intelligence. At other times watching
from the observatory of some cliff or tree, to telegraph any new
arrival; or waiting at evening on the hill-tops for the sky to fall,
that I might catch something, though I never caught much, and
that, manna-wise, would dissolve again in the sun.

For a long time I was reporter to a journal,[6] of no very wide
circulation, whose editor has never yet seen fit to print the bulk
of my contributions, and, as is too common with writers, I got
only my labor for my pains. However, in this case my pains were
their own reward.

4. Probably symbols for the unattainable
things of life; critics differ over whether the
symbols have specific references.
5. A common name for a newspaper, including the *Yeoman's Gazette* of Concord; by extension, any newspaper.

6. The *Dial*, a Transcendentalist magazine
(1840–44), published some of Thoreau's writing; he may refer as well to his own Journal,
which remained unpublished during his
lifetime.

For many years I was self-appointed inspector of snow storms and rain storms, and did my duty faithfully; surveyor, if not of highways, then of forest paths and all across-lot routes, keeping them open, and ravines bridged and passable at all seasons, where the public heel had testified to their utility.

I have looked after the wild stock of the town, which give a faithful herdsman a good deal of trouble by leaping fences; and I have had an eye to the unfrequented nooks and corners of the farm; though I did not always know whether Jonas or Solomon worked in a particular field to-day; that was none of my business. I have watered the red huckleberry, the sand cherry and the nettle tree, the red pine and the black ash, the white grape and the yellow violet, which might have withered else in dry seasons.

In short, I went on thus for a long time, I may say it without boasting, faithfully minding my business, till it became more and more evident that my townsmen would not after all admit me into the list of town officers, nor make my place a sinecure with a moderate allowance. My accounts, which I can swear to have kept faithfully, I have, indeed, never got audited, still less accepted, still less paid and settled. However, I have not set my heart on that.

Not long since, a strolling Indian went to sell baskets at the house of a well-known lawyer in my neighborhood. "Do you wish to buy any baskets?" he asked. "No, we do not want any," was the reply. "What!" exclaimed the Indian as he went out the gate, "do you mean to starve us?" Having seen his industrious white neighbors so well off,—that the lawyer had only to weave arguments, and by some magic wealth and standing followed, he had said to himself; I will go into business; I will weave baskets; it is a thing which I can do. Thinking that when he had made the baskets he would have done his part, and then it would be the white man's to buy them. He had not discovered that it was necessary for him to make it worth the other's while to buy them, or at least make him think that it was so, or to make something else which it would be worth his while to buy. I too had woven a kind of basket of a delicate texture, but I had not made it worth any one's while to buy them.[7] Yet not the less, in my case, did I think it worth my while to weave them, and instead of studying how to make it worth men's while to buy my baskets, I studied rather how to avoid the necessity of selling them. The life which men praise and regard as successful is but one kind. Why should we exaggerate any one kind at the expense of the others?

Finding that my fellow-citizens were not likely to offer me any

---

7. Thoreau's first book, *A Week on the Concord and Merrimack Rivers* (1849), sold poorly. It took him four years to repay the debt of $290 to his publisher.

room in the court house, or any curacy or living any where else, but I must shift for myself, I turned my face more exclusively than ever to the woods, where I was better known. I determined to go into business at once, and not wait to acquire the usual capital, using such slender means as I had already got. My purpose in going to Walden Pond was not to live cheaply nor to live dearly there, but to transact some private business with the fewest obstacles; to be hindered from accomplishing which for want of a little common sense, a little enterprise and business talent, appeared not so sad as foolish.

I have always endeavored to acquire strict business habits; they are indispensable to every man. If your trade is with the Celestial Empire,[8] then some small counting house on the coast, in some Salem[9] harbor, will be fixture enough. You will export such articles as the country affords, purely native products, much ice and pine timber and a little granite, always in native bottoms. These will be good ventures. To oversee all the details yourself in person; to be at once pilot and captain, and owner and underwriter; to buy and sell and keep the accounts; to read every letter received, and write or read every letter sent; to superintend the discharge of imports night and day; to be upon many parts of the coast almost at the same time;—often the richest freight will be discharged upon a Jersey shore;[1]—to be your own telegraph, unweariedly sweeping the horizon, speaking all passing vessels bound coastwise; to keep up a steady despatch of commodities, for the supply of such a distant and exorbitant market; to keep yourself informed of the state of the markets, prospects of war and peace every where, and anticipate the tendencies of trade and civilization,—taking advantage of the results of all exploring expeditions, using new passages and all improvements in navigation;—charts to be studied, the position of reefs and new lights and buoys to be ascertained, and ever, and ever, the logarithmic tables to be corrected, for by the error of some calculator the vessel often splits upon a rock that should have reached a friendly pier,—there is the untold fate of La Perouse;[2]—universal science to be kept pace with, studying the lives of all great discoverers and navigators, great adventurers and merchants, from Hanno[3] and the Phœnicians down to our day; in fine, account of stock to be taken from time to time, to know how you stand. It is a labor to task the faculties of a man,—such problems of profit and loss, of interest,

8. China.
9. An important port on the Massachusetts coast.
1. The coast of New Jersey, on which many ships were wrecked.

2. French explorer (1741–88) whose ship was lost in the south Pacific.
3. Carthaginian explorer and navigator (ca. 500 B.C.)

of tare and tret,[4] and gauging of all kinds in it, as demand a universal knowledge.

I have thought that Walden Pond would be a good place for business, not solely on account of the railroad and the ice trade; it offers advantages which it may not be good policy to divulge; it is a good port and a good foundation. No Neva [5] marshes to be filled; though you must every where build on piles of your own driving. It is said that a flood-tide, with a westerly wind, and ice in the Neva, would sweep St. Petersburg from the face of the earth.

As this business was to be entered into without the usual capital, it may not be easy to conjecture where those means, that will still be indispensable to every such undertaking, were to be obtained. As for Clothing, to come at once to the practical part of the question, perhaps we are led oftener by the love of novelty, and a regard for the opinions of men, in procuring it, than by a true utility. Let him who has work to do recollect that the object of clothing is, first, to retain the vital heat, and secondly, in this state of society, to cover nakedness, and he may judge how much of any necessary or important work may be accomplished without adding to his wardrobe. Kings and queens who wear a suit but once, though made by some tailor or dressmaker to their majesties, cannot know the comfort of wearing a suit that fits. They are no better than wooden horses to hang the clean clothes on. Every day our garments become more assimilated to ourselves, receiving the impress of the wearer's character, until we hesitate to lay them aside, without such delay and medical appliances and some such solemnity even as our bodies. No man ever stood the lower in my estimation for having a patch in his clothes; yet I am sure that there is greater anxiety, commonly, to have fashionable, or at least clean and unpatched clothes, than to have a sound conscience. But even if the rent is not mended, perhaps the worst vice betrayed is improvidence. I sometimes try my acquaintances by such tests as this;—who could wear a patch, or two extra seams only, over the knee? Most behave as if they believed that their prospects for life would be ruined if they should do it. It would be easier for them to hobble to town with a broken leg than with a broken pantaloon. Often if an accident happens to a gentleman's legs, they can be mended; but if a similar accident happens to the legs of his pantaloons, there is no help for it; for he considers, not what is truly respectable, but what is respected. We know but few men,

4. In shipping, "tare" is a deduction for the weight of the container; "tret" is an allowance made to buyers for waste or damage.

5. St. Petersburg (from 1914 to 1991, called Leningrad) in Russia was built on the delta of the Neva River.

a great many coats and breeches. Dress a scarecrow in your last
shift, you standing shiftless by, who would not soonest salute the
scarecrow? Passing a cornfield the other day, close by a hat and
coat on a stake, I recognized the owner of the farm. He was only
a little more weather-beaten than when I saw him last. I have
heard of a dog that barked at every stranger who approached his
master's premises with clothes on, but was easily quieted by a
naked thief. It is an interesting question how far men would retain their relative rank if they were divested of their clothes.
Could you, in such a case, tell surely of any company of civilized
men, which belonged to the most respected class? When Madam
Pfeiffer, in her adventurous travels round the world, from east
to west, had got so near home as Asiatic Russia, she says that she
felt the necessity of wearing other than a travelling dress, when
she went to meet the authorities, for she "was now in a civilized
country, where——people are judged of by their clothes."[6]
Even in our democratic New England towns the accidental possession of wealth, and its manifestation in dress and equipage alone,
obtain for the possessor almost universal respect. But they who
yield such respect, numerous as they are, are so far heathen, and
need to have a missionary sent to them. Beside, clothes introduced sewing, a kind of work which you may call endless; a
woman's dress, at least, is never done.

A man who has at length found something to do will not need
to get a new suit to do it in; for him the old will do, that has
lain dusty in the garret for an indeterminate period. Old shoes will
serve a hero longer than they have served his valet,—if a hero
ever has a valet,—bare feet are older than shoes, and he can make
them do. Only they who go to soirées and legislative halls must
have new coats, coats to change as often as the man changes in
them. But if my jacket and trousers, my hat and shoes, are fit to
worship God in, they will do; will they not? Who ever saw his old
clothes,—his old coat, actually worn out, resolved into its primitive elements, so that it was not a deed of charity to bestow it on
some poor boy, by him perchance to be bestowed on some poorer
still, or shall we say richer, who could do with less? I say, beware
of all enterprises that require new clothes, and not rather a new
wearer of clothes. If there is not a new man, how can the new
clothes be made to fit? If you have any enterprise before you, try
it in your old clothes. All men want, not something to *do with*,
but something to *do*, or rather something to *be*. Perhaps we should
never procure a new suit, however ragged or dirty the old, until
we have so conducted, so enterprised or sailed in some way, that

6. Ida Pfeiffer (1797–1858), Austrian traveler; from her A *Lady's Voyage Round the World*
(1852).

we feel like new men in the old, and that to retain it would be like keeping new wine in old bottles.[7] Our moulting season, like that of the fowls, must be a crisis in our lives. The loon retires to solitary ponds to spend it. Thus also the snake casts its slough, and the caterpillar its wormy coat, by an internal industry and expansion; for clothes are but our outmost cuticle and mortal coil. Otherwise we shall be found sailing under false colors, and be inevitably cashiered at last by our own opinion, as well as that of mankind. We don garment after garment, as if we grew like exogenous plants by addition without. Our outside and often thin and fanciful clothes are our epidermis or false skin, which partakes not of our life, and may be stripped off here and there without fatal injury; our thicker garments, constantly worn, are our cellular integument, or cortex; but our shirts are our liber or true bark, which cannot be removed without girdling and so destroying the man. I believe that all races at some seasons wear something equivalent to the shirt. It is desirable that a man be clad so simply that he can lay his hands on himself in the dark, and that he live in all respects so compactly and preparedly, that, if an enemy take the town, he can, like the old philosopher, walk out the gate empty-handed without anxiety. While one thick garment is, for most purposes, as good as three thin ones, and cheap clothing can be obtained at prices really to suit customers; while a thick coat can be bought for five dollars, which will last as many years, thick pantaloons for two dollars, cowhide boots for a dollar and a half a pair, a summer hat for a quarter of a dollar, and a winter cap for sixty-two and a half cents, or a better be made at home at a nominal cost, where is he so poor that, clad in such a suit, *of his own earning*, there will not be found wise men to do him reverence?

When I ask for a garment of a particular form, my tailoress tells me gravely, "They do not make them so now," not emphasizing the "They" at all, as if she quoted an authority as impersonal as the Fates,[8] and I find it difficult to get made what I want, simply because she cannot believe that I mean what I say, that I am so rash. When I hear this oracular sentence, I am for a moment absorbed in thought, emphasizing to myself each word separately that I may come at the meaning of it, that I may find out by what degree of consanguinity *They* are related to *me*, and what authority they may have in an affair which affects me so

---

7. An echo of Jesus' words to his disciples in Matthew 9.17: "Neither do men put new wine into old bottles, else the bottles break, and the wine runneth out, . . . : but they put new wine into new bottles, and both are preserved."
8. In classical mythology, the three goddesses who control human destiny.

nearly; and, finally, I am inclined to answer her with equal mystery, and without any more emphasis of the "they,"—"It is true, they did not make them so recently, but they do now." Of what use this measuring of me if she does not measure my character, but only the breadth of my shoulders, as it were a peg to hang the coat on? We worship not the Graces, nor the Parcæ,[9] but Fashion. She spins and weaves and cuts with full authority. The head monkey at Paris puts on a traveller's cap, and all the monkeys in America do the same. I sometimes despair of getting any thing quite simple and honest done in this world by the help of men. They would have to be passed through a powerful press first, to squeeze their old notions out of them, so that they would not soon get upon their legs again, and then there would be some one in the company with a maggot in his head, hatched from an egg deposited there nobody knows when, for not even fire kills these things, and you would have lost your labor. Nevertheless, we will not forget that some Egyptian wheat is said to have been handed down to us by a mummy.

On the whole, I think that it cannot be maintained that dressing has in this or any country risen to the dignity of an art. At present men make shift to wear what they can get. Like shipwrecked sailors, they put on what they can find on the beach, and at a little distance, whether of space or time, laugh at each other's masquerade. Every generation laughs at the old fashions, but follows religiously the new. We are amused at beholding the costume of Henry VIII., or Queen Elizabeth, as much as if it was that of the King and Queen of the Cannibal Islands. All costume off a man is pitiful or grotesque. It is only the serious eye peering from and the sincere life passed within it, which restrain laughter and consecrate the costume of any people. Let Harlequin[1] be taken with a fit of the colic and his trappings will have to serve that mood too. When the soldier is hit by a cannon ball rags are as becoming as purple.

The childish and savage taste of men and women for new patterns keeps how many shaking and squinting through kaleidoscopes that they may discover the particular figure which this generation requires to-day. The manufacturers have learned that this taste is merely whimsical. Of two patterns which differ only by a few threads more or less of a particular color, the one will be sold readily, the other lie on the shelf, though it frequently happens that after the lapse of a season the latter becomes the

9. The Fates in Roman mythology; the Graces were minor goddesses and personifications of grace and beauty in classical mythology.

1. A standard character in old Italian comedy, traditionally dressed in multicolored tights.

most fashionable. Comparatively, tattooing is not the hideous
custom which it is called. It is not barbarous merely because the
printing is skin-deep and unalterable.

I cannot believe that our factory system is the best mode by
which men may get clothing. The condition of the operatives is
becoming every day more like that of the English; and it cannot be
wondered at, since, as far as I have heard or observed, the
principal object is, not that mankind may be well and honestly
clad, but, unquestionably, that the corporations may be enriched.
In the long run men hit only what they aim at. Therefore, though
they should fail immediately, they had better aim at something
high.

As for a Shelter, I will not deny that this is now a necessary of
life, though there are instances of men having done without it
for long periods in colder countries than this. Samuel Laing
says that "The Laplander in his skin dress, and in a skin bag
which he puts over his head and shoulders, will sleep night after
night on the snow——in a degree of cold which would extinguish
the life of one exposed to it in any woollen clothing." He had seen
them asleep thus. Yet he adds, "They are not hardier than other
people."[2] But, probably, man did not live long on the earth without discovering the convenience which there is in a house, the
domestic comforts, which phrase may have originally signified the
satisfactions of the house more than of the family; though these
must be extremely partial and occasional in those climates where
the house is associated in our thoughts with winter or the rainy
season chiefly, and two thirds of the year, except for a parasol, is
unnecessary. In our climate, in the summer, it was formerly almost solely a covering at night. In the Indian gazettes a wigwam
was the symbol of a day's march, and a row of them cut or painted
on the bark of a tree signified that so many times they had
camped. Man was not made so large limbed and robust but that
he must seek to narrow his world, and wall in a space such as
fitted him. He was at first bare and out of doors; but though this
was pleasant enough in serene and warm weather, by daylight,
the rainy season and the winter, to say nothing of the torrid sun,
would perhaps have nipped his race in the bud if he had not made
haste to clothe himself with the shelter of a house. Adam and
Eve, according to the fable, wore the bower before other clothes.
Man wanted a home, a place of warmth, or comfort, first of
physical warmth, then the warmth of the affections.
We may imagine a time when, in the infancy of the human

2. British traveler (1780–1868); from his *Journal of a Residence in Norway* (1837).

race, some enterprising mortal crept into a hollow in a rock for shelter. Every child begins the world again, to some extent, and loves to stay out doors, even in wet and cold. It plays house, as well as horse, having an instinct for it. Who does not remember the interest with which when young he looked at shelving rocks, or any approach to a cave? It was the natural yearning of that portion of our most primitive ancestor which still survived in us. From the cave we have advanced to roofs of palm leaves, of bark and boughs, of linen woven and stretched, of grass and straw, of boards and shingles, of stones and tiles. At last, we know not what it is to live in the open air, and our lives are domestic in more senses than we think. From the hearth to the field is a great distance. It would be well perhaps if we were to spend more of our days and nights without any obstruction between us and the celestial bodies, if the poet did not speak so much from under a roof, or the saint dwell there so long. Birds do not sing in caves, nor do doves cherish their innocence in dovecots.

However, if one designs to construct a dwelling house, it behooves him to exercise a little Yankee shrewdness, lest after all he find himself in a workhouse, a labyrinth without a clew, a museum, an almshouse, a prison, or a splendid mausoleum instead. Consider first how slight a shelter is absolutely necessary. I have seen Penobscot Indians,[3] in this town, living in tents of thin cotton cloth, while the snow was nearly a foot deep around them, and I thought that they would be glad to have it deeper to keep out the wind. Formerly, when how to get my living honestly, with freedom left for my proper pursuits, was a question which vexed me even more than it does now, for unfortunately I am become somewhat callous, I used to see a large box by the railroad, six feet long by three wide, in which the laborers locked up their tools at night, and it suggested to me that every man who was hard pushed might get such a one for a dollar, and, having bored a few auger holes in it, to admit the air at least, get into it when it rained and at night, and hook down the lid, and so have freedom in his love, and in his soul be free. This did not appear the worst, nor by any means a despicable alternative. You could sit up as late as you pleased, and, whenever you got up, go abroad without any landlord or house-lord dogging you for rent. Many a man is harassed to death to pay the rent of a larger and more luxurious box who would not have frozen to death in such a box as this. I am far from jesting. Economy is a subject which admits of being treated with levity, but it cannot so be disposed of. A comfortable house for a rude and hardy race, that lived mostly out of doors,

3. A tribe originally from northern Maine.

was once made here almost entirely of such materials as Nature
furnished ready to their hands. Gookin, who was superintendent
of the Indians subject to the Massachusetts Colony, writing in
1674, says, "The best of their houses are covered very neatly, tight
and warm, with barks of trees, slipped from their bodies at those
seasons when the sap is up, and made into great flakes, with
pressure of weighty timber, when they are green. . . . The meaner
sort are covered with mats which they make of a kind of bulrush,
and are also indifferently tight and warm, but not so good as the
former. . . . Some I have seen, sixty or a hundred feet long and
thirty feet broad. . . . I have often lodged in their wigwams, and
found them as warm as the best English houses."[4] He adds, that
they were commonly carpeted and lined within with well-wrought
embroidered mats, and were furnished with various utensils. The
Indians had advanced so far as to regulate the effect of the wind by
a mat suspended over the hole in the roof and moved by a string.
Such a lodge was in the first instance constructed in a day or
two at most, and taken down and put up in a few hours; and every
family owned one, or its apartment in one.

In the savage state every family owns a shelter as good as the
best, and sufficient for its coarser and simpler wants; but I think
that I speak within bounds when I say that, though the birds of
the air have their nests, and the foxes their holes, and the savages
their wigwams, in modern civilized society not more than one
half the families own a shelter.[5] In the large towns and cities, where
civilization especially prevails, the number of those who own a
shelter is a very small fraction of the whole. The rest pay an
annual tax for this outside garment of all, become indispensable
summer and winter, which would buy a village of Indian wigwams,
but now helps to keep them poor as long as they live. I do not
mean to insist here on the disadvantage of hiring compared with
owning, but it is evident that the savage owns his shelter because
it costs so little, while the civilized man hires his commonly because he cannot afford to own it; nor can he, in the long run, any
better afford to hire. But, answers one, by merely paying this tax
the poor civilized man secures an abode which is a palace compared with the savage's. An annual rent of from twenty-five to
a hundred dollars, these are the country rates, entitles him to the
benefit of the improvements of centuries, spacious apartments,
clean paint and paper, Rumford[6] fireplace, back plastering, Vene-
tian blinds, copper pump, spring lock, a commodious cellar, and

4. Daniel Gookin (1612–87), *Historical Collections of the Indians in New England* (1792).
5. Compare Matthew 8.20: "The foxes have
holes, and the birds of the air have nests; but

the Son of man hath not where to lay his head."
6. Benjamin Thompson, Count Rumford
(1753–1814), designed a nonsmoking stove.

many other things. But how happens it that he who is said to enjoy these things is so commonly a *poor* civilized man, while the savage, who has them not, is rich as a savage? If it is asserted that civilization is a real advance in the condition of man,—and I think that it is, though only the wise improve their advantages,— it must be shown that it has produced better dwellings without making them more costly; and the cost of a thing is the amount of what I will call life which is required to be exchanged for it, immediately or in the long run. An average house in this neighborhood costs perhaps eight hundred dollars, and to lay up this sum will take from ten to fifteen years of the laborer's life, even if he is not encumbered with a family;—estimating the pecuniary value of every man's labor at one dollar a day, for if some receive more, others receive less;—so that he must have spent more than half his life commonly before *his* wigwam will be earned. If we suppose him to pay a rent instead, this is but a doubtful choice of evils. Would the savage have been wise to exchange his wigwam for a palace on these terms?

It may be guessed that I reduce almost the whole advantage of holding this superfluous property as a fund in store against the future, so far as the individual is concerned, mainly to the defraying of funeral expenses. But perhaps a man is not required to bury himself. Nevertheless this points to an important distinction between the civilized man and the savage; and, no doubt, they have designs on us for our benefit, in making the life of a civilized people an *institution*, in which the life of the individual is to a great extent absorbed, in order to preserve and perfect that of the race. But I wish to show at what a sacrifice this advantage is at present obtained, and to suggest that we may possibly so live as to secure all the advantage without suffering any of the disadvantage. What mean ye by saying that the poor ye have always with you, or that the fathers have eaten sour grapes, and the children's teeth are set on edge?

"As I live, saith the Lord God, ye shall not have occasion any more to use this proverb in Israel."

"Behold all souls are mine; as the soul of the father, so also the soul of the son is mine: the soul that sinneth it shall die." [7]

When I consider my neighbors, the farmers of Concord, who are at least as well off as the other classes, I find that for the most part they have been toiling twenty, thirty, or forty years, that they may become the real owners of their farms, which commonly they have inherited with encumbrances, or else bought with hired money,—and we may regard one third of that toil as the cost of

7. Matthew 26.11, Ezekiel 18.2–4.

their houses,—but commonly they have not paid for them yet. It is true, the encumbrances sometimes outweigh the value of the farm, so that the farm itself becomes one great encumbrance, and still a man is found to inherit it, being well acquainted with it, as he says. On applying to the assessors, I am surprised to learn that they cannot at once name a dozen in the town who own their farms free and clear. If you would know the history of these homesteads, inquire at the bank where they are mortgaged. The man who has actually paid for his farm with labor on it is so rare that every neighbor can point to him. I doubt if there are three such men in Concord. What has been said of the merchants, that a very large majority, even ninety-seven in a hundred, are sure to fail, is equally true of the farmers. With regard to the merchants, however, one of them says pertinently that a great part of their failures are not genuine pecuniary failures, but merely failures to fulfil their engagements, because it is inconvenient; that is, it is the moral character that breaks down. But this puts an infinitely worse face on the matter, and suggests, beside, that probably not even the other three succeed in saving their souls, but are perchance bankrupt in a worse sense than they who fail honestly. Bankruptcy and repudiation are the spring-boards from which much of our civilization vaults and turns its somersets, but the savage stands on the unelastic plank of famine. Yet the Middlesex Cattle Show [8] goes off here with *éclat* [9] annually, as if all the joints of the agricultural machine were suent.[1]

The farmer is endeavoring to solve the problem of a livelihood by a formula more complicated than the problem itself. To get his shoestrings he speculates in herds of cattle. With consummate skill he has set his trap with a hair springe to catch comfort and independence, and then, as he turned away, got his own leg into it. This is the reason he is poor; and for a similar reason we are all poor in respect to a thousand savage comforts, though surrounded by luxuries. As Chapman sings,—

> "The false society of men —
> — for earthly greatness
> All heavenly comforts rarefies to air." [2]

And when the farmer has got his house, he may not be the richer but the poorer for it, and it be the house that has got him. As I understand it, that was a valid objection urged by Momus [3] against the house which Minerva made, that she "had not made it

---

8. Middlesex is the county of which Concord is a part; the Agricultural Fair was an annual event.
9. Conspicuous success.
1. Also spelled "suant"; a dialect term meaning "running smoothly."
2. George Chapman (1559?–1634), English dramatist, translator and poet; from his *The Tragedy of Caesar and Pompey* 5.2.
3. The Greek god of pleasure.

movable, by which means a bad neighborhood might be avoided;" and it may still be urged, for our houses are such unwieldy property that we are often imprisoned rather than housed in them; and the bad neighborhood to be avoided is our own scurvy selves. I know one or two families, at least, in this town, who, for nearly a generation, have been wishing to sell their houses in the outskirts and move into the village, but have not been able to accomplish it, and only death will set them free.

Granted that the *majority* are able at last either to own or hire the modern house with all its improvements. While civilization has been improving our houses, it has not equally improved the men who are to inhabit them. It has created palaces, but it was not so easy to create noblemen and kings. And *if the civilized man's pursuits are no worthier than the savage's, if he is employed the greater part of his life in obtaining gross necessaries and comforts merely, why should he have a better dwelling than the former?*

But how do the poor *minority* fare? Perhaps it will be found, that just in proportion as some have been placed in outward circumstances above the savage, others have been degraded below him. The luxury of one class is counterbalanced by the indigence of another. On the one side is the palace, on the other are the almshouse and "silent poor."[4] The myriads who built the pyramids to be the tombs of the Pharaohs were fed on garlic, and it may be were not decently buried themselves. The mason who finishes the cornice of the palace returns at night perchance to a hut not so good as a wigwam. It is a mistake to suppose that, in a country where the usual evidences of civilization exist, the condition of a very large body of the inhabitants may not be as degraded as that of savages. I refer to the degraded poor, not now to the degraded rich. To know this I should not need to look farther than to the shanties which every where border our railroads, that last improvement in civilization; where I see in my daily walks human beings living in sties, and all winter with an open door, for the sake of light, without any visible, often imaginable, wood pile, and the forms of both old and young are permanently contracted by the long habit of shrinking from cold and misery, and the development of all their limbs and faculties is checked. It certainly is fair to look at that class by whose labor the works which distinguish this generation are accomplished. Such too, to a greater or less extent, is the condition of the operatives of every denomination in England, which is the great workhouse of the world. Or I could refer you to Ireland, which is marked as

---

4. Those who keep their debts secret to avoid being sent to the almshouse, or poorhouse.

one of the white or enlightened spots on the map. Contrast the physical condition of the Irish with that of the North American Indian, or the South Sea Islander, or any other savage race before it was degraded by contact with the civilized man. Yet I have no doubt that that people's rulers are as wise as the average of civilized rulers. Their condition only proves what squalidness may consist with civilization. I hardly need refer now to the laborers in our Southern States who produce the staple exports of this country, and are themselves a staple production of the South. But to confine myself to those who are said to be in *moderate* circumstances.

Most men appear never to have considered what a house is, and are actually though needlessly poor all their lives because they think that they must have such a one as their neighbors have. As if one were to wear any sort of coat which the tailor might cut out for him, or, gradually leaving off palmleaf hat or cap of woodchuck skin, complain of hard times because he could not afford to buy him a crown! It is possible to invent a house still more convenient and luxurious than we have, which yet all would admit that man could not afford to pay for. Shall we always study to obtain more of these things, and not sometimes to be content with less? Shall the respectable citizen thus gravely teach, by precept and example, the necessity of the young man's providing a certain number of superfluous glowshoes,[5] and umbrellas, and empty guest chambers for empty guests, before he dies? Why should not our furniture be as simple as the Arab's or the Indian's? When I think of the benefactors of the race, whom we have apotheosized as messengers from heaven, bearers of divine gifts to man, I do not see in my mind any retinue at their heels, any car-load of fashionable furniture. Or what if I were to allow— would it not be a singular allowance?—that our furniture should be more complex than the Arab's, in proportion as we are morally and intellectually his superiors! At present our houses are cluttered and defiled with it, and a good housewife would sweep out the greater part into the dust hole, and not leave her morning's work undone. Morning work! By the blushes of Aurora and the music of Memnon,[6] what should be man's *morning work* in this world? I had three pieces of limestone on my desk, but I was terrified to find that they required to be dusted daily, when the furniture of my mind was all undusted still, and I threw them out the window in disgust. How, then, could I have a furnished house? I would rather sit in the open air, for no dust gathers on the grass, unless where man has broken ground.

It is the luxurious and dissipated who set the fashions which the

---

5. Galoshes, waterproof overshoes.
6. In Roman mythology, the goddess of dawn and her son. A statue of Memnon near Thebes supposedly emitted musical sounds at dawn.

herd so diligently follow. The traveller who stops at the best houses, so called, soon discovers this, for the publicans presume him to be a Sardanapalus,[7] and if he resigned himself to their tender mercies he would soon be completely emasculated. I think that in the railroad car we are inclined to spend more on luxury than on safety and convenience, and it threatens without attaining these to become no better than a modern drawing room, with its divans, and ottomans, and sunshades, and a hundred other oriental things, which we are taking west with us, invented for the ladies of the harem and the effeminate natives of the Celestial Empire, which Jonathan [8] should be ashamed to know the names of. I would rather sit on a pumpkin and have it all to myself, than be crowded on a velvet cushion. I would rather ride on earth in an ox cart with a free circulation, than go to heaven in the fancy car of an excursion train and breathe a *malaria* all the way.

The very simplicity and nakedness of man's life in the primitive ages imply this advantage at least, that they left him still but a sojourner in nature. When he was refreshed with food and sleep he contemplated his journey again. He dwelt, as it were, in a tent in this world, and was either threading the valleys, or crossing the plains, or climbing the mountain tops. But lo! men have become the tools of their tools. The man who independently plucked the fruits when he was hungry is become a farmer; and he who stood under a tree for shelter, a housekeeper. We now no longer camp as for a night, but have settled down on earth and forgotten heaven. We have adopted Christianity merely as an improved method of *agri*-culture. We have built for this world a family mansion, and for the next a family tomb. The best works of art are the expression of man's struggle to free himself from this condition, but the effect of our art is merely to make this low state comfortable and that higher state to be forgotten. There is actually no place in this village for a work of *fine* art, if any had come down to us, to stand, for our lives, our houses and streets, furnish no proper pedestal for it. There is not a nail to hang a picture on, nor a shelf to receive the bust of a hero or a saint. When I consider how our houses are built and paid for, or not paid for, and their internal economy managed and sustained, I wonder that the floor does not give way under the visitor while he is admiring the gewgaws upon the mantel-piece, and let him through into the cellar, to some solid and honest though earthy foundation. I cannot but perceive that this so called rich and refined life is a thing jumped at, and I do not get on in the enjoy-

7. A corrupt king of ancient Assyria (d. 880 B.C.).
8. A common nineteenth-century name for an inhabitant of the United States; also, "Brother Jonathan."

ment of the *fine* arts which adorn it, my attention being wholly occupied with the jump; for I remember that the greatest genuine leap, due to human muscles alone, on record, is that of certain wandering Arabs, who are said to have cleared twenty-five feet on level ground. Without factitious support, man is sure to come to earth again beyond that distance. The first question which I am tempted to put to the proprietor of such great impropriety is, Who bolsters you? Are you one of the ninety-seven who fail, or the three who succeed? Answer me these questions, and then perhaps I may look at your bawbles and find them ornamental. The cart before the horse is neither beautiful nor useful. Before we can adorn our houses with beautiful objects the walls must be stripped, and our lives must be stripped, and beautiful house-keeping and beautiful living be laid for a foundation: now, a taste for the beautiful is most cultivated out of doors, where there is no house and no housekeeper.

Old Johnson, in his "Wonder-Working Providence," speaking of the first settlers of this town, with whom he was contemporary, tells us that "they burrow themselves in the earth for their first shelter under some hillside, and, casting the soil aloft upon timber, they make a smoky fire against the earth, at the highest side." They did not "provide them houses," says he, "till the earth, by the Lord's blessing, brought forth bread to feed them," and the first year's crop was so light that "they were forced to cut their bread very thin for a long season."[9] The secretary of the Province of New Netherland, writing in Dutch, in 1650, for the information of those who wished to take up land there, states more particularly, that "those in New Netherland, and especially in New England, who have no means to build farm houses at first according to their wishes, dig a square pit in the ground, cellar fashion, six or seven feet deep, as long and as broad as they think proper, case the earth inside with wood all round the wall, and line the wood with the bark of trees or something else to prevent the caving in of the earth; floor this cellar with plank, and wainscot it overhead for a ceiling, raise a roof of spars clear up, and cover the spars with bark or green sods, so that they can live dry and warm in these houses with their entire families for two, three, and four years, it being understood that partitions are run through those cellars which are adapted to the size of the family. The wealthy and principal men in New England, in the beginning of the colonies, commenced their first dwelling houses in this fashion for two reasons; firstly, in order not to waste time in building, and not to want food the next season; secondly, in order not to dis-

9. Edward Johnson (1598–1672), *Wonder-working Providence of Sion's Saviour in New England* (1654).

courage poor laboring people whom they brought over in numbers from Fatherland. In the course of three or four years, when the country became adapted to agriculture, they built themselves handsome houses, spending on them several thousands."[1]

In this course which our ancestors took there was a show of prudence at least, as if their principle were to satisfy the more pressing wants first. But are the more pressing wants satisfied now? When I think of acquiring for myself one of our luxurious dwellings, I am deterred, for, so to speak, the country is not yet adapted to *human* culture, and we are still forced to cut our *spiritual* bread far thinner than our forefathers did their wheaten. Not that all architectural ornament is to be neglected even in the rudest periods; but let our houses first be lined with beauty, where they come in contact with our lives, like the tenement of the shellfish, and not overlaid with it. But, alas! I have been inside one or two of them, and know what they are lined with.

Though we are not so degenerate but that we might possibly live in a cave or a wigwam or wear skins to-day, it certainly is better to accept the advantages, though so dearly bought, which the invention and industry of mankind offer. In such a neighborhood as this, boards and shingles, lime and bricks, are cheaper and more easily obtained than suitable caves, or whole logs, or bark in sufficient quantities, or even well-tempered clay or flat stones. I speak understandingly on this subject, for I have made myself acquainted with it both theoretically and practically. With a little more wit we might use these materials so as to become richer than the richest now are, and make our civilization a blessing. The civilized man is a more experienced and wiser savage. But to make haste to my own experiment.

Near the end of March, 1845, I borrowed an axe and went down to the woods by Walden Pond, nearest to where I intended to build my house, and began to cut down some tall arrowy white pines, still in their youth, for timber. It is difficult to begin without borrowing, but perhaps it is the most generous course thus to permit your fellow-men to have an interest in your enterprise. The owner of the axe, as he released his hold on it, said that it was the apple of his eye; but I returned it sharper than I received it. It was a pleasant hillside where I worked, covered with pine woods, through which I looked out on the pond, and a small open field in the woods where pines and hickories were springing up. The ice in the pond was not yet dissolved, though there were some open spaces, and it was all dark colored and saturated with water. There were some slight flurries of snow during the days that I

1. Edmund Bailey O'Callaghan, *Documentary History of the State of New-York* (1851).

worked there; but for the most part when I came out on to the
railroad, on my way home, its yellow sand heap stretched away
gleaming in the hazy atmosphere, and the rails shone in the spring
sun, and I heard the lark and pewee [2] and other birds already
come to commence another year with us. They were pleasant
spring days, in which the winter of man's discontent was thawing
as well as the earth, and the life that had lain torpid began to
stretch itself. One day, when my axe had come off and I had cut
a green hickory for a wedge, driving it with a stone, and had
placed the whole to soak in a pond hole in order to swell the
wood, I saw a striped snake run into the water, and he lay on the
bottom, apparently without inconvenience, as long as I staid
there, or more than a quarter of an hour; perhaps because he had
not yet fairly come out of the torpid state. It appeared to me that
for a like reason men remain in their present low and primitive
condition; but if they should feel the influence of the spring of
springs arousing them, they would of necessity rise to a higher and
more ethereal life. I had previously seen the snakes in frosty
mornings in my path with portions of their bodies still numb and
inflexible, waiting for the sun to thaw them. On the 1st of April
it rained and melted the ice, and in the early part of the day, which
was very foggy, I heard a stray goose groping about over the
pond and cackling as if lost, or like the spirit of the fog.

So I went on for some days cutting and hewing timber, and also
studs and rafters, all with my narrow axe, not having many
communicable or scholar-like thoughts, singing to myself,— [3]

> Men say they know many things;
> But lo! they have taken wings, —
> The arts and sciences,
> And a thousand appliances;
> The wind that blows
> Is all that any body knows.

I hewed the main timbers six inches square, most of the studs on
two sides only, and the rafters and floor timbers on one side,
leaving the rest of the bark on, so that they were just as straight
and much stronger than sawed ones. Each stick was carefully
mortised or tenoned by its stump, for I had borrowed other tools
by this time. My days in the woods were not very long ones; yet
I usually carried my dinner of bread and butter, and read the
newspaper in which it was wrapped, at noon, sitting amid the
green pine boughs which I had cut off, and to my bread was imparted some of their fragrance, for my hands were covered with a

2. The meadowlark and the phoebe.
3. This poem, like all poems not enclosed within quotation marks, was written by Thoreau himself.

thick coat of pitch. Before I had done I was more the friend than the foe of the pine tree, though I had cut down some of them, having become better acquainted with it. Sometimes a rambler in the wood was attracted by the sound of my axe, and we chatted pleasantly over the chips which I had made.

By the middle of April, for I made no haste in my work, but rather made the most of it, my house was framed and ready for the raising. I had already bought the shanty of James Collins, an Irishman who worked on the Fitchburg Railroad,[4] for boards. James Collins' shanty was considered an uncommonly fine one. When I called to see it he was not at home. I walked about the outside, at first unobserved from within, the window was so deep and high. It was of small dimensions, with a peaked cottage roof, and not much else to be seen, the dirt being raised five feet all around as if it were a compost heap. The roof was the soundest part, though a good deal warped and made brittle by the sun. Doorsill there was none, but a perennial passage for the hens under the door board. Mrs. C. came to the door and asked me to view it from the inside. The hens were driven in by my approach. It was dark, and had a dirt floor for the most part, dank, clammy, and aguish, only here a board and there a board which would not bear removal. She lighted a lamp to show me the inside of the roof and the walls, and also that the board floor extended under the bed, warning me not to step into the cellar, a sort of dust hole two feet deep. In her own words, they were "good boards overhead, good boards all around, and a good window,"—of two whole squares originally, only the cat had passed out that way lately. There was a stove, a bed, and a place to sit, an infant in the house where it was born, a silk parasol, gilt-framed looking-glass, and a patent new coffee mill nailed to an oak sapling, all told. The bargain was soon concluded, for James had in the mean while returned. I to pay four dollars and twenty-five cents to-night, he to vacate at five to-morrow morning, selling to nobody else meanwhile: I to take possession at six. It were well, he said, to be there early, and anticipate certain indistinct but wholly unjust claims on the score of ground rent and fuel. This he assured me was the only encumbrance. At six I passed him and his family on the road. One large bundle held their all,—bed, coffee-mill, looking-glass, hens,—all but the cat, she took to the woods and became a wild cat, and, as I learned afterward, trod in a trap set for woodchucks, and so became a dead cat at last.

I took down this dwelling the same morning, drawing the nails, and removed it to the pond side by small cartloads, spreading the

4. The Boston & Fitchburg Railroad, which ran near Walden Pond.

boards on the grass there to bleach and warp back again in the sun. One early thrush gave me a note or two as I drove along the woodland path. I was informed treacherously by a young Patrick [5] that neighbor Seeley, an Irishman, in the intervals of the carting, transferred the still tolerable, straight, and drivable nails, staples, and spikes to his pocket, and then stood when I came back to pass the time of day, and look freshly up, unconcerned, with spring thoughts, at the devastation; there being a dearth of work, as he said. He was there to represent spectatordom, and help make this seemingly insignificant event one with the removal of the gods of Troy.[6]

I dug my cellar in the side of a hill sloping to the south, where a woodchuck had formerly dug his burrow, down through sumach and blackberry roots, and the lowest stain of vegetation, six feet square by seven deep, to a fine sand where potatoes would not freeze in any winter. The sides were left shelving, and not stoned; but the sun having never shone on them, the sand still keeps its place. It was but two hours' work. I took particular pleasure in this breaking of ground, for in almost all latitudes men dig into the earth for an equable temperature. Under the most splendid house in the city is still to be found the cellar where they store their roots as of old, and long after the superstructure has disappeared posterity remark its dent in the earth. The house is still but a sort of porch at the entrance of a burrow.

At length, in the beginning of May, with the help of some of my acquaintances, rather to improve so good an occasion for neighborliness than from any necessity, I set up the frame of my house. No man was ever more honored in the character of his raisers than I. They are destined, I trust, to assist at the raising of loftier structures one day. I began to occupy my house on the 4th of July, as soon as it was boarded and roofed, for the boards were carefully feather-edged and lapped, so that it was perfectly impervious to rain; but before boarding I laid the foundation of a chimney at one end, bringing two cartloads of stones up the hill from the pond in my arms. I built the chimney after my hoeing in the fall, before a fire became necessary for warmth, doing my cooking in the mean while out of doors on the ground, early in the morning: which mode I still think is in some respects more convenient and agreeable than the usual one. When it stormed before my bread was baked, I fixed a few boards over the fire, and sat under them to watch my loaf, and passed some pleasant hours in that way. In those days, when my hands were much em-

5. A common name for any Irishman.
6. The removal of the images of gods from

Troy precedes the defeat of the city in Virgil's *Aeneid*, Book 2.

ployed, I read but little, but the least scraps of paper which lay on the ground, my holder, or tablecloth, afforded me as much entertainment, in fact answered the same purpose as the Iliad.[7]

It would be worth the while to build still more deliberately than I did, considering, for instance, what foundation a door, a window, a cellar, a garret, have in the nature of man, and perchance never raising any superstructure until we found a better reason for it than our temporal necessities even. There is some of the same fitness in a man's building his own house that there is in a bird's building its own nest. Who knows but if men constructed their dwellings with their own hands, and provided food for themselves and families simply and honestly enough, the poetic faculty would be universally developed, as birds universally sing when they are so engaged? But alas! we do like cowbirds and cuckoos, which lay their eggs in nests which other birds have built, and cheer no traveller with their chattering and unmusical notes. Shall we forever resign the pleasure of construction to the carpenter? What does architecture amount to in the experience of the mass of men? I never in all my walks came across a man engaged in so simple and natural an occupation as building his house. We belong to the community. It is not the tailor alone who is the ninth part of a man; it is as much the preacher, and the merchant, and the farmer. Where is this division of labor to end? and what object does it finally serve? No doubt another *may* also think for me; but it is not therefore desirable that he should do so to the exclusion of my thinking for myself.

True, there are architects so called in this country, and I have heard of one at least possessed with the idea of making architectural ornaments have a core of truth, a necessity, and hence a beauty, as if it were a revelation to him.[8] All very well perhaps from his point of view, but only a little better than the common dilettantism. A sentimental reformer in architecture, he began at the cornice, not at the foundation. It was only how to put a core of truth within the ornaments, that every sugar plum in fact might have an almond or caraway seed in it,—though I hold that almonds are most wholesome without the sugar,—and not how the inhabitant, the indweller, might build truly within and without, and let the ornaments take care of themselves. What reasonable man ever supposed that ornaments were something outward and in the skin merely,—that the tortoise got his spotted shell, or the shell-

7. Epic poem by Homer that tells of the siege of Troy by the Greeks, and the tragic consequences of the wrath of Achilles, a great mythological Greek warrior.

8. The sculptor Horatio Greenough (1805–52), an early proponent of the idea that architectural decoration should be functional.

fish its mother-o'-pearl tints, by such a contract as the inhabitants of Broadway their Trinity Church?[9] But a man has no more to do with the style of architecture of his house than a tortoise with that of its shell: nor need the soldier be so idle as to try to paint the precise *color* of his virtue on his standard. The enemy will find it out. He may turn pale when the trial comes. This man seemed to me to lean over the cornice, and timidly whisper his half truth to the rude occupants who really knew it better than he. What of architectural beauty I now see, I know has gradually grown from within outward, out of the necessities and character of the indweller, who is the only builder,—out of some unconscious truthfulness, and nobleness, without ever a thought for the appearance; and whatever additional beauty of this kind is destined to be produced will be preceded by a like unconscious beauty of life. The most interesting dwellings in this country, as the painter knows, are the most unpretending, humble log huts and cottages of the poor commonly; it is the life of the inhabitants whose shells they are, and not any peculiarity in their surfaces merely, which makes them *picturesque*; and equally interesting will be the citizen's suburban box, when his life shall be as simple and as agreeable to the imagination, and there is as little straining after effect in the style of his dwelling. A great proportion of architectural ornaments are literally hollow, and a September gale would strip them off, like borrowed plumes, without injury to the substantials. They can do without *architecture* who have no olives nor wines in the cellar. What if an equal ado were made about the ornaments of style in literature, and the architects of our bibles spent as much time about their cornices as the architects of our churches do? So are made the *belles-lettres* and the *beaux-arts* [1] and their professors. Much it concerns a man, forsooth, how a few sticks are slanted over him or under him, and what colors are daubed upon his box. It would signify somewhat, if, in any earnest sense, *he* slanted them and daubed it; but the spirit having departed out of the tenant, it is of a piece with constructing his own coffin, —the architecture of the grave, and "carpenter," is but another name for "coffin-maker." One man says, in his despair or indifference to life, take up a handful of the earth at your feet, and paint your house that color. Is he thinking of his last and narrow house? Toss up a copper[2] for it as well. What an abundance of leisure he must have! Why do you take up a handful of dirt? Better paint your house your own complexion; let it turn pale or

9. A famous church in New York City built by Richard Upjohn in the Gothic Revival style and completed in 1846.

1. Esthetic or polite literature and the fine arts.

2. A coin; perhaps a reference to the ancient Greek belief about giving a coin to the spirit who guides a corpse to the land of the dead.

blush for you. An enterprise to improve the style of cottage architecture! When you have got my ornaments ready I will wear them.

Before winter I built a chimney, and shingled the sides of my house, which were already impervious to rain, with imperfect and sappy shingles made of the first slice of the log, whose edges I was obliged to straighten with a plane.

I have thus a tight shingled and plastered house, ten feet wide by fifteen long, and eight-feet posts, with a garret and a closet, a large window on each side, two trap doors, one door at the end, and a brick fireplace opposite. The exact cost of my house, paying the usual price for such materials as I used, but not counting the work, all of which was done by myself. was as follows; and I give the details because very few are able to tell exactly what their houses cost, and fewer still, if any, the separate cost of the various materials which compose them:—

Boards,	$8 03½,	mostly shanty boards.
Refuse shingles for roof and sides,	. 4 00	
Laths,	1 25	
Two second-hand windows with glass,	2 43	
One thousand old brick,	4 00	
Two casks of lime,	2 40	That was high.
Hair,	0 31	˙More than I needed.
Mantle-tree iron,	0 15	
Nails,	3 90	
Hinges and screws,	0 14	
Latch,	0 10	
Chalk,	0 01	
Transportation,	1 40	I carried a good part on my back.
In all,	$28 12½	

These are all the materials excepting the timber, stones and sand, which I claimed by squatter's right. I have also a small wood-shed adjoining, made chiefly of the stuff which was left after building the house.

I intend to build me a house which will surpass any on the main street in Concord in grandeur and luxury, as soon as it pleases me as much and will cost me no more than my present one.

I thus found that the student who wishes for a shelter can obtain one for a lifetime at an expense not greater than the rent which he now pays annually. If I seem to boast more than is becoming, my excuse is that I brag for humanity rather than for myself; and my shortcomings and inconsistencies do not affect the truth of my statement. Notwithstanding much cant and hypocrisy,—chaff which I find it difficult to separate from my wheat, but for which I am as sorry as any man,—I will breathe freely and stretch myself in this respect, it is such a relief to both the moral and physical system; and I am resolved that I will not through humility become the devil's attorney. I will endeavor to speak a good word for the truth. At Cambridge College [3] the mere rent of a student's room, which is only a little larger than my own, is thirty dollars each year, though the corporation had the advantage of building thirty-two side by side and under one roof, and the occupant suffers the inconvenience of many and noisy neighbors, and perhaps a residence in the fourth story. I cannot but think that if we had more true wisdom in these respects, not only less education would be needed, because, forsooth, more would already have been acquired, but the pecuniary expense of getting an education would in a great measure vanish. Those conveniences which the student requires at Cambridge or elsewhere cost him or somebody else ten times as great a sacrifice of life as they would with proper management on both sides. Those things for which the most money is demanded are never the things which the student most wants. Tuition, for instance, is an important item in the term bill, while for the far more valuable education which he gets by associating with the most cultivated of his contemporaries no charge is made. The mode of founding a college is, commonly, to get up a subscription of dollars and cents, and then following blindly the principles of a division of labor to its extreme, a principle which should never be followed but with circumspection, —to call in a contractor who makes this a subject of speculation, and he employs Irishmen or other operatives actually to lay the foundations, while the students that are to be are said to be fitting themselves for it; and for these oversights successive generations have to pay. I think that it would be *better than this*, for the students, or those who desire to be benefited by it, even to lay the foundation themselves. The student who secures his coveted leisure and retirement by systematically shirking any labor necessary to man obtains but an ignoble and unprofitable leisure, defrauding himself of the experience which alone can make leisure fruitful. "But," says one, "you do not mean that the students should go to work with their hands instead of their heads?" I do not mean that exactly, but I mean something which he might think a good deal like that; I mean that they should not *play* life, or *study* it merely, while the community supports them at this expensive game, but earnestly *live* it from beginning to end. How could youths better learn to live than by at once trying the experiment of living? Methinks this would exercise their minds as much as mathematics. If I wished a boy to know something about the arts and sciences, for instance, I would not pursue the common course,

3. Harvard College, Cambridge, Massachusetts; Thoreau's own college.

which is merely to send him into the neighborhood of some professor, where any thing is professed and practised but the art of life;—to survey the world through a telescope or a microscope, and never with his natural eye; to study chemistry, and not learn how his bread is made, or mechanics, and not learn how it is earned; to discover new satellites to Neptune, and not detect the motes in his eyes, or to what vagabond he is a satellite himself; or to be devoured by the monsters that swarm all around him, while contemplating the monsters in a drop of vinegar. Which would have advanced the most at the end of a month,—the boy who had made his own jackknife from the ore which he had dug and smelted, reading as much as would be necessary for this,—or the boy who had attended the lectures on metallurgy at the Institute in the mean while, and had received a Rogers'[4] penknife from his father? Which would be most likely to cut his fingers? . . . To my astonishment I was informed on leaving college that I had studied navigation!—why, if I had taken one turn down the harbor I should have known more about it. Even the *poor* student studies and is taught only *political* economy, while that economy of living which is synonymous with philosophy is not even sincerely professed in our colleges. The consequence is, that while he is reading Adam Smith, Ricardo, and Say,[5] he runs his father in debt irretrievably.

As with our colleges, so with a hundred "modern improvements;" there is an illusion about them; there is not always a positive advance. The devil goes on exacting compound interest to the last for his early share and numerous succeeding investments in them. Our inventions are wont to be pretty toys, which distract our attention from serious things. They are but improved means to an unimproved end, an end which it was already but too easy to arrive at; as railroads lead to Boston or New York. We are in great haste to construct a magnetic telegraph from Maine to Texas; but Maine and Texas, it may be, have nothing important to communicate. Either is in such a predicament as the man who was earnest to be introduced to a distinguished deaf woman, but when he was presented, and one end of her ear trumpet was put into his hand, had nothing to say. As if the main object were to talk fast and not to talk sensibly. We are eager to tunnel under the Atlantic and bring the old world some weeks nearer to the new; but perchance the first news that will leak through into the broad, flapping American ear will be that the Princess Adelaide[6] has the

4. A relatively costly knife manufactured by Joseph Rodgers & Sons in Sheffield, England.
5. Three economists: Scottish Adam Smith (1723–90), English David Ricardo (1772–1823), and French Jean Baptiste Say (1767–1823).
6. Perhaps the Princess of Orleans, the sister of King Louis Phillipe of France; figuratively, any famous but inconsequential person.

whooping cough. After all, the man whose horse trots a mile in a minute does not carry the most important messages; he is not an evangelist, nor does he come round eating locusts and wild honey. I doubt if Flying Childers [7] ever carried a peck of corn to mill. One says to me, "I wonder that you do not lay up money; you love to travel; you might take the cars and go to Fitchburg [8] to-day and see the country." But I am wiser than that. I have learned that the swiftest traveller is he that goes afoot. I say to my friend, Suppose we try who will get there first. The distance is thirty miles; the fare ninety cents. That is almost a day's wages. I remember when wages were sixty cents a day for laborers on this very road. Well, I start now on foot, and get there before night; I have travelled at that rate by the week together. You will in the mean while have earned your fare, and arrive there some time to-morrow, or possibly this evening, if you are lucky enough to get a job in season. Instead of going to Fitchburg, you will be working here the greater part of the day. And so, if the railroad reached round the world, I think that I should keep ahead of you; and as for seeing the country and getting experience of that kind, I should have to cut your acquaintance altogether.

Such is the universal law, which no man can ever outwit, and with regard to the railroad even we may say it is as broad as it is long. To make a railroad round the world available to all mankind is equivalent to grading the whole surface of the planet. Men have an indistinct notion that if they keep up this activity of joint stocks and spades long enough all will at length ride somewhere, in next to no time, and for nothing; but though a crowd rushes to the depot, and the conductor shouts "All aboard!" when the smoke is blown away and the vapor condensed, it will be perceived that a few are riding, but the rest are run over,—and it will be called, and will be, "A melancholy accident." No doubt they can ride at last who shall have earned their fare, that is, if they survive so long, but they will probably have lost their elasticity and desire to travel by that time. This spending of the best part of one's life earning money. in order to enjoy a questionable liberty during the least valuable part of it, reminds me of the Englishman who went to India to make a fortune first, in order that he might return to England and live the life of a poet. He should have gone up garret at once. "What!" exclaim a million Irishmen starting up from all the shanties in the land, "is not this railroad which we have built a good thing?" Yes, I answer, *comparatively* good, that is, you might have done worse; but I wish, as you are brothers of mine, that you could have spent your time better than digging in this dirt.

7. A famous English racehorse.   8. A town west of Concord.

Before I finished my house, wishing to earn ten or twelve dollars by some honest and agreeable method, in order to meet my unusual expenses, I planted about two acres and a half of light and sandy soil near it chiefly with beans, but also a small part with potatoes, corn, peas, and turnips. The whole lot contains eleven acres, mostly growing up to pines and hickories, and was sold the preceding season for eight dollars and eight cents an acre. One farmer said that it was "good for nothing but to raise cheeping squirrels on." I put no manure whatever on this land, not being the owner, but merely a squatter, and not expecting to cultivate so much again, and I did not quite hoe it all once. I got out several cords of stumps in ploughing, which supplied me with fuel for a long time, and left small circles of virgin mould, easily distinguishable through the summer by the greater luxuriance of the beans there. The dead and for the most part unmerchantable wood behind my house, and the driftwood from the pond, have supplied the remainder of my fuel. I was obliged to hire a team and a man for the ploughing, though I held the plough myself. My farm outgoes for the first season were, for implements, seed, work, &c., $14 72½. The seed corn was given me. This never costs any thing to speak of, unless you plant more than enough. I got twelve bushels of beans, and eighteen bushels of potatoes, beside some peas and sweet corn. The yellow corn and turnips were too late to come to any thing. My whole income from the farm was

$23 44.
Deducting the outgoes, ... 14 72½
There are left, ... $8 71½,

beside produce consumed and on hand at the time this estimate was made of the value of $4 50,—the amount on hand much more than balancing a little grass which I did not raise. All things considered, that is, considering the importance of a man's soul and of to-day, notwithstanding the short time occupied by my experiment, nay, partly even because of its transient character, I believe that that was doing better than any farmer in Concord did that year.

The next year I did better still, for I spaded up all the land which I required, about a third of an acre, and I learned from the experience of both years, not being in the least awed by many celebrated works on husbandry, Arthur Young [9] among the rest, that if one would live simply and eat only the crop which he raised, and raise no more than he ate, and not exchange it for an insufficient quantity of more luxurious and expensive things, he would need to cultivate only a few rods of ground, and that it

9. British agricultural author.

would be cheaper to spade up that than to use oxen to plough it, and to select a fresh spot from time to time than to manure the old, and he could do all his necessary farm work as it were with his left hand at odd hours in the summer; and thus he would not be tied to an ox, or horse, or cow, or pig, as at present. I desire to speak impartially on this point, and as one not interested in the success or failure of the present economical and social arrangements. I was more independent than any farmer in Concord, for I was not anchored to a house or farm, but could follow the bent of my genius, which is a very crooked one, every moment. Beside being better off than they already, if my house had been burned or my crops had failed, I should have been nearly as well off as before.

I am wont to think that men are not so much the keepers of herds as herds are the keepers of men, the former are so much the freer. Men and oxen exchange work; but if we consider necessary work only, the oxen will be seen to have greatly the advantage, their farm is so much the larger. Man does some of his part of the exchange work in his six weeks of haying, and it is no boy's play. Certainly no nation that lived simply in all respects, that is, no nation of philosophers, would commit so great a blunder as to use the labor of animals. True, there never was and is not likely soon to be a nation of philosophers, nor am I certain it is desirable that there should be. However, I should never have broken a horse or bull and taken him to board for any work he might do for me, for fear I should become a horse-man or a herds-man merely; and if society seems to be the gainer by so doing, are we certain that what is one man's gain is not another's loss, and that the stable-boy has equal cause with his master to be satisfied? Granted that some public works would not have been constructed without this aid, and let man share the glory of such with the ox and horse; does it follow that he could not have accomplished works yet more worthy of himself in that case? When men begin to do, not merely unnecessary or artistic, but luxurious and idle work, with their assistance, it is inevitable that a few do all the exchange work with the oxen, or, in other words, become the slaves of the strongest. Man thus not only works for the animal within him, but, for a symbol of this, he works for the animal without him. Though we have many substantial houses of brick or stone, the prosperity of the farmer is still measured by the degree to which the barn overshadows the house. This town is said to have the largest houses for oxen, cows, and horses hereabouts, and it is not behindhand in its public buildings; but there are very few halls for free worship or free speech in this country. It should not be by their architecture, but why not even by their power of abstract thought, that nations should seek to commemorate themselves? How much more admirable the Bhagvat-Geeta [1] than all the ruins of the East! Towers and temples are the luxury of princes. A simple and independent mind does not toil at the bidding of any prince. Genius is not a retainer to any emperor, nor is its material silver, or gold, or marble, except to a trifling extent. To what end, pray, is so much stone hammered? In Arcadia,[2] when I was there, I did not see any hammering stone. Nations are possessed with an insane ambition to perpetuate the memory of themselves by the amount of hammered stone they leave. What if equal pains were taken to smooth and polish their manners? One piece of good sense would be more memorable than a monument as high as the moon. I love better to see stones in place. The grandeur of Thebes [3] was a vulgar grandeur. More sensible is a rod of stone wall that bounds an honest man's field than a hundred-gated Thebes that has wandered farther from the true end of life. The religion and civilization which are barbaric and heathenish build splendid temples; but what you might call Christianity does not. Most of the stone a nation hammers goes toward its tomb only. It buries itself alive. As for the Pyramids, there is nothing to wonder at in them so much as the fact that so many men could be found degraded enough to spend their lives constructing a tomb for some ambitious booby, whom it would have been wiser and manlier to have drowned in the Nile, and then given his body to the dogs. I might possibly invent some excuse for them and him, but I have no time for it. As for the religion and love of art of the builders, it is much the same all the world over, whether the building be an Egyptian temple or the United States Bank. It costs more than it comes to. The mainspring is vanity, assisted by the love of garlic and bread and butter. Mr. Balcom, a promising young architect, designs it on the back of his Vitruvius,[4] with hard pencil and ruler, and the job is let out to Dobson & Sons, stonecutters. When the thirty centuries begin to look down on it, mankind begin to look up at it. As for your high towers and monuments, there was a crazy fellow once in this town who undertook to dig through to China, and he got so far that, as he said, he heard the Chinese pots and kettles rattle; but I think that I shall not go out of my way to admire the hole which he made. Many are concerned about the monuments of the West and

1. A sacred Hindu text, frequently cited by Thoreau; also spelled "Bhagavad Gita."
2. Ancient Greek pastoral region; figuratively, any ideal land.
3. Ancient capital of Upper Egypt, a standard symbol of grandeur.
4. Roman architect and author of a book on design, *De Architectura*.

the East,—to know who built them. For my part, I should like to know who in those days did not build them,—who were above such trifling. But to proceed with my statistics.

By surveying, carpentry, and day-labor of various other kinds in the village in the mean while, for I have as many trades as fingers, I had earned $13 34. The expense of food for eight months, namely, from July 4th to March 1st, the time when these estimates were made, though I lived there more than two years,—not counting potatoes, a little green corn, and some peas, which I had raised, nor considering the value of what was on hand at the last date, was

Rice, ...	$1 73½	
Molasses, . . .	1 73	Cheapest form of the saccharine.
Rye meal, . .	1 04¾	
Indian meal, .	0 99¾	Cheaper than rye.
Pork, ...	0 22	
Flour, ...	0 88 }	Costs more than Indian meal, both money and trouble.
Sugar, ...	0 80	
Lard, ...	0 65	
Apples, . . .	0 25	
Dried apple, . .	0 22	
Sweet potatoes,	0 10	
One pumpkin,	0 6	
One watermelon,	0 2	
Salt, ...	0 3	

All experiments which failed.

Yes, I did eat $8 74 all told; but I should not thus unblushingly publish my guilt, if I did not know that most of my readers were equally guilty with myself, and that their deeds would look no better in print. The next year I sometimes caught a mess of fish for my dinner, and once I went so far as to slaughter a woodchuck which ravaged my bean-field,—effect his transmigration, as a Tartar [5] would say,—and devour him, partly for experiment's sake; but though it afforded me a momentary enjoyment, notwithstanding a musky flavor, I saw that the longest use would not make that a good practice, however it might seem to have your woodchucks ready dressed by the village butcher.

Clothing and some incidental expenses within the same dates, though little can be inferred from this item, amounted to

$8 40¾

Oil and some household utensils, . . . 2 00

So that all the pecuniary outgoes, excepting for washing and mending, which for the most part were done out of the house, and

---

5. A resident of Tartary, a region of Central Asia, and believer in the transmigration of souls.

their bills have not yet been received,—and these are all and more than all the ways by which money necessarily goes out in this part of the world,—were

House, ...	$28 12½
Farm one year, ...	14 72½
Food eight months, ...	8 74
Clothing, &c., eight months, ...	8 40¾
Oil, &c., eight months, ...	2 00
In all, ...	$61 99¾

I address myself now to those of my readers who have a living to get. And to meet this I have for farm produce sold

	$23 44
Earned by day-labor, ...	13 34
In all, ...	$36 78,

which subtracted from the sum of the outgoes leaves a balance of $25 21¾ on the one side,—this being very nearly the means with which I started, and the measure of expenses to be incurred,—and on the other, beside the leisure and independence and health thus secured, a comfortable house for me as long as I choose to occupy it.

These statistics, however accidental and therefore uninstructive they may appear, as they have a certain completeness, have a certain value also. Nothing was given me of which I have not rendered some account. It appears from the above estimate, that my food alone cost me in money about twenty-seven cents a week. It was, for nearly two years after this, rye and Indian meal without yeast, potatoes, rice, a very little salt pork, molasses, and salt, and my drink water. It was fit that I should live on rice, mainly, who loved so well the philosophy of India. To meet the objections of some inveterate cavillers, I may as well state, that if I dined out occasionally, as I always had done, and I trust shall have opportunities to do again, it was frequently to the detriment of my domestic arrangements. But the dining out, being, as I have stated, a constant element, does not in the least affect a comparative statement like this.

I learned from my two years' experience that it would cost incredibly little trouble to obtain one's necessary food, even in this latitude; that a man may use as simple a diet as the animals, and yet retain health and strength. I have made a satisfactory dinner, satisfactory on several accounts, simply off a dish of purslane (*Portulaca oleracea*) which I gathered in my cornfield, boiled and salted. I give the Latin on account of the savoriness of the trivial name. And pray what more can a reasonable man desire, in peaceful times, in ordinary noons, than a sufficient number of ears of green sweet-corn boiled, with the addition of salt? Even the little variety which I used was a yielding to the demands of appetite, and not of health. Yet men have come to such a pass that they frequently starve, not for want of necessaries, but for want of luxuries; and I know a good woman who thinks that her son lost his life because he took to drinking water only.

The reader will perceive that I am treating the subject rather from an economic than a dietetic point of view, and he will not venture to put my abstemiousness to the test unless he has a well-stocked larder.

Bread I at first made of pure Indian meal and salt, genuine hoe-cakes, which I baked before my fire out of doors on a shingle or the end of a stick of timber sawed off in building my house; but it was wont to get smoked and to have a piny flavor. I tried flour also; but have at last found a mixture of rye and Indian meal most convenient and agreeable. In cold weather it was no little amusement to bake several small loaves of this in succession, tending and turning them as carefully as an Egyptian his hatching eggs. They were a real cereal fruit which I ripened, and they had to my senses a fragrance like that of other noble fruits, which I kept in as long as possible by wrapping them in cloths. I made a study of the ancient and indispensable art of bread-making, consulting such authorities as offered, going back to the primitive days and first invention of the unleavened kind, when from the wildness of nuts and meats men first reached the mildness and refinement of this diet, and travelling gradually down in my studies through that accidental souring of the dough which, it is supposed, taught the leavening process, and through the various fermentations there-after, till I came to "good, sweet, wholesome bread," the staff of life. Leaven, which some deem the soul of bread, the *spiritus* which fills its cellular tissue, which is religiously preserved like the vestal fire,—some precious bottle-full, I suppose, first brought over in the Mayflower, did the business for America, and its in-fluence is still rising, swelling, spreading, in cerealian billows over the land,—this seed I regularly and faithfully procured from the village, till at length one morning I forgot the rules, and scalded my yeast; by which accident I discovered that even this was not indis-pensable,—for my discoveries were not by the synthetic but analytic process,—and I have gladly omitted it since, though most housewives earnestly assured me that safe and wholesome bread without yeast might not be, and elderly people prophesied a speedy decay of the vital forces. Yet I find it not to be an essential in-gredient, and after going without it for a year am still in the land of the living; and I am glad to escape the trivialness of carrying a bottle-full in my pocket, which would sometimes pop and discharge its contents to my discomfiture. It is simpler and more respectable to omit it. Man is an animal who more than any other can adapt himself to all climates and circumstances. Neither did I put any sal soda, or other acid or alkali, into my bread. It would seem that I made it according to the recipe which Marcus Porcius Cato gave about two centuries before Christ. "Panem depsticium sic facito. Manus mortariumque bene lavato. Farinam in mortarium indito, aquæ paulatim addito, subigitoque pulchre. Ubi bene subegeris, defingito, coquitoque sub testu."[6] Which I take to mean— "Make kneaded bread thus. Wash your hands and trough well. Put the meal into the trough, add water gradually, and knead it thoroughly. When you have kneaded it well, mould it, and bake it under a cover," that is, in a baking-kettle. Not a word about leaven. But I did not always use this staff of life. At one time, owing to the emptiness of my purse, I saw none of it for more than a month.

Every New Englander might easily raise all his own breadstuffs in this land of rye and Indian corn, and not depend on distant and fluctuating markets for them. Yet so far are we from simplicity and independence that, in Concord, fresh and sweet meal is rarely sold in the shops, and hominy and corn in a still coarser form are hardly used by any. For the most part the farmer gives to his cattle and hogs the grain of his own producing, and buys flour, which is at least no more wholesome, at a greater cost, at the store. I saw that I could easily raise my bushel or two of rye and Indian corn, for the former will grow on the poorest land, and the latter does not require the best, and grind them in a hand-mill, and so do without rice and pork; and if I must have some concentrated sweet, I found by experiment that I could make a very good molasses either of pumpkins or beets, and I knew that I needed only to set out a few maples to obtain it more easily still, and while these were growing I could use various substitutes beside those which I have named. "For," as the Forefathers sang,—

> "we can make liquor to sweeten our lips
> Of pumpkins and parsnips and walnut-tree chips."[7]

Finally, as for salt, that grossest of groceries, to obtain this might be a fit occasion for a visit to the seashore, or, if I did without it altogether, I should probably drink the less water. I do not learn that the Indians ever troubled themselves to go after it.

Thus I could avoid all trade and barter, so far as my food was concerned, and having a shelter already, it would only remain to

---

6. Roman statesman and agriculturalist (239–149 B.C.); from his *De Agri Cultura*; also called *De Re Rustica*.

7. From John Warner Barber, *Historical Collections* (1839).

get clothing and fuel. The pantaloons which I now wear were woven in a farmer's family,—thank Heaven there is so much virtue still in man; for I think the fall from the farmer to the operative as great and memorable as that from the man to the farmer;—and in a new country fuel is an encumbrance. As for a habitat, if I were not permitted still to squat, I might purchase one acre at the same price for which the land I cultivated was sold—namely, eight dollars and eight cents. But as it was, I considered that I enhanced the value of the land by squatting on it.

There is a certain class of unbelievers who sometimes ask me such questions as, if I think that I can live on vegetable food alone; and to strike at the root of the matter at once,—for the root is faith,—I am accustomed to answer such, that I can live on board nails. If they cannot understand that, they cannot understand much that I have to say. For my part, I am glad to hear of experiments of this kind being tried; as that a young man tried for a fortnight to live on hard, raw corn on the ear, using his teeth for all mortar. The squirrel tribe tried the same and succeeded. The human race is interested in these experiments, though a few old women who are incapacitated for them, or who own their thirds[8] in mills, may be alarmed.

My furniture, part of which I made myself, and the rest cost me nothing of which I have not rendered an account, consisted of a bed, a table, a desk, three chairs, a looking-glass three inches in diameter, a pair of tongs and andirons, a kettle, a skillet, and a frying-pan, a dipper, a wash-bowl, two knives and forks, three plates, one cup, one spoon, a jug for oil, a jug for molasses, and a japanned lamp. None is so poor that he need sit on a pumpkin. That is shiftlessness. There is a plenty of such chairs as I like best in the village garrets to be had for taking them away. Furniture! Thank God, I can sit and I can stand without the aid of a furniture warehouse. What man but a philosopher would not be ashamed to see his furniture packed in a cart and going up country exposed to the light of heaven and the eyes of men, a beggarly account of empty boxes? That is Spaulding's furniture. I could never tell from inspecting such a load whether it belonged to a so called rich man or a poor one; the owner always seemed poverty-stricken. Indeed, the more you have of such things the poorer you are. Each load looks as if it contained the contents of a dozen shanties; and if one shanty is poor, this is a dozen times as poor. Pray, for what do we *move* ever but to get rid of our furniture, our *exuviæ*;[9] at last to go from this world to another

8. A widow's legal share of an inheritance was one-third.   9. Things cast off.

newly furnished, and leave this to be burned? It is the same as if all these traps were buckled to a man's belt, and he could not move over the rough country where our lines are cast without dragging them,—dragging his trap. He was a lucky fox that left his tail in the trap. The muskrat will gnaw his third leg off to be free. No wonder man has lost his elasticity. How often he is at a dead set! "Sir, if I may be so bold, what do you mean by a dead set?" If you are a seer, whenever you meet a man you will see all that he owns, ay, and much that he pretends to disown, behind him, even to his kitchen furniture and all the trumpery which he saves and will not burn, and he will appear to be harnessed to it and making what headway he can. I think that the man is at a dead set who has got through a knot hole or gateway where his sledge load of furniture cannot follow him. I cannot but feel compassion when I hear some trig, compact-looking man, seemingly free, all girded and ready, speak of his "furniture," as whether it is insured or not. "But what shall I do with my furniture?" My gay butterfly is entangled in a spider's web then. Even those who seem for a long while not to have any, if you inquire more narrowly you will find have some stored in somebody's barn. I look upon England to-day as an old gentleman who is travelling with a great deal of baggage, trumpery which has accumulated from long housekeeping, which he has not the courage to burn; great trunk, little trunk, bandbox and bundle. Throw away the first three at least. It would surpass the powers of a well man nowadays to take up his bed and walk, and I should certainly advise a sick one to lay down his bed and run. When I have met an immigrant tottering under a bundle which contained his all—looking like an enormous wen which had grown out of the nape of his neck—I have pitied him, not because that was his all, but because he had all *that* to carry. If I have got to drag my trap, I will take care that it be a light one and do not nip me in a vital part. But perchance it would be wisest never to put one's paw into it.

I would observe, by the way, that it costs me nothing for curtains, for I have no gazers to shut out but the sun and moon, and I am willing that they should look in. The moon will not sour milk nor taint meat of mine, nor will the sun injure my furniture or fade my carpet, and if he is sometimes too warm a friend, I find it still better economy to retreat behind some curtain which nature has provided, than to add a single item to the details of housekeeping. A lady once offered me a mat, but as I had no room to spare within the house, nor time to spare within or without to shake it, I declined it, preferring to wipe my feet on the sod before my door. It is best to avoid the beginnings of evil.

Not long since I was present at the auction of a deacon's effects, for his life had not been ineffectual:—

"The evil that men do lives after them." [1]

As usual, a great proportion was trumpery which had begun to accumulate in his father's day. Among the rest was a dried tapeworm. And now, after lying half a century in his garret and other dust holes, these things were not burned; instead of a *bonfire*, or purifying destruction of them, there was an *auction*, or increasing of them. The neighbors eagerly collected to view them, bought them all, and carefully transported them to their garrets and dust holes, to lie there till their estates are settled, when they will start again. When a man dies he kicks the dust.

The customs of some savage nations might, perchance, be profitably imitated by us, for they at least go through the semblance of casting their slough annually; they have the idea of the thing, whether they have the reality or not. Would it not be well if we were to celebrate such a "busk," or "feast of first fruits," as Bartram describes to have been the custom of the Mucclasse Indians? "When a town celebrates the busk," says he, "having previously provided themselves with new clothes, new pots, pans, and other household utensils and furniture, they collect all their worn out clothes and other despicable things, sweep and cleanse their houses, squares, and the whole town, of their filth, which with all the remaining grain and other old provisions they cast together into one common heap, and consume it with fire. After having taken medicine, and fasted for three days, all the fire in the town is extinguished. During this fast they abstain from the gratification of every appetite and passion whatever. A general amnesty is proclaimed; all malefactors may return to their town.—"

"On the fourth morning, the high priest, by rubbing dry wood together, produces new fire in the public square, from whence every habitation in the town is supplied with the new and pure flame."

They then feast on the new corn and fruits and dance and sing for three days, "and the four following days they receive visits and rejoice with their friends from neighboring towns who have in like manner purified and prepared themselves." [2]

The Mexicans also practised a similar purification at the end of every fifty-two years, in the belief that it was time for the world to come to an end.

I have scarcely heard of a truer sacrament, that is, as the

1. From Antony's speech after the death of Caesar in Shakespeare's *Julius Caesar* 3.3.
2. William Bartram (1739–1823), early American naturalist; from his *Travels through North and South Carolina . . .* (1791).

dictionary defines it, "outward and visible sign of an inward and spiritual grace," than this, and I have no doubt that they were originally inspired directly from Heaven to do thus, though they have no biblical record of the revelation.

For more than five years I maintained myself thus solely by the labor of my hands, and I found, that by working about six weeks in a year, I could meet all the expenses of living. The whole of my winters, as well as most of my summers, I had free and clear for study. I have thoroughly tried school-keeping, and found that my expenses were in proportion, or rather out of proportion, to my income, for I was obliged to dress and train, not to say think and believe, accordingly, and I lost my time into the bargain. As I did not teach for the good of my fellow-men, but simply for a livelihood, this was a failure. I have tried trade; but I found that it would take ten years to get under way in that, and that then I should probably be on my way to the devil. I was actually afraid that I might by that time be doing what is called a good business. When formerly I was looking about to see what I could do for a living, some sad experience in conforming to the wishes of friends being fresh in my mind to tax my ingenuity, I thought often and seriously of picking huckleberries; that surely I could do, and its small profits might suffice,—for my greatest skill has been to want but little,—so little capital it required, so little distraction from my wonted moods, I foolishly thought. While my acquaintances went unhesitatingly into trade or the professions, I contemplated this occupation as most like theirs; ranging the hills all summer to pick the berries which came in my way, and thereafter carelessly dispose of them; so, to keep the flocks of Admetus.[3] I also dreamed that I might gather the wild herbs, or carry evergreens to such villagers as loved to be reminded of the woods, even to the city, by hay-cart loads. But I have since learned that trade curses every thing it handles; and though you trade in messages from heaven, the whole curse of trade attaches to the business.

As I preferred some things to others, and especially valued my freedom, as I could fare hard and yet succeed well, I did not wish to spend my time in earning rich carpets or other fine furniture, or delicate cookery, or a house in the Grecian or the Gothic[4] style just yet. If there are any to whom it is no interruption to acquire these things, and who know how to use them when acquired, I relinquish to them the pursuit. Some are "industrious," and appear

3. In Greek mythology, Apollo, the god of music, poetry, and prophecy, was forced to tend the flocks of Admetus, king of Pherae, when the god was banished from heaven for nine years.
4. Architectural styles popular in the nineteenth century—revivals of classical Greek and medieval European architecture, respectively.

to love labor for its own sake, or perhaps because it keeps them out of worse mischief; to such I have at present nothing to say. Those who would not know what to do with more leisure than they now enjoy, I might advise to work twice as hard as they do,—work till they pay for themselves, and get their free papers. For myself I found that the occupation of a day-laborer was the most independent of any, especially as it required only thirty or forty days in a year to support one. The laborer's day ends with the going down of the sun, and he is then free to devote himself to his chosen pursuit, independent of his labor; but his employer, who speculates from month to month, has no respite from one end of the year to the other.

In short, I am convinced, both by faith and experience, that to maintain one's self on this earth is not a hardship but a pastime, if we will live simply and wisely; as the pursuits of the simpler nations are still the sports of the more artificial. It is not necessary that a man should earn his living by the sweat of his brow, unless he sweats easier than I do.

One young man of my acquaintance, who has inherited some acres, told me that he thought he should live as I did, *if he had the means.* I would not have any one adopt *my* mode of living on any account; for, beside that before he has fairly learned it I may have found out another for myself, I desire that there may be as many different persons in the world as possible; but I would have each one be very careful to find out and pursue *his own* way, and not his father's or his mother's or his neighbor's instead. The youth may build or plant or sail, only let him not be hindered from doing that which he tells me he would like to do. It is by a mathematical point only that we are wise, as the sailor or the fugitive slave keeps the polestar in his eye; but that is sufficient guidance for all our life. We may not arrive at our port within a calculable period, but we would preserve the true course.

Undoubtedly, in this case, what is true for one is truer still for a thousand, as a large house is not proportionally more expensive than a small one, since one roof may cover, one cellar underlie, and one wall separate several apartments. But for my part, I preferred the solitary dwelling. Moreover, it will commonly be cheaper to build the whole yourself than to convince another of the advantage of the common wall; and when you have done this, the common partition, to be much cheaper, must be a thin one, and that other may prove a bad neighbor, and also not keep his side in repair. The only coöperation which is commonly possible is exceedingly partial and superficial; and what little true coöperation there is, is as if it were not, being a harmony inaudible to men. If a man has faith he will coöperate with equal faith every where; if he has not faith, he will continue to live like the rest of the world, whatever company he is joined to. To coöperate, in the highest as well as the lowest sense, means *to get our living together.* I heard it proposed lately that two young men should travel together over the world, the one without money, earning his means as he went, before the mast and behind the plough, the other carrying a bill of exchange in his pocket. It was easy to see that they could not long be companions or coöperate, since one would not *operate* at all. They would part at the first interesting crisis in their adventures. Above all, as I have implied, the man who goes alone can start to-day; but he who travels with another must wait till that other is ready, and it may be a long time before they get off.

But all this is very selfish, I have heard some of my townsmen say. I confess that I have hitherto indulged very little in philanthropic enterprises. I have made some sacrifices to a sense of duty, and among others have sacrificed this pleasure also. There are those who have used all their arts to persuade me to undertake the support of some poor family in the town; and if I had nothing to do,—for the devil finds employment for the idle,—I might try my hand at some such pastime as that. However, when I have thought to indulge myself in this respect, and lay their Heaven under an obligation by maintaining certain poor persons in all respects as comfortably as I maintain myself, and have even ventured so far as to make them the offer, they have one and all unhesitatingly preferred to remain poor. While my townsmen and women are devoted in so many ways to the good of their fellows, I trust that one at least may be spared to other and less humane pursuits. You must have a genius for charity as well as for any thing else. As for Doing-good, that is one of the professions which are full. Moreover, I have tried it fairly, and, strange as it may seem, am satisfied that it does not agree with my constitution. Probably I should not consciously and deliberately forsake my particular calling to do the good which society demands of me, to save the universe from annihilation; and I believe that a like but infinitely greater steadfastness elsewhere is all that now preserves it. But I would not stand between any man and his genius; and to him who does this work, which I decline, with his whole heart and soul and life, I would say, Persevere, even if the world call it doing evil, as it is most likely they will.

I am far from supposing that my case is a peculiar one; no doubt many of my readers would make a similar defence. At doing something,—I will not engage that my neighbors shall pronounce it good,—I do not hesitate to say that I should be a capital fellow to hire; but what that is, it is for my employer to find out. What *good* I do, in the common sense of that word, must be aside from my main path, and for the most part wholly unintended. Men say, practically, Begin where you are and such as you are, without aiming mainly to become of more worth, and with kindness aforethought go about doing good. If I were to preach at all in this strain, I should say rather, Set about being good. As if the sun should stop when he had kindled his fires up to the splendor of a moon or a star of the sixth magnitude, and go about like a Robin Goodfellow,[5] peeping in at every cottage window, inspiring lunatics, and tainting meats, and making darkness visible, instead of steadily increasing his genial heat and beneficence till he is of such brightness that no mortal can look him in the face, and then, and in the mean while too, going about the world in his own orbit, doing it good, or rather, as a truer philosophy has discovered, the world going about him getting good. When Phaeton,[6] wishing to prove his heavenly birth by his beneficence, had the sun's chariot but one day, and drove out of the beaten track, he burned several blocks of houses in the lower streets of heaven, and scorched the surface of the earth, and dried up every spring, and made the great desert of Sahara, till at length Jupiter hurled him headlong to the earth with a thunderbolt, and the sun, through grief at his death, did not shine for a year.[7]

There is no odor so bad as that which arises from goodness tainted. It is human, it is divine, carrion. If I knew for a certainty that a man was coming to my house with the conscious design of doing me good, I should run for my life, as from that dry and parching wind of the African deserts called the simoom, which fills the mouth and nose and ears and eyes with dust till you are suffocated, for fear that I should get some of his good done to me,—some of its virus mingled with my blood. No,—in this case I would rather suffer evil the natural way. A man is not a good *man* to me because he will feed me if I should be starving, or warm me if I should be freezing, or pull me out of a ditch if I should ever fall into one. I can find you a Newfoundland dog that will do as much. Philanthropy is not love for one's fellow-man in the broadest sense. Howard[8] was no doubt an exceedingly kind and worthy man in his way, and has his reward; but, comparatively speaking, what are a hundred Howards to *us*, if their

5. In English folklore, a mischievous elf; also known as Puck.
6. In Greek mythology, the son of Helios (the sun).
7. From Ovid's *Metamorphoses* 2.1–400; Jupiter is the chief god in Roman mythology.
8. John Howard (1726?–90), English prison reformer.

philanthropy do not help *us* in our best estate, when we are most worthy to be helped? I never heard of a philanthropic meeting in which it was sincerely proposed to do any good to me, or the like of me.

The Jesuits [9] were quite balked by those Indians who, being burned at the stake, suggested new modes of torture to their tormentors. Being superior to physical suffering, it sometimes chanced that they were superior to any consolation which the missionaries could offer; and the law to do as you would be done by fell with less persuasiveness on the ears of those, who, for their part, did not care how they were done by, who loved their enemies after a new fashion, and came very near freely forgiving them all they did.

Be sure that you give the poor the aid they most need, though it be your example which leaves them far behind. If you give money, spend yourself with it, and do not merely abandon it to them. We make curious mistakes sometimes. Often the poor man is not so cold and hungry as he is dirty and ragged and gross. It is partly his taste, and not merely his misfortune. If you give him money, he will perhaps buy more rags with it. I was wont to pity the clumsy Irish laborers who cut ice on the pond, in such mean and ragged clothes, while I shivered in my more tidy and somewhat more fashionable garments, till, one bitter cold day, one who had slipped into the water came to my house to warm him, and I saw him strip off three pairs of pants and two pairs of stockings ere he got down to the skin, though they were dirty and ragged enough, it is true, and that he could afford to refuse the *extra* garments which I offered him, he had so many *intra* ones. This ducking was the very thing he needed. Then I began to pity myself, and I saw that it would be a greater charity to bestow on me a flannel shirt than a whole slop-shop on him. There are a thousand hacking at the branches of evil to one who is striking at the root, and it may be that he who bestows the largest amount of time and money on the needy is doing the most by his mode of life to produce that misery which he strives in vain to relieve. It is the pious slave-breeder devoting the proceeds of every tenth slave to buy a Sunday's liberty for the rest. Some show their kindness to the poor by employing them in their kitchens. Would they not be kinder if they employed themselves there? You boast of spending a tenth part of your income in charity; may be you should spend the nine tenths so, and done with it. Society recovers only a tenth part of the property then. Is this owing to the generosity of him in

9. A religious order of the Roman Catholic faith, which attempted to convert the Indians to Christianity.

whose possession it is found, or to the remissness of the officers of justice?

Philanthropy is almost the only virtue which is sufficiently appreciated by mankind. Nay, it is greatly overrated; and it is our selfishness which overrates it. A robust poor man, one sunny day here in Concord, praised a fellow-townsman to me, because, as he said, he was kind to the poor; meaning himself. The kind uncles and aunts of the race are more esteemed than its true spiritual fathers and mothers. I once heard a reverend lecturer on England, a man of learning and intelligence, after enumerating her scientific, literary, and political worthies, Shakspeare, Bacon, Cromwell, Milton, Newton, and others, speak next of her Christian heroes, whom, as if his profession required it of him, he elevated to a place far above all the rest, as the greatest of the great. They were Penn, Howard, and Mrs. Fry.[1] Every one must feel the falsehood and cant of this. The last were not England's best men and women; only, perhaps, her best philanthropists.

I would not subtract any thing from the praise that is due to philanthropy, but merely demand justice for all who by their lives and works are a blessing to mankind. I do not value chiefly a man's uprightness and benevolence, which are, as it were, his stem and leaves. Those plants of whose greenness withered we make herb tea for the sick, serve but a humble use, and are most employed by quacks. I want the flower and fruit of a man; that some fragrance be wafted over from him to me, and some ripeness flavor our intercourse. His goodness must not be a partial and transitory act, but a constant superfluity, which costs him nothing and of which he is unconscious. This is a charity that hides a multitude of sins. The philanthropist too often surrounds mankind with the remembrance of his own cast-off griefs as an atmosphere, and calls it sympathy. We should impart our courage, and not our despair, our health and ease, and not our disease, and take care that this does not spread by contagion. From what southern plains comes up the voice of wailing? Under what latitudes reside the heathen to whom we would send light? Who is that intemperate and brutal man whom we would redeem? If any thing ail a man, so that he does not perform his functions, if he have a pain in his bowels even,—for that is the seat of sympathy,—he forthwith sets about reforming—the world. Being a microcosm himself, he discovers, and it is a true discovery, and he is the man to make it,— that the world has been eating green apples; to his eyes, in fact, the globe itself is a great green apple, which there is danger awful to

1. William Penn (1644–1718), humanitarian and founder of Pennsylvania; John Howard (1726?–90), English prison reformer; Elizabeth Fry (1780–1845), English prison reformer.

think of that the children of men will nibble before it is ripe; and straightway his drastic philanthropy seeks out the Esquimaux and the Patagonian,[2] and embraces the populous Indian and Chinese villages; and thus, by a few years of philanthropic activity, the powers in the mean while using him for their own ends, no doubt, he cures himself of his dyspepsia, the globe acquires a faint blush on one or both of its cheeks, as if it were beginning to be ripe, and life loses its crudity and is once more sweet and wholesome to live. I never dreamed of any enormity greater than I have committed. I never knew, and never shall know, a worse man than myself.

I believe that what so saddens the reformer is not his sympathy with his fellows in distress, but, though he be the holiest son of God, is his private ail. Let this be righted, let the spring come to him, the morning rise over his couch, and he will forsake his generous companions without apology. My excuse for not lecturing against the use of tobacco is, that I never chewed it; that is a penalty which reformed tobacco-chewers have to pay; though there are things enough I have chewed, which I could lecture against. If you should ever be betrayed into any of these philanthropies, do not let your left hand know what your right hand does, for it is not worth knowing. Rescue the drowning and tie your shoe-strings. Take your time, and set about some free labor.

Our manners have been corrupted by communication with the saints. Our hymn-books resound with a melodious cursing of God and enduring him forever. One would say that even the prophets and redeemers had rather consoled the fears than confirmed the hopes of man. There is nowhere recorded a simple and irrepressible satisfaction with the gift of life, any memorable praise of God. All health and success does me good, however far off and withdrawn it may appear; all disease and failure helps to make me sad and does me evil, however much sympathy it may have with me or I with it. If, then, we would indeed restore mankind by truly Indian, botanic, magnetic, or natural means, let us first be as simple and well as Nature ourselves, dispel the clouds which hang over our own brows, and take up a little life into our pores. Do not stay to be an overseer of the poor, but endeavor to become one of the worthies of the world.

I read in the Gulistan, or Flower Garden, of Sheik Sadi of Shiraz, that "They asked a wise man, saying; Of the many celebrated trees which the Most High God has created lofty and umbrageous, they call none azad, or free, excepting the cypress, which bears no fruit; what mystery is there in this? He replied;

2. A native of the southernmost part of South America.

Each has its appropriate produce, and appointed season, during the continuance of which it is fresh and blooming, and during their absence dry and withered; to neither of which states is the cypress exposed, being always flourishing; and of this nature are the azads, or religious independents.—Fix not thy heart on that which is transitory; for the Dijlah, or Tigris, will continue to flow through Bagdad after the race of caliphs [3] is extinct: if thy hand has plenty, be liberal as the date tree; but if it affords nothing to give away, be an azad, or free man, like the cypress."[4]

COMPLEMENTAL VERSES.[5]

THE PRETENSIONS OF POVERTY.

"Thou dost presume too much, poor needy wretch,
To claim a station in the firmament,
Because thy humble cottage, or thy tub,
Nurses some lazy or pedantic virtue
In the cheap sunshine or by shady springs,
With roots and pot-herbs; where thy right hand,
Tearing those humane passions from the mind,
Upon whose stocks fair blooming virtues flourish,
Degradeth nature, and benumbeth sense,
And, Gorgon-like, turns active men to stone.
We not require the dull society
Of your necessitated temperance,
Or that unnatural stupidity
That knows nor joy nor sorrow; nor your forc'd
Falsely exalted passive fortitude
Above the active. This low abject brood,
That fix their seats in mediocrity,
Become your servile minds; but we advance
Such virtues only as admit excess,
Brave, bounteous acts, regal magnificence,
All-seeing prudence, magnanimity
That knows no bound, and that heroic virtue
For which antiquity hath left no name,
But patterns only, such as Hercules,
Achilles, Theseus. Back to thy loath'd cell;
And when thou seest the new enlightened sphere,
Study to know but what those worthies were."

T. Carew.

---

3. Bagdad is the capital of Iraq, located on the Dijlah (or Tigris) river; a caliph is a Moslem ruler.
4. Muslih-ud-Din (Saadi) (1184?–1291), Persian poet; from his *The Gulistan, or Rose Garden*.
5. By Thomas Carew (1595?–1645), from *Coelum Britannicum*; Thoreau added the title and modernized the spelling.

Where I Lived, and What I Lived for

At a certain season of our life we are accustomed to consider every spot as the possible site of a house. I have thus surveyed the country on every side within a dozen miles of where I live. In imagination I have bought all the farms in succession, for all were to be bought, and I knew their price. I walked over each farmer's premises, tasted his wild apples, discoursed on husbandry with him, took his farm at his price, at any price, mortgaging it to him in my mind; even put a higher price on it,—took every thing but a deed of it,—took his word for his deed, for I dearly love to talk,—cultivated it, and him too to some extent, I trust, and withdrew when I had enjoyed it long enough, leaving him to carry it on. This experience entitled me to be regarded as a sort of real-estate broker by my friends. Wherever I sat, there I might live, and the landscape radiated from me accordingly. What is a house but a *sedes*, a seat?—better if a country seat. I discovered many a site for a house not likely to be soon improved, which some might have thought too far from the village, but to my eyes the village was too far from it. Well, there I might live, I said; and there I did live, for an hour, a summer and a winter life; saw how I could let the years run off, buffet the winter through, and see the spring come in. The future inhabitants of this region, wherever they may place their houses, may be sure that they have been anticipated. An afternoon sufficed to lay out the land into orchard, woodlot, and pasture, and to decide what fine oaks or pines should be left to stand before the door, and whence each blasted tree could be seen to the best advantage; and then I let it lie, fallow perchance, for a man is rich in proportion to the number of things which he can afford to let alone.

My imagination carried me so far that I even had the refusal of several farms,—the refusal was all I wanted,—but I never got my fingers burned by actual possession. The nearest that I came to actual possession was when I bought the Hollowell place, and had begun to sort my seeds, and collected materials with which to make a wheelbarrow to carry it on or off with; but before the owner gave me a deed of it, his wife—every man has such a wife—changed her mind and wished to keep it, and he offered me ten dollars to release him. Now, to speak the truth, I had but ten cents in the world, and it surpassed my arithmetic to tell, if I was that man who had ten cents, or who had a farm, or ten dollars, or all together. However, I let him keep the ten dollars and the farm too, for I had carried it far enough; or rather, to be generous, I sold him the farm for just what I gave for it, and, as he was not a rich man, made him a present of ten dollars, and still had my ten cents, and seeds, and materials for a wheelbarrow left. I found thus that I had been a rich man without any damage to my poverty. But I retained the landscape, and I have since annually carried off what it yielded without a wheelbarrow. With respect to landscapes,—

"I am monarch of all I *survey*,
My right there is none to dispute."[1]

I have frequently seen a poet withdraw, having enjoyed the most valuable part of a farm, while the crusty farmer supposed that he had got a few wild apples only. Why, the owner does not know it for many years when a poet has put his farm in rhyme, the most admirable kind of invisible fence, has fairly impounded it, milked it, skimmed it, and got all the cream, and left the farmer only the skimmed milk.

The real attractions of the Hollowell farm, to me, were; its complete retirement, being about two miles from the village, half a mile from the nearest neighbor, and separated from the highway by a broad field; its bounding on the river, which the owner said protected it by its fogs from frosts in the spring, though that was nothing to me; the gray color and ruinous state of the house and barn, and the dilapidated fences, which put such an interval between me and the last occupant; the hollow and lichen-covered apple trees, gnawed by rabbits, showing what kind of neighbors I should have; but above all, the recollection I had of it from my earliest voyages up the river, when the house was concealed behind a dense grove of red maples, through which I heard the house-dog bark. I was in haste to buy it, before the proprietor finished getting out some rocks, cutting down the hollow apple trees, and grubbing up some young birches which had sprung up in the pasture, or, in short, had made any more of his improvements. To enjoy these advantages I was ready to carry it on; like Atlas,[2] to take the world on my shoulders,—I never heard what compensation he received for that,—and do all those things which had no other motive or excuse but that I might pay for it and be unmolested in my possession of it; for I knew all the while that it would yield the most abundant crop of the kind I wanted if I could only afford to let it alone. But it turned out as I have said.

All that I could say, then, with respect to farming on a large scale, (I have always cultivated a garden,) was, that I had had

1. William Cowper (1731–1800), from his "Verses Supposed to Be Written by Alexander Selkirk"; Selkirk was Daniel Defoe's model for Robinson Crusoe. Thoreau, a surveyor, italicized the final word of the first line to emphasize the pun.

2. According to Greek mythology, Atlas supported the sky on his shoulders as punishment for having taken part in the revolt of the Titans against Zeus.

my seeds ready. Many think that seeds improve with age. I have no doubt that time discriminates between the good and the bad; and when at last I shall plant, I shall be less likely to be disappointed. But I would say to my fellows, once for all, As long as possible live free and uncommitted. It makes but little difference whether you are committed to a farm or the county jail.

Old Cato, whose "De Re Rusticâ" is my "Cultivator," says, and the only translation I have seen makes sheer nonsense of the passage, "When you think of getting a farm, turn it thus in your mind, not to buy greedily; nor spare your pains to look at it, and do not think it enough to go round it once. The oftener you go there the more it will please you, if it is good." I think I shall not buy greedily, but go round and round it as long as I live, and be buried in it first, that it may please me the more at last.

The present was my next experiment of this kind, which I purpose to describe more at length; for convenience, putting the experience of two years into one. As I have said, I do not propose to write an ode to dejection, but to brag as lustily as chanticleer in the morning, standing on his roost, if only to wake my neighbors up.

When first I took up my abode in the woods, that is, began to spend my nights as well as days there, which, by accident, was on Independence day, or the fourth of July, 1845, my house was not finished for winter, but was merely a defence against the rain, without plastering or chimney, the walls being of rough weather-stained boards, with wide chinks, which made it cool at night. The upright white hewn studs and freshly planed door and window casings gave it a clean and airy look, especially in the morning, when its timbers were saturated with dew, so that I fancied that by noon some sweet gum would exude from them. To my imagination it retained throughout the day more or less of this auroral character, reminding me of a certain house on a mountain which I had visited the year before. This was an airy and unplastered cabin, fit to entertain a travelling god, and where a goddess might trail her garments. The winds which passed over my dwelling were such as sweep over the ridges of mountains, bearing the broken strains, or celestial parts only, of terrestrial music. The morning wind forever blows, the poem of creation is uninterrupted; but few are the ears that hear it. Olympus[3] is but the outside of the earth every where.

The only house I had been the owner of before, if I except a boat, was a tent, which I used occasionally when making excursions in the summer, and this is still rolled up in my garret; but the

---

3. Mount Olympus; in Greek mythology, the residence of the gods.

boat, after passing from hand to hand, has gone down the stream of time. With this more substantial shelter about me, I had made some progress toward settling in the world. This frame, so slightly clad, was a sort of crystallization around me, and reacted on the builder. It was suggestive somewhat as a picture in outlines. I did not need to go out doors to take the air, for the atmosphere within had lost none of its freshness. It was not so much within doors as behind a door where I sat, even in the rainiest weather. The Harivansa [4] says, "An abode without birds is like a meat without seasoning." Such was not my abode, for I found myself suddenly neighbor to the birds; not by having imprisoned one, but having caged myself near them. I was not only nearer to some of those which commonly frequent the garden and the orchard, but to those wilder and more thrilling songsters of the forest which never, or rarely, serenade a villager,—the wood-thrush, the veery, the scarlet tanager, the field-sparrow, the whippoorwill, and many others.

I was seated by the shore of a small pond, about a mile and a half south of the village of Concord and somewhat higher than it, in the midst of an extensive wood between that town and Lincoln, and about two miles south of that our only field known to fame, Concord Battle Ground; [5] but I was so low in the woods that the opposite shore, half a mile off, like the rest, covered with wood, was my most distant horizon. For the first week, whenever I looked out on the pond it impressed me like a tarn high up on the side of a mountain, its bottom far above the surface of other lakes, and, as the sun arose, I saw it throwing off its nightly clothing of mist, and here and there, by degrees, its soft ripples or its smooth reflecting surface was revealed, while the mists, like ghosts, were stealthily withdrawing in every direction into the woods, as at the breaking up of some nocturnal conventicle. The very dew seemed to hang upon the trees later into the day than usual, as on the sides of mountains.

This small lake was of most value as a neighbor in the intervals of a gentle rain storm in August, when, both air and water being perfectly still, but the sky overcast, mid-afternoon had all the serenity of evening, and the wood-thrush sang around, and was heard from shore to shore. A lake like this is never smoother than at such a time; and the clear portion of the air above it being shallow and darkened by clouds, the water, full of light and re-flections, becomes a lower heaven itself so much the more im-portant. From a hill top near by, where the wood had been re-cently cut off, there was a pleasing vista southward across the

4. Hindu epic poem concerning the god Krishna, written about the fifth century A.D.

5. Site of the opening battle of the American Revolution, April 19, 1775.

pond, through a wide indentation in the hills which form the
shore there, where their opposite sides sloping toward each other
suggested a stream flowing out in that direction through a wooded
valley, but stream there was none. That way I looked between and
over the near green hills to some distant and higher ones in the
horizon, tinged with blue. Indeed, by standing on tiptoe I could
catch a glimpse of some of the peaks of the still bluer and more
distant mountain ranges in the north-west, those true-blue coins
from heaven's own mint, and also of some portion of the village.
But in other directions, even from this point, I could not see over
or beyond the woods which surrounded me. It is well to have
some water in your neighborhood, to give buoyancy to and float
the earth. One value even of the smallest well is, that when you
look into it you see that earth is not continent but insular. This is as
important as that it keeps butter cool. When I looked across the
pond from this peak toward the Sudbury meadows, which in time
of flood I distinguished elevated perhaps by a mirage in their seeth-
ing valley, like a coin in a basin, all the earth beyond the pond
appeared like a thin crust insulated and floated even by this small
sheet of intervening water, and I was reminded that this on which
I dwelt was but *dry land.*

Though the view from my door was still more contracted, I did
not feel crowded or confined in the least. There was pasture
enough for my imagination. The low shrub-oak plateau to which
the opposite shore arose, stretched away toward the prairies of
the West and the steppes of Tartary, affording ample room for all
the roving families of men. "There are none happy in the world
but beings who enjoy freely a vast horizon,"—said Damodara,[6]
when his herds required new and larger pastures.

Both place and time were changed, and I dwelt nearer to those
parts of the universe and to those eras in history which had most
attracted me. Where I lived was as far off as many a region
viewed nightly by astronomers. We are wont to imagine rare and
delectable places in some remote and more celestial corner of the
system, behind the constellation of Cassiopeia's Chair, far from
noise and disturbance. I discovered that my house actually had its
site in such a withdrawn, but forever new and unprofaned, part of
the universe. If it were worth the while to settle in those parts near
to the Pleiades or the Hyades, to Aldebaran or Altair,[7] then I was
really there, or at an equal remoteness from the life which I had
left behind, dwindled and twinkling with as fine a ray to my
nearest neighbor, and to be seen only in moonless nights by him.
Such was that part of creation where I had squatted;—

6. Quoted from the *Harivansa.* Damodara is
another name for Krishna.

7. Like Cassiopeia's Chair, Pleiades and Aldebaran are constellations of stars.

"There was a shepherd that did live,
    And held his thoughts as high
As were the mounts whereon his flocks
    Did hourly feed him by." [8]

What should we think of the shepherd's life if his flocks always
wandered to higher pastures than his thoughts?

Every morning was a cheerful invitation to make my life of
equal simplicity, and I may say innocence, with Nature herself. I
have been as sincere a worshipper of Aurora as the Greeks. I got
up early and bathed in the pond; that was a religious exercise, and
one of the best things which I did. They say that characters were
engraven on the bathing tub of king Tching-thang to this effect:
"Renew thyself completely each day; do it again, and again, and
forever again." [9] I can understand that. Morning brings back the
heroic ages. I was as much affected by the faint hum of a mosquito making its invisible and unimaginable tour through my apartment at earliest dawn, when I was sitting with door and windows
open, as I could be by any trumpet that ever sang of fame. It was
Homer's requiem; itself an Iliad and Odyssey in the air, singing its
own wrath and wanderings. There was something cosmical about
it; a standing advertisement, till forbidden, of the everlasting vigor
and fertility of the world. The morning, which is the most memorable season of the day, is the awakening hour. Then there is
least somnolence in us; and for an hour, at least, some part of us
awakes which slumbers all the rest of the day and night. Little is
to be expected of that day, if it can be called a day, to which we
are not awakened by our Genius, but by the mechanical nudgings
of some servitor, are not awakened by our own newly-acquired
force and aspirations from within, accompanied by the undulations
of celestial music, instead of factory bells, and a fragrance filling
the air—to a higher life than we fell asleep from; and thus the
darkness bear its fruit, and prove itself to be good, no less than
the light. That man who does not believe that each day contains
an earlier, more sacred, and auroral hour than he has yet profaned, has despaired of life, and is pursuing a descending and
darkening way. After a partial cessation of his sensuous life, the
soul of man, or its organs rather, are reinvigorated each day, and
his Genius tries again what noble life it can make. All memorable
events, I should say, transpire in morning time and in a morning
atmosphere. The Vedas [1] say, "All intelligences awake with the
morning." Poetry and art, and the fairest and most memorable of
the actions of men, date from such an hour. All poets and heroes,
like Memnon, are the children of Aurora, and emit their music

---

8. An anonymous Jacobean poem set to music
and published in *The Muses Garden* (1610).

9. Confucius, *The Great Learning*.
1. Ancient Hindu scriptures.

at sunrise. To him whose elastic and vigorous thought keeps pace with the sun, the day is a perpetual morning. It matters not what the clocks say or the attitudes and labors of men. Morning is when I am awake and there is a dawn in me. Moral reform is the effort to throw off sleep. Why is it that men give so poor an account of their day if they have not been slumbering? They are not such poor calculators. If they had not been overcome with drowsiness they would have performed something. The millions are awake enough for physical labor; but only one in a million is awake enough for effective intellectual exertion, only one in a hundred millions to a poetic or divine life. To be awake is to be alive. I have never yet met a man who was quite awake. How could I have looked him in the face?

We must learn to reawaken and keep ourselves awake, not by mechanical aids, but by an infinite expectation of the dawn, which does not forsake us in our soundest sleep. I know of no more encouraging fact than the unquestionable ability of man to elevate his life by a conscious endeavor. It is something to be able to paint a particular picture, or to carve a statue, and so to make a few objects beautiful; but it is far more glorious to carve and paint the very atmosphere and medium through which we look, which morally we can do. To affect the quality of the day, that is the highest of arts. Every man is tasked to make his life, even in its details, worthy of the contemplation of his most elevated and critical hour. If we refused, or rather used up, such paltry information as we get, the oracles would distinctly inform us how this might be done.

I went to the woods because I wished to live deliberately, to front only the essential facts of life, and see if I could not learn what it had to teach, and not, when I came to die, discover that I had not lived. I did not wish to live what was not life, living is so dear; nor did I wish to practise resignation, unless it was quite necessary. I wanted to live deep and suck out all the marrow of life, to live so sturdily and Spartan-like[2] as to put to rout all that was not life, to cut a broad swath and shave close, to drive life into a corner, and reduce it to its lowest terms, and, if it proved to be mean, why then to get the whole and genuine meanness of it, and publish its meanness to the world; or if it were sublime, to know it by experience, and be able to give a true account of it in my next excursion. For most men, it appears to me, are in a strange uncertainty about it, whether it is of the devil or of God, and have *somewhat hastily* concluded that it is the chief end of man here to "glorify God and enjoy him forever."[3]

---

2. The Spartans of ancient Greece were courageous warriors who lived hardy and rigorous
lives.
3. Quoted from the Shorter Catechism.

Still we live meanly, like ants; though the fable tells us that we were long ago changed into men; like pygmies we fight with cranes;[4] it is error upon error, and clout upon clout, and our best virtue has for its occasion a superfluous and evitable wretchedness. Our life is frittered away by detail. An honest man has hardly need to count more than his ten fingers, or in extreme cases he may add his ten toes, and lump the rest. Simplicity, simplicity, simplicity! I say, let your affairs be as two or three, and not a hundred or a thousand; instead of a million count half a dozen, and keep your accounts on your thumb nail. In the midst of this chopping sea of civilized life, such are the clouds and storms and quicksands and thousand-and-one items to be allowed for, that a man has to live, if he would not founder and go to the bottom and not make his port at all, by dead reckoning, and he must be a great calculator indeed who succeeds. Simplify, simplify. Instead of three meals a day, if it be necessary eat but one; instead of a hundred dishes, five; and reduce other things in proportion. Our life is like a German Confederacy,[5] made up of petty states, with its boundary forever fluctuating, so that even a German cannot tell you how it is bounded at any moment. The nation itself, with all its so called internal improvements, which, by the way, are all external and superficial, is just such an unwieldy and overgrown establishment, cluttered with furniture and tripped up by its own traps, ruined by luxury and heedless expense, by want of calculation and a worthy aim, as the million households in the land; and the only cure for it as for them is in a rigid economy, a stern and more than Spartan simplicity of life and elevation of purpose. It lives too fast. Men think that it is essential that the *Nation* have commerce, and export ice, and talk through a telegraph, and ride thirty miles an hour, without a doubt, whether *they* do or not; but whether we should live like baboons or like men, is a little uncertain. If we do not get out sleepers,[6] and forge rails, and devote days and nights to the work, but go to tinkering upon our *lives* to improve *them*, who will build railroads? And if railroads are not built, how shall we get to heaven in season? But if we stay at home and mind our business, who will want railroads? We do not ride on the railroad; it rides upon us. Did you ever think what those sleepers are that underlie the railroad? Each one is a man, an Irishman, or a Yankee man. The rails are laid on them, and they are covered with sand, and the cars run smoothly over them. They are sound sleepers, I assure you. And every few years a new

4. According to Greek mythology, Zeus turned ants into men. The Trojans are compared to cranes fighting pygmies in the *Iliad*, Book 3.

5. A loose collection of states from 1815 to 1866, Germany was unified later in the century under Prince Otto von Bismarck.
6. Wooden railroad ties.

lot is laid down and run over; so that, if some have the pleasure of riding on a rail, others have the misfortune to be ridden upon. And when they run over a man that is walking in his sleep, a supernumerary sleeper in the wrong position, and wake him up, they suddenly stop the cars, and make a hue and cry about it, as if this were an exception. I am glad to know that it takes a gang of men for every five miles to keep the sleepers down and level in their beds as it is, for this is a sign that they may sometime get up again.

Why should we live with such hurry and waste of life? We are determined to be starved before we are hungry. Men say that a stitch in time saves nine, and so they take a thousand stitches to-day to save nine to-morrow. As for *work*, we haven't any of any consequence. We have the Saint Vitus' dance,[7] and cannot possibly keep our heads still. If I should only give a few pulls at the parish bell-rope, as for a fire, that is, without setting the bell, there is hardly a man on his farm in the outskirts of Concord, notwith-standing that press of engagements which was his excuse so many times this morning, nor a boy, nor a woman, I might almost say, but would forsake all and follow that sound, not mainly to save property from the flames, but, if we will confess the truth, much more to see it burn, since burn it must, and we, be it known, did not set it on fire,—or to see it put out, and have a hand in it, if that is done as handsomely; yes, even if it were the parish church itself. Hardly a man takes a half hour's nap after dinner, but when he wakes he holds up his head and asks, "What's the news?" as if the rest of mankind had stood his sentinels. Some give directions to be waked every half hour, doubtless for no other purpose; and then, to pay for it, they tell what they have dreamed. After a night's sleep the news is as indispensable as the breakfast. "Pray tell me any thing new that has happened to a man any where on this globe,"—and he reads it over his coffee and rolls, that a man has had his eyes gouged out this morning on the Wachito River;[8] never dreaming the while that he lives in the dark unfathomed mammoth cave of this world, and has but the rudiment of an eye himself.

For my part, I could easily do without the post-office. I think that there are very few important communications made through it. To speak critically, I never received more than one or two letters in my life—I wrote this some years ago—that were worth the postage. The penny-post is, commonly, an institution through which you seriously offer a man that penny for his thoughts which

7. Chorea, a nervous disease accompanied by involuntary movements, depression, and emotional instability.

8. Now called the Ouachita River; it begins in Arkansas and empties into the Red River in Louisana.

is so often safely offered in jest. And I am sure that I never read any memorable news in a newspaper. If we read of one man robbed, or murdered, or killed by accident, or one house burned, or one vessel wrecked, or one steamboat blown up, or one cow run over on the Western Railroad, or one mad dog killed, or one lot of grasshoppers in the winter,—we never need read of another. One is enough. If you are acquainted with the principle, what do you care for a myriad instances and applications? To a philosopher all *news*, as it is called, is gossip, and they who edit and read it are old women over their tea. Yet not a few are greedy after this gossip. There was such a rush, as I hear, the other day at one of the offices to learn the foreign news by the last arrival, that several large squares of plate glass belonging to the establishment were broken by the pressure,—news which I seriously think a ready wit might write a twelvemonth or twelve years beforehand with sufficient accuracy. As for Spain, for instance, if you know how to throw in Don Carlos and the Infanta, and Don Pedro and Seville and Granada,[9] from time to time in the right proportions,— they may have changed the names a little since I saw the papers,— and serve up a bull-fight when other entertainments fail, it will be true to the letter, and give us as good an idea of the exact state or ruin of things in Spain as the most succinct and lucid reports under this head in the newspapers: and as for England, almost the last significant scrap of news from that quarter was the revolution of 1649; and if you have learned the history of her crops for an average year, you never need attend to that thing again, unless your speculations are of a merely pecuniary character. If one may judge who rarely looks into the newspapers, nothing new does ever happen in foreign parts, a French revolution not excepted.

What news! how much more important to know what that is which was never old! "Kieou-he-yu (great dignitary of the state of Wei) sent a man to Khoung-tseu to know his news. Khoung-tseu caused the messenger to be seated near him, and questioned him in these terms: What is your master doing? The messenger answered with respect: My master desires to diminish the number of his faults, but he cannot accomplish it. The messenger being gone, the philosopher remarked: What a worthy messenger! What a worthy messenger!"[1] The preacher, instead of vexing the ears of drowsy farmers on their day of rest at the end of the week,—for Sunday is the fit conclusion of an ill-spent week, and not the fresh and brave beginning of a new one,—with this one other

9. Thoreau names persons involved in Portuguese and Spanish politics in the 1830s and '40s: Dom Pedro was emperor of Brazil whose daughter became queen of Portugal; Don Car-

los connived against his niece, the Infanta, for the Spanish throne.
1. Confucius, *Analects* 14.

draggletail of a sermon, should shout with thundering voice,—
"Pause! Avast! Why so seeming fast, but deadly slow?"

Shams and delusions are esteemed for soundest truths, while
reality is fabulous. If men would steadily observe realities only,
and not allow themselves to be deluded, life, to compare it with
such things as we know, would be like a fairy tale and the
Arabian Nights' Entertainments.[2] If we respected only what is
inevitable and has a right to be, music and poetry would resound
along the streets. When we are unhurried and wise, we perceive
that only great and worthy things have any permanent and absolute
existence,—that petty fears and petty pleasures are but the shadow
of the reality. This is always exhilarating and sublime. By closing
the eyes and slumbering, and consenting to be deceived by shows,
men establish and confirm their daily life of routine and habit
every where, which still is built on purely illusory foundations.
Children, who play life, discern its true law and relations more
clearly than men, who fail to live it worthily, but who think that
they are wiser by experience, that is, by failure. I have read in a
Hindoo book, that "there was a king's son, who, being expelled
in infancy from his native city, was brought up by a forester, and,
growing up to maturity in that state, imagined himself to belong
to the barbarous race with which he lived. One of his father's
ministers having discovered him, revealed to him what he was,
and the misconception of his character was removed, and he knew
himself to be a prince. So soul," continues the Hindoo philosopher,
"from the circumstances in which it is placed, mistakes its own
character, until the truth is revealed to it by some holy teacher,
and then it knows itself to be *Brahme*."[3] I perceive that we inhabitants of New England live this mean life that we do because
our vision does not penetrate the surface of things. We think that
that *is* which *appears* to be. If a man should walk through this
town and see only the reality, where, think you, would the "Mill-
dam"[4] go to? If he should give us an account of the realities he
beheld there, we should not recognize the place in his description.
Look at a meeting-house, or a court-house, or a jail, or a shop, or
a dwelling-house, and say what that thing really is before a true
gaze, and they would all go to pieces in your account of them.
Men esteem truth remote, in the outskirts of the system, behind
the farthest star, before Adam and after the last man. In eternity
there is indeed something true and sublime. But all these times and
places and occasions are now and here. God himself culminates

---

2. A collection of ancient Persian, Indian, and
Arabian tales compiled about the tenth century
and including, among others, tales of Aladdin,
Ali Baba, and Sinbad the Sailor.

3. The essence of spiritual being in Hindu
thought.
4. The general meeting place and business
center of Concord.

in the present moment, and will never be more divine in the lapse of all the ages. And we are enabled to apprehend at all what is sublime and noble only by the perpetual instilling and drenching of the reality that surrounds us. The universe constantly and obediently answers to our conceptions; whether we travel fast or slow, the track is laid for us. Let us spend our lives in conceiving then. The poet or the artist never yet had so fair and noble a design but some of his posterity at least could accomplish it.

Let us spend one day as deliberately as Nature, and not be thrown off the track by every nutshell and mosquito's wing that falls on the rails. Let us rise early and fast, or break fast, gently and without perturbation; let company come and let company go, let the bells ring and the children cry,—determined to make a day of it. Why should we knock under and go with the stream? Let us not be upset and overwhelmed in that terrible rapid and whirlpool called a dinner, situated in the meridian shallows. Weather this danger and you are safe, for the rest of the way is down hill. With unrelaxed nerves, with morning vigor, sail by it, looking another way, tied to the mast like Ulysses.[5] If the engine whistles, let it whistle till it is hoarse for its pains. If the bell rings, why should we run? We will consider what kind of music they are like. Let us settle ourselves, and work and wedge our feet downward through the mud and slush of opinion, and prejudice, and tradition, and delusion, and appearance, that alluvion which covers the globe, through Paris and London, through New York and Boston and Concord, through church and state, through poetry and philosophy and religion, till we come to a hard bottom and rocks in place, which we can call *reality*, and say, This is, and no mistake; and then begin, having a *point d'appui*,[6] below freshet and frost and fire, a place where you might found a wall or a state, or set a lamp-post safely, or perhaps a gauge, not a Nilometer,[7] but a Realometer, that future ages might know how deep a freshet of shams and appearances had gathered from time to time. If you stand right fronting and face to face to a fact, you will see the sun glimmer on both its surfaces, as if it were a cimeter, and feel its sweet edge dividing you through the heart and marrow, and so you will happily conclude your mortal career. Be it life or death, we crave only reality. If we are really dying, let us hear the rattle in our throats and feel cold in the extremities; if we are alive, let us go about our business.

Time is but the stream I go a-fishing in. I drink at it; but while

5. The Roman name of Odysseus, who had himself tied to the mast so that he might both hear and resist the alluring and fatal song of the Sirens.

6. A base; a point of support.
7. An ancient instrument for recording the rise and fall of the Nile River in Egypt.

I drink I see the sandy bottom and detect how shallow it is. Its thin current slides away, but eternity remains. I would drink deeper; fish in the sky, whose bottom is pebbly with stars. I cannot count one. I know not the first letter of the alphabet. I have always been regretting that I was not as wise as the day I was born. The intellect is a cleaver; it discerns and rifts its way into the secret of things. I do not wish to be any more busy with my hands than is necessary. My head is hands and feet. I feel all my best faculties concentrated in it. My instinct tells me that my head is an organ for burrowing, as some creatures use their snout and fore-paws, and with it I would mine and burrow my way through these hills. I think that the richest vein is somewhere hereabouts; so by the divining rod and thin rising vapors I judge; and here I will begin to mine.

Reading

With a little more deliberation in the choice of their pursuits, all men would perhaps become essentially students and observers, for certainly their nature and destiny are interesting to all alike. In accumulating property for ourselves or our posterity, in founding a family or a state, or acquiring fame even, we are mortal; but in dealing with truth we are immortal, and need fear no change nor accident. The oldest Egyptian or Hindoo philosopher raised a corner of the veil from the statue of the divinity; and still the trembling robe remains raised, and I gaze upon as fresh a glory as he did, since it was I in him that was then so bold, and it is he in me that now reviews the vision. No dust has settled on that robe; no time has elapsed since that divinity was revealed. That time which we really improve, or which is improvable, is neither past, present, nor future.

My residence was more favorable, not only to thought, but to serious reading, than a university; and though I was beyond the range of the ordinary circulating library, I had more than ever come within the influence of those books which circulate round the world, whose sentences were first written on bark, and are now merely copied from time to time on to linen paper. Says the poet Mîr Camar Uddîn Mast,[1] "Being seated to run through the region of the spiritual world; I have had this advantage in books. To be intoxicated by a single glass of wine; I have experienced this pleasure when I have drunk the liquor of the esoteric doctrines." I kept Homer's Iliad on my table through the summer, though I

---

1. An eighteenth-century Persian poet; quoted from Garcin de Tassy, *Histoire de la Litterature Hindoui* (1839).

looked at his page only now and then. Incessant labor with my hands, at first, for I had my house to finish and my beans to hoe at the same time, made more study impossible. Yet I sustained myself by the prospect of such reading in future. I read one or two shallow books of travel in the intervals of my work, till that employment made me ashamed of myself, and I asked where it was then that *I* lived.

The student may read Homer or Æschylus [2] in the Greek without danger of dissipation or luxuriousness, for it implies that he in some measure emulate their heroes, and consecrate morning hours to their pages. The heroic books, even if printed in the character of our mother tongue, will always be in a language dead to degenerate times; and we must laboriously seek the meaning of each word and line, conjecturing a larger sense than common use permits out of what wisdom and valor and generosity we have. The modern cheap and fertile press, with all its translations, has done little to bring us nearer to the heroic writers of antiquity. They seem as solitary, and the letter in which they are printed as rare and curious, as ever. It is worth the expense of youthful days and costly hours, if you learn only some words of an ancient language, which are raised out of the trivialness of the street, to be perpetual suggestions and provocations. It is not in vain that the farmer remembers and repeats the few Latin words which he has heard. Men sometimes speak as if the study of the classics would at length make way for more modern and practical studies; but the adventurous student will always study classics, in whatever language they may be written and however ancient they may be. For what are the classics but the noblest recorded thoughts of man? They are the only oracles which are not decayed, and there are such answers to the most modern inquiry in them as Delphi and Dodona [3] never gave. We might as well omit to study Nature because she is old. To read well, that is, to read true books in a true spirit, is a noble exercise, and one that will task the reader more than any exercise which the customs of the day esteem. It requires a training such as the athletes underwent, the steady intention almost of the whole life to this object. Books must be read as deliberately and reservedly as they were written. It is not enough even to be able to speak the language of that nation by which they are written, for there is a memorable interval between the spoken and the written language, the language heard and the language read. The one is commonly transitory, a sound, a tongue, a dialect merely, almost brutish, and we learn it unconsciously, like the brutes, of our mothers. The other is the

2. Greek dramatist (525–456 B.C.) whose tragedies *Prometheus Bound* and *Seven Against Thebes* Thoreau translated in the early 1840s.

3. Famous oracles of ancient Greece.

maturity and experience of that; if that is our mother tongue, this is our father tongue, a reserved and select expression, too significant to be heard by the ear, which we must be born again in order to speak. The crowds of men who merely *spoke* the Greek and Latin tongues in the middle ages were not entitled by the accident of birth to *read* the works of genius written in those languages; for these were not written in that Greek or Latin which they knew, but in the select language of literature. They had not learned the nobler dialects of Greece and Rome, but the very materials on which they were written were waste paper to them, and they prized instead a cheap contemporary literature. But when the several nations of Europe had acquired distinct though rude written languages of their own, sufficient for the purposes of their rising literatures, then first learning revived, and scholars were enabled to discern from that remoteness the treasures of antiquity. What the Roman and Grecian multitude could not *hear*, after the lapse of ages a few scholars *read*, and a few scholars only are still reading it.

However much we may admire the orator's occasional bursts of eloquence, the noblest written words are commonly as far behind or above the fleeting spoken language as the firmament with its stars is behind the clouds. *There* are the stars, and they who can may read them. The astronomers forever comment on and observe them. They are not exhalations like our daily colloquies and vaporous breath. What is called eloquence in the forum is commonly found to be rhetoric in the study. The orator yields to the inspiration of a transient occasion, and speaks to the mob before him, to those who can *hear* him; but the writer, whose more equable life is his occasion, and who would be distracted by the event and the crowd which inspire the orator, speaks to the intellect and heart of mankind, to all in any age who can *understand* him.

No wonder that Alexander[4] carried the Iliad with him on his expeditions in a precious casket. A written word is the choicest of relics. It is something at once more intimate with us and more universal than any other work of art. It is the work of art nearest to life itself. It may be translated into every language, and not only be read but actually breathed from all human lips;—not be represented on canvas or in marble only, but be carved out of the breath of life itself. The symbol of an ancient man's thought becomes a modern man's speech. Two thousand summers have imparted to the monuments of Grecian literature, as to her marbles, only a maturer golden and autumnal tint, for they have carried their own serene and

4. Alexander the Great of Macedon (356–323 B.C.), king and conqueror of the Persian empire. The practice Thoreau describes is recorded in Plutarch's *Lives*.

celestial atmosphere into all lands to protect them against the corrosion of time. Books are the treasured wealth of the world and the
fit inheritance of generations and nations. Books, the oldest and the
best, stand naturally and rightfully on the shelves of every cottage.
They have no cause of their own to plead, but while they enlighten
and sustain the reader his common sense will not refuse them.
Their authors are a natural and irresistible aristocracy in every
society, and, more than kings or emperors, exert an influence on
mankind. When the illiterate and perhaps scornful trader has
earned by enterprise and industry his coveted leisure and independence, and is admitted to the circles of wealth and fashion,
he turns inevitably at last to those still higher but yet inaccessible
circles of intellect and genius, and is sensible only of the imperfection of his culture and the vanity and insufficiency of all his
riches, and further proves his good sense by the pains which he
takes to secure for his children that intellectual culture whose
want he so keenly feels; and thus it is that he becomes the founder
of a family.

Those who have not learned to read the ancient classics in the
language in which they were written must have a very imperfect
knowledge of the history of the human race; for it is remarkable
that no transcript of them has ever been made into any modern
tongue, unless our civilization itself may be regarded as such a
transcript. Homer has never yet been printed in English, nor
Æschylus, nor Virgil even,—works as refined, as solidly done, and
as beautiful almost as the morning itself; for later writers, say
what we will of their genius, have rarely, if ever, equalled the
elaborate beauty and finish and the lifelong and heroic literary
labors of the ancients. They only talk of forgetting them who never
knew them. It will be soon enough to forget them when we have
the learning and the genius which will enable us to attend to and
appreciate them. That age will be rich indeed when those relics
which we call Classics, and the still older and more than classic
but even less known Scriptures of the nations, shall have still
further accumulated, when the Vaticans shall be filled with Vedas
and Zendavestas [5] and Bibles, with Homers and Dantes and
Shakspeares, and all the centuries to come shall have successively
deposited their trophies in the forum of the world. By such a pile
we may hope to scale heaven at last.

The works of the great poets have never yet been read by mankind, for only great poets can read them. They have only been
read as the multitude read the stars, at most astrologically, not
astronomically. Most men have learned to read to serve a paltry

5. The scripture of Zoroastrianism, a religion that began in Iran in the sixth or seventh
century B.C.

convenience, as they have learned to cipher in order to keep accounts and not be cheated in trade; but of reading as a noble intellectual exercise they know little or nothing; yet this only is reading, in a high sense, not that which lulls us as a luxury and suffers the nobler faculties to sleep the while, but what we have to stand on tiptoe to read and devote our most alert and wakeful hours to.

I think that having learned our letters we should read the best that is in literature, and not be forever repeating our a b abs, and words of one syllable, in the fourth or fifth classes, sitting on the lowest and foremost form all our lives.[6] Most men are satisfied if they read or hear read, and perchance have been convicted by the wisdom of one good book, the Bible, and for the rest of their lives vegetate and dissipate their faculties in what is called easy reading. There is a work in several volumes in our Circulating Library entitled Little Reading, which I thought referred to a town of that name which I had not been to. There are those who, like cormorants and ostriches, can digest all sorts of this, even after the fullest dinner of meats and vegetables, for they suffer nothing to be wasted. If others are the machines to provide this provender, they are the machines to read it. They read the nine thousandth tale about Zebulon and Sephronia, and how they loved as none had ever loved before, and neither did the course of their true love run smooth,—at any rate, how it did run and stumble, and get up again and go on! how some poor unfortunate got up on to a steeple, who had better never have gone up as far as the belfry; and then, having needlessly got him up there, the happy novelist rings the bell for all the world to come together and hear, O dear! how he did get down again! For my part, I think that they had better metamorphose all such aspiring heroes of universal noveldom into man weathercocks, as they used to put heroes among the constellations, and let them swing round there till they are rusty, and not come down at all to bother honest men with their pranks. The next time the novelist rings the bell I will not stir though the meeting-house burn down. "The Skip of the Tip-Toe-Hop, a Romance of the Middle Ages, by the celebrated author of 'Tittle-Tol-Tan,' to appear in monthly parts; a great rush; don't all come together." All this they read with saucer eyes, and erect and primitive curiosity, and with unwearied gizzard, whose corrugations even yet need no sharpening, just as some little four-year-old bencher his two-cent gilt-covered edition of Cinderella,—without any improvement, that I can see, in the pronunciation, or accent, or emphasis, or any more skill in ex-

6. I.e., with the youngest children on the front row of the schoolroom.

tracting or inserting the moral. The result is dulness of sight, a stagnation of the vital circulations, and a general deliquium and sloughing off of all the intellectual faculties. This sort of gingerbread is baked daily and more sedulously than pure wheat or rye-and-Indian in almost every oven, and finds a surer market.

The best books are not read even by those who are called good readers. What does our Concord culture amount to? There is in this town, with a very few exceptions, no taste for the best or for very good books even in English literature, whose words all can read and spell. Even the college-bred and so called liberally educated men here and elsewhere have really little or no acquaintance with the English classics; and as for the recorded wisdom of mankind, the ancient classics and Bibles, which are accessible to all who will know of them, there are the feeblest efforts any where made to become acquainted with them. I know a woodchopper, of middle age, who takes a French paper, not for news as he says, for he is above that, but to "keep himself in practice," he being a Canadian by birth; and when I asked him what he considers the best thing he can do in this world, he says, beside this, to keep up and add to his English. This is about as much as the college bred generally do or aspire to do, and they take an English paper for the purpose. One who has just come from reading perhaps one of the best English books will find how many with whom he can converse about it? Or suppose he comes from reading a Greek or Latin classic in the original, whose praises are familiar even to the so called illiterate; he will find nobody at all to speak to, but must keep silence about it. Indeed, there is hardly the professor in our colleges, who, if he has mastered the difficulties of the language, has proportionally mastered the difficulties of the wit and poetry of a Greek poet, and has any sympathy to impart to the alert and heroic reader; and as for the sacred Scriptures, or Bibles of mankind, who in this town can tell me even their titles? Most men do not know that any nation but the Hebrews have had a scripture. A man, any man, will go considerably out of his way to pick up a silver dollar; but here are golden words, which the wisest men of antiquity have uttered, and whose worth the wise of every succeeding age have assured us of, —and yet we learn to read only as far as Easy Reading, the primers and class-books, and when we leave school, the "Little Reading," and story books, which are for boys and beginners; and our reading, our conversation and thinking, are all on a very low level, worthy only of pygmies and manikins.

I aspire to be acquainted with wiser men than this our Concord soil has produced, whose names are hardly known here. Or shall I hear the name of Plato and never read his book? As if Plato were my townsman and I never saw him,—my next neighbor and I never heard him speak or attended to the wisdom of his words. But how actually is it? His Dialogues, which contain what was immortal in him, lie on the next shelf, and yet I never read them. We are under-bred and low-lived and illiterate; and in this respect I confess I do not make any very broad distinction between the illiterateness of my townsman who cannot read at all, and the illiterateness of him who has learned to read only what is for children and feeble intellects. We should be as good as the worthies of antiquity, but partly by first knowing how good they were. We are a race of tit-men,[7] and soar but little higher in our intellectual flights than the columns of the daily paper.

It is not all books that are as dull as their readers. There are probably words addressed to our condition exactly, which, if we could really hear and understand, would be more salutary than the morning or the spring to our lives, and possibly put a new aspect on the face of things for us. How many a man has dated a new era in his life from the reading of a book. The book exists for us perchance which will explain our miracles and reveal new ones. The at present unutterable things we may find somewhere uttered. These same questions that disturb and puzzle and confound us have in their turn occurred to all the wise men; not one has been omitted; and each has answered them, according to his ability, by his words and his life. Moreover, with wisdom we shall learn liberality. The solitary hired man on a farm in the outskirts of Concord, who has had his second birth and peculiar religious experience, and is driven as he believes into silent gravity and exclusiveness by his faith, may think it is not true; but Zoroaster, thousands of years ago, travelled the same road and had the same experience; but he, being wise, knew it to be universal, and treated his neighbors accordingly, and is even said to have invented and established worship among men. Let him humbly commune with Zoroaster then, and, through the liberalizing influence of all the worthies, with Jesus Christ himself, and let "our church" go by the board.

We boast that we belong to the nineteenth century and are making the most rapid strides of any nation. But consider how little this village does for its own culture. I do not wish to flatter my townsmen, nor to be flattered by them, for that will not advance either of us. We need to be provoked,—goaded like oxen, as we are, into a trot. We have a comparatively decent system of common schools, schools for infants only; but excepting the half-starved Lyceum [8] in the winter, and latterly the puny beginning

7. Runts, intellectually small.
8. An organization that sponsored public lectures.

of a library suggested by the state, no school for ourselves. We spend more on almost any article of bodily aliment or ailment than on our mental aliment. It is time that we had uncommon schools, that we did not leave off our education when we begin to be men and women. It is time that villages were universities, and their elder inhabitants the fellows of universities, with leisure—if they are indeed so well off—to pursue liberal studies the rest of their lives. Shall the world be confined to one Paris or one Oxford forever? Cannot students be boarded here and get a liberal education under the skies of Concord? Can we not hire some Abelard[9] to lecture to us? Alas! what with foddering the cattle and tending the store, we are kept from school too long, and our education is sadly neglected. In this country, the village should in some respects take the place of the nobleman of Europe. It should be the patron of the fine arts. It is rich enough. It wants only the magnanimity and refinement. It can spend money enough on such things as farmers and traders value, but it is thought Utopian to propose spending money for things which more intelligent men know to be of far more worth. This town has spent seventeen thousand dollars on a town-house, thank fortune or politics, but probably it will not spend so much on living wit, the true meat to put into that shell, in a hundred years. The one hundred and twenty-five dollars annually subscribed for a Lyceum in the winter is better spent than any other equal sum raised in the town. If we live in the nineteenth century, why should we not enjoy the advantages which the nineteenth century offers? Why should our life be in any respect provincial? If we will read newspapers, why not skip the gossip of Boston and take the best newspaper in the world at once?—not be sucking the pap of "neutral family" papers, or browsing "Olive-Branches"[1] here in New England. Let the reports of all the learned societies come to us, and we will see if they know any thing. Why should we leave it to Harper & Brothers and Redding & Co.[2] to select our reading? As the nobleman of cultivated taste surrounds himself with whatever conduces to his culture,—genius—learning—wit—books—paintings—statuary—music—philosophical instruments, and the like; so let the village do,—not stop short at a pedagogue, a parson, a sexton, a parish library, and three selectmen, because our pilgrim forefathers got through a cold winter once on a bleak rock with these. To act collectively is according to the spirit of our institutions; and I am confident that, as our circumstances are more flourishing, our

---

9. Peter Abelard (1079–1142), a French philosopher, theologian, and teacher.
1. A Methodist weekly newspaper; neutral family newspapers avoided discussion of political issues in favor of family entertainment.
2. Book publishers, located in New York and Boston, respectively.

means are greater than the nobleman's. New England can hire all the wise men in the world to come and teach her, and board them round the while, and not be provincial at all. That is the *uncommon* school we want. Instead of noblemen, let us have noble villages of men. If it is necessary, omit one bridge over the river, go round a little there, and throw one arch at least over the darker gulf of ignorance which surrounds us.

Sounds

But while we are confined to books, though the most select and classic, and read only particular written languages, which are themselves but dialects and provincial, we are in danger of forgetting the language which all things and events speak without metaphor, which alone is copious and standard. Much is published, but little printed. The rays which stream through the shutter will be no longer remembered when the shutter is wholly removed. No method nor discipline can supersede the necessity of being forever on the alert. What is a course of history, or philosophy, or poetry, no matter how well selected, or the best society, or the most admirable routine of life, compared with the discipline of looking always at what is to be seen? Will you be a reader, a student merely, or a seer? Read your fate, see what is before you, and walk on into futurity.

I did not read books the first summer; I hoed beans. Nay, I often did better than this. There were times when I could not afford to sacrifice the bloom of the present moment to any work, whether of the head or hands. I love a broad margin to my life. Sometimes, in a summer morning, having taken my accustomed bath, I sat in my sunny doorway from sunrise till noon, rapt in a revery, amidst the pines and hickories and sumachs, in undisturbed solitude and stillness, while the birds sang around or flitted noiseless through the house, until by the sun falling in at my west window, or the noise of some traveller's wagon on the distant highway, I was reminded of the lapse of time. I grew in those seasons like corn in the night, and they were far better than any work of the hands would have been. They were not time subtracted from my life, but so much over and above my usual allowance. I realized what the Orientals mean by contemplation and the forsaking of works. For the most part, I minded not how the hours went. The day advanced as if to light some work of mine; it was morning, and lo, now it is evening, and nothing memorable is accomplished. Instead of singing like the birds, I silently smiled at my incessant good fortune. As the sparrow had its trill, sitting on the hickory before my door, so had I my chuckle or suppressed warble which he might hear out of my nest. My days were not days of the week, bearing the stamp of any heathen deity, nor were they minced into hours and fretted by the ticking of a clock; for I lived like the Puri Indians, of whom it is said that "for yesterday, to-day, and to-morrow they have only one word, and they express the variety of meaning by pointing backward for yesterday, forward for to-morrow, and overhead for the passing day."[1] This was sheer idleness to my fellow-townsmen, no doubt; but if the birds and flowers had tried me by their standard, I should not have been found wanting. A man must find his occasions in himself, it is true. The natural day is very calm, and will hardly reprove his indolence.

I had this advantage, at least, in my mode of life, over those who were obliged to look abroad for amusement, to society and the theatre, that my life itself was become my amusement and never ceased to be novel. It was a drama of many scenes and without an end. If we were always indeed getting our living, and regulating our lives according to the last and best mode we had learned, we should never be troubled with ennui. Follow your genius closely enough, and it will not fail to show you a fresh prospect every hour. Housework was a pleasant pastime. When my floor was dirty, I rose early, and, setting all my furniture out of doors on the grass, bed and bedstead making but one budget, dashed water on the floor, and sprinkled white sand from the pond on it, and then with a broom scrubbed it clean and white; and by the time the villagers had broken their fast the morning sun had dried my house sufficiently to allow me to move in again, and my meditations were almost uninterrupted. It was pleasant to see my whole household effects out on the grass, making a little pile like a gypsy's pack, and my three-legged table, from which I did not remove the books and pen and ink, standing amid the pines and hickories. They seemed glad to get out themselves, and as if unwilling to be brought in. I was sometimes tempted to stretch an awning over them and take my seat there. It was worth the while to see the sun shine on these things, and hear the free wind blow on them; so much more interesting most familiar objects look out of doors than in the house. A bird sits on the next bough, life-everlasting grows under the table, and blackberry vines run round its legs; pine cones, chestnut burs, and strawberry leaves are strewn about. It looked as if this was the way these forms came to be transferred to our furniture, to tables, chairs, and bedsteads,—because they once stood in their midst.

1. From Ida Pfeiffer, *A Lady's Voyage Round the World* (1852); the Puris are a tribe in eastern Brazil.

My house was on the side of a hill, immediately on the edge of the larger wood, in the midst of a young forest of pitch pines and hickories, and half a dozen rods from the pond, to which a narrow footpath led down the hill. In my front yard grew the strawberry, blackberry, and life-everlasting, johnswort and golden-rod, shrub-oaks and sand-cherry, blueberry and groundnut. Near the end of May, the sand-cherry, (*cerasus pumila,*) adorned the sides of the path with its delicate flowers arranged in umbels cylindrically about its short stems, which last, in the fall, weighed down with good sized and handsome cherries, fell over in wreaths like rays on every side. I tasted them out of compliment to Nature, though they were scarcely palatable. The sumach, (*rhus glabra,*) grew luxuriantly about the house, pushing up through the embankment which I had made, and growing five or six feet the first season. Its broad pinnate tropical leaf was pleasant though strange to look on. The large buds, suddenly pushing out late in the spring from dry sticks which had seemed to be dead, developed themselves as by magic into graceful green and tender boughs, an inch in diameter; and sometimes, as I sat at my window, so heedlessly did they grow and tax their weak joints, I heard a fresh and tender bough suddenly fall like a fan to the ground, when there was not a breath of air stirring, broken off by its own weight. In August, the large masses of berries, which, when in flower, had attracted many wild bees, gradually assumed their bright velvety crimson hue, and by their weight again bent down and broke the tender limbs.

As I sit at my window this summer afternoon, hawks are circling about my clearing; the tantivy of wild pigeons, flying by twos and threes athwart my view, or perching restless on the white-pine boughs behind my house, gives a voice to the air; a fishhawk dimples the glassy surface of the pond and brings up a fish; a mink steals out of the marsh before my door and seizes a frog by the shore; the sedge is bending under the weight of the reed-birds flitting hither and thither; and for the last half hour I have heard the rattle of railroad cars, now dying away and then reviving like the beat of a partridge, conveying travellers from Boston to the country. For I did not live so out of the world as that boy, who, as I hear, was put out to a farmer in the east part of the town, but ere long ran away and came home again, quite down at the heel and homesick. He had never seen such a dull and out-of-the-way place; the folks were all gone off; why, you couldn't even hear the whistle! I doubt if there is such a place in Massachusetts now:—

" In truth, our village has become a butt
    For one of those fleet railroad shafts, and o'er
    Our peaceful plain its soothing sound is—Concord." [2]

The Fitchburg Railroad touches the pond about a hundred rods
south of where I dwell. I usually go to the village along its causeway, and am, as it were, related to society by this link. The men on
the freight trains, who go over the whole length of the road, bow
to me as to an old acquaintance, they pass me so often, and
apparently they take me for an employee; and so I am. I too
would fain be a track-repairer somewhere in the orbit of the earth.

The whistle of the locomotive penetrates my woods summer and
winter, sounding like the scream of a hawk sailing over some
farmer's yard, informing me that many restless city merchants are
arriving within the circle of the town, or adventurous country
traders from the other side. As they come under one horizon, they
shout their warning to get off the track to the other, heard sometimes through the circles of two towns. Here come your groceries,
country; your rations, countrymen! Nor is there any man so independent on his farm that he can say them nay. And here's your
pay for them! screams the countryman's whistle; timber like long
battering rams going twenty miles an hour against the city's walls,
and chairs enough to seat all the weary and heavy laden that
dwell within them. With such huge and lumbering civility the
country hands a chair to the city. All the Indian huckleberry hills
are stripped, all the cranberry meadows are raked into the city.
Up comes the cotton, down goes the woven cloth; up comes the
silk, down goes the woollen; up come the books, but down goes
the wit that writes them.

When I meet the engine with its train of cars moving off with
planetary motion,—or, rather, like a comet, for the beholder
knows not if with that velocity and with that direction it will ever
revisit this system, since its orbit does not look like a returning
curve,—with its steam cloud like a banner streaming behind in
golden and silver wreaths, like many a downy cloud which I
have seen, high in the heavens, unfolding its masses to the light,
—as if this travelling demigod, this cloud-compeller, would ere
long take the sunset sky for the livery of his train; when I hear the
iron horse make the hills echo with his snort like thunder, shaking
the earth with his feet, and breathing fire and smoke from his
nostrils, (what kind of winged horse or fiery dragon they will put
into the new Mythology I don't know,) it seems as if the earth
had got a race now worthy to inhabit it. If all were as it seems,

2. From "Walden Spring," in *The Woodman* (1818–1901), Thoreau's close friend and
and Other Poems (1849), by Ellery Channing biographer.

and men made the elements their servants for noble ends! If the cloud that hangs over the engine were the perspiration of heroic deeds, or as beneficent as that which floats over the farmer's fields, then the elements and Nature herself would cheerfully accompany men on their errands and be their escort.

I watch the passage of the morning cars with the same feeling that I do the rising of the sun, which is hardly more regular. Their train of clouds stretching far behind and rising higher and higher, going to heaven while the cars are going to Boston, conceals the sun for a minute and casts my distant field into the shade, a celestial train beside which the petty train of cars which hugs the earth is but the barb of the spear. The stabler of the iron horse was up early this winter morning by the light of the stars amid the mountains, to fodder and harness his steed. Fire, too, was awakened thus early to put the vital heat in him and get him off. If the enterprise were as innocent as it is early! If the snow lies deep, they strap on his snow-shoes, and with the giant plough plough a furrow from the mountains to the seaboard, in which the cars, like a following drill-barrow, sprinkle all the restless men and floating merchandise in the country for seed. All day the fire-steed flies over the country, stopping only that his master may rest, and I am awakened by his tramp and defiant snort at midnight, when in some remote glen in the woods he fronts the elements incased in ice and snow; and he will reach his stall only with the morning star, to start once more on his travels without rest or slumber. Or perchance, at evening, I hear him in his stable blowing off the superfluous energy of the day, that he may calm his nerves and cool his liver and brain for a few hours of iron slumber. If the enterprise were as heroic and commanding as it is protracted and unwearied!

Far through unfrequented woods on the confines of towns, where once only the hunter penetrated by day, in the darkest night dart these bright saloons without the knowledge of their inhabitants; this moment stopping at some brilliant station-house in town or city, where a social crowd is gathered, the next in the Dismal Swamp,[3] scaring the owl and fox. The startings and arrivals of the cars are now the epochs in the village day. They go and come with such regularity and precision, and their whistle can be heard so far, that the farmers set their clocks by them, and thus one well conducted institution regulates a whole country. Have not men improved somewhat in punctuality since the railroad was invented? Do they not talk and think faster in the depot than they did in the stage-office? There is something electrifying

---

3. A coastal swamp in southeastern Virginia and northeastern North Carolina.

in the atmosphere of the former place. I have been astonished at the miracles it has wrought; that some of my neighbors, who, I should have prophesied, once for all, would never get to Boston by so prompt a conveyance, were on hand when the bell rang. To do things "railroad fashion" is now the by-word; and it is worth the while to be warned so often and so sincerely by any power to get off its track. There is no stopping to read the riot act, no firing over the heads of the mob, in this case. We have constructed a fate, an *Atropos*,[4] that never turns aside. (Let that be the name of your engine.) Men are advertised that at a certain hour and minute these bolts will be shot toward particular points of the compass; yet it interferes with no man's business, and the children go to school on the other track. We live the steadier for it. We are all educated thus to be sons of Tell.[5] The air is full of invisible bolts. Every path but your own is the path of fate. Keep on your own track, then.

What recommends commerce to me is its enterprise and bravery. It does not clasp its hands and pray to Jupiter. I see these men every day go about their business with more or less courage and content, doing more even than they suspect, and perchance better employed than they could have consciously devised. I am less affected by their heroism who stood up for half an hour in the front line at Buena Vista,[6] than by the steady and cheerful valor of the men who inhabit the snow-plough for their winter quarters; who have not merely the three-o'-clock in the morning courage, which Bonaparte[7] thought was the rarest, but whose courage does not go to rest so early, who go to sleep only when the storm sleeps or the sinews of their iron steed are frozen. On this morning of the Great Snow,[8] perchance, which is still raging and chilling men's blood, I hear the muffled tone of their engine bell from out the fog bank of their chilled breath, which announces that the cars *are coming*, without long delay, notwithstanding the veto of a New England north-east snow storm, and I behold the ploughmen covered with snow and rime, their heads peering above the mould-board which is turning down other than daisies and the nests of field-mice, like bowlders of the Sierra Nevada, that occupy an outside place in the universe.

Commerce is unexpectedly confident and serene, alert, adventurous, and unwearied. It is very natural in its methods withal, far

4. In Greek mythology, one of the three Fates who determined when a person was to die.
5. I.e., one of the sons of William Tell who, according to legend, shot an arrow through an apple that rested on his son's head.
6. Site of a victory in 1847, celebrated by many of Thoreau's contemporaries, of the United States' forces over those of Mexico during the Mexican War.
7. I.e., spontaneous courage.
8. According to Walter Harding, the "Great snow" of February 1717, described by Cotton Mather.

more so than many fantastic enterprises and sentimental experiments, and hence its singular success. I am refreshed and expanded when the freight train rattles past me, and I smell the stores which go dispensing their odors all the way from Long Wharf to Lake Champlain,[9] reminding me of foreign parts, of coral reefs, and Indian oceans, and tropical climes, and the extent of the globe. I feel more like a citizen of the world at the sight of the palm-leaf which will cover so many flaxen New England heads the next summer, the Manilla hemp and cocoa-nut husks, the old junk, gunny bags, scrap iron, and rusty nails. This car-load of torn sails is more legible and interesting now than if they should be wrought into paper and printed books. Who can write so graphically the history of the storms they have weathered as these rents have done? They are proof-sheets which need no correction. Here goes lumber from the Maine woods, which did not go out to sea in the last freshet, risen four dollars on the thousand because of what did go out or was split up; pine, spruce, cedar, —first, second, third and fourth qualities, so lately all of one quality, to wave over the bear, and moose, and caribou. Next rolls Thomaston [1] lime, a prime lot, which will get far among the hills before it gets slacked. These rags in bales, of all hues and qualities, the lowest condition to which cotton and linen descend, the final result of dress,—of patterns which are now no longer cried up, unless it be in Milwaukie, as those splendid articles, English, French, or American prints, ginghams, muslins, &c., gathered from all quarters both of fashion and poverty, going to become paper of one color or a few shades only, on which forsooth will be written tales of real life, high and low, and founded on fact! This closed car smells of salt fish, the strong New England and commercial scent, reminding me of the Grand Banks [2] and the fisheries. Who has not seen a salt fish, thoroughly cured for this world, so that nothing can spoil it, and putting the perseverance of the saints to the blush? with which you may sweep or pave the streets, and split your kindlings, and the teamster shelter himself and his lading against sun wind and rain behind it,—and the trader, as a Concord trader once did, hang it up by his door for a sign when he commences business, until at last his oldest customer cannot tell surely whether it be animal, vegetable, or mineral, and yet it shall be as pure as a snowflake, and if it be put into a pot and boiled, will come out an excellent dun fish for a Saturday's dinner. Next Spanish hides, with the tails still preserving their twist and the angle of elevation they had when the oxen that

9. I.e., from Boston Harbor to the New York–Vermont border.
1. A town in southern Maine, known for its lime deposits.
2. A major fishing ground in the northern Atlantic Ocean, southeast of Newfoundland.

wore them were careering over the pampas of the Spanish main,
—a type of all obstinacy, and evincing how almost hopeless and
incurable aie all constitutional vices. I confess, that practically
speaking, when I have learned a man's real disposition, I have no
hopes of changing it for the better or worse in this state of
existence. As the Orientals say, "A cur's tail may be warmed, and
pressed, and bound round with ligatures, and after a twelve years'
labor bestowed upon it, still it will retain its natural form."[3] The
only effectual cure for such inveteracies as these tails exhibit is to
make glue of them, which I believe is what is usually done with
them, and then they will stay put and stick. Here is a hogshead of
molasses or of brandy directed to John Smith, Cuttingsville, Vermont, some trader among the Green Mountains, who imports for
the farmers near his clearing, and now perchance stands over
his bulk-head and thinks of the last arrivals on the coast, how
they may affect the price for him, telling his customers this moment, as he has told them twenty times before this morning, that
he expects some by the next train of prime quality. It is advertised
in the Cuttingsville Times.

While these things go up other things come down. Warned by
the whizzing sound, I look up from my book and see some tall
pine, hewn on far northern hills, which has winged its way over
the Green Mountains and the Connecticut, shot like an arrow
through the township within ten minutes, and scarce another eye
beholds it; going

> "to be the mast
> Of some great ammiral."[4]

And hark! here comes the cattle-train bearing the cattle of a
thousand hills, sheepcots, stables, and cowyards in the air, drovers
with their sticks, and shepherd boys in the midst of their flocks, all
but the mountain pastures, whirled along like leaves blown from
the mountains by the September gales. The air is filled with the
bleating of calves and sheep, and the hustling of oxen, as if a
pastoral valley were going by. When the old bell-weather at the
head rattles his bell, the mountains do indeed skip like rams and
the little hills like lambs. A car-load of drovers, too, in the
midst, on a level with their droves now, their vocation gone, but
still clinging to their useless sticks as their badge of office. But
their dogs, where are they? It is a stampede to them; they are
quite thrown out; they have lost the scent. Methinks I hear them
barking behind the Peterboro' Hills, or panting up the western

3. Quoted from Charles Wilkins's translation of *Hitopadesa: Fables and Proverbs from the Sanskrit* (1787), the fable of the lion and the rabbit.

4. John Milton, *Paradise Lost* 1.293–94.

slope of the Green Mountains.[5] They will not be in at the death. Their vocation, too, is gone. Their fidelity and sagacity are below par now. They will slink back to their kennels in disgrace, or perchance run wild and strike a league with the wolf and the fox. So is your pastoral life whirled past and away. But the bell rings, and I must get off the track and let the cars go by;—

> What's the railroad to me?
> I never go to see
> Where it ends.
> It fills a few hollows,
> And makes banks for the swallows,
> It sets the sand a-blowing,
> And the blackberries a-growing,

but I cross it like a cart-path in the woods. I will not have my eyes put out and my ears spoiled by its smoke and steam and hissing.

Now that the cars are gone by and all the restless world with them, and the fishes in the pond no longer feel their rumbling, I am more alone than ever. For the rest of the long afternoon, perhaps, my meditations are interrupted only by the faint rattle of a carriage or team along the distant highway.

Sometimes, on Sundays, I heard the bells, the Lincoln, Acton, Bedford,[6] or Concord bell, when the wind was favorable, a faint, sweet, and, as it were, natural melody, worth importing into the wilderness. At a sufficient distance over the woods this sound acquires a certain vibratory hum, as if the pine needles in the horizon were the strings of a harp which it swept. All sound heard at the greatest possible distance produces one and the same effect, a vibration of the universal lyre, just as the intervening atmosphere makes a distant ridge of earth interesting to our eyes by the azure tint it imparts to it. There came to me in this case a melody which the air had strained, and which had conversed with every leaf and needle of the wood, that portion of the sound which the elements had taken up and modulated and echoed from vale to vale. The echo is, to some extent, an original sound, and therein is the magic and charm of it. It is not merely a repetition of what was worth repeating in the bell, but partly the voice of the wood; the same trivial words and notes sung by a wood-nymph.

At evening, the distant lowing of some cow in the horizon beyond the woods sounded sweet and melodious, and at first I

5. The Peterboro' Hills are in southern New Hampshire, visible from Concord; the Green Mountains run from northern Vermont to western Massachusetts.
6. Towns near Concord.

would mistake it for the voices of certain minstrels by whom I was sometimes serenaded, who might be straying over hill and dale; but soon I was not unpleasantly disappointed when it was prolonged into the cheap and natural music of the cow. I do not mean to be satirical, but to express my appreciation of those youths' singing, when I state that I perceived clearly that it was akin to the music of the cow, and they were at length one articulation of Nature.

Regularly at half past seven, in one part of the summer, after the evening train had gone by, the whippoorwills chanted their vespers for half an hour, sitting on a stump by my door, or upon the ridge pole of the house. They would begin to sing almost with as much precision as a clock, within five minutes of a particular time, referred to the setting of the sun, every evening. I had a rare opportunity to become acquainted with their habits. Sometimes I heard four or five at once in different parts of the wood, by accident one a bar behind another, and so near me that I distinguished not only the cluck after each note, but often that singular buzzing sound like a fly in a spider's web, only proportionally louder. Sometimes one would circle round and round me in the woods a few feet distant as if tethered by a string, when probably I was near its eggs. They sang at intervals throughout the night, and were again as musical as ever just before and about dawn.

When other birds are still the screech owls take up the strain, like mourning women their ancient u-lu-lu. Their dismal scream is truly Ben Jonsonian.[7] Wise midnight hags! It is no honest and blunt tu-whit tu-who of the poets, but, without jesting, a most solemn graveyard ditty, the mutual consolations of suicide lovers remembering the pangs and the delights of supernal love in the infernal groves. Yet I love to hear their wailing, their doleful responses, trilled along the woodside; reminding me sometimes of music and singing birds; as if it were the dark and tearful side of music, the regrets and sighs that would fain be sung. They are the spirits, the low spirits and melancholy forebodings, of fallen souls that once in human shape night-walked the earth and did the deeds of darkness, now expiating their sins with their wailing hymns or threnodies in the scenery of their transgressions. They give me a new sense of the variety and capacity of that nature which is our common dwelling. *Oh-o-o-o-o that I never had been bor-r-r-r-n!* sighs one on this side of the pond, and circles with the restlessness of despair to some new perch on the gray oaks. Then—*that I never had been bor-r-r-r-n!* echoes another on the farther side with

7. Ben Jonson (1572–1637), English dramatist; the reference may be to his "Witches' Song."

tremulous sincerity, and—*bor-r-r-r-n!* comes faintly from far in the Lincoln woods.

I was also serenaded by a hooting owl. Near at hand you could fancy it the most melancholy sound in Nature, as if she meant by this to stereotype and make permanent in her choir the dying moans of a human being,—some poor weak relic of mortality who has left hope behind, and howls like an animal, yet with human sobs, on entering the dark valley, made more awful by a certain gurgling melodiousness,—I find myself beginning with the letters gl when I try to imitate it,—expressive of a mind which has reached the gelatinous mildewy stage in the mortification of all healthy and courageous thought. It reminded me of ghouls and idiots and insane howlings. But now one answers from far woods in a strain made really melodious by distance,—*Hoo hoo hoo, hoorer hoo;* and indeed for the most part it suggested only pleasing associations, whether heard by day or night, summer or winter.

I rejoice that there are owls. Let them do the idiotic and maniacal hooting for men. It is a sound admirably suited to swamps and twilight woods which no day illustrates, suggesting a vast and undeveloped nature which men have not recognized. They represent the stark twilight and unsatisfied thoughts which all have. All day the sun has shone on the surface of some savage swamp, where the double spruce stands hung with usnea lichens, and small hawks circulate above, and the chicadee lisps amid the evergreens, and the partridge and rabbit skulk beneath; but now a more dismal and fitting day dawns, and a different race of creatures awakes to express the meaning of Nature there.

Late in the evening I heard the distant rumbling of wagons over bridges,—a sound heard farther than almost any other at night,— the baying of dogs, and sometimes again the lowing of some disconsolate cow in a distant barn-yard. In the mean while all the shore rang with the trump of bullfrogs, the sturdy spirits of ancient winebibbers and wassailers, still unrepentant, trying to sing a catch in their Stygian lake,[8]—if the Walden nymphs will pardon the comparison, for though there are almost no weeds, there are frogs there,—who would fain keep up the hilarious rules of their old festal tables, though their voices have waxed hoarse and solemnly grave, mocking at mirth, and the wine has lost its flavor, and become only liquor to distend their paunches, and sweet intoxication never comes to drown the memory of the past, but mere saturation and waterloggedness and distention. The most aldermanic, with his chin upon a heart-leaf, which serves for a napkin to his drooling chaps, under this northern shore quaffs a

8. I.e., any gloomy lake; in Greek mythology, the Styx was one of five rivers surrounding the land of the dead.

deep draught of the once scorned water, and passes round the cup with the ejaculation *tr-r-r-oonk, tr-r-r-oonk, tr-r-r-oonk!* and straightway comes over the water from some distant cove the same password repeated, where the next in seniority and girth has gulped down to his mark; and when this observance has made the circuit of the shores, then ejaculates the master of ceremonies, with satisfaction, *tr-r-r-oonk!* and each in his turn repeats the same down to the least distended, leakiest, and flabbiest paunched, that there be no mistake; and then the bowl goes round again and again, until the sun disperses the morning mist, and only the patriarch is not under the pond, but vainly bellowing *troonk* from time to time, and pausing for a reply.

I am not sure that I ever heard the sound of cock-crowing from my clearing, and I thought that it might be worth the while to keep a cockerel for his music merely, as a singing bird. The note of this once wild Indian pheasant is certainly the most remarkable of any bird's, and if they could be naturalized without being domesticated, it would soon become the most famous sound in our woods, surpassing the clangor of the goose and the hooting of the owl; and then imagine the cackling of the hens to fill the pauses when their lords' clarions rested! No wonder that man added this bird to his tame stock,—to say nothing of the eggs and drumsticks. To walk in a winter morning in a wood where these birds abounded, their native woods, and hear the wild cockerels crow on the trees, clear and shrill for miles over the resounding earth, drowning the feebler notes of other birds,—think of it! It would put nations on the alert. Who would not be early to rise, and rise earlier and earlier every successive day of his life, till he became unspeakably healthy, wealthy, and wise? This foreign bird's note is celebrated by the poets of all countries along with the notes of their native songsters. All climates agree with brave Chanticleer. He is more indigenous even than the natives. His health is ever good, his lungs are sound, his spirits never flag. Even the sailor on the Atlantic and Pacific is awakened by his voice; but its shrill sound never roused me from my slumbers. I kept neither dog, cat, cow, pig, nor hens, so that you would have said there was a deficiency of domestic sounds; neither the churn, nor the spinning wheel, nor even the singing of the kettle, nor the hissing of the urn, nor children crying, to comfort one. An old-fashioned man would have lost his senses or died of ennui before this. Not even rats in the wall, for they were starved out, or rather were never baited in,—only squirrels on the roof and under the floor, a whippoorwill on the ridge pole, a blue-jay screaming beneath the window, a hare or woodchuck under the house, a screech-owl or a cat-owl behind it, a flock of wild geese or a laughing loon on the pond, and a fox to bark in the night. Not even a lark or an oriole, those mild plantation birds, ever visited my clearing. No cockerels to crow nor hens to cackle in the yard. No yard! but unfenced Nature reaching up to your very sills. A young forest growing up under your windows, and wild sumachs and blackberry vines breaking through into your cellar; sturdy pitch-pines rubbing and creaking against the shingles for want of room, their roots reaching quite under the house. Instead of a scuttle or a blind blown off in the gale,—a pine tree snapped off or torn up by the roots behind your house for fuel. Instead of no path to the front-yard gate in the Great Snow,—no gate—no front-yard,—and no path to the civilized world!

Solitude

This is a delicious evening, when the whole body is one sense, and imbibes delight through every pore. I go and come with a strange liberty in Nature, a part of herself. As I walk along the stony shore of the pond in my shirt sleeves, though it is cool as well as cloudy and windy, and I see nothing special to attract me, all the elements are unusually congenial to me. The bullfrogs trump to usher in the night, and the note of the whippoorwill is borne on the rippling wind from over the water. Sympathy with the fluttering alder and poplar leaves almost takes away my breath; yet, like the lake, my serenity is rippled but not ruffled. These small waves raised by the evening wind are as remote from storm as the smooth reflecting surface. Though it is now dark, the wind still blows and roars in the wood, the waves still dash, and some creatures lull the rest with their notes. The repose is never complete. The wildest animals do not repose, but seek their prey now; the fox, and skunk, and rabbit, now roam the fields and woods without fear. They are Nature's watchmen,—links which connect the days of animated life.

When I return to my house I find that visitors have been there and left their cards, either a bunch of flowers, or a wreath of evergreen, or a name in pencil on a yellow walnut leaf or a chip. They who come rarely to the woods take some little piece of the forest into their hands to play with by the way, which they leave, either intentionally or accidentally. One has peeled a willow wand, woven it into a ring, and dropped it on my table. I could always tell if visitors had called in my absence, either by the bended twigs or grass, or the print of their shoes, and generally of what sex or age or quality they were by some slight trace left, as a flower dropped, or a bunch of grass plucked and thrown away, even as far off as the railroad, half a mile distant, or by the lingering odor of a cigar or pipe. Nay, I was frequently notified of the passage of a traveller along the highway sixty rods off by the scent of his pipe.

There is commonly sufficient space about us. Our horizon is never quite at our elbows. The thick wood is not just at our door, nor the pond, but somewhat is always clearing, familiar and worn by us, appropriated and fenced in some way, and reclaimed from Nature. For what reason have I this vast range and circuit, some square miles of unfrequented forest, for my privacy, abandoned to me by men? My nearest neighbor is a mile distant, and no house is visible from any place but the hill-tops within half a mile of my own. I have my horizon bounded by woods all to myself; a distant view of the railroad where it touches the pond on the one hand, and of the fence which skirts the woodland road on the other. But for the most part it is as solitary where I live as on the prairies. It is as much Asia or Africa as New England. I have, as it were, my own sun and moon and stars, and a little world all to myself. At night there was never a traveller passed my house, or knocked at my door, more than if I were the first or last man; unless it were in the spring, when at long intervals some came from the village to fish for pouts,—they plainly fished much more in the Walden Pond of their own natures, and baited their hooks with darkness,—but they soon retreated, usually with light baskets, and left "the world to darkness and to me,"[1] and the black kernel of the night was never profaned by any human neighborhood. I believe that men are generally still a little afraid of the dark, though the witches are all hung, and Christianity and candles have been introduced.

Yet I experienced sometimes that the most sweet and tender, the most innocent and encouraging society may be found in any natural object, even for the poor misanthrope and most melancholy man. There can be no very black melancholy to him who lives in the midst of Nature and has his senses still. There was never yet such a storm but it was Æolian music[2] to a healthy and innocent ear. Nothing can rightly compel a simple and brave man to a vulgar sadness. While I enjoy the friendship of the seasons I trust that nothing can make life a burden to me. The gentle rain which waters my beans and keeps me in the house to-day is not drear and melancholy, but good for me too. Though it prevents my hoeing them, it is of far more worth than my hoeing. If it should continue so long as to cause the seeds to rot in the ground and destroy the potatoes in the low lands, it would still be good for the grass on the uplands, and, being good for the grass,

1. From Thomas Gray, "Elegy Written in a Country Churchyard."
2. Music produced by a stringed instrument when placed in a window casement or otherwise exposed to a current of air; in Greek mythology Aeolus was the god of the winds.

it would be good for me. Sometimes, when I compare myself with other men, it seems as if I were more favored by the gods than they, beyond any deserts that I am conscious of; as if I had a warrant and surety at their hands which my fellows have not, and were especially guided and guarded. I do not flatter myself, but if it be possible they flatter me. I have never felt lonesome, or in the least oppressed by a sense of solitude, but once, and that was a few weeks after I came to the woods, when, for an hour, I doubted if the near neighborhood of man was not essential to a serene and healthy life. To be alone was something unpleasant. But I was at the same time conscious of a slight insanity in my mood, and seemed to foresee my recovery. In the midst of a gentle rain while these thoughts prevailed, I was suddenly sensible of such sweet and beneficent society in Nature, in the very pattering of the drops, and in every sound and sight around my house, an infinite and unaccountable friendliness all at once like an atmosphere sustaining me, as made the fancied advantages of human neighborhood insignificant, and I have never thought of them since. Every little pine needle expanded and swelled with sympathy and befriended me. I was so distinctly made aware of the presence of something kindred to me, even in scenes which we are accustomed to call wild and dreary, and also that the nearest of blood to me and humanest was not a person nor a villager, that I thought no place could ever be strange to me again.—

> "Mourning untimely consumes the sad;
> Few are their days in the land of the living,
> Beautiful daughter of Toscar." [3]

Some of my pleasantest hours were during the long rain storms in the spring or fall, which confined me to the house for the afternoon as well as the forenoon, soothed by their ceaseless roar and pelting; when an early twilight ushered in a long evening in which many thoughts had time to take root and unfold themselves. In those driving north-east rains which tried the village houses so, when the maids stood ready with mop and pail in front entries to keep the deluge out, I sat behind my door in my little house, which was all entry, and thoroughly enjoyed its protection. In one heavy thunder shower the lightning struck a large pitch-pine across the pond, making a very conspicuous and perfectly regular spiral groove from top to bottom, an inch or more deep, and four or five inches wide, as you would groove a walking-stick. I passed it again the other day, and was struck with awe on looking up and beholding that mark, now more distinct than ever, where a

---

3. From "Croma," in *The Genuine Remains of Ossian* by James Macpherson; the poem's hero is attempting to console Malvina, daughter of Toscar, after the death of her lover.

terrific and resistless bolt came down out of the harmless sky eight years ago. Men frequently say to me, "I should think you would feel lonesome down there, and want to be nearer to folks, rainy and snowy days and nights especially." I am tempted to reply to such,—This whole earth which we inhabit is but a point in space. How far apart, think you, dwell the two most distant inhabitants of yonder star, the breadth of whose disk cannot be appreciated by our instruments? Why should I feel lonely? is not our planet in the Milky Way? This which you put seems to me not to be the most important question. What sort of space is that which separates a man from his fellows and makes him solitary? I have found that no exertion of the legs can bring two minds much nearer to one another. What do we want most to dwell near to? Not to many men surely, the depot, the post-office, the barroom, the meeting-house, the school-house, the grocery, Beacon Hill, or the Five Points,[4] where men most congregate, but to the perennial source of our life, whence in all our experience we have found that to issue, as the willow stands near the water and sends out its roots in that direction. This will vary with different natures, but this is the place where a wise man will dig his cellar. . . . I one evening overtook one of my townsmen, who has accumulated what is called "a handsome property,"—though I never got a *fair* view of it,—on the Walden road, driving a pair of cattle to market, who inquired of me how I could bring my mind to give up so many of the comforts of life. I answered that I was very sure I liked it passably well; I was not joking. And so I went home to my bed, and left him to pick his way through the darkness and the mud to Brighton,[5]—or Bright-town,—which place he would reach some time in the morning.

Any prospect of awakening or coming to life to a dead man makes indifferent all times and places. The place where that may occur is always the same, and indescribably pleasant to all our senses. For the most part we allow only outlying and transient circumstances to make our occasions. They are, in fact, the cause of our distraction. Nearest to all things is that power which fashions their being. *Next* to us the grandest laws are continually being executed. *Next* to us is not the workman whom we have hired, with whom we love so well to talk, but the workman whose work we are.

"How vast and profound is the influence of the subtle powers of Heaven and of Earth!"

"We seek to perceive them, and we do not see them; we seek to

4. Beacon Hill was the fashionable section of Boston; Five Points, in New York City, was known for its crime.
5. A suburb of Boston.

hear them, and we do not hear them; identified with the substance of things, they cannot be separated from them."

"They cause that in all the universe men purify and sanctify their hearts, and clothe themselves in their holiday garments to offer sacrifices and oblations to their ancestors. It is an ocean of subtile intelligences. They are every where, above us, on our left, on our right; they environ us on all sides." [6]

We are the subjects of an experiment which is not a little interesting to me. Can we not do without the society of our gossips a little while under these circumstances,—have our own thoughts to cheer us? Confucius says truly, "Virtue does not remain as an abandoned orphan; it must of necessity have neighbors." [7]

With thinking we may be beside ourselves in a sane sense. By a conscious effort of the mind we can stand aloof from actions and their consequences; and all things, good and bad, go by us like a torrent. We are not wholly involved in Nature. I may be either the driftwood in the stream, or Indra [8] in the sky looking down on it. I *may* be affected by a theatrical exhibition; on the other hand, I *may not* be affected by an actual event which appears to concern me much more. I only know myself as a human entity; the scene, so to speak, of thoughts and affections; and am sensible of a certain doubleness by which I can stand as remote from myself as from another. However intense my experience, I am conscious of the presence and criticism of a part of me, which, as it were, is not a part of me, but spectator, sharing no experience, but taking note of it; and that is no more I than it is you. When the play, it may be the tragedy, of life is over, the spectator goes his way. It was a kind of fiction, a work of the imagination only, so far as he was concerned. This doubleness may easily make us poor neighbors and friends sometimes.

I find it wholesome to be alone the greater part of the time. To be in company, even with the best, is soon wearisome and dissipating. I love to be alone. I never found the companion that was so companionable as solitude. We are for the most part more lonely when we go abroad among men than when we stay in our chambers. A man thinking or working is always alone, let him be where he will. Solitude is not measured by the miles of space that intervene between a man and his fellows. The really diligent student in one of the crowded hives of Cambridge College is as solitary as a dervis in the desert. The farmer can work alone in the field or the woods all day, hoeing or chopping, and not feel

6. Confucius, *The Doctrine of the Mean* 14.
7. *Analects* 4.
8. In the Hindu Vedas, the god of air, thunder, and rain.

lonesome, because he is employed; but when he comes home at
night he cannot sit down in a room alone, at the mercy of his
thoughts, but must be where he can "see the folks," and recreate,
and as he thinks remunerate himself for his day's solitude; and
hence he wonders how the student can sit alone in the house all
night and most of the day without ennui and "the blues;" but he
does not realize that the student, though in the house, is still at
work in *his* field, and chopping in *his* woods, as the farmer in his,
and in turn seeks the same recreation and society that the latter
does, though it may be a more condensed form of it.

Society is commonly too cheap. We meet at very short intervals, not having had time to acquire any new value for each
other. We meet at meals three times a day, and give each other
a new taste of that old musty cheese that we are. We have had to
agree on a certain set of rules, called etiquette and politeness, to
make this frequent meeting tolerable and that we need not come
to open war. We meet at the post-office, and at the sociable, and
about the fireside every night; we live thick and are in each
other's way, and stumble over one another, and I think that we thus
lose some respect for one another. Certainly less frequency would
suffice for all important and hearty communications. Consider the
girls in a factory,—never alone, hardly in their dreams. It would
be better if there were but one inhabitant to a square mile, as
where I live. The value of a man is not in his skin, that we should
touch him.

I have heard of a man lost in the woods and dying of famine
and exhaustion at the foot of a tree, whose loneliness was relieved by the grotesque visions with which, owing to bodily weakness, his diseased imagination surrounded him, and which he believed to be real. So also, owing to bodily and mental health and
strength, we may be continually cheered by a like but more normal and natural society, and come to know that we are never
alone.

I have a great deal of company in my house; especially in the
morning, when nobody calls. Let me suggest a few comparisons,
that some one may convey an idea of my situation. I am no more
lonely than the loon in the pond that laughs so loud, or than
Walden Pond itself. What company has that lonely lake, I pray?
And yet it has not the blue devils, but the blue angels in it, in the
azure tint of its waters. The sun is alone, except in thick weather,
when there sometimes appear to be two, but one is a mock sun.
God is alone,—but the devil, he is far from being alone; he sees a
great deal of company; he is legion. I am no more lonely than a
single mullein or dandelion in a pasture, or a bean leaf, or sorrel,
or a horse-fly, or a humble-bee. I am no more lonely than the

Mill Brook, or a weathercock, or the north star, or the south wind, or an April shower, or a January thaw, or the first spider in a new house.

I have occasional visits in the long winter evenings, when the snow falls fast and the wind howls in the wood, from an old settler and original proprietor, who is reported to have dug Walden Pond, and stoned it, and fringed it with pine woods; who tells me stories of old time and of new eternity; and between us we manage to pass a cheerful evening with social mirth and pleasant views of things, even without apples or cider,—a most wise and humorous friend, whom I love much, who keeps himself more secret than ever did Goffe or Whalley;[9] and though he is thought to be dead, none can show where he is buried. An elderly dame, too, dwells in my neighborhood, invisible to most persons, in whose odorous herb garden I love to stroll sometimes, gathering simples and listening to her fables; for she has a genius of unequalled fertility, and her memory runs back farther than mythology, and she can. tell me the original of every fable, and on what fact every one is founded, for the incidents occurred when she was young. A ruddy and lusty old dame, who delights in all weathers and seasons, and is likely to outlive all her children yet.

The indescribable innocence and beneficence of Nature,—of sun and wind and rain, of summer and winter,—such health, such cheer, they afford forever! and such sympathy have they ever with our race, that all Nature would be affected, and the sun's brightness fade, and the winds would sigh humanely, and the clouds rain tears, and the woods shed their leaves and put on mourning in midsummer, if any man should ever for a just cause grieve. Shall I not have intelligence with the earth? Am I not partly leaves and vegetable mould myself?

What is the pill which will keep us well, serene, contented? Not my or thy great-grandfather's, but our great-grandmother Nature's universal, vegetable, botanic medicines, by which she has kept herself young always, outlived so many old Parrs[1] in her day, and fed her health with their decaying fatness. For my panacea, instead of one of those quack vials of a mixture dipped from Acheron[2] and the Dead Sea, which come out of those long shallow black-schooner looking wagons which we sometimes see made to carry bottles, let me have a draught of undiluted morning air. Morning air! If men will not drink of this at the fountainhead of the day, why, then, we must even bottle up some and

9. William Goffe (d. ca. 1679) and Edward Whalley (1615?–75?), two of the men indicted for killing Charles I of England, fled to America, where they lived in hiding.
1. Thomas Parr, an Englishman born in 1483 who reputedly lived 152 years.
2. In Greek mythology, Acheron was one of the five rivers surrounding the land of the dead; the Dead Sea is a large salt lake on the Israel-Jordan border.

sell it in the shops, for the benefit of those who have lost their subscription ticket to morning time in this world. But remember, it will not keep quite till noonday even in the coolest cellar, but drive out the stopples long ere that and follow westward the steps of Aurora. I am no worshipper of Hygeia,[3] who was the daughter of that old herb-doctor Æsculapius, and who is represented on monuments holding a serpent in one hand, and in the other a cup out of which the serpent sometimes drinks; but rather of Hebe,[4] cupbearer to Jupiter, who was the daughter of Juno and wild lettuce, and who had the power of restoring gods and men to the vigor of youth. She was probably the only thoroughly sound-conditioned, healthy, and robust young lady that ever walked the globe, and wherever she came it was spring.

Visitors

I think that I love society as much as most, and am ready enough to fasten myself like a bloodsucker for the time to any full-blooded man that comes in my way. I am naturally no hermit, but might possibly sit out the sturdiest frequenter of the bar-room, if my business called me thither.

I had three chairs in my house; one for solitude, two for friendship, three for society. When visitors came in larger and unexpected numbers there was but the third chair for them all, but they generally economized the room by standing up. It is surprising how many great men and women a small house will contain. I have had twenty-five or thirty souls, with their bodies, at once under my roof, and yet we often parted without being aware that we had come very near to one another. Many of our houses, both public and private, with their almost innumerable apartments, their huge halls and their cellars for the storage of wines and other munitions of peace, appear to me extravagantly large for their inhabitants. They are so vast and magnificent that the latter seem to be only vermin which infest them. I am surprised when the herald blows his summons before some Tremont or Astor or Middlesex House,[1] to see come creeping out over the piazza for all inhabitants a ridiculous mouse, which soon again slinks into some hole in the pavement.

One inconvenience I sometimes experienced in so small a house, the difficulty of getting to a sufficient distance from my guest when we began to utter the big thoughts in big words. You want room

3. In Greek mythology, the goddess of health and daughter of Æsculapius, the god of medical arts.
4. In Greek mythology, Hebe was the goddess of youth, the daughter of Zeus (called "Jupiter" by the Romans) and Hera (called "Juno" by the Romans); according to some legends, Hebe was conceived after Hera ate some wild lettuce.
1. Prosperous hotels in Boston, New York, and Concord, respectively.

for your thoughts to get into sailing trim and run a course or two before they make their port. The bullet of your thought must have overcome its lateral and ricochet motion and fallen into its last and steady course before it reaches the ear of the hearer, else it may plough out again through the side of his head. Also, our sentences wanted room to unfold and form their columns in the interval. Individuals, like nations, must have suitable broad and natural boundaries, even a considerable neutral ground, between them. I have found it a singular luxury to talk across the pond to a companion on the opposite side. In my house we were so near that we could not begin to hear,—we could not speak low enough to be heard; as when you throw two stones into calm water so near that they break each other's undulations. If we are merely loquacious and loud talkers, then we can afford to stand very near together, cheek by jowl, and feel each other's breath; but if we speak reservedly and thoughtfully, we want to be farther apart, that all animal heat and moisture may have a chance to evaporate. If we would enjoy the most intimate society with that in each of us which is without, or above, being spoken to, we must not only be silent, but commonly so far apart bodily that we cannot possibly hear each other's voice in any case. Referred to this standard, speech is for the convenience of those who are hard of hearing; but there are many fine things which we cannot say if we have to shout. As the conversation began to assume a loftier and grander tone, we gradually shoved our chairs farther apart till they touched the wall in opposite corners, and then commonly there was not room enough.

My "best" room, however, my withdrawing room, always ready for company, on whose carpet the sun rarely fell, was the pine wood behind my house. Thither in summer days, when distinguished guests came, I took them, and a priceless domestic swept the floor and dusted the furniture and kept the things in order.

If one guest came he sometimes partook of my frugal meal, and it was no interruption to conversation to be stirring a hasty-pudding, or watching the rising and maturing of a loaf of bread in the ashes, in the mean while. But if twenty came and sat in my house there was nothing said about dinner, though there might be bread enough for two, more than if eating were a forsaken habit; but we naturally practised abstinence; and this was never felt to be an offence against hospitality, but the most proper and considerate course. The waste and decay of physical life, which so often needs repair, seemed miraculously retarded in such a case, and the vital vigor stood its ground. I could entertain thus a thousand as well as twenty; and if any ever went away disappointed or hungry from my house when they found me at home, they may

depend upon it that I sympathized with them at least. So easy is
it, though many housekeepers doubt it, to establish new and better
customs in the place of the old. You need not rest your reputation
on the dinners you give. For my own part, I was never so
effectually deterred from frequenting a man's house, by any kind
of Cerberus [2] whatever, as by the parade one made about dining
me, which I took to be a very polite and roundabout hint never
to trouble him so again. I think I shall never revisit those scenes.
I should be proud to have for the motto of my cabin those lines
of Spenser which one of my visitors inscribed on a yellow
walnut leaf for a card:—

> "Arrivéd there, the little house they fill,
> Ne looke for entertainment where none was;
> Rest is their feast, and all things at their will:
> The noblest mind the best contentment has." [3]

When Winslow afterward governor of the Plymouth Colony,
went with a companion on a visit of ceremony to Massassoit on
foot through the woods, and arrived tired and hungry at his
lodge, they were well received by the king, but nothing was said
about eating that day. When the night arrived, to quote their
own words,—"He laid us on the bed with himself and his wife,
they at the one end and we at the other, it being only plank, laid
a foot from the ground, and a thin mat upon them. Two more of
his chief men, for want of room, pressed by and upon us; so that
we were worse weary of our lodging than of our journey." At one
o'clock the next day Massassoit "brought two fishes that he had
shot," about thrice as big as a bream; "these being boiled, there
were at least forty looked for a share in them. The most ate of
them. This meal only we had in two nights and a day; and had
not one of us bought a partridge, we had taken our journey
fasting." Fearing that they would be light-headed for want of
food and also sleep, owing to "the savages' barbarous singing,
(for they used to sing themselves asleep,)" and that they might get
home while they had strength to travel, they departed. [4] As for
lodging, it is true they were but poorly entertained, though what
they found an inconvenience was no doubt intended for an honor;
but as far as eating was concerned, I do not see how the Indians
could have done better. They had nothing to eat themselves, and
they were wiser than to think that apologies could supply the
place of food to their guests; so they drew their belts tighter and

2. In Greek mythology, a three-headed dog who guarded the entrance to the land of the dead.
3. Edmund Spenser, *The Fairie Queen* 1.1.35.
4. From Edward Winslow, *The English Plantation at Plymouth* (1622); Massassoit (1590–1661) was a Wampanoag chief friendly to the Plymouth settlers.

said nothing about it. Another time when Winslow visited them, it being a season of plenty with them, there was no deficiency in this respect.

As for men, they will hardly fail one any where. I had more visitors while I lived in the woods than at any other period of my life; I mean that I had some. I met several there under more favorable circumstances than I could any where else. But fewer came to see me upon trivial business. In this respect, my company was winnowed by my mere distance from town. I had withdrawn so far within the great ocean of solitude, into which the rivers of society empty, that for the most part, so far as my needs were concerned, only the finest sediment was deposited around me. Beside, there were wafted to me evidences of unexplored and uncultivated continents on the other side.

Who should come to my lodge this morning but a true Homeric or Paphlagonian [5] man,—he had so suitable and poetic a name that I am sorry I cannot print it here,—a Canadian, a wood-chopper and post-maker, who can hole fifty posts in a day, who made his last supper on a woodchuck which his dog caught. He, too, has heard of Homer, and, "if it were not for books," would "not know what to do rainy days," though perhaps he has not read one wholly through for many rainy seasons. Some priest who could pronounce the Greek itself taught him to read his verse in the testament in his native parish far away; and now I must translate to him, while he holds the book, Achilles' reproof to Patroclus for his sad countenance.—"Why are you in tears, Patroclus, like a young girl?"—

> "Or have you alone heard some news from Phthia?
> They say that Mencetius lives yet, son of Actor,
> And Peleus lives, son of Æacus, among the Myrmidons,
> Either of whom having died, we should greatly grieve." [6]

He says, "That's good." He has a great bundle of white-oak bark under his arm for a sick man, gathered this Sunday morning. "I suppose there's no harm in going after such a thing to-day," says he. To him Homer was a great writer, though what his writing was about he did not know. A more simple and natural man it would be hard to find. Vice and disease, which cast such a sombre moral hue over the world, seemed to have hardly any existence for him. He was about twenty-eight years old, and had left Canada and his father's house a dozen years before to work in the States, and earn money to buy a farm with at last, perhaps in his

---

5. Paphlagonia was a heavily wooded country in northern Asia Minor whose inhabitants were known for their heaviness and dullness; the woodchopper was Alek Therien.
6. The *Iliad* 16.13–16; Patroclus is Achilles' closest friend, whose death Achilles avenges.

native country. He was cast in the coarsest mould; a stout but sluggish body, yet gracefully carried, with a thick sunburnt neck, dark bushy hair, and dull sleepy blue eyes, which were occasionally lit up with expression. He wore a flat gray cloth cap, a dingy wool-colored greatcoat, and cowhide boots. He was a great consumer of meat, usually carrying his dinner to his work a couple of miles past my house,—for he chopped all summer,—in a tin pail; cold meats, often cold woodchucks, and coffee in a stone bottle which dangled by a string from his belt; and sometimes he offered me a drink. He came along early, crossing my bean-field, though without anxiety or haste to get to his work, such as Yankees exhibit. He wasn't a-going to hurt himself. He didn't care if he only earned his board. Frequently he would leave his dinner in the bushes, when his dog had caught a woodchuck by the way, and go back a mile and a half to dress it and leave it in the cellar of the house where he boarded, after deliberating first for half an hour whether he could not sink it in the pond safely till nightfall,— loving to dwell long upon these themes. He would say, as he went by in the morning, "How thick the pigeons are! If working every day were not my trade, I could get all the meat I should want by hunting,—pigeons, woodchucks, rabbits, partridges,—by gosh! I could get all I should want for a week in one day."

He was a skilful chopper, and indulged in some flourishes and ornaments in his art. He cut his trees level and close to the ground, that the sprouts which came up afterward might be more vigorous and a sled might slide over the stumps; and instead of leaving a whole tree to support his corded wood, he would pare it away to a slender stake or splinter which you could break off with your hand at last.

He interested me because he was so quiet and solitary and so happy withal; a well of good humor and contentment which overflowed at his eyes. His mirth was without alloy. Sometimes I saw him at his work in the woods, felling trees, and he would greet me with a laugh of inexpressible satisfaction, and a salutation in Canadian French, though he spoke English as well. When I approached him he would suspend his work, and with half-suppressed mirth lie along the trunk of a pine which he had felled, and, peeling off the inner bark, roll it up into a ball and chew it while he laughed and talked. Such an exuberance of animal spirits had he that he sometimes tumbled down and rolled on the ground with laughter at any thing which made him think and tickled him. Looking round upon the trees he would exclaim,— "By George! I can enjoy myself well enough here chopping; I want no better sport." Sometimes, when at leisure, he amused himself all day in the woods with a pocket pistol, firing salutes to himself at regular intervals as he walked. In the winter he had a fire by which at noon he warmed his coffee in a kettle; and as he sat on a log to eat his dinner the chicadees would sometimes come round and alight on his arm and peck at the potato in his fingers; and he said that he "liked to have the little *fellers* about him."

In him the animal man chiefly was developed. In physical endurance and contentment he was cousin to the pine and the rock. I asked him once if he was not sometimes tired at night, after working all day; and he answered, with a sincere and serious look, "Gorrappit, I never was tired in my life." But the intellectual and what is called spiritual man in him were slumbering as in an infant. He had been instructed only in that innocent and ineffectual way in which the Catholic priests teach the aborigines, by which the pupil is never educated to the degree of consciousness, but only to the degree of trust and reverence, and a child is not made a man, but kept a child. When Nature made him, she gave him a strong body and contentment for his portion, and propped him on every side with reverence and reliance, that he might live out his threescore years and ten a child. He was so genuine and unsophisticated that no introduction would serve to introduce him, more than if you introduced a woodchuck to your neighbor. He had got to find him out as you did. He would not play any part. Men paid him wages for work, and so helped to feed and clothe him; but he never exchanged opinions with them. He was so simply and naturally humble—if he can be called humble who never aspires—that humility was no distinct quality in him, nor could he conceive of it. Wiser men were demigods to him. If you told him that such a one was coming, he did as if he thought that any thing so grand would expect nothing of himself, but take all the responsibility on itself, and let him be forgotten still. He never heard the sound of praise. He particularly reverenced the writer and the preacher. Their performances were miracles. When I told him that I wrote considerably, he thought for a long time that it was merely the handwriting which I meant, for he could write a remarkably good hand himself. I sometimes found the name of his native parish handsomely written in the snow by the highway, with the proper French accent, and knew that he had passed. I asked him if he ever wished to write his thoughts. He said that he had read and written letters for those who could not, but he never tried to write thoughts,—no, he could not, he could not tell what to put first, it would kill him, and then there was spelling to be attended to at the same time!

I heard that a distinguished wise man and reformer asked him if he did not want the world to be changed; but he answered with a chuckle of surprise in his Canadian accent, not knowing that the

question had ever been entertained before, "No, I like it well
enough." It would have suggested many things to a philosopher to
have dealings with him. To a stranger he appeared to know nothing
of things in general; yet I sometimes saw in him a man whom I
had not seen before, and I did not know whether he was as wise
as Shakspeare or as simply ignorant as a child, whether to suspect
him of a fine poetic consciousness or of stupidity. A townsman
told me that when he met him sauntering through the village in
his small close-fitting cap, and whistling to himself, he reminded
him of a prince in disguise.

His only books were an almanac and an arithmetic, in which
last he was considerably expert. The former was a sort of cyclo-
pædia to him, which he supposed to contain an abstract of human
knowledge, as indeed it does to a considerable extent. I loved to
sound him on the various reforms of the day, and he never failed
to look at them in the most simple and practical light. He had
never heard of such things before. Could he do without factories?
I asked. He had worn the home-made Vermont gray, he said, and
that was good. Could he dispense with tea and coffee? Did this
country afford any beverage beside water? He had soaked hemlock
leaves in water and drank it, and thought that was better than
water in warm weather. When I asked him if he could do without
money, he showed the convenience of money in such a way as to
suggest and coincide with the most philosophical accounts of the
origin of this institution, and the very derivation of the word
pecunia.[7] If an ox were his property, and he wished to get needles
and thread at the store, he thought it would be inconvenient and
impossible soon to go on mortgaging some portion of the creature
each time to that amount. He could defend many institutions better
than any philosopher, because, in describing them as they concerned him, he gave the true reason for their prevalence, and
speculation had not suggested to him any other. At another time,
hearing Plato's definition of a man,—a biped without feathers,—
and that one exhibited a cock plucked and called it Plato's man,
he thought it an important difference that the *knees* bent the
wrong way. He would sometimes exclaim, "How I love to talk!
By George, I could talk all day!" I asked him once, when I had
not seen him for many months, if he had got a new idea this
summer. "Good Lord," said he, "a man that has to work as I do,
if he does not forget the ideas he has had, he will do well. May be
the man you hoe with is inclined to race; then, by gorry, your
mind must be there; you think of weeds." He would sometimes
ask me first on such occasions, if I had made any improvement.
One winter day I asked him if he was always satisfied with him-

7. Latin for "money"; derived from *pecus*, "cattle."

self, wishing to suggest a substitute within him for the priest without, and some higher motive for living. "Satisfied!" said he;
"some men are satisfied with one thing, and some with another.
One man, perhaps, if he has got enough, will be satisfied to sit
all day with his back to the fire and his belly to the table, by
George!" Yet I never, by any manœuvring, could get him to take
the spiritual view of things; the highest that he appeared to conceive of was a simple expediency, such as you might expect an
animal to appreciate; and this, practically, is true of most men. If
I suggested any improvement in his mode of life, he merely
answered, without expressing any regret, that it was too late. Yet
he thoroughly believed in honesty and the like virtues.

There was a certain positive originality, however slight, to be
detected in him, and I occasionally observed that he was thinking
for himself and expressing his own opinion, a phenomenon so rare
that I would any day walk ten miles to observe it, and it amounted
to the re-origination of many of the institutions of society. Though
he hesitated, and perhaps failed to express himself distinctly, he
always had a presentable thought behind. Yet his thinking was so
primitive and immersed in his animal life, that, though more
promising than a merely learned man's, it rarely ripened to any
thing which can be reported. He suggested that there might be
men of genius in the lowest grades of life, however permanently
humble and illiterate, who take their own view always, or do not
pretend to see at all; who are as bottomless even as Walden Pond
was thought to be, though they may be dark and muddy.

Many a traveller came out of his way to see me and the inside
of my house, and, as an excuse for calling, asked for a glass of
water. I told them that I drank at the pond, and pointed thither,
offering to lend them a dipper. Far off as I lived, I was not ex-
empted from that annual visitation which occurs, methinks, about
the first of April, when every body is on the move; and I had my
share of good luck, though there were some curious specimens
among my visitors. Half-witted men from the almshouse and elsewhere came to see me; but I endeavored to make them exercise all
the wit they had, and make their confessions to me; in such cases
making wit the theme of our conversation; and so was compen-
sated. Indeed, I found some of them to be wiser than the so
called *overseers* of the poor and selectmen of the town, and
thought it was time that the tables were turned. With respect to
wit, I learned that there was not much difference between the half
and the whole. One day, in particular, an inoffensive, simple-
minded pauper, whom with others I had often seen used as fenc-
ing stuff, standing or sitting on a bushel in the fields to keep cattle

and himself from straying, visited me, and expressed a wish to live as I did. He told me, with the utmost simplicity and truth, quite superior, or rather *inferior*, to any thing that is called humility, that he was "deficient in intellect." These were his words. The Lord had made him so, yet he supposed the Lord cared as much for him as for another. "I have always been so," said he, "from my childhood; I never had much mind; I was not like other children; I am weak in the head. It was the Lord's will, I suppose." And there he was to prove the truth of his words. He was a metaphysical puzzle to me. I have rarely met a fellow-man on such promising ground,—it was so simple and sincere and so true all that he said. And, true enough, in proportion as he appeared to humble himself was he exalted. I did not know at first but it was the result of a wise policy. It seemed that from such a basis of truth and frankness as the poor weak-headed pauper had laid, our intercourse might go forward to something better than the intercourse of sages.

I had some guests from those not reckoned commonly among the town's poor, but who should be; who are among the world's poor, at any rate; guests who appeal, not to your hospitality, but to your *hospitalality*; who earnestly wish to be helped, and preface their appeal with the information that they are resolved, for one thing, never to help themselves. I require of a visitor that he be not actually starving, though he may have the very best appetite in the world, however he got it. Objects of charity are not guests. Men who did not know when their visit had terminated, though I went about my business again, answering them from greater and greater remoteness. Men of almost every degree of wit called on me in the migrating season. Some who had more wits than they knew what to do with; runaway slaves with plantation manners, who listened from time to time, like the fox in the fable, as if they heard the hounds a-baying on their track, and looked at me beseechingly, as much as to say,—

"O Christian, will you send me back?"

One real runaway slave, among the rest, whom I helped to forward toward the northstar. Men of one idea, like a hen with one chicken, and that a duckling; men of a thousand ideas, and unkempt heads, like those hens which are made to take charge of a hundred chickens, all in pursuit of one bug, a score of them lost in every morning's dew,—and become frizzled and mangy in consequence; men of ideas instead of legs, a sort of intellectual centipede that made you crawl all over. One man proposed a book in which visitors should write their names, as at the White Mountains; but, alas! I have too good a memory to make that necessary.

I could not but notice some of the peculiarities of my visitors. Girls and boys and young women generally seemed glad to be in the woods. They looked in the pond and at the flowers, and improved their time. Men of business, even farmers, thought only of solitude and employment, and of the great distance at which I dwelt from something or other; and though they said that they loved a ramble in the woods occasionally, it was obvious that they did not. Restless committed men, whose time was all taken up in getting a living or keeping it; ministers who spoke of God as if they enjoyed a monopoly of the subject, who could not bear all kinds of opinions; doctors, lawyers, uneasy housekeepers who pried into my cupboard and bed when I was out,—how came Mrs. —— to know that my sheets were not as clean as hers?—young men who had ceased to be young, and had concluded that it was safest to follow the beaten track of the professions,—all these generally said that it was not possible to do so much good in my position. Ay! there was the rub. The old and infirm and the timid, of whatever age or sex, thought most of sickness, and sudden accident and death; to them life seemed full of danger,—what danger is there if you don't think of any?—and they thought that a prudent man would carefully select the safest position, where Dr. B.[8] might be on hand at a moment's warning. To them the village was literally a *com-munity*, a league for mutual defence, and you would suppose that they would not go a-huckleberrying without a medicine chest. The amount of it is, if a man is alive, there is always *danger* that he may die, though the danger must be allowed to be less in proportion as he is dead-and-alive to begin with. A man sits as many risks as he runs. Finally, there were the self-styled reformers, the greatest bores of all, who thought that I was forever singing,—

> This is the house that I built;
> This is the man that lives in the house that I built;

but they did not know that the third line was,—

> These are the folks that worry the man
> That lives in the house that I built.

I did not fear the hen-harriers, for I kept no chickens; but I feared the men-harriers rather.

I had more cheering visitors than the last. Children come a-berrying, railroad men taking a Sunday morning walk in clean shirts, fishermen and hunters, poets and philosophers, in short, all

---

8. Josiah Bartlett II, a physician from Concord.

honest pilgrims, who came out to the woods for freedom's sake, and really left the village behind, I was ready to greet with,— "Welcome, Englishmen! welcome, Englishmen!" [9] for I had had communication with that race.

The Bean-Field

Meanwhile my beans, the length of whose rows, added together, was seven miles already planted, were impatient to be hoed, for the earliest had grown considerably before the latest were in the ground; indeed they were not easily to be put off. What was the meaning of this so steady and self-respecting, this small Herculean labor, I knew not. I came to love my rows, my beans, though so many more than I wanted. They attached me to the earth, and so I got strength like Antæus.[1] But why should I raise them? Only Heaven knows. This was my curious labor all summer, —to make this portion of the earth's surface, which had yielded only cinquefoil, blackberries, johnswort, and the like, before, sweet wild fruits and pleasant flowers, produce instead this pulse. What shall I learn of beans or beans of me? I cherish them, I hoe them, early and late I have an eye to them; and this is my day's work. It is a fine broad leaf to look on. My auxiliaries are the dews and rains which water this dry soil, and what fertility is in the soil itself, which for the most part is lean and effete. My enemies are worms, cool days, and most of all woodchucks. The last have nibbled for me a quarter of an acre clean. But what right had I to oust johnswort and the rest, and break up their ancient herb garden? Soon, however, the remaining beans will be too tough for them, and go forward to meet new foes.

When I was four years old, as I well remember, I was brought from Boston to this my native town, through these very woods and this field, to the pond. It is one of the oldest scenes stamped on my memory. And now to-night my flute has waked the echoes over that very water. The pines still stand here older than I; or, if some have fallen, I have cooked my supper with their stumps, and a new growth is rising all around, preparing another aspect for new infant eyes. Almost the same johnswort springs from the same perennial root in this pasture, and even I have at length helped to clothe that fabulous landscape of my infant dreams, and one of the results of my presence and influence is seen in these bean leaves, corn blades, and potato vines.

9. Reputedly the greeting of the Indian, Samoset, to the Pilgrims who landed at Plymouth.
1. A mythical giant in Greek mythology who got his strength from touching the earth; he was strangled by Hercules, who held him off the ground.

I planted about two acres and a half of upland; and as it was only about fifteen years since the land was cleared, and I myself had got out two or three cords of stumps, I did not give it any manure; but in the course of the summer it appeared by the arrow-heads which I turned up in hoeing, that an extinct nation had anciently dwelt here and planted corn and beans ere white men came to clear the land, and so, to some extent, had exhausted the soil for this very crop.

Before yet any woodchuck or squirrel had run across the road, or the sun had got above the shrub-oaks, while all the dew was on, though the farmers warned me against it,—I would advise you to do all your work if possible while the dew is on,—I began to level the ranks of haughty weeds in my bean-field and throw dust upon their heads. Early in the morning I worked barefooted, dabbling like a plastic artist in the dewy and crumbling sand, but later in the day the sun blistered my feet. There the sun lighted me to hoe beans, pacing slowly backward and forward over that yellow gravelly upland, between the long green rows, fifteen rods, the one end terminating in a shrub oak copse where I could rest in the shade, the other in a blackberry field where the green berries deepened their tints by the time I had made another bout. Removing the weeds, putting fresh soil about the bean stems, and encouraging this weed which I had sown, making the yellow soil express its summer thought in bean leaves and blossoms rather than in wormwood and piper and millet grass, making the earth say beans instead of grass,—this was my daily work. As I had little aid from horses or cattle, or hired men or boys, or improved implements of husbandry, I was much slower, and became much more intimate with my beans than usual. But labor of the hands, even when pursued to the verge of drudgery, is perhaps never the worst form of idleness. It has a constant and imperishable moral, and to the scholar it yields a classic result. A very *agricola laboriosus*[2] was I to travellers bound westward through Lincoln and Wayland to nobody knows where; they sitting at their ease in gigs, with elbows on knees, and reins loosely hanging in festoons; I the home-staying, laborious native of the soil. But soon my homestead was out of their sight and thought. It was the only open and cultivated field for a great distance on either side of the road; so they made the most of it; and sometimes the man in the field heard more of travellers' gossip and comment than was meant for his ear: "Beans so late! peas so late!"—for I continued to plant when others had began to hoe,—the ministerial husbandman had not suspected it. "Corn, my boy, for fodder; corn for

2. "Hard-working farmer"; Lincoln and Wayland are towns near Concord.

fodder." "Does he *live* there?" asks the black bonnet of the gray coat; and the hard-featured farmer reins up his grateful dobbin to inquire what you are doing where he sees no manure in the furrow, and recommends a little chip dirt, or any little waste stuff, or it may be ashes or plaster. But here were two acres and a half of furrows, and only a hoe for cart and two hands to draw it,—there being an aversion to other carts and horses,—and chip dirt far away. Fellow-travellers as they rattled by compared it aloud with the fields which they had passed, so that I came to know how I stood in the agricultural world. This was one field not in Mr. Coleman's report.[3] And, by the way, who estimates the value of the crop which Nature yields in the still wilder fields unimproved by man? The crop of *English* hay is carefully weighed, the moisture calculated, the silicates and the potash; but in all dells and pond holes in the woods and pastures and swamps grows a rich and various crop only unreaped by man. Mine was, as it were, the connecting link between wild and cultivated fields; as some states are civilized, and others half-civilized, and others savage or barbarous, so my field was, though not in a bad sense, a half-cultivated field. They were beans cheerfully returning to their wild and primitive state that I cultivated, and my hoe played the *Rans des Vaches* [4] for them.

Near at hand, upon the topmost spray of a birch, sings the brown-thrasher—or red mavis, as some love to call him—all the morning, glad of your society, that would find out another farmer's field if yours were not here. While you are planting the seed, he cries,—"Drop it, drop it,—cover it up, cover it up,—pull it up, pull it up, pull it up." But this was not corn, and so it was safe from such enemies as he. You may wonder what his rigmarole, his amateur Paganini [5] performances on one string or on twenty, have to do with your planting, and yet prefer it to leached ashes or plaster. It was a cheap sort of top dressing in which I had entire faith.

As I drew a still fresher soil about the rows with my hoe, I disturbed the ashes of unchronicled nations who in primeval years lived under these heavens, and their small implements of war and hunting were brought to the light of this modern day. They lay mingled with other natural stones, some of which bore the marks of having been burned by Indian fires, and some by the sun, and also bits of pottery and glass brought hither by the recent culti-

---

3. Henry Coleman (1785–1849), State Commissioner for the Agricultural Survey of Massachusetts.
4. A song for calling cattle, sung or played by Swiss cowherds.
5. Nicolo Paganini (1782–1840), Italian violinist and composer.

vators of the soil. When my hoe tinkled against the stones, that
music echoed to the woods and the sky, and was an accompani-
ment to my labor which yielded an instant and immeasurable crop.
It was no longer beans that I hoed, nor I that hoed beans; and I
remembered with as much pity as pride, if I remembered at all, my
acquaintances who had gone to the city to attend the oratorios. The
night-hawk circled overhead in the sunny afternoons—for I sometimes made a day of it—like a mote in the eye, or in heaven's
eye, falling from time to time with a swoop and a sound as if
the heavens were rent, torn at last to very rags and tatters, and yet
a seamless cope remained; small imps that fill the air and lay their
eggs on the ground on bare sand or rocks on the tops of hills,
where few have found them; graceful and slender like ripples
caught up from the pond, as leaves are raised by the wind to
float in the heavens; such kindredship is in Nature. The hawk is
aerial brother of the wave which he sails over and surveys, those
his perfect air-inflated wings answering to the elemental unfledged
pinions of the sea. Or sometimes I watched a pair of hen-hawks
circling high in the sky, alternately soaring and descending,
approaching and leaving one another, as if they were the imbodiment of my own thoughts. Or I was attracted by the passage of
wild pigeons from this wood to that, with a slight quivering winnowing sound and carrier haste; or from under a rotten stump my
hoe turned up a sluggish portentous and outlandish spotted sala-
mander, a trace of Egypt and the Nile, yet our contemporary.
When I paused to lean on my hoe, these sounds and sights I
heard and saw any where in the row, a part of the inexhaustible
entertainment which the country offers.

On gala days the town fires its great guns, which echo like
popguns to these woods, and some waifs of martial music occasionally penetrate thus far. To me, away there in my bean-field at
the other end of the town, the big guns sounded as if a puff ball
had burst; and when there was a military turnout of which I was
ignorant, I have sometimes had a vague sense all the day of some
sort of itching and disease in the horizon, as if some eruption
would break out there soon, either scarlatina or canker-rash, until
at length some more favorable puff of wind, making haste over
the fields and up the Wayland road, brought me information of
the "trainers."[6] It seemed by the distant hum as if somebody's bees
had swarmed, and that the neighbors, according to Virgil's advice,
by a faint *tintinnabulum* upon the most sonorous of their domestic utensils, were endeavoring to call them down into the hive

6. Members of the Concord Artillery, a unit of the state militia.

again. And when the sound died quite away, and the hum had ceased, and the most favorable breezes told no tale, I knew that they had got the last drone of them all safely into the Middlesex hive, and that now their minds were bent on the honey with which it was smeared.

I felt proud to know that the liberties of Massachusetts and of our fatherland were in such safe keeping; and as I turned to my hoeing again I was filled with an inexpressible confidence, and pursued my labor cheerfully with a calm trust in the future.

When there were several bands of musicians, it sounded as if all the village was a vast bellows, and all the buildings expanded and collapsed alternately with a din. But sometimes it was a really noble and inspiring strain that reached these woods, and the trumpet that sings of fame, and I felt as if I could spit a Mexican with a good relish,—for why should we always stand for trifles?—and looked round for a woodchuck or a skunk to exercise my chivalry upon. These martial strains seemed as far away as Palestine, and reminded me of a march of crusaders in the horizon, with a slight tantivy and tremulous motion of the elm-tree tops which overhang the village. This was one of the *great* days; though the sky had from my clearing only the same everlastingly great look that it wears daily, and I saw no difference in it.

It was a singular experience that long acquaintance which I cultivated with beans, what with planting, and hoeing, and harvesting, and threshing, and picking over, and selling them,—the last was the hardest of all,—I might add eating, for I did taste. I was determined to know beans. When they were growing, I used to hoe from five o'clock in the morning till noon, and commonly spent the rest of the day about other affairs. Consider the intimate and curious acquaintance one makes with various kinds of weeds,—it will bear some iteration in the account, for there was no little iteration in the labor,—disturbing their delicate organizations so ruthlessly, and making such invidious distinctions with his hoe, levelling whole ranks of one species, and sedulously cultivating another. That's Roman wormwood,—that's pigweed,— that's sorrel,—that's piper-grass,—have at him, chop him up, turn his roots upward to the sun, don't let him have a fibre in the shade, if you do he'll turn himself t'other side up and be as green as a leek in two days. A long war, not with cranes, but with weeds, those Trojans who had sun and rain and dews on their side. Daily the beans saw me come to their rescue armed with a hoe, and thin the ranks of their enemies, filling up the trenches with weedy dead. Many a lusty crest-waving Hector,[7] that towered a

7. In the *Iliad*, the bravest of the Trojan warriors, killed by Achilles.

whole foot above his crowding comrades, fell before my weapon and rolled in the dust.

Those summer days which some of my contemporaries devoted to the fine arts in Boston or Rome, and others to contemplation in India, and others to trade in London or New York, I thus, with the other farmers of New England, devoted to husbandry. Not that I wanted beans to eat, for I am by nature a Pythagorean,[8] so far as beans are concerned, whether they mean porridge or voting, and exchanged them for rice; but, perchance, as some must work in fields if only for the sake of tropes and expression, to serve a parable-maker one day. It was on the whole a rare amusement, which continued too long, might have become a dissipation. Though I gave them no manure, and did not hoe them all once, I hoed them unusually well as far as I went, and was paid for it in the end, "there being in truth," as Evelyn says, "no compost or lætation whatsoever comparable to this continual motion, repastination, and turning of the mould with the spade." "The earth," he adds elsewhere, "especially if fresh, has a certain magnetism in it, by which it attracts the salt, power, or virtue (call it either) which gives it life, and is the logic of all the labor and stir we keep about it, to sustain us; all dungings and other sordid temperings being but the vicars succedaneous to this improvement."[9] Moreover, this being one of those "worn-out and exhausted lay fields which enjoy their sabbath," had perchance, as Sir Kenelm Digby[1] thinks likely, attracted "vital, spirits" from the air. I harvested twelve bushels of beans.

But to be more particular, for it is complained that Mr. Coleman has reported chiefly the expensive experiments of gentlemen farmers, my outgoes were,—

For a hoe, ...	$ 0 54	
Ploughing, harrowing, and furrowing, . . .	7 50,	Too much.
Beans for seed, ...	3 12½	
Potatoes "	1 33	
Peas "	0 40	
Turnip seed, ...	0 06	
White line for crow fence, ...	0 02	
Horse cultivator and boy three hours, . . .	1 00	
Horse and cart to get crop, ...	0 75	
In all, ...	$14 72½	

8. A follower of the Greek philosopher and mathematician, Pythagoras (582—507? B.C.), who reputedly forbade his disciples to eat beans.
9. John Evelyn (1620–1706), English horticulturalist and author; from *Terra, a Philosophical Discourse of Earth* (1729).
1. English philosopher and naturalist (1603–65); quoted in Evelyn's *Sylva, or a Discourse of Forest-Trees* (1679), 303.

My income was, (patrem familias vendacem, non emacem esse oportet,) [2] from

Nine bushels and twelve quarts of beans sold, . . $16 94
Five   "   large potatoes, ... 2 50
Nine   "   small, ... 2 25
Grass, ... 1 00
Stalks, ... 0 75

     In all, ... $23 44
Leaving a pecuniary profit, as I have elsewhere said, of $8 71½.

This is the result of my experience in raising beans. Plant the common small white bush bean about the first of June, in rows three feet by eighteen inches apart, being careful to select fresh round and unmixed seed. First look out for worms, and supply vacancies by planting anew. Then look out for woodchucks, if it is an exposed place, for they will nibble off the earliest tender leaves almost clean as they go; and again, when the young tendrils make their appearance, they have notice of it, and will shear them off with both buds and young pods, sitting erect like a squirrel. But above all harvest as early as possible, if you would escape frosts and have a fair and salable crop; you may save much loss by this means.

This further experience also I gained. I said to myself, I will not plant beans and corn with so much industry another summer, but such seeds, if the seed is not lost, as sincerity, truth, simplicity, faith, innocence, and the like, and see if they will not grow in this soil, even with less toil and manurance, and sustain me, for surely it has not been exhausted for these crops. Alas! I said this to myself; but now another summer is gone, and another, and another, and I am obliged to say to you, Reader, that the seeds which I planted, if indeed they *were* the seeds of those virtues, were wormeaten or had lost their vitality, and so did not come up. Commonly men will only be brave as their fathers were brave, or timid. This generation is very sure to plant corn and beans each new year precisely as the Indians did centuries ago and taught the first settlers to do, as if there were a fate in it. I saw an old man the other day, to my astonishment, making the holes with a hoe for the seventieth time at least, and not for himself to lie down in! But why should not the New Englander try new adventures, and not lay so much stress on his grain, his potato and grass crop, and his orchards,—raise other crops than these? Why concern ourselves so much about our beans for seed, and not be concerned at all about a new generation of men? We should really be fed and

2. "A householder should be one who sells, not one who buys" (from Cato, *De Agri Cultura*).

cheered if when we met a man we were sure to see that some of the qualities which I have named, which we all prize more than those other productions, but which are for the most part broadcast and floating in the air, had taken root and grown in him. Here comes such a subtile and ineffable quality, for instance, as truth or justice, though the slightest amount or new variety of it, along the road. Our ambassadors should be instructed to send home such seeds as these, and Congress help to distribute them over all the land. We should never stand upon ceremony with sincerity. We should never cheat and insult and banish one another by our meanness, if there were present the kernel of worth and friendliness. We should not meet thus in haste. Most men I do not meet at all, for they seem not to have time; they are busy about their beans. We would not deal with a man thus plodding ever, leaning on a hoe or a spade as a staff between his work, not as a mushroom, but partially risen out of the earth, something more than erect, like swallows alighted and walking on the ground:—

"And as he spake, his wings would now and then
Spread, as he meant to fly, then close again," [3]

so that we should suspect that we might be conversing with an angel. Bread may not always nourish us; but it always does us good, it even takes stiffness out of our joints, and makes us supple and buoyant, when we knew not what ailed us, to recognize any generosity in man or Nature, to share any unmixed and heroic joy.

Ancient poetry and mythology suggest, at least, that husbandry was once a sacred art; but it is pursued with irreverent haste and heedlessness by us, our object being to have large farms and large crops merely. We have no festival, nor procession, nor ceremony, not excepting our Cattle-shows and so called Thanksgivings, by which the farmer expresses a sense of the sacredness of his calling, or is reminded of its sacred origin. It is the premium and the feast which tempt him. He sacrifices not to Ceres and the Terrestrial Jove, but to the infernal Plutus rather.[4] By avarice and selfishness, and a grovelling habit, from which none of us is free, of regarding the soil as property, or the means of acquiring property chiefly, the landscape is deformed, husbandry is degraded with us, and the farmer leads the meanest of lives. He knows Nature but as a robber. Cato says that the profits of agriculture are particularly pious or just, (*maximeque pius quæstus,*) and according to Varro[5] the old Romans "called the same earth

3. Francis Quarles (1592–1644), English poet; from "The Shepherd's Oracles," eclogue 5.
4. In Roman mythology, the goddess of corn and harvests; "Jove" is another name for the Roman "Jupiter"; Plutus is the god of riches.
5. Marcus Terrentius Varro (116—27 B.C.), Roman scholar and satirist; from his *Rerum Rusticarum.*

Mother and Ceres, and thought that they who cultivated it led a pious and useful life, and that they alone were left of the race of King Saturn."[6]

We are wont to forget that the sun looks on our cultivated fields and on the prairies and forests without distinction. They all reflect and absorb his rays alike, and the former make but a small part of the glorious picture which he beholds in his daily course. In his view the earth is all equally cultivated like a garden. Therefore we should receive the benefit of his light and heat with a corresponding trust and magnanimity. What though I value the seed of these beans, and harvest that in the fall of the year? This broad field which I have looked at so long looks not to me as the principal cultivator, but away from me to influences more genial to it, which water and make it green. These beans have results which are not harvested by me. Do they not grow for woodchucks partly? The ear of wheat, (in Latin *spica*, obsoletely *speca*, from *spe*, hope,) should not be the only hope of the husbandman; its kernel or grain (*granum*, from *gerendo*, bearing,) is not all that it bears. How, then, can our harvest fail? Shall I not rejoice also at the abundance of the weeds whose seeds are the granary of the birds? It matters little comparatively whether the fields fill the farmer's barns. The true husbandman will cease from anxiety, as the squirrels manifest no concern whether the woods will bear chestnuts this year or not, and finish his labor with every day, relinquishing all claim to the produce of his fields, and sacrificing in his mind not only his first but his last fruits also.

The Village

After hoeing, or perhaps reading and writing, in the forenoon, I usually bathed again in the pond, swimming across one of its coves for a stint, and washed the dust of labor from my person, or smoothed out the last wrinkle which study had made, and for the afternoon was absolutely free. Every day or two I strolled to the village to hear some of the gossip which is incessantly going on there, circulating either from mouth to mouth, or from newspaper to newspaper, and which, taken in homœopathic doses, was really as refreshing in its way as the rustle of leaves and the peeping of frogs. As I walked in the woods to see the birds and squirrels, so I walked in the village to see the men and boys; instead of the wind among the pines I heard the carts rattle. In one direction from my house there was a colony of muskrats in the river meadows; under the grove of elms and buttonwoods in the

6. In Roman mythology, the god of agriculture (called "Cronus" by the Greeks).

other horizon was a village of busy men, as curious to me as if they had been prairie dogs, each sitting at the mouth of its burrow, or running over to a neighbor's to gossip. I went there frequently to observe their habits. The village appeared to me a great news room; and on one side, to support it, as once at Redding & Company's on State Street, they kept nuts and raisins, or salt and meal and other groceries. Some have such a vast appetite for the former commodity, that is, the news, and such sound digestive organs, that they can sit forever in public avenues without stirring, and let it simmer and whisper through them like the Etesian winds,[1] or as if inhaling ether, it only producing numbness and insensibility to pain,—otherwise it would often be painful to hear,—without affecting the consciousness. I hardly ever failed, when I rambled through the village, to see a row of such worthies, either sitting on a ladder sunning themselves, with their bodies inclined forward and their eyes glancing along the line this way and that, from time to time, with a voluptuous expression, or else leaning against a barn with their hands in their pockets, like caryatides, as if to prop it up. They, being commonly out of doors, heard whatever was in the wind. These are the coarsest mills, in which all gossip is first rudely digested or cracked up before it is emptied into finer and more delicate hoppers within doors. I observed that the vitals of the village were the grocery, the bar-room, the post-office, and the bank; and, as a necessary part of the machinery, they kept a bell, a big gun, and a fire-engine, at convenient places; and the houses were so arranged as to make the most of mankind, in lanes and fronting one another, so that every traveller had to run the gantlet, and every man, woman, and child might get a lick at him. Of course, those who were stationed nearest to the head of the line, where they could most see and be seen, and have the first blow at him, paid the highest prices for their places; and the few straggling inhabitants in the outskirts, where long gaps in the line began to occur, and the traveller could get over walls or turn aside into cow paths, and so escape, paid a very slight ground or window tax. Signs were hung out on all sides to allure him; some to catch him by the appetite, as the tavern and victualling cellar; some by the fancy, as the dry goods store and the jeweller's; and others by the hair or the feet or the skirts, as the barber, the shoemaker, or the tailor. Besides, there was a still more terrible standing invitation to call at every one of these houses, and company expected about these times. For the most part I escaped wonderfully from these dangers, either by proceeding at once boldly and without delibera-

<hr />

1. Northerly Mediterranean summer winds that recur annually.

tion to the goal, as is recommended to those who run the gantlet, or by keeping my thoughts on high things, like Orpheus,[2] who, "loudly singing the praises of the gods to his lyre, drowned the voices of the Sirens, and kept out of danger." Sometimes I bolted suddenly, and nobody could tell my whereabouts, for I did not stand much about gracefulness, and never hesitated at a gap in a fence. I was even accustomed to make an irruption into some houses, where I was well entertained, and after learning the kernels and very last sieve-ful of news, what had subsided, the prospects of war and peace, and whether the world was likely to hold together much longer, I was let out through the rear avenues, and so escaped to the woods again.

It was very pleasant, when I staid late in town, to launch myself into the night, especially if it was dark and tempestuous, and set sail from some bright village parlor or lecture room, with a bag of rye or Indian meal upon my shoulder, for my snug harbor in the woods, having made all tight without and withdrawn under hatches with a merry crew of thoughts, leaving only my outer man at the helm, or even tying up the helm when it was plain sailing. I had many a genial thought by the cabin fire "as I sailed." I was never cast away nor distressed in any weather, though I encountered some severe storms. It is darker in the woods, even in common nights, than most suppose. I frequently had to look up at the opening between the trees above the path in order to learn my route, and, where there was no cart-path, to feel with my feet the faint track which I had worn, or steer by the known relation of particular trees which I felt with my hands, passing between two pines for instance, not more than eighteen inches apart, in the midst of the woods, invariably, in the darkest night. Sometimes, after coming home thus late in a dark and muggy night, when my feet felt the path which my eyes could not see, dreaming and absent-minded all the way, until I was aroused by having to raise my hand to lift the latch, I have not been able to recall a single step of my walk, and I have thought that perhaps my body would find its way home if its master should forsake it, as the hand finds its way to the mouth without assistance. Several times, when a visitor chanced to stay into evening, and it proved a dark night, I was obliged to conduct him to the cart-path in the rear of the house, and then point out to him the direction he was to pursue, and in keeping which he was to be guided rather by his feet than his eyes. One very dark night I directed thus on their way two young men who had been fishing in the pond. They lived about a mile off through the woods, and were quite used to the route. A

2. In Greek mythology, the son of a Muse whose music had supernatural powers and whose singing could charm animals and inanimate objects.

day or two after one of them told me that they wandered about
the greater part of the night, close by their own premises, and did
not get home till toward morning, by which time, as there had
been several heavy showers in the mean while, and the leaves were
very wet, they were drenched to their skins. I have heard of many
going astray even in the village streets, when the darkness was so
thick that you could cut it with a knife, as the saying is. Some who
live in the outskirts, having come to town a-shopping in their
wagons, have been obliged to put up for the night; and gentlemen
and ladies making a call have gone half a mile out of their way,
feeling the sidewalk only with their feet, and not knowing when
they turned. It is a surprising and memorable, as well as valuable
experience, to be lost in the woods any time. Often in a snow
storm, even by day, one will come out upon a well-known road
and yet find it impossible to tell which way leads to the village.
Though he knows that he has travelled it a thousand times, he
cannot recognize a feature in it, but it is as strange to him as if it
were a road in Siberia. By night, of course, the perplexity is infinitely greater. In our most trivial walks, we are constantly,
though unconsciously, steering like pilots by certain well-known
beacons and headlands, and if we go beyond our usual course we
still carry in our minds the bearing of some neighboring cape;
and not till we are completely lost, or turned round,—for a man
needs only to be turned round once with his eyes shut in this world
to be lost,—do we appreciate the vastness and strangeness of
Nature. Every man has to learn the points of compass again as
often as he awakes, whether from sleep or any abstraction. Not
till we are lost, in other words, not till we have lost the world, do
we begin to find ourselves, and realize where we are and the
infinite extent of our relations.

One afternoon, near the end of the first summer, when I went
to the village to get a shoe from the cobbler's, I was seized and
put into jail, because, as I have elsewhere related,[3] I did not pay a
tax to, or recognize the authority of, the state which buys and
sells men, women, and children, like cattle at the door of its
senate-house. I had gone down to the woods for other purposes.
But, wherever a man goes, men will pursue and paw him with
their dirty institutions, and, if they can, constrain him to belong to
their desperate odd-fellow society. It is true, I might have resisted
forcibly with more or less effect, might have run "amok" against
society; but I preferred that society should run "amok" against
me, it being the desperate party. However, I was released the next
day, obtained my mended shoe, and returned to the woods in

3. I.e., in "Resistance to Civil Government" (1849).

season to get my dinner of huckleberries on Fair-Haven Hill. I was never molested by any person but those who represented the state. I had no lock nor bolt but for the desk which held my papers, not even a nail to put over my latch or windows. I never fastened my door night or day, though I was to be absent several days; not even when the next fall I spent a fortnight in the woods of Maine. And yet my house was more respected than if it had been surrounded by a file of soldiers. The tired rambler could rest and warm himself by my fire, the literary amuse himself with the few books on my table, or the curious, by opening my closet door, see what was left of my dinner, and what prospect I had of a supper. Yet, though many people of every class came this way to the pond, I suffered no serious inconvenience from these sources, and I never missed any thing but one small book, a volume of Homer, which perhaps was improperly gilded, and this I trust a soldier of our camp has found by this time. I am convinced, that if all men were to live as simply as I then did, thieving and robbery would be unknown. These take place only in communities where some have got more than is sufficient while others have not enough. The Pope's Homers [4] would soon get properly distributed.—

"Nec bella fuerunt,
Faginus astabat dum scyphus ante dapes." [5]
"Nor wars did men molest,
When only beechen bowls were in request."

"You who govern public affairs, what need have you to employ punishments? Love virtue, and the people will be virtuous. The virtues of a superior man are like the wind; the virtues of a common man are like the grass; the grass, when the wind passes over it, bends." [6]

The Ponds

Sometimes, having had a surfeit of human society and gossip, and worn out all my village friends, I rambled still farther westward than I habitually dwell, into yet more unfrequented parts of the town, "to fresh woods and pastures new," [1] or, while the sun was setting, made my supper of huckleberries and blueberries on Fair Haven Hill, and laid up a store for several days. The fruits do not yield their true flavor to the purchaser of them, nor to him who raises them for the market. There is but one way to obtain it,

4. Alexander Pope (1688–1744) translated Homer's *Iliad* and *Odyssey* into English.
5. From Albius Tibullus, *Elegies* 3.11.7–8.
6. From Confucius, *Analects* 12.
1. John Milton, "Lycidas" 194.

yet few take that way. If you would know the flavor of huckleberries, ask the cow-boy or the partridge. It is a vulgar error to suppose that you have tasted huckleberries who never plucked them. A huckleberry never reaches Boston; they have not been known there since they grew on her three hills. The ambrosial and essential part of the fruit is lost with the bloom which is rubbed off in the market cart, and they become mere provender. As long as Eternal Justice reigns, not one innocent huckleberry can be transported thither from the country's hills.

Occasionally, after my hoeing was done for the day, I joined some impatient companion who had been fishing on the pond since morning, as silent and motionless as a duck or a floating leaf, and, after practising various kinds of philosophy, had concluded commonly, by the time I arrived, that he belonged to the ancient sect of Cœnobites.[2] There was one older man, an excellent fisher and skilled in all kinds of woodcraft, who was pleased to look upon my house as a building erected for the convenience of fishermen; and I was equally pleased when he sat in my doorway to arrange his lines. Once in a while we sat together on the pond, he at one end of the boat, and I at the other; but not many words passed between us, for he had grown deaf in his later years, but he occasionally hummed a psalm, which harmonized well enough with my philosophy. Our intercourse was thus altogether one of unbroken harmony, far more pleasing to remember than if it had been carried on by speech. When, as was commonly the case, I had none to commune with, I used to raise the echoes by striking with a paddle on the side of my boat, filling the surrounding woods with circling and dilating sound, stirring them up as the keeper of a menagerie his wild beasts, until I elicited a growl from every wooded vale and hill-side.

In warm evenings I frequently sat in the boat playing the flute, and saw the perch, which I seemed to have charmed, hovering around me, and the moon travelling over the ribbed bottom, which was strewed with the wrecks of the forest. Formerly I had come to this pond adventurously, from time to time, in dark summer nights, with a companion, and making a fire close to the water's edge, which we thought attracted the fishes, we caught pouts with a bunch of worms strung on a thread; and when we had done, far in the night, threw the burning brands high into the air like skyrockets, which, coming down into the pond, were quenched with a loud hissing, and we were suddenly groping in total darkness. Through this, whistling a tune, we took our way to the haunts of men again. But now I had made my home by the shore.

2. A religious community, and a pun ("See no bites").

Sometimes, after staying in a village parlor till the family had all retired, I have returned to the woods, and, partly with a view to the next day's dinner, spent the hours of midnight fishing from a boat by moonlight, serenaded by owls and foxes, and hearing, from time to time, the creaking note of some unknown bird close at hand. These experiences were very memorable and valuable to me, —anchored in forty feet of water, and twenty or thirty rods from the shore, surrounded sometimes by thousands of small perch and shiners, dimpling the surface with their tails in the moonlight, and communicating by a long flaxen line with mysterious nocturnal fishes which had their dwelling forty feet below, or sometimes dragging sixty feet of line about the pond as I drifted in the gentle night breeze, now and then feeling a slight vibration along it, indicative of some life prowling about its extremity, of dull uncertain blundering purpose there, and slow to make up its mind. At length you slowly raise, pulling hand over hand, some horned pout squeaking and squirming to the upper air. It was very queer, especially in dark nights, when your thoughts had wandered to vast and cosmogonal themes in other spheres, to feel this faint jerk, which came to interrupt your dreams and link you to Nature again. It seemed as if I might next cast my line upward into the air, as well as downward into this element which was scarcely more dense. Thus I caught two fishes as it were with one hook.

The scenery of Walden is on a humble scale, and, though very beautiful, does not approach to grandeur, nor can it much concern one who has not long frequented it or lived by its shore; yet this pond is so remarkable for its depth and purity as to merit a particular description. It is a clear and deep green well, half a mile long and a mile and three quarters in circumference, and contains about sixty-one and a half acres; a perennial spring in the midst of pine and oak woods, without any visible inlet or outlet except by the clouds and evaporation. The surrounding hills rise abruptly from the water to the height of forty to eighty feet, though on the south-east and east they attain to about one hundred and one hundred and fifty feet respectively, within a quarter and a third of a mile. They are exclusively woodland. All our Concord waters have two colors at least, one when viewed at a distance, and another, more proper, close at hand. The first depends more on the light, and follows the sky. In clear weather, in summer, they appear blue at a little distance, especially if agitated, and at a great distance all appear alike. In stormy weather they are sometimes of a dark slate color. The sea, however, is said to be blue one day and green another without any perceptible change in the atmosphere. I have seen our river, when, the landscape being covered with snow, both water and ice were almost as green as grass. Some consider blue "to be the color of pure water, whether liquid or solid." But, looking directly down into our waters from a boat, they are seen to be of very different colors. Walden is blue at one time and green at another, even from the same point of view. Lying between the earth and the heavens, it partakes of the color of both. Viewed from a hill-top it reflects the color of the sky, but near at hand it is of a yellowish tint next the shore where you can see the sand, then a light green, which gradually deepens to a uniform dark green in the body of the pond. In some lights, viewed even from a hill-top, it is of a vivid green next the shore. Some have referred this to the reflection of the verdure; but it is equally green there against the railroad sand-bank, and in the spring, before the leaves are expanded, and it may be simply the result of the prevailing blue mixed with the yellow of the sand. Such is the color of its iris. This is that portion, also, where in the spring, the ice being warmed by the heat of the sun reflected from the bottom, and also transmitted through the earth, melts first and forms a narrow canal about the still frozen middle. Like the rest of our waters, when much agitated, in clear weather, so that the surface of the waves may reflect the sky at the right angle, or because there is more light mixed with it, it appears at a little distance of a darker blue than the sky itself; and at such a time, being on its surface, and looking with divided vision, so as to see the reflection, I have discerned a matchless and indescribable light blue, such as watered or changeable silks and sword blades suggest, more cerulean than the sky itself, alternating with the original dark green on the opposite sides of the waves, which last appeared but muddy in comparison. It is a vitreous greenish blue, as I remember it, like those patches of the winter sky seen through cloud vistas in the west before sundown. Yet a single glass of its water held up to the light is as colorless as an equal quantity of air. It is well known that a large plate of glass will have a green tint, owing, as the makers say, to its "body," but a small piece of the same will be colorless. How large a body of Walden water would be required to reflect a green tint I have never proved. The water of our river is black or a very dark brown to one looking directly down on it, and, like that of most ponds, imparts to the body of one bathing in it a yellowish tinge; but this water is of such crystalline purity that the body of the bather appears of an alabaster whiteness, still more unnatural, which, as the limbs are magnified and distorted withal, produces a monstrous effect, making fit studies for a Michael Angelo.[3]

3. Italian painter, sculptor, and architect (1475–1564). Known for oversized and muscular figures.

The water is so transparent that the bottom can easily be discerned at the depth of twenty-five or thirty feet. Paddling over it, you may see many feet beneath the surface the schools of perch and shiners, perhaps only an inch long, yet the former easily distinguished by their transverse bars, and you think that they must be ascetic fish that find a subsistence there. Once, in the winter, many years ago, when I had been cutting holes through the ice in order to catch pickerel, as I stepped ashore I tossed my axe back on to the ice, but, as if some evil genius had directed it, it slid four or five rods directly into one of the holes, where the water was twenty-five feet deep. Out of curiosity, I lay down on the ice and looked through the hole, until I saw the axe a little on one side, standing on its head, with its helve erect and gently swaying to and fro with the pulse of the pond; and there it might have stood erect and swaying till in the course of time the handle rotted off, if I had not disturbed it. Making another hole directly over it with an ice chisel which I had, and cutting down the longest birch which I could find in the neighborhood with my knife, I made a slip-noose, which I attached to its end, and, letting it down carefully, passed it over the knob of the handle, and drew it by a line along the birch, and so pulled the axe out again.

The shore is composed of a belt of smooth rounded white stones like paving stones, excepting one or two short sand beaches, and is so steep that in many places a single leap will carry you into water over your head; and were it not for its remarkable transparency, that would be the last to be seen of its bottom till it rose on the opposite side. Some think it is bottomless. It is nowhere muddy, and a casual observer would say that there were no weeds at all in it; and of noticeable plants, except in the little meadows recently overflowed, which do not properly belong to it, a closer scrutiny does not detect a flag nor a bulrush, nor even a lily, yellow or white, but only a few small heart-leaves and potamogetons, and perhaps a water-target or two; all which however a bather might not perceive; and these plants are clean and bright like the element they grow in. The stones extend a rod or two into the water, and then the bottom is pure sand, except in the deepest parts, where there is usually a little sediment, probably from the decay of the leaves which have been wafted on to it so many successive falls, and a bright green weed is brought up on anchors even in midwinter.

We have one other pond just like this, White Pond in Nine Acre Corner, about two and a half miles westerly; but, though I am acquainted with most of the ponds within a dozen miles of this centre, I do not know a third of this pure and well-like character. Successive nations perchance have drank at, admired, and fathomed it, and passed away, and still its water is green and pellucid as ever. Not an intermitting spring! Perhaps on that spring morning when Adam and Eve were driven out of Eden Walden Pond was already in existence, and even then breaking up in a gentle spring rain accompanied with mist and a southerly wind, and covered with myriads of ducks and geese, which had not heard of the fall, when still such pure lakes sufficed them. Even then it had commenced to rise and fall, and had clarified its waters and colored them of the hue they now wear, and obtained a patent of heaven to be the only Walden Pond in the world and distiller of celestial dews. Who knows in how many unremembered nations' literatures this has been the Castalian Fountain? [4] or what nymphs presided over it in the Golden Age? It is a gem of the first water which Concord wears in her coronet.

Yet perchance the first who came to this well have left some trace of their footsteps. I have been surprised to detect encircling the pond, even where a thick wood has just been cut down on the shore, a narrow shelf-like path in the steep hill-side, alternately rising and falling, approaching and receding from the water's edge, as old probably as the race of man here, worn by the feet of aboriginal hunters, and still from time to time unwittingly trodden by the present occupants of the land. This is particularly distinct to one standing on the middle of the pond in winter, just after a light snow has fallen, appearing as a clear undulating white line, unobscured by weeds and twigs, and very obvious a quarter of a mile off in many places where in summer it is hardly distinguishable close at hand. The snow reprints it, as it were, in clear white type alto-relievo.[5] The ornamented grounds of villas which will one day be built here may still preserve some trace of this.

The pond rises and falls, but whether regularly or not, and within what period, nobody knows, though, as usual, many pretend to know. It is commonly higher in the winter and lower in the summer, though not corresponding to the general wet and dryness. I can remember when it was a foot or two lower, and also when it was at least five feet higher, than when I lived by it. There is a narrow sand-bar running into it, with very deep water on one side, on which I helped boil a kettle of chowder, some six rods from the main shore, about the year 1824, which it has not been possible to do for twenty-five years; and on the other hand, my friends used to listen with incredulity when I told them, that a

4. In Greek mythology, a fountain on Mount Parnassus, the source of poetic inspiration.
5. A sculptural term referring to the projection of a figure from the background; also called "high relief."

few years later I was accustomed to fish from a boat in a secluded
cove in the woods, fifteen rods from the only shore they knew,
which place was long since converted into a meadow. But the pond
has risen steadily for two years, and now, in the summer of '52,
is just five feet higher than when I lived there, or as high as it was
thirty years ago, and fishing goes on again in the meadow. This
makes a difference of level, at the outside, of six or seven feet;
and yet the water shed by the surrounding hills is insignificant in
amount, and this overflow must be referred to causes which
affect the deep springs. This same summer the pond has begun to
fall again. It is remarkable that this fluctuation, whether periodical or not, appears thus to require many years for its accomplishment. I have observed one rise and a part of two falls, and I expect that a dozen or fifteen years hence the water will again be as
low as I have ever known it. Flints' Pond, a mile eastward,
allowing for the disturbance occasioned by its inlets and outlets,
and the smaller intermediate ponds also, sympathize with Walden,
and recently attained their greatest height at the same time with
the latter. The same is true, as far as my observation goes, of
White Pond.

This rise and fall of Walden at long intervals serves this use at
least; the water standing at this great height for a year or more,
though it makes it difficult to walk round it, kills the shrubs and
trees which have sprung up about its edge since the last rise,
pitch-pines, birches, alders, aspens, and others, and, falling again,
leaves an unobstructed shore; for, unlike many ponds and all
waters which are subject to a daily tide, its shore is cleanest when
the water is lowest. On the side of the pond next my house, a row
of pitch pines fifteen feet high has been killed and tipped over as if
by a lever, and thus a stop put to their encroachments; and their
size indicates how many years have elapsed since the last rise to
this height. By this fluctuation the pond asserts its title to a shore,
and thus the *shore* is *shorn*, and the trees cannot hold it by right
of possession. These are the lips of the lake on which no beard
grows. It licks its chaps from time to time. When the water is at
its height, the alders, willows, and maples send forth a mass of
fibrous red roots several feet long from all sides of their stems in
the water, and to the height of three or four feet from the ground,
in the effort to maintain themselves; and I have known the high-
blueberry bushes about the shore, which commonly produce no
fruit, bear an abundant crop under these circumstances.

Some have been puzzled to tell how the shore became so regularly paved. My townsmen have all heard the tradition, the oldest
people tell me that they heard it in their youth, that anciently the
Indians were holding a pow-wow upon a hill here, which rose as

high into the heavens as the pond now sinks deep into the earth, and they used much profanity, as the story goes, though this vice is one of which the Indians were never guilty, and while they were thus engaged the hill shook and suddenly sank, and only one old squaw, named Walden, escaped, and from her the pond was named.[6] It has been conjectured that when the hill shook these stones rolled down its side and became the present shore. It is very certain, at any rate, that once there was no pond here, and now there is one; and this Indian fable does not in any respect conflict with the account of that ancient settler whom I have mentioned, who remembers so well when he first came here with his divining rod, saw a thin vapor rising from the sward, and the hazel pointed steadily downward, and he concluded to dig a well here. As for the stones, many still think that they are hardly to be accounted for by the action of the waves on these hills; but I observe that the surrounding hills are remarkably full of the same kind of stones, so that they have been obliged to pile them up in walls on both sides of the railroad cut nearest the pond; and, moreover, there are most stones where the shore is most abrupt; so that, unfortunately, it is no longer a mystery to me. I detect the paver. If the name was not derived from that of some English locality,—Saffron Walden,[7] for instance,—one might suppose that it was called, originally, *Walled-in* Pond.

The pond was my well ready dug. For four months in the year its water is as cold as it is pure at all times; and I think that it is then as good as any, if not the best, in the town. In the winter, all water which is exposed to the air is colder than springs and wells which are protected from it. The temperature of the pond water which had stood in the room where I sat from five o'clock in the afternoon till noon the next day, the sixth of March, 1846, the thermometer having been up to 65° or 70° some of the time, owing partly to the sun on the roof, was 42°, or one degree colder than the water of one of the coldest wells in the village just drawn. The temperature of the Boiling Spring[8] the same day was 45°, or the warmest of any water tried, though it is the coldest that I know of in summer, when, beside, shallow and stagnant surface water is not mingled with it. Moreover, in summer, Walden never becomes so warm as most water which is exposed to the sun, on account of its depth. In the warmest weather I usually placed a pailful in my cellar, where it became cool in the night,

6. This is told of Alexander's Lake in Killingly Ct. by Barber. v *his* Con. Hist. Coll. [*Thoreau's note*].

7. Evelyn in his Diary (1654) mentions "the parish of Saffron Walden, famous for the abundance of Saffron there cultivated, and esteemed the best of any foreign country" [*Thoreau's note*]. Saffron Walden is a town forty miles from London, England.

8. A "bubbling" spring (not a "hot spring") located half a mile west of Walden Pond.

and remained so during the day; though I also resorted to a spring in the neighborhood. It was as good when a week old as the day it was dipped, and had no taste of the pump. Whoever camps for a week in summer by the shore of a pond, needs only bury a pail of water a few feet deep in the shade of his camp to be independent on the luxury of ice.

There have been caught in Walden, pickerel, one weighing seven pounds, to say nothing of another which carried off a reel with great velocity, which the fisherman safely set down at eight pounds because he did not see him, perch and pouts, some of each weighing over two pounds, shiners, chivins or roach, (*Leuciscus pulchellus*,) a very few breams, (*Pomotis obesus*,) one trout weighing a little over five pounds,[9] and a couple of eels, one weighing four pounds,—I am thus particular because the weight of a fish is commonly its only title to fame, and these are the only eels I have heard of here;— also, I have a faint recollection of a little fish some five inches long, with silvery sides and a greenish back, somewhat dace-like in its character, which I mention here chiefly to link my facts to fable. Nevertheless, this pond is not very fertile in fish. Its pickerel, though not abundant, are its chief boast. I have seen at one time lying on the ice pickerel of at least three different kinds; a long and shallow one, steel-colored, most like those caught in the river; a bright golden kind, with greenish reflections and remarkably deep, which is the most common here; and another, golden-colored, and shaped like the last, but peppered on the sides with small dark brown or black spots, intermixed with a few faint blood-red ones, very much like a trout. The specific name *reticulatus* would not apply to this; it should be *guttatus* rather. These are all very firm fish, and weigh more than their size promises. The shiners, pouts, and perch also, and indeed all the fishes which inhabit this pond, are much cleaner, handsomer, and firmer fleshed than those in the river and most other ponds, as the water is purer, and they can easily be distinguished from them. Probably many ichthyologists would make new varieties of some of them. There are also a clean race of frogs and tortoises, and a few muscles in it; muskrats and minks leave their trace about it, and occasionally a travelling mud-turtle visits it. Sometimes, when I pushed off my boat in the morning, I disturbed a great mud-turtle which had secreted himself under the boat in the night. Ducks and geese frequent it in the spring and fall, the white-bellied swallows (*Hirundo bicolor*) skim over it, kingfishers dart away from its coves, and the peet-weets (*Totanus macularius*) "teter" along its stony shores all summer. I have sometimes disturbed a fishhawk sitting on a white-pine over the water; but I doubt if it is ever profaned by the wing

9. *Pomotis obesus* [v Nov 26–58] one trout weighing a little over 5 lbs—(Nov. 14–57) [*Thoreau's note*].

of a gull, like Fair Haven.[1] At most, it tolerates one annual loon. These are all the animals of consequence which frequent it now.

You may see from a boat, in calm weather, near the sandy eastern shore, where the water is eight or ten feet deep, and also in some other parts of the pond, some circular heaps half a dozen feet in diameter by a foot in height, consisting of small stones less than a hen's egg in size, where all around is bare sand. At first you wonder if the Indians could have formed them on the ice for any purpose, and so, when the ice melted, they sank to the bottom; but they are too regular and some of them plainly too fresh for that. They are similar to those found in rivers; but as there are no suckers nor lampreys here, I know not by what fish they could be made. Perhaps they are the nests of the chivin. These lend a pleasing mystery to the bottom.

The shore is irregular enough not to be monotonous. I have in my mind's eye the western indented with deep bays, the bolder northern, and the beautifully scolloped southern shore, where successive capes overlap each other and suggest unexplored coves between. The forest has never so good a setting, nor is so distinctly beautiful, as when seen from the middle of a small lake amid hills which rise from the water's edge; for the water in which it is reflected not only makes the best foreground in such a case, but, with its winding shore, the most natural and agreeable boundary to it. There is no rawness nor imperfection in its edge there, as where the axe has cleared a part, or a cultivated field abuts on it. The trees have ample room to expand on the water side, and each sends forth its most vigorous branch in that direction. There Nature has woven a natural selvage, and the eye rises by just gradations from the low shrubs of the shore to the highest trees. There are few traces of man's hand to be seen. The water laves the shore as it did a thousand years ago.

A lake is the landscape's most beautiful and expressive feature. It is earth's eye; looking into which the beholder measures the depth of his own nature. The fluviatile trees next the shore are the slender eyelashes which fringe it, and the wooded hills and cliffs around are its overhanging brows.

Standing on the smooth sandy beach at the east end of the pond, in a calm September afternoon, when a slight haze makes the opposite shore line indistinct, I have seen whence came the expression, "the glassy surface of a lake." When you invert your head, it looks like a thread of finest gossamer stretched across the valley, and gleaming against the distant pine woods, separat-

---

1. A wide bay in the Sudbury River about a mile south of Walden Pond.

ing one stratum of the atmosphere from another. You would think that you could walk dry under it to the opposite hills, and that the swallows which skim over might perch on it. Indeed, they sometimes dive below the line, as it were by mistake, and are undeceived. As you look over the pond westward you are obliged to employ both your hands to defend your eyes against the reflected as well as the true sun, for they are equally bright; and if, between the two, you survey its surface critically, it is literally as smooth as glass, except where the skater insects at equal intervals scattered over its whole extent, by their motions in the sun produce the finest imaginable sparkle on it, or, perchance, a duck plumes itself, or, as I have said, a swallow skims so low as to touch it. It may be that in the distance a fish describes an arc of three or four feet in the air, and there is one bright flash where it emerges, and another where it strikes the water; sometimes the whole silvery arc is revealed; or here and there, perhaps, is a thistle-down floating on its surface, which the fishes dart at and so dimple it again. It is like molten glass cooled but not congealed, and the few motes in it are pure and beautiful like the imperfections in glass. You may often detect a yet smoother and darker water, separated from the rest as if by an invisible cobweb, boom of the water nymphs, resting on it. From a hill-top you can see a fish leap in almost any part; for not a pickerel or shiner picks an insect from this smooth surface but it manifestly disturbs the equilibrium of the whole lake. It is wonderful with what elaborateness this simple fact is advertised,—this piscine murder will out,—and from my distant perch I distinguish the circling undulations when they are half a dozen rods in diameter. You can even detect a water-bug (*Gyrinus*) ceaselessly progressing over the smooth surface a quarter of a mile off; for they furrow the water slightly, making a conspicuous ripple bounded by two diverging lines, but the skaters glide over it without rippling it perceptibly. When the surface is considerably agitated there are no skaters nor water-bugs on it, but apparently, in calm days, they leave their havens and adventurously glide forth from the shore by short impulses till they completely cover it. It is a soothing employment, on one of those fine days in the fall when all the warmth of the sun is fully appreciated, to sit on a stump on such a height as this, overlooking the pond, and study the dimpling circles which are incessantly inscribed on its otherwise invisible surface amid the reflected skies and trees. Over this great expanse there is no disturbance but it is thus at once gently smoothed away and assuaged, as, when a vase of water is jarred, the trembling circles seek the shore and all is smooth again. Not a fish can leap or an insect fall on the pond but it is thus reported in circling dimples, in lines of beauty, as it were the constant welling up of its fountain, the gentle pulsing of its life, the heaving of its breast. The thrills of joy and thrills of pain are undistinguishable. How peaceful the phenomena of the lake! Again the works of man shine as in the spring. Ay, every leaf and twig and stone and cobweb sparkles now at mid-afternoon as when covered with dew in a spring morning. Every motion of an oar or an insect produces a flash of light; and if an oar falls, how sweet the echo!

In such a day, in September or October, Walden is a perfect forest mirror, set round with stones as precious to my eye as if fewer or rarer. Nothing so fair, so pure, and at the same time so large, as a lake, perchance, lies on the surface of the earth. Sky water. It needs no fence. Nations come and go without defiling it. It is a mirror which no stone can crack, whose quicksilver will never wear off, whose gilding Nature continually repairs; no storms, no dust, can dim its surface ever fresh;—a mirror in which all impurity presented to it sinks, swept and dusted by the sun's hazy brush,—this the light dust-cloth,—which retains no breath that is breathed on it, but sends its own to float as clouds high above its surface, and be reflected in its bosom still.

A field of water betrays the spirit that is in the air. It is continually receiving new life and motion from above. It is intermediate in its nature between land and sky. On land only the grass and trees wave, but the water itself is rippled by the wind. I see where the breeze dashes across it by the streaks or flakes of light. It is remarkable that we can look down on its surface. We shall, perhaps, look down thus on the surface of air at length, and mark where a still subtler spirit sweeps over it.

The skaters and water-bugs finally disappear in the latter part of October, when the severe frosts have come; and then and in November, usually, in a calm day, there is absolutely nothing to ripple the surface. One November afternoon, in the calm at the end of a rain storm of several days' duration, when the sky was still completely overcast and the air was full of mist, I observed that the pond was remarkably smooth, so that it was difficult to distinguish its surface; though it no longer reflected the bright tints of October, but the sombre November colors of the surrounding hills. Though I passed over it as gently as possible, the slight undulations produced by my boat extended almost as far as I could see, and gave a ribbed appearance to the reflections. But, as I was looking over the surface, I saw here and there at a distance a faint glimmer, as if some skater insects which had escaped the frosts might be collected there, or, perchance, the surface, being so smooth, betrayed where a spring welled up from the bottom.

Paddling gently to one of these places, I was surprised to find myself surrounded by myriads of small perch, about five inches long, of a rich bronze color in the green water, sporting there and constantly rising to the surface and dimpling it, sometimes leaving bubbles on it. In such transparent and seemingly bottomless water, reflecting the clouds, I seemed to be floating through the air as in a balloon, and their swimming impressed me as a kind of flight or hovering, as if they were a compact flock of birds passing just beneath my level on the right or left, their fins, like sails, set all around them. There were many such schools in the pond, apparently improving the short season before winter would draw an icy shutter over their broad skylight, sometimes giving to the surface an appearance as if a slight breeze struck it, or a few rain-drops fell there. When I approached carelessly and alarmed them, they made a sudden plash and rippling with their tails, as if one had struck the water with a brushy bough, and instantly took refuge in the depths. At length the wind rose, the mist increased, and the waves began to run, and the perch leaped much higher than before, half out of water, a hundred black points, three inches long, at once above the surface. Even as late as the fifth of December, one year, I saw some dimples on the surface, and thinking it was going to rain hard immediately, the air being full of mist, I made haste to take my place at the oars and row homeward; already the rain seemed rapidly increasing, though I felt none on my cheek, and I anticipated a thorough soaking. But suddenly the dimples ceased, for they were produced by the perch, which the noise of my oars had scared into the depths, and I saw their schools dimly disappearing; so I spent a dry afternoon after all.

An old man who used to frequent this pond nearly sixty years ago, when it was dark with surrounding forests, tells me that in those days he sometimes saw it all alive with ducks and other water fowl, and that there were many eagles about it. He came here a-fishing, and used an old log canoe which he found on the shore. It was made of two white-pine logs dug out and pinned together, and was cut off square at the ends. It was very clumsy, but lasted a great many years before it became water-logged and perhaps sank to the bottom. He did not know whose it was; it belonged to the pond. He used to make a cable for his anchor of strips of hickory bark tied together. An old man, a potter, who lived by the pond before the Revolution, told him once that there was an iron chest at the bottom, and that he had seen it. Sometimes it would come floating up to the shore; but when you went toward it, it would go back into deep water and disappear. I was pleased to hear of the old log canoe, which took the place of an Indian one of the same material but more graceful construction, which perchance had first been a tree on the bank, and then, as it were, fell into the water, to float there for a generation, the most proper vessel for the lake. I remember that when I first looked into these depths there were many large trunks to be seen indistinctly lying on the bottom, which had either been blown over formerly, or left on the ice at the last cutting, when wood was cheaper; but now they have mostly disappeared.

When I first paddled a boat on Walden, it was completely surrounded by thick and lofty pine and oak woods, and in some of its coves grape vines had run over the trees next the water and formed bowers under which a boat could pass. The hills which form its shores are so steep, and the woods on them were then so high, that, as you looked down from the west end, it had the appearance of an amphitheatre for some kind of sylvan spectacle. I have spent many an hour, when I was younger, floating over its surface as the zephyr willed, having paddled my boat to the middle, and lying on my back across the seats, in a summer forenoon, dreaming awake, until I was aroused by the boat touching the sand, and I arose to see what shore my fates had impelled me to; days when idleness was the most attractive and productive industry. Many a forenoon have I stolen away, preferring to spend thus the most valued part of the day; for I was rich, if not in money, in sunny hours and summer days, and spent them lavishly; nor do I regret that I did not waste more of them in the workshop or the teacher's desk. But since I left those shores the woodchoppers have still further laid them waste, and now for many a year there will be no more rambling through the aisles of the wood, with occasional vistas through which you see the water. My Muse may be excused if she is silent henceforth. How can you expect the birds to sing when their groves are cut down?

Now the trunks of trees on the bottom, and the old log canoe, and the dark surrounding woods, are gone, and the villagers, who scarcely know where it lies, instead of going to the pond to bathe or drink, are thinking to bring its water, which should be as sacred as the Ganges [2] at least, to the village in a pipe, to wash their dishes with!—to earn their Walden by the turning of a cock or drawing of a plug! That devilish Iron Horse, whose ear-rending neigh is heard throughout the town, has muddied the Boiling Spring with his foot, and he it is that has browsed off all the woods on Walden shore; that Trojan horse, with a thousand men in his belly, introduced by mercenary Greeks! Where is the country's champion, the Moore of Moore Hall,[3] to meet him at the

2. A river in northern India, believed to be sacred by the Hindus.
3. According to an old English ballad, "The Dragon of Wantley," a hero who killed a dragon.

Deep Cut and thrust an avenging lance between the ribs of the bloated pest?

Nevertheless, of all the characters I have known, perhaps Walden wears best, and best preserves its purity. Many men have been likened to it, but few deserve that honor. Though the wood-choppers have laid bare first this shore and then that, and the Irish have built their sties by it, and the railroad has infringed on its border, and the ice-men have skimmed it once, it is itself un-changed, the same water which my youthful eyes fell on; all the change is in me. It has not acquired one permanent wrinkle after all its ripples. It is perennially young, and I may stand and see a swallow dip apparently to pick an insect from its surface as of yore. It struck me again to-night, as if I had not seen it almost daily for more than twenty years,—Why, here is Walden, the same woodland lake that I discovered so many years ago; where a forest was cut down last winter another is springing up by its shore as lustily as ever; the same thought is welling up to its surface that was then; it is the same liquid joy and happiness to itself and its Maker, ay, and it *may* be to me. It is the work of a brave man surely, in whom there was no guile! He rounded this water with his hand, deepened and clarified it in his thought, and in his will bequeathed it to Concord. I see by its face that it is visited by the same reflection; and I can almost say, Walden, is it you?

> It is no dream of mine,
> To ornament a line;
> I cannot come nearer to God and Heaven
> Than I live to Walden even.
> I am its stony shore,
> And the breeze that passes o'er;
> In the hollow of my hand
> Are its water and its sand,
> And its deepest resort
> Lies high in my thought.

The cars never pause to look at it; yet I fancy that the engineers and firemen and brakemen, and those passengers who have a season ticket and see it often, are better men for the sight. The engineer does not forget at night, or his nature does not, that he has beheld this vision of serenity and purity once at least during the day. Though seen but once, it helps to wash out State-street [4] and the engine's soot. One proposes that it be called "God's Drop."

I have said that Walden has no visible inlet nor outlet, but it is on the one hand distantly and indirectly related to Flints' Pond, which is more elevated, by a chain of small ponds coming from

4. The financial district of Boston.

that quarter, and on the other directly and manifestly to Concord River, which is lower, by a similar chain of ponds through which in some other geological period it may have flowed, and by a little digging, which God forbid, it can be made to flow thither again. If by living thus reserved and austere, like a hermit in the woods, so long, it has acquired such wonderful purity, who would not regret that the comparatively impure waters of Flints' Pond should be mingled with it, or itself should ever go to waste its sweetness in the ocean wave?

Flints', or Sandy Pond, in Lincoln, our greatest lake and inland sea, lies about a mile east of Walden. It is much larger, being said to contain one hundred and ninety-seven acres, and is more fertile in fish; but it is comparatively shallow, and not remarkably pure. A walk through the woods thither was often my recreation. It was worth the while, if only to feel the wind blow on your cheek freely, and see the waves run, and remember the life of mariners. I went a-chestnutting there in the fall, on windy days, when the nuts were dropping into the water and were washed to my feet; and one day, as I crept along its sedgy shore, the fresh spray blowing in my face, I came upon the mouldering wreck of a boat, the sides gone, and hardly more than the impression of its flat bottom left amid the rushes; yet its model was sharply defined, as if it were a large decayed pad, with its veins. It was as impressive a wreck as one could imagine on the sea-shore, and had as good a moral. It is by this time mere vegetable mould and undistinguishable pond shore, through which rushes and flags have pushed up. I used to admire the ripple marks on the sandy bottom, at the north end of this pond, made firm and hard to the feet of the wader by the pressure of the water, and the rushes which grew in Indian file, in waving lines, corresponding to these marks, rank behind rank, as if the waves had planted them. There also I have found, in considerable quantities, curious balls, composed apparently of fine grass or roots, of pipewort perhaps, from half an inch to four inches in diameter, and perfectly spherical. These wash back and forth in shallow water on a sandy bottom, and are sometimes cast on the shore. They are either solid grass, or have a little sand in the middle. At first you would say that they were formed by the action of the waves, like a pebble; yet the smallest are made of equally coarse materials, half an inch long, and they are produced only at one season of the year. Moreover, the waves, I suspect, do not so much construct as wear down a material which has already acquired consistency. They preserve their form when dry for an indefinite period.

Flints' Pond! Such is the poverty of our nomenclature. What right had the unclean and stupid farmer, whose farm abutted on this sky water, whose shores he has ruthlessly laid bare, to give his name to it? Some skin-flint, who loved better the reflecting surface of a dollar, or a bright cent, in which he could see his own brazen face; who regarded even the wild ducks which settled in it as trespassers; his fingers grown into crooked and horny talons from the long habit of grasping harpy-like;—so it is not named for me. I go not there to see him nor to hear of him; who never *saw* it, who never bathed in it, who never loved it, who never protected it, who never spoke a good word for it, nor thanked God that he had made it. Rather let it be named from the fishes that swim in it, the wild fowl or quadrupeds which frequent it, the wild flowers which grow by its shores, or some wild man or child the thread of whose history is interwoven with its own; not from him who could show no title to it but the deed which a like-minded neighbor or legislature gave him,—him who thought only of its money value; whose presence perchance cursed all the shore; who exhausted the land around it, and would fain have exhausted the waters within it; who regretted only that it was not English hay or cranberry meadow,—there was nothing to redeem it, forsooth, in his eyes,—and would have drained and sold it for the mud at its bottom. It did not turn his mill, and it was no *privilege* to him to behold it. I respect not his labors, his farm where every thing has its price; who would carry the landscape, who would carry his God, to market, if he could get any thing for him; who goes to market *for* his god as it is; on whose farm nothing grows free, whose fields bear no crops, whose meadows no flowers, whose trees no fruits, but dollars; who loves not the beauty of his fruits, whose fruits are not ripe for him till they are turned to dollars. Give me the poverty that enjoys true wealth. Farmers are respectable and interesting to me in proportion as they are poor,— poor farmers. A model farm! where the house stands like a fungus in a muck-heap, chambers for men, horses, oxen, and swine, cleansed and uncleansed, all contiguous to one another! Stocked with men! A great grease-spot, redolent of manures and buttermilk! Under a high state of cultivation, being manured with the hearts and brains of men! As if you were to raise your potatoes in the church-yard! Such is a model farm.

No, no; if the fairest features of the landscape are to be named after men, let them be the noblest and worthiest men alone. Let our lakes receive as true names at least as the Icarian Sea, where "still the shore" a "brave attempt resounds." [5]

<hr>

5. According to Greek mythology, the Icarian Sea was named for Icarus, who, while attempting to escape Crete on wings made of wax, fell into the sea when he flew too near the sun; Thoreau quotes from "Icarus" by William of Hawthornden (1585–1649).

Goose Pond, of small extent, is on my way to Flints'; Fair-Haven, an expansion of Concord River, said to contain some seventy acres, is a mile south-west; and White Pond, of about forty acres, is a mile and a half beyond Fair-Haven. This is my lake country.[6] These, with Concord River, are my water privileges; and night and day, year in year out, they grind such grist as I carry to them.

Since the woodcutters, and the railroad, and I myself have profaned Walden, perhaps the most attractive, if not the most beautiful, of all our lakes, the gem of the woods, is White Pond; —a poor name from its commonness, whether derived from the remarkable purity of its waters or the color of its sands. In these as in other respects, however, it is a lesser twin of Walden. They are so much alike that you would say they must be connected under ground. It has the same stony shore, and its waters are of the same hue. As at Walden, in sultry dog-day weather, looking down through the woods on some of its bays which are not so deep but that the reflection from the bottom tinges them, its waters are of a misty bluish-green or glaucous color. Many years since I used to go there to collect the sand by cart-loads, to make sand-paper with, and I have continued to visit it ever since. One who frequents it proposes to call it Virid Lake. Perhaps it might be called Yellow-Pine Lake, from the following circumstance. About fifteen years ago you could see the top of a pitch-pine, of the kind called yellow-pine hereabouts, though it is not a distinct species, projecting above the surface in deep water, many rods from the shore. It was even supposed by some that the pond had sunk, and this was one of the primitive forest that formerly stood there. I find that even so long ago as 1792, in a "Topographical Description of the Town of Concord," by one of its citizens, in the Collections of the Massachusetts Historical Society, the author,[7] after speaking of Walden and White Ponds, adds: "In the middle of the latter may be seen, when the water is very low, a tree which appears as if it grew in the place where it now stands, although the roots are fifty feet below the surface of the water; the top of this tree is broken off, and at that place measures fourteen inches in diameter." In the spring of '49 I talked with the man who lives nearest the pond in Sudbury, who told me that it was he who got out this tree ten or fifteen years before. As near as he could remember, it stood twelve or fifteen rods from the shore, where the water was thirty or forty feet deep. It was in the winter, and he had been getting out ice in the forenoon, and had resolved that in

6. The English Lake Country, associated with William Wordsworth and other English Ro-mantic poets.
7. William Jones.

the afternoon, with the aid of his neighbors, he would take out the old yellow-pine. He sawed a channel in the ice toward the shore, and hauled it over and along and out on to the ice with oxen; but, before he had gone far in his work, he was surprised to find that it was wrong end upward, with the stumps of the branches pointing down, and the small end firmly fastened in the sandy bottom. It was about a foot in diameter at the big end, and he had expected to get a good saw-log, but it was so rotten as to be fit only for fuel, if for that. He had some of it in his shed then. There were marks of an axe and of woodpeckers on the but. He thought that it might have been a dead tree on the shore, but was finally blown over into the pond, and after the top had become water-logged, while the but-end was still dry and light, had drifted out and sunk wrong end up. His father, eighty years old, could not remember when it was not there. Several pretty large logs may still be seen lying on the bottom, where, owing to the undulation of the surface, they look like huge water snakes in motion.

This pond has rarely been profaned by a boat, for there is little in it to tempt a fisherman. Instead of the white lily, which requires mud, or the common sweet flag, the blue flag (*Iris versicolor*) grows thinly in the pure water, rising from the stony bottom all around the shore, where it is visited by humming birds in June, and the color both of its bluish blades and its flowers, and especially their reflections, are in singular harmony with the glaucous water.

White Pond and Walden are great crystals on the surface of the earth, Lakes of Light. If they were permanently congealed, and small enough to be clutched, they would, perchance, be carried off by slaves, like precious stones, to adorn the heads of emperors; but being liquid, and ample, and secured to us and our successors forever, we disregard them, and run after the diamond of Kohinoor.[8] They are too pure to have a market value; they contain no muck. How much more beautiful than our lives, how much more transparent than our characters, are they! We never learned meanness of them. How much fairer than the pool before the farmer's door, in which his ducks swim! Hither the clean wild ducks come. Nature has no human inhabitant who appreciates her. The birds with their plumage and their notes are in harmony with the flowers, but what youth or maiden conspires with the wild luxuriant beauty of Nature? She flourishes most alone, far from the towns where they reside. Talk of heaven! ye disgrace earth.

8. A famous diamond from India, weighing 106 carats, now part of the British crown jewels.

Baker Farm

Sometimes I rambled to pine groves, standing like temples, or like fleets at sea, full-rigged, with wavy boughs, and rippling with light, so soft and green and shady that the Druids [1] would have forsaken their oaks to worship in them; or to the cedar wood beyond Flints' Pond, where the trees, covered with hoary blue berries, spiring higher and higher, are fit to stand before Valhalla,[2] and the creeping juniper covers the ground with wreaths full of fruit; or to swamps where the usnea lichen hangs in festoons from the black-spruce trees, and toad-stools, round tables of the swamp gods, cover the ground, and more beautiful fungi adorn the stumps, like butterflies or shells, vegetable winkles; where the swamp-pink and dogwood grow, the red alder-berry glows like eyes of imps, the waxwork grooves and crushes the hardest woods in its folds, and the wild-holly berries make the beholder forget his home with their beauty, and he is dazzled and tempted by nameless other wild forbidden fruits, too fair for mortal taste. Instead of calling on some scholar, I paid many a visit to particular trees, of kinds which are rare in this neighborhood, standing far away in the middle of some pasture, or in the depths of a wood or swamp, or on a hill-top; such as the black-birch, of which we have some handsome specimens two feet in diameter; its cousin the yellow-birch, with its loose golden vest, perfumed like the first; the beech, which has so neat a bole and beautifully lichen-painted, perfect in all its details, of which, excepting scattered specimens, I know but one small grove of sizable trees left in the township, supposed by some to have been planted by the pigeons that were once baited with beech nuts near by; it is worth the while to see the silver grain sparkle when you split this wood; the bass; the hornbeam; the *celtis occidentalis*, or false elm, of which we have but one well-grown; some taller mast of a pine, a shingle tree, or a more perfect hemlock than usual, standing like a pagoda in the midst of the woods; and many others I could mention. These were the shrines I visited both summer and winter.

Once it chanced that I stood in the very abutment of a rainbow's arch, which filled the lower stratum of the atmosphere, tinging the grass and leaves around, and dazzling me as if I looked through colored crystal. It was a lake of rainbow light, in which, for a short while, I lived like a dolphin. If it had lasted longer it might have tinged my employments and life. As I walked on the

---

1. An ancient Celtic priesthood that worshipped in oak groves.

2. In Norse mythology, a great hall in which the souls of dead warriors live.

railroad causeway, I used to wonder at the halo of light around my shadow, and would fain fancy myself one of the elect. One who visited me declared that the shadows of some Irishmen before him had no halo about them, that it was only natives that were so distinguished. Benvenuto Cellini [3] tells us in his memoirs, that, after a certain terrible dream or vision which he had during his confinement in the castle of St. Angelo, a resplendent light appeared over the shadow of his head at morning and evening, whether he was in Italy or France, and it was particularly conspicuous when the grass was moist with dew. This was probably the same phenomenon to which I have referred, which is especially observed in the morning, but also at other times, and even by moonlight. Though a constant one, it is not commonly noticed, and, in the case of an excitable imagination like Cellini's, it would be basis enough for superstition. Beside, he tells us that he showed it to very few. But are they not indeed distinguished who are conscious that they are regarded at all?

I set out one afternoon to go a-fishing to Fair-Haven, through the woods, to eke out my scanty fare of vegetables. My way led through Pleasant Meadow, an adjunct of the Baker Farm, that retreat of which a poet has since sung, beginning,—

> "Thy entry is a pleasant field,
> Which some mossy fruit trees yield
> Partly to a ruddy brook,
> By gliding musquash undertook,
> And mercurial trout,
> Darting about." [4]

I thought of living there before I went to Walden. I "hooked" the apples, leaped the brook, and scared the musquash and the trout. It was one of those afternoons which seem indefinitely long before one, in which many events may happen, a large portion of our natural life, though it was already half spent when I started. By the way there came up a shower, which compelled me to stand half an hour under a pine, piling boughs over my head, and wearing my handkerchief for a shed; and when at length I had made one cast over the pickerel-weed, standing up to my middle in water, I found myself suddenly in the shadow of a cloud, and the thunder began to rumble with such emphasis that I could do no more than listen to it. The gods must be proud, thought I, with such forked flashes to rout a poor unarmed fisherman. So I made haste

3. Italian sculptor and goldsmith (1500–71), known for his autobiography.
4. All the poetic excerpts in this chapter are from "Baker Farm," in *The Woodman and Other Poems* (1849), by Ellery Channing.

for shelter to the nearest hut, which stood half a mile from any road, but so much the nearer to the pond, and had long been uninhabited:—

> "And here a poet builded,
> In the completed years,
> For behold a trival cabin
> That to destruction steers."

So the Muse fables. But therein, as I found, dwelt now John Field, an Irishman, and his wife, and several children, from the broad-faced boy who assisted his father at his work, and now came running by his side from the bog to escape the rain, to the wrinkled, sibyl-like,[5] cone-headed infant that sat upon its father's knee as in the palaces of nobles, and looked out from its home in the midst of wet and hunger inquisitively upon the stranger, with the privilege of infancy, not knowing but it was the last of a noble line, and the hope and cynosure of the world, instead of John Field's poor starveling brat. There we sat together under that part of the roof which leaked the least, while it showered and thundered without. I had sat there many times of old before the ship was built that floated this family to America. An honest, hard-working, but shiftless man plainly was John Field; and his wife, she too was brave to cook so many successive dinners in the recesses of that lofty stove; with round greasy face and bare breast, still thinking to improve her condition one day; with the never absent mop in one hand, and yet no effects of it visible any where. The chickens, which had also taken shelter here from the rain, stalked about the room like members of the family, too humanized methought to roast well. They stood and looked in my eye or pecked at my shoe significantly. Meanwhile my host told me his story, how hard he worked "bogging" for a neighboring farmer, turning up a meadow with a spade or bog hoe at the rate of ten dollars an acre and the use of the land with manure for one year, and his little broad-faced son worked cheerfully at his father's side the while, not knowing how poor a bargain the latter had made. I tried to help him with my experience, telling him that he was one of my nearest neighbors, and that I too, who came a-fishing here, and looked like a loafer, was getting my living like himself; that I lived in a tight, light, and clean house, which hardly cost more than the annual rent of such a ruin as his commonly amounts to; and how, if he chose, he might in a month or two build himself a palace of his own; that I did not use tea, nor coffee, nor butter, nor milk, nor fresh meat, and so did not have to work to get them; again, as I did not work hard, I did not have to eat hard, and it

---

5. In ancient Greece, a sibyl was a fortune-teller who lived to be very old.

cost me but a trifle for my food; but as he began with tea, and coffee, and butter, and milk, and beef, he had to work hard to pay for them, and when he had worked hard he had to eat hard again to repair the waste of his system,—and so it was as broad as it was long, indeed it was broader than it was long, for he was discontented and wasted his life into the bargain; and yet he had rated it as a gain in coming to America, that here you could get tea, and coffee, and meat every day. But the only true America is that country where you are at liberty to pursue such a mode of life as may enable you to do without these, and where the state does not endeavor to compel you to sustain the slavery and war and other superfluous expenses which directly or indirectly result from the use of such things. For I purposely talked to him as if he were a philosopher, or desired to be one. I should be glad if all the meadows on the earth were left in a wild state, if that were the consequence of men's beginning to redeem themselves. A man will not need to study history to find out what is best for his own culture. But alas! the culture of an Irishman is an enterprise to be undertaken with a sort of moral bog hoe. I told him, that as he worked so hard at bogging, he required thick boots and stout clothing, which yet were soon soiled and worn out, but I wore light shoes and thin clothing, which cost not half so much, though he might think that I was dressed like a gentleman, (which, however, was not the case,) and in an hour or two, without labor, but as a recreation, I could, if I wished, catch as many fish as I should want for two days, or earn enough money to support me a week. If he and his family would live simply, they might all go a-huckleberrying in the summer for their amusement. John heaved a sigh at this, and his wife stared with arms a-kimbo, and both appeared to be wondering if they had capital enough to begin such a course with, or arithmetic enough to carry it through. It was sailing by dead reckoning to them, and they saw not clearly how to make their port so; therefore I suppose they still take life bravely, after their fashion, face to face, giving it tooth and nail, not having skill to split its massive columns with any fine entering wedge, and rout it in detail;—thinking to deal with it roughly, as one should handle a thistle. But they fight at an overwhelming disadvantage,—living, John Field, alas! without arithmetic, and failing so.

"Do you ever fish?" I asked. "O yes, I catch a mess now and then when I am lying by; good perch I catch." "What's your bait?" "I catch shiners with fish-worms, and bait the perch with them." "You'd better go now, John," said his wife with glistening and hopeful face; but John demurred.

The shower was now over, and a rainbow above the eastern woods promised a fair evening; so I took my departure. When I had got without I asked for a dish, hoping to get a sight of the well bottom, to complete my survey of the premises; but there, alas! are shallows and quicksands, and rope broken withal, and bucket irrecoverable. Meanwhile the right culinary vessel was selected, water was seemingly distilled, and after consultation and long delay passed out to the thirsty one,—not yet suffered to cool, not yet to settle. Such gruel sustains life here, I thought; so, shutting my eyes, and excluding the motes by a skilfully directed undercurrent, I drank to genuine hospitality the heartiest draught I could. I am not squeamish in such cases when manners are concerned.

As I was leaving the Irishman's roof after the rain, bending my steps again to the pond, my haste to catch pickerel, wading in retired meadows, in sloughs and bog-holes, in forlorn and savage places, appeared for an instant trivial to me who had been sent to school and college; but as I ran down the hill toward the reddening west, with the rainbow over my shoulder, and some faint tinkling sounds borne to my ear through the cleansed air, from I know not what quarter, my Good Genius seemed to say,—Go fish and hunt far and wide day by day,—farther and wider,—and rest thee by many brooks and hearth-sides without misgiving. Remember thy Creator in the days of thy youth.[6] Rise free from care before the dawn, and seek adventures. Let the noon find thee by other lakes, and the night overtake thee every where at home. There are no larger fields than these, no worthier games than may here be played. Grow wild according to thy nature, like these sedges and brakes, which will never become English hay. Let the thunder rumble; what if it threaten ruin to farmers crops? that is not its errand to thee. Take shelter under the cloud, while they flee to carts and sheds. Let not to get a living be thy trade, but thy sport. Enjoy the land, but own it not. Through want of enterprise and faith men are where they are, buying and selling, and spending their lives like serfs.

O Baker Farm!

> "Landscape where the richest element
> Is a little sunshine innocent." * *

> "No one runs to revel
> On thy rail-fenced lea." * *

> "Debate with no man hast thou,
>   With questions art never perplexed,
> As tame at the first sight as now,
>   In thy plain russet gabardine dressed." * *

6. Ecclesiastes 12.1.

> "Come ye who love,
>   And ye who hate,
> Children of the Holy Dove,
>   And Guy Faux[7] of the state,
> And hang conspiracies
> From the tough rafters of the trees!"

Men come tamely home at night only from the next field or street, where their household echoes haunt, and their life pines because it breathes its own breath over again; their shadows morning and evening reach farther than their daily steps. We should come home from far, from adventures, and perils, and discoveries every day, with new experience and character.

Before I had reached the pond some fresh impulse had brought out John Field, with altered mind, letting go "bogging" ere this sunset. But he, poor man, disturbed only a couple of fins while I was catching a fair string, and he said it was his luck; but when we changed seats in the boat luck changed seats too. Poor John Field!—I trust he does not read this, unless he will improve by it, —thinking to live by some derivative old country mode in this primitive new country,—to catch perch with shiners. It is good bait sometimes, I allow. With his horizon all his own, yet he a poor man, born to be poor, with his inherited Irish poverty or poor life, his Adam's grandmother and boggy ways, not to rise in this world, he nor his posterity, till their wading webbed bog-trotting feet get *talaria*[8] to their heels.

Higher Laws

As I came home through the woods with my string of fish, trailing my pole, it being now quite dark, I caught a glimpse of a woodchuck stealing across my path, and felt a strange thrill of savage delight, and was strongly tempted to seize and devour him raw; not that I was hungry then, except for that wildness which he represented. Once or twice, however, while I lived at the pond, I found myself ranging the woods, like a half-starved hound, with a strange abandonment, seeking some kind of venison which I might devour, and no morsel could have been too savage for me. The wildest scenes had become unaccountably familiar. I found in myself, and still find, an instinct toward a higher, or, as it is named, spiritual life, as do most men, and another toward a primitive rank and savage one, and I reverence them both. I love

7. Guy Fawkes (1570–1606) was an English Catholic executed for attempting to blow up the House of Lords.

8. Winged sandals, or wings growing directly from the ankles.

the wild not less than the good. The wildness and adventure that
are in fishing still recommended it to me. I like sometimes to take
rank hold on life and spend my day more as the animals do. Perhaps I have owed to this employment and to hunting, when quite
young, my closest acquaintance with Nature. They early introduce
us to and detain us in scenery with which otherwise, at that age,
we should have little acquaintance. Fishermen, hunters, wood-
choppers, and others, spending their lives in the fields and woods,
in a peculiar sense a part of Nature themselves, are often in a
more favorable mood for observing her, in the intervals of their
pursuits, than philosophers or poets even, who approach her with
expectation. She is not afraid to exhibit herself to them. The traveller on the prairie is naturally a hunter, on the head waters of the
Missouri and Columbia a trapper, and at the Falls of St. Mary [1]
a fisherman. He who is only a traveller learns things at second-
hand and by the halves, and is poor authority. We are most interested when science reports what those men already know
practically or instinctively, for that alone is a true *humanity*, or
account of human experience.

They mistake who assert that the Yankee has few amusements,
because he has not so many public holidays, and men and boys do
not play so many games as they do in England, for here the more
primitive but solitary amusements of hunting fishing and the like
have not yet given place to the former. Almost every New
England boy among my contemporaries shouldered a fowling
piece between the ages of ten and fourteen; and his hunting and
fishing grounds were not limited like the preserves of an English
nobleman, but were more boundless even than those of a savage.
No wonder, then, that he did not oftener stay to play on the
common. But already a change is taking place, owing, not to an
increased humanity, but to an increased scarcity of game, for
perhaps the hunter is the greatest friend of the animals hunted, not
excepting the Humane Society.

Moreover, when at the pond, I wished sometimes to add fish
to my fare for variety. I have actually fished from the same kind of
necessity that the first fishers did. Whatever humanity I might
conjure up against it was all factitious, and concerned my philosophy more than my feelings. I speak of fishing only now, for I
had long felt differently about fowling, and sold my gun before I
went to the woods. Not that I am less humane than others, but I
did not perceive that my feelings were much affected. I did not
pity the fishes nor the worms. This was habit. As for fowling, dur-

1. St. Marys River flows out of Lake Superior,   now permit ships to circumvent the falls and
forming part of the boundary between Michi-   the rapids.
gan and Ontario; the Sault Sainte Marie Canals

ing the last years that I carried a gun my excuse was that I was studying ornithology, and sought only new or rare birds. But I confess that I am now inclined to think that there is a finer way of studying ornithology than this. It requires so much closer attention to the habits of the birds, that, if for that reason only, I have been willing to omit the gun. Yet notwithstanding the objection on the score of humanity, I am compelled to doubt if equally valuable sports are ever substituted for these; and when some of my friends have asked me anxiously about their boys, whether they should let them hunt, I have answered, yes,—remembering that it was one of the best parts of my education,—*make* them hunters, though sportsmen only at first, if possible, mighty hunters at last, so that they shall not find game large enough for them in this or any vegetable wilderness,—hunters as well as fishers of men.[2] Thus far I am of the opinion of Chaucer's nun, who

> "yave not of the text a pulled hen
> That saith that hunters ben not holy men."[3]

There is a period in the history of the individual, as of the race, when the hunters are the "best men," as the Algonquins[4] called them. We cannot but pity the boy who has never fired a gun; he is no more humane, while his education has been sadly neglected. This was my answer with respect to those youths who were bent on this pursuit, trusting that they would soon outgrow it. No humane being, past the thoughtless age of boyhood, will wantonly murder any creature, which holds its life by the same tenure that he does. The hare in its extremity cries like a child. I warn you, mothers, that my sympathies do not always make the usual philanthropic distinctions.

Such is oftenest the young man's introduction to the forest, and the most original part of himself. He goes thither at first as a hunter and fisher, until at last, if he has the seeds of a better life in him, he distinguishes his proper objects, as a poet or naturalist it may be, and leaves the gun and fish-pole behind. The mass of men are still and always young in this respect. In some countries a hunting parson is no uncommon sight. Such a one might make a good shepherd's dog, but is far from being the Good Shepherd. I have been surprised to consider that the only obvious employment, except wood-chopping, ice-cutting, or the like business, which ever to my knowledge detained at Walden Pond for a whole half day any of my fellow-citizens, whether fathers or children of the town,

2. Jesus' call to the fishermen Simon and Andrew in Mark 1.17: "Come ye after me, and I will make you to become fishers of men."
3. From the "Prologue" to Geoffrey Chaucer's *Canterbury Tales*; the lines (177–78) describe the monk, however, not the nun.
4. A tribe of Indians formerly inhabiting the area north of the St. Lawrence River in Canada.

with just one exception, was fishing. Commonly they did not think that they were lucky, or well paid for their time, unless they got a long string of fish, though they had the opportunity of seeing the pond all the while. They might go there a thousand times before the sediment of fishing would sink to the bottom and leave their purpose pure; but no doubt such a clarifying process would be going on all the while. The governor and his council faintly remember the pond, for they went a-fishing there when they were boys; but now they are too old and dignified to go a-fishing, and so they know it no more forever. Yet even they expect to go to heaven at last. If the legislature regards it, it is chiefly to regulate the number of hooks to be used there; but they know nothing about the hook of hooks with which to angle for the pond itself, impaling the legislature for a bait. Thus, even in civilized communities, the embryo man passes through the hunter stage of development.

I have found repeatedly, of late years, that I cannot fish without falling a little in self-respect. I have tried it again and again. I have skill at it, and, like many of my fellows, a certain instinct for it, which revives from time to time, but always when I have done I feel that it would have been better if I had not fished. I think that I do not mistake. It is a faint intimation, yet so are the first streaks of morning. There is unquestionably this instinct in me which belongs to the lower orders of creation; yet with every year I am less a fisherman, though without more humanity or even wisdom; at present I am no fisherman at all. But I see that if I were to live in a wilderness I should again be tempted to become a fisher and hunter in earnest. Beside, there is something essentially unclean about this diet and all flesh, and I began to see where housework commences, and whence the endeavor, which costs so much, to wear a tidy and respectable appearance each day, to keep the house sweet and free from all ill odors and sights. Having been my own butcher and scullion and cook, as well as the gentleman for whom the dishes were served up, I can speak from an unusually complete experience. The practical objection to animal food in my case was its uncleanness; and, besides, when I had caught and cleaned and cooked and eaten my fish, they seemed not to have fed me essentially. It was insignificant and unnecessary, and cost more than it came to. A little bread or a few potatoes would have done as well, with less trouble and filth. Like many of my contemporaries, I had rarely for many years used animal food, or tea, or coffee, &c.; not so much because of any ill effects which I had traced to them, as because they were not agreeable to my imagination. The repugnance to animal food is not the effect of experience, but is an instinct. It appeared more beautiful to live

low and fare hard in many respects; and though I never did so,
I went far enough to please my imagination. I believe that every
man who has ever been earnest to preserve his higher or poetic
faculties in the best condition has been particularly inclined to
abstain from animal food, and from much food of any kind. It is
a significant fact, stated by entomologists, I find it in Kirby and
Spence, that "some insects in their perfect state, though furnished
with organs of feeding, make no use of them;" and they lay it
down as "a general rule, that almost all insects in this state eat
much less than in that of larvæ. The voracious caterpillar when
transformed into a butterfly," . . "and the gluttonous maggot when
become a fly," content themselves with a drop or two of honey
or some other sweet liquid.[5] The abdomen under the wings of the
butterfly still represents the larva. This is the tid-bit which tempts
his insectivorous fate. The gross feeder is a man in the larva state;
and there are whole nations in that condition, nations without
fancy or imagination, whose vast abdomens betray them.

It is hard to provide and cook so simple and clean a diet as will
not offend the imagination; but this, I think, is to be fed when we
feed the body; they should both sit down at the same table. Yet
perhaps this may be done. The fruits eaten temperately need not
make us ashamed of our appetites, nor interrupt the worthiest pursuits. But put an extra condiment into your dish, and it will poison
you. It is not worth the while to live by rich cookery. Most men
would feel shame if caught preparing with their own hands precisely such a dinner, whether of animal or vegetable food, as is
every day prepared for them by others. Yet till this is otherwise
we are not civilized, and, if gentlemen and ladies, are not true
men and women. This certainly suggests what change is to be
made. It may be vain to ask why the imagination will not be
reconciled to flesh and fat. I am satisfied that it is not. Is it not a
reproach that man is a carniverous animal? True, he can and does
live, in a great measure, by preying on other animals; but this is a
miserable way,—as any one who will go to snaring rabbits, or
slaughtering lambs, may learn,—and he will be regarded as a benefactor of his race who shall teach man to confine himself to a
more innocent and wholesome diet. Whatever my own practice
may be, I have no doubt that it is a part of the destiny of the
human race, in its gradual improvement, to leave off eating animals, as surely as the savage tribes have left off eating each other
when they came in contact with the more civilized.

If one listens to the faintest but constant suggestions of his

5. From William Kirby and William Spence, *An Introduction to Entomology* (1815–26).

genius, which are certainly true, he sees not to what extremes, or even insanity, it may lead him; and yet that way, as he grows more resolute and faithful, his road lies. The faintest assured objection which one healthy man feels will at length prevail over the arguments and customs of mankind. No man ever followed his genius till it misled him. Though the result were bodily weakness, yet perhaps no one can say that the consequences were to be regretted, for these were a life in conformity to higher principles. If the day and the night are such that you greet them with joy, and life emits a fragrance like flowers and sweet-scented herbs, is more elastic, more starry, more immortal,—that is your success. All nature is your congratulation, and you have cause momentarily to bless yourself. The greatest gains and values are farthest from being appreciated. We easily come to doubt if they exist. We soon forget them. They are the highest reality. Perhaps the facts most astounding and most real are never communicated by man to man. The true harvest of my daily life is somewhat as intangible and indescribable as the tints of morning or evening. It is a little stardust caught, a segment of the rainbow which I have clutched.

Yet, for my part, I was never unusually squeamish; I could sometimes eat a fried rat with a good relish, if it were necessary. I am glad to have drunk water so long, for the same reason that I prefer the natural sky to an opium-eater's heaven. I would fain keep sober always; and there are infinite degrees of drunkenness. I believe that water is the only drink for a wise man; wine is not so noble a liquor; and think of dashing the hopes of a morning with a cup of warm coffee, or of an evening with a dish of tea! Ah, how low I fall when I am tempted by them! Even music may be intoxicating. Such apparently slight causes destroyed Greece and Rome, and will destroy England and America. Of all ebriosity, who does not prefer to be intoxicated by the air he breathes? I have found it to be the most serious objection to coarse labors long continued, that they compelled me to eat and drink coarsely also. But to tell the truth, I find myself at present somewhat less particular in these respects. I carry less religion to the table, ask no blessing; not because I am wiser than I was, but, I am obliged to confess, because, however much it is to be regretted, with years I have grown more coarse and indifferent. Perhaps these questions are entertained only in youth, as most believe of poetry. My practice is "nowhere," my opinion is here. Nevertheless I am far from regarding myself as one of those privileged ones to whom the Ved refers when it says, that "he who has true faith in the Omnipresent Supreme Being may eat all that exists," that is, is not bound to inquire what is his food, or who prepares it; and even in their case it is to be observed, as a Hindoo commentator has remarked, that the Vedant limits this privilege to "the time of distress."[6]

Who has not sometimes derived an inexpressible satisfaction from his food in which appetite had no share? I have been thrilled to think that I owed a mental perception to the commonly gross sense of taste, that I have been inspired through the palate, that some berries which I had eaten on a hill-side had fed my genius. "The soul not being mistress of herself," says Thseng-tseu, "one looks, and one does not see; one listens, and one does not hear; one eats, and one does not know the savor of food."[7] He who distinguishes the true savor of his food can never be a glutton; he who does not cannot be otherwise. A puritan may go to his brown-bread crust with as gross an appetite as ever an alderman to his turtle. Not that food which entereth into the mouth defileth a man, but the appetite with which it is eaten.[8] It is neither the quality nor the quantity, but the devotion to sensual savors; when that which is eaten is not a viand to sustain our animal, or inspire our spiritual life, but food for the worms that possess us. If the hunter has a taste for mud-turtles, muskrats, and other such savage tid-bits, the fine lady indulges a taste for jelly made of a calf's foot, or for sardines from over the sea, and they are even. He goes to the mill-pond, she to her preserve-pot. The wonder is how they, how you and I, can live this slimy beastly life, eating and drinking.

Our whole life is startlingly moral. There is never an instant's truce between virtue and vice. Goodness is the only investment that never fails. In the music of the harp which trembles round the world it is the insisting on this which thrills us. The harp is the travelling patterer for the Universe's Insurance Company, recommending its laws, and our little goodness is all the assessment that we pay. Though the youth at last grows indifferent, the laws of the universe are not indifferent, but are forever on the side of the most sensitive. Listen to every zephyr for some reproof, for it is surely there, and he is unfortunate who does not hear it. We cannot touch a string or move a stop but the charming moral transfixes us. Many an irksome noise, go a long way off, is heard as music, a proud sweet satire on the meanness of our lives.

We are conscious of an animal in us, which awakens in proportion as our higher nature slumbers. It is reptile and sensual, and perhaps cannot be wholly expelled; like the worms which, even in

6. From *Translation of . . . the Veds* (1832) by Raja Rammohun Roy.
7. Confucius, *The Great Learning* 7.
8. Compare Matthew 15.11: "Not that which goeth into the mouth defileth a man: but that which cometh out of the mouth, this defileth a man."

life and health, occupy our bodies. Possibly we may withdraw from it, but never change its nature. I fear that it may enjoy a certain health of its own; that we may be well, yet not pure. The other day I picked up the lower jaw of a hog, with white and sound teeth and tusks, which suggested that there was an animal health and vigor distinct from the spiritual. This creature succeeded by other means than temperance and purity. "That in which men differ from brute beasts," says Mencius,[9] "is a thing very inconsiderable; the common herd lose it very soon; superior men preserve it carefully." Who knows what sort of life would result if we had attained to purity? If I knew so wise a man as could teach me purity I would go to seek him forthwith. "A command over our passions, and over the external senses of the body, and good acts, are declared by the Ved to be indispensable in the mind's approximation to God." Yet the spirit can for the time pervade and control every member and function of the body, and transmute what in form is the grossest sensuality into purity and devotion. The generative energy, which, when we are loose, dissipates and makes us unclean, when we are continent invigorates and inspires us. Chastity is the flowering of man; and what are called Genius, Heroism, Holiness, and the like, are but various fruits which succeed it. Man flows at once to God when the channel of purity is open. By turns our purity inspires and our impurity casts us down. He is blessed who is assured that the animal is dying out in him day by day, and the divine being established. Perhaps there is none but has cause for shame on account of the inferior and brutish nature to which he is allied. I fear that we are such gods or demigods only as fauns and satyrs, the divine allied to beasts, the creatures of appetite, and that, to some extent, our very life is our disgrace.—

> "How happy's he who hath due place assigned
> To his beasts and disaforested his mind!
>
> *   *   *   *   *
>
> Can use his horse, goat, wolf, and ev'ry beast,
> And is not ass himself to all the rest!
> Else man not only is the herd of swine,
> But he's those devils too which did incline
> Them to a headlong rage, and made them worse."[1]

All sensuality is one, though it takes many forms; all purity is one. It is the same whether a man eat, or drink, or cohabit, or sleep sensually. They are but one appetite, and we only need to

9. Latinized name of Meng-tse, Chinese philosopher (d. 289? B.C.); from his *Works*.

1. From "To Sir Edward Herbert," by John Donne (1573–1631).

see a person do any one of these things to know how great a
sensualist he is. The impure can neither stand nor sit with purity.
When the reptile is attacked at one mouth of his burrow, he
shows himself at another. If you would be chaste, you must be
temperate. What is chastity? How shall a man know if he is
chaste? He shall not know it. We have heard of this virtue, but we
know not what it is. We speak conformably to the rumor which
we have heard. From exertion come wisdom and purity; from
sloth ignorance and sensuality. In the student sensuality is a sluggish habit of mind. An unclean person is universally a slothful one,
one who sits by a stove, whom the sun shines on prostrate, who
reposes without being fatigued. If you would avoid uncleanness,
and all the sins, work earnestly, though it be at cleaning a stable.
Nature is hard to be overcome, but she must be overcome. What
avails it that you are Christian, if you are not purer than the
heathen, if you deny yourself no more, if you are not more
religious? I know of many systems of religion esteemed heathenish
whose precepts fill the reader with shame, and provoke him to new
endeavors, though it be to the performance of rites merely.

I hesitate to say these things, but it is not because of the subject,—
I care not how obscene my *words* are,—but because I cannot
speak of them without betraying my impurity. We discourse freely
without shame of one form of sensuality, and are silent about
another. We are so degraded that we cannot speak simply of the
necessary functions of human nature. In earlier ages, in some
countries, every function was reverently spoken of and regulated
by law. Nothing was too trivial for the Hindoo lawgiver, however
offensive it may be to modern taste. He teaches how to eat, drink,
cohabit, void excrement and urine, and the like, elevating what
is mean, and does not falsely excuse himself by calling these things
trifles.

Every man is the builder of a temple, called his body, to the
god he worships, after a style purely his own, nor can he get off
by hammering marble instead. We are all sculptors and painters,
and our material is our own flesh and blood and bones. Any nobleness begins at once to refine a man's features, any meanness or
sensuality to imbrute them.

John Farmer sat at his door one September evening, after a
hard day's work, his mind still running on his labor more or less.
Having bathed he sat down to recreate his intellectual man. It was
a rather cool evening, and some of his neighbors were apprehend-
ing a frost. He had not attended to the train of his thoughts long
when he heard some one playing on a flute, and that sound harmonized with his mood. Still he thought of his work; but the burden
of his thought was, that though this kept running in his head, and

he found himself planning and contriving it against his will, yet it concerned him very little. It was no more than the scurf of his skin, which was constantly shuffled off. But the notes of the flute came home to his ears out of a different sphere from that he worked in, and suggested work for certain faculties which slumbered in him. They gently did away with the street, and the village, and the state in which he lived. A voice said to him,— Why do you stay here and live this mean moiling life, when a glorious existence is possible for you? Those same stars twinkle over other fields than these.—But how to come out of this condition and actually migrate thither? All that he could think of was to practise some new austerity, to let his mind descend into his body and redeem it, and treat himself with ever increasing respect.

Brute Neighbors

Sometimes I had a companion in my fishing,[1] who came through the village to my house from the other side of the town, and the catching of the dinner was as much a social exercise as the eating of it.

Hermit. I wonder what the world is doing now. I have not heard so much as a locust over the sweet-fern these three hours. The pigeons are all asleep upon their roosts,—no flutter from them. Was that a farmer's noon horn which sounded from beyond the woods just now? The hands are coming in to boiled salt beef and cider and Indian bread. Why will men worry themselves so? He that does not eat need not work. I wonder how much they have reaped. Who would live there where a body can never think for the barking of Bose?[2] And O, the housekeeping! to keep bright the devil's door-knobs, and scour his tubs this bright day! Better not keep a house. Say, some hollow tree; and then for morning calls and dinner-parties! Only a wood-pecker tapping. O, they swarm; the sun is too warm there; they are born too far into life for me. I have water from the spring, and a loaf of brown bread on the shelf.—Hark! I hear a rustling of the leaves. Is it some ill-fed village hound yielding to the instinct of the chase? or the lost pig which is said to be in these woods, whose tracks I saw after the rain? It comes on apace; my sumachs and sweet-briers tremble.—Eh, Mr. Poet, is it you? How do you like the world to-day?

Poet. See those clouds; how they hang! That's the greatest thing I have seen to-day. There's nothing like it in old paintings,

---

1. Thoreau's frequent companion, and the model for the poet of the following dialogue, was Ellery Channing.

2. In Thoreau's time, a generic name for any dog.

nothing like it in foreign lands,—unless when we were off the coast of Spain. That's a true Mediterranean sky. I thought, as I have my living to get, and have not eaten to-day, that I might go a-fishing. That's the true industry for poets. It is the only trade I have learned. Come, let's along.

Hermit. I cannot resist. My brown bread will soon be gone. I will go with you gladly soon, but I am just concluding a serious meditation. I think that I am near the end of it. Leave me alone, then, for a while. But that we may not be delayed, you shall be digging the bait meanwhile. Angle-worms are rarely to be met with in these parts, where the soil was never fattened with manure; the race is nearly extinct. The sport of digging the bait is nearly equal to that of catching the fish, when one's appetite is not too keen; and this you may have all to yourself to-day. I would advise you to set in the spade down yonder among the ground-nuts, where you see the johnswort waving. I think that I may warrant you one worm to every three sods you turn up, if you look well in among the roots of the grass, as if you were weeding. Or, if you choose to go farther, it will not be unwise, for I have found the increase of fair bait to be very nearly as the squares of the distances.

Hermit alone. Let me see; where was I? Methinks I was nearly in this frame of mind; the world lay about at this angle. Shall I go to heaven or a-fishing? If I should soon bring this meditation to an end, would another so sweet occasion be likely to offer? I was as near being resolved into the essence of things as ever I was in my life. I fear my thoughts will not come back to me. If it would do any good, I would whistle for them. When they make us an offer, is it wise to say, We will think of it? My thoughts have left no track, and I cannot find the path again. What was it that I was thinking of? It was a very hazy day. I will just try these three sentences of Con-fut-see; [3] they may fetch that state about again. I know not whether it was the dumps or a budding ecstasy. Mem.[4] There never is but one opportunity of a kind.

Poet. How now, Hermit, is it too soon? I have got just thirteen whole ones, beside several which are imperfect or under-sized; but they will do for the smaller fry; they do not cover up the hook so much. Those village worms are quite too large; a shiner may make a meal off one without finding the skewer.

Hermit. Well, then, let's be off. Shall we to the Concord? There's good sport there if the water be not too high.

Why do precisely these objects which we behold make a world? Why has man just these species of animals for his neighbors; as if

3. Confucius. 4. Memorandum.

nothing but a mouse could have filled this crevice? I suspect that Pilpay & Co.[5] have put animals to their best use, for they are all beasts of burden, in a sense, made to carry some portion of our thoughts.

The mice which haunted my house were not the common ones, which are said to have been introduced into the country, but a wild native kind (*Mus leucopus*) not found in the village. I sent one to a distinguished naturalist,[6] and it interested him much. When I was building, one of these had its nest underneath the house, and before I had laid the second floor, and swept out the shavings, would come out regularly at lunch time and pick up the crums at my feet. It probably had never seen a man before; and it soon became quite familiar, and would run over my shoes and up my clothes. It could readily ascend the sides of the room by short impulses, like a squirrel, which it resembled in its motions. At length, as I leaned with my elbow on the bench one day, it ran up my clothes, and along my sleeve, and round and round the paper which held my dinner, while I kept the latter close, and dodged and played at bo-peep with it; and when at last I held still a piece of cheese between my thumb and finger, it came and nibbled it, sitting in my hand, and afterward cleaned its face and paws, like a fly, and walked away.

A phœbe soon built in my shed, and a robin for protection in a pine which grew against the house. In June the partridge, (*Tetrao umbellus,*) which is so shy a bird, led her brood past my windows, from the woods in the rear to the front of my house, clucking and calling to them like a hen, and in all her behavior proving herself the hen of the woods. The young suddenly disperse on your approach, at a signal from the mother, as if a whirlwind had swept them away, and they so exactly resemble the dried leaves and twigs that many a traveller has placed his foot in the midst of a brood, and heard the whir of the old bird as she flew off, and her anxious calls and mewing, or seen her trail her wings to attract his attention, without suspecting their neighborhood. The parent will sometimes roll and spin round before you in such a dishabille, that you cannot, for a few moments, detect what kind of creature it is. The young squat still and flat, often running their heads under a leaf, and mind only their mother's directions given from a distance, nor will your approach make them run again and betray themselves. You may even tread on them, or have your eyes on them for a minute, without discovering them. I have held them in my open hand at such a time,

5. Pilpay was erroneously supposed to have been the author of a collection of Sanskrit fables translated by Charles Wilkins, the *Hitopadesa*. Hence, tellers of fables.

6. Louis Agassiz (1807–73), for whom Thoreau occasionally worked as a collector of specimens.

and still their only care, obedient to their mother and their instinct, was to squat there without fear or trembling. So perfect is this instinct, that once, when I had laid them on the leaves again, and one accidentally fell on its side, it was found with the rest in exactly the same position ten minutes afterward. They are not callow like the young of most birds, but more perfectly developed and precocious even than chickens. The remarkably adult yet innocent expression of their open and serene eyes is very memorable. All intelligence seems reflected in them. They suggest not merely the purity of infancy, but a wisdom clarified by experience. Such an eye was not born when the bird was, but is coeval with the sky it reflects. The woods do not yield another such a gem. The traveller does not often look into such a limpid well. The ignorant or reckless sportsman often shoots the parent at such a time, and leaves these innocents to fall a prey to some prowling beast or bird, or gradually mingle with the decaying leaves which they so much resemble. It is said that when hatched by a hen they will directly disperse on some alarm, and so are lost, for they never hear the mother's call which gathers them again. These were my hens and chickens.

It is remarkable how many creatures live wild and free though secret in the woods, and still sustain themselves in the neighborhood of towns, suspected by hunters only. How retired the otter manages to live here! He grows to be four feet long, as big as a small boy, perhaps without any human being getting a glimpse of him. I formerly saw the raccoon in the woods behind where my house is built, and probably still heard their whinnering at night. Commonly I rested an hour or two in the shade at noon, after planting, and ate my lunch, and read a little by a spring which was the source of a swamp and of a brook, oozing from under Brister's Hill, half a mile from my field. The approach to this was through a succession of descending grassy hollows, full of young pitch-pines, into a larger wood about the swamp. There, in a very secluded and shaded spot, under a spreading white-pine, there was yet a clean firm sward to sit on. I had dug out the spring and made a well of clear gray water, where I could dip up a pailful without roiling it, and thither I went for this purpose almost every day in midsummer, when the pond was warmest. Thither too the wood-cock led her brood, to probe the mud for worms, flying but a foot above them down the bank, while they ran in a troop beneath; but at last, spying me, she would leave her young and circle round and round me, nearer and nearer till within four or five feet, pretending broken wings and legs, to attract my attention, and get off her young, who would already have taken up their march, with faint wiry peep, single file through the swamp, as she directed. Or I heard the peep of the young when I could not see the parent bird. There too the turtle-doves sat over the spring, or fluttered from bough to bough of the soft white-pines over my head; or the red squirrel, coursing down the nearest bough, was particularly familiar and inquisitive. You only need sit still long enough in some attractive spot in the woods that all its inhabitants may exhibit themselves to you by turns.

I was witness to events of a less peaceful character. One day when I went out to my wood-pile, or rather my pile of stumps, I observed two large ants, the one red, the other much larger, nearly half an inch long, and black, fiercely contending with one another. Having once got hold they never let go, but struggled and wrestled and rolled on the chips incessantly. Looking farther, I was surprised to find that the chips were covered with such combatants, that it was not a *duellum*, but a *bellum*,[7] a war between two races of ants, the red always pitted against the black, and frequently two red ones to one black. The legions of these Myrmidons [8] covered all the hills and vales in my wood-yard, and the ground was already strewn with the dead and dying, both red and black. It was the only battle which I have ever witnessed, the only battle-field I ever trod while the battle was raging; internecine war; the red republicans on the one hand, and the black imperialists on the other. On every side they were engaged in deadly combat, yet without any noise that I could hear, and human soldiers never fought so resolutely. I watched a couple that were fast locked in each other's embraces, in a little sunny valley amid the chips, now at noon-day prepared to fight till the sun went down, or life went out. The smaller red champion had fastened himself like a vice to his adversary's front, and through all the tumblings on that field never for an instant ceased to gnaw at one of his feelers near the root, having already caused the other to go by the board; while the stronger black one dashed him from side to side, and, as I saw on looking nearer, had already divested him of several of his members. They fought with more pertinacity than bull-dogs. Neither manifested the least disposition to retreat. It was evident that their battle-cry was Conquer or die. In the mean while there came along a single red ant on the hill-side of this valley, evidently full of excitement, who either had despatched his foe, or had not yet taken part in the battle; probably the latter, for he had lost none of his limbs; whose mother

7. Not a duel, "a combat between two," but a war.

8. In Greek legend, a warlike people who fought with Achilles in the Trojan War.

had charged him to return with his shield or upon it. Or perchance he was some Achilles, who had nourished his wrath apart,
and had now come to avenge or rescue his Patroclus. He saw this
unequal combat from afar,—for the blacks were nearly twice the
size of the red,—he drew near with rapid pace till he stood on
his guard within half an inch of the combatants; then, watching his
opportunity, he sprang upon the black warrior, and commenced
his operations near the root of his right fore-leg, leaving the foe to
select among his own members; and so there were three united for
life, as if a new kind of attraction had been invented which put all
other locks and cements to shame. I should not have wondered by
this time to find that they had their respective musical bands
stationed on some eminent chip, and playing their national airs the
while, to excite the slow and cheer the dying combatants. I was
myself excited somewhat even as if they had been men. The more
you think of it, the less the difference. And certainly there is not the
fight recorded in Concord history, at least, if in the history of
America, that will bear a moment's comparison with this, whether
for the numbers engaged in it, or for the patriotism and heroism
displayed. For numbers and for carnage it was an Austerlitz or
Dresden.[9] Concord Fight! Two killed on the patriots' side,
and Luther Blanchard wounded! Why here every ant was a
Buttrick,—"Fire! for God's sake fire!"—and thousands shared
the fate of Davis and Hosmer.[1] There was not one hireling there.
I have no doubt that it was a principle they fought for, as much
as our ancestors, and not to avoid a three-penny tax on their tea;
and the results of this battle will be as important and memorable to those whom it concerns as those of the battle of Bunker
Hill, at least.

I took up the chip on which the three I have particularly
described were struggling, carried it into my house, and placed it
under a tumbler on my window-sill, in order to see the issue. Holding a microscope to the first-mentioned red ant, I saw that, though
he was assiduously gnawing at the near fore-leg of his enemy, having
severed his remaining feeler, his own breast was all torn away,
exposing what vitals he had there to the jaws of the black warrior,
whose breast-plate was apparently too thick for him to pierce; and
the dark carbuncles of the sufferer's eyes shone with ferocity such
as war only could excite. They struggled half an hour longer under
the tumbler, and when I looked again the black soldier had
severed the heads of his foes from their bodies, and the still
living heads were hanging on either side of him like ghastly trophies

9. Two battles fought by Napoleon.
1. The first major battle of the American Revolution. The five hundred "minutemen" were
under the command of Major John Buttrick;
Isaac Davis and David Hosmer were the only
two Americans killed.

at his saddle-bow, still apparently as firmly fastened as ever, and he was endeavoring with feeble struggles, being without feelers and with only the remnant of a leg, and I know not how many other wounds, to divest himself of them; which at length, after half an hour more, he accomplished. I raised the glass, and he went off over the window-sill in that crippled state. Whether he finally survived that combat, and spent the remainder of his days in some Hotel des Invalides,[2] I do not know; but I thought that his industry would not be worth much thereafter. I never learned which party was victorious, nor the cause of the war; but I felt for the rest of that day as if I had had my feelings excited and harrowed by witnessing the struggle, the ferocity and carnage, of a human battle before my door.

Kirby and Spence tell us that the battles of ants have long been celebrated and the date of them recorded, though they say that Huber[3] is the only modern author who appears to have witnessed them. "Æneas Sylvius,"[4] say they, "after giving a very circumstantial account of one contested with great obstinacy by a great and small species on the trunk of a pear tree," adds that " 'This action was fought in the pontificate of Eugenius the Fourth,[5] in the presence of Nicholas Pistoriensis, an eminent lawyer, who related the whole history of the battle with the greatest fidelity.' A similar engagement between great and small ants is recorded by Olaus Magnus,[6] in which the small ones, being victorious, are said to have buried the bodies of their own soldiers, but left those of their giant enemies a prey to the birds. This event happened previous to the expulsion of the tyrant Christiern the Second from Sweden." The battle which I witnessed took place in the Presidency of Polk, five years before the passage of Webster's Fugitive-Slave Bill.[7]

Many a village Bose, fit only to course a mud-turtle in a victualling cellar, sported his heavy quarters in the woods, without the knowledge of his master, and ineffectually smelled at old fox burrows and woodchucks' holes; led perchance by some slight cur which nimbly threaded the wood, and might still inspire a natural terror in its denizens;—now far behind his guide, barking like a canine bull toward some small squirrel which had treed itself for scrutiny, then, cantering off, bending the bushes with his weight, imagining that he is on the track of some stray member of the jerbilla family. Once I was surprised to see a cat walking along the

2. A veterans' hospital in Paris.
3. Francois Huber (1750–1831), a Swiss entomologist.
4. The pen name of Pope Pius II (1405–64), poet and historian.
5. Pope from 1431 to 1437.

6. Swedish historian (1490–1558).
7. James K. Polk (1795–1849), president from 1845 to 1849. Daniel Webster (1782–1852), senator from Massachusetts; he did not introduce the Fugitive Slave Bill, passed in 1850, but he assisted in its passage.

stony shore of the pond, for they rarely wander so far from home. The surprise was mutual. Nevertheless the most domestic cat, which has lain on a rug all her days, appears quite at home in the woods, and, by her sly and stealthy behavior, proves herself more native there than the regular inhabitants. Once, when berrying, I met with a cat with young kittens in the woods, quite wild, and they all, like their mother, had their backs up and were fiercely spitting at me. A few years before I lived in the woods there was what was called a "winged cat" in one of the farm-houses in Lincoln nearest the pond, Mr. Gilian Baker's. When I called to see her in June, 1842, she was gone a-hunting in the woods, as was her wont, (I am not sure whether it was a male or female, and so use the more common pronoun,) but her mistress told me that she came into the neighborhood a little more than a year before, in April, and was finally taken into their house; that she was of a dark brownish-gray color, with a white spot on her throat, and white feet, and had a large bushy tail like a fox; that in the winter the fur grew thick and flatted out along her sides, forming strips ten or twelve inches long by two and a half wide, and under her chin like a muff, the upper side loose, the under matted like felt, and in the spring these appendages dropped off. They gave me a pair of her "wings," which I keep still. There is no appearance of a membrane about them. Some thought it was part flying-squirrel or some other wild animal, which is not impossible, for, according to naturalists, prolific hybrids have been produced by the union of the marten and domestic cat. This would have been the right kind of cat for me to keep, if I had kept any; for why should not a poet's cat be winged as well as his horse? [8]

In the fall the loon (*Colymbus glacialis*) came, as usual, to moult and bathe in the pond, making the woods ring with his wild laughter before I had risen. At rumor of his arrival all the Mill-dam sportsmen are on the alert, in gigs and on foot, two by two and three by three, with patent rifles and conical balls and spy-glasses. They come rustling through the woods like autumn leaves, at least ten men to one loon. Some station themselves on this side of the pond, some on that, for the poor bird cannot be omnipresent; if he dive here he must come up there. But now the kind October wind rises, rustling the leaves and rippling the surface of the water, so that no loon can be heard or seen, though his foes sweep the pond with spy-glasses, and make the woods resound with their discharges. The waves generously rise and dash angrily, taking sides with all waterfowl, and our sportsmen must beat a retreat to town and shop and unfinished jobs. But they

8. Inspired poets are said to ride on Pegasus, a winged horse in Greek mythology.

were too often successful. When I went to get a pail of water early in the morning I frequently saw this stately bird sailing out of my cove within a few rods. If I endeavored to overtake him in a boat, in order to see how he would manœuvre, he would dive and be completely lost, so that I did not discover him again, sometimes, till the latter part of the day. But I was more than a match for him on the surface. He commonly went off in a rain.

As I was paddling along the north shore one very calm October afternoon, for such days especially they settle on to the lakes, like the milkweed down, having looked in vain over the pond for a loon, suddenly one, sailing out from the shore toward the middle a few rods in front of me, set up his wild laugh and betrayed himself. I pursued with a paddle and he dived, but when he came up I was nearer than before. He dived again, but I miscalculated the direction he would take, and we were fifty rods apart when he came to the surface this time, for I had helped to widen the interval; and again he laughed long and loud, and with more reason than before. He manœuvred so cunningly that I could not get within half a dozen rods of him. Each time, when he came to the surface, turning his head this way and that, he coolly surveyed the water and the land, and apparently chose his course so that he might come up where there was the widest expanse of water and at the greatest distance from the boat. It was surprising how quickly he made up his mind and put his resolve into execution. He led me at once to the widest part of the pond, and could not be driven from it. While he was thinking one thing in his brain, I was endeavoring to divine his thought in mine. It was a pretty game, played on the smooth surface of the pond, a man against a loon. Suddenly your adversary's checker disappears beneath the board, and the problem is to place yours nearest to where his will appear again. Sometimes he would come up unexpectedly on the opposite side of me, having apparently passed directly under the boat. So long-winded was he and so unweariable, that when he had swum farthest he would immediately plunge again, nevertheless; and then no wit could divine where in the deep pond, beneath the smooth surface, he might be speeding his way like a fish, for he had time and ability to visit the bottom of the pond in its deepest part. It is said that loons have been caught in the New York lakes eighty feet beneath the surface, with hooks set for trout,—though Walden is deeper than that. How surprised must the fishes be to see this ungainly visitor from another sphere speeding his way amid their schools! Yet he appeared to know his course as surely under water as on the surface, and swam much faster there. Once or twice I saw a ripple where he approached the surface, just put his head out to reconnoitre, and instantly dived again. I found that it was as well for me to rest on my oars and wait his reappearing as to endeavor to calculate where he would rise; for again and again, when I was straining my eyes over the surface one way, I would suddenly be startled by his unearthly laugh behind me. But why, after displaying so much cunning, did he invariably betray himself the moment he came up by that loud laugh? Did not his white breast enough betray him? He was indeed a silly loon, I thought. I could commonly hear the plash of the water when he came up, and so also detected him. But after an hour he seemed as fresh as ever, dived as willingly and swam yet farther than at first. It was surprising to see how serenely he sailed off with unruffled breast when he came to the surface, doing all the work with his webbed feet beneath. His usual note was this demoniac laughter, yet somewhat like that of a water-fowl; but occasionally, when he had balked me most successfully and come up a long way off, he uttered a long-drawn unearthly howl, probably more like that of a wolf than any bird; as when a beast puts his muzzle to the ground and deliberately howls. This was his looning,—perhaps the wildest sound that is ever heard here, making the woods ring far and wide. I concluded that he laughed in derision of my efforts, confident of his own resources. Though the sky was by this time overcast, the pond was so smooth that I could see where he broke the surface when I did not hear him. His white breast, the stillness of the air, and the smoothness of the water were all against him. At length, having come up fifty rods off, he uttered one of those prolonged howls, as if calling on the god of loons to aid him, and immediately there came a wind from the east and rippled the surface, and filled the whole air with misty rain, and I was impressed as if it were the prayer of the loon answered, and his god was angry with me; and so I left him disappearing far away on the tumultuous surface.

For hours, in fall days, I watched the ducks cunningly tack and veer and hold the middle of the pond, far from the sportsman; tricks which they will have less need to practise in Louisiana bayous. When compelled to rise they would sometimes circle round and round and over the pond at a considerable height, from which they could easily see to other ponds and the river, like black motes in the sky; and, when I thought they had gone off thither long since, they would settle down by a slanting flight of a quarter of a mile on to a distant part which was left free; but what beside safety they got by sailing in the middle of Walden I do not know, unless they love its water for the same reason that I do.

House-Warming

In October I went a-graping to the river meadows, and loaded myself with clusters more precious for their beauty and fragrance than for food. There too I admired, though I did not gather, the cranberries, small waxen gems, pendants of the meadow grass, pearly and red, which the farmer plucks with an ugly rake, leaving the smooth meadow in a snarl, heedlessly measuring them by the bushel and the dollar only, and sells the spoils of the meads to Boston and New York; destined to be *jammed*, to satisfy the tastes of lovers of Nature there. So butchers rake the tongues of bison out of the prairie grass, regardless of the torn and drooping plant. The barberry's brilliant fruit was likewise food for my eyes merely; but I collected a small store of wild apples for coddling, which the proprietor and travellers had overlooked. When chestnuts were ripe I laid up half a bushel for winter. It was very exciting at that season to roam the then boundless chestnut woods of Lincoln,— they now sleep their long sleep under the railroad,—with a bag on my shoulder, and a stick to open burrs with in my hand, for I did not always wait for the frost, amid the rustling of leaves and the loud reproofs of the red-squirrels and the jays, whose half-consumed nuts I sometimes stole, for the burrs which they had selected were sure to contain sound ones. Occasionally I climbed and shook the trees. They grew also behind my house, and one large tree which almost overshadowed it, was, when in flower, a bouquet which scented the whole neighborhood, but the squirrels and the jays got most of its fruit; the last coming in flocks early in the morning and picking the nuts out of the burrs before they fell. I relinquished these trees to them and visited the more distant woods composed wholly of chestnut. These nuts, as far as they went, were a good substitute for bread. Many other substitutes might, perhaps, be found. Digging one day for fish-worms I discovered the ground-nut (*Apios tuberosa*) on its string, the potato of the aborigines, a sort of fabulous fruit, which I had begun to doubt if I had ever dug and eaten in childhood, as I had told, and had not dreamed it. I had often since seen its crimpled red velvety blossom supported by the stems of other plants without knowing it to be the same. Cultivation has well nigh exterminated it. It has a sweetish taste, much like that of a frostbitten potato, and I found it better boiled than roasted. This tuber seemed like a faint promise of Nature to rear her own children and feed them simply here at some future period. In these days of fatted cattle and waving grain-fields, this humble root, which was once the *totem* of an Indian tribe,[1] is quite forgotten, or known only by its flowering vine; but let wild Nature reign here once more, and the tender and luxurious English grains will probably disappear before a myriad of foes, and without the care of man the crow may carry back even the last seed of corn to the great corn-field of the Indian's God in the south-west, whence he is said to have brought it; but the now almost exterminated ground-nut will perhaps revive and flourish in spite of frosts and wildness, prove itself indigenous, and resume its ancient importance and dignity as the diet of the hunter tribe. Some Indian Ceres or Minerva [2] must have been the inventor and bestower of it; and when the reign of poetry commences here, its leaves and string of nuts may be represented on our works of art.

Already, by the first of September, I had seen two or three small maples turned scarlet across the pond, beneath where the white stems of three aspens diverged, at the point of a promontory, next the water. Ah, many a tale their color told! And gradually from week to week the character of each tree came out, and it admired itself reflected in the smooth mirror of the lake. Each morning the manager of this gallery substituted some new picture, distinguished by more brilliant or harmonious coloring, for the old upon the walls.

The wasps came by thousands to my lodge in October, as to winter quarters, and settled on my windows within and on the walls over-head, sometimes deterring visitors from entering. Each morning, when they were numbed with cold, I swept some of them out, but I did not trouble myself much to get rid of them; I even felt complimented by their regarding my house as a desirable shelter. They never molested me seriously, though they bedded with me; and they gradually disappeared, into what crevices I do not know, avoiding winter and unspeakable cold.

Like the wasps, before I finally went into winter quarters in November, I used to resort to the north-east side of Walden, which the sun, reflected from the pitch-pine woods and the stony shore, made the fire-side of the pond; it is so much pleasanter and wholesomer to be warmed by the sun while you can be, than by an artificial fire. I thus warmed myself by the still glowing embers which the summer, like a departed hunter, had left.

When I came to build my chimney I studied masonry. My bricks being second-hand ones required to be cleaned with a trowel, so that I learned more than usual of the qualities of bricks and

---

1. According to some authorities, the potato was believed by some Indians to bear a spiritual relation to their tribe.

2. In Roman mythology, goddesses of agriculture and wisdom, respectively.

trowels. The mortar on them was fifty years old, and was said to be still growing harder; but this is one of those sayings which men love to repeat whether they are true or not. Such sayings themselves grow harder and adhere more firmly with age, and it would take many blows with a trowel to clean an old wiseacre of them. Many of the villages of Mesopotamia are built of second-hand bricks of a very good quality, obtained from the ruins of Babylon, and the cement on them is older and probably harder still. However that may be, I was struck by the peculiar toughness of the steel which bore so many violent blows without being worn out. As my bricks had been in a chimney before, though I did not read the name of Nebuchadnezzar[3] on them, I picked out as many fireplace bricks as I could find, to save work and waste, and I filled the spaces between the bricks about the fireplace with stones from the pond shore, and also made my mortar with the white sand from the same place. I lingered most about the fireplace, as the most vital part of the house. Indeed, I worked so deliberately, that though I commenced at the ground in the morning, a course of bricks raised a few inches above the floor served for my pillow at night; yet I did not get a stiff neck for it that I remember; my stiff neck is of older date. I took a poet[4] to board for a fortnight about those times, which caused me to be put to it for room. He brought his own knife, though I had two, and we used to scour them by thrusting them into the earth. He shared with me the labors of cooking. I was pleased to see my work rising so square and solid by degrees, and reflected, that, if it proceeded slowly, it was calculated to endure a long time. The chimney is to some extent an independent structure, standing on the ground and rising through the house to the heavens; even after the house is burned it still stands sometimes, and its importance and independence are apparent. This was toward the end of summer. It was now November.

The north wind had already begun to cool the pond, though it took many weeks of steady blowing to accomplish it, it is so deep. When I began to have a fire at evening, before I plastered my house, the chimney carried smoke particularly well, because of the numerous chinks between the boards. Yet I passed some cheerful evenings in that cool and airy apartment, surrounded by the rough brown boards full of knots, and rafters with the bark on high over-head. My house never pleased my eye so much after it was plastered, though I was obliged to confess that it was more comfortable. Should not every apartment in which man dwells be lofty enough to create some obscurity over-head, where flickering

---

3. King of ancient Babylonia (604–561 B.C.).　　4. Ellery Channing.

shadows may play at evening about the rafters? These forms are more agreeable to the fancy and imagination than fresco paintings or other the most expensive furniture. I now first began to inhabit my house, I may say, when I began to use it for warmth as well as shelter. I had got a couple of old fire-dogs to keep the wood from the hearth, and it did me good to see the soot form on the back of the chimney which I had built, and I poked the fire with more right and more satisfaction than usual. My dwelling was small, and I could hardly entertain an echo in it; but it seemed larger for being a single apartment and remote from neighbors. All the attractions of a house were concentrated in one room; it was kitchen, chamber, parlor, and keeping-room; [5] and whatever satisfaction parent or child, master or servant, derive from living in a house, I enjoyed it all. Cato says, the master of a family (*patremfamilias*) must have in his rustic villa "cellam oleariam, vinariam, dolia multa, uti lubeat caritatem expectare, et rei, et virtuti, et gloriæ erit," that is, "an oil and wine cellar, many casks, so that it may be pleasant to expect hard times; it will be for his advantage, and virtue, and glory." [6] I had in my cellar a firkin of potatoes, about two quarts of peas with the weevil in them, and on my shelf a little rice, a jug of molasses, and of rye and Indian meal a peck each.

I sometimes dream of a larger and more populous house, standing in a golden age, of enduring materials, and without gingerbread work, which shall still consist of only one room, a vast, rude, substantial, primitive hall, without ceiling or plastering, with bare rafters and purlins supporting a sort of lower heaven over one's head,—useful to keep off rain and snow; where the king and queen posts stand out to receive your homage, when you have done reverence to the prostrate Saturn [7] of an older dynasty on stepping over the sill; a cavernous house, wherein you must reach up a torch upon a pole to see the roof; where some may live in the fire-place, some in the recess of a window, and some on settles, some at one end of the hall, some at another, and some aloft on rafters with the spiders, if they choose; a house which you have got into when you have opened the outside door, and the ceremony is over; where the weary traveller may wash, and eat, and converse, and sleep, without further journey; such a shelter as you would be glad to reach in a tempestuous night, containing all the essentials of a house, and nothing for house-keeping; where you can see all the treasures of the house at one view, and every thing hangs upon its peg that a man should use; at once kitchen,

5. A New England dialect term for a sitting-room.
6. From *De Agri Cultura*.

7. A Roman god (known to the Greeks as "Cronus"), overthrown by Jupiter (Greek: "Zeus").

pantry, parlor, chamber, store-house, and garret; where you can
see so necessary a thing as a barrel or a ladder, so convenient a
thing as a cupboard, and hear the pot boil, and pay your respects
to the fire that cooks your dinner and the oven that bakes your
bread, and the necessary furniture and utensils are the chief ornaments; where the washing is not put out, nor the fire, nor the mistress, and perhaps you are sometimes requested to move from off
the trap-door, when the cook would descend into the cellar, and so
learn whether the ground is solid or hollow beneath you without
stamping. A house whose inside is as open and manifest as a
bird's nest, and you cannot go in at the front door and out at the
back without seeing some of its inhabitants; where to be a guest
is to be presented with the freedom of the house, and not to be
carefully excluded from seven eighths of it, shut up in a particular
cell, and told to make yourself at home there,—in solitary confinement. Nowadays the host does not admit you to *his* hearth, but
has got the mason to build one for yourself somewhere in his alley,
and hospitality is the art of *keeping* you at the greatest distance.
There is as much secrecy about the cooking as if he had a design
to poison you. I am aware that I have been on many a man's
premises, and might have been legally ordered off, but I am not
aware that I have been in many men's houses. I might visit in my
old clothes a king and queen who lived simply in such a house as
I have described, if I were going their way; but backing out of a
modern palace will be all that I shall desire to learn, if ever I
am caught in one.

It would seem as if the very language of our parlors would lose
all its nerve and degenerate into *parlaver* [8] wholly, our lives pass at
such remoteness from its symbols, and its metaphors and tropes
are necessarily so far fetched, through slides and dumb-waiters, as
it were; in other words, the parlor is so far from the kitchen and
workshop. The dinner even is only the parable of a dinner, commonly. As if only the savage dwelt near enough to Nature and
Truth to borrow a trope from them. How can the scholar, who
dwells away in the North West Territory [9] or the Isle of Man,
tell what is parliamentary in the kitchen?

However, only one or two of my guests were ever bold enough
to stay and eat a hasty-pudding with me; but when they saw that
crisis approaching they beat a hasty retreat rather, as if it would
shake the house to its foundations. Nevertheless, it stood through a
great many hasty-puddings.

I did not plaster till it was freezing weather. I brought over some

8. A punning combination of "parlor" and
"palaver," i.e., empty, profuse talk.
9. The area included within the current states
of Ohio, Indiana, Michigan, Wisconsin, and
Minnesota. The Isle of Man is in the Irish Sea.

whiter and cleaner sand for this purpose from the opposite shore
of the pond in a boat, a sort of conveyance which would have
tempted me to go much farther if necessary. My house had in
the mean while been shingled down to the ground on every side.
In lathing I was pleased to be able to send home each nail with a
single blow of the hammer, and it was my ambition to transfer
the plaster from the board to the wall neatly and rapidly. I
remembered the story of a conceited fellow, who, in fine clothes,
was wont to lounge about the village once, giving advice to workmen. Venturing one day to substitute deeds for words, he turned
up his cuffs, seized a plasterer's board, and having loaded his
trowel without mishap, with a complacent look toward the lathing
overhead, made a bold gesture thitherward; and straightway, to his
complete discomfiture, received the whole contents in his ruffled
bosom. I admired anew the economy and convenience of plastering, which so effectually shuts out the cold and takes a handsome finish, and I learned the various casualties to which the
plasterer is liable. I was surprised to see how thirsty the bricks
were which drank up all the moisture in my plaster before I had
smoothed it, and how many pailfuls of water it takes to christen a
new hearth. I had the previous winter made a small quantity of
lime by burning the shells of the *Unio fluviatilis*, which our river
affords, for the sake of the experiment; so that I knew where my
materials came from. I might have got good limestone within a
mile or two and burned it myself, if I had cared to do so.

The pond had in the mean while skimmed over in the shadiest
and shallowest coves, some days or even weeks before the general freezing. The first ice is especially interesting and perfect,
being hard, dark, and transparent, and affords the best opportunity
that ever offers for examining the bottom where it is shallow; for
you can lie at your length on ice only an inch thick, like a skater
insect on the surface of the water, and study the bottom at your
leisure, only two or three inches distant, like a picture behind a
glass, and the water is necessarily always smooth then. There are
many furrows in the sand where some creature has travelled about
and doubled on its tracks; and, for wrecks, it is strewn with the
cases of cadis worms made of minute grains of white quartz. Perhaps these have creased it, for you find some of their cases in the
furrows, though they are deep and broad for them to make. But
the ice itself is the object of most interest, though you must improve the earliest opportunity to study it. If you examine it closely
the morning after it freezes, you find that the greater part of the
bubbles, which at first appeared to be within it, are against its
under surface, and that more are continually rising from the

bottom; while the ice is as yet comparatively solid and dark, that is, you see the water through it. These bubbles are from an eightieth to an eighth of an inch in diameter, very clear and beautiful, and you see your face reflected in them through the ice. There may be thirty or forty of them to a square inch. There are also already within the ice narrow oblong perpendicular bubbles about half an inch long, sharp cones with the apex upward; or oftener, if the ice is quite fresh, minute spherical bubbles one directly above another, like a string of beads. But these within the ice are not so numerous nor obvious as those beneath. I sometimes used to cast on stones to try the strength of the ice, and those which broke through carried in air with them, which formed very large and conspicuous white bubbles beneath. One day when I came to the same place forty-eight hours afterward, I found that those large bubbles were still perfect, though an inch more of ice had formed, as I could see distinctly by the seam in the edge of a cake. But as the last two days had been very warm, like an Indian summer, the ice was not now transparent, showing the dark green color of the water, and the bottom, but opaque and whitish or gray, and though twice as thick was hardly stronger than before, for the air bubbles had greatly expanded under this heat and run together, and lost their regularity; they were no longer one directly over another, but often like silvery coins poured from a bag, one overlapping another, or in thin flakes, as if occupying slight cleavages. The beauty of the ice was gone, and it was too late to study the bottom. Being curious to know what position my great bubbles occupied with regard to the new ice, I broke out a cake containing a middling sized one, and turned it bottom upward. The new ice had formed around and under the bubble, so that it was included between the two ices. It was wholly in the lower ice, but close against the upper, and was flattish, or perhaps slightly lenticular, with a rounded edge, a quarter of an inch deep by four inches in diameter; and I was surprised to find that directly under the bubble the ice was melted with great regularity in the form of a saucer reversed, to the height of five eighths of an inch in the middle, leaving a thin partition there between the water and the bubble, hardly an eighth of an inch thick; and in many places the small bubbles in this partition had burst out downward, and probably there was no ice at all under the largest bubbles, which were a foot in diameter. I inferred that the infinite number of minute bubbles which I had first seen against the under surface of the ice were now frozen in likewise, and that each, in its degree, had operated like a burning glass on the ice beneath to melt and rot it. These are the little air-guns which contribute to make the ice crack and whoop.

At length the winter set in in good earnest, just as I had finished plastering, and the wind began to howl around the house as it had not had permission to do so till then. Night after night the geese came lumbering in in the dark with a clangor and a whistling of wings, even after the ground was covered with snow, some to alight in Walden, and some flying low over the woods toward Fair Haven, bound for Mexico. Several times, when returning from the village at ten or eleven o'clock at night, I heard the tread of a flock of geese, or else ducks, on the dry leaves in the woods by a pond-hole behind my dwelling, where they had come up to feed, and the faint honk or quack of their leader as they hurried off. In 1845 Walden froze entirely over for the first time on the night of the 22d of December, Flints' and other shallower ponds and the river having been frozen ten days or more; in '46, the 16th; in '49, about the 31st; and in '50, about the 27th of December; in '52, the 5th of January; in '53, the 31st of December. The snow had already covered the ground since the 25th of November, and surrounded me suddenly with the scenery of winter. I withdrew yet farther into my shell, and endeavored to keep a bright fire both within my house and within my breast. My employment out of doors now was to collect the dead wood in the forest, bringing it in my hands or on my shoulders, or sometimes trailing a dead pine tree under each arm to my shed. An old forest fence which had seen its best days was a great haul for me. I sacrificed it to Vulcan, for it was past serving the god Terminus.[1] How much more interesting an event is that man's supper who has just been forth in the snow to hunt, nay, you might say, steal, the fuel to cook it with! His bread and meat are sweet. There are enough fagots and waste wood of all kinds in the forests of most of our towns to support many fires, but which at present warm none, and, some think, hinder the growth of the young wood. There was also the drift-wood of the pond. In the course of the summer I had discovered a raft of pitch-pine logs with the bark on, pinned together by the Irish when the railroad was built. This I hauled up partly on the shore. After soaking two years and then lying high six months it was perfectly sound, though waterlogged past drying. I amused myself one winter day with sliding this piece-meal across the pond, nearly half a mile, skating behind with one end of a log fifteen feet long on my shoulder, and the other on the ice; or I tied several logs together with a birch withe, and then, with a longer birch or alder which had a hook at the end, dragged them across. Though completely waterlogged and almost as heavy as lead, they not only burned long, but made a very hot fire; nay, I

1. In Roman mythology, the gods of fire and boundaries, respectively.

thought that they burned better for the soaking, as if the pitch, being confined by the water, burned longer as in a lamp.

Gilpin, in his account of the forest borderers of England, says that "the encroachments of trespassers, and the houses and fences thus raised on the borders of the forest," were "considered as great nuisances by the old forest law, and were severely punished under the name of *purprestures,* as tending *ad terrorem ferarum— ad nocumentum forestæ,* &c.," to the frightening of the game and the detriment of the forest.[2] But I was interested in the preservation of the venison and the vert more than the hunters or wood-choppers, and as much as though I had been the Lord Warden[3] himself; and if any part was burned, though I burned it myself by accident, I grieved with a grief that lasted longer and was more inconsolable than that of the proprietors; nay, I grieved when it was cut down by the proprietors themselves. I would that our farmers when they cut down a forest felt some of that awe which the old Romans did when they came to thin, or let in the light to, a consecrated grove, (*lucum conlucare,*) that is, would believe that it is sacred to some god. The Roman made an expiatory offering, and prayed, Whatever god or goddess thou art to whom this grove is sacred, be propitious to me, my family, and children, &c.

It is remarkable what a value is still put upon wood even in this age and in this new country, a value more permanent and universal than that of gold. After all our discoveries and inventions no man will go by a pile of wood. It is as precious to us as it was to our Saxon and Norman ancestors. If they made their bows of it, we make our gun-stocks of it. Michaux, more than thirty years ago, says that the price of wood for fuel in New York and Philadelphia "nearly equals, and sometimes exceeds, that of the best wood in Paris, though this immense capital annually requires more than three hundred thousand cords, and is surrounded to the distance of three hundred miles by cultivated plains."[4] In this town the price of wood rises almost steadily, and the only question is, how much higher it is to be this year than it was the last. Mechanics and tradesmen who come in person to the forest on no other errand, are sure to attend the wood auction, and even pay a high price for the privilege of gleaning after the wood-chopper. It is now many years that men have resorted to the forest for fuel and the materials of the arts; the New Englander and the New Hollander, the Parisian and the Celt, the farmer and Robinhood, Goody

2. William Gilpin (1724–1804), English author and landscape artist; from his *Remarks on Forest Scenery* (1834).
3. A person who has the responsibility of protecting the wildlife and preserving the greenery of a forest.
4. François André Michaux (1770–1855), French naturalist; from his *North American Sylva* (1819).

Blake and Harry Gill,[5] in most parts of the world the prince and the peasant, the scholar and the savage, equally require still a few sticks from the forest to warm them and cook their food. Neither could I do without them.

Every man looks at his wood-pile with a kind of affection. I loved to have mine before my window, and the more chips the better to remind me of my pleasing work. I had an old axe which nobody claimed, with which by spells in winter days, on the sunny side of the house, I played about the stumps which I had got out of my bean-field. As my driver prophesied when I was ploughing, they warmed me twice, once while I was splitting them, and again when they were on the fire, so that no fuel could give out more heat. As for the axe, I was advised to get the village blacksmith to "jump" it;[6] but I jumped him, and, putting a hickory helve from the woods into it, made it do. If it was dull, it was at least hung true.

A few pieces of fat pine were a great treasure. It is interesting to remember how much of this food for fire is still concealed in the bowels of the earth. In previous years I had often gone "prospecting" over some bare hill-side, where a pitch-pine wood had formerly stood, and got out the fat pine roots. They are almost indestructible. Stumps thirty or forty years old, at least, will still be sound at the core, though the sap-wood has all become vegetable mould, as appears by the scales of the thick bark forming a ring level with the earth four or five inches distant from the heart. With axe and shovel you explore this mine, and follow the marrowy store, yellow as beef tallow, or as if you had struck on a vein of gold, deep into the earth. But commonly I kindled my fire with the dry leaves of the forest, which I had stored up in my shed before the snow came. Green hickory finely split makes the wood-chopper's kindlings, when he has a camp in the woods. Once in a while I got a little of this. When the villagers were lighting their fires beyond the horizon, I too gave notice to the various wild inhabitants of Walden vale, by a smoky streamer from my chimney, that I was awake.—

> Light-winged Smoke, Icarian bird,
> Melting thy pinions in thy upward flight,
> Lark without song, and messenger of dawn,
> Circling above the hamlets as thy nest;
> Or else, departing dream, and shadowy form
> Of midnight vision, gathering up thy skirts;
> By night star-veiling, and by day

---

5. In a poem of this title by William Wordsworth (1770–1850), Harry Gill denies fuel to Goody Blake, whereupon she curses him to eternal cold.

6. To flatten or lengthen the end of a piece of metal by hammering it.

Darkening the light and blotting out the sun;
Go thou my incense upward from this hearth,
And ask the gods to pardon this clear flame.

Hard green wood just cut, though I used but little of that, answered my purpose better than any other. I sometimes left a good fire when I went to take a walk in a winter afternoon; and when I returned, three or four hours afterward, it would be still alive and glowing. My house was not empty though I was gone. It was as if I had left a cheerful housekeeper behind. It was I and Fire that lived there; and commonly my housekeeper proved trustworthy. One day, however, as I was splitting wood, I thought that I would just look in at the window and see if the house was not on fire; it was the only time I remember to have been particularly anxious on this score; so I looked and saw that a spark had caught my bed, and I went in and extinguished it when it had burned a place as big as my hand. But my house occupied so sunny and sheltered a position, and its roof was so low, that I could afford to let the fire go out in the middle of almost any winter day.

The moles nested in my cellar, nibbling every third potato, and making a snug bed even there of some hair left after plastering and of brown paper; for even the wildest animals love comfort and warmth as well as man, and they survive the winter only because they are so careful to secure them. Some of my friends spoke as if I was coming to the woods on purpose to freeze myself. The animal merely makes a bed, which he warms with his body in a sheltered place; but man, having discovered fire, boxes up some air in a spacious apartment, and warms that, instead of robbing himself, makes that his bed, in which he can move about divested of more cumbrous clothing, maintain a kind of summer in the midst of winter, and by means of windows even admit the light, and with a lamp lengthen out the day. Thus he goes a step or two beyond instinct, and saves a little time for the fine arts. Though, when I had been exposed to the rudest blasts a long time, my whole body began to grow torpid, when I reached the genial atmosphere of my house I soon recovered my faculties and prolonged my life. But the most luxuriously housed has little to boast of in this respect, nor need we trouble ourselves to speculate how the human race may be at last destroyed. It would be easy to cut their threads any time with a little sharper blast from the north. We go on dating from Cold Fridays and Great Snows; but a little colder Friday, or greater snow, would put a period to man's existence on the globe.

The next winter I used a small cooking-stove for economy, since I did not own the forest; but it did not keep fire so well as the open fire-place. Cooking was then, for the most part, no longer a poetic, but merely a chemic process. It will soon be forgotten, in these days of stoves, that we used to roast potatoes in the ashes, after the Indian fashion. The stove not only took up room and scented the house, but it concealed the fire, and I felt as if I had lost a companion. You can always see a face in the fire. The laborer, looking into it at evening, purifies his thoughts of the dross and earthiness which they have accumulated during the day. But I could no longer sit and look into the fire, and the pertinent words of a poet recurred to me with new force.—

> "Never, bright flame, may be denied to me
> Thy dear, life imaging, close sympathy.
> What but my hopes shot upward e'er so bright?
> What but my fortunes sunk so low in night?
>
> Why art thou banished from our hearth and hall,
> Thou who art welcomed and beloved by all?
> Was thy existence then too fanciful
> For our life's common light, who are so dull?
> Did thy bright gleam mysterious converse hold
> With our congenial souls? secrets too bold?
> Well, we are safe and strong, for now we sit
> Beside a hearth where no dim shadows flit,
> Where nothing cheers nor saddens, but a fire
> Warms feet and hands—nor does to more aspire;
> By whose compact utilitarian heap
> The present may sit down and go to sleep,
> Nor fear the ghosts who from the dim past walked,
> And with us by the unequal light of the old wood fire
>   talked."
>
> (Mrs. Hooper)[7]

Former Inhabitants; and Winter Visitors

I weathered some merry snow storms, and spent some cheerful winter evenings by my fire-side, while the snow whirled wildly without, and even the hooting of the owl was hushed. For many weeks I met no one in my walks but those who came occasionally to cut wood and sled it to the village. The elements, however, abetted me in making a path through the deepest snow in the woods, for when I had once gone through the wind blew the oak leaves into my tracks, where they lodged, and by absorbing the rays of the sun melted the snow, and so not only made a dry

7. From "The Wood-Fire" by Ellen Sturgis Hooper (1812–48), an American poet widely admired by the Transcendentalists.

bed for my feet, but in the night their dark line was my guide. For human society I was obliged to conjure up the former occupants of these woods. Within the memory of many of my townsmen the road near which my house stands resounded with the laugh and gossip of inhabitants, and the woods which border it were notched and dotted here and there with their little gardens and dwellings, though it was then much more shut in by the forest than now. In some places, within my own remembrance, the pines would scrape both sides of a chaise at once, and women and children who were compelled to go this way to Lincoln alone and on foot did it with fear, and often ran a good part of the distance. Though mainly but a humble route to neighboring villages, or for the woodman's team, it once amused the traveller more than now by its variety, and lingered longer in his memory. Where now firm open fields stretch from the village to the woods, it then ran through a maple swamp on a foundation of logs, the remnants of which, doubtless, still underlie the present dusty highway, from the Stratton, now the Alms House, Farm to Brister's Hill.

East of my bean-field, across the road, lived Cato Ingraham, slave of Duncan Ingraham, Esquire, gentleman of Concord village; who built his slave a house, and gave him permission to live in Walden Woods;—Cato, not Uticensis, but Concordiensis.[1] Some say that he was a Guinea Negro. There are a few who remember his little patch among the walnuts, which he let grow up till he should be old and need them; but a younger and whiter speculator got them at last. He too, however, occupies an equally narrow house at present. Cato's half-obliterated cellar hole still remains, though known to few, being concealed from the traveller by a fringe of pines. It is now filled with the smooth sumach, (*Rhus glabra*,) and one of the earliest species of goldenrod (*Solidago stricta*) grows there luxuriantly.

Here, by the very corner of my field, still nearer to town, Zilpha, a colored woman, had her little house, where she spun linen for the townsfolk, making the Walden Woods ring with her shrill singing, for she had a loud and notable voice. At length, in the war of 1812, her dwelling was set on fire by English soldiers, prisoners on parole, when she was away, and her cat and dog and hens were all burned up together. She led a hard life, and somewhat inhumane. One old frequenter of these woods remembers, that as he passed her house one noon he heard her muttering to herself over her gurgling pot,—"Ye are all bones, bones!" I have seen bricks amid the oak copse there.

1. I.e., not the Roman statesman, Marcus Porcius Cato (95–46 B.C.), who died in the town of Utica in north Africa, but Cato of Concord.

Down the road, on the right hand, on Brister's Hill, lived Brister Freeman, "a handy Negro," slave of Squire Cummings once,—there where grow still the apple-trees which Brister planted and tended; large old trees now, but their fruit still wild and ciderish to my taste. Not long since I read his epitaph in the old Lincoln burying-ground, a little on one side, near the un-marked graves of some British grenadiers who fell in the retreat from Concord,—where he is styled "Sippio Brister,"—Scipio Afri-canus [2] he had some title to be called,—"a man of color," as if he were discolored. It also told me, with staring emphasis, when he died; which was but an indirect way of informing me that he ever lived. With him dwelt Fenda, his hospitable wife, who told for-tunes, yet pleasantly,—large, round, and black, blacker than any of the children of night, such a dusky orb as never rose on Concord before or since.

Farther down the hill, on the left, on the old road in the woods, are marks of some homestead of the Stratton family; whose orchard once covered all the slope of Brister's Hill, but was long since killed out by pitch-pines, excepting a few stumps, whose old roots furnish still the wild stocks of many a thrifty village tree.[3]

Nearer yet to town, you come to Breed's location, on the other side of the way, just on the edge of the wood; ground famous for the pranks of a demon not distinctly named in old my-thology, who has acted a prominent and astounding part in our New England life, and deserves, as much as any mythological character, to have his biography written one day; who first comes in the guise of a friend or hired man, and then robs and murders the whole family,—New-England Rum. But history must not yet tell the tragedies enacted here; let time intervene in some measure to assuage and lend an azure tint to them. Here the most indistinct and dubious tradition says that once a tavern stood; the well the same, which tempered the traveller's beverage and refreshed his steed. Here then men saluted one another, and heard and told the news, and went their ways again.

Breed's hut was standing only a dozen years ago, though it had long been unoccupied. It was about the size of mine. It was set on fire by mischievous boys, one Election night, if I do not mistake. I lived on the edge of the village then, and had just lost myself over Davenant's Gondibert,[4] that winter that I labored

---

2. Roman general (237–183 B.C.) who was awarded the honorary name "Africanus" after he defeated the Carthaginian general, Han-nibal.
3. Surveying for Cyrus Jarvis Dec. 23d 56— he shows me a deed of this lot containing 6 A. 52 rods all on the W. of the Wayland Road—

& "consisting of plowland, orcharding & wood-land." sold by Joseph Stratton to Samuel Swan of Concord In holder Aug. 11th 1777 [*Tho-reau's note*].
4. William D'Avenant (1606–68), English dramatist and poet; *Gondibert* is an unfinished romantic epic of chivalry.

with a lethargy,—which, by the way, I never knew whether to regard as a family complaint, having an uncle who goes to sleep shaving himself, and is obliged to sprout potatoes in a cellar Sundays, in order to keep awake and keep the Sabbath, or as the consequence of my attempt to read Chalmers' collection of English poetry [5] without skipping. It fairly overcame my Nervii.[6] I had just sunk my head on this when the bells rung fire, and in hot haste the engines rolled that way, led by a straggling troop of men and boys, and I among the foremost, for I had leaped the brook. We thought it was far south over the woods,—we who had run to fires before,—barn, shop, or dwelling-house, or all together. "It's Baker's barn," cried one. "It is the Codman Place," affirmed another. And then fresh sparks went up above the wood, as if the roof fell in, and we all shouted "Concord to the rescue!" Wagons shot past with furious speed and crushing loads, bearing, perchance, among the rest, the agent of the Insurance Company, who was bound to go however far; and ever and anon the engine bell tinkled behind, more slow and sure, and rearmost of all, as it was afterward whispered, came they who set the fire and gave the alarm. Thus we kept on like true idealists, rejecting the evidence of our senses, until at a turn in the road we heard the crackling and actually felt the heat of the fire from over the wall, and realized, alas! that we were there. The very nearness of the fire but cooled our ardor. At first we thought to throw a frog-pond on to it; but concluded to let it burn, it was so far gone and so worthless. So we stood round our engine, jostled one another, expressed our sentiments through speaking trumpets, or in lower tone referred to the great conflagrations which the world has witnessed, including Bascom's shop, and, between ourselves, we thought that, were we there in season with our "tub," [7] and a full frog-pond by, we could turn that threatened last and universal one into another flood. We finally retreated without doing any mischief,—returned to sleep and Gondibert. But as for Gondibert, I would except that passage in the preface about wit being the soul's powder,—"but most of mankind are strangers to wit, as Indians are to powder."[8]

It chanced that I walked that way across the fields the following night, about the same hour, and hearing a low moaning at this spot, I drew near in the dark, and discovered the only survivor of the family that I know, the heir of both its virtues and its vices, who alone was interested in this burning, lying on his

5. Alexander Chalmers, *The Works of the English Poets from Chaucer to Cowper* (1810), 21 vols.

6. A punning reference to a northern European tribe that was defeated by Julius Caesar in 57 B.C..

7. A hand-drawn fire engine.

8. From "The Author's Preface."

stomach and looking over the cellar wall at the still smouldering cinders beneath, muttering to himself, as is his wont. He had been working far off in the river meadows all day, and had improved the first moments that he could call his own to visit the home of his fathers and his youth. He gazed into the cellar from all sides and points of view by turns, always lying down to it, as if there was some treasure, which he remembered, concealed between the stones, where there was absolutely nothing but a heap of bricks and ashes. The house being gone, he looked at what there was left. He was soothed by the sympathy which my mere presence implied, and showed me, as well as the darkness permitted, where the well was covered up; which, thank Heaven, could never be burned; and he groped long about the wall to find the well-sweep which his father had cut and mounted, feeling for the iron hook or staple by which a burden had been fastened to the heavy end,— all that he could now cling to,—to convince me that it was no common "rider."[9] I felt it, and still remark it almost daily in my walks, for by it hangs the history of a family.

Once more, on the left, where are seen the well and lilac bushes by the wall, in the now open field, lived Nutting and Le Grosse. But to return toward Lincoln.

Farther in the woods than any of these, where the road approaches nearest to the pond, Wyman the potter squatted, and furnished his townsmen with earthen ware, and left descendants to succeed him. Neither were they rich in worldly goods, holding the land by sufferance while they lived; and there often the sheriff came in vain to collect the taxes, and "attached a chip,"[1] for form's sake, as I have read in his accounts, there being nothing else that he could lay his hands on. One day in midsummer, when I was hoeing, a man who was carrying a load of pottery to market stopped his horse against my field and inquired concerning Wyman the younger. He had long ago bought a potter's wheel of him, and wished to know what had become of him. I had read of the potter's clay and wheel in Scripture, but it had never occurred to me that the pots we use were not such as had come down unbroken from those days, or grown on trees like gourds somewhere, and I was pleased to hear that so fictile an art was ever practised in my neighborhood.

The last inhabitant of these woods before me was an Irishman, Hugh Quoil, (if I have spelt his name with coil enough,) who occupied Wyman's tenement,—Col. Quoil, he was called. Rumor said that he had been a soldier at Waterloo.[2] If he had lived I should have made him fight his battles over again. His

9. The top rail of a fence.
1. Confiscated a worthless item.

2. A Belgian village, scene of Napoleon's defeat by the duke of Wellington, June 18, 1815.

trade here was that of a ditcher. Napoleon went to St. Helena; Quoil came to Walden Woods. All I know of him is tragic. He was a man of manners, like one who had seen the world, and was capable of more civil speech than you could well attend to. He wore a great coat in mid-summer, being affected with the trembling delirium, and his face was the color of carmine. He died in the road at the foot of Brister's Hill shortly after I came to the woods, so that I have not remembered him as a neighbor. Before his house was pulled down, when his comrades avoided it as "an unlucky castle," I visited it. There lay his old clothes curled up by use, as if they were himself, upon his raised plank bed. His pipe lay broken on the hearth, instead of a bowl broken at the fountain. The last could never have been the symbol of his death, for he confessed to me that, though he had heard of Brister's Spring, he had never seen it; and soiled cards, kings of diamonds spades and hearts, were scattered over the floor. One black chicken which the administrator could not catch, black as night and as silent, not even croaking, awaiting Reynard, still went to roost in the next apartment. In the rear there was the dim outline of a garden, which had been planted but had never received its first hoeing, owing to those terrible shaking fits, though it was now harvest time. It was over-run with Roman wormwood and beggar-ticks, which last stuck to my clothes for all fruit. The skin of a woodchuck was freshly stretched upon the back of the house, a trophy of his last Waterloo; but no warm cap or mittens would he want more.

Now only a dent in the earth marks the site of these dwellings, with buried cellar stones, and strawberries, raspberries, thimbleberries, hazel-bushes, and sumachs growing in the sunny sward there; some pitch-pine or gnarled oak occupies what was the chimney nook, and a sweet-scented black-birch, perhaps, waves where the door-stone was. Sometimes the well dent is visible, where once a spring oozed; now dry and tearless grass; or it was covered deep,— not to be discovered till some late day,—with a flat stone under the sod, when the last of the race departed. What a sorrowful act must that be,—the covering up of wells! coincident with the opening of wells of tears. These cellar dents, like deserted fox burrows, old holes, are all that is left where once were the stir and bustle of human life, and "fate, free-will, foreknowledge absolute," [3] in some form and dialect or other were by turns discussed. But all I can learn of their conclusions amounts to just this, that "Cato and Brister pulled wool;" [4] which is about as edifying as the history of more famous schools of philosophy.

Still grows the vivacious lilac a generation after the door and lintel and the sill are gone, unfolding its sweet-scented flowers each

3. Milton, *Paradise Lost* 2.560.   4. I.e., performed menial tasks.

spring, to be plucked by the musing traveller; planted and tended once by children's hands, in front-yard plots,—now standing by wall-sides in retired pastures, and giving place to new-rising forests; —the last of that stirp, sole survivor of that family. Little did the dusky children think that the puny slip with its two eyes only, which they stuck in the ground in the shadow of the house and daily watered, would root itself so, and outlive them, and house itself in the rear that shaded it, and grown man's garden and orchard, and tell their story faintly to the lone wanderer a half century after they had grown up and died,—blossoming as fair, and smelling as sweet, as in that first spring. I mark its still tender, civil, cheerful, lilac colors.

But this small village, germ of something more, why did it fail while Concord keeps its ground? Were there no natural advantages,—no water privileges, forsooth? Ay, the deep Walden Pond and cool Brister's Spring,—privilege to drink long and healthy draughts at these, all unimproved by these men but to dilute their glass. They were universally a thirsty race. Might not the basket, stable-broom, mat-making, corn-parching, linen-spinning, and pottery business have thrived here, making the wilderness to blossom like the rose, and a numerous posterity have inherited the land of their fathers? The sterile soil would at least have been proof against a low-land degeneracy. Alas! how little does the memory of these human inhabitants enhance the beauty of the landscape! Again, perhaps, Nature will try, with me for a first settler, and my house raised last spring to be the oldest in the hamlet.

I am not aware that any man has ever built on the spot which I occupy. Deliver me from a city built on the site of a more ancient city, whose materials are ruins, whose gardens cemeteries. The soil is blanched and accursed there, and before that becomes necessary the earth itself will be destroyed. With such reminiscences I repeopled the woods and lulled myself asleep.

At this season I seldom had a visitor. When the snow lay deepest no wanderer ventured near my house for a week or fortnight at a time, but there I lived as snug as a meadow mouse, or as cattle and poultry which are said to have survived for a long time buried in drifts, even without food; or like that early settler's family in the town of Sutton, in this state, whose cottage was completely covered by the great snow of 1717 when he was absent, and an Indian found it only by the hole which the chimney's breath made in the drift, and so relieved the family. But no friendly Indian concerned himself about me; nor needed he, for the master of the house was at home. The Great Snow! How cheerful it is to hear of! When the farmers could not get to the woods and swamps with their teams, and were obliged to cut down the shade trees before their houses, and when the crust was harder cut off the trees in the swamps ten feet from the ground, as it appeared the next spring.

In the deepest snows, the path which I used from the highway to my house, about half a mile long, might have been represented by a meandering dotted line, with wide intervals between the dots. For a week of even weather I took exactly the same number of steps, and of the same length, coming and going, stepping deliberately and with the precision of a pair of dividers in my own deep tracks,—to such routine the winter reduces us,—yet often they were filled with heaven's own blue. But no weather interfered fatally with my walks, or rather my going abroad, for I frequently tramped eight or ten miles through the deepest snow to keep an appointment with a beech-tree, or a yellow-birch, or an old acquaintance among the pines; when the ice and snow causing their limbs to droop, and so sharpening their tops, had changed the pines into fir-trees; wading to the tops of the highest hills when the snow was nearly two feet deep on a level, and shaking down another snow-storm on my head at every step; or sometimes creeping and floundering thither on my hands and knees, when the hunters had gone into winter quarters. One afternoon I amused myself by watching a barred owl (*Strix nebulosa*) sitting on one of the lower dead limbs of a white-pine, close to the trunk, in broad daylight, I standing within a rod of him. He could hear me when I moved and cronched the snow with my feet, but could not plainly see me. When I made most noise he would stretch out his neck, and erect his neck feathers, and open his eyes wide; but their lids soon fell again, and he began to nod. I too felt a slumberous influence after watching him half an hour, as he sat thus with his eyes half open, like a cat, winged brother of the cat. There was only a narrow slit left between their lids, by which he preserved a peninsular relation to me; thus, with half-shut eyes, looking out from the land of dreams, and endeavoring to realize me, vague object or mote that interrupted his visions. At length, on some louder noise or my nearer approach, he would grow uneasy and sluggishly turn about on his perch, as if impatient at having his dreams disturbed; and when he launched himself off and flapped through the pines, spreading his wings to unexpected breadth, I could not hear the slightest sound from them. Thus, guided amid the pine boughs rather by a delicate sense of their neighborhood than by sight, feeling his twilight way as it were with his sensitive pinions, he found a new perch, where he might in peace await the dawning of his day.

As I walked over the long causeway made for the railroad through the meadows, I encountered many a blustering and nipping wind, for nowhere has it freer play; and when the frost had smitten me on one cheek, heathen as I was, I turned to it the other also.[5] Nor was it much better by the carriage road from Brister's Hill. For I came to town still, like a friendly Indian, when the contents of the broad open fields were all piled up between the walls of the Walden road, and half an hour sufficed to obliterate the tracks of the last traveller. And when I returned new drifts would have formed, through which I floundered, where the busy north-west wind had been depositing the powdery snow round a sharp angle in the road, and not a rabbit's track, nor even the fine print, the small type, of a meadow (deer) mouse was to be seen. Yet I rarely failed to find, even in mid-winter, some warm and springy swamp where the grass and the skunk-cabbage still put forth with perennial verdure, and some hardier bird occasionally awaited the return of spring.

Sometimes, notwithstanding the snow, when I returned from my walk at evening I crossed the deep tracks of a woodchopper leading from my door, and found his pile of whittlings on the hearth, and my house filled with the odor of his pipe. Or on a Sunday afternoon, if I chanced to be at home, I heard the cronching of the snow made by the step of a long-headed farmer, who from far through the woods sought my house, to have a social "crack;" one of the few of his vocation who are "men on their farms;"[6] who donned a frock instead of a professor's gown, and is as ready to extract the moral out of church or state as to haul a load of manure from his barn-yard. We talked of rude and simple times, when men sat about large fires in cold bracing weather, with clear heads; and when other dessert failed, we tried our teeth on many a nut which wise squirrels have long since abandoned, for those which have the thickest shells are commonly empty.

The one who came from farthest to my lodge, through deepest snows and most dismal tempests, was a poet.[7] A farmer, a hunter, a soldier, a reporter, even a philosopher, may be daunted; but nothing can deter a poet, for he is actuated by pure love. Who can predict his comings and goings? His business calls him out at all hours, even when doctors sleep. We made that small house ring with boisterous mirth and resound with the murmur of much sober talk, making amends then to Walden vale for the long silences.

5. Compare Jesus' Sermon on the Mount: "I say unto you, That ye resist not evil: but whosoever shall smite thee on they right cheek, turn to him the other also" (Matthew 5.39).
6. In "The American Scholar," Ralph Waldo Emerson distinguishes the ideal individual ("Man on the farm") from the social being (the farmer).
7. Ellery Channing.

Broadway was still and deserted in comparison. At suitable intervals there were regular salutes of laughter, which might have
been referred indifferently to the last uttered or the forth-coming
jest. We made many a "bran new" theory of life over a thin dish
of gruel, which combined the advantages of conviviality with the
clear-headedness which philosophy requires.

I should not forget that during my last winter at the pond
there was another welcome visitor,[8] who at one time came through
the village, through snow and rain and darkness, till he saw my
lamp through the trees, and shared with me some long winter
evenings. One of the last of the philosophers,—Connecticut gave
him to the world,—he peddled first her wares, afterwards, as he
declares, his brains. These he peddles still, prompting God and
disgracing man, bearing for fruit his brain only, like the nut its
kernel. I think that he must be the man of the most faith of
any alive. His words and attitude always suppose a better state of
things than other men are acquainted with, and he will be the
last man to be disappointed as the ages revolve. He has no
venture in the present. But though comparatively disregarded now,
when his day comes, laws unsuspected by most will take effect,
and masters of families and rulers will come to him for advice.—

"How blind that cannot see serenity!"[9]

A true friend of man; almost the only friend of human progress.
An Old Mortality,[1] say rather an Immortality, with unwearied
patience and faith making plain the image engraven in men's bodies,
the God of whom they are but defaced and leaning monuments.
With his hospitable intellect he embraces children, beggars, insane,
and scholars, and entertains the thought of all, adding to it commonly some breadth and elegance. I think that he should keep a
caravansary on the world's highway, where philosophers of all
nations might put up, and on his sign should be printed,
"Entertainment for man, but not for his beast. Enter ye that have
leisure and a quiet mind, who earnestly seek the right road." He
is perhaps the sanest man and has the fewest crotchets of any I
chance to know; the same yesterday and to-morrow. Of yore we
had sauntered and talked, and effectually put the world behind us;
for he was pledged to no institution in it, freeborn, *ingenuus*.
Whichever way we turned, it seemed that the heavens and the
earth had met together, since he enhanced the beauty of the landscape. A blue-robed man, whose fittest roof is the overarching

8. Amos Bronson Alcott (1799–1888), Transcendentalist and educator.
9. From *The Life and Death of Thomas Wol-
sey, Cardinal* (1599) by Thomas Storer.

1. The title of a novel by Sir Walter Scott
(1771–1832); the leading character wanders
through Scotland repairing and cleaning
gravestones.

sky which reflects his serenity. I do not see how he can ever die; Nature cannot spare him.

Having each some shingles of thought well dried, we sat and whittled them, trying our knives, and admiring the clear yellowish grain of the pumpkin pine. We waded so gently and reverently, or we pulled together so smoothly, that the fishes of thought were not scared from the stream, nor feared any angler on the bank, but came and went grandly, like the clouds which float through the western sky, and the mother-o'-pearl flocks which sometimes form and dissolve there. There we worked, revising mythology, rounding a fable here and there, and building castles in the air for which earth offered no worthy foundation. Great Looker! Great Expecter! to converse with whom was a New England Night's Entertainment. Ah! such discourse we had, hermit and philosopher, and the old settler I have spoken of,—we three,— it expanded and racked my little house; I should not dare to say how many pounds' weight there was above the atmospheric pressure on every circular inch; it opened its seams so that they had to be calked with much dulness thereafter to stop the consequent leak;—but I had enough of that kind of oakum already picked.

There was one other [2] with whom I had "solid seasons," long to be remembered, at his house in the village, and who looked in upon me from time to time; but I had no more for society there.

There too, as every where, I sometimes expected the Visitor who never comes. The Vishnu Purana [3] says, "The house-holder is to remain at eventide in his court-yard as long as it takes to milk a cow, or longer if he pleases, to await the arrival of a guest." I often performed this duty of hospitality, waited long enough to milk a whole herd of cows, but did not see the man approaching from the town.

Winter Animals

When the ponds were firmly frozen, they afforded not only new and shorter routes to many points, but new views from their surfaces of the familiar landscape around them. When I crossed Flints' Pond, after it was covered with snow, though I had often paddled about and skated over it, it was so unexpectedly wide and so strange that I could think of nothing but Baffin's Bay.[1] The Lincoln hills rose up around me at the extremity of a snowy plain, in which I did not remember to have stood before; and the fishermen, at an indeterminable distance over the ice, moving slowly

2. Ralph Waldo Emerson (1803–82), a leading Transcendentalist and a close friend of
Thoreau.

3. A Hindu scripture.
1. A part of the north Atlantic Ocean between
Greenland and Canada.

about with their wolfish dogs, passed for sealers or Esquimaux, or in misty weather loomed like fabulous creatures, and I did not know whether they were giants or pygmies. I took this course when I went to lecture in Lincoln in the evening, travelling in no road and passing no house between my own hut and the lecture room. In Goose Pond, which lay in my way, a colony of muskrats dwelt, and raised their cabins high above the ice, though none could be seen abroad when I crossed it. Walden, being like the rest usually bare of snow, or with only shallow and interrupted drifts on it, was my yard, where I could walk freely when the snow was nearly two feet deep on a level elsewhere and the villagers were confined to their streets. There, far from the village street, and except at very long intervals, from the jingle of sleigh-bells, I slid and skated, as in a vast moose-yard well trodden, overhung by oak woods and solemn pines bent down with snow or bristling with icicles.

For sounds in winter nights, and often in winter days, I heard the forlorn but melodious note of a hooting owl indefinitely far; such a sound as the frozen earth would yield if struck with a suitable plectrum, the very *lingua vernacula* [2] of Walden Wood, and quite familiar to me at last, though I never saw the bird while it was making it. I seldom opened my door in a winter evening without hearing it; *Hoo hoo hoo, hoorer hoo,* sounded sonorously, and the first three syllables accented somewhat like *how der do;* or sometimes *hoo hoo* only. One night in the beginning of winter, before the pond froze over, about nine o'clock, I was startled by the loud honking of a goose, and, stepping to the door, heard the sound of their wings like a tempest in the woods as they flew low over my house. They passed over the pond toward Fair Haven, seemingly deterred from settling by my light, their commodore honking all the while with a regular beat. Suddenly an unmistakable cat-owl from very near me, with the most harsh and tremendous voice I ever heard from any inhabitant of the woods, responded at regular intervals to the goose, as if determined to expose and disgrace this intruder from Hudson's Bay [3] by exhibiting a greater compass and volume of voice in a native, and *boo-hoo* him out of Concord horizon. What do you mean by alarming the citadel at this time of night consecrated to me? Do you think I am ever caught napping at such an hour, and that I have not got lungs and a larynx as well as yourself? *Boo-hoo, boo-hoo, boo-hoo!* It was one of the most thrilling discords I ever heard. And yet, if you had a discriminating ear, there were in it the elements of a concord such as these plains never saw nor heard.

I also heard the whooping of the ice in the pond, my great

2. The native language of a locality.   3. An inland sea in north central Canada.

bed-fellow in that part of Concord, as if it were restless in its bed and would fain turn over, were troubled with flatulency and bad dreams; or I was waked by the cracking of the ground by the frost, as if some one had driven a team against my door, and in the morning would find a crack in the earth a quarter of a mile long and a third of an inch wide.

Sometimes I heard the foxes as they ranged over the snow crust, in moonlight nights, in search of a partridge or other game, barking raggedly and demoniacally like forest dogs, as if laboring with some anxiety, or seeking expression, struggling for light and to be dogs outright and run freely in the streets; for if we take the ages into our account, may there not be a civilization going on among brutes as well as men? They seemed to me to be rudimental, burrowing men, still standing on their defence, awaiting their transformation. Sometimes one came near to my window, attracted by my light, barked a vulpine curse at me, and then retreated.

Usually the red squirrel (*Sciurus Hudsonius*) waked me in the dawn, coursing over the roof and up and down the sides of the house, as if sent out of the woods for this purpose. In the course of the winter I threw out half a bushel of ears of sweet-corn, which had not got ripe, on to the snow crust by my door, and was amused by watching the motions of the various animals which were baited by it. In the twilight and the night the rabbits came regularly and made a hearty meal. All day long the red squirrels came and went, and afforded me much entertainment by their manœuvres. One would approach at first warily through the shrub-oaks, running over the snow crust by fits and starts like a leaf blown by the wind, now a few paces this way, with wonderful speed and waste of energy, making inconceivable haste with his "trotters," as if it were for a wager, and now as many paces that way, but never getting on more than half a rod at a time; and then suddenly pausing with a ludicrous expression and a gratuitous somerset, as if all the eyes in the universe were fixed on him,—for all the motions of a squirrel, even in the most solitary recesses of the forest, imply spectators as much as those of a dancing girl,—wasting more time in delay and circumspection than would have sufficed to walk the whole distance,—I never saw one walk,—and then suddenly, before you could say Jack Robinson, he would be in the top of a young pitch-pine, winding up his clock and chiding all imaginary spectators, soliloquizing and talking to all the universe at the same time,—for no reason that I could ever detect, or he himself was aware of, I suspect. At length he would reach the corn, and selecting a suitable ear, frisk about in the same uncertain trigonometrical way to the top-most stick of my wood-pile, before my window, where he looked me in the face, and there sit for hours, supplying himself with a new ear from time to time, nibbling at first voraciously and throwing the half-naked cobs about; till at length he grew more dainty still and played with his food, tasting only the inside of the kernel, and the ear, which was held balanced over the stick by one paw, slipped from his careless grasp and fell to the ground, when he would look over at it with a ludicrous expression of uncertainty, as if suspecting that it had life, with a mind not made up whether to get it again, or a new one, or be off; now thinking of corn, then listening to hear what was in the wind. So the little impudent fellow would waste many an ear in a forenoon; till at last, seizing some longer and plumper one, considerably bigger than himself, and skilfully balancing it, he would set out with it to the woods, like a tiger with a buffalo, by the same zig-zag course and frequent pauses, scratching along with it as if it were too heavy for him and falling all the while, making its fall a diagonal between a perpendicular and horizontal, being determined to put it through at any rate;—a singularly frivolous and whimsical fellow;—and so he would get off with it to where he lived, perhaps carry it to the top of a pine tree forty or fifty rods distant, and I would afterwards find the cobs strewn about the woods in various directions.

At length the jays arrive, whose discordant screams were heard long before, as they were warily making their approach an eighth of a mile off, and in a stealthy and sneaking manner they flit from tree to tree, nearer and nearer, and pick up the kernels which the squirrels have dropped. Then, sitting on a pitch-pine bough, they attempt to swallow in their haste a kernel which is too big for their throats and chokes them; and after great labor they disgorge it, and spend an hour in the endeavor to crack it by repeated blows with their bills. They were manifestly thieves, and I had not much respect for them; but the squirrels, though at first shy, went to work as if they were taking what was their own.

Meanwhile also came the chicadees in flocks, which, picking up the crums the squirrels had dropped, flew to the nearest twig, and, placing them under their claws, hammered away at them with their little bills, as if it were an insect in the bark, till they were sufficiently reduced for their slender throats. A little flock of these tit-mice came daily to pick a dinner out of my wood-pile, or the crums at my door, with faint flitting lisping notes, like the tinkling of icicles in the grass, or else with sprightly *day day day*, or more rarely, in spring-like days, a wiry summery *phe-be* from the woodside. They were so familiar that at length one alighted on an armful of wood which I was carrying in, and pecked at the sticks without fear. I once had a sparrow alight upon my shoulder for a moment while I was hoeing in a village garden, and I felt that I was more distinguished by that circumstance than I should have been by any epaulet I could have worn. The squirrels also grew at last to be quite familiar, and occasionally stepped upon my shoe, when that was the nearest way.

When the ground was not yet quite covered, and again near the end of winter, when the snow was melted on my south hill-side and about my wood-pile, the partridges came out of the woods morning and evening to feed there. Whichever side you walk in the woods the partridge bursts away on whirring wings, jarring the snow from the dry leaves and twigs on high, which comes sifting down in the sun-beams like golden dust; for this brave bird is not to be scared by winter. It is frequently covered up by drifts, and, it is said, "sometimes plunges from on wing into the soft snow, where it remains concealed for a day or two." I used to start them in the open land also, where they had come out of the woods at sunset to "bud" the wild apple-trees. They will come regularly every evening to particular trees, where the cunning sportsman lies in wait for them, and the distant orchards next the woods suffer thus not a little. I am glad that the partridge gets fed, at any rate. It is Nature's own bird which lives on buds and diet-drink.

In dark winter mornings, or in short winter afternoons, I sometimes heard a pack of hounds threading all the woods with hounding cry and yelp, unable to resist the instinct of the chase, and the note of the hunting horn at intervals, proving that man was in the rear. The woods ring again, and yet no fox bursts forth on to the open level of the pond, nor following pack pursuing their Actæon.[4] And perhaps at evening I see the hunters returning with a single brush trailing from their sleigh for a trophy, seeking their inn. They tell me that if the fox would remain in the bosom of the frozen earth he would be safe, or if he would run in a straight line away no fox-hound could overtake him; but, having left his pursuers far behind, he stops to rest and listen till they come up, and when he runs he circles round to his old haunts, where the hunters await him. Sometimes, however, he will run upon a wall many rods, and then leap off far to one side, and he appears to know that water will not retain his scent. A hunter told me that he once saw a fox pursued by hounds burst out on to Walden when the ice was covered with shallow puddles, run part way across, and then return to the same shore. Ere long the hounds arrived, but here they lost the

---

4. In Greek mythology a hunter who was transformed into a stag, then pursued and killed by his own dogs.

scent. Sometimes a pack hunting by themselves would pass my door, and circle round my house, and yelp and hound without regarding me, as if afflicted by a species of madness, so that nothing could divert them from the pursuit. Thus they circle until they fall upon the recent trail of a fox, for a wise hound will forsake every thing else for this. One day a man came to my hut from Lexington to inquire after his hound that made a large track, and had been hunting for a week by himself. But I fear that he was not the wiser for all I told him, for every time I attempted to answer his questions he interrupted me by asking, "What do you do here?" He had lost a dog, but found a man.

One old hunter who has a dry tongue, who used to come to bathe in Walden once every year when the water was warmest, and at such times looked in upon me, told me, that many years ago he took his gun one afternoon and went out for a cruise in Walden Wood; and as he walked the Wayland road he heard the cry of hounds approaching, and ere long a fox leaped the wall into the road, and as quick as thought leaped the other wall out of the road, and his swift bullet had not touched him. Some way behind came an old hound and her three pups in full pursuit, hunting on their own account, and disappeared again in the woods. Late in the afternoon, as he was resting in the thick woods south of Walden, he heard the voice of the hounds far over toward Fair Haven still pursuing the fox; and on they came, their hounding cry which made all the woods ring sounding nearer and nearer, now from Well-Meadow, now from the Baker Farm. For a long time he stood still and listened to their music, so sweet to a hunter's ear, when suddenly the fox appeared, threading the solemn aisles with an easy coursing pace, whose sound was concealed by a sympathetic rustle of the leaves, swift and still, keeping the ground, leaving his pursuers far behind; and, leaping upon a rock amid the woods, he sat erect and listening, with his back to the hunter. For a moment compassion restrained the latter's arm; but that was a short-lived mood, and as quick as thought can follow thought his piece was levelled, and *whang!*—the fox rolling over the rock lay dead on the ground. The hunter still kept his place and listened to the hounds. Still on they came, and now the near woods resounded through all their aisles with their demoniac cry. At length the old hound burst into view with muzzle to the ground, and snapping the air as if possessed, and ran directly to the rock; but spying the dead fox she suddenly ceased her hounding, as if struck dumb with amazement, and walked round and round him in silence; and one by one her pups arrived, and, like their mother, were sobered into silence by the mystery. Then the hunter came forward and stood in their midst, and the mystery was solved. They waited in silence while he skinned the fox, then followed the brush a while, and at length turned off into the woods again. That evening a Weston [5] Squire came to the Concord hunter's cottage to inquire for his hounds, and told how for a week they had been hunting on their own account from Weston woods. The Concord hunter told him what he knew and offered him the skin; but the other declined it and departed. He did not find his hounds that night, but the next day learned that they had crossed the river and put up at a farm-house for the night, whence, having been well fed, they took their departure early in the morning.

The hunter who told me this could remember one Sam Nutting, who used to hunt bears on Fair Haven Ledges, and exchange their skins for rum in Concord village; who told him, even, that he had seen a moose there. Nutting had a famous fox-hound named Burgoyne,—he pronounced it Bugine,—which my informant used to borrow. In the "Wast Book" [6] of an old trader of this town, who was also a captain, town-clerk, and representative, I find the following entry. Jan. 18th, 1742–3, "John Melven Cr. by 1 Grey Fox 0—2—3;" they are not now found here; and in his leger, Feb. 7th, 1743, Hezekiah Stratton has credit "by ½ a Catt [7] skin 0—1—4½;" of course, a wild-cat, for Stratton was a sergeant in the old French war, and would not have got credit for hunting less noble game. Credit is given for deer skins also, and they were daily sold. One man still preserves the horns of the last deer that was killed in this vicinity, and another has told me the particulars of the hunt in which his uncle was engaged. The hunters were formerly a numerous and merry crew here. I remember well one gaunt Nimrod [8] who would catch up a leaf by the road-side and play a strain on it wilder and more melodious, if my memory serves me, than any hunting horn.

At midnight, when there was a moon, I sometimes met with hounds in my path prowling about the woods, which would skulk out of my way, as if afraid, and stand silent amid the bushes till I had passed.

Squirrels and wild mice disputed for my store of nuts. There were scores of pitch-pines around my house, from one to four inches in diameter, which had been gnawed by mice the previous winter,—a Norwegian winter for them, for the snow lay long and deep, and they were obliged to mix a large proportion of pine bark with their other diet. These trees were alive and apparently

---

5. A town near Concord.
6. An account book, or daybook.
7. can it be Calf? v. Mott ledger near beginning [*Thoreau's note*]. Thoreau also underlined the word "Catt" in his copy.
8. Described in Genesis 10.9 as "a mighty hunter."

flourishing at mid-summer, and many of them had grown a foot, though completely girdled; but after another winter such were without exception dead. It is remarkable that a single mouse should thus be allowed a whole pine tree for its dinner, gnawing round instead of up and down it; but perhaps it is necessary in order to thin these trees, which are wont to grow up densely.

The hares (*Lepus Americanus*) were very familiar. One had her form under my house all winter, separated from me only by the flooring, and she startled me each morning by her hasty departure when I began to stir,—thump, thump, thump, striking her head against the floor timbers in her hurry. They used to come round my door at dusk to nibble the potato parings which I had thrown out, and were so nearly the color of the ground that they could hardly be distinguished when still. Sometimes in the twilight I alternately lost and recovered sight of one sitting motionless under my window. When I opened my door in the evening, off they would go with a squeak and a bounce. Near at hand they only excited my pity. One evening one sat by my door two paces from me, at first trembling with fear, yet unwilling to move; a poor wee thing, lean and bony, with ragged ears and sharp nose, scant tail and slender paws. It looked as if Nature no longer contained the breed of nobler bloods, but stood on her last toes. Its large eyes appeared young and unhealthy, almost dropsical. I took a step, and lo, away it scud with an elastic spring over the snow crust, straightening its body and its limbs into graceful length, and soon put the forest between me and itself,—the wild free venison, asserting its vigor and the dignity of Nature. Not without reason was its slenderness. Such then was its nature. (*Lepus, levipes,* light-foot, some think.)

What is a country without rabbits and partridges? They are among the most simple and indigenous animal products; ancient and venerable families known to antiquity as to modern times; of the very hue and substance of Nature, nearest allied to leaves and to the ground,—and to one another; it is either winged or it is legged. It is hardly as if you had seen a wild creature when a rabbit or a partridge bursts away, only a natural one, as much to be expected as rustling leaves. The partridge and the rabbit are still sure to thrive, like true natives of the soil, whatever revolutions occur. If the forest is cut off, the sprouts and bushes which spring up afford them concealment, and they become more numerous than ever. That must be a poor country indeed that does not support a hare. Our woods teem with them both, and around every swamp may be seen the partridge or rabbit walk, beset with twiggy fences and horse-hair snares, which some cowboy tends.

The Pond in Winter

After a still winter night I awoke with the impression that some question had been put to me, which I had been endeavoring in vain to answer in my sleep, as what—how—when—where? But there was dawning Nature, in whom all creatures live, looking in at my broad windows with serene and satisfied face, and no question on *her* lips. I awoke to an answered question, to Nature and daylight. The snow lying deep on the earth dotted with young pines, and the very slope of the hill on which my house is placed, seemed to say, Forward! Nature puts no question and answers none which we mortals ask. She has long ago taken her resolution. "O Prince, our eyes contemplate with admiration and transmit to the soul the wonderful and varied spectacle of this universe. The night veils without doubt a part of this glorious creation; but day comes to reveal to us this great work, which extends from earth even into the plains of the ether."[1]

Then to my morning work. First I take an axe and pail and go in search of water, if that be not a dream. After a cold and snowy night it needed a divining rod to find it. Every winter the liquid and trembling surface of the pond, which was so sensitive to every breath, and reflected every light and shadow, becomes solid to the depth of a foot or a foot and a half, so that it will support the heaviest teams, and perchance the snow covers it to an equal depth, and it is not to be distinguished from any level field. Like the marmots in the surrounding hills, it closes its eye-lids and becomes dormant for three months or more. Standing on the snow-covered plain, as if in a pasture amid the hills, I cut my way first through a foot of snow, and then a foot of ice, and open a window under my feet, where, kneeling to drink, I look down into the quiet parlor of the fishes, pervaded by a softened light as through a window of ground glass, with its bright sanded floor the same as in summer; there a perennial waveless serenity reigns as in the amber twilight sky, corresponding to the cool and even temperament of the inhabitants. Heaven is under our feet as well as over our heads.

Early in the morning, while all things are crisp with frost, men come with fishing reels and slender lunch, and let down their fine lines through the snowy field to take pickerel and perch; wild men, who instinctively follow other fashions and trust other authorities than their townsmen, and by their goings and comings

1. From *Mahabharata. Harivansa, ou Historie de la Famille de Hari* (1834–35), translated by S. A. Langlois.

stitch towns together in parts where else they would be ripped. They sit and eat their luncheon in stout fear-naughts[2] on the dry oak leaves on the shore, as wise in natural lore as the citizen is in artificial. They never consulted with books, and know and can tell much less than they have done. The things which they practise are said not yet to be known. Here is one fishing for pickerel with grown perch for bait. You look into his pail with wonder as into a summer pond, as if he kept summer locked up at home, or knew where she had retreated. How, pray, did he get these in mid-winter? O, he got worms out of rotten logs since the ground froze, and so he caught them. His life itself passes deeper in Nature than the studies of the naturalist penetrate; himself a subject for the naturalist. The latter raises the moss and bark gently with his knife in search of insects; the former lays open logs to their core with his axe, and moss and bark fly far and wide. He gets his living by barking trees. Such a man has some right to fish, and I love to see Nature carried out in him. The perch swallows the grub-worm, the pickerel swallows the perch, and the fisherman swallows the pickerel; and so all the chinks in the scale of being are filled.

When I strolled around the pond in misty weather I was some-times amused by the primitive mode which some ruder fisherman had adopted. He would perhaps have placed alder branches over the narrow holes in the ice, which were four or five rods apart and an equal distance from the shore, and having fastened the end of the line to a stick to prevent its being pulled through, have passed the slack line over a twig of the alder, a foot or more above the ice, and tied a dry oak leaf to it, which, being pulled down, would show when he had a bite. These alders loomed through the mist at regular intervals as you walked half way round the pond.

Ah, the pickerel of Walden! when I see them lying on the ice, or in the well which the fisherman cuts in the ice, making a little hole to admit the water, I am always surprised by their rare beauty, as if they were fabulous fishes, they are so foreign to the streets, even to the woods, foreign as Arabia to our Concord life. They possess a quite dazzling and transcendent beauty which separates them by a wide interval from the cadaverous cod and haddock whose fame is trumpeted[3] in our streets. They are not green like the pines, nor gray like the stones, nor blue like the sky; but they have, to my eyes, if possible, yet rarer colors, like flowers and precious stones, as if they were the pearls, the animal-ized *nuclei* or crystals of the Walden water. They, of course,

2. A coat made of heavy woolen material.
3. In the nineteenth century, fish sellers blew horns as they went through the streets.

are Walden all over and all through; are themselves small Waldens in the animal kingdom, Waldenses.[4] It is surprising that they are caught here,—that in this deep and capacious spring, far beneath the rattling teams and chaises and tinkling sleighs that travel the Walden road, this great gold and emerald fish swims. I never chanced to see its kind in any market; it would be the cynosure of all eyes there. Easily, with a few convulsive quirks, they give up their watery ghosts, like a mortal translated before his time to the thin air of heaven.

As I was desirous to recover the long lost bottom of Walden Pond, I surveyed it carefully, before the ice broke up, early in '46, with compass and chain and sounding line. There have been many stories told about the bottom, or rather no bottom, of this pond, which certainly had no foundation for themselves. It is remarkable how long men will believe in the bottomlessness of a pond without taking the trouble to sound it. I have visited two such Bottomless Ponds in one walk in this neighborhood. Many have believed that Walden reached quite through to the other side of the globe. Some who have lain flat on the ice for a long time, looking down through the illusive medium, perchance with watery eyes into the bargain, and driven to hasty conclusions by the fear of catching cold in their breasts, have seen vast holes "into which a load of hay might be driven," if there were any body to drive it, the undoubted source of the Styx and entrance to the Infernal Regions from these parts. Others have gone down from the village with a "fifty-six" [5] and a wagon load of inch rope, but yet have failed to find any bottom; for while the "fifty-six" was resting by the way, they were paying out the rope in the vain attempt to fathom their truly immeasurable capacity for marvellousness. But I can assure my readers that Walden has a reasonably tight bottom at a not unreasonable, though at an unusual, depth. I fathomed it easily with a cod-line and a stone weighing about a pound and a half, and could tell accurately when the stone left the bottom, by having to pull so much harder before the water got underneath to help me. The greatest depth was exactly one hundred and two feet; to which may be added the five feet which it has risen since, making one hundred and seven. This is a remarkable depth for so small an area; yet not an inch of it can be spared by the imagination. What if all ponds were shallow? Would it not react on the minds of men? I am thankful that this pond was made deep and pure for a symbol. While men believe in the infinite some ponds will be thought to be bottomless.

4. A sect of religious dissenters founded about 1170 by Peter Waldo in France.

5. A fifty-six-pound iron weight.

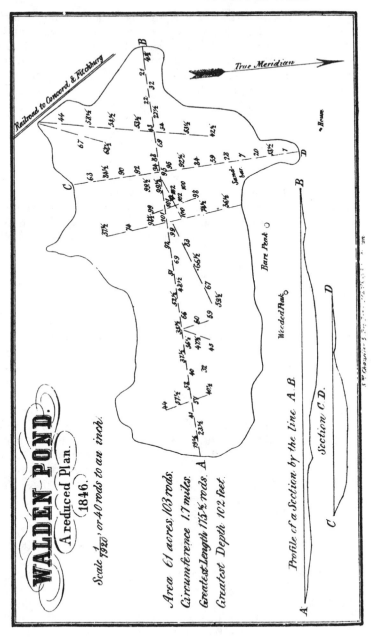

WALDEN POND.
A reduced Plan.
1846.

Scale $\frac{1}{7920}$, or 40 rods to an inch.

Area 61 acres, 103 rods.
Circumference 1.7 miles.
Greatest Length 175½ rods.
Greatest Depth 102 feet.

Profile of a Section by the line. A. B.

Section C. D.

A factory owner, hearing what depth I had found, thought that it could not be true, for, judging from his acquaintance with dams, sand would not lie at so steep an angle. But the deepest ponds are not so deep in proportion to their area as most suppose, and, if drained, would not leave very remarkable valleys. They are not like cups between the hills; for this one, which is so unusually deep for its area, appears in a vertical section through its centre not deeper than a shallow plate. Most ponds, emptied, would leave a meadow no more hollow than we frequently see. William Gilpin, who is so admirable in all that relates to landscapes, and usually so correct, standing at the head of Loch Fyne, in Scotland, which he describes as "a bay of salt water, sixty or seventy fathoms deep, four miles in breadth," and about fifty miles long, surrounded by mountains, observes, "If we could have seen it immediately after the diluvian crash, or whatever convulsion of Nature occasioned it, before the waters gushed in, what a horrid chasm it must have appeared!

> So high as heaved the tumid hills, so low
> Down sunk a hollow bottom, broad, and deep,
> Capacious bed of waters—." [6]

But if, using the shortest diameter of Loch Fyne, we apply these proportions to Walden, which, as we have seen, appears already in a vertical section only like a shallow plate, it will appear four times as shallow. So much for the *increased* horrors of the chasm of Loch Fyne when emptied. No doubt many a smiling valley with its stretching cornfields occupies exactly such a "horrid chasm," from which the waters have receded, though it requires the insight and the far sight of the geologist to convince the unsuspecting inhabitants of this fact. Often an inquisitive eye may detect the shores of a primitive lake in the low horizon hills, and no subsequent elevation of the plain has been necessary to conceal their history. But it is easiest, as they who work on the highways know, to find the hollows by the puddles after a shower. The amount of it is, the imagination, give it the least license, dives deeper and soars higher than Nature goes. So, probably, the depth of the ocean will be found to be very inconsiderable compared with its breadth.

As I sounded through the ice I could determine the shape of the bottom with greater accuracy than is possible in surveying harbors which do not freeze over, and I was surprised at its general regularity. In the deepest part there are several acres more level than almost any field which is exposed to the sun wind and

6. From *Observations on Several Parts of Great Britain* (1808); Gilpin quotes from Milton, *Paradise Lost*, 7.288–90.

plough. In one instance, on a line arbitrarily chosen, the depth did not vary more than one foot in thirty rods; and generally, near the middle, I could calculate the variation for each one hundred feet in any direction beforehand within three or four inches. Some are accustomed to speak of deep and dangerous holes even in quiet sandy ponds like this, but the effect of water under these circumstances is to level all inequalities. The regularity of the bottom and its conformity to the shores and the range of the neighboring hills were so perfect that a distant promontory betrayed itself in the soundings quite across the pond, and its direction could be determined by observing the opposite shore. Cape becomes bar, and plain shoal, and valley and gorge deep water and channel.

When I had mapped the pond by the scale of ten rods to an inch, and put down the soundings, more than a hundred in all, I observed this remarkable coincidence. Having noticed that the number indicating the greatest depth was apparently in the centre of the map, I laid a rule on the map lengthwise, and then breadthwise, and found, to my surprise, that the line of greatest length intersected the line of greatest breadth *exactly* at the point of greatest depth, notwithstanding that the middle is so nearly level, the outline of the pond far from regular, and the extreme length and breadth were got by measuring into the coves; and I said to myself, Who knows but this hint would conduct to the deepest part of the ocean as well as of a pond or puddle? Is not this the rule also for the height of mountains, regarded as the opposite of valleys? We know that a hill is not highest at its narrowest part.

Of five coves, three, or all which had been sounded, were observed to have a bar quite across their mouths and deeper water within, so that the bay tended to be an expansion of water within the land not only horizontally but vertically, and to form a basin or independent pond, the direction of the two capes showing the course of the bar. Every harbor on the sea-coast, also, has its bar at its entrance. In proportion as the mouth of the cove was wider compared with its length, the water over the bar was deeper compared with that in the basin. Given, then, the length and breadth of the cove, and the character of the surrounding shore, and you have almost elements enough to make out a formula for all cases.

In order to see how nearly I could guess, with this experience, at the deepest point in a pond, by observing the outlines of its surface and the character of its shores alone, I made a plan of White Pond, which contains about forty-one acres, and, like this, has no island in it, nor any visible inlet or outlet; and as the line of greatest breadth fell very near the line of least breadth, where two opposite capes approached each other and two opposite bays receded, I ventured to mark a point a short distance from the latter line, but still on the line of greatest length, as the deepest. The deepest part was found to be within one hundred feet of this, still farther in the direction to which I had inclined, and was only one foot deeper, namely, sixty feet. Of course, a stream running through, or an island in the pond, would make the problem much more complicated.

If we knew all the laws of Nature, we should need only one fact, or the description of one actual phenomenon, to infer all the particular results at that point. Now we know only a few laws, and our result is vitiated, not, of course, by any confusion or irregularity in Nature, but by our ignorance of essential elements in the calculation. Our notions of law and harmony are commonly confined to those instances which we detect; but the harmony which results from a far greater number of seemingly conflicting, but really concurring, laws, which we have not detected, is still more wonderful. The particular laws are as our points of view, as, to the traveller, a mountain outline varies with every step, and it has an infinite number of profiles, though absolutely but one form. Even when cleft or bored through it is not comprehended in its entireness.

What I have observed of the pond is no less true in ethics. It is the law of average. Such a rule of the two diameters not only guides us toward the sun in the system and the heart in man, but draw lines through the length and breadth of the aggregate of a man's particular daily behaviors and waves of life into his coves and inlets, and where they intersect will be the height or depth of his character. Perhaps we need only to know how his shores trend and his adjacent country or circumstances, to infer his depth and concealed bottom. If he is surrounded by mountainous circumstances, an Achillean shore,[7] whose peaks overshadow and are reflected in his bosom, they suggest a corresponding depth in him. But a low and smooth shore proves him shallow on that side. In our bodies, a bold projecting brow falls off to and indicates a corresponding depth of thought. Also there is a bar across the entrance of our every cove, or particular inclination; each is our harbor for a season, in which we are detained and partially land-locked. These inclinations are not whimsical usually, but their form, size, and direction are determined by the promontories of the shore, the ancient axes of elevation. When this bar is gradually increased by storms, tides, or currents, or there is a subsidence of the waters, so that it reaches to the surface, that which was at first but an inclination in the shore in which a thought was harbored

7. The Greek hero Achilles was reportedly born in Thessaly, a mountainous region in northeastern Greece.

becomes an individual lake, cut off from the ocean, wherein the thought secures its own conditions, changes, perhaps, from salt to fresh, becomes a sweet sea, dead sea, or a marsh. At the advent of each individual into this life, may we not suppose that such a bar has risen to the surface somewhere? It is true, we are such poor navigators that our thoughts, for the most part, stand off and on upon a harborless coast, are conversant only with the bights of the bays of poesy, or steer for the public ports of entry, and go into the dry docks of science, where they merely refit for this world, and no natural currents concur to individualize them.

As for the inlet or outlet of Walden, I have not discovered any but rain and snow and evaporation, though perhaps, with a thermometer and a line, such places may be found, for where the water flows into the pond it will probably be coldest in summer and warmest in winter. When the ice-men were at work here in '46–7, the cakes sent to the shore were one day rejected by those who were stacking them up there, not being thick enough to lie side by side with the rest; and the cutters thus discovered that the ice over a small space was two or three inches thinner than elsewhere, which made them think that there was an inlet there. They also showed me in another place what they thought was a "leach hole," through which the pond leaked out under a hill into a neighboring meadow, pushing me out on a cake of ice to see it. It was a small cavity under ten feet of water; but I think that I can warrant the pond not to need soldering till they find a worse leak than that. One has suggested, that if such a "leach hole" should be found, its connection with the meadow, if any existed, might be proved by conveying some colored powder or sawdust to the mouth of the hole, and then putting a strainer over the spring in the meadow, which would catch some of the particles carried through by the current.

While I was surveying, the ice, which was sixteen inches thick, undulated under a slight wind like water. It is well known that a level cannot be used on ice. At one rod from the shore its greatest fluctuation, when observed by means of a level on land directed toward a graduated staff on the ice, was three quarters of an inch, though the ice appeared firmly attached to the shore. It was probably greater in the middle. Who knows but if our instruments were delicate enough we might detect an undulation in the crust of the earth? When two legs of my level were on the shore and the third on the ice, and the sights were directed over the latter, a rise or fall of the ice of an almost infinitesimal amount made a difference of several feet on a tree across the pond. When I began to cut holes for sounding, there were three or four inches of water on the ice under a deep snow which had sunk it thus far; but the water began immediately to run into these holes, and continued to run for two days in deep streams, which wore away the ice on every side, and contributed essentially, if not mainly, to dry the surface of the pond; for, as the water ran in, it raised and floated the ice. This was somewhat like cutting a hole in the bottom of a ship to let the water out. When such holes freeze, and a rain succeeds, and finally a new freezing forms a fresh smooth ice over all, it is beautifully mottled internally by dark figures, shaped somewhat like a spider's web, what you may call ice rosettes, produced by the channels worn by the water flowing from all sides to a centre. Sometimes, also, when the ice was covered with shallow puddles, I saw a double shadow of myself, one standing on the head of the other, one on the ice, the other on the trees or hill-side.

While yet it is cold January, and snow and ice are thick and solid, the prudent landlord comes from the village to get ice to cool his summer drink; impressively, even pathetically wise, to foresee the heat and thirst of July now in January,—wearing a thick coat and mittens! when so many things are not provided for. It may be that he lays up no treasures in this world which will cool his summer drink in the next.[8] He cuts and saws the solid pond, unroofs the house of fishes, and carts off their very element and air, held fast by chains and stakes like corded wood, through the favoring winter air, to wintry cellars, to underlie the summer there. It looks like solidified azure, as, far off, it is drawn through the streets. These ice-cutters are a merry race, full of jest and sport, and when I went among them they were wont to invite me to saw pit-fashion with them, I standing underneath.

In the winter of '46-7 there came a hundred men of Hyperborean [9] extraction swoop down on to our pond one morning, with many car-loads of ungainly-looking farming tools, sleds, ploughs, drill-barrows, turf-knives, spades, saws, rakes, and each man was armed with a double-pointed pike-staff, such as is not described in the New-England Farmer or the Cultivator.[1] I did not know whether they had come to sow a crop of winter rye, or some other kind of grain recently introduced from Iceland. As I saw no manure, I judged that they meant to skim the land, as I had done, thinking the soil was deep and had lain fallow long enough. They said that a gentleman farmer, who was behind the scenes, wanted to double his money, which, as I understood, amounted to half a million already; but in order to cover each one of his dollars with another, he took off the only coat, ay, the skin itself, of Walden

8. Matthew 6.19–21.
9. According to Greek mythology, a tribe that

lived far north of Greece.
1. Nineteenth-century farm journals.

Pond in the midst of a hard winter. They went to work at once, ploughing, harrowing, rolling, furrowing, in admirable order, as if they were bent on making this a model farm; but when I was looking sharp to see what kind of seed they dropped into the furrow, a gang of fellows by my side suddenly began to hook up the virgin mould itself, with a peculiar jerk, clean down to the sand, or rather the water,—for it was a very springy soil,—indeed all the *terra firma*[2] there was,—and haul it away on sleds, and then I guessed that they must be cutting peat in a bog. So they came and went every day, with a peculiar shriek from the locomotive, from and to some point of the polar regions, as it seemed to me, like a flock of arctic snow-birds. But sometimes Squaw Walden had her revenge, and a hired man, walking behind his team, slipped through a crack in the ground down toward Tartarus,[3] and he who was so brave before suddenly became but the ninth part of a man, almost gave up his animal heat, and was glad to take refuge in my house, and acknowledge that there was some virtue in a stove; or sometimes the frozen soil took a piece of steel out of a ploughshare, or a plough got set in the furrow and had to be cut out.

To speak literally, a hundred Irishmen, with Yankee overseers, came from Cambridge every day to get out the ice. They divided it into cakes by methods too well known to require description, and these, being sledded to the shore, were rapidly hauled off on to an ice platform, and raised by grappling irons and block and tackle, worked by horses, on to a stack, as surely as so many barrels of flour, and there placed evenly side by side, and row upon row, as if they formed the solid base of an obelisk designed to pierce the clouds. They told me that in a good day they could get out a thousand tons, which was the yield of about one acre. Deep ruts and "cradle holes" were worn in the ice, as on *terra firma*, by the passage of the sleds over the same track, and the horses invariably ate their oats out of cakes of ice hollowed out like buckets. They stacked up the cakes thus in the open air in a pile thirty-five feet high on one side and six or seven rods square, putting hay between the outside layers to exclude the air; for when the wind, though never so cold, finds a passage through, it will wear large cavities, leaving slight supports or studs only here and there, and finally topple it down. At first it looked like a vast blue fort or Valhalla; but when they began to tuck the coarse meadow hay into the crevices, and this became covered with rime and icicles, it looked like a venerable moss-grown and hoary ruin, built of azure-tinted marble, the abode of Winter, that old man we see in the almanac,—his shanty, as if he had a design to estivate with

2. Solid ground.
3. In Greek mythology, a dark region far beneath the surface of the earth.

us. They calculated that not twenty-five per cent. of this would reach its destination, and that two or three per cent. would be wasted in the cars. However, a still greater part of this heap had a different destiny from what was intended; for, either because the ice was found not to keep so well as was expected, containing more air than usual, or for some other reason, it never got to market. This heap, made in the winter of '46–7 and estimated to contain ten thousand tons, was finally covered with hay and boards; and though it was unroofed the following July, and a part of it carried off, the rest remaining exposed to the sun, it stood over that summer and the next winter, and was not quite melted till September 1848. Thus the pond recovered the greater part.

Like the water, the Walden ice, seen near at hand, has a green tint, but at a distance is beautifully blue, and you can easily tell it from the white ice of the river, or the merely greenish ice of some ponds, a quarter of a mile off. Sometimes one of those great cakes slips from the ice-man's sled into the village street, and lies there for a week like a great emerald, an object of interest to all passers. I have noticed that a portion of Walden which in the state of water was green will often, when frozen, appear from the same point of view blue. So the hollows about this pond will, sometimes, in the winter, be filled with a greenish water somewhat like its own, but the next day will have frozen blue. Perhaps the blue color of water and ice is due to the light and air they contain, and the most transparent is the bluest. Ice is an interesting subject for contemplation. They told me that they had some in the ice-houses at Fresh Pond five years old which was as good as ever. Why is it that a bucket of water soon becomes putrid, but frozen remains sweet forever? It is commonly said that this is the difference between the affections and the intellect.

Thus for sixteen days I saw from my window a hundred men at work like busy husbandmen, with teams and horses and apparently all the implements of farming, such a picture as we see on the first page of the almanac; and as often as I looked out I was reminded of the fable of the lark and the reapers, or the parable of the sower, and the like;[4] and now they are all gone, and in thirty days more, probably, I shall look from the same window on the pure sea-green Walden water there, reflecting the clouds and the trees, and sending up its evaporations in solitude, and no traces will appear that a man has ever stood there. Perhaps I shall hear a solitary loon laugh as he dives and plumes himself, or shall see a lonely fisher in his boat, like a floating leaf, beholding his form

4. The Lark and Her Young, in Jean La Fontaine's *Fables* (4.22); and the Parable of the Sower, Matthew 13.3–9, 18–23.

reflected in the waves, where lately a hundred men securely labored.

Thus it appears that the sweltering inhabitants of Charleston and New Orleans, of Madras and Bombay and Calcutta,[5] drink at my well. In the morning I bathe my intellect in the stupendous and cosmogonal philosophy of the Bhagvat Geeta, since whose composition years of the gods have elapsed, and in comparison with which our modern world and its literature seem puny and trivial; and I doubt if that philosophy is not to be referred to a previous state of existence, so remote is its sublimity from our conceptions. I lay down the book and go to my well for water, and lo! there I meet the servant of the Bramin, priest of Brahma and Vishnu and Indra,[6] who still sits in his temple on the Ganges reading the Vedas, or dwells at the root of a tree with his crust and water jug. I meet his servant come to draw water for his master, and our buckets as it were grate together in the same well. The pure Walden water is mingled with the sacred water of the Ganges. With favoring winds it is wafted past the site of the fabulous islands of Atlantis and the Hesperides,[7] makes the periplus of Hanno, and, floating by Ternate and Tidore[8] and the mouth of the Persian Gulf, melts in the tropic gales of the Indian seas, and is landed in ports of which Alexander[9] only heard the names.

Spring

The opening of large tracts by the ice-cutters commonly causes a pond to break up earlier; for the water, agitated by the wind, even in cold weather, wears away the surrounding ice. But such was not the effect on Walden that year, for she had soon got a thick new garment to take the place of the old. This pond never breaks up so soon as the others in this neighborhood, on account both of its greater depth and its having no stream passing through it to melt or wear away the ice. I never knew it to open in the course of a winter, not excepting that of '52–3, which gave the ponds so severe a trial. It commonly opens about the first of April, a week or ten days later than Flints' Pond and Fair-Haven,

5. Madras, Bombay, and Calcutta, all major cities in India, were three of the many places that bought ice from New England merchants.
6. The three major Hindu deities.
7. Paradisiacal islands of the west in Greek mythology.
8. Follows the route of the Carthaginian explorer Hanno, who traveled to west Africa; Ter-nate and Tidore are islands in the Molucca Sea, south of the Philippines.
9. Alexander the Great (356–323 B.C.) extended his empire, and Greek culture, into northwestern India. There he heard fabulous stories of the Ganges in eastern India but was unable to reach it.

beginning to melt on the north side and in the shallower parts
where it began to freeze. It indicates better than any water hereabouts the absolute progress of the season, being least affected
by transient changes of temperature. A severe cold of a few days'
duration in March may very much retard the opening of the
former ponds, while the temperature of Walden increases almost
uninterruptedly. A thermometer thrust into the middle of Walden
on the 6th of March, 1847, stood at 32°, or freezing point; near
the shore at 33°; in the middle of Flints' Pond, the same day, at
32½°; at a dozen rods from the shore, in shallow water, under ice
a foot thick, at 36°. This difference of three and a half degrees
between the temperature of the deep water and the shallow in the
latter pond, and the fact that a great proportion of it is comparatively shallow, show why it should break up so much sooner than
Walden. The ice in the shallowest part was at this time several
inches thinner than in the middle. In mid-winter the middle had
been the warmest and the ice thinnest there. So, also, every one
who has waded about the shores of a pond in summer must have
perceived how much warmer the water is close to the shore, where
only three or four inches deep, than a little distance out, and on
the surface where it is deep, than near the bottom. In spring the
sun not only exerts an influence through the increased temperature
of the air and earth, but its heat passes through ice a foot or more
thick, and is reflected from the bottom in shallow water, and so
also warms the water and melts the under side of the ice, at the
same time that it is melting it more directly above, making it un-
even, and causing the air bubbles which it contains to extend
themselves upward and downward until it is completely honey-
combed, and at last disappears suddenly in a single spring rain.
Ice has its grain as well as wood, and when a cake begins to rot
or "comb," that is, assume the appearance of honey-comb, whatever may be its position, the air cells are at right angles with
what was the water surface. Where there is a rock or a log rising
near to the surface the ice over it is much thinner, and is frequently
quite dissolved by this reflected heat; and I have been told that in
the experiment at Cambridge to freeze water in a shallow wooden
pond, though the cold air circulated underneath, and so had
access to both sides, the reflection of the sun from the bottom more
than counterbalanced this advantage. When a warm rain in the
middle of the winter melts off the snow-ice from Walden, and
leaves a hard dark or transparent ice on the middle, there will
be a strip of rotten though thicker white ice, a rod or more wide,
about the shores, created by this reflected heat. Also, as I have
said, the bubbles themselves within the ice operate as burning
glasses to melt the ice beneath.

The phenomena of the year take place every day in a pond on a small scale. Every morning, generally speaking, the shallow water is being warmed more rapidly than the deep, though it may not be made so warm after all, and every evening it is being cooled more rapidly until the morning. The day is an epitome of the year. The night is the winter, the morning and evening are the spring and fall, and the noon is the summer. The cracking and booming of the ice indicate a change of temperature. One pleasant morning after a cold night, February 24th, 1850, having gone to Flints' Pond to spend the day, I noticed with surprise, that when I struck the ice with the head of my axe, it resounded like a gong for many rods around, or as if I had struck on a tight drum-head. The pond began to boom about an hour after sunrise, when it felt the influence of the sun's rays slanted upon it from over the hills; it stretched itself and yawned like a waking man with a gradually increasing tumult, which was kept up three or four hours. It took a short siesta at noon, and boomed once more toward night, as the sun was withdrawing his influence. In the right stage of the weather a pond fires its evening gun with great regularity. But in the middle of the day, being full of cracks, and the air also being less elastic, it had completely lost its resonance, and probably fishes and muskrats could not then have been stunned by a blow on it. The fishermen say that the "thundering of the pond" scares the fishes and prevents their biting. The pond does not thunder every evening, and I cannot tell surely when to expect its thundering; but though I may perceive no difference in the weather, it does. Who would have suspected so large and cold and thick-skinned a thing to be so sensitive? Yet it has its law to which it thunders obedience when it should as surely as the buds expand in the spring. The earth is all alive and covered with papillæ. The largest pond is as sensitive to atmospheric changes as the globule of mercury in its tube.

One attraction in coming to the woods to live was that I should have leisure and opportunity to see the spring come in. The ice in the pond at length begins to be honey-combed, and I can set my heel in it as I walk. Fogs and rains and warmer suns are gradually melting the snow; the days have grown sensibly longer; and I see how I shall get through the winter without adding to my wood-pile, for large fires are no longer necessary. I am on the alert for the first signs of spring, to hear the chance note of some arriving bird, or the striped squirrel's chirp, for his stores must be now nearly exhausted, or see the woodchuck venture out of his winter quarters. On the 13th of March, after I had heard the bluebird, song-sparrow, and red-wing, the ice was still nearly a foot thick.

As the weather grew warmer, it was not sensibly worn away by the water, nor broken up and floated off as in rivers, but, though it was completely melted for half a rod in width about the shore, the middle was merely honey-combed and saturated with water, so that you could put your foot through it when six inches thick; but by the next day evening, perhaps, after a warm rain followed by fog, it would have wholly disappeared, all gone off with the fog, spirited away. One year I went across the middle only five days before it disappeared entirely. In 1845 Walden was first completely open on the 1st of April; in '46, the 25th of March; in '47, the 8th of April; in '51, the 28th of March; in '52, the 18th of April; in '53, the 23d of March; in '54, about the 7th of April.

Every incident connected with the breaking up of the rivers and ponds and the settling of the weather is particularly interesting to us who live in a climate of so great extremes. When the warmer days come, they who dwell near the river hear the ice crack at night with a startling whoop as loud as artillery, as if its icy fetters were rent from end to end, and within a few days see it rapidly going out. So the alligator comes out of the mud with quakings of the earth. One old man, who has been a close observer of Nature, and seems as thoroughly wise in regard to all her operations as if she had been put upon the stocks when he was a boy, and he had helped to lay her keel,—who has come to his growth, and can hardly acquire more of natural lore if he should live to the age of Methuselah,[1]—told me, and I was surprised to hear him express wonder at any of Nature's operations, for I thought that there were no secrets between them, that one spring day he took his gun and boat, and thought that he would have a little sport with the ducks. There was ice still on the meadows, but it was all gone out of the river, and he dropped down without obstruction from Sudbury, where he lived, to Fair-Haven Pond, which he found, unexpectedly, covered for the most part with a firm field of ice. It was a warm day, and he was surprised to see so great a body of ice remaining. Not seeing any ducks, he hid his boat on the north or back side of an island in the pond, and then concealed himself in the bushes on the south side, to await them. The ice was melted for three or four rods from the shore, and there was a smooth and warm sheet of water, with a muddy bottom, such as the ducks love, within, and he thought it likely that some would be along pretty soon. After he had lain still there about an hour he heard a low and seemingly very distant sound, but singularly grand and impressive, unlike any thing he had ever heard, gradually swelling and increasing as if it would have a

---

1. According to Genesis 5.27, Methuselah lived to be 969 years old.

universal and memorable ending, a sullen rush and roar, which seemed to him all at once like the sound of a vast body of fowl coming in to settle there, and, seizing his gun, he started up in haste and excited; but he found, to his surprise, that the whole body of the ice had started while he lay there, and drifted in to the shore, and the sound he had heard was made by its edge grating on the shore,—at first gently nibbled and crumbled off, but at length heaving up and scattering its wrecks along the island to a considerable height before it came to a stand still.

At length the sun's rays have attained the right angle, and warm winds blow up mist and rain and melt the snow banks, and the sun dispersing the mist smiles on a checkered landscape of russet and white smoking with incense, through which the traveller picks his way from islet to islet, cheered by the music of a thousand tinkling rills and rivulets whose veins are filled with the blood of winter which they are bearing off.

Few phenomena gave me more delight than to observe the forms which thawing sand and clay assume in flowing down the sides of a deep cut on the railroad through which I passed on my way to the village, a phenomenon not very common on so large a scale, though the number of freshly exposed banks of the right material must have been greatly multiplied since railroads were invented. The material was sand of every degree of fineness and of various rich colors, commonly mixed with a little clay. When the frost comes out in the spring, and even in a thawing day in the winter, the sand begins to flow down the slopes like lava, sometimes bursting out through the snow and overflowing it where no sand was to be seen before. Innumerable little streams overlap and interlace one with another, exhibiting a sort of hybrid product, which obeys half way the law of currents, and half way that of vegetation. As it flows it takes the forms of sappy leaves or vines, making heaps of pulpy sprays a foot or more in depth, and resembling, as you look down on them, the laciniated lobed and imbricated thalluses of some lichens; or you are reminded of coral, of leopards' paws or birds' feet, of brains or lungs or bowels, and excrements of all kinds. It is a truly *grotesque* vegetation, whose forms and color we see imitated in bronze, a sort of architectural foliage more ancient and typical than acanthus, chiccory, ivy, vine, or any vegetable leaves; destined perhaps, under some circumstances, to become a puzzle to future geologists. The whole cut impressed me as if it were a cave with its stalactites laid open to the light. The various shades of the sand are singularly rich and agreeable, embracing the different iron colors, brown, gray, yellowish, and reddish. When the flowing mass reaches the drain at the foot of the bank it spreads out flatter into *strands*, the separate streams losing their semi-cylindrical form and gradually becoming more flat and broad, running together as they are more moist, till they form an almost flat *sand*, still variously and beautifully shaded, but in which you can trace the original forms of vegetation; till at length, in the water itself, they are converted into *banks*, like those formed off the mouths of rivers, and the forms of vegetation are lost in the ripple marks on the bottom.

The whole bank, which is from twenty to forty feet high, is sometimes overlaid with a mass of this kind of foliage, or sandy rupture, for a quarter of a mile on one or both sides, the produce of one spring day. What makes this sand foliage remarkable is its springing into existence thus suddenly. When I see on the one side the inert bank,—for the sun acts on one side first,—and on the other this luxuriant foliage, the creation of an hour, I am affected as if in a peculiar sense I stood in the laboratory of the Artist who made the world and me,—had come to where he was still at work, sporting on this bank, and with excess of energy strewing his fresh designs about. I feel as if I were nearer to the vitals of the globe, for this sandy overflow is something such a foliaceous mass as the vitals of the animal body. You find thus in the very sands an anticipation of the vegetable leaf. No wonder that the earth expresses itself outwardly in leaves, it so labors with the idea inwardly. The atoms have already learned this law, and are pregnant by it. The overhanging leaf sees here its prototype. *Internally*, whether in the globe or animal body, it is a moist thick *lobe*, a word especially applicable to the liver and lungs and the *leaves* of fat, (λείβω, labor, *lapsus*, to flow or slip downward, a lapsing; λοβος, *globus*, lobe, globe; also lap, flap, and many other words,) *externally* a dry thin *leaf*, even as the *f* and *v* are a pressed and dried *b*. The radicals of lobe are *lb*, the soft mass of the *b* (single lobed, or B, double lobed,) with a liquid *l* behind it pressing it forward. In globe, *glb*, the guttural g adds to the meaning the capacity of the throat. The feathers and wings of birds are still drier and thinner leaves. Thus, also, you pass from the lumpish grub in the earth to the airy and fluttering butterfly. The very globe continually transcends and translates itself, and becomes winged in its orbit. Even ice begins with delicate crystal leaves, as if it had flowed into moulds which the fronds of water plants have impressed on the watery mirror. The whole tree itself is but one leaf, and rivers are still vaster leaves whose pulp is intervening earth, and towns and cities are the ova of insects in their axils.

When the sun withdraws the sand ceases to flow, but in the morning the streams will start once more and branch and branch again into a myriad of others. You here see perchance how blood vessels are formed. If you look closely you observe that first there pushes forward from the thawing mass a stream of softened sand with a drop-like point, like the ball of the finger, feeling its way slowly and blindly downward, until at last with more heat and moisture, as the sun gets higher, the most fluid portion, in its effort to obey the law to which the most inert also yields, separates from the latter and forms for itself a meandering channel or artery within that, in which is seen a little silvery stream glancing like lightning from one stage of pulpy leaves or branches to another, and ever and anon swallowed up in the sand. It is wonderful how rapidly yet perfectly the sand organizes itself as it flows, using the best material its mass affords to form the sharp edges of its channel. Such are the sources of rivers. In the silicious matter which the water deposits is perhaps the bony system, and in the still finer soil and organic matter the fleshy fibre or cellular tissue. What is man but a mass of thawing clay? The ball of the human finger is but a drop congealed. The fingers and toes flow to their extent from the thawing mass of the body. Who knows what the human body would expand and flow out to under a more genial heaven? Is not the hand a spreading *palm* leaf with its lobes and veins? The ear may be regarded, fancifully, as a lichen, *umbilicaria*, on the side of the head, with its lobe or drop. The lip—*labium*, from *labor* (?)—laps or lapses from the sides of the cavernous mouth. The nose is a manifest congealed drop or stalactite. The chin is a still larger drop, the confluent dripping of the face. The cheeks are a slide from the brows into the valley of the face, opposed and diffused by the cheek bones. Each rounded lobe of the vegetable leaf, too, is a thick and now loitering drop, larger or smaller; the lobes are the fingers of the leaf; and as many lobes as it has, in so many directions it tends to flow, and more heat or other genial influences would have caused it to flow yet farther.

Thus it seemed that this one hillside illustrated the principle of all the operations of Nature. The Maker of this earth but patented a leaf. What Champollion [2] will decipher this hieroglyphic for us, that we may turn over a new leaf at last? This phenomenon is more exhilarating to me than the luxuriance and fertility of vineyards. True, it is somewhat excrementitious in its character, and there is no end to the heaps of liver lights and bowels, as if the globe were turned wrong side outward; but this suggests at least that Nature has some bowels, and there again is mother of humanity. This is the frost coming out of the ground; this is Spring. It precedes the green and flowery spring, as mythology precedes

2. Jean Francois Champollion (1790–1832), French Egyptologist, deciphered the Rosetta stone that provided a key to the ancient inscriptions of Egypt.

regular poetry. I know of nothing more purgative of winter fumes and indigestions. It convinces me that Earth is still in her swaddling clothes, and stretches forth baby fingers on every side. Fresh curls spring from the baldest brow. There is nothing inorganic. These foliaceous heaps lie along the bank like the slag of a furnace, showing that Nature is "in full blast" within. The earth is not a mere fragment of dead history, stratum upon stratum like the leaves of a book, to be studied by geologists and antiquaries chiefly, but living poetry like the leaves of a tree, which precede flowers and fruit,—not a fossil earth, but a living earth; compared with whose great central life all animal and vegetable life is merely parasitic. Its throes will heave our exuviæ from their graves. You may melt your metals and cast them into the most beautiful moulds you can; they will never excite me like the forms which this molten earth flows out into. And not only it, but the institutions upon it, are plastic like clay in the hands of the potter.

Ere long, not only on these banks, but on every hill and plain and in every hollow, the frost comes out of the ground like a dormant quadruped from its burrow, and seeks the sea with music, or migrates to other climes in clouds. Thaw with his gentle persuasion is more powerful than Thor [3] with his hammer. The one melts, the other but breaks in pieces.

When the ground was partially bare of snow, and a few warm days had dried its surface somewhat, it was pleasant to compare the first tender signs of the infant year just peeping forth with the stately beauty of the withered vegetation which had withstood the winter,—life-everlasting, golden-rods, pinweeds, and graceful wild grasses, more obvious and interesting frequently than in summer even, as if their beauty was not ripe till then; even cotton-grass, cat-tails, mulleins, johns-wort, hard-hack, meadow-sweet, and other strong stemmed plants, those unexhausted granaries which entertain the earliest birds,—decent weeds, at least, which widowed Nature wears. I am particularly attracted by the arching and sheaf-like top of the wool-grass; it brings back the summer to our winter memories, and is among the forms which art loves to copy, and which, in the vegetable kingdom, have the same relation to types already in the mind of man that astronomy has. It is an antique style older than Greek or Egyptian. Many of the phenomena of Winter are suggestive of an inexpressible tenderness and fragile delicacy. We are accustomed to hear this king described as a rude and boisterous tyrant; but with the gentleness of a lover he adorns the tresses of Summer.

3. In Norse mythology, the god of war and thunder.

At the approach of spring the red-squirrels got under my house, two at a time, directly under my feet as I sat reading or writing, and kept up the queerest chuckling and chirruping and vocal pirouetting and gurgling sounds that ever were heard; and when I stamped they only chirruped the louder, as if past all fear and respect in their mad pranks, defying humanity to stop them. No you don't—chickaree—chickaree. They were wholly deaf to my arguments, or failed to perceive their force, and fell into a strain of invective that was irresistible.

The first sparrow of spring! The year beginning with younger hope than ever! The faint silvery warblings heard over the partially bare and moist fields from the blue-bird, the song-sparrow, and the red-wing, as if the last flakes of winter tinkled as they fell! What at such a time are histories, chronologies, traditions, and all written revelations? The brooks sing carols and glees to the spring. The marsh-hawk sailing low over the meadow is already seeking the first slimy life that awakes. The sinking sound of melting snow is heard in all dells, and the ice dissolves apace in the ponds. The grass flames up on the hillsides like a spring fire,—"et primitus oritur herba imbribus primoribus evocata," [4]—as if the earth sent forth an inward heat to greet the returning sun; not yellow but green is the color of its flame;—the symbol of perpetual youth, the grass-blade, like a long green ribbon, streams from the sod in-to the summer, checked indeed by the frost, but anon pushing on again, lifting its spear of last year's hay with the fresh life below. It grows as steadily as the rill oozes out of the ground. It is almost identical with that, for in the growing days of June, when the rills are dry, the grass blades are their channels, and from year to year the herds drink at this perennial green stream, and the mower draws from it betimes their winter supply. So our human life but dies down to its root, and still puts forth its green blade to eternity.

Walden is melting apace. There is a canal two rods wide along the northerly and westerly sides, and wider still at the east end. A great field of ice has cracked off from the main body. I hear a song-sparrow singing from the bushes on the shore,—*olit, olit, olit,—chip, chip, chip, che char,—che wiss, wiss, wiss.* He too is helping to crack it. How handsome the great sweeping curves in the edge of the ice, answering somewhat to those of the shore, but more regular! It is unusually hard, owing to the recent severe but transient cold, and all watered or waved like a palace floor. But the wind slides eastward over its opaque surface in vain, till it reaches the living surface beyond. It is glorious to behold this

---

4. From Varro, *Rerum Rusticarum*: "And for the first time, the grass rises, called forth by the first rains."

ribbon of water sparkling in the sun, the bare face of the pond full of glee and youth, as if it spoke the joy of the fishes within it, and of the sands on its shore,—a silvery sheen as from the scales of a *leuciscus*,[5] as it were all one active fish. Such is the contrast between winter and spring. Walden was dead and is alive again. But this spring it broke up more steadily, as I have said.

The change from storm and winter to serene and mild weather, from dark and sluggish hours to bright and elastic ones, is a memorable crisis which all things proclaim. It is seemingly instantaneous at last. Suddenly an influx of light filled my house, though the evening was at hand, and the clouds of winter still overhung it, and the eaves were dripping with sleety rain. I looked out the window, and lo! where yesterday was cold gray ice there lay the transparent pond already calm and full of hope as in a summer evening, reflecting a summer evening sky in its bosom, though none was visible overhead, as if it had intelligence with some remote horizon. I heard a robin in the distance, the first I had heard for many a thousand years, methought, whose note I shall not forget for many a thousand more,—the same sweet and powerful song as of yore. O the evening robin, at the end of a New England summer day! If I could ever find the twig he sits upon! I mean *he*; I mean *the twig*. This at least is not the *Turdus migratorius*.[6] The pitch-pines and shrub-oaks about my house, which had so long drooped, suddenly resumed their several characters, looked brighter, greener, and more erect and alive, as if effectually cleansed and restored by the rain. I knew that it would not rain any more. You may tell by looking at any twig of the forest, ay, at your very wood-pile, whether its winter is past or not. As it grew darker, I was startled by the *honking* of geese flying low over the woods, like weary travellers getting in late from southern lakes, and indulging at last in unrestrained complaint and mutual consolation. Standing at my door, I could hear the rush of their wings; when, driving toward my house, they suddenly spied my light, and with hushed clamor wheeled and settled in the pond. So I came in, and shut the door, and passed my first spring night in the woods.

In the morning I watched the geese from the door through the mist, sailing in the middle of the pond, fifty rods off, so large and tumultuous that Walden appeared like an artificial pond for their amusement. But when I stood on the shore they at once rose up with a great flapping of wings at the signal of their commander, and when they had got into rank circled about over my head, twenty-nine of them, and then steered straight to Canada, with a regular *honk* from the leader at intervals, trusting to break their

5. A small freshwater fish, probably the shiner.   6. Migratory thrush.

fast in muddier pools. A "plump" of ducks rose at the same time and took the route to the north in the wake of their noisier cousins.

For a week I heard the circling groping clangor of some solitary goose in the foggy mornings, seeking its companion, and still peopling the woods with the sound of a larger life than they could sustain. In April the pigeons were seen again flying express in small flocks, and in due time I heard the martins twittering over my clearing, though it had not seemed that the township contained so many that it could afford me any, and I fancied that they were peculiarly of the ancient race that dwelt in hollow trees ere white men came. In almost all climes the tortoise and the frog are among the precursors and heralds of this season, and birds fly with song and glancing plumage, and plants spring and bloom, and winds blow, to correct this slight oscillation of the poles and preserve the equilibrium of Nature.

As every season seems best to us in its turn, so the coming in of spring is like the creation of Cosmos out of Chaos and the realization of the Golden Age.—[7]

"Eurus ad Auroram, Nabathacaque regna recessit,
    Persidaque, et radiis juga subdita matutinis."

"The East-Wind withdrew to Aurora and the Nabathæan
        kingdom,
    And the Persian, and the ridges placed under the morning rays.

*   *   *   *

Man was born. Whether that Artificer of things,
    The origin of a better world, made him from the divine seed;
Or the earth being recent and lately sundered from the high
    Ether, retained some seeds of cognate heaven." [8]

A single gentle rain makes the grass many shades greener. So our prospects brighten on the influx of better thoughts. We should be blessed if we lived in the present always, and took advantage of every accident that befell us, like the grass which confesses the influence of the slightest dew that falls on it; and did not spend our time in atoning for the neglect of past opportunities, which we call doing our duty. We loiter in winter while it is already spring. In a pleasant spring morning all men's sins are forgiven. Such a day is a truce to vice. While such a sun holds out to burn, the vilest sinner may return. Through our own recovered innocence we discern the innocence of our neighbors. You may have known your

7. According to Greek mythology, the universe ("Cosmos") was created from some un-formed original state ("Chaos"); the Golden Age of innocence, peace and happiness occurred soon after creation.
8. Ovid, *Metamorphoses* 1.61–62, 78–81.

neighbor yesterday for a thief, a drunkard, or a sensualist, and merely pitied or despised him, and despaired of the world; but the sun shines bright and warm this first spring morning, recreating the world, and you meet him at some serene work, and see how his exhausted and debauched veins expand with still joy and bless the new day, feel the spring influence with the innocence of infancy, and all his faults are forgotten. There is not only an atmosphere of good will about him, but even a savor of holiness groping for expression, blindly and ineffectually perhaps, like a new-born instinct, and for a short hour the south hill-side echoes to no vulgar jest. You see some innocent fair shoots preparing to burst from his gnarled rind and try another year's life, tender and fresh as the youngest plant. Even he has entered into the joy of his Lord. Why the jailer does not leave open his prison doors,—why the judge does not dismiss his case,—why the preacher does not dismiss his congregation! It is because they do not obey the hint which God gives them, nor accept the pardon which he freely offers to all.

"A return to goodness produced each day in the tranquil and beneficent breath of the morning, causes that in respect to the love of virtue and the hatred of vice, one approaches a little the primitive nature of man, as the sprouts of the forest which has been felled. In like manner the evil which one does in the interval of a day prevents the germs of virtues which began to spring up again from developing themselves and destroys them.

"After the germs of virtue have thus been prevented many times from developing themselves, then the beneficent breath of evening does not suffice to preserve them. As soon as the breath of evening does not suffice longer to preserve them, then the nature of man does not differ much from that of the brute. Men seeing the nature of this man like that of the brute, think that he has never possessed the innate faculty of reason. Are those the true and natural sentiments of man?" [9]

"The Golden Age was first created, which without any avenger
Spontaneously without law cherished fidelity and rectitude.
Punishment and fear were not; nor were threatening words read
On suspended brass; nor did the suppliant crowd fear
The words of their judge; but were safe without an avenger.
Not yet the pine felled on its mountains had descended
To the liquid waves that it might see a foreign world,
And mortals knew no shores but their own.

      *   *   *   *

There was eternal spring, and placid zephyrs with warm
Blasts soothed the flowers born without seed." [1]

9. From the Chinese philosopher Meng-tse;   1. Ovid, *Metamorphoses* 1.89–96, 107–8.
Works 6.1.

On the 29th of April, as I was fishing from the bank of the river near the Nine-Acre-Corner bridge, standing on the quaking grass and willow roots, where the muskrats lurk, I heard a singular rattling sound, somewhat like that of the sticks which boys play with their fingers, when, looking up, I observed a very slight and graceful hawk, like a night-hawk, alternately soaring like a ripple and tumbling a rod or two over and over, showing the underside of its wings, which gleamed like a satin ribbon in the sun, or like the pearly inside of a shell. This sight reminded me of falconry and what nobleness and poetry are associated with that sport. The Merlin it seemed to me it might be called: but I care not for its name. It was the most ethereal flight I had ever witnessed. It did not simply flutter like a butterfly, nor soar like the larger hawks, but it sported with proud reliance in the fields of air; mounting again and again with its strange chuckle, it repeated its free and beautiful fall, turning over and over like a kite, and then recovering from its lofty tumbling, as if it had never set its foot on *terra firma*. It appeared to have no companion in the universe,—sporting there alone,—and to need none but the morning and the ether with which it played. It was not lonely, but made all the earth lonely beneath it. Where was the parent which hatched it, its kindred, and its father in the heavens? The tenant of the air, it seemed related to the earth but by an egg hatched some time in the crevice of a crag;—or was its native nest made in the angle of a cloud, woven of the rainbow's trimmings and the sunset sky, and lined with some soft midsummer haze caught up from earth? Its eyry now some cliffy cloud.

Beside this I got a rare mess of golden and silver and bright cupreous fishes, which looked like a string of jewels. Ah! I have penetrated to those meadows on the morning of many a first spring day, jumping from hummock to hummock, from willow root to willow root, when the wild river valley and the woods were bathed in so pure and bright a light as would have waked the dead, if they had been slumbering in their graves, as some suppose. There needs no stronger proof of immortality. All things must live in such a light. O Death, where was thy sting? O Grave, where was thy victory, then?[2]

Our village life would stagnate if it were not for the unexplored forests and meadows which surround it. We need the tonic of wildness,—to wade sometimes in marshes where the bittern and the meadow-hen lurk, and hear the booming of the snipe; to smell the whispering sedge where only some wilder and more solitary fowl builds her nest, and the mink crawls with its belly close to the ground. At the same time that we are earnest to explore and

2. 1 Corinthians 15.55.

learn all things, we require that all things be mysterious and un-explorable, that land and sea be infinitely wild, unsurveyed and unfathomed by us because unfathomable. We can never have enough of Nature. We must be refreshed by the sight of inex-haustible vigor, vast and Titanic features, the sea-coast with its wrecks, the wilderness with its living and its decaying trees, the thunder cloud, and the rain which lasts three weeks and produces freshets. We need to witness our own limits transgressed, and some life pasturing freely where we never wander. We are cheered when we observe the vulture feeding on the carrion which disgusts and disheartens us and deriving health and strength from the repast. There was a dead horse in the hollow by the path to my house, which compelled me sometimes to go out of my way, especially in the night when the air was heavy, but the assurance it gave me of the strong appetite and inviolable health of Nature was my com-pensation for this. I love to see that Nature is so rife with life that myriads can be afforded to be sacrificed and suffered to prey on one another; that tender organizations can be so serenely squashed out of existence like pulp,—tadpoles which herons gobble up, and tortoises and toads run over in the road; and that some-times it has rained flesh and blood! With the liability to accident, we must see how little account is to be made of it. The impression made on a wise man is that of universal innocence. Poison is not poisonous after all, nor are any wounds fatal. Compassion is a very untenable ground. It must be expeditious. Its pleadings will not bear to be stereotyped.

Early in May, the oaks, hickories, maples, and other trees, just putting out amidst the pine woods around the pond, imparted a brightness like sunshine to the landscape, especially in cloudy days, as if the sun were breaking through mists and shining faintly on the hill-sides here and there. On the third or fourth of May I saw a loon in the pond, and during the first week of the month I heard the whippoorwill, the brown-thrasher, the veery, the wood-pewee, the chewink, and other birds. I had heard the wood-thrush long before. The phœbe had already come once more and looked in at my door and window, to see if my house was cavern-like enough for her, sustaining herself on humming wings with clinched talons, as if she held by the air, while she surveyed the premises. The sulphur-like pollen of the pitch-pine soon covered the pond and the stones and rotten wood along the shore, so that you could have collected a barrel-ful. This is the "sulphur showers" we hear of. Even in Calidas' drama of Sacontala, we read of "rills dyed yellow with the golden dust of the lotus."[3] And so the seasons

3. From Sir William Jones's translation of *Sacontala* by Calidas, a fifth-century Hindu poet and dramatist.

went rolling on into summer, as one rambles into higher and higher grass.

Thus was my first year's life in the woods completed; and the second year was similar to it. I finally left Walden September 6th, 1847.

Conclusion

To the sick the doctors wisely recommend a change of air and scenery. Thank Heaven, here is not all the world. The buck-eye does not grow in New England, and the mocking-bird is rarely heard here. The wild-goose is more of a cosmopolite than we; he breaks his fast in Canada, takes a luncheon in the Ohio, and plumes himself for the night in a southern bayou. Even the bison, to some extent, keeps pace with the seasons, cropping the pastures of the Colorado only till a greener and sweeter grass awaits him by the Yellowstone. Yet we think that if rail-fences are pulled down, and stone-walls piled up on our farms, bounds are henceforth set to our lives and our fates decided. If you are chosen town-clerk, forsooth, you cannot go to Tierra del Fuego this summer: but you may go to the land of infernal fire nevertheless. The universe is wider than our views of it.

Yet we should oftener look over the tafferel of our craft, like curious passengers, and not make the voyage like stupid sailors picking oakum.[1] The other side of the globe is but the home of our correspondent. Our voyaging is only great-circle sailing,[2] and the doctors prescribe for diseases of the skin merely. One hastens to Southern Africa to chase the giraffe; but surely that is not the game he would be after. How long, pray, would a man hunt giraffes if he could? Snipes and woodcocks also may afford rare sport; but I trust it would be nobler game to shoot one's self.—

> "Direct your eye right inward, and you'll find
> A thousand regions in your mind
> Yet undiscovered. Travel them, and be
> Expert in home-cosmography." [3]

What does Africa,—what does the West stand for? Is not our own interior white on the chart? black though it may prove, like the coast, when discovered. Is it the source of the Nile, or the

---

1. Oakum, a hemp fiber obtained by untwisting and picking out the fibers of old rope, is used for caulking seams in a ship; picking oakum is a dull and monotonous job.
2. In geometry, a great circle is a circle formed on the surface of a sphere by a plane that passes through the center of the sphere; great-circle sailing is navigation along the arc of any great circle on the earth's surface.
3. William Habbington (1605–64), "To My Honoured Friend Sir Ed. P. Knight." Thoreau modernized the spelling and changed "eye-sight" to "eye right."

Niger, or the Mississippi, or a North-West Passage around this continent, that we would find? Are these the problems which most concern mankind? Is Franklin the only man who is lost, that his wife should be so earnest to find him? Does Mr. Grinnell [4] know where he himself is? Be rather the Mungo Park, the Lewis and Clarke and Frobisher,[5] of your own streams and oceans; explore your own higher latitudes,—with shiploads of preserved meats to support you, if they be necessary; and pile the empty cans sky-high for a sign. Were preserved meats invented to preserve meat merely? Nay, be a Columbus to whole new continents and worlds within you, opening new channels, not of trade, but of thought. Every man is the lord of a realm beside which the earthly empire of the Czar is but a petty state, a hummock left by the ice. Yet some can be patriotic who have no *self*-respect, and sacrifice the greater to the less. They love the soil which makes their graves, but have no sympathy with the spirit which may still animate their clay. Patriotism is a maggot in their heads. What was the meaning of that South-Sea Exploring Expedition,[6] with all its parade and expense, but an indirect recognition of the fact, that there are continents and seas in the moral world, to which every man is an isthmus or an inlet, yet unexplored by him, but that it is easier to sail many thousand miles through cold and storm and cannibals, in a government ship, with five hundred men and boys to assist one, than it is to explore the private sea, the Atlantic and Pacific Ocean of one's being alone.—

> "Erret, et extremos alter scrutetur Iberos.
> Plus habet hic vitæ, plus habet ille viæ." [7]

Let them wander and scrutinize the outlandish Australians. I have more of God, they more of the road.

It is not worth the while to go round the world to count the cats in Zanzibar.[8] Yet do this even till you can do better, and

---

4. John Franklin (1786–1847), English explorer who disappeared in 1847 attempting to find the Northwest Passage; his remains were finally discovered in 1859. Henry Grinnell (1799–1874), a wealthy New York merchant, financed two searches for Franklin, in 1850 and 1853.

5. Mungo Park (1771–1806), Scottish explorer who traced the course of the Niger River; Meriwether Lewis (1774–1809) and William Clark (1770–1838) led an expedition to discover a land route to the Pacific Ocean (1804–6); Martin Frobisher (1535?—94), English explorer who attempted three times to find the Northwest Passage.

6. An expedition sponsored by the U.S. Navy and led by Charles Wilkes (1798–1877), which explored the South Pacific and Antarctic Oceans in 1838–42.

7. From Claudian (fl. 400 A.D.), "The Old Man of Verona." In his translation, Thoreau substitutes "Australians" for "Iberians" (i.e., those living in the part of Europe now comprising Spain and Portugal).

8. An island off the coast of eastern Africa; Thoreau read about Zanzibar cats in Charles Pickering's *The Races of Man* (1851).

you may perhaps find some "Symmes' Hole"[9] by which to get at the inside at last. England and France, Spain and Portugal, Gold Coast and Slave Coast, all front on this private sea; but no bark from them has ventured out of sight of land, though it is without doubt the direct way to India. If you would learn to speak all tongues and conform to the customs of all nations, if you would travel farther than all travellers, be naturalized in all climes, and cause the Sphinx[1] to dash her head against a stone, even obey the precept of the old philospher,[2] and Explore thyself. Herein are demanded the eye and the nerve. Only the defeated and deserters go to the wars, cowards that run away and enlist. Start now on that farthest western way, which does not pause at the Mississippi or the Pacific, nor conduct toward a worn-out China or Japan, but leads on direct a tangent to this sphere, summer and winter, day and night, sun down, moon down, and at last earth down too.

It is said that Mirabeau[3] took to highway robbery "to ascertain what degree of resolution was necessary in order to place one's self in formal opposition to the most sacred laws of society." He declared that "a soldier who fights in the ranks does not require half so much courage as a foot-pad,"—"that honor and religion have never stood in the way of a well-considered and a firm resolve." This was manly, as the world goes; and yet it was idle, if not desperate. A saner man would have found himself often enough "in formal opposition" to what are deemed "the most sacred laws of society," through obedience to yet more sacred laws, and so have tested his resolution without going out of his way. It is not for a man to put himself in such an attitude to society, but to maintain himself in whatever attitude he find himself through obedience to the laws of his being, which will never be one of opposition to a just government, if he should chance to meet with such.

I left the woods for as good a reason as I went there. Perhaps it seemed to me that I had several more lives to live, and could not spare any more time for that one. It is remarkable how easily and insensibly we fall into a particular route, and make a beaten track for ourselves. I had not lived there a week before my feet wore a path from my door to the pond-side; and though it is five or six years since I trod it, it is still quite distinct.

9. According to John Symmes, a retired army officer, "the earth is hollow and habitable within"; from 1818 until his death in 1829, he tried to raise support for an expedition.
1. In Greek mythology, a winged monster with a woman's head and a lion's body that destroyed anyone unable to guess her riddle; according to legend, Oedipus guessed the riddle, and the Sphinx killed herself.
2. The dictum "Know thyself" has been attributed to several Greek philosophers.
3. Honore Riqueti, Count de Mirabeau (1749–91), French revolutionary statesman.

It is true, I fear that others may have fallen into it, and so helped to keep it open. The surface of the earth is soft and impressible by the feet of men; and so with the paths which the mind travels. How worn and dusty, then, must be the highways of the world, how deep the ruts of tradition and conformity! I did not wish to take a cabin passage, but rather to go before the mast and on the deck of the world, for there I could best see the moonlight amid the mountains. I do not wish to go below now.

I learned this, at least, by my experiment; that if one advances confidently in the direction of his dreams, and endeavors to live the life which he has imagined, he will meet with a success unexpected in common hours. He will put some things behind, will pass an invisible boundary; new, universal, and more liberal laws will begin to establish themselves around and within him; or the old laws be expanded, and interpreted in his favor in a more liberal sense, and he will live with the license of a higher order of beings. In proportion as he simplifies his life, the laws of the universe will appear less complex, and solitude will not be solitude, nor poverty poverty, nor weakness weakness. If you have built castles in the air, your work need not be lost; that is where they should be. Now put the foundations under them.

It is a ridiculous demand which England and America make, that you shall speak so that they can understand you. Neither men nor toad-stools grow so. As if that were important, and there were not enough to understand you without them. As if Nature could support but one order of understandings, could not sustain birds as well as quadrupeds, flying as well as creeping things, and *hush* and *who*, which Bright [4] can understand, were the best English. As if there were safety in stupidity alone. I fear chiefly lest my expression may not be *extra- vagant* enough, may not wander far enough beyond the narrow limits of my daily experience, so as to be adequate to the truth of which I have been convinced. *Extra vagance!* it depends on how you are yarded. The migrating buffalo, which seeks new pastures in another latitude, is not extravagant like the cow which kicks over the pail, leaps the cow-yard fence, and runs after her calf, in milking time. I desire to speak somewhere *without* bounds; like a man in a waking moment, to men in their waking moments; for I am convinced that I cannot exaggerate enough even to lay the foundation of a true expression. Who that has heard a strain of music feared then lest he should speak extravagantly any more forever? In view of the future or possible, we should live quite laxly and undefined in front, our outlines dim and misty on that side; as our shadows

4. A common name for an ox.

reveal an insensible perspiration toward the sun. The volatile truth of our words should continually betray the inadequacy of the residual statement. Their truth is instantly *translated*; its literal monument alone remains. The words which express our faith and piety are not definite; yet they are significant and fragrant like frankincense to superior natures.

Why level downward to our dullest perception always, and praise that as common sense? The commonest sense is the sense of men asleep, which they express by snoring. Sometimes we are inclined to class those who are once-and-a-half witted with the half-witted, because we appreciate only a third part of their wit. Some would find fault with the morning-red, if they ever got up early enough. "They pretend," as I hear, "that the verses of Kabir have four different senses; illusion, spirit, intellect, and the exoteric doctrine of the Vedas;" [5] but in this part of the world it is considered a ground for complaint if a man's writings admit of more than one interpretation. While England endeavors to cure the potato-rot, will not any endeavor to cure the brain-rot, which prevails so much more widely and fatally?

I do not suppose that I have attained to obscurity, but I should be proud if no more fatal fault were found with my pages on this score than was found with the Walden ice. Southern customers objected to its blue color, which is the evidence of its purity, as if it were muddy, and preferred the Cambridge ice, which is white, but tastes of weeds. The purity men love is like the mists which envelop the earth, and not like the azure ether beyond.

Some are dinning in our ears that we Americans, and moderns generally, are intellectual dwarfs compared with the ancients, or even the Elizabethan men. But what is that to the purpose? A living dog is better than a dead lion.[6] Shall a man go and hang himself because he belongs to the race of pygmies, and not be the biggest pygmy that he can? Let every one mind his own business, and endeavor to be what he was made.

Why should we be in such desperate haste to succeed, and in such desperate enterprises? If a man does not keep pace with his companions, perhaps it is because he hears a different drummer. Let him step to the music which he hears, however measured or far away. It is not important that he should mature as soon as an apple-tree or an oak. Shall he turn his spring into summer? If the condition of things which we were made for is not yet, what were any reality which we can substitute? We will not be

---

5. From Garcin de Tassy, *History of Hindu Literature* (1839); Kabir was an Indian mystic of the fifteenth century who tried to reconcile the religions of the Hindus and Moslems.
6. Ecclesiastes 9.4.

shipwrecked on a vain reality. Shall we with pains erect a heaven of blue glass over ourselves, though when it is done we shall be sure to gaze still at the true ethereal heaven far above, as if the former were not?

There was an artist[7] in the city of Kouroo who was disposed to strive after perfection. One day it came into his mind to make a staff. Having considered that in an imperfect work time is an ingredient, but into a perfect work time does not enter, he said to himself, It shall be perfect in all respects, though I should do nothing else in my life. He proceeded instantly to the forest for wood, being resolved that it should not be made of unsuitable material; and as he searched for and rejected stick after stick, his friends gradually deserted him, for they grew old in their works and died, but he grew not older by a moment. His singleness of purpose and resolution, and his elevated piety, endowed him, without his knowledge, with perennial youth. As he made no compromise with Time, Time kept out of his way, and only sighed at a distance because he could not overcome him. Before he had found a stock in all respects suitable the city of Kouroo was a hoary ruin, and he sat on one of its mounds to peel the stick. Before he had given it the proper shape the dynasty of the Candahars was at an end, and with the point of the stick he wrote the name of the last of that race in the sand, and then resumed his work. By the time he had smoothed and polished the staff Kalpa was no longer the pole-star; and ere he had put on the ferule and the head adorned with precious stones, Brahma had awoke and slumbered many times. But why do I stay to mention these things? When the finishing stroke was put to his work, it suddenly expanded before the eyes of the astonished artist into the fairest of all the creations of Brahma. He had made a new system in making a staff, a world with full and fair proportions; in which, though the old cities and dynasties had passed away, fairer and more glorious ones had taken their places. And now he saw by the heap of shavings still fresh at his feet, that, for him and his work, the former lapse of time had been an illusion, and that no more time had elapsed than is required for a single scintillation from the brain of Brahma to fall on and inflame the tinder of a mortal brain. The material was pure, and his art was pure; how could the result be other than wonderful?

No face which we can give to a matter will stead us so well at last as the truth. This alone wears well. For the most part,

7. Scholars generally agree that this "legend" was probably composed by Thoreau. In the Hindu scripture, Bhagavad-Gita, there is a nation of Kooroo; Kalpa is not a star but the period of time between the creation and destruction of the world, said to be more than four billion years; Brahma, the supreme Hindu deity, reputedly has a day and night equal to one Kalpa: at the end of every Kalpa, the world is absorbed into Brahma and then recreated.

we are not where we are, but in a false position. Through an infirmity of our natures, we suppose a case, and put ourselves into it, and hence are in two cases at the same time, and it is doubly difficult to get out. In sane moments we regard only the facts, the case that is. Say what you have to say, not what you ought. Any truth is better than make-believe. Tom Hyde, the tinker, standing on the gallows, was asked if he had any thing to say. "Tell the tailors," said he, "to remember to make a knot in their thread before they take the first stitch." His companion's prayer is forgotten.

However mean your life is, meet it and live it; do not shun it and call it hard names. It is not so bad as you are. It looks poorest when you are richest. The fault-finder will find faults even in paradise. Love your life, poor as it is. You may perhaps have some pleasant, thrilling, glorious hours, even in a poor-house. The setting sun is reflected from the windows of the alms-house as brightly as from the rich man's abode; the snow melts before its door as early in the spring. I do not see but a quiet mind may live as contentedly there, and have as cheering thoughts, as in a palace. The town's poor seem to me often to live the most independent lives of any. May be they are simply great enough to receive without misgiving. Most think that they are above being supported by the town; but it oftener happens that they are not above supporting themselves by dishonest means, which should be more disreputable. Cultivate poverty like a garden herb, like sage. Do not trouble yourself much to get new things, whether clothes or friends. Turn the old; return to them. Things do not change; we change. Sell your clothes and keep your thoughts. God will see that you do not want society. If I were confined to a corner of a garret all my days, like a spider, the world would be just as large to me while I had my thoughts about me. The philosopher said: "From an army of three divisions one can take away its general, and put it in disorder; from the man the most abject and vulgar one cannot take away his thought."[8] Do not seek so anxiously to be developed, to subject yourself to many influences to be played on; it is all dissipation. Humility like darkness reveals the heavenly lights. The shadows of poverty and meanness gather around us, "and lo! creation widens to our view."[9] We are often reminded that if there were bestowed on us the wealth of Crœsus,[1] our aims must still be the same, and our means essentially the same. Moreover, if you are restricted in

8. Confucius, *Analects* 9.25.
9. From "Night and Death," by Joseph Blanco White, English ecclesiastic and poet (1775–1841). According to White, both night and death reveal knowledge of a wider universe to us. In the poem, the line is "lo! creation widened in man's view."
1. King of Lydia, in western Asia Minor, in the sixth century B.C., famed for his wealth.

your range by poverty, if you cannot buy books and newspapers, for instance, you are but confined to the most significant and vital experiences; you are compelled to deal with the material which yields the most sugar and the most starch. It is life near the bone where it is sweetest. You are defended from being a trifler. No man loses ever on a lower level by magnanimity on a higher. Superfluous wealth can buy superfluities only. Money is not required to buy one necessary of the soul.

I live in the angle of a leaden wall, into whose composition was poured a little alloy of bell metal. Often, in the repose of my mid-day, there reaches my ears a confused *tintinnabulum*[2] from without. It is the noise of my contemporaries. My neighbors tell me of their adventures with famous gentlemen and ladies, what notabilities they met at the dinner-table; but I am no more interested in such things than in the contents of the Daily Times. The interest and the conversation are about costume and manners chiefly; but a goose is a goose still, dress it as you will. They tell me of California and Texas, of England and the Indies, of the Hon. Mr. —— of Georgia or of Massachusetts, all transient and fleeting phenomena, till I am ready to leap from their court-yard like the Mameluke bey.[3] I delight to come to my bearings,—not walk in procession with pomp and parade, in a conspicuous place, but to walk even with the Builder of the universe, if I may,—not to live in this restless, nervous, bustling, trivial Nineteenth Century, but stand or sit thoughtfully while it goes by. What are men celebrating? They are all on a committee of arrangements, and hourly expect a speech from somebody. God is only the president of the day, and Webster[4] is his orator. I love to weigh, to settle, to gravitate toward that which most strongly and rightfully attracts me;—not hang by the beam of the scale and try to weigh less,—not suppose a case, but take the case that is; to travel the only path I can, and that on which no power can resist me. It affords me no satisfaction to commence to spring an arch before I have got a solid foundation. Let us not play at kittlybenders.[5] There is a solid bottom every where. We read that the traveller asked the boy if the swamp before him had a hard bottom. The boy replied that it had. But presently the traveller's horse sank in up to the girths, and he observed to the boy, "I thought you said that this bog had a hard bottom." "So it has," answered the latter, "but you have not got half way to

2. Literally, a small tinkling bell; here, a ringing of bells.
3. The Mamelukes, a military caste in Egypt, were massacred in 1811 by Mehemet Ali, viceroy of Egypt; a story holds that one man, an officer (or "bey"), leaped from a wall to his horse and escaped.
4. Daniel Webster, senator from Massachusetts and a noted orator.
5. A game in which children attempt to run or skate on thin ice without breaking it.

it yet." So it is with the bogs and quicksands of society; but he is an old boy that knows it. Only what is thought said or done at a certain rare coincidence is good. I would not be one of those who will foolishly drive a nail into mere lath and plastering; such a deed would keep me awake nights. Give me a hammer, and let me feel for the furrowing. Do not depend on the putty. Drive a nail home and clinch it so faithfully that you can wake up in the night and think of your work with satisfaction,—a work at which you would not be ashamed to invoke the Muse.[6] So will help you God, and so only. Every nail driven should be as another rivet in the machine of the universe, you carrying on the work.

Rather than love, than money, than fame, give me truth. I sat at a table where were rich food and wine in abundance, and obsequious attendance, but sincerity and truth were not; and I went away hungry from the inhospitable board. The hospitality was as cold as the ices. I thought that there was no need of ice to freeze them. They talked to me of the age of the wine and the fame of the vintage; but I thought of an older, a newer, and purer wine, of a more glorious vintage, which they had not got, and could not buy. The style, the house and grounds and "entertainment" pass for nothing with me. I called on the king, but he made me wait in his hall, and conducted like a man incapacitated for hospitality. There was a man in my neighborhood who lived in a hollow tree. His manners were truly regal. I should have done better had I called on him.

How long shall we sit in our porticoes practising idle and musty virtues, which any work would make impertinent? As if one were to begin the day with long-suffering, and hire a man to hoe his potatoes; and in the afternoon go forth to practise Christian meekness and charity with goodness aforethought! Consider the China pride [7] and stagnant self-complacency of mankind. This generation reclines a little to congratulate itself on being the last of an illustrious line; and in Boston and London and Paris and Rome, thinking of its long descent, it speaks of its progress in art and science and literature with satisfaction. There are the Records of the Philosophical Societies, and the public Eulogies of *Great Men!* It is the good Adam contemplating his own virtue. "Yes, we have done great deeds, and sung divine songs, which shall never die,"—that is, as long as *we* can remember them. The learned societies and great men of Assyria,[8]—where are they? What youthful philosophers and experimentalists we

---

6. In Greek mythology, one of the nine goddesses of poetry, music, dance, and other arts; epic poems traditionally begin with an invocation of the Muse.

7. The Chinese empire was commonly believed to be smug and self-satisfied.
8. An ancient empire in western Asia.

are! There is not one of my readers who has yet lived a whole human life. These may be but the spring months in the life of the race. If we have had the seven-years' itch, we have not seen the seventeen-year locust yet in Concord. We are acquainted with a mere pellicle of the globe on which we live. Most have not delved six feet beneath the surface, nor leaped as many above it. We know not where we are. Beside, we are sound asleep nearly half our time. Yet we esteem ourselves wise, and have an established order on the surface. Truly, we are deep thinkers, we are ambitious spirits! As I stand over the insect crawling amid the pine needles on the forest floor, and endeavoring to conceal itself from my sight, and ask myself why it will cherish those humble thoughts, and hide its head from me who might, perhaps, be its benefactor, and impart to its race some cheering information, I am reminded of the greater Benefactor and Intelligence that stands over me the human insect.

There is an incessant influx of novelty into the world, and yet we tolerate incredible dulness. I need only suggest what kind of sermons are still listened to in the most enlightened countries. There are such words as joy and sorrow, but they are only the burden of a psalm, sung with a nasal twang, while we believe in the ordinary and mean. We think that we can change our clothes only. It is said that the British Empire is very large and respectable, and that the United States are a first-rate power. We do not believe that a tide rises and falls behind every man which can float the British Empire like a chip, if he should ever harbor it in his mind. Who knows what sort of seventeen-year locust will next come out of the ground? The government of the world I live in was not framed, like that of Britain, in after-dinner conversations over the wine.

The life in us is like the water in the river. It may rise this year higher than man has ever known it, and flood the parched uplands; even this may be the eventful year, which will drown out all our muskrats. It was not always dry land where we dwell. I see far inland the banks which the stream anciently washed, before science began to record its freshets. Every one has heard the story which has gone the rounds of New England, of a strong and beautiful bug which came out of the dry leaf of an old table of apple-tree wood, which had stood in a farmer's kitchen for sixty years, first in Connecticut, and afterward in Massachusetts,— from an egg deposited in the living tree many years earlier still, as appeared by counting the annual layers beyond it; which was heard gnawing out for several weeks, hatched perchance by the heat of an urn. Who does not feel his faith in a resurrection and immortality strengthened by hearing of this? Who knows what beautiful and winged life, whose egg has been buried for ages under many concentric layers of woodenness in the dead dry life of society, deposited at first in the alburnum of the green and living tree, which has been gradually converted into the semblance of its well-seasoned tomb,—heard perchance gnawing out now for years by the astonished family of man, as they sat round the festive board,—may unexpectedly come forth from amidst society's most trivial and handselled furniture, to enjoy its perfect summer life at last!

I do not say that John or Jonathan [9] will realize all this; but such is the character of that morrow which mere lapse of time can never make to dawn. The light which puts out our eyes is darkness to us. Only that day dawns to which we are awake. There is more day to dawn. The sun is but a morning star.

THE END.

---

9. Common mid-nineteenth-century names for an Englishman and an American respectively.

TEXTUAL APPENDIX TO *WALDEN*

The present text is based on the first edition of *Walden*, published by Ticknor and Fields on August 9, 1854. Emendations have been made either according to Thoreau's corrections and additions to his own copy of the first edition (and, in the case of the title, Thoreau's correspondence with his publisher requesting that the subtitle be dropped in future printings) or in a few cases according to the editor's judgment. Decisions to emend have been made after consulting and comparing the proof sheets corrected by Thoreau and relevant manuscript versions with a copy of the first edition in the Knight Library, University of Oregon. All changes to the 1854 edition of *Walden*, whether initiated by Thoreau or by the editor, are summarized in the list below.

Annotations Thoreau made in his copy of *Walden* are included among the editor's annotations at the foot of pages 123, 124, 172, and 186, identified by the bracketed statement: [*Thoreau's note*]. One of these annotations ("breams, . . . 5lbs—" on 124) contains material apparently intended as an addition to the *Walden* text, for in Thoreau's copy the note is marked for insertion with a caret. For the present edition, therefore, the scientific name for the bream, the trout, and its weight have been treated as additions to the text and rendered to conform to printing conventions and the surrounding text, while Thoreau's bracketed and parenthetical cross-references to the Journal in his note have been treated as annotations and not included in the *Walden* text.

In addition to these emendations, there are a few nonsubstantive differences between the present text and the first edition of *Walden*. Since the Norton edition was completely reset, end-line hyphens generally do not conform in placement to those found in the 1854 edition, and one possibly substantive hyphenation in the first edition ("re-/create") has been resolved to nonhyphenated form ("recreate", 148.40). Two misspellings not detected by Thoreau or his printer have been corrected ("occcasionally", 103.08, and "neighhorhood", 120.18), as has a grammatical error ("have" corrected to "has", 192.31) and an error in spelling a family name ("Stratton", 171.18). In the latter case, Thoreau made the correction in his copy at 172.17 but neglected to correct the previous occurrence at 171.18. Other variant or irregular spellings have been preserved since they might reflect Thoreau's preferences. A period inadvertently omitted in the 1854 edition has been restored (160.40).

Textual Variants

All variants between the Norton Critical Edition and the first edition of *Walden* are summarized in the table below. Page and line number and the word or phrase as printed in the Norton Critical Edition are in boldface, followed by the first edition reading. (T) refers to changes authorized by Thoreau's corrections or additions in his copy of the first edition, now in the Abernethy Library, Middlebury College, Middlebury, Vermont, or by his correspondence with the publisher; (Ed) refers to changes made by the present editor for reasons explained above.

Title page Walden *Walden; Or, Life in the Woods* (T)
14.06 port post (T)
17.17 wheat is said to have been handed wheat was handed (T)
64.37 accomplish it come to the end of them (T)
80.04 were are (T)
80.04 rang rings (T)
85.23 double single (T)
92.04 remunerate remunerate, (T)
103.08 occasionally occcasionally (Ed)
114.29 invariably, invariably (T)
120.18 neighborhood neighhorhood (Ed)
124.12 breams, (Pomotis obesus,) one trout weighing a little over five pounds, breams, (T/Ed)
124.39 it, kingfishers dart away from its coves, it, (T)
135.10 black white (T)
148.40 re-create rec/reate (Ed)
151.07 kind (Mus leucopus) kind (T)
160.40 masonry. masonry (Ed)
170.29 (Mrs. Hooper) (T)
171.18 Stratton Stratten (Ed)
172.17 Stratton Stratten (T)
178.13 meadow (deer) meadow (T)
182.43 frisk brisk (T)
192.31 has have (Ed)

Resistance to Civil Government

I heartily accept the motto,—"That government is best which governs least;"[1] and I should like to see it ǎcted up to more rapidly and systematically. Carried out, it finally amounts to this, which also I believe,—"That government is best which governs not at all;" and when men are prepared for it, that will be the kind of government which they will have. Government is at best but an expedient; but most governments are usually, and all governments are sometimes, inexpedient. The objections which have been brought against a standing army, and they are many and weighty, and deserve to prevail, may also at last be brought against a standing government. The standing army is only an arm of the standing government. The government itself, which is only the mode which the people have chosen to execute their will, is equally liable to be abused and perverted before the people can act through it. Witness the present Mexican war,[2] the work of comparatively a few individuals using the standing government as their tool; for, in the outset, the people would not have consented to this measure.

This American government,—what is it but a tradition, though a recent one, endeavoring to transmit itself unimpaired to posterity, but each instant losing some of its integrity? It has not the vitality and force of a single living man; for a single man can bend it to his will. It is a sort of wooden gun to the people themselves; and, if ever they should use it in earnest as a real one against each other, it will surely split. But it is not the less necessary for this; for the people must have some complicated machinery or other, and hear its din, to satisfy that idea of government which they have. Governments show thus how successfully men can be imposed on, even impose on themselves, for their own advantage. It is excellent, we must all allow; yet this government never of itself furthered any enterprise, but by the alacrity with which it got out of its way. *It* does not keep the country free. *It* does not settle the West. *It* does not educate. The character inherent in the American people has done all that

1. The motto of the *United States Magazine and Democratic Review*, a monthly literary-political journal; a similar statement occurs in Emerson's essay "Politics."

2. Between Mexico and the United States (1846–48); the issues included slavery and the annexation of Texas.

has been accomplished; and it would have done somewhat more, if the government had not sometimes got in its way. For government is an expedient by which men would fain succeed in letting one another alone; and, as has been said, when it is most expedient, the governed are most let alone by it. Trade and commerce, if they were not made of India rubber,[3] would never manage to bounce over the obstacles which legislators are continually putting in their way; and, if one were to judge these men wholly by the effects of their actions, and not partly by their intentions, they would deserve to be classed and punished with those mischievous persons who put obstructions on the railroads.

But, to speak practically and as a citizen, unlike those who call themselves no-government men, I ask for, not at once no government, but *at once* a better government. Let every man make known what kind of government would command his respect, and that will be one step toward obtaining it.

After all, the practical reason why, when the power is once in the hands of the people, a majority are permitted, and for a long period continue, to rule, is not because they are most likely to be in the right, nor because this seems fairest to the minority, but because they are physically the strongest. But a government in which the majority rule in all cases cannot be based on justice, even as far as men understand it. Can there not be a government in which majorities do not virtually decide right and wrong, but conscience?—in which majorities decide only those questions to which the rule of expediency is applicable? Must the citizen ever for a moment, or in the least degree, resign his conscience to the legislator? Why has every man a conscience, then? I think that we should be men first, and subjects afterward. It is not desirable to cultivate a respect for the law, so much as for the right. The only obligation which I have a right to assume, is to do at any time what I think right. It is truly enough said, that a corporation has no conscience; but a corporation of conscientious men is a corporation *with* a conscience. Law never made men a whit more just; and, by means of their respect for it, even the well-disposed are daily made the agents of injustice. A common and natural result of an undue respect for law is, that you may see a file of soldiers, colonel, captain, corporal, privates, powder-monkeys [4] and all, marching in admirable order over hill and dale to the wars, against their wills, aye, against their common sense and consciences, which makes it very steep marching indeed, and produces a palpitation of the heart. They have no doubt that it is a damnable business in which they are

3. A form of crude rubber made from latex.
4. A young boy in military service who carries gunpowder from a storehouse to the guns.

concerned; they are all peaceably inclined. Now, what are they?
Men at all? or small moveable forts and magazines, at the service
of some unscrupulous man in power? Visit the Navy Yard,[5]
and behold a marine, such a man as an American government
can make, or such as it can make a man with its black arts, a
mere shadow and reminiscence of humanity, a man laid out
alive and standing, and already, as one may say, buried under
arms with funeral accompaniments, though it may be

> "Not a drum was heard, not a funeral note,
>   As his corse to the rampart we hurried;
> Not a soldier discharged his farewell shot
>   O'er the grave where our hero we buried." [6]

The mass of men serve the State thus, not as men mainly,
but as machines, with their bodies. They are the standing army,
and the militia, jailers, constables, *posse comitatus*,[7] &c. In
most cases there is no free exercise whatever of the judgment
or of the moral sense; but they put themselves on a level with
wood and earth and stones; and wooden men can perhaps be
manufactured that will serve the purpose as well. Such command
no more respect than men of straw, or a lump of dirt. They have
the same sort of worth only as horses and dogs. Yet such as these
even are commonly esteemed good citizens. Others, as most
legislators, politicians, lawyers, ministers, and office-holders, serve
the State chiefly with their heads; and, as they rarely make
any moral distinctions, they are as likely to serve the devil, without
intending it, as God. A very few, as heroes, patriots, martyrs,
reformers in the great sense, and *men*, serve the State with their
consciences also, and so necessarily resist it for the most part;
and they are commonly treated by it as enemies. A wise man
will only be useful as a man, and will not submit to be "clay,"
and "stop a hole to keep the wind away," [8] but leave that office
to his dust at least:—

> "I am too high-born to be propertied,
> To be a secondary at control,
> Or useful serving-man and instrument
> To any sovereign state throughout the world." [9]

He who gives himself entirely to his fellow-men appears to
them useless and selfish; but he who gives himself partially to
them is pronounced a benefactor and philanthropist.

How does it become a man to behave toward this American

5. Probably the U.S. Navy Yard in Boston, Massachusetts.
6. From "The Burial of Sir John Moore at Corunna" by Charles Wolfe (1791–1823).
7. A body of men summoned by a sheriff to assist in keeping peace.
8. Shakespeare, *Hamlet* 5.1.236–7.
9. Shakespeare, *King John* 5.2.79–82.

government to-day? I answer that he cannot without disgrace be associated with it. I cannot for an instant recognize that political organization as *my* government which is the *slave's* government also.

All men recognize the right of revolution; that is, the right to refuse allegiance to and to resist the government, when its tyranny or its inefficiency are great and unendurable. But almost all say that such is not the case now. But such was the case, they think, in the Revolution of '75.[1] If one were to tell me that this was a bad government because it taxed certain foreign commodities brought to its ports, it is most probable that I should not make an ado about it, for I can do without them: all machines have their friction; and possibly this does enough good to counterbalance the evil. At any rate, it is a great evil to make a stir about it. But when the friction comes to have its machine, and oppression and robbery are organized, I say, let us not have such a machine any longer. In other words, when a sixth of the population of a nation which has undertaken to be the refuge of liberty are slaves, and a whole country is unjustly overrun and conquered by a foreign army, and subjected to military law, I think that it is not too soon for honest men to rebel and revolutionize. What makes this duty the more urgent is the fact, that the country so overrun is not our own, but ours is the invading army.

Paley, a common authority with many on moral questions, in his chapter on the "Duty of Submission to Civil Government," resolves all civil obligation into expediency; and he proceeds to say, "that so long as the interest of the whole society requires it, that is, so long as the established government cannot be resisted or changed without public inconveniency, it is the will of God that the established government be obeyed, and no longer."—"This principle being admitted, the justice of every particular case of resistance is reduced to a computation of the quantity of the danger and grievance on the one side, and of the probability and expense of redressing it on the other."[2] Of this, he says, every man shall judge for himself. But Paley appears never to have contemplated those cases to which the rule of expediency does not apply, in which a people, as well as an individual, must do justice, cost what it may. If I have unjustly wrested a plank from a drowning man, I must restore it to him though I drown myself. This, according to Paley, would be inconvenient. But he that would save his life, in such a case, shall lose it.[3] This people must

1. The American Revolution, begun with the Battle of Lexington and Concord on April 19, 1775.
2. William Paley (1743–1805), English theologian and philosopher; from his *Principles of Moral and Political Philosophy* (1785).
3. Luke 9.24.

cease to hold slaves, and to make war on Mexico, though it cost them their existence as a people.

In their practice, nations agree with Paley; but does any one think that Massachusetts does exactly what is right at the present crisis?

"A drab of state, a cloth-o'-silver slut,
    To have her train borne up, and her soul trail in the dirt." [4]

Practically speaking, the opponents to a reform in Massachusetts are not a hundred thousand politicians at the South, but a hundred thousand merchants and farmers here, who are more interested in commerce and agriculture than they are in humanity, and are not prepared to do justice to the slave and to Mexico, *cost what it may*. I quarrel not with far-off foes, but with those who, near at home, co-operate with, and do the bidding of those far away, and without whom the latter would be harmless. We are accustomed to say, that the mass of men are unprepared; but improvement is slow, because the few are not materially wiser or better than the many. It is not so important that many should be as good as you, as that there be some absolute goodness somewhere; for that will leaven the whole lump.[5] There are thousands who are *in opinion* opposed to slavery and to the war, who yet in effect do nothing to put an end to them; who, esteeming themselves children of Washington and Franklin, sit down with their hands in their pockets, and say that they know not what to do, and do nothing; who even postpone the question of freedom to the question of free-trade, and quietly read the prices-current along with the latest advices from Mexico, after dinner, and, it may be, fall asleep over them both. What is the price-current of an honest man and patriot to-day? They hesitate, and they regret, and sometimes they petition; but they do nothing in earnest and with effect. They will wait, well disposed, for others to remedy the evil, that they may no longer have it to regret. At most, they give only a cheap vote, and a feeble countenance and God-speed, to the right, as it goes by them. There are nine hundred and ninety-nine patrons of virtue to one virtuous man; but it is easier to deal with the real possessor of a thing than with the temporary guardian of it.

All voting is a sort of gaming, like chequers or backgammon, with a slight moral tinge to it, a playing with right and wrong, with moral questions; and betting naturally accompanies it. The character of the voters is not staked. I cast my vote, perchance, as I think right; but I am not vitally concerned that that right

---

4. Cyril Tourneur (1575?–1626), *The Revenger's Tragedy* 4.4.72–73.   5. 1 Corinthians 5.6–8.

should prevail. I am willing to leave it to the majority. Its obligation, therefore, never exceeds that of expediency. Even voting *for the right* is *doing* nothing for it. It is only expressing to men feebly your desire that it should prevail. A wise man will not leave the right to the mercy of chance, nor wish it to prevail through the power of the majority. There is but little virtue in the action of masses of men. When the majority shall at length vote for the abolition of slavery, it will be because they are indifferent to slavery, or because there is but little slavery left to be abolished by their vote. *They* will then be the only slaves. Only *his* vote can hasten the abolition of slavery who asserts his own freedom by his vote.

I hear of a convention to be held at Baltimore, or elsewhere, for the selection of a candidate for the Presidency, made up chiefly of editors, and men who are politicians by profession; but I think, what is it to any independent, intelligent, and respectable man what decision they may come to, shall we not have the advantage of his wisdom and honesty, nevertheless? Can we not count·upon some independent votes? Are there not many individuals in the country who do not attend conventions? But no: I find that the respectable man, so called, has immediately drifted from his position, and despairs of his country, when his country has more reason to despair of him. He forthwith adopts one of the candidates thus selected as the only *available* one, thus proving that he is himself *available* for any purposes of the demagogue. His vote is of no more worth than that of any unprincipled foreigner or hireling native, who may have been bought. Oh for a man who is a *man*, and, as my neighbor says, has a bone in his back which you cannot pass your hand through! Our statistics are at fault: the population has been returned too large. How many *men* are there to a square thousand miles in this country? Hardly one. Does not America offer any inducement for men to settle here? The American has dwindled into an Odd Fellow,[6]—one who may be known by the development of his organ of gregariousness, and a manifest lack of intellect and cheerful self-reliance; whose first and chief concern, on coming into the world, is to see that the alms-houses are in good repair; and, before yet he has lawfully donned the virile garb,[7] to collect a fund for the support of the widows and orphans that may be; who, in short, ventures to live only by the aid of the mutual insurance company, which has promised to bury him decently.

It is not a man's duty, as a matter of course, to devote himself to the eradication of any, even the most enormous wrong; he

---

6. A member of the Independent Order of Odd Fellows, a secret fraternal organization.

7. Adult clothing a Roman boy was permitted to wear upon reaching age fourteen.

may still properly have other concerns to engage him; but it is his duty, at least, to wash his hands of it, and, if he gives it no thought longer, not to give it practically his support. If I devote myself to other pursuits and contemplations, I must first see, at least, that I do not pursue them sitting upon another man's shoulders. I must get off him first, that he may pursue his contemplations too. See what gross inconsistency is tolerated. I have heard some of my townsmen say, "I should like to have them order me out to help put down an insurrection of the slaves, or to march to Mexico,—see if I would go;" and yet these very men have each, directly by their allegiance, and so indirectly, at least, by their money, furnished a substitute. The soldier is applauded who refuses to serve in an unjust war by those who do not refuse to sustain the unjust government which makes the war; is applauded by those whose own act and authority he disregards and sets at nought; as if the State were penitent to that degree that it hired one to scourge it while it sinned, but not to that degree that it left off sinning for a moment. Thus, under the name of order and civil government, we are all made at last to pay homage to and support our own meanness. After the first blush of sin, comes its indifference; and from im-moral it becomes, as it were, *un*moral, and not quite unnecessary to that life which we have made.

The broadest and most prevalent error requires the most disin-terested virtue to sustain it. The slight reproach to which the virtue of patriotism is commonly liable, the noble are most likely to incur. Those who, while they disapprove of the character and measures of a government, yield to it their allegiance and support, are undoubtedly its most conscientious supporters, and so frequently the most serious obstacles to reform. Some are petitioning the State to dissolve the Union, to disregard the requisitions of the President. Why do they not dissolve it themselves,—the union between themselves and the State,—and refuse to pay their quota into its treasury? Do not they stand in the same relation to the State, that the State does to the Union? And have not the same reasons prevented the State from resisting the Union, which have prevented them from resisting the State?

How can a man be satisfied to entertain an opinion merely, and enjoy *it*? Is there any enjoyment in it, if his opinion is that he is aggrieved? If you are cheated out of a single dollar by your neighbor, you do not rest satisfied with knowing that you are cheated, or with saying that you are cheated, or even with peti-tioning him to pay you your due; but you take effectual steps at once to obtain the full amount, and see that you are never cheated again. Action from principle,—the perception and the performance of right,—changes things and relations; it is essentially revolutionary, and does not consist wholly with any thing which was. It not only divides states and churches, it divides families; aye, it divides the *individual*, separating the diabolical in him from the divine.

Unjust laws exist: shall we be content to obey them, or shall we endeavor to amend them, and obey them until we have succeeded, or shall we transgress them at once? Men generally, under such a government as this, think that they ought to wait until they have persuaded the majority to alter them. They think that, if they should resist, the remedy would be worse than the evil. But it is the fault of the government itself that the remedy *is* worse than the evil. *It* makes it worse. Why is it not more apt to anticipate and provide for reform? Why does it not cherish its wise minority? Why does it cry and resist before it is hurt? Why does it not encourage its citizens to be on the alert to point out its faults, and *do* better than it would have them? Why does it always crucify Christ, and excommunicate Copernicus and Luther,[8] and pronounce Washington and Franklin rebels?

One would think, that a deliberate and practical denial of its authority was the only offence never contemplated by government; else, why has it not assigned its definite, its suitable and proportionate penalty? If a man who has no property refuses but once to earn nine shillings[9] for the State, he is put in prison for a period unlimited by any law that I know, and determined only by the discretion of those who placed him there; but if he should steal ninety times nine shillings from the State, he is soon permitted to go at large again.

If the injustice is part of the necessary friction of the machine of government, let it go, let it go: perchance it will wear smooth, —certainly the machine will wear out. If the injustice has a spring, or a pulley, or a rope, or a crank, exclusively for itself, then perhaps you may consider whether the remedy will not be worse than the evil; but if it is of such a nature that it requires you to be the agent of injustice to another, then, I say, break the law. Let your life be a counter friction to stop the machine. What I have to do is to see, at any rate, that I do not lend myself to the wrong which I condemn.

As for adopting the ways which the State has provided for remedying the evil, I know not of such ways. They take too much time, and a man's life will be gone. I have other affairs

---

8. Nicolaus Copernicus (1473–1543), Polish astronomer; he was not excommunicated, but his dissertation on the solar system was banned by the Roman Catholic Church; Martin Luther (1483–1546), German theologian, leader of the Protestant Reformation.
9. The amount of poll tax Thoreau refused to pay.

to attend to. I came into this world, not chiefly to make this a good place to live in, but to live in it, be it good or bad. A man has not every thing to do, but something; and because he cannot do *every thing*, it is not necessary that he should do *something* wrong. It is not my business to be petitioning the governor or the legislature any more than it is theirs to petition me; and, if they should not hear my petition, what should I do then? But in this case the State has provided no way: its very Constitution is the evil. This may seem to be harsh and stubborn and unconciliatory; but it is to treat with the utmost kindness and consideration the only spirit that can appreciate or deserves it. So is all change for the better, like birth and death which convulse the body.

I do not hesitate to say, that those who call themselves abolitionists should at once effectually withdraw their support, both in person and property, from the government of Massachusetts, and not wait till they constitute a majority of one, before they suffer the right to prevail through them. I think that it is enough if they have God on their side, without waiting for that other one. Moreover, any man more right than his neighbors, constitutes a majority of one already.

I meet this American government, or its representative the State government, directly, and face to face, once a year, no more, in the person of its tax-gatherer; this is the only mode in which a man situated as I am necessarily meets it; and it then says distinctly, Recognize me; and the simplest, the most effectual, and, in the present posture of affairs, the indispensablest mode of treating with it on this head, of expressing your little satisfaction with and love for it, is to deny it then. My civil neighbor, the tax-gatherer, is the very man I have to deal with,—for it is, after all, with men and not with parchment that I quarrel,— and he has voluntarily chosen to be an agent of the government. How shall he ever know well what he is and does as an officer of the government, or as a man, until he is obliged to consider whether he shall treat me, his neighbor, for whom he has respect, as a neighbor and well-disposed man, or as a maniac and disturber of the peace, and see if he can get over this obstruction to his neighborliness without a ruder and more impetuous thought or speech corresponding with his action? I know this well, that if one thousand, if one hundred, if ten men whom I could name, —if ten *honest* men only,—aye, if *one* HONEST man, in this State of Massachusetts, *ceasing to hold slaves*, were actually to withdraw from this copartnership, and be locked up in the county jail therefor, it would be the abolition of slavery in America. For it matters not how small the beginning may seem to be:

what is once well done is done for ever. But we love better to talk about it: that we say is our mission. Reform keeps many scores of newspapers in its service, but not one man. If my esteemed neighbor, the State's ambassador,[1] who will devote his days to the settlement of the question of human rights in the Council Chamber, instead of being threatened with the prisons of Carolina, were to sit down the prisoner of Massachusetts, that State which is so anxious to foist the sin of slavery upon her sister,—though at present she can discover only an act of inhospitality to be the ground of a quarrel with her,—the Legislature would not wholly waive the subject the following winter.

Under a government which imprisons any unjustly, the true place for a just man is also a prison. The proper place to-day, the only place which Massachusetts has provided for her freer and less desponding spirits, is in her prisons, to be put out and locked out of the State by her own act, as they have already put themselves out by their principles. It is there that the fugitive slave, and the Mexican prisoner on parole, and the Indian come to plead the wrongs of his race, should find them; on that separate, but more free and honorable ground, where the State places those who are not *with* her but *against* her,—the only house in a slave-state in which a free man can abide with honor. If any think that their influence would be lost there, and their voices no longer afflict the ear of the State, that they would not be as an enemy within its walls, they do not know by how much truth is stronger than error, nor how much more eloquently and effectively he can combat injustice who has experienced a little in his own person. Cast your whole vote, not a strip of paper merely, but your whole influence. A minority is powerless while it conforms to the majority; it is not even a minority then; but it is irresistible when it clogs by its whole weight. If the alternative is to keep all just men in prison, or give up war and slavery, the State will not hesitate which to choose. If a thousand men were not to pay their tax-bills this year, that would not be a violent and bloody measure, as it would be to pay them, and enable the State to commit violence and shed innocent blood. This is, in fact, the definition of a peaceable revolution, if any such is possible. If the tax-gatherer, or any other public officer, asks me, as one has done, "But what shall I do?" my answer is, "If you really wish to do any thing, resign your office." When the subject has refused allegiance, and the officer has resigned his office, then the revolution is accomplished. But even suppose

1. Samuel Hoar (1778–1856), a congressman from Concord, was sent to Charleston, South Carolina, to protest the treatment accorded Negro seamen from Massachusetts. Hoar was expelled from Charleston by the legislature of South Carolina.

blood should flow. Is there not a sort of blood shed when the conscience is wounded? Through this wound a man's real manhood and immortality flow out, and he bleeds to an everlasting death. I see this blood flowing now.

I have contemplated the imprisonment of the offender, rather than the seizure of his goods,—though both will serve the same purpose,—because they who assert the purest right, and consequently are most dangerous to a corrupt State, commonly have not spent much time in accumulating property. To such the State renders comparatively small service, and a slight tax is wont to appear exorbitant, particularly if they are obliged to earn it by special labor with their hands. If there were one who lived wholly without the use of money, the State itself would hesitate to demand it of him. But the rich man—not to make any invidious comparison—is always sold to the institution which makes him rich. Absolutely speaking, the more money, the less virtue; for money comes between a man and his objects, and obtains them for him; and it was certainly no great virtue to obtain it. It puts to rest many questions which he would otherwise be taxed to answer; while the only new question which it puts is the hard but superfluous one, how to spend it. Thus his moral ground is taken from under his feet. The opportunities of living are diminished in proportion as what are called the "means" are increased. The best thing a man can do for his culture when he is rich is to endeavour to carry out those schemes which he entertained when he was poor. Christ answered the Herodians according to their condition. "Show me the tribute-money," said he;—and one took a penny out of his pocket;—If you use money which has the image of Cæsar on it, and which he has made current and valuable, that is, *if you are men of the State,* and gladly enjoy the advantages of Cæsar's government, then pay him back some of his own when he demands it; "Render therefore to Cæsar that which is Cæsar's, and to God those things which are God's," [2] —leaving them no wiser than before as to which was which; for they did not wish to know.

When I converse with the freest of my neighbors, I perceive that, whatever they may say about the magnitude and seriousness of the question, and their regard for the public tranquillity, the long and the short of the matter is, that they cannot spare the protection of the existing government, and they dread the consequences of disobedience to it to their property and families. For

2. Matthew 22.15–22. Herodians were followers of Herod Antipas, tetrarch of Galilee from 4 B.C. to A.D. 39.

my own part, I should not like to think that I ever rely on the protection of the State. But, if I deny the authority of the State when it presents its tax-bill, it will soon take and waste all my property, and so harass me and my children without end. This is hard. This makes it impossible for a man to live honestly and at the same time confortably in outward respects. It will not be worth the while to accumulate property; that would be sure to go again. You must hire or squat somewhere, and raise but a small crop, and eat that soon. You must live within yourself, and depend upon yourself, always tucked up and ready for a start, and not have many affairs. A man may grow rich in Turkey even, if he will be in all respects a good subject of the Turkish government. Confucius said,—"If a State is governed by the principles of reason, poverty and misery are subjects of shame; if a State is not governed by the principles of reason, riches and honors are the subjects of shame."[3] No: until I want the protection of Massachusetts to be extended to me in some distant southern port, where my liberty is endangered, or until I am bent solely on building up an estate at home by peaceful enterprise, I can afford to refuse allegiance to Massachusetts, and her right to my property and life. It costs me less in every sense to incur the penalty of disobedience to the State, than it would to obey. I should feel as if I were worth less in that case.

Some years ago, the State met me in behalf of the church, and commanded me to pay a certain sum toward the support of a clergyman whose preaching my father attended, but never I myself. "Pay it," it said, "or be locked up in the jail." I declined to pay. But, unfortunately, another man saw fit to pay it. I did not see why the schoolmaster should be taxed to support the priest, and not the priest the schoolmaster; for I was not the State's schoolmaster, but I supported myself by voluntary subscription. I did not see why the lyceum should not present its tax-bill, and have the State to back its demand, as well as the church. However, at the request of the selectmen, I conde-scended to make some such statement as this in writing:—"Know all men by these presents, that I, Henry Thoreau, do not wish to be regarded as a member of any incorporated society which I have not joined." This I gave to the town-clerk; and he has it. The State, having thus learned that I did not wish to be re-garded as a member of that church, has never made a like demand on me since; though it said that it must adhere to its original presumption that time. If I had known how to name them, I

3. *Analects* 8.13.

should then have signed off in detail from all the societies which I never signed on to; but I did not know where to find a complete list.

I have paid no poll-tax for six years. I was put into a jail once on this account, for one night; and, as I stood considering the walls of solid stone, two or three feet thick, the door of wood and iron, a foot thick, and the iron grating which strained the light, I could not help being struck with the foolishness of that institution which treated me as if I were mere flesh and blood and bones, to be locked up. I wondered that it should have concluded at length that this was the best use it could put me to, and had never thought to avail itself of my services in some way. I saw that, if there was a wall of stone between me and my townsmen, there was a still more difficult one to climb or break through, before they could get to be as free as I was. I did not for a moment feel confined, and the walls seemed a great waste of stone and mortar. I felt as if I alone of all my townsmen had paid my tax. They plainly did not know how to treat me, but behaved like persons who are underbred. In every threat and in every compliment there was a blunder; for they thought that my chief desire was to stand the other side of that stone wall. I could not but smile to see how industriously they locked the door on my meditations, which followed them out again without let or hinderance, and *they* were really all that was dangerous. As they could not reach me, they had resolved to punish my body; just as boys, if they cannot come at some person against whom they have a spite, will abuse his dog. I saw that the State was half-witted, that it was timid as a lone woman with her silver spoons, and that it did not know its friends from its foes, and I lost all my remaining respect for it, and pitied it.

Thus the State never intentionally confronts a man's sense, intellectual or moral, but only his body, his senses. It is not armed with superior wit or honesty, but with superior physical strength. I was not born to be forced. I will breathe after my own fashion. Let us see who is the strongest. What force has a multitude? They only can force me who obey a higher law than I. They force me to become like themselves. I do not hear of *men* being *forced* to live this way or that by masses of men. What sort of life were that to live? When I meet a government which says to me, "Your money or your life," why should I be in haste to give it my money? It may be in a great strait, and not know what to do: I cannot help that. It must help itself; do as I do. It is not worth the while to snivel about it. I am not responsible for the successful working of the machinery of society.

I am not the son of the engineer. I perceive that, when an acorn and a chestnut fall side by side, the one does not remain inert to make way for the other, but both obey their own laws, and spring and grow and flourish as best they can, till one, perchance, overshadows and destroys the other. If a plant cannot live according to its nature, it dies; and so a man.

The night in prison was novel and interesting enough. The prisoners in their shirt-sleeves were enjoying a chat and the evening air in the door-way, when I entered. But the jailer said, "Come, boys, it is time to lock up;" and so they dispersed, and I heard the sound of their steps returning into the hollow apartments. My room-mate was introduced to me by the jailer, as "a first-rate fellow and a clever man." When the door was locked, he showed me where to hang my hat, and how he managed matters there. The rooms were whitewashed once a month; and this one, at least, was the whitest, most simply furnished, and probably the neatest apartment in the town. He naturally wanted to know where I came from, and what brought me there; and, when I had told him, I asked him in my turn how he came there, presuming him to be an honest man, of course; and, as the world goes, I believe he was. "Why," said he, "they accuse me of burning a barn; but I never did it." As near as I could discover, he had probably gone to bed in a barn when drunk, and smoked his pipe there; and so a barn was burnt. He had the reputation of being a clever man, had been there some three months waiting for his trial to come on, and would have to wait as much longer; but he was quite domesticated and contented, since he got his board for nothing, and thought that he was well treated.

He occupied one window, and I the other; and I saw, that if one stayed there long, his principal business would be to look out the window. I had soon read all the tracts that were left there, and examined where former prisoners had broken out, and where a grate had been sawed off, and heard the history of the various occupants of that room; for I found that even here there was a history and a gossip which never circulated beyond the walls of the jail. Probably this is the only house in the town where verses are composed, which are afterward printed in a circular form, but not published. I was shown quite a long list of verses which were composed by some young men who had been detected in an attempt to escape, who avenged themselves by singing them.

I pumped my fellow-prisoner as dry as I could, for fear I should never see him again; but at length he showed me which was my bed, and left me to blow out the lamp.

It was like travelling into a far country, such as I had never expected to behold, to lie there for one night. It seemed to me that I never had heard the town-clock strike before, nor the evening sounds of the village; for we slept with the windows open, which were inside the grating. It was to see my native village in the light of the middle ages, and our Concord was turned into a Rhine stream, and visions of knights and castles passed before me. They were the voices of old burghers that I heard in the streets. I was an involuntary spectator and auditor of whatever was done and said in the kitchen of the adjacent village-inn,—a wholly new and rare experience to me. It was a closer view of my native town. I was fairly inside of it. I never had seen its institutions before. This is one of its peculiar institutions; for it is a shire [4] town. I began to comprehend what its inhabitants were about.

In the morning, our breakfasts were put through the hole in the door, in small oblong-square tin pans, made to fit, and holding a pint of chocolate, with brown bread, and an iron spoon. When they called for the vessels again, I was green enough to return what bread I had left; but my comrade seized it, and said that I should lay that up for lunch or dinner. Soon after, he was let out to work at haying in a neighboring field, whither he went every day, and would not be back till noon; so he bade me good-day, saying that he doubted if he should see me again.

When I came out of prison,—for some one [5] interfered, and paid the tax,—I did not perceive that great changes had taken place on the common, such as he observed who went in a youth, and emerged a tottering and gray-headed man; and yet a change had to my eyes come over the scene,— the town, and State, and country,—greater than any that mere time could effect. I saw yet more distinctly the State in which I lived. I saw to what extent the people among whom I lived could be trusted as good neighbors and friends; that their friendship was for summer weather only; that they did not greatly purpose to do right; that they were a distinct race from me by their prejudices and superstitions, as the Chinamen and Malays are; that, in their sacrifices to humanity, they ran no risks, not even to their property; that, after all, they were not so noble but they treated the thief as he had treated them, and hoped, by a certain outward observance and a few prayers, and by walking in a particular straight though useless path from time to time, to save their souls. This may be to judge my neighbors harshly; for I believe that most of them are not aware that they have such an institution as the jail in their village.

It was formerly the custom in our village, when a poor debtor came out of jail, for his acquaintances to salute him, looking through their fingers, which were crossed to represent the grating of a jail window, "How do ye do?" My neighbors did not thus salute me, but first looked at me, and then at one another, as

---

4. The seat of government in a county.   5. Probably Thoreau's aunt, Maria Thoreau.

if I had returned from a long journey. I was put into jail as I
was going to the shoemaker's to get a shoe which was mended.
When I was let out the next morning, I proceeded to finish
my errand, and, having put on my mended shoe, joined a huckleberry party, who were impatient to put themselves under my
conduct; and in half an hour,—for the horse was soon tackled,[6]
—was in the midst of a huckleberry field, on one of our highest
hills, two miles off; and then the State was nowhere to be seen.
This is the whole history of "My Prisons." [7]

I have never declined paying the highway tax, because I
am as desirous of being a good neighbor as I am of being a
bad subject; and, as for supporting schools, I am doing my part
to educate my fellow-countrymen now. It is for no particular
item in the tax-bill that I refuse to pay it. I simply wish to
refuse allegiance to the State, to withdraw and stand aloof from
it effectually. I do not care to trace the course of my dollar, if
I could, till it buys a man, or a musket to shoot one with,—the
dollar is innocent,—but I am concerned to trace the effects of
my allegiance. In fact, I quietly declare war with the State, after
my fashion, though I will still make what use and get what advantage of her I can, as is usual in such cases.

If others pay the tax which is demanded of me, from a sympathy with the State, they do but what they have already done
in their own case, or rather they abet injustice to a greater extent
than the State requires. If they pay the tax from a mistaken interest
in the individual taxed, to save his property or prevent his going
to jail, it is because they have not considered wisely how far
they let their private feelings interfere with the public good.

This, then, is my position at present. But one cannot be too
much on his guard in such a case, lest his action be biassed by
obstinacy, or an undue regard for the opinions of men. Let him
see that he does only what belongs to himself and to the hour.

I think sometimes, Why, this people mean well; they are
only ignorant; they would do better if they knew how: why give
your neighbors this pain to treat you as they are not inclined
to? But I think, again, this is no reason why I should do as
they do, or permit others to suffer much greater pain of a different
kind. Again, I sometimes say to myself, When many millions
of men, without heat, without ill-will, without personal feeling
of any kind, demand of you a few shillings only, without the
possibility, such is their constitution, of retracting or altering
their present demand, and without the possibility, on your side,
of appeal to any other millions, why expose yourself to this

6. Harnessed.
7. An ironic reference to *Le Mie Prigioni*, the

memoirs of Italian patriot Silvio Pellico (1789–
1854).

overwhelming brute force? You do not resist cold and hunger, the winds and the waves, thus obstinately; you quietly submit to a thousand similar necessities. You do not put your head into the fire. But just in proportion as I regard this as not wholly a brute force, but partly a human force, and consider that I have relations to those millions as to so many millions of men, and not of mere brute or inanimate things, I see that appeal is possible, first and instantaneously, from them to the Maker of them, and, secondly, from them to themselves. But, if I put my head deliberately into the fire, there is no appeal to fire or to the Maker of fire, and I have only myself to blame. If I could convince myself that I have any right to be satisfied with men as they are, and to treat them accordingly, and not according, in some respects, to my requisitions and expectations of what they and I ought to be, then, like a good Mussulman [8] and fatalist, I should endeavor to be satisfied with things as they are, and say it is the will of God. And, above all, there is this difference between resisting this and a purely brute or natural force, that I can resist this with some effect; but I cannot expect, like Orpheus,[9] to change the nature of the rocks and trees and beasts.

I do not wish to quarrel with any man or nation. I do not wish to split hairs, to make fine distinctions, or set myself up as better than my neighbors. I seek rather, I may say, even an excuse for conforming to the laws of the land. I am but too ready to conform to them. Indeed I have reason to suspect myself on this head; and each year, as the tax-gatherer comes round, I find myself disposed to review the acts and position of the general and state governments, and the spirit of the people, to discover a pretext for conformity. I believe that the State will soon be able to take all my work of this sort out of my hands, and then I shall be no better a patriot than my fellow-countrymen. Seen from a lower point of view, the Constitution, with all its faults, is very good; the law and the courts are very respectable; even this State and this American government are, in many respects, very admirable and rare things, to be thankful for, such as a great many have described them; but seen from a point of view a little higher, they are what I have described them; seen from a higher still, and the highest, who shall say what they are, or that they are worth looking at or thinking of at all?

8. A Moslem, a Mohammedan; generally spelled "Musselman."
9. In Greek mythology Orpheus, son of the Muse Calliope, charmed wild animals and moved stones and trees with his music and singing.

However, the government does not concern me much, and I shall bestow the fewest possible thoughts on it. It is not many moments that I live under a government, even in this world. If a man is thought-free, fancy-free, imagination-free, that which *is not* never for a long time appearing *to be* to him, unwise rulers or reformers cannot fatally interrupt him.

I know that most men think differently from myself; but those whose lives are by profession devoted to the study of these or kindred subjects, content me as little as any. Statesmen and legislators, standing so completely within the institution, never distinctly and nakedly behold it. They speak of moving society, but have no resting-place without it. They may be men of a certain experience and discrimination, and have no doubt invented ingenious and even useful systems, for which we sincerely thank them; but all their wit and usefulness lie within certain not very wide limits. They are wont to forget that the world is not governed by policy and expediency. Webster[1] never goes behind government, and so cannot speak with authority about it. His words are wisdom to those legislators who contemplate no essential reform in the existing government; but for thinkers, and those who legislate for all time, he never once glances at the subject. I know of those whose serene and wise speculations on this theme would soon reveal the limits of his mind's range and hospitality. Yet, compared with the cheap professions of most reformers, and the still cheaper wisdom and eloquence of politicians in general, his are almost the only sensible and valuable words, and we thank Heaven for him. Comparatively, he is always strong, original, and, above all, practical. Still his quality is not wisdom, but prudence. The lawyer's truth is not Truth, but consistency, or a consistent expediency. Truth is always in harmony with herself, and is not concerned chiefly to reveal the justice that may consist with wrong-doing. He well deserves to be called, as he has been called, the Defender of the Constitution. There are really no blows to be given by him but defensive ones. He is not a leader, but a follower. His leaders are the men of '87.[2] "I have never made an effort," he says, "and never propose to make an effort; I have never countenanced an effort, and never mean to countenance an effort, to disturb the arrangement as originally made, by which the various States came into the Union."[3] Still thinking of the sanction which the Constitution gives to slavery, he says, "Because it was a part of the original

---

1. Daniel Webster (1782–1852), senator from Massachusetts and noted orator.
2. Members of the Federal Constitutional Convention, held in Philadelphia in 1787 and presided over by George Washington.
3. From Webster's speech in the Senate, "The Admission of Texas," delivered December 22, 1845.

compact,—let it stand." [4] Notwithstanding his special acuteness and ability, he is unable to take a fact out of its merely political relations, and behold it as it lies absolutely to be disposed of by the intellect,—what, for instance, it behoves a man to do here in America to-day with regard to slavery, but ventures, or is driven, to make some such desperate answer as the following, while professing to speak absolutely, and as a private man,—from which what new and singular code of social duties might be inferred?—"The manner," says he, "in which the governments of those States where slavery exists are to regulate it, is for their own consideration, under their responsibility to their constituents, to the general laws of propriety, humanity, and justice, and to God. Associations formed elsewhere, springing from a feeling of humanity, or any other cause, have nothing whatever to do with it. They have never received any encouragement from me, and they never will." [5]

They who know of no purer sources of truth, who have traced up its stream no higher, stand, and wisely stand, by the Bible and the Constitution, and drink at it there with reverence and humility; but they who behold where it comes trickling into this lake or that pool, gird up their loins once more, and continue their pilgrimage toward its fountain-head.

No man with a genius for legislation has appeared in America. They are rare in the history of the world. There are orators, politicians, and eloquent men, by the thousand; but the speaker has not yet opened his mouth to speak, who is capable of settling the much-vexed questions of the day. We love eloquence for its own sake, and not for any truth which it may utter, or any heroism it may inspire. Our legislators have not yet learned the comparative value of free-trade and of freedom, of union, and of rectitude, to a nation. They have no genius or talent for comparatively humble questions of taxation and finance, commerce and manufactures and agriculture. If we were left solely to the wordy wit of legislators in Congress for our guidance, uncorrected by the seasonable experience and the effectual complaints of the people, America would not long retain her rank among the nations. For eighteen hundred years, though perchance I have no right to say it, the New Testament has been written; yet where is the legislator who has wisdom and practical talent enough

4. No source in Webster's works has been found for this quotation. In *Reform Papers* (Princeton: Princeton UP, 1973), editor Wendell Glick suggests that Thoreau may be quoting from memory a line in Webster's speech, "The Constitution and the Union," delivered in the Senate, March 7, 1850 (p. 325).
5. These extracts have been inserted since the Lecture was read [*Thoreau's note*]. I.e., "The manner . . . will."; quoted from Webster's speech, "Exclusion of Slavery from the Territories," delivered August 12, 1848.

to avail himself of the light which it sheds on the science of legislation?

The authority of government, even such as I am willing to submit to,—for I will cheerfully obey those who know and can do better than I, and in many things even those who neither know nor can do so well,—is still an impure one: to be strictly just, it must have the sanction and consent of the governed. It can have no pure right over my person and property but what I concede to it. The progress from an absolute to a limited monarchy, from a limited monarchy to a democracy, is a progress toward a true respect for the individual. Is a democracy, such as we know it, the last improvement possible in government? Is it not possible to take a step further towards recognizing and organizing the rights of man? There will never be a really free and enlightened State, until the State comes to recognize the individual as a higher and independent power, from which all its own power and authority are derived, and treats him accordingly. I please myself with imagining a State at last which can afford to be just to all men, and to treat the individual with respect as a neighbor; which even would not think it inconsistent with its own repose, if a few were to live aloof from it, not meddling with it, nor embraced by it, who fulfilled all the duties of neighbors and fellow-men. A State which bore this kind of fruit, and suffered it to drop off as fast as it ripened, would prepare the way for a still more perfect and glorious State, which also I have imagined, but not yet anywhere seen.

A TEXTUAL NOTE ON
"RESISTANCE TO CIVIL GOVERNMENT"

Thoreau first delivered a lecture version of his famous essay at the Concord Lyceum on January 26, 1848, and either repeated or gave a second installment of it there about three weeks later. The next spring, 1849, it was solicited by Elizabeth P. Peabody for her *Aesthetic Papers*, where the essay was published in May as "Resistance to Civil Government." After Thoreau died, it appeared again in A *Yankee in Canada, with Anti-Slavery and Reform Papers* (Boston: Ticknor and Fields, 1866), edited by Thoreau's sister, Sophia Thoreau, and his friend Ellery Channing. In addition to minor alterations of wording and sentence structure, the 1866 printing contained a quotation from George Peele's *Battle of Alcazar* at 242.30 (following "conformity."), a sentence about Confucius at 245.11 (following "individual."), and carried the title "Civil Disobedience." Although Thoreau prepared a number of his essays for posthumous publication during the last few months of his life, no evidence exists indicating that "Resistance to Civil Government" was among them. Despite the fact that the 1866 title has acquired the force of tradition, neither the title nor other alterations of the text for the 1866 printing have any authority.

The present edition, therefore, reprints the 1849 text with four corrections. In the first edition, "he" was misprinted as "be" at 234.3; and Thoreau apparently mistranscribed lines from Wolfe at 228.9 and 228.10 (writing "nor" for "not" and "ramparts" for "rampart") and from Webster at 242.9 ("government" for "governments").

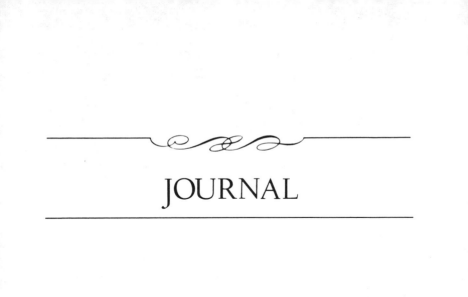

JOURNAL

THE JOURNAL AND WALDEN

Thoreau began keeping a journal in 1837 at the age of twenty, soon after he graduated from Harvard College, and he continued the practice until August 1861, nine months before his death. A massive work to which in the last eleven years of his life he typically devoted numerous hours a week, the Journal is at the same time an illuminating source of information about his imaginative life and published writings and a remarkable literary creation in its own right. The passages that comprise the present collection have been selected from what survives of the twenty one journal volumes (or over forty-six hundred manuscript pages) Thoreau filled between July 1845, when he moved to Walden Pond, and May 1854, when he sent the last of his *Walden* manuscript to the printer. Although highly selective, this collection may serve to illustrate the central role played by the Journal in Thoreau's creation and recreation of his Walden experience and to suggest the complex, interdependent relation that developed between the two works-in-progress.

During the nine years in which *Walden* developed from journal reflections into lectures and then through a series of drafts, the Journal was undergoing a metamorphosis of its own.[1] Successively, and at times simultaneously, in these years the Journal assumed the forms of a source book for future writings; a draft book for *Walden* and other writing in progress; a record of daily walks and reflections, incorporating Thoreau's increasingly detailed exploration into natural and local history; and, finally, a distinct work with an aesthetic integrity and unconventional life of its own, now broadly conceived as "the record of . . . my affection for any aspect of the world" (289). In the early 1850s Thoreau recognized that as a work perpetually in process the Journal could be more faithful to the "life" he sought to represent than could any conventional literary structure assembled from Journal fragments.[2] In this sense, the Journal project became quite distinct from *Walden*. Yet, the difference between these two works can be overemphasized. To a significant degree, *Walden* turned out as it did because in these years the Journal

1. Seven partial manuscript versions of *Walden* were first distinguished by J. Lyndon Shanley and analyzed in *The Making of* Walden (Chicago: U of Chicago, 1957), which also prints Shanley's reconstruction of the first version of *Walden*. For two recent studies of the composition of *Walden*, see Stephen Adams and Donald A. Ross, *Revising Mythologies: The Composition of Thoreau's Major Works* (Charlottesville: UP of Virginia, 1988), 51–63; 165–91; and Robert Sattelmeyer, "The Remaking of Walden," in James Barbour and Tom Quirk, eds., *Writing the American Classics* (Chapel Hill: U of North Carolina P, 1990), 53–78,

reprinted on pp. 428–44 of this volume.
2. See Sharon Cameron, *Writing Nature: Henry Thoreau's Journal* (New York: Oxford UP, 1985) for a persuasive reading of the Journal "against" *Walden*. While acknowledging the different formal qualities and constraints in *Walden* and the Journal, H. Daniel Peck sees them (together with A *Week*) as "emergences one from another, and all of them" part of a larger project he calls Thoreau's "morning work" (x). See *Thoreau's Morning Work: Memory and Perception in* A Week on the Concord and Merrimack Rivers, the Journal, and Walden (New Haven: Yale UP, 1990).

provided a means of perpetuating, even as it transformed, the *Walden* enterprise and the Walden experiment.

Two circumstances have combined to obscure the Journal's intimate relation to *Walden*: the unavailability until recently of much of the Walden-period Journal, and a prevalent misconception about the kind of work the Journal is. The misconception involves a deep-seated belief that, owing to the supposed spontaneous composition and private character of diaries and journals, this form of writing is "a mode of spontaneous utterance wholly unshaped by convention," and therefore more like a natural production than an artistic or "literary" one.[3] According to this belief, journal writing may therefore provide the stuff of which literature is made, or a useful "background" for understanding literature, but, apparently lacking the formal design of works intended for publication, this writing must be disqualified as literature itself. As a corollary of their supposed mode of production, journals and diaries may be thought as well to mirror raw experience (or "fact," or "nature") more closely. Inevitably, perhaps, this notion of the artless journal mirroring nature has especially colored understanding of a writer famous for wanting to "front" the "facts" of nature, and whose "rare descriptive powers" have long been celebrated.[4] Knowing that Thoreau kept a journal and that *Walden* is in part based on his experiences at the pond, readers have thus often assumed that in writing his book Thoreau simply drew upon the journal record of his thoughts and activities there, filling out the "account" with recollections after his return.[5]

But rather than an artless private record, free from convention, Thoreau's journal was initially, and in important ways remained, the product of a highly refined theory of journal writing shared by other members of the Transcendentalist circle in Concord, one that effectively defined the parameters of both its form and content. Moreover, because members of the circle often exchanged their journals, the writing of them was to a certain extent a public matter, certainly a social one. In Transcendentalist theory, post-Puritan self-examination and romantic self-expression combine in a conception of the primary function of journal composition as a means of giving form to those moments of insight that define the journalist's imaginative and spiritual life. The writer's journal thus bears witness to an on-going process of "self-culture," or the discovery and expression of transpersonal truth in his or her deeper "nature," a process epitomized in the creation of

3. Lawrence Rosenwald, *Emerson and the Art of the Diary* (New York: Oxford UP 1988), 21.
4. John Burroughs, *Indoor Studies* (Boston: Houghton Mifflin, 1902), 37. An example of the conclusions to which this notion has led critics is Perry Miller's influential dismissal of the mature Journal as a mere dry compilation of "facts without metaphors." Miller's reading has seemed to serve as presumptive evidence for the argument (already present in Emerson's eulogy) that Thoreau suffered a creative decline after *Walden*, and thus had "a career . . . as tragic as that of King Lear." "Thoreau in the Context of International Romanticism," *The New England Quarterly* 34 (1961): 158.
5. Shanley, for instance, in arguing for the importance of studying the *Walden* manuscript for an understanding of Thoreau's aesthetic achievement, contrasts it with the Journal as follows: "Although the journals made it clear that Thoreau added to *Walden* between 1847 and 1854, and especially after 1850, only the manuscript could reveal to how great an extent *Walden* is the result of a gradual re-creation of his experience rather than simply a recounting of that experience as he had entered it in his journal when it happened" (5).

poetry.[6] As Emerson puts it in "The Poet," "The man is only half himself, the other half is his expression."[7]

Thoreau's early journal has been aptly described as a "display case" of such self-consciously crafted thoughts and "moments."[8] But by the time he moved to Walden Pond he had learned to "winnow" for his literary compositions the kernels of insight recorded in his journal—to rely on them, that is, as "sources" in a double sense—as well as to draft new material there for immediate use.[9] Since a primary motive for moving to the Pond was to complete a draft of his first book, *A Week on the Concord and Merrimack Rivers* (and thereby to build a literary reputation as well as a hut by the shore of Walden), Thoreau took with him two journal volumes to use as literary workbooks in this way. Initially, he seems to have intended to use a third volume, from which the first nine entries in the present collection are taken (255–63), as a regular dated record of his thoughts. Thoreau may well have gone to Walden with a new literary project in mind, or he may have discovered the literary potential inherent in his new pastoral standpoint after settling in. In any case, rather quickly the distinction between regular journal and draft book, between self-culture and explicitly "literary" composition, began to fade (at least as a matter of journal record) and with it the distance between Thoreau's experience and its literary representation. The Journal shows Thoreau to have begun his new work much earlier than he himself suggests in *Walden*. The "very particular inquiries . . . made by my townsmen concerning my mode of life," which he claims prompted his "simple and sincere account" in response, in actuality only provided him "a convenient rhetorical pretext for explaining the purpose of a lecture [on his life at the Pond which] he had already begun to write" in the fall of 1845.[1]

With respect to work on what was becoming *Walden*, then, the original function of the Journal as a means of cultivating inspiration and insight is transformed with Thoreau's discovery of his "present condition" as subject. And in this way the field of the Journal is also extended to the representation of his engagement with the local and natural history of Concord environs (features that will dominate the mature Journal), in, for instance, his reconstruction of former inhabitants' lives and study of the thawing sandbank (264–66, 279–81). But while the original function is transformed, it is not abandoned. The original disposition may still be seen in the close resemblance between the journal versions of several passages that end up in *Walden*

6. On Transcendentalist journal-keeping, see *Journal 1: 1837–1844*, ed. Elizabeth Hall Witherell, William L. Howarth, Robert Sattelmeyer, and Thomas Blanding (Princeton UP, 1981), 592–95; Lawrence Buell, *Literary Transcendentalism: Style and Vision in the American Renaissance* (Ithaca: Cornell UP, 1973), 265–83; and Rosenwald, *Emerson and the Art of the Diary*, 83–98. An excellent study of Emerson's development of the doctrine of self-culture is David M. Robinson's *Apostle of Culture: Emerson as Preacher and Lecturer* (Philadelphia: U of Pennsylvania P, 1982). For a more detailed discussion of the Journal and self-culture, see William Rossi, "The Journal, Self-Culture, and the Genesis of 'Walking,'" *Thoreau Quarterly* 16 (1984) : 138–55.

7. Ralph Waldo Emerson, *Essays: Second Series*, ed. Alfred R. Ferguson and Jean Ferguson Carr (Cambridge: Harvard UP, 1983), 4.

8. *Journal 1*, 592.

9. See *Journal 2: 1842–1848*, ed. Robert Sattelmeyer (Princeton: Princeton UP, 1986), 452–54, and p. 264 in the Journal selections in this volume.

1. *Journal 2: 1842–1848*, 454–55; 457.

and their final published form, as if Thoreau wished to preserve the bloom of that particular kind of experience the Journal was designed to help cultivate.[2] Yet, if Thoreau took care to preserve these individual kernels in his developing book manuscript (there to expand them further), he apparently did not so treasure the Journal *as* journal at this time. In preparing for publication various writings begun or continued at the Pond, he did not hesitate to remove pages from his journal as he needed them for draft.[3] Apparently, at this point Thoreau thought of his journal primarily as a collection of discrete fragments to be assembled into larger wholes in the process of winnowing them "into Lectures" and then "in due time from Lectures into Essays" (264).

But the commercial failure of A *Week on the Concord and Merrimack Rivers*, evident within a few months of its publication in May 1849, and the debt Thoreau incurred as a result, rendered the *Walden* manuscript he had been working to complete unpublishable for the time being and a conventional literary career doubtful at best. In order to make a living and still to carry out his determination to make "letters my profession," Thoreau fashioned a daily routine of reading, writing, or making pencils for the family business in the morning, while walking and occasionally surveying in the afternoon.[4] Adopting the methods of the serious naturalist he was in fact becoming, Thoreau made field notes on his daily walks, and then anywhere from a few hours to several days later he composed the scrupulously dated accounts of his rambles that characterize the mature Journal. This method appears thus to have satisfied both the working naturalist's requirements for a reliable record of detailed observations and the writer's desire for aesthetic integrity and literary vitality.[5] As a result, the Journal grew and prospered. "As you *see* so at length will you *say*" (292), Thoreau told himself in November 1851. And this conviction eventually made *Walden*, as it had already begun to make the Journal, the natural beneficiary of that reciprocal deepening of perception and expression.

Considering the observation, thought, and time Thoreau committed to

2. Readers who desire to locate for comparison the final (i.e., the *Walden*) version of Journal passages reprinted in the Norton Critical Edition may do so by consulting the tables of Cross-References to Published Versions in the Princeton Journal volumes beginning with *Journal 2*.

3. See the Historical Introduction and 467–75 in the Textual Introduction of *Journal 2*. In addition to much of A *Week*, two lectures on his Walden life, and a first draft of *Walden*, these various writings included a long essay on "Thomas Carlyle and His Works," published in 1847 in *Graham's American Monthly Magazine*, the excursion "Ktaadn, and the Maine Woods," published the following year in the *Union Magazine of Literature and Art*, and a lecture on each of these two topics.

4. *The Correspondence of Henry David Thoreau*, ed. Walter Harding and Carl Bode (New York: New York UP, 1958), 249; and see Robert D. Richardson, Jr., *Henry Thoreau: A Life of The Mind* (Berkeley: U of California P,

1986), 194–97. Thoreau describes his daily routine in a letter dated November 20, 1849 (*Correspondence*, 250–51).

5. See William L. Howarth, *The Book of Concord: Thoreau's Life as a Writer* (New York: Viking, 1982), 59–64. Both the notes and the interval Thoreau deliberately allowed to intervene between the walks and their literary representation were important. "I succeed best," he wrote in May 1852, "when I *recur* to my experience not too late, but within a day or two; when there is some distance, but enough of freshness." *The Journal of Henry D. Thoreau* (1906; New York: Dover, 1962) 4.20.

For analyses of Thoreau's literary art in the mature Journal, see Howarth, *The Book of Concord*; Sharon Cameron, *Writing Nature*; Joan Burbick, *Thoreau's Alternative History: Changing Perspectives on Nature, Culture, and Language* (Philadelphia: U of Pennsylvania P, 1987); and H. Daniel Peck, *Thoreau's Morning Work*.

the Journal's keeping in the early 1850s, then, it is not surprising that he began to preserve his volumes intact, making careful indexes and numbering the volumes sequentially. Rather than removing pages for literary draft, as he had done during and for some time after his stay at Walden, he now recopied passages deemed appropriate (and in several cases apparently drafted intentionally) for *Walden* and transferred them to a separate draft-in-progress. The private success of the Journal led in January 1852 to Thoreau's recognition that, rather than supplying "parts" from which "wholes" might "at last" be made, the Journal itself supplied the "proper frame" for his "disconnected thoughts" (295). While he continued to transcribe Journal passages for *Walden* and other writings intended for publication, he saw that he could never transcribe all that those passages suggested within their Journal habitat, for there they were "allied to life." "Perhaps I can never find so good a setting for my thoughts as I shall thus have taken them out of" (297). From this time on Thoreau consciously developed this Journal "setting" as an original perspective from which to view present society, history, and, especially, nature, a perspective not subject to the constraints upon vision and representation imposed by conventional literary form and by Thoreau's methods of constructing that form.[6]

But the Journal clearly continued to play a no less crucial role in furthering the *Walden* project. Indeed, that Thoreau's discovery of the Journal's unique form in January 1852 should be accompanied by renewed and intensive work on his book suggests that the independent Journal perspective helped in some way to stimulate the substantial revision and even reconception of *Walden* that followed in the next two years. At the same time, the profuse emergence of *Walden* draft in the Journal about this time also hints at a deeper, long-standing intimacy between the Walden experiment and the Journal, as does the surfacing now of the fundamental question "Why I left the woods?" (294). More than merely unable, Thoreau seems unwilling to answer this question. "Perhaps," he says, "it is none of my business—even if it is your's" (294). And no wonder. For this is the same question, or tension, that the Journal[7] had kept in play, sustaining it as a kind of "vital heat," since late 1849 or early 1850. When, in the wake of the commercial failure of *A Week*, the Journal became an integral part of the new routine Thoreau then established, it became the means of perpetuating—now as a potentially revitalizing daily event—precisely the dialectic of pastoral withdrawl and return that was the Walden experiment. The complex dual perspective figured in *Walden* as that of "civilized" sojourner and perpetual Walden dweller is thus inseparable from the maintenance of that vital and necessary duality in the Journal. If, as form and project, the Journal assumed a kind of independent existence, then, it did so by virtue of the germinal memory of the Walden experiment and pastoral perspective that Thoreau carried on by means of the Journal and that the Journal, as it were, carried within itself.

Finally, as an accumulating phenological record of seasonal patterns and

6. Cameron's book presents a detailed analysis of the Journal form and language as a non-anthropocentric alternative to writing nature. See *Writing Nature*, especially 108–54.

7. Or, more precisely, the whole Journal project—the walking, natural and historical study, field notes, and journal entries—which each act of journal composition provisionally completed and furthered.

rhythms, the Journal project fostered in Thoreau an increasingly concrete perception of the seasonal cycle of which he strove to see his own particular life as part and parcel.[8] To the working out of precise correspondences between the larger rhythms of his chosen place and those in his own life and consciousness the Journal is increasingly devoted in the years after *Walden*. It seems appropriate, therefore, that when the time finally arrived for the book to be published, that "fact" should be registered in the Journal among other late summer phenomena: "Walden published. Elder berries. Waxwork yellowing" (307).

Entry dates for the following excerpted Journal passages are given in footnotes. Dates enclosed in brackets represent the Princeton Journal editors' conjectures based on proximity to dated material and other relevant information; unbracketed dates are Thoreau's. Passages dated before August 1851 have been reprinted with permission from *Journal 2: 1842–1848* and *Journal 3: 1848–1851* in the Princeton University Press edition of the Writings of Henry D. Thoreau; those dated after July 1851 have been edited for the Norton Critical Edition from photocopies and transcripts of the manuscript Journal maintained at the Thoreau Edition and used with the permission of Elizabeth Hall Witherell, Editor-in-Chief. Individual words or letters enclosed in brackets indicate illegible words or letters, or doubtful readings in the manuscript. Thoreau's errors of spelling, grammar, and punctuation have been allowed to stand without comment unless serious ambiguity might result from doing so.

8. See Peck, *Thoreau's Morning Work*, 42–49, 112–14.

Selections from the Journal, 1845-54

Walden Sat. July 5th—45

Yesterday I came here to live. My house makes me think of some mountain houses I have seen, which seemed to have a fresher auroral atmosphere about them as I fancy of the halls of Olympus.[1] I lodged at the house of a saw-miller last summer, on the Caatskills mountains, high up as Pine orchard in the blue-berry & raspberry region, where the quiet and cleanliness & coolness seemed to be all one, which had this ambrosial character. He was the miller of the Kaaterskill Falls, They were a clean & wholesome family inside and out—like their house. The latter was not plastered—only lathed and the inner doors were not hung. The house seemed high placed, airy, and perfumed, fit to entertain a travelling God. It was so high indeed that all the music, the broken strains, the waifs & accompaniments of tunes, that swept over the ridge of the Caatskills, passed through its aisles. Could not man be man in such an abode? And would he ever find out this grovelling life?

It was the very light & atmosphere in which the works of Grecian art were composed, and in which they rest. They have appropriated to themselves a loftier hall than mortals ever occupy, at least on a level with the mountain brows of the world.

There was wanting a little of the glare of the lower vales and in its place a pure twilight as became the precincts of heaven   Yet so equable and calm was the season there that you could not tell whether it was morning or noon or evening. Always there was the sound of the morning cricket

July 6th

I wish to meet the facts of life—the vital facts, which where [sic] the phenomena or actuality the Gods meant to show us,—face to face, And so I came down here. Life! who knows what it is—what it does? If I am not quite right here I am less wrong than before—and now let us see what they will have. The preacher, instead of vexing the ears of drowsy farmers on their day of rest, at the end of the week, (for sunday always seemed to me like a fit conclusion of an ill spent week and not the fresh and brave beginning of a new one) with this one other draggletail and postponed affair of a sermon, from thirdly to 15thly, should teach them with a thundering voice—pause & simplicity.

1. Mount Olympus; in Greek mythology the residence of the gods.

stop— Avast— Why so fast? In all studies we go not forward but rather backward with redoubled pauses, we always study *antiques*—with silence and *reflection*. Even time has a depth, and below its surface the waves do not lapse and roar. I wonder men can be so frivolous almost as to attend to the gross form of negro slavery—there are so many keen and subtle masters, who subject us both. Self-emancipation in the West Indies of a man's thinking and imagining provinces, which should be more than his island territory   One emancipated heart & intellect— It would knock off the fetters from a million slaves.

July 7th

I am glad to remember tonight as I sit by my door that I too am at least a remote descendent of that heroic race of men of whom there is tradition. I too sit here on the shore of my Ithaca a fellow wanderer and survivor of Ulysses.[2] How Symbolical, significant of I know not what the pitch pine stands here before my door unlike any glyph I have seen sculptured or painted yet—   One of nature's later designs. Yet perfect as her Grecian art. There it is, a done tree. Who can mend it? And now where is the generation of heroes whose lives are to pass amid these our northern pines? Whose exploits shall appear to posterity pictured amid these strong and shaggy forms?

Shall there be only arrows and bows to go with these pines on some pipe stone quarry at length.

If we can forget we have done somewhat, if we can remember we have done somewhat. Let us remember this

The Great spirit of course makes indifferent all times & places. The place where he is seen is always the same, and indescribably pleasant to all our senses. We had allowed only near-lying and transient circumstances to make our occasions—   But nearest to all things is that which fashions its being. Next to us the grandest laws are being enacted and administered.

Bread may not always nourish us, but it always does us good   it even takes stiffness out of our joints and makes us supple and boyant when we knew not what ailed us—to share any heroic joy—to recognise any largeness in man or nature, to see and to know—   This is all cure and prevention.

Verily a good house is a temple—   A clean house—pure and undefiled, as the saying is. I have seen such made of white pine. Seasoned and seasoning still to eternity. Where a Goddess might trail her garment. The less dust we bring in to nature, the less we shall have to pick up. It was a place where one would go in, expecting to find something agreeable; as to a shade—or to a shelter—a more natural place.

2. The *Odyssey* tells of the wanderings of Odysseus (Ulysses), returning home to the island of Ithaca after the Trojan War.

I hear the far off lowing of a cow and it seems to heave the firmament. I at first thought it was the voice of a minstrel whom I know, who might be straying over hill and dale this eve—but soon I was not disappointed when it was prolonged into the sweet and natural and withal cheap tone of the cow. This youths brave music is indeed of kin with the music of the cow. They are but one articulation of nature.

Sound was made not so much for convenience, that we might hear when called, as to regale the sense—and fill one of the avenues of life. A healthy organization will never need what are commonly called the sensual gratifications, but will enjoy the daintiest feasts at those tables where there is nothing to tempt the appetite of the sensual.

There are strange affinities in this universe—strange ties stranger harmonies and relationships, what kin am I to some wildest pond among the mountains—high up ones shaggy side—in the gray morning twilight draped with mist—suspended in low wreathes from the dead willows and bare firs that stand here and there in the water, as if here were the evidence of those old contests between the land and water which we read of. But why should I find anything to welcome me in such a nook as this— This faint reflection this dim watery eye—where in some angle of the hills the woods meet the waters edge and a grey tarn lies sleeping

My beans—whose continuous length of row is 7 miles, already planted and now so impatient of be howed—not easily to be put off. What is the meaning of this service this small Hercules labor—of this small warfare—I know not. I come to love my rows—they attatch me to the earth—and so I get new strength and health like Antaeus

—My beans, so many more than I want. This has been my curious labor— Why only heaven knows—to make this surface of the earth, which yielded only blackberries & Johnswort—& cinqfoil—sweet wild fruits & pleasant flowers produce instead this pulse   What shall I learn of beans or beans of me— I cherish them— I hoe them early & late I have an eye to them.— And this is my days work. It is a fine broad leaf to look upon.

My auxiliaries are the dews and rains—to water this dry soil—and genial fatness in the soil itself, which for the most part is lean and effoete. My enemies are worms cool days—and most of all woodchucks. They have nibbled for me an eigth of an acre clean. I plant in faith—and they reap— this is the tax I pay—for ousting jonswort & the rest   But soon the surviving beans will be too tough for woodchucks and then—they will go forward to meet new foes.

July 14th 1845
What sweet and tender, the most innocent and divinely encouraging society there is in every natural object, and so in universal nature even for the poor misanthrope and most melancholy man. There can be no really

black melan-choly to him who lives in the midst of nature, and has still his senses. There never was yet such a storm but it was Aeolian music[3] to the innocent ear. Nothing can compel to a vulgar sadness a simple & brave man. While I enjoy the sweet friendship of the seasons I trust that nothing can make life a burden to me. This rain which is now watering my beans, and keeping me in the house waters me too. I needed it as much. And what if most are not hoed—those who send the rain whom I chiefly respect will pardon me.

Sometimes when I compare myself with other men methinks I am favored by the Gods. They seem to whisper joy to me beyond my deserts and that I do have a solid warrant and surety at their hands, which my fellows do not. I do not flatter myself but if it were possible *they* flatter me. I am especially guided and guarded.

And now I think of it—let me remember—

What was seen true once—and sanctioned by the flash of Jove—will always be true, and nothing can hinder it. I have the warrant that no fair dream I have had need fail of its fulfilment.

Here I know I am in good company—here is the world its centre and metropolis, and all the palms of Asia—and the laurels of Greece—and the firs of the Arctic Zones incline thither.

Here I can read Homer if I would have books, as well as in Ionia, and not wish myself in Boston or New-york or London or Rome or Greece— In such place as this he wrote or sang. Who should come to my lodge Just now—but a true Homeric boor—one of those Paphlagonian men?[4] Alek Therien—he called himself— A Canadian now, a woodchopper—a post maker—makes fifty posts—holes them i.e. in a day, and who made his last supper on a woodchuck which his dog caught— And he too has heard of Homer and *if it were not for books would not know what to do*—rainy days. Some priest once who could read glibly from the Greek itself—taught him reading in a measure his verse at least in his turn—at Nicolet away by the Trois Riviers once.

* * *

Therien said this morning (July 16th Wednesday) If those beans were mine I should'nt like to hoe them till the dew was off—" He was going to his wood chopping. Ah said I that is one of the notions the farmers have got—but I don't believe it.

"How thick the pigeons are" said he, "if working every day were not my trade I could get all the meat I should want by hunting. Pigeons wood-chucks—Rabbits—Partridges—by George I could get all I should want for a week in one day."

---

3. Music produced by a stringed instrument when placed in a window casement or otherwise exposed to a current of air; in Greek myth-ology Aeolus was the god of the winds.
4. Inhabitants of a wooded region in Asia Minor, known for their heaviness and dullness.

I imagine it to be some advantage to live a primitive and frontier life—though in the midst of an outward civilization. Of course all the improvements of the ages do not carry a man backward nor forward in relation to the great facts of his existence.

Our furniture should be as simple as the Arab's or the Indians'— At first the thoughtful wondering man plucked in haste the fruits which the boughs extended to him—and found in the sticks and stones around him his implements ready. And he still remembered that he was a sojourner in nature. When he was refreshed with food and sleep he contemplated his journey again. He dwelt in a tent in this world. He was either threading the vallies or crossing the plains or climbing the mountain tops

Now the best works of art serve comparatively but to dissipate the mind—for they are themselves transitionary and paroxismal and not free and absolute thoughts.

Men have become the tools of their tools—the man who independently plucked the fruits when he was hungry—is become a *farmer*

There are scores of pitch pine in my field—from one to three inches in diameter, girdled by the mice last winter— A Norwegian winter it was for them—for the snow lay long and deep—and they had to mix much pine meal with their usual diet— Yet these trees have not many of them died even in midsummer—and laid bare for a foot—but have grown a foot. They seem to do all their gnawing beneath the snow. There is not much danger of the mouse tribe becoming extinct in hard winters for their granary is a cheap and extensive one.

Here is one has had her nest under my house, and came when I took my luncheon to pick the crumbs at my feet. It had never seen the race of man before, and so the sooner became familiar— It ran over my shoes and up my pantaloons inside clinging to my flesh with its sharp claws. It would run up the side of the room by short impulses like a squirrel—which resembles—coming between the house mouse and the former— Its belly is a little reddish and its ears a little longer. At length as I leaned my elbow on the bench it ran over my arm and round the paper which contained my dinner. And when I held it a piece of cheese it came and nibled between my fingers and then cleaned its face and paws like a fly.

There[5] is a memorable intervale between the written and the spoken language—the language read and the language heard. The one is transient—a sound—a tongue—a dialect—and all men learn it of their mothers—

It is loquacious, fragmentary—raw material— The other is a reserved select matured expression—a deliberate word addressed to the ear of nations & generations. The one is natural & convenient—the other divine & instructive— The clouds flit here below—genial refreshing with their show-

5. [After July 16, 1845.]

ers—and gratifying with their tints—alternate sun & shade— A grosser heaven adapted to our trivial wants—but above them—repose the blue firmament and the stars. The stars are written words & sterotyped on the blue parchment of the skies—the fickle clouds that hide them from our view—which we on this side need though heaven does not These are our daily colloquies our vaporous garrulous breath.

Books must be read as deliberately and reservedly as they were written. The herd of men the generations who speak the Greek and Latin, are not entitled by the accident of birth to read the works of Genius whose mother tongue speaks every where, and is learned by every child who hears.

*   *   *

Walden Aug 6—45

I have just been reading a book called "The Crescent & the Cross"[6] till now I am somewhat ashamed of myself. Am I sick, or idle—that I can sacrifice my energy—America—and to-day—to this mans ill remembered and indolent story— Carnac and Luxor[7] are but names, and still more desert sand and at length a wave of the great ocean itself are needed to wash away the filth that attaches to their grandeur. Carnac—Carnac—this is carnac for me and I behold the columns of a larger and a purer temple.

May our childish and fickle aspirations be divine, while we descend to this mean intercourse. Our reading should be heroic—in an unknown tongue—a dialect always but imperfectly learned—through which we stammer line by line, catching but a glimmering of the sense—and still afterward admiring its unexhausted hieroglyphics—its untranslated columns.

Here grow around me nameless trees and shrubs each morning freshly sculptured—rising new stories day by day—instead of hideous ruins— Their myriad-handed worker—uncompelled as uncompelling.

This is my carnac—that its unmeasured dome—the measuring art man has invented flourishes and dies upon this temples floor nor ever dreams to reach that ceilings height. Carnac & Luxor crumble underneath—their shadowy roofs let in the light once more reflected from the ceiling of the sky

Behold these flowers—let us be up with Time not dreaming of 3000 years ago. Erect ourselves and let those columns lie—not stoop to raise a foil against the sky— Where is the *spirit* of that time but in this present day— this present line 3000 years ago are not agone—they are still lingering here aye every one,

---

6. Eliot Warburton, *The Crescent and the Cross; or, Romance and Realities of Eastern Travel* (1845).
7. Sites of ruins of the ancient city of Thebes on the Nile River in Upper Egypt. The ruined temple of Amon-Re at Karnak contains massive columns decorated with hieroglyphics.

And Memnon's mother[8] sprightly greets us now
Wears still her youthful blushes on her brow
And Carnac's columns why stand they on the plain?
T'enjoy our Opportunities they would fain remain

This is my Carnac whose unmeasured dome
Shelters the measuring art & measurer's home
Whose propylaeum is the system nigh
And sculptured facade the visible sky

Where there is memory which compelleth time the muse's mother and the muses nine—there are all ages—past and future time unwearied memory that does not forget the actions of the past—that does not forego—to stamp them freshly—   That old mortality industrious to retouch the monuments of time, in the world's cemetery through out every clime

The student may read Homer or Aeschylus in the original Greek—for to do so implies to emulate their heroes—the consecration of morning hours to their page—

The heroic books though printed in the character of our mother tongue—are always written in a foreign language dead to idle & degenerate times, and we must laboriously seek the meaning of each word and line, conjecturing a larger sense than the text renders us at last out of our own valor and generosity.

A man must find his own occasions in himself. The natural day is very calm, and will hardly reproove our indolence. If there is no elevation in our spirits—the pond will not seem elevated like a mountain tarn, but a low pool a silent muddy water—a place for fishermen.

I sit here at my window like a priest of Isis[9]—and observe the phenomena of 3000 years ago, yet unimpaired. The tantivy of wild pigeons, an ancient race of birds—gives a voice to the air—flying by twos and threes athwart my view or perching restless on the white pine boughs occasionally—a fish-hawk dimples the glassy surface of the pond and brings up a fish   And for the last half hour I have heard the rattle of rail-road cars conveying travellers from Boston to the country.

*   *   *

All[1] nature is classic and akin to art—   The sumack and pine and hickory which surround my house remind me of the most graceful sculpture. Some times the trees do not make merely a vague impression—but their tops or a single limb or leaf seems to have grown to a distinct expression and invites my life to a like distinctness and emphasis.

---

8. I.e., Eos, goddess of the dawn in Greek mythology; in Roman mythology called Aurora. Memnon was a Theban king whose statue was supposed to emit musical sounds at dawn.

9. An Egyptian goddess capable of transforming herself into any kind of creature; Isis was worshipped until the sixth century A.D.

1. [After August 6, 1845.]

Poetry Painting Sculpture claim at once and associate with themselves those perfect pieces of art—leaves—vines acorns—

The critic must at last stand as mute though contented before a true poem—as before an acorn or a vine leaf. The perfect work of art is received again into the bosom of nature whence its material proceeded—and that criticism which can only detect its unnaturalness has no longer any office to fulfill.

The choicest maxims that have come down to us are more beautiful or integrally wise—than they are wise to our understandings— This wisdom which we are inclined to pluck from their stalk is the fruit only of a single association. Every natural form—palm leaves and acorns—oak-leaves and sumack and dodder—are untranslateable aphorisms

* * *

Twenty three years since when I was 5 years old, I was brought from Boston to this pond, away in the country which was then but another name for the extended world for me—one of the most ancient scenes stamped on the tablets of my memory—the oriental asiatic valley of my world—whence so many races and inventions have gone forth in recent times. That woodland vision for a long time made the drapery of my dreams. That sweet solitude my spirit seemed so early to require that I might have room to entertain my thronging guests, and that speaking silence that my ears might distinguish the significant sounds. Some how or other it at once gave the preference to this recess among the pines where almost sunshine & shadow were the only inhabitants that varied the scene, over that tumultuous and varied city—as if it had found its proper nursery.

Well now to-night my flute awakes the echoes over this very water, but one generation of pines has fallen and with their stumps I have cooked my supper, And a lusty growth of oaks and pines is rising all around its brim and preparing its wilder aspect for new infant eyes.

Almost the same johnswort springs from the same perennial root in this pasture.—

Even I have at length helped to clothe that fabulous landscape of my imagination— —and one result of my presence and influence is seen in the bean leaves and corn blades and potatoe vines.

Seek to preserve the tenderness of your nature as you would the bloom upon a peach.

Most men are so taken up with the cares and rude practice of life—that its finer fruits can not be plucked by them. Literally the laboring man has not leisure for a strict and lofty integrity day by day he cannot afford to sustain the fairest and nobelest relations. His labor will depreciate in the market.

How can he remember well his ignorance who has so often to use his knowledge

August 15th

The sounds heard at this hour 8 ½ are the distant rumbling of wagons over bridges—a sound farthest heard of any human at night—the baying of dogs—the lowing of cattle in distant yards

What if we were to obey these fine dictates these divine suggestions which are addressed to the mind & not to the body—which are certainly true—not to eat meat—not to buy or sell or barter &c &c &c?

I will not plant beans another summer but sincerity—truth—simplicity—faith—trust—innocence—and see if they will not grow in this soil with such manure as I have, and sustain me. When a man meets a man—it should not be some uncertain appearance and falsehood—but the personification of great qualities. Here comes truth perchance personified along the road—Let me see how Truth behaves— I have not seen enough of her— He shall utter no foreign word—no doubtful sentence—and I shall not make haste to part with him.

I would not forget that I deal with infinite and divine qualities in my fellow. All men indeed are divine in their core of light but that is indistinct and distant to me, like the stars of the least magnitude—or the galaxy itself—but my kindred planets show their round disks and even their attendant moons to my eye.

Even the tired laborers I meet on the road, I really meet as travelling Gods, but it is as yet and must be for a long season, without speech.

* * *

I[2] find an instinct in me conducting to a mystic spiritual life—and also another—to a primitive savage life—

Toward evening—as the world waxes darker I am permitted to see the woodchuck stealing across my path, and tempted to seize and devour it. The wildest most desolate scenes are strangely familiar to me

Why not live a hard and emphatic life? not to be avoided—full of adventures and work! Learn much—in it. travel much though it be only in these woods I some-times walk across a field with unexpected expansion and long-missed content—as if there were a field worthy of me. The usual daily boundaries of life are dispersed and I see in what field I stand.

* * *

Exaggeration[3]—was ever any virtue attributed to a man without exaggeration—was ever any vice—without infinite exagggeration? Do we not exaggerate ourselves to ourselves—or Do we often recognise ourselves for the actual men we are— The lightning is an exaggeration of light. We live by exaggeration Exaggerated history is poetry—and is truth referred to a new standard. To a small man every greater one is an exaggeration. No

2. August 23, 1845. 3. [Summer 1845.]

truth was ever expressed but with this sort of emphasis—so that for the time there was no other truth. The value of what is really valuable can never be exaggerated. You must speak loud to those who are hard of hearing—so you acquire a habit of speaking loud to those who are not. In order to appreciate any even the humblest man—you must not only understand but you must first love him— And there never was such an exaggerator as love— Who are we are we not all of us great men And yet what actually— Nothing certainly to speak of— By an immense exaggeration we appreciate our Greek—Poetry—& Philosophy—Egyptian Ruins—our shakspears & Miltons our liberty & christianity. We give importance to this hour over all other hours— We do not live by justice—but[4]

* * *

From all points of the compass from the earth beneath and the heavens above have come these inspirations and been entered duly in such order as they came in the Journal. Thereafter when the time arrived they were winnowed into Lectures—and again in due time from Lectures into Essays— And at last they stand like the cubes of Pythagoras firmly on either basis— like statues on their pedestals—but the statues rarely take hold of hands— There is only such connexion and series as is attainable in the galleries. And this affects their immediate practical & popular influence.

* * *

I[5] went over to neighbor Hugh Quoil's the waterloo soldier—the Colonels house the other day. He lay lately dead at the foot of the hill—the house locked up—and wife at work in town but before key reaches padlock or news wife—another door is unlocked for him and news is carried farther than to wife in town—

In his old house—an "unlucky castle now" pervious to wind & snow— lay his old clothes his outmost cuticle curled up by habit as it were like himself upon his raised plank bed. One black chicken still goes to roost lonely in the next apartment—stepping silent over the floor—frightened by the sound of its own wings—never—croaking—black as night and silent too, awaiting reynard—its God actually dead.

And in his garden never to be harvested where corn and beans and potatoes had grown tardily unwillingly as if foreknowing that the planter would die— —how how luxurious the weeds—cockles and burs stick to your clothes, and beans are hard to find—corn never got its first hoeing

I never was much acquainted with Hugh Quoil—the Ditcher dubbed Colonel sometime—killed a Colonel in some war and rode off his horse? Soldier at Waterloo—son of Erin. though sometimes I met him in the path, and can vouch for it that he verily lived and was once an inhabitant

4. Two-thirds page removed from manuscript   5. [Fall 1845.]
at this point.

of this earth—fought toiled joyed sorrowed drank—experienced life and at length Death—and do believe that a solid shank bone or skull which no longer aches lie somewhere and can still be produced which once with garment of flesh and broad-cloth were called and hired to do work as Hugh Quoil.

I say I have met him—got and given the nod—as when man meets man and not ghost— At distance seemingly a ruddy face as of cold biting January—but nearer—clear bright carmine with signs of inward combustion It would have made the ball of your finger burn to touch his cheek—with sober reflecting eye that had seen other sights. Straight-bodied snuff colored coat long familiar with him, he with it, axe or turf knife in hand—no sword nor firelock now—fought his battles through still but did not conquer—on the Napoleon side at last—and exiled to this st Helena Rock— A man of manners—gentleman like—who had seen this world—more civil speech than you could well attend to.

He and I at length came to be neighbors not speaking nor ever visiting hardly seeing neighbors—but nearest inhabitants mutually.

He was thirstier than I—drank more—probably—but not out of the pond— It was never the lower for him—perhaps I ate more than he. The last time I met him the only time I spoke with him it was at the foot of the hill in the highway where I was crossing to the spring one warm afternoon in summer—the pond water being too warm for me— I was crossing pail in hand—when Quoil came down the hill still in snuff colored coat as last winter—shivering as with cold rather with heat—delirium tremens they name it— I greeted him and told him my errand to get water at the spring close by only at the foot of the hill over the fence— he answered with stuttering parched lips—bloodshot eye—staggering gesture—he'd like to see it— Follow me there then. But I had got my pail full and back before he scaled the fence— And he drawing his coat about him to warm him to cool him answered in delirium tremens—hydrophobia dialect not easy to be written here he'd heard of it but had never seen it—and so shivered his way along toward the town—not to work there nor transact special business—but to get whack at a sweet remote hour to liquor & to oblivion.

*   *   *

Over eastward of my bean field lived Cato Ingraham slave—born slave perhaps of Duncan Ingraham Esqr—gentleman of Concord village—who built him a house and gave him permission to live in Walden woods— — and then on the N E corner Zilpha—colored woman of fame—and down the road on the right hand Bristow—colored man—on Bristow's hill—where grow still those little wild apples he tended now large trees but still wild—and farther still you come to Breeds location and again on the left by well and roadside Hilda lived Farther up the road at the ponds end Wyeman the potter who furnished his towns men earthen ware—the squatter—

Now only a dent in the earth marks the site of most of those human dwellings—sometimes the well dent where a spring oozed now dry and tearless grass—or covered deep not to be discovered till late days by accident with a flat stone under the sod.

* * *

For[6] every inferior earthly pleasure we forego a superior celestial one is substituted.

To purify our lives requires simply to weed out what is foul & noxious— And the sound and innocent is supplied—as nature purifies the blood—if we will but reject impurities.

Nature and human life are as various to our several experiences as our constitutions are various— Who shall say what prospect life offers to another? Could a greater miracle take place than if we should look through each other's eyes for an instant. What I have read of Rhapsodists[7]—of the primitive poets—Argonautic expeditions[8]—the life of demigods & heroes— Eleusinian mysteries[9]—&c—suggests nothing so ineffably grand and informing as this would be.

We know not what it is to live in the open air—our lives are domestic in more senses than we had thought. From the hearth to the field is a great distance. A man should always speak as if there were no obstruction not even a mote or a shadow between him & the celestial bodies. The voices of men sound hoarse and cavernous—tinkling as from out of the recesses of caves—enough to frighten bats & toads—not like bells—not like the music of birds, not a natural melody.

Of all the Inhabitants of Concord I know not one that dwells in nature.— If one were to inhabit her forever he would never meet a man. This country is not settled nor discovered yet

Circumstances & employment have but little effect on the finer qualities of our nature. I observe among the rail-road men—such inextinguishable ineradicable refinement & delicacy of nature—older and of more worth than the sun & moon. A genuine magnanimity—more than Greek or Roman— equal to the least occasion—of unexplored of uncontaminated descent. Greater traits I observe in them—in the shortest intercourse—than are recorded of Epaminondas Socrates—or Cato— The most famous philosophers & poets seem infantile—in comparison with these easy profligate giants. with faces homely—hard and scarred like the rocks—but human & wise—embracing—copt & musselman—all races & nations. One is a famous pacha—or sultan in disguise

A fineness which is commonly thought to adorn the drawing rooms

6. [Fall–Winter 1845–46.]
7. Professional reciters of poetry in ancient Greece.
8. According to Greek mythology, journeys made by fifty Greek heroes and their leader, Jason, aboard the *Argo* in search of a golden

ram's fleece.
9. The best known of several such religious cults that flourished in ancient Greece as private forms of worship, available only to specially initiated persons.

only There is no more real rudeness in laborers—and washerwomen than in Gentlemen & ladies Under some ancient wrinkled—almost forlorn visage—as of a Indian chieftain slumber the world famous humanities of man. There is the race—& you need look no farther. You can tell a nobleman's head among a million—though he may be shovelling gravel six rods off in the midst of a gang—with a cotton handkerchief tied about it— Such as are to succeed the worthies of history— It seems no disadvantage, their humble occupation and that they take no airs upon themselves Civilization seems to make bright the superficial film of the eye

Most men are wrecked upon their consciousness—morally—intellectually—and humanly.

———

A place of pines—of forest scenes and events visited by successive nations of men all of whom have successively fathomed it— And still its water is green & pellucid not an intermittent spring—somewhat perennial in it— While the nations pass away. A true well—a gem of the first water—which concord wears in her coronet.

looking blue as amethyst or solidified azure far off as it is drawn through the streets. Green in the deeps—blue in the shallows— Perhaps the grass is a denser deeper heaven

———

*   *   *

My house is 10 feet wide by 15 long—with a garret & closet—2 windows one door at the end—and a fire place A cellar six feet square and seven deep with shelving sides not stoned—but having never come to the sun the sand still keeps its place.

I laid up a half bushel of chestnuts which were an important item in the winter's store—which cost me only a pleasant ramble in the October woods.

Flints pond lies east a mile or more—a walk to which through the woods by such paths as the Indians used is a pleasant diversion summer or winter— Our greatest lake— Worth the while if only to feel the wind blow—and see the waves run—and remember those that go down upon the sea— I went a nutting there in the fall—one windy day—when the nuts were dropping into the water & were washed ashore— and as I crawled along its long sedgey shore the fresh spray flung in my face—I came upon what seemed a large pad amid the reeds—which proved the mouldering wreck of a boat still distinctly preserving its well modelled outline—as when it was first cast up upon that beach—but ready to furnish the substance of new pads and reeds.

*   *   *

I expect of any lecturer[1] that he will read me a more or less simple & sincere account of his life—of what he has done & thought. Not so much what he has read or heard of other mens lives—and actions— But some such account as he would put into a letter to his kindred if in a distant land—describing his outward circumstance and any little adventures that he might have—and also his thoughts and feelings about them there.

He who gives us only the results of other men's living though with brilliant temporary success—we may in some measure justly accuse of having defrauded us of our time— We want a man to give us that which was most precious to him—not his lifes blood but even that for which his life's blood circulated what he has got by living—

If any thing ever yielded him pure pleasure or instruction—let him communicate it. The Miser must tell us how much he loves wealth and what means he takes to accumulate it— He must describe those facts which he knows & loves better than any body else.

He must not lecture on Missions & the Temperance   The mechanic will naturally lecture about his trade the farmer about his farm and every man about that which he compared with other men—knows best.

Yet incredible mistakes are made— I have heard an Owl lecture with a perverse show of learning upon the solar microscope—and chanticlere upon nebulous stars   When both ought to have been sound asleep in a hollow tree—or upon a hen roost. When I lectured here before this winter I heard that some of my towns men had expected of me some account of my life at the pond—this I will endeavor to give tonight.

I find that no way of doing or thinking however ancient is to be trusted. What every body echoes or in silence passes by may turn out to be sheer falsehood at last— As it were the mere smoke of opinion falling back in cinders which some thought—a cloud that would sprinkle fertile rain upon their fields.

One says you cant live so and so—it is madness—on vegetable food solely—or mainly—for it furnishes nothing to make bones with—walking behind his oxen—and so religiously devotes a part of his day to supplying his system with the raw material of bones.

Certain things are absolute necessaries of life in some circles—the most helpless and diseased—in others certain other or fewer things—and in others fewer still—and still what the absolutely indispensible are has never been determined   I know a robust and hearty mother who thinks that her son who died abroad—came to his end by living too low, as she had since learned that he drank only water— Men are not inclined to leave off hanging men—today—though they will be to-morrow. I heard of a family

1. Lecture draft in the Journal at this point and above indicates that Thoreau expected to lecture on his Walden experience during his first winter there, or about six months after he had moved to the pond. The opportunity to do so, however, did not arrive until the following winter, February 10, 1847, when he spoke before the Concord Lyceum on "The History of Myself."

in Concord this winter which would have starved, if it had not been for potatoes—& tea & coffee.

——

It has not been my design to live cheaply but only to live as I could not devoting much time to getting a living— I made the most of what means were already got.

——

To determine the character of our life and how adequate it is to the occasion—just try it by any test—as for instance that this same sun is seen in Europe & in America at the same time—that these same stars are visible in 24 hours to ⅔ the inhabitants of the globe—and who shall say to how many inhabitants of the universe—
What farmer in his field lives according even to this somewhat trivial material fact.
I just looked up at a fine twinkling star—and thought that a voyager whom I know now many days sail from this coast—might possibly be looking up at that same star with me— The stars are the apexes of important triangles.
There is always the possibility—the possibility I say of being *all*—or remaining a particle in the universe

Perhaps we may distribute the necessaries of life under the several heads of food—clothing—shelter—& fuel And this suggests how nearly the expression "animal heat"—is to being synonymous with animal life.

* * *

The philosopher is in advance of his age not merely in his discourse but in his life—in the form & outward mode of it. He is not fed—clothed—warmed—sheltered like other men—
How can a man be a philosopher and not maintain his vital heat by better methods than other men.
The body is so perfectly subjugated by the mind that it prophecies the sovereignty of the latter over the whole of nature. The instincts are to a certain extent a sort of independent nobility—of equal date with the crown. They are perhaps the mind of our ancestors subsided in us. The experience of the race—
I have thought sometimes when going home through the woods at night—star-gazing all the way—till I was aroused from my reflections by finding my door before me—that perhaps my body would find its way home if its master should have forsaken it— As the hand finds its way to the mouth without assistance.
All matter indeed is capable of entertaining thought.

——

Why do men degenerate— what makes families run-out? What is the nature of that luxury that ennervates nations and is there none of it in our lives? Are we the founders of a race.

Men frequently say to me I should think you would feel lonely down there— I should think you would want to be nearer to folks rainy days & nights especially. How far apart dwell the most distant inhabitants of those stars the breadth of whose disks cannot be appreciated by our instruments.

But what after all do we want to dwell near to?— not mainly to the depot or to many men—not to the post office or the bar room—or the meeting house or school house—or Beacon hill or the Five points where men are more numerous than any where— —but rather I should say to the source of our life—whence in all our experience we have found that to issue. As the willow stands near the water and sends out its roots in that direction.

But most men are not so wise as a tree or rather are like those trees which being badly located make only wood & leaves and bear no fruit.

This will vary with different natures of course—but this is the place where a wise man will dig his cellar.

What is the great attraction in cities? It is universally admitted that human beings invariably degenerate there—and do not propagate their kind.— Yet the prevailing tendency is to the city life—whether we move to Boston or stay in Concord.

We are restless to pack up our furniture and move into a more bustling neighborhood but we are proportionally slow to rent a new mode of living— or rather to rend the old.

* * *

March 13th 1846 The Songsparrow & Black bird heard today—the snow going off—the ice in the pond 1 foot thick.

———

Men speak—or at least think much of cooperation nowadays—of working together to some worthy end— But what little there is, is as if it were not—being a simple result of which the means are hidden—a harmony inaudible to men— If a man has faith—he will cooperate with equal faith every where— If he has not faith he will continue to live like the rest of the world. To cooperate in the lowest & in the highest sense—thoroughly— is simply to get your living together. I heard it proposed lately that two young men should travel together over the world—the one making his way as he went, seeking his fortune,—before the mast—behind the plow— walking and sleeping on the ground—living from hand to mouth—and so come in immediate contact with all lands and nations—the other carrying a bill of exchange in his pocket as a resource in case of extremity— It was easy to see that they could not be companions to one another—or cooperate.

They would part company at the first interesting crisis the most interesting point in their adventures

I live about a mile from any neighbor no house is visible within a quarter of a mile or more—

The pond furnishes my water which 8 or 9 months in the year I think is the best in the town— In the summer I set it in my cellar and found that it became sufficiently cool.—

It seemed to me that it would become colder—than well water under the same circumstances—but I never tried the experiment

* * *

In[2] due time in the spring I heard the martins twittering over my clearing though it had not appeared that the town contained so many that it could afford any to me   They were rather of the ancient stock that dwelt in hollow trees before the white man came than the modern village race that live in boxes.

Let a man live in any part of the globe and he will hear the same simple spring sounds to cheer him. Along the Nile and the Orinoco and the Mississippi birds of the same genus—migrate. Everywhere the frog and the turtle greet the season   The temperate and Frigid salute the Torrid zone again—and birds fly & plants and winds blow to correct this oscillation of the poles and preserve the equilibrium of nature. This slight oscillation how it is painted by the seasons and heralded by the songs and the glancing plumage of migrating birds—

The Pewee (Phoebe?) came and look in at my door or window to see if my house were cave like enough for her—sustaining herself on humming wings—with clenched talons as if she held by the air—while she surveyed the premises.

Girls and boys generally seemed glad to be in the woods & young women they looked in the pond and at the flowers and improved their time.

But men of business only thought of Solitude and employment.   though they said they loved a ramble in the woods occasionally it was obvious that they did not.

Restless committed men whose time is all taken up in getting a living— Ministers Doctors—lawyers generally suggested in one way or another the importance of doing good.

Conscientious preachers—(the way of their profession)—uneasy house keepers—young men who had ceased to be young and had concluded that it was safest to follow the beaten track of the professions generally said it was not possible to do so much good in my position.

The old and infirm thought of sickness & sudden death—to them life

2. [After March 13, 1846.]

seemed full of danger—any where—and a prudent man would carefully
select the safest position

* * *

Husbandry[3] is universally a sacred art—pursued with too much heedlessness and haste by us— To have large farms and large crops is our
object. Our thoughts on this subject should be as slow and deliberate as the
pace of the ox.

"According to the early laws of Greece, the ploughing ox was held sacred,
& was entitled, when past service, to range the pastures in freedom & repose.
It was forbidden, by the decrees of Triptolemus, to put to death this faithful
ally of the labors of the husbandman, who shared the toils of ploughing &
threshing. Whenever, therefore, an ox was slaughtered, he must first be
consecrated or devoted as a sacrifice (ἱερεῖον), by the sprinkling of the
sacrificial barley; this was a precaution against the barbarous practice of
eating raw flesh (βουφόαγια). A peculiar sacrifice (Διιπόλια) at Athens,
at which the slayer of the ox fled, and the guilty axe was thrown into the
sea, on the sentence of the Prytanes, yearly placed before the people a visible
type of the first beginnings of their social institutions."[4]

Ap 18th The morning
must remind every one of his ideal life— Then if ever we can realize the
life of the Greeks   We see then Aurora. The morning brings back the heroic
ages.

I get up early and bathe in the pond—that is one of the best things I do—
so far the day is well spent.

In some unrecorded hours of solitude whether of morning or evening
whose stillness was audible—when the atmosphere contained an auroral
perfume the hum of a mosquito was a trumpet that recalled what I had read
of most ancient history and heroic ages. There was somewhat that I fancy
the Greeks meant by ambrosial about it—more than Sybilline or Delphic[5]—
It expressed the infinite fertility and fragrance and the everlastingness of the
κοςμος   It was θειον[6]   Only Homer could name it. The faintest is the
most significant sound.

* * *

The[7] struggle in me is between a love of contemplation and a love of
action—the life of a philosopher & of a hero. The poetic & philosophic
have my constant vote—the practic hinders & unfits me for the former.

3. April 17, 1846.
4. According to Greek mythology, Triptolemus was chosen by Demeter, goddess of agriculture, to teach the skills of farming; the
Prytanes were members of a governing body
chosen each year in ancient Athens. Thoreau's
source has not been identified.
5. I.e., prophetic or inspirational.
6. κοςμος, cosmos; θειον, divine.
7. [After April 18, 1846.]

How many things that my neighbors do bunglingly could I do skilfully & effectually—but I fain would not have leisure— My tendency is, on the one hand to the poetic life—on the other to the practic—and the result is the indifference[8] of both—or the philosophic.

In the practic the poetic loses its intensity—and fineness but gains in health & assurance—

The practical life is the poetic making for itself a basis—and in proportion to the breadth of the base will be the quantity of material at the apex— The angle of slope for various materials is determined by science. The fabric of life is pyramidal.

The man of practice is laying the foundations of a poetic life

The poet of great sensibility is rearing a superstructure without foundation.

To make a perfect man—the Soul must be much like the body not too unearthly & the body like the soul. The one must not deny & oppress the other.

The line of greatest breadth intersects the line of greatest length at the point of greatest depth or height

A law so universal—and to be read in all material—in Ethics as well as mechanics—that it remains its own most final statement.

—It is the heart in man— It is the sun in the system—it is the result of forces— In the case of the pond it is the law operating without friction. Draw lines through the length & breadth of the aggregate of a man's particular daily experiences and volumes of life into his coves and inlets—and where they intersect will be the height or depth of his character.

You only need to know how his shores trend & the character of the adjacent country to know his depth and concealed bottom.

There is a bar too across the entrance of his every cove—every cove is his harbor for a season—and in each successively is he detained—land locked.

There is no exclusively moral law—there is no exclusively physical law.

* * *

For the most part I know not how the hours go. Certainly I am not living that heroic life I had dreamed of— And yet all my veins are full of life— and nature whispers no reproach— The day advances as if to light some work of mine—and I defer in my thought as if there were some where busier men— It was morning & lo! it is now evening— And nothing memorable is accomplished— Yet my nature is *almost* content with this— It hears no reproach in nature.

What are these pines & these birds about? What is this pond a-doing? I must know a little more—& be forever ready. Instead of singing as the birds I silently smile at my incessant good fortune but I dont know that I bear any flowers or fruits— Methinks if they try me by their standards I shall

8. In magnetism, the indifference point is the middle region of a magnet where the two powers neutralize each other.

not be found wanting—but men try one another not so. The elements are working their will with me.

As the fields sparrow has its trill sitting on the hickory before my door— so have I my chuckle as happy as he—which he may hear out of my nest.

Man is like a plant and his satisfactions are like those of a vegetable—his rarest life is least his own— One or two persons come to my house—there being proposed it may be to their vision the faint possibility of intercourse— & joyous communion. They are as full as they are silent and wait for your plectrum or your spirit to stir the strings of their lyre. If they could ever come to the length of a sentence or hear one—on that ground they are thinking of!! They speak faintly—they do not obtrude themselves They have heard some news which none, not even they themselves can impart. What come they out for to seek? If you will strike my chord?

They come with somethings in their minds no particular fact or infor- mation—which yet is ready to take any form of expression on the proper impulse It is a wealth they bear about them which can be expended in various ways. Laden with its honey the bee straightway flies to the hive to make its treasure common stock— The poet is impelled to communicate at every risk and at any sacrifice.

I think I have this advantage in my present mode of life over those who are obliged to look abroad for amusement—to theatres & society—that my life itself is my amusement and never ceases to be novel—the commence- ment of an experiment—or a drama which will never end.

Sunday May 3d
I heard the whippoorwill last night for the first time.

Carlyle's books[9] are not to be studied but read with a swift satisfaction— rather— Their flavor & charm—their gust is like the froth of wine which can only be tasted once & that hastily. On a review I never can find the pages I had read— The book has done its work when once I have reached the conclusion, and will never inspire me again.

They are calculated to make one strong and lively impression—and en- tertain us for the while more entirely than any—but that is the last we shall know of them They have not that stereotyped success & accomplishment which we name classic—

It is an easy and inexpensive entertainment—and we are not pained by the author's straining & impoverishing himself to feed his readers.

It is plain that the reviewers and politicians do not know how to dispose of him— They take it too easily & must try again a loftier pitch— They speak of him within the passing hour as if he too were one other ephemeral

9. Thomas Carlyle (1795–1881), Scottish es- sayist and historian. Thoreau lectured on Car- lyle's writings before the Concord Lyceum on February 4, 1846, and published an essay, "Thomas Carlyle and His Works," the follow- ing year.

man of letters about town who lives under Mr. Somebody's administration.
Who will not vex the world after burial—

But he does not depend on the favor of reviewers—nor the honesty of booksellers—nor on popularity— He has more to impart than to receive from his generation

He is a strong & finished journeyman in his craft—& reminds us oftener of Samuel Johnsson[1] than of any other. So few writers are respectable—ever get out of their apprenticeship—

* * *

When[2] my friends reprove me for not devoting myself to some trade or profession, and acquiring property I feel not the reproach— I am guiltless & safe comparatively on that score— But when they remind me of the advantages of society of worthy and earnest helpful relations to people I am convicted—and yet not I only but they also.

But I am advised by thee Friend of friends to strive singly for the highest—without concern for the lower— The integrity of life is otherwise sacrificed to factitious virtues—and frittered away in morbid efforts & despair.

Disturb not the sailor with too many details—but let him be sure that he keep his guiding star in his eye. It is by a mathematical point that we are wise—but that is a sufficient guidance for all our lives— The blind are led by the slightest clue.

When I am reproved for being what I am I find the only resource is being still more entirely what I am.

Carry yourself as you should and your garments will trail as they should.

I am useless for keeping flocks & herds, for I am on the trail of a rarer game.

To the mariner the faint star is the chief light though he will avail himself of the light in the binnacle.

* * *

In[3] my short experience of human life I have found that the outward obstacles which stood in my way were not living men—but dead institutions It has been unspeakably grateful & refreshing to make my way through the crowd of this latest generation honest & dishonest virtuous & vicious as through the dewy grass—men are as innocent as the morning to the early riser—and unsuspicious pilgrim and many an early traveller which he met on his way v poetry[4]—but the institutions as church—state—the school property &c are grim and ghostly phantoms like Moloch &

1. Samuel Johnson (1709–84), English author, lexicographer, and critic.
2. May 15, 1846.
3. [After July 24, 1846.] Thoreau was arrested for several years' nonpayment of poll tax on July 24, 1846, and, though unwilling, was released the next day.

4. Thoreau's notation to himself to insert lines of an old ballad, "The Lordling Peasant": "The early pilgrim blithe he hailed / That o'er the hills did stray; / And many an early husband-man, / That he met on his way."

Juggernaut[5] because of the blind reverence paid to them. When I have indulged a poets dream of a terrestrial paradise I have not foreseen that any cossack or Chipeway—would disturb it—but some monster institution would swallow it— The only highway man I ever met was the state itself—When I have refused to pay the tax which it demanded for that protection I did not want itself has robbed me— When I have asserted the freedom it declared it has imprisoned me.

I love mankind I hate the institutions of their forefathers—

What are the sermons of the church but the Dudleian lectures[6]—against long extinct perhaps always imaginary evils, which the dead generations have *willed* and so the bell still tolls to call us to the funeral services which a generation can rightly demand but once.

It is singular that not the Devil himself—has been in my way but these cobwebs—which tradition says were originally spun to obstruct the fiend.

If I will not fight—if I will not pray—if I will not be taxed—if I will not bury the unsettled prairie—my neighbor will still tolerate me and sometimes even sustains me—but not the state.

And should our piety derive its origin still from that exploit of pius Aenaeus who bore his father Anchises on his shoulders from the ruins of Troy.

Not thieves & highwaymen but Constables & judges—not sinners but priests—not the ignorant but pedants & pedagogues—not foreign foes but standing armies—not pirates but men of war. Not free malevolence—but organized benevolence.

For instance the jailer or constable as a mere man and neighbor—with life in him intended for this particular 3 score years & ten—maybe a right worthy man with a thought in the brain of him—but as the officer & tool of the state he has no more understanding or heart than his prison key or his staff— This is what is saddest that men should voluntarily assume the character & office of brute nature.— Certainly there are modes enough by which a man may put bread into his mouth which will not prejudice him as a companion & neighbor. There are stones enough in the path of the traveller with out a man's adding his own body to the number.

There probably never were worse crimes committed since time began than in the present Mexican war—to take a single instance— And yet I have not yet learned the name or residence and probably never should of the reckless vilain who should father them— all concerned—from the political contriver to the latest recruit possess an average share of virtue & of vice the vilainy is in the readiness with which men, doing outrage to their proper natures—lend themselves to perform the office of inferior & brutal ones.

---

5. Gods described in the Old Testament and Hindu myth, respectively, to whose images their devotees blindly sacrificed themselves or others.

6. Lectures given at Harvard by speakers who frequently took conservative positions on religious issues.

The stern command is—move or ye shall be moved—be the master of your own action—or you shall unawares become the tool of the meanest slave. Any can command him who doth not command himself. Let men be men & stones be stones and we shall see if majorities *do* rule.

Countless reforms are called for because society is not animated or instinct enough with life, but like snakes I have seen in early spring—with alternate portions torpid & flexible—so that they could wriggle neither way.

All men more or less are buried partially in the grave of custom, and of some we see only a few hairs upon the crown above ground.

Better are the physically dead for they more lively rot.

*   *   *

Of[7] Emerson's Essays I should say that they were not poetry—that they were not written exactly at the right crisis though inconceivably near to it. Poetry is simply a miracle & we only recognize it receding from us not coming toward us— It yields only tints & hues of thought like the clouds which reflect the sun—& not distinct propositions—

In poetry the sentence is as one word—whose syllables are words— They do not convey thoughts but some of the health which he had inspired— It does not deal in thoughts—they are indifferent to it—

A poem is one undivided unimpeded expression—fallen ripe into literature The poet has opened his heart and still lives— And it is undividedly and unimpededly received by those for whom it was matured—but mortal eye can never dissect it— while it sees it is blinded.

The wisest *man*—though he should get all the academies in the world to help him cannot add to or subtract one syllable from a line of poetry.

*   *   *

When[8] I am stimulated by reading the biographies of literary men to adopt some method of educating myself and directing my studies—I can only resolve to keep unimpaired the freedom & wakefulness of my genius. I will not seek to accomplish much in breadth and bulk and loose my self in industry but keep my celestial relations fresh.

No method or discipline can supersede the necessity of being forever on the alert— What is a course of History—no matter how well selected—or the most admirable routine of life—and fairest relation to society—when one is reminded that he may be a *Seer* that to keep his eye constantly on the true and real is a discipline that will absorb every other.

How can he appear or be seen to be well employed to the mass of men whose profession it is to climb resolutely the heights of life—and never lose a step he has taken

7. December 2, 1846. Emerson's *Essays* was published in 1841 and *Essays: Second Series* in 1844.
8. [After December 2, 1846.] Quotations from the *Auto-Biography* of Johann Wolfgang von Goethe immediately precede this excerpt. See *Journal 2*, 356–57.

Let the youth seize upon the finest and most memorable experience in his life—that which most reconciled him to his unknown destiny—and seek to discover in it his future path. Let him be sure that that way is his only true and worthy career.

Every mortal sent into this world has a star in the heavens appointed to guide him— Its ray he cannot mistake— It has sent its beam to him either through clouds and mists faintly or through a serene heaven— He knows better than to seek advice of any.

This world is no place for the exercise of what is called common sense. This world would be denied.

Of how much improvement a man is susceptible—and what are the methods?

* * *

The[9] best books are not read even by those who have learned their letters. What does our Concord culture amount to? There is in this town—with a very few exceptions, no taste for the best or the very good books even in English literature which all can read— Even college bred—& so called liberally educated men here & elsewhere have no acquaintance with the English Classics.— and as for the recorded wisdom of mankind—which accessible to all who will know of it—there are but the feeblest efforts made to study or to become acquainted with it. One who has just come from reading perhaps the best of English books will find how few to converse with respecting it! It is for the most part foreign & unheard of. One who comes from reading a Greek—or Latin book—in the original—whose praisies are familiar even to the illiterate will find nobody at all to speak to and must keep silence about it.

Indeed there is hardly the professor in our colleges who if he has mastered the difficulties of the language has in any like proportion mastered the difficulty of the wisdom & the poetry. And the zealous morning reader of Homer or of the Greek Dramatic poets might find no more valuable sympathy in the atmosphere of Cambridge A man—any man will go considerably[1]

your gone—pull it up—pull it up But this—was Beans and not corn & so it was safe from such enemies as he

—In summer days which some devoted to the fine arts—away in Italy—and others to contemplation away in India and some to trade in London & New York—I with other farmers of N.E. devoted to field-labor.

When my hoe tinkled on a stone it was no longer beans that I hoed nor I that hoed beans.— By such sugar plums they tempt us to live this life of man—however mean and trivial.

---

9. [Winter 1846–47.]
1. Thirty-four pages removed from manuscript at this point, some or all of it, perhaps, containing draft for *Walden*.

Or it was my amusement when I rested in the shrub oaks to watch a pair of hen-hawks circling high in the sky as silently as the humors on my eye— alternately soaring and descending—approaching and leaving one another— the imbodiment of some of my own thoughts which some times soar as high & sail & circle as majestically there.

*   *   *

Mythology[2] is ancient history or biography   The oldest history still memorable becomes a mythus—   It is the fruit which history at last bears— The fable so far from being false contains only the essential parts of the history—   What is today a diffuse biography—was anciently before printing was discovered—   —a short & pithy tradition   a century was equal to a thousand years. To day you have the story told at length with all its accompaniments   In mythology you have the essential & memorable parts alone—the you & I the here & there the now & then being omitted—   In how few words for instance the Greeks would have told the story of Abelard & Heloise[3]   instead of a volume They would have made a mythus of it among the fables of their gods and demigods or mortals—and then have stuck up their names to shine in some corner of the firmament—   And who knows what Greeks may come again at last to mythologize their Love.— and our own deeds.

How many Vols folio must the life and labors of Prometheus[4] have filled if perchance it fell in days of cheap printing!—   What shape at length will assume the fable of Columbus—to be confounded at last with that of Jason— & the expedition of the Argonauts—and future Homers quoted as authority. And Franklin[5] there may be a line for him in the future Classical dictionary recording what that demigod did.—   & referring him to some new genealogy—

I see already the naked fables scattered up & down the history of modern— Europe—   A small volume of mythology preparing in the press of time— The hero tell—with his bow—Shakespeare—the new Apollo—   —Cromwell—Napoleon.

The most comprehensive the most pithy & significant book is the mythology

Few[6] phenomena give me more delight in the spring of the year than to observe the forms which thawing clay and sand assume on flowing down the sides of a deep cut on the rail road through which I walk.

The clay especially assumes an infinite variety of forms—

2. [Spring 1848.]
3. The tragic love affair between Peter Abelard (1079–1142), famed teacher and theologian of Notre Dame in Paris, and Heloise (d. 1163), a woman of learning and Abelard's pupil.
4. In Greek mythology, a Titan whose labors included creating humans out of clay and stealing fire for the human race from heaven, against the hostility of the gods.
5. Benjamin Franklin (1706–90), American statesman, scientist, and philosopher.
6. Thoreau later extensively revised the following description of the thawing sandbank. For these revisions, see *Journal 2*, 576–79.

There lie the sand and clay all winter on this shelving surface an inert mass but when the spring sun comes to thaw the ice which binds them they begin to flow down the bank like lava—

These little streams & ripples of lava like clay over flow & interlace one another like some mythological vegetation—like the forms which I seem to have seen imitated in bronze— What affects me is the presence of the law—between the inert mass and the luxuriant vegetation what interval is there? Here is an artist at work—as it were not at work but—a-playing designing — — It begins to flow & immediately it takes the forms of vines—or of the feet & claws of animals—or of the human brain or lungs or bowels— Now it is bluish clay now clay mixed with reddish sand—now pure iron sand—and sand and clay of every degree of fineness and every shade of color— The whole bank for a quarter of a mile on both sides is sometimes overlaid with a mass of plump & sappy verdure of this kind—I am startled probably because it grows so fast—it is produced in one spring day. The lobe of these leaves—perchance of all leaves—is a thick—now loitering drop like the ball of the finger larger or smaller   so perchance the fingers & toes flow to their extent from the thawing mass of the body—& then are congealed for a night.

—Whither may the sun of new spring lead them on— These roots of ours— In the mornings these resting streams start again and branch & branch again into a myriad others— Here it is coarse red sand & even pebbles—there fine adhesive clay—

—And where the flowing mass reaches the drain at the foot of the bank on either side it spreads out flatter in to sands like those formed at the mouths of rivers—the separate streams losing their semicilindrical form—and gradually growing more and more flat—and running together as it is more moist till they form an almost flat sand—variously & beautifully shaded—& in which you can still trace the forms of vegetation till at length in the water itself they become the ripple marks on the bottom

The lobes are the fingers of the leaf as many lobes as it has in so many directions it inclines to flow—more genial heat or other influences in its springs might have caused it flow farther.

—So it seemed as if this one hill side contained an epitome of all the operations in nature.

So the stream is but a leaf   What is the river with all its branches—but a leaf divested of its pulp— — but its pulp is intervening earth—forests & fields & town & cities— What is the river but a tree on oak or pine—& its leaves perchance are ponds & lakes & meadows innumerable as the springs which feed it.

I perceive that there is the same power that made me my brain my lungs my bowels my fingers & toes working in other clay this very day— I am in the studio of an artist.

This cut is about a quarter of a mile long—& 30 or 40 feet deep—and in several places clay occurs which rises to within a dozen feet of the surface.— Where there is sand only the slope is great & uniform—but the clay being more adhesive inclines to stand out longer from the sand as in boulders—which are continually washing & coming down.

Flowing down it of course runs together and forms masses and conglomerations but if flowed upward it would disperesed itself more—& grow more freely—& unimpeded

* * *

Is[7] it a use I make of my friends which necessarily transcends their privity (consciousness)?— They sometimes even demand to be admitted to my solitary joy—ask why I smile—but I see too plainly—that if I degraded my ideal to an identity with any actual mortal whose hand is to be grasped there would be an end of our fine relations. I would be related to my friend by the most etherial part of our natures alone—and what else is quite obedient to this.

I learned this by my experiments in the woods, of more value perhaps than all the rest—that if one will advance confidently in the direction of his dreams, and live that life which he has imagined— If he will walk the water, if he will step forth on to the clouds if he will heartily embrace the true, if in his life he will transend the temporal— (He shall walk securely—perfect success shall attend him, there shall be the terra firma or the coelum firmior—) If he will do that in which alone he has faith, if he will yield to love and go whither it leads him) He shall be translated—he shall know no interval he shall be surrounded by new environments, new and more universal & libereal laws shall {MS torn} establish themselves around & within[8]

It is not enough that my friend is good—he must be wise— Our intercourse is likely to be a tragedy with that one who cannot measure us Where there is not discernment the behavior even of a pure soul may in effect amount to coarseness.— In a difference with a friend I have felt that our intercourse was prophaned when that friend made haste come to speech about it. I am more grieved that my friend can so easily give utterance to his wounded feelings—than by what he says. Such a wound cannot be permanently healed. There is a certain vulgarity & coarseness in that sentiment that is liable to a common difference—such wordy reproaches as are heard in street & the kitchen.[9]

as it were in a new world in which these laws prevailed— All things were miraculously changed— Nature was unexpectedly kind. I lived with the license of a higher order of beings— Some restrictions were taken off. I was met. Solitude, was not solitude—nor silence—silence—nor poverty

7. [After May 26, 1849.]
8. Two-fifths page removed from the manuscript at this point.
9. Two-fifths page removed from the manuscript at this point. The "friend" with whom Thoreau had a falling-out at this time is believed to have been Emerson. See *Journal 3*, 485–88.

poverty nor weakness weakness. I had travelled things {*MS torn*}t as they had been. I had died to a life {*MS torn*} my life,[1]

* * *

The[2] Hindoos by constitution possess in in a wonderful degree the faculty of contemplation—they can speculate—they have imagination & invention & fancy. The western man thinks only with ruinous interruptions & friction—his contemplative faculty is rusty & does not work. He is soon aground in the shallows of the practical— It gives him indigestion to think. His cowardly *legs* run away with him—but the Hindoo bravely cuts off his legs in the first place. To him his imagination is a distinct & honorable faculty as valuable as the understanding or the legs— The legs were made to transport it—& it does not merely direct the legs. How incredibly poor in speculation is the western world!— one would have thought that a drop of thought & a single afternoon would have set afloat more speculations—
What has Europe been *thinking* of these two thousand years. A child put to bed half an hour before its time would have invented more systems— would have had more theories set afloat would have amused itself with more thoughts. But instead of going to bed and thinking Europe has got up and gone to work, and when she goes to bed she goes to sleep. We cannot go to bed & think as children do The Yankee cannot sit but he sleeps— I have an uncle who is obliged to sprout potatoes on sundays to keep him awake. The Hindoo thinks so vividly & intensely that he can think sitting or on his back—far into a siesta He can dream awake.

* * *

Feb 24th 1850 Saw red wing blackbirds & heard them sing & whistle— & also cherry birds on the cedar trees by Flints Pond in company with hundreds of lisping robins Feb. 28th heard blue birds & saw a striped squirrel—and a caterpillar

He is a happy man who is assured that the animal is dying out in him day by day & the spiritual being established.
What a strange alliance of the divine & brutish there is in a man
Man has a gross animal & unreasoning nature which puts to shame his spiritual.
We would fain esteem a person for what he is absolutely & not relatively to us alone,—and be so esteemed ourselves. There is no safety or progress in the love which is identical with partiality.
We would love universal and absolute qualities, all other love is transient & factitious & impure

* * *

1. Three-fifths page removed from the man-   2. [After September 11, 1849.]
uscript at this point.

The[3] calmness & gentleness with which the Hindoo philosophers approach & discourse on forbidden themes is admirable

What extracts from the vedas I have read fall on me like the light of a higher & purer luminary which describes a loftier curve through a purer stratum—free from particulars—simple—universal— It rises on me like the full moon after the stars have come out wading through some far summer stratum of the sky.

The Vedant teaches how "by forsaking religious rites" the votary may "obtain purification of mind."[4]

One wise sentence is worth the state of Massachusetts, many times over.

The Vedas contain a sensible account of God.

The religion & phil. of the Hebrews are those of a wilder & ruder tribe—wanting the civility & intellectual refinements & subtlety of the Hindoos.

Man flows at once to God as soon as the channel of purity, physical, intellectual & moral, is open.

with the Hindoos virtue is an intellectual exercise—not a social & *practical* one— It is a knowing not a doing.

I do not prefer one religion or philosophy to another— I have no sympathy with the bigotry & ignorance which make transient & partial & puerile distinctions between one man's faith or form of faith & anothers—as christian & heathen— I pray to be delivered from narrowness partiality exaggeration—bigotry. To the philosopher all sects all nations are alike. I like Brahma—Hare Buddha—the Great spirit as well as God.

* * *

A page with as true & inevitable & deep a meaning as a hill-side. A book which nature shall own as her own flower her own leaves—with whose leaves her own shall rustle in sympathy imperishable & russet—which shall push out with the skunk cabbage in the spring

I am not offended by the odor of the skunk in passing by sacred places— I am invigorated rather. It is a reminiscence of immortality borne on the gale O thou partial world, when wilt thou know God?

I would as soon transplant this vegetable to Polynesia or to heaven with me as the violet.

Shoes are commonly too narrow. If you should take off a gentleman's shoes you would find that his foot was wider than his shoe. Think of his wearing such an engine—walking in it many miles year after year. A shoe which presses aagainst the sides of the foot is to be condemned— To compress the foot like the Chinese is as bad as to compress the head—like

3. [After April 26, 1850.]
4. The Vedas are Hindu scriptures; Thoreau
quotes from *Translation of . . .the Veds* (1832) by Raja Rammohun Roy.

the Flat heads—for the Head & the foot are one body. A sensible man will
not follow fashion in this respect but reason. Better moccasins or Sandals
or even bare feet, than a tight shoe.

A wise man will wear a shoe wide & large enough shaped somewhat like
the foot & tied with a leather string.   & so go his way in peace letting his
foot fall at every step.

When your shoe chafes your feet put in a mullein leaf.

When I ask for a garment of a particular form my tailoress tells me gravely
'They do not make them so now," and I find it difficult to get made what
I want—simply because she cannot believe that I mean what I say—   It
surpasses her credulity—   Properly speaking my style is as fashionable as
theirs. "They do not make them so now"!   as if she quoted the Fates. I am
for a moment absorbed in thought—thinking wondering who they are &
where *they* live. It is some Oak Hall[5] O Call—   O K all correct establishment which she knows but I do not. Oliver Cromwell—   I emphasize &
in imagination italicize each word separately of that sentence to come at
the meaning of it

*   *   *

Jewett's[6] steam mill is profitable because the planing machine alone while
that is running makes shavings & waste enough to feed the engine—to say
nothing of the saw-dust—from the saw mill & the Engine had not required
the least repair for several years. Perhaps as there is not so much sawing &
planing to be done in England they therefore may not find steam so cheap
as water.

A single gentle rain in the spring makes the grass look many shades greener.

It is wisest to live without any definite & recognised object from day to
day,—any particular object for the world is round and we are not to live on
a tangent or a radius to the sphere—   As an old poet says Though man
proposeth, God disposeth all.

Our thoughts are wont to run in muddy or dusty ruts

I too revive as does the grass after rain—   We are never so flourishing
our day is never so fair but that the sun may come out a little brighter
through mists & we yearn to live a better life—   What have we to boast
of?   we are made the very sewers the cloacae of nature.

If the hunter has a taste for mud turtles & muskrats & skunks and other
such savage tit bits—the fine lady indulges a taste for some form of potted
cheese or jelly made of a calf's foot or anchovies from over the water—&
they are even. He goes to the mill pond—she to her preserve pot. I wonder
how he—I wonder how I can live this slimy beastly kind of life—eating &
drinking—

5. A Boston clothing store.   6. May 12, 1850.

The fresh foliage of the woods in May—when the leaves are about as big as a mouse's ear—putting out like taller grasses & herbs

In all my rambles I have seen no landscape which can make me forget Fair Haven. I still sit on its Cliff in a new spring day & look over the awakening woods & the river & hear the new birds sing with the same delight as ever— It is as sweet a mystery to me as ever what this world is— Wild Fair Haven lake in the South with its pine covered island & its meadows— the hickories putting out fresh young yellowish leaves—and the oaks light greyish ones while the oven bird thrums his sawyer-like strain & the chewink rustles through the dry leaves or repeats his jingle on a tree top—& the wood thrush, the genius of the wood, whistles for the first time his clear & thrilling strain— It sounds as it did the first time I heard it. The sight of these budding woods intoxicates me—this diet drink.

The strong colored pine—the grass of trees—in the midst of which other trees are but as weeds or flowers.   a little exotic.

*   *   *

Today June 4th I have been tending a burning in the woods. Ray was there. It is a pleasant fact that you will know no man long however low in the social scale however poor miserable, intemperate & worthless he may appear to be a mere burden to society—but you will find at last that there is something which he understands & can do better than any other. I was pleased to hear that one man had sent Ray as the one who had had the most experience in setting fires of any man in Lincoln— He had experience & skill as a burner of brush. You must burn against the wind always & burn slowly— When the fire breaks over the hoed line—a little system & perseverance will accomplish more toward quelling it than any man would believe.

—It fortunately happens that the experience acquired is oftentimes worth more than the wages. When a fire breaks out in the woods & a man fights it too near & on the side—in the heat of the moment without the systematic cooperation of others he is disposed to think it a desperate case & that this relentless fiend will run through the forests till it is glutted with food; but let the company rest from their labors a moment—& then proceed more deliberately & systematically giving the fire a wider berth—and the company will be astonished to find how soon & easily they will subdue it. The woods themselves furnish one of the best weapons with which to contend with the fires that destroy them—a pitch pine bow. It is the best instrument to thrash it with. There are few men who do not love better to give advice than to give assistance.

*   *   *

Men go to a fire for entertainment. When I see how eagerly men will run to a fire whether in warm or in cold weather by day or by night dragging an engine at their heels, I am astonished to perceive how good a purpose the love of excitement is made to serve.— What other force pray—what offered pay—what disinterested neighborliness could ever effect so much. No these are boys who are to be dealt with—& these are the motives that prevail.

There is no old man or woman dropping into the grave but covets excitement.

* * *

Olive or red seems the fittest color for a man—a denizen of the woods. The *pale white man* I do not wonder that the African pitied him.

The white-pine cones which are earlier than the pitch are now two inches long curved sickle-like from the top most branches—reminding you of the tropical trees which bear their fruit at their heads.

The life in us is like the water in the river, it may rise this year higher than ever it was known to before and flood the uplands—even this may be the eventful year—& drown out all our muskrats   There are as many strata at different levels of life as there are leaves in a book   Most men probably have lived in two or three. When on the higher levels we can remember the lower levels, but when on the lower we cannot remember the higher.

My imagination, my love & reverance & admiration, my sense of the miraculous is not so excited by any event as by the remembrance of my youth. Men talk about bible miracles because there is no miracle in their lives. Cease to gnaw that crust. There is ripe fruit over your head   Wo to him who wants a companion—for he is unfit to be the companion even of himself.

We inspire friendship in men when we have contracted friendship with the gods.

When we cease to sympathise with and to be personally related to men, and begin to be universally related—then we are capable of inspiring others with the sentiment of love for us.

I have been into a village and there was not a man of a large soul in it— In what respect was it better than a village of prairie dogs?

We hug the earth—how rare we mount!   how rarely, we climb a tree! We might get a little higher methinks   That pine would make us dizzy. You can see the *Mts* from it as you never did before.

Shall not a man have his spring as well as the plants?

The halo around the shadow is visible both morning & evening.

* * *

However mean your life is meet it & live—do not shun it and call it hard names. It is not so bad as you are. It looks poorest when you are richest   The fault finder will find faults even in paradise   Love your life, poor as it is. You may perchance have some pleasant—thrilling glorious hours even in a poor-house—   The setting sun is reflected from the windows of the alms-house as brightly as from the rich man's house.

The snow melts before its door as early in the spring. I do not see but a quiet mind may live as contentedly there, and have as cheering thoughts as any where—& indeed the towns poor seem to live the most independent lives of any. they are simply great enough to receive—without misgiving. Cultivate poverty like sage like a garden herb. Do not trouble yourself to get new things—whether clothes—or friends— That is dissipation. Turn the old—return to them. Things do not change, we change. If I were confined to a corner—in a garret all my days like a spider—the world would be just as large to me—while I had my thoughts

In all my travels I never came to the abode of the present

I live in the angle of a leaden wall into whose alloy was poured a littl bell metal. Some times in the repose of my midday there reaches my ears a confused tintinnabulum from without— It is the noise of my contemporaries.

That the brilliant leaves of Autumn are not withered ones is proved by the fact, that they wilt when gathered as soon as the green.

But now, Oct 31st, they are all withered. This has been the most perfect afternoon in the year. The air quite warm enough—perfectly still & dry & clear, and not a cloud in the sky. Scarcely the song of a cricket is heard to disturb the stillness When they ceased their song I do not know— I wonder that the impetus which our hearing had got did not hurry us into deafness over a precipitous silence There must have been a thick web of cobwebs on the grass this morning promising this fair day—for I see them still through the afternoon covering not only the grass but the bushes & the trees. They are stretched across the unfrequented roads from weed to weed & broken by the legs of the horses

*   *   *

This[7] is a peculiar season—peculiar for its stillness—the crickets have ceased their song. The few birds are well nigh silent— The tinted & gay leaves are now sere and dead and the woods wear a sombre aspect. A carpet of snow under the pines & shrub-oaks will make it look more cheerful— Very few plants have now their spring But thoughts still spring in man's brain. There are no flowers nor berries to speak of. The grass begins to die at top— In the morning it is stiff with frost. Ice has been discovered in somebody's tub very early this morn of the thickness of a dollar. The flies are betwixt life & death. The wasps come into the houses & settle on the walls & windows All insects go into crevices. The fly is entangled in a web and struggles vainly to escape—but there is no spider to secure him— The corner of the pane is a deserted camp.

When I lived in the woods the wasps came by thousands to my lodge in November—as to winter quarters, and settled on my—windows & on the walls over my head sometimes deterring visitors from entering— Each

7. November 2, 1850.

morning when they were numbed with cold I swept some of them out. But I did not trouble myself to get rid of them   they never molested me, though they bedded with me—and they gradually disappeared into what crevices I do not know.—   avoiding winter

I saw a squash-bug go slowly behind a clapboard to avoid winter—as some of these melon-seeds come up in the garden again in the spring—so some of these squash bugs come forth—   The flies are for a long time in a somnambulic state—   They have too littl energy or vis vitae to clean their wings or heads which are covered with dust. They buzz and bump their heads against the windows or lie on their backs and that is all—two or three short spurts—   One of these mornings we shall hear that Mr Minot had to break the ice to water his cow. And so it will go on till the ground freezes. If the race had never lived through a winter what would they think was coming?

Walden Pond has at last fallen a little—   It has been so high over the stones quite into the bushes that walkers have been excluded from it. There has been no accessible shore—   All Ponds have been high—   The water stood higher than usual in the distant ponds which I visited & had never seen before. It has been a peculiar season. At Goose-Pond I notice that the birches of one years growth from the stumps standing in the water are all dead apparently killed by the water—unless like the pine they die down after springing from the stump.

It is warm somewhere anyday in the year—   You will find some nook in the woods generally at midforenoon of the most blustering day where you may forget the cold. I used to resort to the North east shore of Walden where the sun reflected from the pine woods on the stoney shore made it as warm as a fireside. It is so much pleasanter and wholsomer to be warmed by the sun when you can than by a fire.

* * *

The[8] era of wild apples will soon be over—   I wander through old orchards of great extent now all gone to decay all of native fruit which for the most part went to the cider mill—   But since the temperance reform—and the general introduction of grafted fruit—no wild apples such as I see every where in deserted pastures and where the woods have grown up among them—are set out. I fear that he who walks over these hills a century hence will not know the pleasure of knocking off wild apples—   Ah poor man!   there are many pleasures which he will be debarred from. Notwithstanding the prevalence of the Baldwin & the porter,[9] I doubt if as extensive orchards are set out to day in this town as there were a century ago when these vast straggling cider orchards were set out. Men stuck in a tree then by every wall side & let it take its chance—   I see nobody planting trees

---

8. November 16, 1850.   9. Common varieties of eating apples.

today in such out of the way places along almost every road & lane & wall side, and at the bottom of dells in the wood. Now that they have grafted trees & pay a price for them they collect them into a plot by their houses & fence them in.

My Journal should be the record of my love. I would write in it only of the things I love. My affection for any aspect of the world. What I love to think of. I have no more distinctness or pointedness in my yearnings than an expanding bud—which does indeed point to flower & fruit to summer & autumn—but is aware of the warm sun & spring influence only. I feel ripe for something yet do nothing—cant discover what that thing is. I feel fertile merely. It is seed time with me— I have lain fallow long enough.

Notwithstanding a sense of unworthiness which possesses me not without reason—notwithstanding that I regard myself as a good deal of a scamp— yet for the most part the spirit of the universe is unaccountably kind to me— and I enjoy perhaps an unusual share of happiness. Yet I question sometimes if there is not some settlement to come.

*　　*　　*

Dec 31st

I observe that in the cut by Walden Pond the sand and stones fall from the overhanging bank and rest on the snow below— And thus perchance the stratum deposited by the side of the road in the winter can permanently be distinguished from the summer one by some faint seam to be referred to the peculiar conditions under which it was deposited.

The Pond has been frozen over since I was there last.

Certain meadows, as Heywoods, contain warmer water than others and are slow to freeze. I do not remember to have crossed this with impunity in all places. The brook that issues from it is still open completely though the thermometer was down to 8 below zero this morning.

The blue-jays evidently notify each other of the presence of an intruder, and will sometimes make a great chattering about it, & so communicate the alarm to other birds—& to beasts.

*　　*　　*

July 19th

Here I am 34 years old, and yet my life is almost wholly unexpanded. How much is in the germ! There is such an interval between my ideal and the actual in many instances that I may say I am unborn. There is the instinct for society—but no society. Life is not long enough for one success. Within another 34 years that miracle can hardly take place. Methinks my seasons revolve more slowly than those of nature, I am differently timed. I am—contented. This rapid revolution of nature even of nature in me—why should it hurry me. Let a man step to the music which he hears however measured. Is it important that I should mature as soon as an apple tree? Ye, as soon as an oak? May not my life in nature, in proportion as it is super-natural, be only the spring & infantile portion of my spirit's life shall I turn my spring to summer? May I not sacrifice a hasty & petty completeness here—to entireness there? If my curve is large—why bend it to a smaller circle? My spirits unfolding observes not the pace of nature. The society which I was made for is not here, shall I then substitute for the anticipation of that this poor reality. I would have the unmixed expectation of that than this reality.

If life is a waiting—so be it. I will not be shipwrecked on a vain reality. What were any reality which I can substitute. Shall I with pains erect a heaven of blue glass over myself though when it is done I shall be sure to gaze still on the true etherial heaven—far above as if the former were not—that still distant sky oer arching that blue expressive eye of heaven. I am enamored of the blue eyed arch of heaven.

I did not *make* this demand for a more thorough sympathy. This is not my idiosyncrasy or disease. He that made the demand will answer the demand.

My blood flows as slowly as the waves of my native Musketaquid —yet they reach the ocean sooner perchance than those of the Nashua.[1]

Already the golden-rod is budded, but I can make no haste for that.

* * *

It[2] is the fault of some excellent writers—De Quincy's first impressions on seeing London[3] suggest it to me—that they express themselves with too great fullness & detail. They give the most faithful natural & living account of their sensations mental & physical—but they lack moderation and sen-tentiousness—they do not affect us by an ineffectual earnesst and a reserve of meaning—like a stutterer—they say all they mean. Their sentences are not concentrated and nutty. Sentences which suggest far more than they say, which have an atmosphere about them—which do not merely report an old but make a new impression— Sentences which suggest as many things and are as durable as a Roman Acqueduct To frame these that is the *art* of writing. Sentences which are expensive towards which so many volumes—so much life went—which lie like boulders on the page—up & down or across. Not mere repetition but creation. Which a man might sell his grounds & castle to build. If De Quincy had suggested each of his pages in a sentence & passed on it would have been far more excellent writing.— His style is no where kinked and knotted up into something hard & significant which you could swallow like a diamond without digesting.

1. Rivers that flow north into the Merrimack River (at points in northeastern Massachusetts and southeastern New Hampshire, respectively) before it flows into the Atlantic Ocean at Newburyport, Massachusetts. "Musketa quid" is the Indian name for the Concord River.
2. August 22, 1851.
3. Thomas De Quincey (1785–1859), English writer; his impressions are described in *Literary Reminiscences* (1851).

Aug 23ᵈ Sat.

To walden to bathe at 5½ AM   Traces of the heavy rains in the night   The sand and gravel are beaten hard by them. 3 or 4 showers in succession. But the grass is not so wet as after an ordinary dew. The verbena hastata at the pond has reached the top of its spike—a little in advance of what I noticed yesterday—only one or two flowers are adhering. At the commencement of my walk I saw no traces of fog.   but after detected fogs over particular meadows & high up some brooks' valleys—and far in the deep cut—the wood fog   1st muskmelon this morning—

*   *   *

Sep 19th '51

Perambulated Carlisle line   Large flowered bidens or Beggar ticks or Burr–Marygold now abundant by river side. Found the bound-stones on Carlisle by the river—all or mostly tipped over by the ice & water like the pitch pines about Walden pond. Grapes very abundant along that line.

The soap-wort Gentian now—   In an old pasture now grown up to birches & other trees—followed the cow paths to the old apple trees. Mr Isaiah Green of Carlisle who lives nearest to the Kibbe Place—can remember when there were 3 or 4 houses around him (he is nearly 80 years old & has always lived there & was born there) now he is quite retired—& the nearest road is scarcely used at all. He spoke of one old field, now grown up—which were going through, as the "hog-pasture", formerly. We found the meadows so dry that it was thought to be a good time to burn out the moss.

Sep. 20th

3 Pm. to Cliffs via Bear Hill. As I go through the fields endeavoring to recover my tone & sanity—& to perceive things truly & simply again, after having been perambulating the bounds of the town all the week, and dealing with the most common place and worldly minded men, and emphatically *trivial* things I feel as if I had committed suicide in a sense. I am again forcibly struck with the truth of the fable of Apollo serving king Admetus⁴— its universal applicability. A fatal coarseness is the result of mixing in the trivial affairs of men. Though I have been associating even with the *select* men⁵ of this and the surrounding towns, I feel inexpressibly begrimmed, my pegasus has lost his wings, he has turned a reptile and gone on his belly. Such things are compatible only with a cheap and superficial life

The poet must keep himself unstained and aloof. Let him perambulate the bounds of Imagination's provinces the realms of faery, and not the insignificant boundaries of towns. The excursions of the imagination are so boundless—the limits of towns are so petty.

I scare up the great bittern in meadow by the Heywood Brook near the

---

4. Apollo, the god of music, poetry, and prophecy, was banished from heaven for nine years and forced to tend the flocks of Admetus, king of Pherae.
5. Pun on "selectmen," a board of town officers elected to manage local affairs.

ivy.— he rises buoyantly as he flies against the wind & sweep south over the willow with outstretched neck surveying.

* * *

It[6] is a rare qualification to be ably to state a fact simply & adequately. To digest some experience cleanly. To say yes and no with authority— To make a square edge. To conceive & suffer the truth to pass through as living & intact—even as a waterfowl an eel—thus peopling new waters. First of all a man must see, before he can say.— Statements are made but partially—Things are said with reference to certain conventions or existing institutions.— not absolutely. A fact truly & absolutely stated is taken out of the region of commonsense and acquires a mythologic or universal significance. Say it & have done with it. Express it without expressing yourself. See not with the eye of science—which is barren—nor of youthful poetry which is impotent. But taste the world. & digest it. It would seem as if things got said but rarely & by chance— As you *see* so at length will you *say*. When facts are seen superficially they are seen as they lie in relation to certain institution's perchance. But I would have them expressed as more deeply seen with deeper references.— so that the hearer or reader cannot recognize them or apprehend their significance from the platform of common life—but it will be necessary that he be in a sense translated in order to understand them.

When the truth respecting *his* things shall naturally exhale from a man like the odor of the muskrat from the coat of the trapper. At first blush a man is not capable of reporting truth—he must be drenched & saturated with it first. What was en*thusiasm* in the young man must become *tem-pera*ment in the mature man. without excitement—heat or passion he will survey the world which excited the youth—& threw him off his balance. As all things are significant; so all words should be significant. It is a fault which attaches to the speaker to speak flippantly or supeficially of anything. Of what use are words which do not move the hearer.— are not oracular & fateful?— A style in which the matter is all in all & the manner nothing at all.

In your thoughts no more than in your walks do you meet men—in moods I find such privacy as in dismal swamps & on mountain tops.

Man recognizes laws little enforced & he condescends to obey them. In the moment that he feels his superiority to them as compulsatory he as it were courteously reenacts them but to obey them.

* * *

Friday Nov 14
Surveying the Ministerial lot in the S W part of the town. Unexpectedly find Heywoods pond frozen over thinly it being shallow & coldly placed.

6. November 1, 1851.

In the evening went to a party. It is a bad place to go to.— 30 or 40 persons mostly young women in a small room—warm & noisy. Was introduced to two young women— The first one was as lively & loquacious as a chic-a-dee—had been accustomed to the society of watering places, and therefore could get no refreshment out of such a dry fellow as I. The other was said to be pretty looking, but I rarely look people in their faces, and moreover I could not hear what she said there was such a clacking—could only see the motion of her lips when I looked that way. I could imagine better places for conversation—where there should be a certain degree of silence surrounding you & less than 40 talking at once. Why this afternoon even I did better. There was old Mr Joseph Hosmer & I ate our luncheon of cracker & cheese together in the woods. I heard all he said, though it was not much to be sure & he could hear me. & then he talked out of such a glorious repose—taking a leisurely bite at the cracker & cheese between his words—& so some of him was communicated to me & some of me to him.

These parties I think are a part of the machinery of modern society—that young people may be brought together to form marriage connections.

What is the use of going to see people whom yet you never see—& who never see you? I begin to suspect that it is not necessary that we should see one another.

Some of my friends make singular blunders. They go out of their way to talk with certain young women of whom they think or have heard that they are pretty—and take pains to introduce me to them. That may be a reason why they should look at them, but it is not a reason why they should talk with them. I confess that I am lacking a sense perchance in this respect— & I derive no pleasure from talking with a young woman half an hour— simply because she has regular features.

The society of young women is the most unprofitably I have ever tried.

They are so light & flighty that you can never be sure whether they are there or not there. I prefer to talk with the more staid & settled—*settled for life*, in every sense.

* * *

Jan 20th

Walked down the Boston road. It was good to look off over the great unspotted fields of snow the walls & fences almost buried in it—& hardly a turf or stake left bare for the starving crows to alight on. There is no track nor mark to mar its purity beyond the single sled track—except where once in half a mile some traveller has stepped aside for a sleigh to pass.

The farmers now a days can cart out peat & muck over the frozen meadows. Somewhat analogous methinks the scholar does—drives in with tight traced energy & winter cheer—onto his now firm meadowy grounds—& carts hauls off the virgin loads of fertilizing soil which he threw up in the warm soft summer. We now bring our muck out of the meadows, but it was thrown up first in summer. The scholars & the farmers work are strictly analogous.

Easily he now conveys sliding over the snow clad ground—great loads of fuel & of lumber which have grown in many summers—from the forest to the town. *He* deals with the dry hay & cows—the spoils of summer meads & fields—stored in his barns doling it out from day to day, & manufactures milk for men.

When I see the farmer driving into his barn yard with a load of muck—whose blackness contrasts strangely with the white snow, I have the thought which I have described. He is doing like myself. My barn-yard is my journal.

* * *

Jan 22nd

Having occasion to get up & light a lamp in the middle of a sultry night I observed a stream of large black ants passing up and down one of the bare corner posts—those descending having their large white eggs or larva in their mouths—the others making haste up for another load. I supposed that they had found the heat so great just under the roof as to compel them to remove their progeny to a cooler place by night. They had evidently taken & communicated the resolution to improve the coolness of the night to remove their young to a cooler & safer locality. One stream running up another down with great industry.

But why I changed—? Why I left the woods? I do not think that I can tell. I have often wished myself back— I do not know any better how I ever came to go there—. Perhaps it is none of my business—even if it is your's. Perhaps I wanted a change— There was a little stagnation it may be—about 2 o'clock in the afternoon the world's axle—creaked as if it needed greasing—as if the oxen labored—& could hardly get their load over the ridge of the day— Perhaps if I lived there much longer I might live there forever— One would think twice before he accepted heaven on such terms— A ticket to Heaven must include tickets to Limbo—Purgatory—& Hell. Your ticket to the boxes admits you to the pit also. And if you take a cabin-passage you can smoke at least forward of the engine.— You have the liberty of the whole boat. But no I do not wish for a ticket to the boxes—nor to take a cabin passage. I will rather go before the mast & on the deck of the world. I have no desire to go "abaft the engine"

What is it that I see from a mile to a mile & a half & 2 miles distant in the horizon on all sides of our villages—the woods.— which still almost without exception encircle the towns.— They at least bound almost every view. They have been driven off only so far. Where still wild creatures haunt. How long will these last? Is this a universal and permanent feature? Is it not an interesting, an important question whether these are decreasing or not. Have the oldest countries retained it?

Look out what window I will my eyes rest in the distance on a forest! Is this fact of no significance— Is this circumstance of no value? Why such pains in old countries to plant gardens & parks?— A certain sample of wild nature—a certain primitiveness.

One man proposed a book in which visitors should write their names— said he would be at the expense of it!!! Did he consider what the expense of it would be? As if it were of any use when a man had failed to make any memorable impression on you—for him to leave his name. But it may be that he writes a good hand.— who had not left any fame. No! I kept a book to put their fames in— I was at the expense of it.

The milk man is now filling his ice-house.

The towns thus bordered—with a fringed & tasselled border—each has its preserves. Methinks the town should have more supervision & control over its parks[7] than it has. It concerns us all whether these proprietors— choose to cut down all the woods this winter or not.

I must say that I do not know what made me leave the pond— I left it as unaccountably as I went to it. To speak sincerely, I went there because I had got ready to go— I left it for the same reason.

* * *

To set down such choice experiences that my own writings may inspire me.— and at last I may make wholes of parts.

Certainly it is a distinct profession to rescue from oblivion & to fix the sentiments & thoughts which visit all men more or less generally. That the contemplation of the unfinished picture may suggest its harmonious completion. Associate reverently, and as much as you can with your loftiest thoughts. Each thought that is welcomed and recorded is a nest egg—by the side of which more will be laid. Thoughts accidentally thrown together become a frame—in which more may be developed—& exhibited. Perhaps this is the main value of a habit of writing—of keeping a journal. That so we remember our best hours—& stimulate ourselves. My thoughts are my company— They have a certain individuality & separate existence—aye personality. Having by chance recorded a few disconnected thoughts and then brought them into juxtaposition—they suggest a whole new field in which it was possible to labor & to think. Thought begat thought.

The mother o' pearl tint is common in the winter sky ½ hour before sundown.

* * *

A[8] tree seen against other trees is a mere dark mass—but against the sky it has parts, has symmetry & expression.

Whatever wit has been produced on the spur of the moment will bear to

---

7. I. e., naturally occurring wooded areas or meadows resembling artificial parks.

8. January 26, 1852.

be reconsidered & reformed with phlegm. The arrow had best not be loosely shot. The most transient & passing remark—must be reconsidered by the writer—made sure & warranted—as if the earth had rested on its axle to back it,—and all the natural forces lay behind it. The writer must direct his sentences as carefully & leisurely as the marks-man his rifle—who shoots sitting & with a rest—with patent sights & conical balls beside. He must not merely seem to speak the truth. He must really speak it. If you foresee that a part of your essay will topple down after the lapse of time, throw it down now. yourself.

The thousand fine points & tops of the trees delight me—they are the plumes & standards & bayonets of a host that march to victory over the earth. The trees are handsome towards the heavens—as well as up their boles—they are good for other things than boards & shingles.

Obey the spur of the moment. These accumulated it is that makes the impulse & the impetus of the life of genius.— These are the spongioles or rootlets by which its trunk is fed. If you neglect the moments—if you cut off your fibrous roots—what but a languishing life is to be expected. Let the spurs of countless moments goad us incessantly into life.

* * *

Let all things give way to the impulse of expression. It is the bud unfolding— The perennial spring. As well stay the spring. Who shall resist the thaw?

What if all the ponds were shallow!—would it not react on the minds of men? If there were no physical deeps. I thank God that he made this pond deep & pure—for a symbol.

The word is well naturalized or rooted that can be traced back to a celtic originnal. It is like getting out stumps & fat pine roots.

While men believe in the infinite some ponds will be thought bottomless.

In winter we will think brave & hardy—& most native thoughts— Then the tender summer birds are flown.

In few countries do they enjoy so fine a contrast of summer & winter— we really have four seasons. each incredible to the other. Winter cannot be mistaken for summer here. Though I see the boat turned up on the shore & half buried under snow—as I walk over the invisible river—summer is far away. with its rustling reeds. It only suggests the want of thrift—the carelessness of its owner.

Nature never indulges in exclamations—never says Ah! or alas! She is not of French descent. She is a plain writer uses few gestures—does not add to her verbs—uses few adverbs. uses no expletives. I find that I use many words for the sake of emphasis—which really add nothing to the force of my sentences—and they look relieved the moment I have cancelled these. Words by which I express my mood, my conviction, rather than the simple truth.

Yesterday though warm it was clear enough for water & windows to sparkle.

*   *   *

I[9] do not know but thoughts written down thus in a journal might be printed in the same form with greater advantage—than if the related ones were brought together into separate essays. They are now allied to life—& are seen by the reader not to be far fetched— It is more simple—less artful— I feel that in the other case I should have no proper frame for my sketches. Mere facts & names & dates communicate more than we suspect— Whether the flower looks better in the nosegay—than in the meadow where it grew—& we had to wet our feet to get it! Is the scholastic air any advantage?

Jan 28

Perhaps I can never find so good a setting for my thoughts as I shall thus have taken them out of. The crystal never sparkles more brightly than in the cavern. The world have always loved best the fable with the moral. The children could read the fable alone—the grown up read both. The truth so told has the best advantages of the most abstract statement—for it is not the less universally applicable. Where also will you ever find the true cement for your thoughts? How will you ever rivet them together without leaving the marks of the file?

Yet Plutarch did not so— Montaigne[1] did not so. Men have written travels in this form—but perhaps no man's daily life has been rich enough to be journalized. Our life should be so active and progressive as to be a journey— Our meals should all be of journey-cake & hasty pudding. We should be more alert—see the sun rise—not keep fashionable hours— Enter a house our own house as a Khan—a caravansery. At noon I did not dine I ate my journey-cake. I quenched my thirst at a spring or a brook. As I sat at the table the hospitality was so perfect & the repast so sumptuous that I seemed to be breaking my fast upon a bank in the midst of an arduous journey—that the water seemed to be a living spring—the napkins grass, the conversation free as the winds. & the servants that waited on us were our simple desires.— Cut off from Pilpay[2] & AEsop the moral alone at the bottom—would that content you?

There will be no more rambling through the aisles of the wood, with occasional vistas through which you see the pond.

In those days when how to get my living honestly with freedom left for my proper pursuits, was a question which vexed me even more than it does now—I used to see a large box by the RR 6 feet long by 3 wide, in which the workmen locked up their tools at night— And it suggested to me that every man who was hard pushed might get him such a one for a dollar,

---

9. January 27, 1852.
1. Greek biographer, historian, and moral philosopher (A.D. 46?–120?); and French essayist (1533–92), respectively. Montaigne modelled his *Essays* on Plutarch's moral history and treatises.
2. Supposed to have been the author of a collection of Sanskrit fables, the *Hitopadesa*.

and having bored a few auger holes in it to admit the air at least—get into it when it rained and at night, & so have freedom in his mind and in his soul be free. This did not seem the worst alternative nor by any means a despicable resource. You could sit up as late as you pleased. & you would not have any creditor dogging you for rent. I should not be in a bad box. Many a man is harassed to death to pay the rent of a larger and more luxurious box—who would not have frozen to death in such a box as this. I should not be in so bad a box as many a man is in now.

* * *

The[3] entertaining a single thought of a certain elevation makes all men of one religion. It is always some base alloy that creates the distinction of sects— Thought greets thought over the widest gulfs of time with unerring free-masonry. I know for instance that Sadi[4] entertained once identically the same thought that I do—and thereafter I can find no essential difference between Sadi and myself. He is not Persian—he is not ancient—he is not strange to me. By the identity of his thought with mine he still survives. It makes no odds what atoms serve us. Sadi possessed no greater privacy or individuality than is thrown open to me. He had no more interior & essential & sacred self than can come naked into my thought this moment. Truth and a true man is something essentially public not private. If Sadi were to come back to claim a *personal* indentity with the historical Sadi he would find there were too many of us—he could not get a skin that would contain us all. The symbol of a personal identity preserved in this sense is a mummy from the Catacombs—a whole skin it may but no life within it. By living the life of a man is made common property. By sympathy with Sadi I have embowelled him. In his thoughts I have a sample of *him* a slice from his core—which makes it unimportant where certain bones which the thinker once employed may lie—but I could not have got this without being equally entitled to it with himself. The difference between any man and that posterity amid whom he is famous is too insignificant to sanction that he should be set up again in any world as distinct from them.

Methinks I can be as intimate with the essence of an ancient worthy as, so to speak, he was with himself.

I only know myself as a human entity—the scene, so to speak, of thoughts & affections—and am sensible of a certain doubleness by which I can stand as remote from myself as from another. However intense my experience— I am conscious of the presence & criticism of a part of me which as it were is not a part of me—but spectator sharing no experience, but taking note of it—and that is no more I than it is you.— When the play—it may be the tragedy—is over, the spectator goes his way. It was a kind of fiction— a work of the imagination—so far as he was concerned. A man *may* be

3. August 8, 1852.
4. Muslih-ud-Din (Saadi) (1184?–1291), famous Persian poet.

affected by a theatrical exhibition; On the other hand he *may not* be affected by an actual event which appears to concern him never so much.

*   *   *

Pm[5] to Walden.

Storm drawing to a close—crickets sound much louder after the rain in this cloudy weather. They are beginning to dig potatoes in earnest. Hips of the early roses are reddening. I have not seen a rose for a week or two. Lower leaves of the smooth sumach are red. Hear chic-a-day-day-day—& crows— But for music reduced almost to the winter quire. Young partridges ⅔ grown burst away. Globular galls on young oaks green on one side red on the other. Elatina (?) Americana   Small crypta in Walden Pond   Paddled *round* the pond— The shore is composed of a belt of smooth rounded white stones like paving stones a rod or two in width—excepting 1 or 2 short sand beaches—and is so steep that much of the way a single leap will carry you into water over your head. It is no where muddy & & the bottom is not to be touched, scarcely even seen again, except for the transparency of the water till it rises on the other side   A casual observer would say that there were no weeds at all in it, and of noticeable plants a closer scrutiny detects only a few small hearts leaves &—potamogetons—& perchance a water target or two—which yet even a bather might not perceive.— Both fishes and plants are clean & bright like the element they live in. Viewed from a hill top it is blue in the depths & green in the shallows—but from a boat it is seen to be a uniform dark green— I can remember when it was 4 or 5 feet higher—also a foot or two lower—than when I lived there   There is a narrow sand bar running into it in one place with very deep water on one side—on which I boiled a kettle of chowder at least 6 rods from the main shore more than 20 years ago—which it has not been possible to do since—and my friends used to listen with incredulity when I told them that a year or two later I was accustomed to fish from a boat in a deep cove in the woods, long since converted into a meadow—but since I left it the pond has risen steadily for a year past ap.[6] unaffected by drouth or rain—& now in the summer of 52 is as high as it was 20 years ago—& fishing goes on again in the meadow—& yet the water shed by the surrounding hills is insignificant in amount & this overflow must be referred to causes which affect the deep springs— The surrounding hills are from 50 to a hundred & in one place perhaps 200 feet high, covered with wood.

*   *   *

Nov 2nd

Tall buttercups—red Clover—houstonias   Polygonum aviculare still. Those handsome red buds on often red-barked twigs with some red leaves

---

5. August 27, 1852.   6. Apparently.

still left appear to be blueberry buds. The prinos berries also now attract me in the scarcity of leaves—its own all gone—its berries are apparently a brighter red for it— The month of chicadees & new swolen buds.— At long intervals I see or hear a robin still.

To Walden.

In the latter part of Oct. the skaters & water bugs entirely disappear from the surface of the pond & then & in november, when the weather is perfectly calm—it is almost absolutely as smooth as glass. This afternoon a 3 days rain storm is drawing to an end. though still overcast— The air is quite still but misty—& from time to time mizzling—and the pond is very smooth & its surface difficult to distinguish. though it no longer reflects the *bright* tints of autumn—but sombre colors only.— Calm at the end of a storm. except here and there a slight glimmer or dimple—as if a few skaters which had escaped the frosts were still collected there—or a faint breeze then struck—or a few rain drops fell there, or perchance the surface being remarkably smooth betrayed by circling dimples where a spring welled up from below. I paddled gently toward one of those places & was surprised to find myriads of small perch about 5 inches long sporting there one after another rising to the surface & dimpling it—leaving bubbles on it. They were very handsome as they surrounded the boat with their distinct tranverse stripes—a rich brown color

There were many such schools in the pond—as it were improving the short season before the ice would close their window. When I approached them suddenly with noise—they made a sudden plash & rippling with their tails in fright & then took refuge in the depths

Slate colored snow birds? with a faint note. Suddenly the wind rose the mist increased & the waves rose and still the perch leaped—but much higher half out of water a hundred black points 3 inches long at once above the surface.

The pond dark before was now a glorious & indescribable blue—mixed with dark—perhaps the opposite side of the wave—a sort of changeable or watered silk blue, more cerulean if possible than the sky itself which was now seen overhead— It required a certain division of the sight however to discern this.—like the colors on a steel sword blade The leaves which are not withered—whose tints are still fresh & bright are now remarked in sheltered places Plucked quite a handsome nose gay from the S side of Heywards' peak. W*ht* & blue stemmed golden rods—asters, undulatus & ?

I do not know whether the perch amuse them selves thus more in the fall than at any other time. In such transparent & apparently bottomless water their swimming impresses the beholder as a kind of flight or hovering like a compact flock of birds passing below one—just beneath his level on the right or left. What a singular experience must be theirs in their winter quarters—their long night—expecting when the sun will open their shutters

If you look discerningly so as to see the reflection only—you see a most glorious light blue in comparison with which the original dark green of the opposite side of the waves is but muddy.

* * *

Jan 6th   Walden froze over apparently last night. It is but little more than an inch thick—& 2 or 3 square rods by Hubbards shore are still open. A dark transparent ice—   It would not have frozen entirely over as it were in one night or may be a little more and yet have been so thin next the shore as well as in the middle, if it had not been so late in the winter, & so ready to freeze. It is a dark transparent ice. But will not bear me without much cracking. As I walked along the edge I started out 3 little pickerel no bigger than my finger from *close* to the shore which went wiggling into deeper water like bloodsuckers or pollywogs. When I lie down on it and examine it closely, I find that the greater part of the bubbles which I had thought were within its own substance are against its under surface, and that they are continually rising up from the bottom.   perfect spheres apparently & very beautiful & clear in which I see my face through this thin ice (perhaps 1 & ⅛ inch) from ¹⁄₃₀ of an inch in diameter or a mere point up to ⅛ of an inch. There are 30 or 40 of these at least to every square inch—   These probably when heated by the sun make it crack & whoop— There are also within the substance of the ice oblong perpendicular bubbles ½ inch long more or less by about ¹⁄₃₀ of an inch & these are commonly widest at the bottom?[7]   —or oftener separate minute spherical bubbles of equal or smaller diameter one directly above another like a string of beads— perhaps the first stage of the former—   But these internal bubbles are not nearly so numerous as those in the water beneath. It may be 24 hours since the ice began to form decidedly.

I see on the sandy bottom a few inches beneath—the white cases of Cadis worms made of the white quartz sand or pebbles—   And the bottom is very much creased or furrowed where some creature has travelled about and doubled on its tracks—perhaps the cadis worm, for I find one or two of the same in the furrows—though the latter are deep & broad for them to make.

* * *

Jan 27

Trench says a wild man is a *willed* man[8]   Well then a man of will who does what he wills—or wishes—a man of hope and of the future tense— for not only the obstinate is willed but far more the constant & persevering— The obstinate man properly speaking is one who will not. The perseverance of the saints is positive willedness—not a mere passive willingness—   The fates are wild for they *will*—& the Almighty is wild above all—.   As fate is.

7. Thoreau made a drawing of the oblong bubble structure at this point in the manuscript.
8. Richard Chenevix Trench (1807–86), Irish author, philologist, and archbishop of Dublin; from his *On the Study of Words* (1852).

What are our fields but felds or felled woods—they bear a more recent name than the woods suggesting that previously the earth was covered with woods.

Always in the new country a field is a clearing.

* * *

Sunday March 20th

8 Am   Via Walden Goose Flints & Beaver Ponds & the valley of Stony Brook to the south end of Lincoln—   A rather cool and breezy morning which was followed by milder day.

We go listening for early birds—with bread & cheese for our dinners * * * It was a question whether we should not go to Fair Haven to see the gulls &c. I notice the downy-swaddled plants now & in the fall, the fragrant life everlasting & the rib-wort—innocents born in a cloud. Those algae I saw the other day in John Hosmers ditch were the most like sea weed of anything I have seen in the county—they made me look at the whole earth as a sea-shore.   reminded me of Nereids—sea nymphs triton—Proteus[9] &c— made the ditches fabulate in an older than the arrowheaded character. Better learn this strange character which nature speaks to day—than the Sanscrit— books in the brooks—   Saw a large dead water bug in walden. I suspect he came out alive. Walden is melting apace—   It has a canal 2 rods wide along the northerly side & the W end—wider at the E end—Yet after running round from W to E it does not keep the S shore but crosses in front of the deep cove in a broad crack to where it started—by the ice ground

It is glorious to behold the life & joy of this ribbon of water sparkling in the sun—   The wind blows eastward over the opaque ice—unusually hard owing to the recent severe though transient cold—all watered or waved like a tesselated floor—a figured carpet—   Yet dead—yet in vain till it slides on to the living water surface where it raises a myriad brilliant sparkles on the bare face of the pond—and expression of glee—of youth—of spring— As if it spoke the joy of the fishes within it—& of the sands on its shore— A silvery sheen like the scales of a leuciscus—   As if it were all one active fish in the spring. It is the contrast between life & death—   There is the difference between winter and spring. The bared face of the pond sparkles with joy. How handsome the curves which the edge of the ice makes an-swering somewhat to those of the shore but more regular—sweeping entirely round the pond—as if defined by a vast bold sweep—

* * *

Dec 22nd 53

A slight whitening of snow last evening—the 2nd whitening of the winter—just enough to spoil the skating now 10 days old on the ponds—

---

9. In Greek mythology the Nereids, or sea nymphs, were fifty daughters of the sea god Nereus; Triton and Proteus were minor sea gods, the latter capable of transforming himself into various natural forms.

Walden skimmed over in the widest part, but some acres still open—will prob. freeze entirely tonight if this weather holds.

Surveying the last 3 days— They have not yielded much that I am aware of— All I find is old bound marks—and the slowness & dullness of farmers reconfirmed— They even complain that I walk too fast for them. Their legs have become stiff from toil. This coarse & hurried out door work compels me to live grossly or be inattentive to my diet—that is the worst of it. Like work—like diet that I find is the rule. Left to my chosen pursuits I should never drink tea nor coffee, nor eat meat. The diet of any class or generation is the natural result of its employment and locality. It is remarkable how unprofitable it is for the most part to talk with farmers. They commonly stand on their good-behavior & attempt to moralize or philosophize in a serious conversation— Sports-men & loafers are better company. For society a man must not be too *good* or well disposed to spoil his natural disposition— The bad are frequently good enough to let you see how bad they are—but the good as frequently endeavor get between you and themselves.— I have dined out 5 times—& tea'd once within a week— 4 times there was tea on the dinner table always meat but once—once baked beans—always pie but no puddings. I suspect tea had taken the place of cider with farmers I am reminded of Haydn the painter's[1] experience when he went about painting the nobility— I go about to the houses of the farmers & squires in like manner— This is my portrait painting—when I would fain be employed on higher subjects. I have offered myself much more earnestly as a lecturer than a surveyor— Yet I do not get any employment as a lecturer was not invited to lecture once last winter and only once (without pay) this winter— but I can get surveying enough—which a hundred others in this county can do as well as I—though it is not boasting much to say that a hundred others in N. England cannot lecture as well as I on my themes. But they who do not make the highest demand on you shall rue it— It is because they make a low demand on themselves. All the while that they use only your humbler faculties—your higher unemployed faculties—like an invisible cimetar are cutting them in twain. Woe be to the generation that lets any higher faculty in its midst go unemployed— that is to deny god & know him not—& he accordingly will know not of them.

✳   ✳   ✳

That[2] sand foliage! It convinces me that nature is still in her youth— That florid fact about which Mythology merely mutters. That the very soil can fabulate as well as you or I. It stretches forth its baby fingers on every side. Fresh curls spring forth from its bald brow— There is nothing in-

1. Benjamin Robert Haydon (1786–1846), ambitious English painter of historical and religious subjects, known for his portraits of William Wordsworth and John Keats, among others. Thoreau alludes to his *Autobiography and Journals* (1853).
2. February 5, 1854.

organic. This earth is not then a mere fragment of dead history—strata upon strata like the leaves of a book—an object for a museum & an Antiquarian but living poetry like the leaves of a tree— —not a fossil earth—but a living specimen. You may melt your metals & cast them into the most beautiful moulds you can— They will never excite me like the forms which this molten earth flows out into— The very earth—as well as the institutions upon it—is plastic like potters clay in the hands of the artist. These florid heaps lie along the bank like the slag of a furnace— Showing that nature is in full-blast within. but there is No admittance except on business. Ye dead & alive preachers Ye have no business here. Ye will enter it only as your tomb

I fear only lest my expressions may not be extravagant enough—may not wander far enough beyond the narrow limits of our ordinary insight & faith— So as to be adequate to the truth of which I have been convinced. I desire to speak somewhere without bounds in order that I may attain to an expression in some degree adequate to truth of which I have been convinced— From a man in a waking moment to men in their waking moments. Wandering toward the more distant boundaries of wider pastures— Nothing is so truly bounded & obedient to law as music— Yet nothing so surely breaks all petty & narrow bonds.

Whenever I hear any music I fear that I may have spoken tamely & within bounds. And I am convinced that I cannot exaggerate enough even to lay the foundation of a true expression— As for books & the adequateness of their statements to the truth—they are as the tower of Babel[3] to the sky.

* * *

Feb 19

Many College text books which were a weakness & a stumbling block— when *studied* I have since read a little in with pleasure & profit. For several weeks the fall has seemed far behind—spring comparatively near— Yet I cannot say that there is any positive sign of spring yet—only we feel that we are sloping toward it. The sky has sometimes a warmth in it colors more like summer. A few birds have possibly strayed northward—further than they have wintered.

Pm to Fair Haven by river, back by RR. Though the wind is cold, the earth feels the heat of the sun higher in the heavens & melts in ploughed fields. The willow twigs rise out of the ice beside the river the silvery down of each catkin just peeping from under each scale in some places—the work probably of last falls sun—like a mouse peeping from under its covert. I incline to walk now in swamps & on the river & ponds—where I cannot walk in summer— I am struck by the greenness of the green briar of this season still covering the alders &c 12 feet high & full of shining & fresh

---

3. In Genesis 11.1–9, God prevents the completion of this tower by rendering the language shared by its builders incomprehensible to them.

berries— The greenness of the sassafrass shoots makes a similar impression.

The large moths ap.[4] love the neighborhood of water—& are wont to suspend their coccoons over the edge of the meadow & river—places more or less inaccessible to men at least. I saw a button bush with what at first sight looked like the open pods of the locust or of the water asclepias attached— They were the light ash-colored coccoons of the A. Promethea 4 or 5—with the completely withered & faded leaves wrapt around them— & so artfully and admirably secured to the twigs by fine silk wound round the leaf-stalk & the twig—which last add nothing to its strength being deciduous, but aid its deception— They are taken at a little distance for a few curled & withered leaves left on. Though the particular twigs on which you find some coccoons may never or very rarely retain any leaves the maple for instance—there are enough leaves left on other shrubs & trees to warrant their adopting this disguise. Yet it is startling to think that the inference has in this case been drawn by some mind that as most other plants retain some leaves the walker will suspect these also to.

Each and all such disguises & other resources remind us that not some poor worms instinct merely, as we call it, but the mind of the universe rather which we share has been intended upon each particular object—All the wit in the world was brought to bear on each case to secure its end— It was long ago in a full senate of all intellects determined how coccoons had best be suspended—kindred mind with mine that admires & approves decided it so. * * *   The snow not only reveals a track but sometimes hands it down—to the ice that succeeds it. The sled track which I saw in the slight snow over the ice here Feb. 2nd—though we have had many snows since—& now there is no snow at all—is still perfectly marked on the ice.

Much study a weariness of the flesh! eh? But did not they intend that we should read & ponder—who covered the whole earth with alphabets— primers or bibles coarse or fine print. The very debris of the cliffs—the [stivers] of the rocks are covered with geographic lichens—no surface is permitted to be bare long— As by an inevitable decree we have come to times at last when our very waste paper is printed. Was not he who created lichens the abetter of Cadmus[5] when he invented letters. Types almost arrange themselves into words & sentences as dust arranges itself under the magnet. Print! it is a close-hugging lichen that forms on a favorable surface— which paper offers— The linen gets itself wrought with paper—that the song of the shirt may be printed on it— Who placed us with eyes between a microscopic and a telescopic world? * * *

I wait till sundown on Fair Haven to hear it[6] boom but am disappointed— though I hear much slight crackling— but as for the previous cracking—

4. Apparently.
5. In Greek mythology, the founder of the city of Thebes, who is said to have introduced the

Phoenician alphabet to Greece.
6. I.e., Fair Haven Pond, about one-half mile southwest of Walden Pond.

it is so disruptive & produces such a commotion that it extends itself through snow drifts six inches deep, and is even more distinct there than in bare ice even to the sharpest angle of its forking. Saw an otter track near Walden.

* * *

In[7] correcting my mss—which I do with sufficient phlegm. I find that I invariably turn out much that is good along with the bad, which it is then impossible for me to distinguish—so much for keeping bad company— but after the lapse of time having purified the main body & thus created a distinct standard for comparison—I can review the rejected sentence & easily detect those which deserve to be readmitted.

Pm to Walden via R W E's[8] I am surprised to see how bare Minott's hillside is already— It is already spring there & Minott is puttering outside in the sun— How wise in his grandfather to select such a site for a house— The summers he has lived have been so much longer.

How pleasant the calm season & the warmth—(The sun is even like a burning glass on my back—) & the sight & sound of melting snow running down the hill. I look in among the withered grass blades for some starting greenness— I listen to hear the first blue-bird in the soft air. I hear the dry clucking of hens which dare come abroad.

The ice at Walden is softened—the skating is gone—with a stick you can loosen it to the depth of an inch or the first freezing & turn it up in cakes. Yesterday you could skate here—now only *close* to the *south* shore. I notice the redness of the andromeda leaves—but not so much as once— The sand foliage is now in its prime.

March 2nd

A Corner man tells me that Witherel has seen a blue-bird & Martial Miles thought that he heard one. I doubt it. It may have been given to Witherel to see the first blue bird—so much has been with-holden from him[9]

What produces the peculiar softness of the air yesterday & today—as if it were the air of the south suddenly pillowed amid our wintry hills— We have suddenly a different sky—a dif. atmosphere. It is as if the subtlest possible soft vapor were diffused through the atmosphere Warm air has come to us from the S, but charged with moisture—which will yet distill in rain or congeal into snow & hail—

The sand foliage is vital in its form—reminding me what are called the vitals of the animal body— I am not sure that its arteries are even hollow They are rather meandering channels with remarkably distinct sharp edges—formed instantaneously as by magic— How rapidly & per-

---

7. March 1, 1854; "mss" is the abbreviation for "manuscripts."
8. Ralph Waldo Emerson's.
9. Thoreau added this sentence later. Both

Witherel and Miles were local fishermen and ne'er-do-wells; the Corner (or Nine Acre Corner) was a relatively populous area in southern Middlesex county.

fectly it organizes itself— The material must be sufficiently cohesive. I suspect that a certain portion of clay is necessary. Mixed Sand & clay being saturated with melted ice & snow—the most liquid portion flows downward through the mass forming for itself instantly a perfect canal—using the best materials the mass—affords for its banks— It digs & builds it in a twinkling— The less fluid portions clog the artery change its course and form thick stems & leaves— The lobe principle—lobe of the ear (labor lapsus?)

On the outside all the life of the earth is expressed in animal or vegetable—but make a deep cut in it & you find it vital— You find in the very sands an anticipation of the vegetable leaf— No wonder then that plants grow & spring in it— The atoms have already learned the law— Let a vegetable sap convey it upwards and you have a vegetable leaf— No wonder that the earth expresses itself outwardly in leaves—which labors with the idea thus inwardly— The overhanging leaf sees here its prototype— The earth is pregnant with law—

The various shades of this sand foliage are very agreeable to the eye. including all the different colors which iron assumes—brown—grey—yellowish reddish—& clay-color. Perhaps it produces the greater effect by arranged the sands of the same color—side by side—bringing them together.

*   *   *

Saw[1] several yellow red poles—(sylvia patechia) on the willows by the Hubbard bridge Am not sure I heard their note— May have mistaken it formerly for the Pine warbler. Its chestnut crown would distinguish it. Hazel the *very first* male open.

I find that I can criticise my composition best when I stand at a little distance from it—when I do not see it, for instance—. I make a little chapter of contents which enables me to recall it page by page to my mind—& judge it more impartially when my MSS is out of the way. The distraction of surveying enables me rapidly to take new points of view. A day or two surveying is equal to a journey.

Pickerel have darted in shallows for nearly a week.

Some poets mature early & die young. Their fruits have a delicious flavor like strawberries—but do not keep till fall or winter— Others are slower in coming to their growth Their fruits maybe less delicious but are a more lasting food & are so hardened by the sun of summer & the coolness [o]f autumn that they keep sound over winter— The first are June eatings—early but soon withering—the last are russets which last till June again.

*   *   *

Wednesday Aug 9th   To Boston
Walden published. Elder berries. Waxwork yellowing

1. P.M., April 8, 1854.

REVIEWS AND
CRITICISM

Reviews and
Posthumous Assessments

In addition to "Resistance to Civil Government," *Aesthetic Papers* contained a few poems and eleven other articles on social, aesthetic, philosophical, and scientific topics, including an essay on "War" by Ralph Waldo Emerson, another on "Language" by Elizabeth Peabody, the editor, and "Main-street," a sketch by Nathaniel Hawthorne. Although planned as the first number of a periodical to be published irregularly "whenever a sufficient quantity of valuable matter shall have accumulated," it was also the last.

Walden seems to have been well-received and widely reviewed, thanks to vigorous promotion by the publishers, Ticknor and Fields. Recent scholarship lists ninety-three contemporary reviews, and reports that of those located the majority were "strongly favorable." (See Bradley P. Dean and Gary Scharnhorst, "The Contemporary Reception of *Walden*," *Studies in the American Renaissance* 1990: 293–328.) But the book sold only modestly and was not reprinted until after Thoreau's death in 1862.

Lengthy extracts from *Walden* in the reviews by Briggs and Eliot below have been omitted.

[Review of *Aesthetic Papers*]†

Here is a pleasant pamphlet to carry up into the country, and read under the elm-trees. It contains many things to admire—some to smile at—and a few that to plain understandings will appear absurd.

* * *

We must dismiss Mr. Thoreau with an earnest prayer that he may become a better subject in time, or else take a trip to France, and preach his doctrine of "Resistance to Civil Government" to the red republicans.

[Review of *Aesthetic Papers*]‡

The purpose this publication (which is to be followed by others, in series) is declared to be "to assemble upon high aesthetic ground (away from the regions of strife) writers of different schools; that antagonistic views of philosophy, etc., may be brought together, and a white radiance

† From *Boston Daily Courier* 19 June 1849: 2.   ‡ From *The Literary World* 5 (29 Sept. 1849): 269–70.

of love and wisdom be evolved from the union of many-colored rays, that shall cultivate an harmonious, intellectual, and moral life in our country."

With this design, the Editor, in the introduction, gives a definition of the "Aesthetic element," which, in her view, is "neither a theory of the beautiful nor a philosophy of art, but a component and indivisible part in all human creations, which are not mere works of necessity; in other words, which are based on idea, as distinguished from appetite."

*   *   *

We have here, indeed, true, and new, and false, and contradictory views of life, morals, and religion; but how they coalesce in a region above strife we are at a loss to see.

There is, for instance, an article on "The Abuse of Representative Government,"[1] wisely teaching the supremacy of the machine of government, when once the people have constructed it by their votes; and inculcating the duty of submission to it, to the exclusion of the disgraceful system of "instruction"—which is followed by another on "Resistance to Civil Government," whose author would make it every man's duty to refuse allegiance to the state, whenever any of its laws violate his conscience. He has carried out his theory in his own case, and been shut up in prison for refusing to pay his "poll-tax." He appeals to the New Testament, even; by which he means, of course, that part of it which may be made to coincide with his own opinions, and not those ugly precepts about the paying of tribute, and submission to the powers that be. This article is about as fit in a volume of "Aesthetic Papers" as would be "the voyage of Gulliver."

[GAMALIEL BAILEY?]

[Review of *Walden*]†

In its narrative, this book is unique, in its philosophy quite Emersonian. It is marked by genius of a certain order, but just as strongly, by pride of intellect. It contains many acute observations on the follies of mankind, but enough of such follies to show that its author has his full share of the infirmities of human nature, without being conscious of it. By precept and example he clearly shows how very little is absolutely necessary to the subsistence of a man, what a Robinson Crusoe life he may lead in Massachusetts, how little labor he need perform, if he will but reduce his wants to the philosophical standard, and how much time he may then have for meditation and study. To go out and squat, all alone, by a pretty pond in

1. By Stephen Higginson Perkins (1804–77), a Boston merchant [*Editor*].   † From *National Era* 8 (28 Sept. 1854):155.

the woods, dig, lay the foundation of a little cabin, and put it up, with borrowed tools, furnish it, raise corn, beans, and potatoes, and do one's own cooking, hermit like, so that the total cost of the whole building, furnishing, purchasing necessaries, and living for eight months, shall not exceed forty or fifty dollars, may do for an experiment, by a highly civilized man, with Yankee versatility, who has had the full benefit of the best civilization of the age. All men are not "up to" everything. But, if they were, if they all had the universal genius of the "Yankee nation," how long would they remain civilized, by squatting upon solitary duck-ponds, es-chewing matrimony, casting off all ties of family, each one setting his wits to work to see how little he could do with, and how much of that little he could himself accomplish? At the end of eight months, Mr. Thoreau might remain a ruminating philosopher, but he would have few but ruminating animals to write books for.

But, with all its extravagances, its sophisms, and its intellectual pride, the book is acute and suggestive, and contains passages of great beauty.

ELIZABETH BARSTOW STODDARD

[Review of *Walden*]†

If my limits would allow, the Book I would most like to expatiate upon, would be Thoreau's *Walden, or Life in the Woods*, published by Ticknor and Fields, Boston. It is the result of a two or three years' sojourn in the woods, and it is a most minute history of Thoreau's external life, and internal speculation. It is the latest effervescence of the peculiar school, at the head of which stands Ralph Waldo Emerson. Of *Walden*, Emerson says, that Thoreau has cornered nature in it. Several years ago Thoreau sought the freedom of the woods, and built him a little house with his two hands, on the margin of Walden Pond, near Concord, Massachusetts. There he con-templated, on "cornered" nature, and hoed beans, determined, as he said, to know them. Notwithstanding an apparent contempt for utility, he seems a sharp accountant, and not a little interest is attached to his bills of expense, they are so ludicrously small. Coarse bread, occasional molasses and rice, now and then a fish taken from Walden Pond, and philosophically matured vegetables, (he sold his beans) were his fare. His ideas of beauty are positive, but limited. The world of art is beyond his wisdom. Individualism is the altar at which he worships. Philanthropy is an opposite term, and he does not scruple to affirm that Philanthropy and he are two. The book is full of talent, curious and interesting. I recommend it as a study to all fops, male and female.

† From *Daily Alta California* 8 Oct. 1854: 2.

A. P. PEABODY†

Critical Notice

The economical details and calculations in this book are more curious than useful; for the author's life in the woods was on too narrow a scale to find imitators. But in describing his hermitage and his forest life, he says so many pithy and brilliant things, and offers so many piquant, and, we may add, so many just, comments on society as it is, that his book is well worth the reading, both for its actual contents and its suggestive capacity.

CHARLES FREDERICK BRIGGS‡

A Yankee Diogenes

The New England character is essentially anti-Diogenic; the Yankee is too shrewd not to comprehend the advantages of living in what we call the world; there are no bargains to be made in the desert, nobody to be taken advantage of in the woods, while the dwellers in tubs and shanties have slender opportunities of bettering their condition by barter. When the New Englander leaves his home, it is not for the pleasure of living by himself; if he is migratory in his habits, it is not from his fondness for solitude, nor from any impatience he feels at living in a crowd. Where there are most men, there is, generally, most money, and there is where the strongest attractions exist for the genuine New Englander. A Yankee Diogenes is a *lusus*,[1] and we feel a peculiar interest in reading the account which an oddity of that kind gives of himself. The name of Thoreau has not a New England sound; but we believe that the author of *Walden* is a genuine New Englander, and of New England antecedents and education. Although he plainly gives the reasons for publishing his book, at the outset, he does not clearly state the causes that led him to live the life of a hermit on the shore of Walden Pond. But we infer from his volume that his aim was the very remarkable one of trying to be something, while he lived upon nothing; in opposition to the general rule of striving to live upon something, while doing nothing. Mr. Thoreau probably tried the experiment long enough to test its success, and then fell back again into his normal condition. But he does not tell us such was the case. He was happy enough to get back among the good people of Concord, we have no doubt; for although he paints his shanty-life in rose-colored tints, we do not believe he liked it, else why not stick to it? We

† From *North American Review* 79 (Oct. 1854): 536.
‡ From *Putnam's Monthly Magazine* 4 (Oct. 1854): 443–48.
1. An oddity or freak of nature. Diogenes (c. 400–325 B.C.), member of a Greek philosophical sect, the Cynics, who stressed stoic self-sufficiency and rejected luxury and conventionalism; he lived in poverty and is said to have inhabited an earthenware tub [*Editor*].

have a mistrust of the sincerity of the St. Simon Stylites',[2] and suspect that they come down from their pillars in the night-time, when nobody is looking at them. Diogenes placed his tub where Alexander would be sure of seeing it, and Mr. Thoreau ingenuously confesses that he occasionally went out to dine, and when the society of woodchucks and chipping-squirrels were insufficient for his amusement, he liked to go into Concord and listen to the village gossips in the stores and taverns. Mr. Thoreau informs us that he lived alone in the woods, by the shore of Walden Pond, in a shanty built by his own hands, a mile from any neighbor, two years and a half. What he did there besides writing the book before us, cultivating beans, sounding Walden Pond, reading Homer, baking johnny-cakes, studying Brahminical theology, listening to chipping-squirrels, receiving visits, and having high imaginations, we do not know. He gives us the results of his bean cultivation with great particularity, and the cost of his shanty; but the actual results of his two years and a half of hermit life he does not give. But there have been a good many lives spent and a good deal of noise made about them, too, from the sum total of whose results not half so much good could be extracted as may be found in this little volume. Many a man will find pleasure in reading it, and many a one, we hope, will be profited by its counsels. A tour in Europe would have cost a good deal more, and not have produced half as much. As a matter of curiosity, to show how cheaply a gentleman of refined tastes, lofty aspirations and cultivated intellect may live, even in these days of high prices, we copy Mr. Thoreau's account of his first year's operations; he did better, he informs us, the second year. The entire cost of his house, which answered all his purposes, and was as comfortable and showy as he desired, was $28 12½. But one cannot live on a house unless he rents it to somebody else, even though he be a philosopher and a believer in Vishnu. Mr. Thoreau felt the need of a little ready money, one of the most convenient things in the world to have by one, even before his house was finished.

"Wishing to earn ten or twelve dollars by some agreeable and honest method," he observes, "I planted about two acres and a half of light and sandy soil, chiefly with beans, but also a small part with potatoes and corn, peas and turnips." As he was a squatter, he paid nothing for rent, and as he was making no calculation for future crops, he expended nothing for manure so that the results of his farming will not be highly instructive to young agriculturists, nor be likely to be held up as excitements to farming pursuits by agricultural periodicals. * * *

* * * according to his figures it cost him twenty-seven cents a week to live, clothes included; and for this sum he lived healthily and happily, received a good many distinguished visitors, who, to humor his style, used to leave their names on a leaf or a chip, when they did not happen to find

---

2. Imitators of Saint Simeon Stylites (c. 390–459), a Syrian monk and reputed miracle-worker who lived on a column fifty feet high, from which he counseled and healed pilgrims [*Editor*].

him at home. But, it strikes us that all the knowledge which the "Hermit of Walden" gained by his singular experiment in living might have been done just as well, and as satisfactorily, without any experiment at all. We know what it costs to feed prisoners, paupers and soldiers; we know what the cheapest and most nutritious food costs, and how little it requires to keep up the bodily health of a full-grown man. A very simple calculation will enable any one to satisfy himself in regard to such points. and those who wish to live upon twenty-seven cents a week, may indulge in that pleasure. The great Abernethy's prescription for the attainment of perfect bodily health was, "live on sixpence a day and earn it." But that would be Sybaritic indulgence compared with Mr. Thoreau's experience, whose daily expenditure hardly amounted to a quarter of that sum. And he lived happily, too, though it don't exactly speak volumes in favor of his system to announce that he only continued his economical mode of life two years. If it was "the thing," why did he not continue it? But, if he did not always live like a hermit, squatting on other people's property, and depending upon chance perch and pickerel for his dinner, he lived enough by his own labor, and carried his system of economy to such a degree of perfection, that he tells us:

> "More than five years I maintained myself thus solely by the labor of my hands, and I found that working about six weeks in a year, I could meet all the expenses of living."

* * *

There is nothing of the mean or sordid in the economy of Mr. Thoreau, though to some his simplicity and abstemiousness may appear trivial and affected; he does not live cheaply for the sake of saving, nor idly to avoid labor; but, that he may live independently and enjoy his great thoughts; that he may read the Hindoo scriptures and commune with the visible forms of nature. We must do him the credit to admit that there is no mock sentiment, nor simulation of piety or philanthropy in his volume. He is not much of a cynic, and though we have called him a Yankee Diogenes, the only personage to whom he bears a decided resemblance is that good humored creation of Dickens, Mark Tapley, whose delight was in being jolly under difficulties.

* * *

There is much excellent good sense delivered in a very comprehensive and by no means unpleasant style in Mr. Thoreau's book, and let people think as they may of the wisdom or propriety of living after his fashion, denying oneself all the luxuries which the earth can afford, for the sake of leading a life of lawless vagabondage, and freedom from starched collars, there are but few readers who will fail to find profit and refreshment in his pages. Perhaps some practical people will think that a philosopher like Mr.

Thoreau might have done the world a better service by purchasing a piece of land, and showing how much it might be made to produce, instead of squatting on another man's premises, and proving how little will suffice to keep body and soul together. But we must allow philosophers, and all other men, to fulfil their missions in their own way. If Mr. Thoreau had been a practical farmer, we should not have been favored with his volume; his corn and cabbage would have done but little towards profiting us, and we might never have been the better for his labors. As it is, we see how much more valuable to mankind is our philosophical vagabond than a hundred sturdy agriculturists; any plodder may raise beans, but it is only one in a million who can write a readable volume.

✳   ✳   ✳

[LYDIA MARIA CHILD?]

[Review of *A Week on the Concord and Merrimack Rivers* and *Walden*]†

These books spring from a depth of thought which will not suffer them to be put by, and are written in a spirit in striking contrast with that which is uppermost in our time and country. Out of the heart of practical, hard-working, progressive New England comes these Oriental utterances. The life exhibited in them teaches us, much more impressively than any number of sermons could, that this Western activity of which we are so proud, these material improvements, this commercial enterprise, this rapid accumulation of wealth, even our external, associated philanthropic action, are very easily overrated. The true glory of the human soul is not to be reached by the most rapid travelling in car or steamboat, by the instant transmission of intelligence however far, by the most speedy accumulation of a fortune, and however efficient measures we may adopt for the reform of the intemperate, the emancipation of the enslaved, &c., it will avail little unless we are ourselves essentially noble enough to inspire those whom we would so benefit with nobleness. External bondage is trifling compared with the bondage of an ignoble soul. Such things are often said, doubtless, in pulpits and elsewhere, but the men who say them are too apt to live just with the crowd, and so their words come more and more to ring with a hollow sound.

It is refreshing to find in these books the sentiments of one man whose aim manifestly is to *live*, and not to waste his time upon the externals of living. Educated at Cambridge, in the way called liberal, he seems determined to make a liberal life of it, and not to become the slave of any calling, for the sake of earning a reputable livelihood or of being regarded as a useful member of society. He evidently considers it his first business to become

† From the *National Anti-Slavery Standard* 16 Dec. 1854: 3.

more and more a living, advancing soul, knowing that thus alone (though he desires to think as little as possible about that) can he be, in any proper sense, useful to others. Mr. Thoreau's view of life has been called selfish. His own words, under the head of "Philanthropy" in Walden, are the amplest defence against this charge, to those who can appreciate them. In a deeper sense than we commonly think, charity begins at home. The man who, with any fidelity, obeys his own genius, serves men infinitely more by so doing, becoming an encouragement, a strengthener, a fountain of inspiration to them, than if he were to turn aside from his path and exhaust his energies in striving to meet their superficial needs. As a thing by the way, aside from our proper work, we may seek to remove external obstacles from the path of our neighbours, but no man can help them much who makes that his main business, instead of seeking evermore, with all his energies, to reach the loftiest point which his imagination sets before him, thus adding to the stock of true nobleness in the world.

But suppose all men should pursue Mr. Thoreau's course, it is asked triumphantly, as though, then, we should be sure to go back to barbarism. Let it be considered, in the first place, that no man could pursue his course who was a mere superficial imitator, any more than it would be a real imitation of Christ if all men were to make it their main business to go about preaching the Gospel to each other. Is it progress toward barbarism to simplify one's outward life for the sake of coming closer to Nature and to the realm of ideas? Is it civilization and refinement to be occupied evermore with adding to our material conveniences, comforts and luxuries, to make ourselves not so much living members as dead tools of society, in some bank, shop, office, pulpit or kitchen? If men were to follow Mr. Thoreau's steps, by being more obedient to their loftiest instincts, there would, indeed, be a falling off in the splendour of our houses, in the richness of our furniture and dress, in the luxury of our tables, but how poor are these things in comparison with the new grandeur and beauty which would appear in the souls of men. What fresh and inspiring conversation should we have, instead of the wearisome gossip which now meets us at every turn. Men toil on, wearing out body or soul, or both, that they may accumulate a needless amount of the externals of living; that they may win the regard of those no wiser than themselves; their natures become warped and hardened to their pursuits; they get fainter and fainter glimpses of the glory of the world, and, by and by, comes into their richly-adorned parlours some wise and beautiful soul, like the writer of these books, who, speaking from the fullness of his inward life, makes their luxuries appear vulgar, showing that, in a direct way, he has obtained the essence of that which his entertainers have been vainly seeking for at such a terrible expense.

It seems remarkable, that these books have received no more adequate notice in our Literary Journals. But the class of scholars are often as blind as others to any new elevation of soul. In Putnam's Magazine, Mr. Thoreau is spoken of as an oddity, as the Yankee Diogenes, as though the really ridiculous oddity were not in us of the "starched shirt-collar" rather than in this devotee of Nature and Thought. Some have praised the originality and profound sympathy with which he views natural objects. We might as well stop with praising Jesus for the happy use he has made of the lilies in the field. The fact of surpassing interest for us is the simple grandeur of Mr. Thoreau's position—a position open to us all, and of which this sympathy with Nature is but a single result. This is seen in the less descriptive, more purely thoughtful passages, such as that upon Friendship in the "Wednesday" of the "Week," and in those upon "Solitude," "What I lived for," and "Higher Laws," in "Walden," as well as in many others in both books. We do not believe that, in the whole course of literature, ancient and modern, so noble a discourse upon Friendship can be produced as that which Mr. Thoreau has given us. It points to a relation, to be sure, which, from the ordinary level of our lives, may seem remote and dreamy. But it is our thirst for, and glimpses of, such things which indicate the greatness of our nature, which give the purest charm and colouring to our lives. The striking peculiarity of Mr. Thoreau's attitude is, that while he is no religionist, and while he is eminently practical in regard to the material economies of life, he yet manifestly feels, through and through, that the loftiest dreams of the imagination are the solidest realities, and so the only foundation for us to build upon, while the affairs in which men are everywhere busying themselves so intensely are comparatively the merest froth and foam.

GEORGE ELIOT

[Review of *Walden*]†

In a volume called *Walden; or, Life in the Woods,* published last year, but quite interesting enough to make it worth while for us to break our rule by a retrospective notice—we have a bit of pure American life (not the 'go a-head' species, but its opposite pole), animated by that energetic, yet calm spirit of innovation, that practical as well as theoretic independence of formulæ, which is peculiar to some of the finer American minds. The writer tells us how he chose, for some years, to be a stoic of the woods; how he built his house, how he earned the necessaries of his simple life by cultivating a bit of ground. He tells his system of diet, his studies, his reflections, and his observations of natural phenomena. These last are not only made by a keen eye, but have their interest enhanced by passing through the medium of a deep poetic sensibility; and, indeed, we feel throughout the book the presence of a refined as well as a hardy mind. People—very wise in their own eyes—who would have every man's life ordered according to a particular pattern, and who are intolerant of every existence the utility of which is not

† From *Westminster Review* 65 (Jan. 1856): 302–3.

palpable to them, may pooh-pooh Mr. Thoreau and this episode in his history, as unpractical and dreamy. Instead of contesting their opinion ourselves, we will let Mr. Thoreau speak for himself. There is plenty of sturdy sense mingled with his unworldliness.

* * *

RALPH WALDO EMERSON

Thoreau†

Henry D. Thoreau was the last male descendent of a French ancestor who came to this country from the isle of Guernsey. His character exhibited occasional traits drawn from this blood in singular combination with a very strong Saxon genius.

He was born in Concord, Massachusetts, on the 12th of July, 1817. He was graduated at Harvard College, in 1837, but without any literary distinction. An iconoclast in literature, he seldom thanked colleges for their service to him, holding them in small esteem, whilst yet his debt to them was important. After leaving the University, he joined his brother in teaching a private school, which he soon renounced. His father was a manufacturer of lead pencils, and Henry applied himself for a time to this craft, believing he could make a better pencil than was then in use. After completing his experiments, he exhibited his work to chemists and artists in Boston, and having obtained their certificates to its excellence and to its equality with the best London manufacture, he returned home contented. His friends congratulated him that he had now opened his way to fortune. But he replied, that he should never make another pencil. "Why should I? I would not do again what I have done once." He resumed his endless walks, and miscellaneous studies, making every day some new acquaintance with Nature, though as yet never speaking of zoology or botany, since, though very studious of natural facts, he was incurious of technical and textual science.

At this time, a strong, healthy youth fresh from college, whilst all his companions were choosing their profession, or eager to begin some lucrative employment, it was inevitable that his thoughts should be exercised on the same question, and it required rare decision to refuse all the accustomed paths, and keep his solitary freedom at the cost of disappointing the natural expectations of his family and friends. All the more difficult that he had a perfect probity, was exact in securing his own independence, and in holding every man to the like duty. But Thoreau never faltered. He was a born protestant. He declined to give up his large ambition of knowledge and action for any narrow craft or profession, aiming at a much more compre-

† Reprinted from Joel Myerson, "Emerson's 'Thoreau': A New Edition from Manuscript," *Studies in the American Renaissance, 1979,* ed. Joel Myerson (Boston: Hall, 1979): 35–55. *Walden* page numbers refer to this Norton Critical Edition.

hensive calling, the art of living well. If he slighted and defied the opinions of others, it was only that he was more intent to reconcile his practice with his own belief. Never idle or self-indulgent, he preferred when he wanted money, earning it by some piece of manual labor agreeable to him, as building a boat or a fence, planting, grafting, surveying, or other short work, to any long engagements. With his hardy habits and few wants, his skill in wood-craft, and his powerful arithmetic, he was very competent to live in any part of the world. It would cost him less time to supply his wants than another. He was therefore secure of his leisure.

A natural skill for mensuration, growing out of his mathematical knowledge, and his habit of ascertaining the measures and distances of objects which interested him, the size of trees, the depth and extent of ponds and rivers, the height of mountains and the air-line distance of his favorite summits,—this, and his intimate knowledge of the territory about Concord, made him drift into the profession of land-surveyor. It had the advantage for him that it led him continually into new and secluded grounds, and helped his studies of nature. His accuracy and skill in this work were readily appreciated, and he found all the employment he wanted.

He could easily solve the problems of the surveyor, but he was daily beset with graver questions which he manfully confronted. He interrogated every custom, and wished to settle all his practice on an ideal foundation. He was a protestant *à l'outrance*[1] and few lives contain so many renunciations. He was bred to no profession; he never married; he lived alone; he never went to church; he never voted; he refused to pay a tax to the state; he ate no flesh, he drank no wine, he never knew the use of tobacco; and, though a naturalist, he used neither trap nor gun. He chose wisely, no doubt, for himself to be the bachelor of thought and nature. He had no talent for wealth, and knew how to be poor without the least hint of squalor or inelegance. Perhaps he fell into his way of living, without forecasting it much, but approved it with later wisdom. "I am often reminded," he wrote in his journal, "that, if I had bestowed on me the wealth of Crœsus, my aims must be still the same, and my means essentially the same." He had no temptation to fight against; no appetites, no passions, no taste for elegant trifles. A fine house, dress, the manners and talk of highly cultivated people were all thrown away on him. He much preferred a good Indian, and considered these refinements as impediments to conversation, wishing to meet his companion on the simplest terms. He declined invitations to dinner-parties, because there each was in every one's way, and he could not meet the individuals to any purpose. "They make their pride," he said, "in making their dinner cost much: I make my pride in making my dinner cost little." When asked at table, what dish he preferred, he answered, "the nearest." He did not like the taste of wine, and never had a vice in his life. He said, "I have a faint recollection of pleasure derived from smoking dried lily stems,

1. In the extreme [*Editor*].

before I was a man. I had commonly a supply of these. I have never smoked any thing more noxious."

He chose to be rich by making his wants few, and supplying them himself. In his travels, he used the railroad only to get over so much country as was unimportant to the present purpose, walking hundreds of miles, avoiding taverns, buying a lodging in farmers' and fishermen's houses, as cheaper, and more agreeable to him, and because there he could better find the men and the information he wanted.

There was somewhat military in his nature not to be subdued, always manly and able, but rarely tender, as if he did not feel himself except in opposition. He wanted a fallacy to expose, a blunder to pillory, I may say, required a little sense of victory, a roll of the drum, to call his powers into full exercise. It cost him nothing to say No; indeed he found it much easier than to say Yes. It seemed as if his first instinct on hearing a proposition was to controvert it, so impatient was he of the limitation of our daily thought. This habit of course is a little chilling to the social affections; and though the companion would in the end acquit him of any malice or untruth, yet it mars conversation. Hence no equal companion stood in affectionate relations with one so pure and guileless. "I love Henry," said one of his friends, "but I cannot like him: and as for taking his arm, I should as soon think of taking the arm of an elm-tree."

Yet hermit and stoic as he was, he was really fond of sympathy, and threw himself heartily and childlike into the company of young people whom he loved, and whom he delighted to entertain, as he only could, with the varied and endless anecdotes of his experiences by field and river. And he was always ready to lead a huckleberry party or a search for chestnuts or grapes. Talking one day of a public discourse, Henry remarked, that whatever succeeded with the audience, was bad. I said, "Who would not like to write something which all can read, like 'Robinson Crusoe'; and who does not see with regret that his page is not solid with a right materialistic treatment, which delights everybody." Henry objected, of course, and vaunted the better lectures which reached only a few persons. But, at supper, a young girl, understanding that he was to lecture at the Lyceum, sharply asked him, "whether his lecture would be a nice, interesting story such as she wished to hear, or whether it was one of those old philosophical things that she did not care about?" Henry turned to her, and bethought himself, and, I saw, was trying to believe that he had matter that might fit her and her brother, who were to sit up and go to the lecture, if it was a good one for them.

He was a speaker and actor of the truth,—born such,—and was ever running into dramatic situations from this cause. In any circumstance, it interested all bystanders to know what part Henry would take, and what he would say: and he did not disappoint expectation, but used an original judgment on each emergency. In 1845, he built himself a small framed house on the shores of Walden Pond, and lived there two years alone, a life of labor and study. This action was quite native and fit for him. No one who knew him would tax him with affectation. He was more unlike his neighbors in his thought, than in his action. As soon as he had exhausted the advantages of that solitude, he abandoned it. In 1847, not approving some uses to which the public expenditure was applied, he refused to pay his town-tax, and was put in jail. A friend paid the tax for him, and he was released. The like annoyance was threatened the next year. But, as his friends paid the tax, notwithstanding his protest, I believe he ceased to resist. No opposition or ridicule had any weight with him. He coldly and fully stated his opinion without affecting to believe that it was the opinion of the company. It was of no consequence if every one present held the opposite opinion. On one occasion he went to the University Library to procure some books. The Librarian refused to lend them. Mr. Thoreau repaired to the President, who stated to him the rules and usages which permitted the loan of books to resident graduates, to clergymen who were alumni, and to some others resident within a circle of ten miles' radius from the College. Mr. Thoreau explained to the President that the railroad had destroyed the old scale of distances,—that the library was useless, yes, and President and College useless, on the terms of his rules,—that the one benefit he owed to the College was its library,—that at this moment, not only his want of books was imperative, but he wanted a large number of books, and assured him that he Thoreau, and not the Librarian, was the proper custodian of these. In short, the President found the petitioner so formidable and the rules getting to look so ridiculous, that he ended by giving him a privilege which in his hands proved unlimited thereafter.

No truer American existed than Thoreau. His preference of his country and condition was genuine, and his aversation from English and European manners and tastes almost reached contempt. He listened impatiently to news or bon mots gleaned from London circles; and, though he tried to be civil, these anecdotes fatigued him. The men were all imitating each other, and on a small mould. Why can they not live as far apart as possible, and each be a man by himself? What he sought was the most energetic nature, and he wished to go to Oregon, not to London. "In every part of Great Britain," he wrote in his diary, "are discovered traces of the Romans, their funereal urns, their camps, their roads, their dwellings. But New England, at least, is not based on any Roman ruins. We have not to lay the foundations of our houses on the ashes of a former civilization."

But idealist as he was, standing for abolition of slavery, abolition of tariffs, almost for abolition of government, it is needless to say he found himself not only unrepresented in actual politics, but almost equally opposed to every class of reformers. Yet he paid the tribute of his uniform respect to the anti-slavery party. One man, whose personal acquaintance he had formed, he honored with exceptional regard. Before the first friendly word had been spoken for Captain John Brown, after the arrest, he sent notices to most houses in Concord, that he would speak in a public hall on the condition and character of John Brown,[2] on Sunday Evening, and invited all people to come. The Republican committee, the abolitionist committee, sent him word that it was premature and not advisable. He replied, "I did not send to you for advice but to announce that I am to speak." The hall was filled at an early hour by people of all parties and his earnest eulogy of the hero was heard by all respectfully, by many with a sympathy that surprised themselves.

It was said of Plotinus, that he was ashamed of his body, and 'tis very likely he had good reason for it; that his body was a bad servant, and he had not skill in dealing with the material world, as happens often to men of abstract intellect. But Mr. Thoreau was equipped with a most adapted and serviceable body. He was of short stature, firmly built, of light complexion, with strong, serious blue eyes, and a grave aspect; his face covered in the late years with a becoming beard. His senses were acute, his frame well-knit and hardy, his hands strong and skilful in the use of tools. And there was a wonderful fitness of body and mind. He could pace sixteen rods more accurately than another man could measure them with rod and chain. He could find his path in the woods at night, he said, better by his feet than his eyes. He could estimate the measure of a tree very well by his eye; he could estimate the weight of a calf or a pig, like a dealer. From a box containing a bushel or more of loose pencils, he could take up with his hands fast enough just a dozen pencils at every grasp. He was a good swimmer, runner, skater, boatman, and would probably out-walk most countrymen in a day's journey. And the relation of body to mind was still finer than we have indicated. He said, he wanted every stride his legs made. The length of his walk uniformly made the length of his writing. If shut up in the house, he did not write at all.

He had a strong common sense, like that which Rose Flammock, the weaver's daughter, in Scott's romance, commends in her father, as resembling a yardstick, which, whilst it measures dowlas and diaper, can equally well measure tapestry and cloth of gold. He had always a new resource. When I was planting forest trees, and had procured half a peck of acorns, he said, that only a small portion of them would be sound, and proceeded to examine them, and select the sound ones. But finding this took time, he said, "I think, if you put them all into water, the good ones will sink," which experiment we tried with success. He could plan a garden, or a house, or a barn; would have been competent to lead a "Pacific Exploring Expedition"; could give judicious counsel in the gravest private or public affairs. He lived for the day, not cumbered and mortified by his memory. If he brought you yesterday a new proposition, he would bring you today another not less revolutionary. A very industrious man, and setting, like all highly

2. "A Plea for Captain John Brown," delivered October 30, 1859. Brown (1800–1859), an American abolitionist, seized a federal arsenal in Harper's Ferry, Virginia; he was arrested and executed two months later for attempting to incite a slave insurrection [*Editor*].

organized men, a high value on his time, he seemed the only man of leisure in town, always ready for any excursion that promised well, or for conversation prolonged into late hours. His trenchant sense was never stopped by his rules of daily prudence, but was always up to the new occasion. He liked and used the simplest food, yet, when some one urged a vegetable diet, Thoreau thought all diets a very small matter; saying, that "the man who shoots the buffalo lives better than the man who boards at the Graham house." He said, "You can sleep near the railroad, and never be disturbed. Nature knows very well what sounds are worth attending to, and has made up her mind not to hear the railroad-whistle. But things respect the devout mind, and a mental ecstacy was never interrupted."

He noted what repeatedly befel him, that, after receiving from a distance a rare plant, he would presently find the same in his own haunts. And those pieces of luck which happen only to good players happened to him. One day walking with a stranger who inquired, where Indian arrowheads could be found, he replied, "Every where," and stooping forward, picked one on the instant from the ground. At Mount Washington, in Tuckerman's Ravine, Thoreau had a bad fall, and sprained his foot. As he was in the act of getting up from his fall, he saw for the first time, the leaves of the *Arnica mollis*.

His robust common sense, armed with stout hands, keen perceptions, and strong will, cannot yet account for the superiority which shone in his simple and hidden life. I must add the cardinal fact that there was an excellent wisdom in him, proper to a rare class of men, which showed him the material world as a means and symbol. This discovery, which sometimes yields to poets a certain casual and interrupted light serving for the ornament of their writing, was in him an unsleeping insight; and, whatever faults or obstructions of temperament might cloud it, he was not disobedient to the heavenly vision. In his youth, he said, one day, "The other world is all my art: my pencils will draw no other; my jack-knife will cut nothing else; I do not use it as a means." This was the muse and genius that ruled his opinions, conversation, studies, work, and course of life. This made him a searching judge of men. At first glance, he measured his companion, and, though insensible to some fine traits of culture, could very well report his weight and calibre. And this made the impression of genius which his conversation often gave.

He understood the matter in hand at a glance, and saw the limitations and poverty of those he talked with, so that nothing seemed concealed from such terrible eyes. I have repeatedly known young men of sensibility converted in a moment to the belief that this was the man they were in search of, the man of men, who could tell them all they should do. His own dealing with them was never affectionate, but superior, didactic; scorning their petty ways; very slowly conceding or not conceding at all the promise of his society at their houses or even at his own. "Would he not walk with them?"—He did not know. There was nothing so important to him as his walk; he had no walks to throw away on company. Visits were offered him from respectful parties, but he declined them. Admiring friends offered to carry him at their own cost to the Yellow Stone River; to the West Indies; to South America. But though nothing could be more grave or considered than his refusals, they remind one in quite new relations of that fop Brummel's reply to the gentleman who offered him his carriage in a shower, "But where will *you* ride then?" And what accusing silences, and what searching and irresistible speeches battering down all defences, his companions can remember!

Mr. Thoreau dedicated his genius with such entire love to the fields, hills, and waters of his native town, that he made them known and interesting to all reading Americans, and to people over the sea. The river on whose banks he was born and died, he knew from its springs to its confluence with the Merrimack. He had made summer and winter observations on it for many years, and at every hour of the day and night. The result of the recent survey of the Water Commissioners appointed by the State of Massachusetts, he had reached by his private experiments, several years earlier. Every fact which occurs in the bed, on the banks, or in the air over it; the fishes, and their spawning and nests, their manners, their food; the shad-flies which fill the air on a certain evening once a year, and which are snapped at by the fishes so ravenously, that many of these die of repletion; the conical heaps of small stones on the river shallows, one of which heaps will sometimes overfill a cart,—these heaps the huge nests of small fishes; the birds which frequent the stream, heron, duck, sheldrake, loon, osprey; the snake, muskrat, otter, woodchuck, and fox, on the banks; the turtle, frog, hyla, and cricket, which make the banks vocal,—were all known to him, and, as it were, townsmen and fellow-creatures: so that he felt an absurdity or violence in any narrative of one of these by itself apart, and still more of its dimensions on an inch-rule, or in the exhibition of its skeleton, or the specimen of a squirrel or a bird in brandy. He liked to speak of the manners of the river, as itself a lawful creature, yet with exactness and always to an observed fact. As he knew the river, so the ponds in this region.

One of the weapons he used, more important than microscope or alcohol receiver, to other investigators, was a whim which grew on him by indulgence, yet appeared in gravest statement, namely, of extolling his own town and neighborhood as the most favored centre for natural observation. He remarked that the Flora of Massachusetts embraced almost all the important plants of America,—most of the oaks, most of the willows, the best pines, the ash, the maple, the beech, the nuts. He returned Kane's "Arctic Voyage" to a friend of whom he had borrowed it with the remark, that "most of the phenomena noted might be observed in Concord." He seemed a little envious of the Pole, for the coincident sunrise and sunset, or five minutes' day after six months. A splendid fact which Annursnuc[3] had never afforded him. He found red snow in one of his walks; and told me that he expected

3. A hill in Concord [*Editor*].

to find yet the *Victoria regia*[4] in Concord. He was the attorney of the indigenous plants, and owned to a preference of the weeds to the imported plants, as of the Indian to the civilized man: and noticed with pleasure that the willow bean-poles of his neighbor had grown more than his beans. "See these weeds," he said, "which have been hoed at by a million farmers all spring and summer, and yet have prevailed, and just now come out triumphant over all lanes, pastures, fields, and gardens, such is their vigor. We have insulted them with low names too, as pigweed, wormwood, chickweed, shad blossom." He says they have brave names too, ambrosia, stellaria, amelanchier, amaranth, etc.

I think his fancy for referring every thing to the meridian of Concord, did not grow out of any ignorance or depreciation of other longitudes or latitudes, but was rather a playful expression of his conviction of the indifferency of all places, and that the best place for each is where he stands. He expressed it once in this wise: "I think nothing is to be hoped from you, if this bit of mould under your feet is not sweeter to you to eat, than any other in this world, or in any world."

The other weapon with which he conquered all obstacles in science was patience. He knew how to sit immoveable, a part of the rock he rested on, until the bird, the reptile, the fish, which had retired from him, should come back, and resume its habits, nay, moved by curiosity should come to him and watch him.

It was a pleasure and a privilege to walk with him. He knew the country like a fox or a bird, and passed through it as freely by paths of his own. He knew every track in the snow, or on the ground, and what creature had taken this path before him. One must submit abjectly to such a guide, and the reward was great. Under his arm he carried an old music book to press plants; in his pocket, his diary and pencil, a spy-glass for birds, microscope, jack-knife, and twine. He wore straw hat, stout shoes, strong gray trowsers, to brave shrub-oaks and smilax, and to climb a tree for a hawk's or a squirrel's nest. He waded into the pool for the water-plants, and his strong legs were no insignificant part of his armour. On the day I speak of he looked for the menyanthes, detected it across the wide pool, and, on examination of the florets, decided that it had been in flower five days. He drew out of his breast-pocket his diary, and read the names of all the plants that should bloom on this day, whereof he kept account as a banker when his notes fall due. The cypripedium not due till tomorrow. He thought, that, if waked up from a trance, in this swamp, he could tell by the plants what time of the year it was within two days. The redstart was flying about and presently the fine grosbeaks, whose brilliant scarlet makes the rash gazer wipe his eye, and whose fine clear note Thoreau compared to that of a tanager which has got rid of its hoarseness. Presently he heard a note which he called that of the night-warbler, a bird he had never identified, had been in search of

4. South American water lily [*Editor*].

twelve years, which always, when he saw it, was in the act of diving down into a tree or bush, and which it was vain to seek; the only bird that sings indifferently by night and by day. I told him he must beware of finding and booking it, lest life should have nothing more to show him. He said, "What you seek in vain for, half your life, one day you come full upon all the family at dinner. You seek it like a dream, and, as soon as you find it, you become its prey."

His interest in the flower or the bird lay very deep in his mind, was connected with Nature,—and the meaning of Nature was never attempted to be defined by him. He would not offer a memoir of his observations to the Natural History Society. "Why should I? To detach the description from its connections in my mind, would make it no longer true or valuable to me: and they do not wish what belongs to it." His power of observation seemed to indicate additional senses. He saw as with microscope, heard as with ear-trumpet, and his memory was a photographic register of all he saw and heard. And yet none knew better than he that it is not the fact that imports, but the impression or effect of the fact on your mind. Every fact lay in glory in his mind, a type of the order and beauty of the whole.

His determination on Natural History was organic. He confessed that he sometimes felt like a hound or a panther, and, if born among Indians, would have been a fell hunter. But, restrained by his Massachusetts culture, he played out the game in this mild form of botany and ichthyology. His intimacy with animals suggested what Thomas Fuller records of Butler the apiologist, that "either he had told the bees things or the bees had told him." Snakes coiled round his leg; the fishes swam into his hand, and he took them out of the water; he pulled the woodchuck out of its hole by the tail, and took the foxes under his protection from the hunters. Our naturalist had perfect magnanimity; he had no secrets: he would carry you to the heron's haunt, or even to his most prized botanical swamp;—possibly knowing that you could never find it again,—yet willing to take his risks.

No college ever offered him a diploma, or a professor's chair; no academy made him its corresponding secretary, its discoverer, or even its member. Whether[5] these learned bodies feared the satire of his presence. Yet so much knowledge of nature's secret and genius few others possessed, none in a more large and religious synthesis. For not a particle of respect had he to the opinions of any man or body of men, but homage solely to the truth itself. And as he discovered everywhere among doctors some leaning of courtesy, it discredited them. He grew to be revered and admired by his townsmen, who had at first known him only as an oddity. The farmers who employed him as a surveyor soon discovered his rare accuracy and skill, his knowledge of their lands, of trees, of birds, of Indian remains, and the like, which enabled him to tell every farmer more than he knew before of his own farm. So that he began to feel as if Mr. Thoreau had better rights in

5. Among other revisions he made to "Thoreau" after Emerson's death, James Eliot Cabot changed this word to "Perhaps." See Myerson, "Emerson's 'Thoreau,' " 20–21, 72 [*Editor*].

his land than he. They felt, too, the superiority of character which addressed all men with a native authority.

Indian relics abound in Concord, arrowheads, stone chisels, pestles, and fragments of pottery; and, on the river bank, large heaps of clam-shells and ashes mark spots which the savages frequented. These, and every circumstance touching the Indian, were important in his eyes. His visits to Maine were chiefly for love of the Indian. He had the satisfaction of seeing the manufacture of the bark-canoe, as well as of trying his hand in its management on the rapids. He was inquisitive about the making of the stone arrowhead, and, in his last days, charged a youth setting out for the Rocky Mountains, to find an Indian who could tell him that: "It was well worth a visit to California, to learn it." Occasionally, a small party of Penobscot Indians would visit Concord, and pitch their tents for a few weeks in summer on the river bank. He failed not to make acquaintance with the best of them, though he well knew that asking questions of Indians is like catechizing beavers and rabbits. In his last visit to Maine, he had great satisfaction from Joseph Polis, an intelligent Indian of Oldtown, who was his guide for some weeks.

He was equally interested in every natural fact. The depth of his perception found likeness of law throughout nature, and, I know not any genius who so swiftly inferred universal law from the single fact. He was no pedant of a department. His eye was open to beauty, and his ear to music. He found these, not in rare conditions, but wheresoever he went. He thought the best of music was in single strains; and he found poetic suggestion in the humming of the telegraph wire.

His poetry might be bad or good; he no doubt wanted a lyric facility, and technical skill; but he had the source of poetry in his spiritual perception. He was a good reader and critic, and his judgment on poetry was to the ground of it. He could not be deceived as to the presence or absence of the poetic element in any composition, and his thirst for this made him negligent and perhaps scornful of superficial graces. He would pass by many delicate rhythms, but he would have detected every live stanza or line in a volume, and knew very well where to find an equal charm in prose. He was so enamoured of the spiritual beauty, that he held all actual written poems in very light esteem in the comparison. He admired Æschylus and Pindar, but when some one was commending them, he said, that, "Æschylus and the Greeks, in describing Apollo and Orpheus, had given no song, or no good one. They ought not to have moved trees, but to have chaunted to the gods such a hymn as would have sung all their old ideas out of their heads, and new ones in." His own verses are often rude and defective. The gold does not yet run pure, is drossy and crude. The thyme and marjoram are not yet honey. But if he want lyric fineness, and technical merits, if he have not the poetic temperament, he never lacks the causal thought, showing that his genius was better than his talent. He knew the worth of the Imagination for the uplifting and consolation of human life, and liked to throw every thought into a symbol. The fact you tell is of no value, but only the impression. For this reason his presence was poetic, always piqued the curiosity to know more deeply the secrets of his mind. He had many reserves,—an unwillingness to exhibit to profane eyes what was still sacred in his own, and knew well how to throw a poetic veil over his experience. All readers of "Walden" will remember his mythical record of his disappointments:—

> "I long ago lost a hound, a bay horse, and a turtle-dove, and am still on their trail. Many are the travellers I have spoken concerning them, describing their tracks, and what calls they answered to. I have met one or two who had heard the hound, and the tramp of the horse, and even seen the dove disappear behind a cloud, and they seemed as anxious to recover them as if they had lost them themselves."[6]

His riddles were worth the reading, and I confide that, if at any time I do not understand the expression, it is yet just. Such was the wealth of his truth, that it was not worth his while to use words in vain.

His poem entitled "Sympathy" reveals the tenderness under that triple steel of stoicism, and the intellectual subtlety it could animate. His classic poem on "Smoke" suggests Simonides, but is better than any poem of Simonides. His biography is in his verses. His habitual thought makes all his poetry a hymn to the Cause of causes, the spirit which vivifies and controls his own.

> "I hearing get, who had but ears,
> And sight, who had but eyes before;
> I moments live, who lived but years,
> And truth discern, who knew but learning's lore."

And still more in these religious lines:—

> "Now chiefly is my natal hour,
> And only now my prime of life;
> I will not doubt the love untold,
> Which not my worth or want hath bought,
> Which wooed me young, and wooes me old,
> And to this evening hath me brought."

Whilst he used in his writings a certain petulance of remark in reference to churches or churchmen, he was a person of a rare, tender, and absolute religion, a person incapable of any profanation, by act or by thought. Of course, the same isolation which belonged to his original thinking and living detached him from the social religious forms. This is neither to be censured nor regretted. Aristotle long ago explained it, when he said, "One who surpasses his fellow citizens in virtue, is no longer a part of the city. Their law is not for him, since he is a law to himself."

6. *Walden* 11 [*Editor*].

Thoreau was sincerity itself, and might fortify the convictions of prophets in the ethical laws, by his holy living. It was an affirmative experience which refused to be set aside. A truth-speaker he, capable of the most deep and strict conversation; a physician to the wounds of any soul; a friend knowing not only the secret of friendship, but almost worshipped by those few persons who resorted to him as their confessor and prophet, and knew the deep value of his mind and great heart. He thought that without religion or devotion of some kind, nothing great was ever accomplished: and he thought that the bigoted sectarian had better bear this in mind.

His virtues of course sometimes ran into extremes. It was easy to trace to the inexorable demand on all for exact truth that austerity which made this willing hermit more solitary even than he wished. Himself of a perfect probity, he required not less of others. He had a disgust at crime, and no worldly success could cover it. He detected paltering as readily in dignified and prosperous persons as in beggars, and with equal scorn. Such dangerous frankness was in his dealing, that his admirers called him "that terrible Thoreau," as if he spoke, when silent, and was still present when he had departed. I think the severity of his ideal interfered to deprive him of a healthy sufficiency of human society.

The habit of a realist to find things the reverse of their appearance inclined him to put every statement in a paradox. A certain habit of antagonism defaced his earlier writings, a trick of rhetoric not quite outgrown in his later, of substituting for the obvious word and thought its diametrical opposite. He praised wild mountains and winter forests for their domestic air; in snow and ice, he would find sultriness; and commended the wilderness for resembling Rome and Paris. "It was so dry, that you might call it wet."

The tendency to magnify the moment, to read all the laws of nature in the one object or one combination under your eye, is of course comic to those who do not share the philosopher's perception of identity. To him there was no such thing as size. The pond was a small ocean; the Atlantic, a large Walden Pond. He referred every minute fact to cosmical laws. Though he meant to be just, he seemed haunted by a certain chronic assumption that the science of the day pretended completeness and he had just found out that the savans had neglected to discriminate a particular botanical variety, had failed to describe the seeds, or count the sepals. "That is to say," we replied, "the blockheads were not born in Concord, but who said they were? It was their unspeakable misfortune to be born in London, or Paris, or Rome; but, poor fellows, they did what they could, considering that they never saw Bateman Pond, or Nine-Acre-Corner, or Becky Stow's Swamp. Besides, what were you sent into the world for, but to add this observation?"

Had his genius been only contemplative, he had been fitted to his life, but with his energy and practical ability he seemed born for great enterprise and for command: and I so much regret the loss of his rare powers of action, that I cannot help counting it a fault in him that he had no ambition.

Wanting this, instead of engineering for all America, he was the captain of a huckleberry party. Pounding beans is good to the end of pounding empires one of these days, but if, at the end of years, it is still only beans!—

But these foibles, real or apparent, were fast vanishing in the incessant growth of a spirit so robust and wise, and which effaced its defects with new triumphs. His study of nature was a perpetual ornament to him, and inspired his friends with curiosity to see the world through his eyes, and to hear his adventures. They possessed every kind of interest. He had many elegances of his own, whilst he scoffed at conventional elegance. Thus he could not bear to hear the sound of his own steps, the grit of gravel; and therefore never willingly walked in the road, but in the grass, on mountains, and in woods. His senses were acute, and he remarked that by night every dwelling-house gives out bad air, like a slaughter-house. He liked the pure fragrance of melilot. He honored certain plants with special regard, and over all the pond-lily,—then the gentian, and the *Mikania scandens*, and "Life Ever-lasting," and a bass tree which he visited every year when it bloomed in the middle of July. He thought the scent a more oracular inquisition than the sight,—more oracular and trustworthy. The scent, of course, reveals what is concealed from the other senses. By it he detected earthiness. He delighted in echoes, and said, they were almost the only kind of kindred voices that he heard. He loved nature so well, was so happy in her solitude, that he became very jealous of cities, and the sad work which their refinements and artifices made with man and his dwelling. The axe was always destroying his forest—"Thank God," he said, "they cannot cut down the clouds. All kinds of figures are drawn on the blue ground, with this fibrous white paint."

I subjoin a few sentences taken from his unpublished manuscripts[7] not only as records of his thought and feeling, but for their power of description and literary excellence.

"Some circumstantial evidence is very strong, as when you find a trout in the milk."

"The chub is a soft fish, and tastes like boiled brown paper salted."

"The youth gets together his materials to build a bridge to the moon, or, perchance, a palace or temple on the earth, and, at length, the middle-aged man concludes to build a woodshed with them."

"The locust z---ing."

"Devil's-needles zig-zagging along the Nut-Meadow brook."

"Sugar is not so sweet to the palate, as sound to the healthy ear."

"I put on some hemlock boughs, and the rich salt crackling of their leaves was like mustard to the ear, the crackling of uncountable regiments. Dead trees love the fire."

"The blue-bird carries the sky on his back."

"The tanager flies through the green foliage, as if it would ignite the leaves."

7. I.e., from Thoreau's Journal [*Editor*].

"If I wish for a horse-hair for my compass-sight, I must go to the stable; but the hair-bird with her sharp eyes goes to the road."

"Immortal water, alive even to the superficies."

"Fire is the most tolerable third party."

"Nature made ferns for pure leaves, to show what she could do in that line."

"No tree has so fair a bole, and so handsome an instep as the beech."

"How did these beautiful rainbow tints get into the shell of the fresh-water clam, buried in the mud at the bottom of our dark river?"

"Hard are the times when the infant's shoes are second-foot."

"We are strictly confined to our men to whom we give liberty."

"Nothing is so much to be feared as fear. Atheism may comparatively be popular with God himself."

"Of what significance the things you can forget? A little thought is sexton to all the world."

"How can we expect a harvest of thought, who have not had a seed-time of character?"

"Only he can be trusted with gifts, who can present a face of bronze to expectations."

"I ask to be melted. You can only ask of the metals that they be tender to the fire that melts them. To nought else can they be tender."

There is a flower known to botanists, one of the same genus with our summer plant called "Life Everlasting," a *Gnaphalium* like that, which grows on the most inaccessible cliffs of the Tyrolese mountains, where the chamois dare hardly venture, and which the hunter, tempted by its beauty, and by his love, (for it is immensely valued by the Swiss maidens,) climbs the cliffs to gather, and is sometimes found dead at the foot, with the flower in his hand. It is called by botanists the *Gnaphalium leontopodium*, but by the Swiss, *Edelweisse*, which signifies, *Noble Purity*. Thoreau seemed to me living in the hope to gather this plant, which belonged to him of right. The scale on which his studies proceeded was so large as to require longevity, and we were the less prepared for his sudden disappearance. The country knows not yet, or in the least part, how great a son it has lost. It seems an injury that he should leave in the midst his broken task, which none else can finish,—a kind of indignity to so noble a soul, that it should depart out of nature before yet he has been really shown to his peers for what he is. But he, at least, is content. His soul was made for the noblest society; he had in a short life exhausted the capabilities of this world; wherever there is knowledge, wherever there is virtue, wherever there is beauty, he will find a home.

JAMES RUSSELL LOWELL

Thoreau†

What contemporary, if he was in the fighting period of his life, (since Nature sets limits about her conscription for spiritual fields, as the state does in physical warfare), will ever forget what was somewhat vaguely called the "Transcendental Movement" of thirty years ago? Apparently set astir by Carlyle's essays on the "Signs of the Times," and on "History," the final and more immediate impulse seemed to be given by "Sartor Resartus."

* * *

Scotch Presbyterianism as a motive of spiritual progress was dead; New England Puritanism was in like manner dead; in other words, Protestantism had made its fortune and no longer protested; but till Carlyle spoke out in the Old World and Emerson in the New, no one had dared to proclaim, *Le roi est mort: vive le roi!* The meaning of which proclamation was essentially this: the vital spirit has long since departed out of this form once so kingly, and the great seal has been in commission long enough; but meanwhile the soul of man, from which all power emanates and to which it reverts, still survives in undiminished royalty; God still survives, little as you gentlemen of the Commission seem to be aware of it,—nay, will possibly outlive the whole of you, incredible as it may appear. The truth is, that both Scotch Presbyterianism and New England Puritanism made their new avatar in Carlyle and Emerson, the heralds of their formal decease, and the tendency of the one toward Authority and of the other toward Independency might have been prophesied by whoever had studied history. The necessity was not so much in the men as in the principles they represented and the traditions which overruled them. The Puritanism of the past found its unwilling poet in Hawthorne, the rarest creative imagination of the century, the rarest in some ideal respects since Shakespeare; but the Puritanism that cannot die, the Puritanism that made New England what it is, and is destined to make America what it should be, found its voice in Emerson. Though holding himself aloof from all active partnership in movements of reform, he has been the sleeping partner who has supplied a great part of their capital.

The artistic range of Emerson is narrow, as every well-read critic must feel at once; and so is that of Æschylus, so is that of Dante, so is that of Montaigne, so is that of Schiller, so is that of nearly every one except Shakespeare; but there is a gauge of height no less than of breadth, of individualty as well as of comprehensiveness, and, above all, there is the standard of genetic power, the test of the masculine as distinguished from

† Written in 1865. From the Riverside Edition of The Writings of James Russell Lowell (Boston, 1890), vol. 1 *Literary Essays*, 361–81. *Walden* page numbers refer to this Norton Critical Edition.

the receptive minds. There are staminate plants in literature, that make no fine show of fruit, but without whose pollen, quintessence of fructifying gold, the garden had been barren. Emerson's mind is emphatically one of these, and there is no man to whom our æsthetic culture owes so much. The Puritan revolt had made us ecclesiastically and the Revolution politically independent, but we were still socially and intellectually moored to English thought, till Emerson cut the cable and gave us a chance at the dangers and the glories of blue water. No man young enough to have felt it can forget or cease to be grateful for the mental and moral *nudge* which he received from the writings of his high-minded and brave-spirited countryman.

* * *

Among the pistillate plants kindled to fruitage by the Emersonian pollen, Thoreau is thus far the most remarkable; and it is something eminently fitting that his posthumous works should be offered us by Emerson, for they are strawberries from his own garden. A singular mixture of varieties, indeed, there is:—alpine, some of them, with the flavor of rare mountain air; others wood, tasting of sunny roadside banks or shy openings in the forest; and not a few seedlings swollen hugely by culture, but lacking the fine natural aroma of the more modest kinds. Strange books these are of his, and interesting in many ways,—instructive chiefly as showing how considerable a crop may be raised on a comparatively narrow close of mind, and how much a man may make of his life if he will assiduously follow it, though perhaps never truly finding it at last.

I have just been renewing my recollection of Mr. Thoreau's writings, and have read through his six volumes in the order of their production.[1] I shall try to give an adequate report of their impression upon me both as critic and as mere reader. He seems to me to have been a man with so high a conceit of himself that he accepted without questioning, and insisted on our accepting, his defects and weaknesses of character as virtues and powers peculiar to himself. Was he indolent, he finds none of the activities which attract or employ the rest of mankind worthy of him. Was he wanting in the qualities that make success, it is success that is contemptible, and not himself that lacks persistency and purpose. Was he poor, money was an unmixed evil. Did his life seem a selfish one, he condemns doing good as one of the weakest of superstitions. To be of use was with him the most killing bait of the wily tempter Uselessness. He had no faculty of generalization from outside of himself, or at least no experience which would supply the material of such, and he makes his own whim the law, his own range the horizon of the universe. He condemns a world, the hollowness of whose satisfactions he had never had the means of testing, and we recognize Ape-

---

1. A *Week on the Concord and Merrimack Rivers* (1849); *Walden; Or, Life in the Woods* (1854); *Excursions* (1863), with Emerson's essay "Thoreau" prefixed to the volume and titled "Biographical Sketch"; *The Maine Woods* (1864); *Cape Cod*, and *Letters to Various Persons* (1865) [*Editor*].

mantus behind the mask of Timon. He had little active imagination; of the receptive he had much. His appreciation is of the highest quality; his critical power, from want of continuity of mind, very limited and inadequate. He somewhere cites a simile from Ossian, as an example of the superiority of the old poetry to the new, though, even were the historic evidence less convincing, the sentimental melancholy of those poems should be conclusive of their modernness. He had none of the artistic mastery which controls a great work to the serene balance of completeness, but exquisite mechanical skill in the shaping of sentences and paragraphs, or (more rarely) short bits of verse for the expression of a detached thought, sentiment, or image. His works give one the feeling of a sky full of stars,—something impressive and exhilarating certainly, something high overhead and freckled thickly with spots of isolated brightness; but whether these have any mutual relation with each other, or have any concern with our mundane matters, is for the most part matter of conjecture,—astrology as yet, and not astronomy.

It is curious, considering what Thoreau afterwards became, that he was not by nature an observer. He only saw the things he looked for, and was less poet than naturalist. Till he built his Walden shanty, he did not know that the hickory grew in Concord. Till he went to Maine, he had never seen phosphorescent wood, a phenomenon early familiar to most country boys. At forty he speaks of the seeding of the pine as a new discovery, though one should have thought that its gold-dust of blowing pollen might have earlier drawn his eye. Neither his attention nor his genius was of the spontaneous kind. He discovered nothing. He thought everything a discovery of his own, from moonlight to the planting of acorns and nuts by squirrels. This is a defect in his character, but one of his chief charms as a writer. Everything grows fresh under his hand. He delved in his mind and nature; he planted them with all manner of native and foreign seeds, and reaped assiduously. He was not merely solitary, he would be isolated, and succeeded at last in almost persuading himself that he was autochthonous. He valued everything in proportion as he fancied it to be exclusively his own. He complains in "Walden" that there is no one in Concord with whom he could talk of Oriental literature, though the man was living within two miles of his hut who had introduced him to it. This intellectual selfishness becomes sometimes almost painful in reading him. He lacked that generosity of "communication" which Johnson admired in Burke. De Quincey tells us that Wordsworth was impatient when any one else spoke of mountains, as if he had a peculiar property in them. And we can readily understand why it should be so: no one is satisfied with another's appreciation of his mistress. But Thoreau seems to have prized a lofty way of thinking (often we should be inclined to call it a remote one) not so much because it was good in itself as because he wished few to share it with him. It seems now and then as if he did not seek to lure others up "above our lower region of turmoil," but to leave his own name cut on the mountain peak as the first climber. This itch of originality infects his thought and style. To be misty is not to be mystic. He turns commonplaces end for end, and fancies it makes something new of them. As we walk down Park Street, our eye is caught by Dr. Winship's dumb-bells, one of which bears an inscription testifying that it is the heaviest ever put up at arm's length by any athlete; and in reading Mr. Thoreau's books we cannot help feeling as if he sometimes invited our attention to a particular sophism or paradox as the biggest yet maintained by any single writer. He seeks, at all risks, for perversity of thought, and revives the age of *concetti* while he fancies himself going back to a preclassical nature. "A day," he says, "passed in the society of those Greek sages, such as described in the Banquet of Xenophon, would not be comparable with the dry wit of decayed cranberry-vines and the fresh Attic salt of the moss-beds." It is not so much the True that he loves as the Out-of-the-Way. As the Brazen Age shows itself in other men by exaggeration of phrase, so in him by extravagance of statement. He wishes always to trump your suit and to *ruff* when you least expect it. Do you love Nature because she is beautiful? He will find a better argument in her ugliness. Are you tired of the artificial man? He instantly dresses you up an ideal in a Penobscot Indian, and attributes to this creature of his otherwise-mindedness as peculiarities things that are common to all woodsmen, white or red, and this simply because he has not studied the pale-faced variety.

This notion of an absolute originality, as if one could have a patent-right in it, is an absurdity. A man cannot escape in thought, any more than he can in language, from the past and the present. As no one ever invents a word, and yet language somehow grows by general contribution and necessity, so it is with thought. Mr. Thoreau seems to me to insist in public on going back to flint and steel, when there is a match-box in his pocket which he knows very well how to use at a pinch. Originality consists in power of digesting and assimilating thoughts, so that they become part of our life and substance. Montaigne, for example, is one of the most original of authors, though he helped himself to ideas in every direction. But they turn to blood and coloring in his style, and give a freshness of complexion that is forever charming. In Thoreau much seems yet to be foreign and unassimilated, showing itself in symptoms of indigestion. A preacher-up of Nature, we now and then detect under the surly and stoic garb something of the sophist and the sentimentalizer. I am far from implying that this was conscious on his part. But it is much easier for a man to impose on himself when he measures only with himself. A greater familiarity with ordinary men would have done Thoreau good, by showing him how many fine qualities are common to the race. The radical vice of his theory of life was that he confounded physical with spiritual remoteness from men. A man is far enough withdrawn from his fellows if he keep himself clear of their weaknesses. He is not so truly withdrawn as exiled, if he refuse to share in their strength. "Solitude," says Cowley, "can be well fitted and set right but upon a very few persons. They must have enough knowledge of the world to see the vanity of it, and enough virtue to despise all vanity." It is morbid self-consciousness that pronounces the world of men empty and worthless before trying it, the instinctive evasion of one who is sensible of some innate weakness, and retorts the accusation of it before any has made it but himself. To a healthy mind, the world is a constant challenge of opportunity. Mr. Thoreau had not a healthy mind, or he would not have been so fond of prescribing. His whole life was a search for the doctor. The old mystics had a wiser sense of what the world was worth. They ordained a severe apprenticeship to law, and even ceremonial, in order to the gaining of freedom and mastery over these. Seven years of service for Rachel were to be rewarded at last with Leah. Seven other years of faithfulness with her were to win them at last the true bride of their souls. Active Life was with them the only path to the Contemplative.

Thoreau had no humor, and this implies that he was a sorry logician. Himself an artist in rhetoric, he confounds thought with style when he undertakes to speak of the latter. He was forever talking of getting away from the world, but he must be always near enough to it, nay, to the Concord corner of it, to feel the impression he makes there. He verifies the shrewd remark of Sainte-Beuve, "On touche encore à son temps et très-fort, même quand on le repousse."[2] This egotism of his is a Stylites pillar after all, a seclusion which keeps him in the public eye. The dignity of man is an excellent thing, but therefore to hold one's self too sacred and precious is the reverse of excellent. There is something delightfully absurd in six volumes addressed to a world of such "vulgar fellows" as Thoreau affirmed his fellowmen to be. I once had a glimpse of a genuine solitary who spent his winters one hundred and fifty miles beyond all human communication, and there dwelt with his rifle as his only confidant. Compared with this, the shanty on Walden Pond has something the air, it must be confessed, of the Hermitage of La Chevrette.[3] I do not believe that the way to a true cosmopolitanism carries one into the woods or the society of musquashes. Perhaps the narrowest provincialism is that of Self; that of Kleinwinkel is nothing to it. The natural man, like the singing birds, comes out of the forest as inevitably as the natural bear and the wildcat stick there. To seek to be natural implies a consciousness that forbids all naturalness forever. It is as easy—and no easier—to be natural in a *salon* as in a swamp, if one do not aim at it, for what we call unnaturalness always has its spring in a man's thinking too much about himself. "It is impossible," said Turgot, "for a vulgar man to be simple."

I look upon a great deal of the modern sentimentalism about Nature as a mark of disease. It is one more symptom of the general liver-complaint. To a man of wholesome constitution the wilderness is well enough for a mood or a vacation, but not for a habit of life. Those who have most loudly advertised their passion for seclusion and their intimacy with nature, from

2. "One is still in touch with one's times and very much so, even when one rejects them" [*Editor*].
3. A cottage occupied by Jean-Jacques Rous-

seau from April 1756 to December 1757 on the grounds of La Chevrette, the country estate of Madame d'Épinay, Rousseau's patron [*Editor*].

Petrarch down, have been mostly sentimentalists, unreal men, misanthropes on the spindle side, solacing an uneasy suspicion of themselves by professing contempt for their kind. They make demands on the world in advance proportioned to their inward measure of their own merit, and are angry that the world pays only by the visible measure of performance. It is true of Rousseau, the modern founder of the sect, true of Saint Pierre, his intellectual child, and of Châteaubriand, his grandchild, the inventor, we might almost say, of the primitive forest, and who first was touched by the solemn falling of a tree from natural decay in the windless silence of the woods. It is a very shallow view that affirms trees and rocks to be healthy, and cannot see that men in communities are just as true to the laws of their organization and destiny; that can tolerate the puffin and the fox, but not the fool and the knave; that would shun politics because of its demagogues, and snuff up the stench of the obscene fungus. The divine life of Nature is more wonderful, more various, more sublime in man than in any other of her works, and the wisdom that is gained by commerce with men, as Montaigne and Shakespeare gained it, or with one's own soul among men, as Dante, is the most delightful, as it is the most precious, of all. In outward nature it is still man that interests us, and we care far less for the things seen than the way in which they are seen by poetic eyes like Wordsworth's or Thoreau's, and the reflections they cast there. To hear the to-do that is often made over the simple fact that a man sees the image of himself in the outward world, one is reminded of a savage when he for the first time catches a glimpse of himself in a looking-glass. "Venerable child of Nature," we are tempted to say, "to whose science in the invention of the tobacco-pipe, to whose art in the tattooing of thine undegenerate hide not yet enslaved by tailors, we are slowly striving to climb back, the miracle thou beholdst is sold in my unhappy country for a shilling!" If matters go on as they have done, and everybody must needs blab of all the favors that have been done him by roadside and river-brink and woodland walk, as if to kiss and tell were no longer treachery, it will be a positive refreshment to meet a man who is as superbly indifferent to Nature as she is to him. By and by we shall have John Smith, of No.–12–12th. Street, advertising that he is not the J. S. who saw a cow-lily on Thursday last, as he never saw one in his life, would not see one if he could, and is prepared to prove an alibi on the day in question.

Solitary communion with Nature does not seem to have been sanitary or sweetening in its influence on Thoreau's character. On the contrary, his letters show him more cynical as he grew older. While he studied with respectful attention the minks and woodchucks, his neighbors, he looked with utter contempt on the august drama of destiny of which his country was the scene, and on which the curtain had already risen. He was converting us back to a state of nature "so eloquently," as Voltaire said of Rousseau, "that he almost persuaded us to go on all fours," while the wiser fates were making it possible for us to walk erect for the first time. Had he conversed more with his fellows, his sympathies would have widened with the assurance that his peculiar genius had more appreciation, and his writings a larger circle of readers, or at least a warmer one, than he dreamed of. We have the highest testimony[4] to the natural sweetness, sincerity, and nobleness of his temper, and in his books an equally irrefragable one to the rare quality of his mind. He was not a strong thinker, but a sensitive feeler. Yet his mind strikes us as cold and wintry in its purity. A light snow has fallen everywhere in which he seems to come on the track of the shier sensations that would elsewhere leave no trace. We think greater compression would have done more for his fame. A feeling of sameness comes over us as we read so much. Trifles are recorded with an over-minute punctuality and conscientiousness of detail. He registers the state of his personal thermometer thirteen times a day. We cannot help thinking sometimes of the man who

> "Watches, starves, freezes, and sweats
> To learn but catechisms and alphabets
> Of unconcerning things, matters of fact,"

and sometimes of the saying of the Persian poet, that "when the owl would boast, he boasts of catching mice at the edge of a hole." We could readily part with some of his affectations. It was well enough for Pythagoras to say, once for all, "When I was Euphorbus at the siege of Troy"; not so well for Thoreau to travesty it into "When I was a shepherd on the plains of Assyria." A naïve thing said over again is anything but naïve. But with every exception, there is no writing comparable with Thoreau's in kind, that is comparable with it in degree where it is best; where it disengages itself, that is, from the tangled roots and dead leaves of a second-hand Orientalism, and runs limpid and smooth and broadening as it runs, a mirror for whatever is grand and lovely in both worlds.

George Sand says neatly, that "Art is not a study of positive reality," (*actuality* were the fitter word,) "but a seeking after ideal truth." It would be doing very inadequate justice to Thoreau if we left it to be inferred that this ideal element did not exist in him, and that too in larger proportion, if less obtrusive, than his nature-worship. He took nature as the mountain-path to an ideal world. If the path wind a good deal, if he record too faithfully every trip over a root, if he botanize somewhat wearisomely, he gives us now and then superb outlooks from some jutting crag, and brings us out at last into an illimitable ether, where the breathing is not difficult for those who have any true touch of the climbing spirit. His shanty-life was a mere impossibility, so far as his own conception of it goes, as an entire independency of mankind. The tub of Diogenes had a sounder bottom. Thoreau's experiment actually presupposed all that complicated civilization which it theoretically abjured. He squatted on another man's land; he borrows an axe; his boards, his nails, his bricks, his mortar, his books, his lamp, his fish-hooks, his plough, his hoe, all turn state's evidence against him as an

4. Mr. Emerson, in his Biographical Sketch.

accomplice in the sin of that artificial civilization which rendered it possible that such a person as Henry D. Thoreau should exist at all. *Magnis tamen excidit ausis.*[5] His aim was a noble and useful one, in the direction of "plain living and high thinking." It was a practical sermon on Emerson's text that "things are in the saddle and ride mankind," an attempt to solve Carlyle's problem (condensed from Johnson) of "lessening your denominator."[6] His whole life was a rebuke of the waste and aimlessness of our American luxury, which is an abject enslavement to tawdry upholstery. He had "fine translunary things" in him. His better style as a writer is in keeping with the simplicity and purity of his life. We have said that his range was narrow, but to be a master is to be a master. He had caught his English at its living source, among the poets and prose-writers of its best days; his literature was extensive and recondite; his quotations are always nuggets of the purest ore: there are sentences of his as perfect as anything in the language, and thoughts as clearly crystallized; his metaphors and images are always fresh from the soil; he had watched Nature like a detective who is to go upon the stand; as we read him, it seems as if all-out-of-doors had kept a diary and become its own Montaigne; we look at the landscape as in a Claude Lorraine glass; compared with his, all other books of similar aim, even White's "Selborne," seem dry as a country clergyman's meteorological journal in an old almanac. He belongs with Donne and Browne and Novalis; if not with the originally creative men, with the scarcely smaller class who are peculiar, and whose leaves shed their invisible thought-seed like ferns.

5. From Ovid, *Metamorphoses* 1.329, the last line of Phaeton's epitaph: "Here Phaeton lies,/ Who drove his father's chariot: if he did not/ Hold it, at least he fell in splendid daring." For the story of Phaeton, see *Walden* 50 [*Editor*].
6. From Emerson's "Ode, Inscribed to W. H.

Channing," lines 50–51; and Carlyle's *Sartor Resartus* 2.9: " 'the Fraction of Life can be increased in value not so much by increasing your Numerator as by lessening your Denominator' " [*Editor*].

Modern Criticism
Since 1941

F. O. MATTHIESSEN

Walden: Craftsmanship *vs.* Technique†

'You can't read any genuine history—as that of Herodotus or the Venerable Bede—without perceiving that our interest depends not on the subject but on the man,—on the manner in which he treats the subject and the importance he gives it. A feeble writer . . . must have what he thinks a great theme, which we are already interested in through the accounts of others, but a genius—a Shakespeare, for instance—would make the history of his parish more interesting than another's history of the world.'

—THOREAU'S *Journal* (March 1861)

It is apparent, in view of this last distinction of Coleridge's,[1] that the real test of whether Thoreau mastered organic form can hardly be made on the basis of accounting for the differences in body and flavor between his portrayal of the natural world and Emerson's, revelatory as these differences are. Nor can it be made by considering one of the rare occasions when his verse was redeemed by virtue of his discipline in translating from the Greek Anthology. Nor is it enough to reckon with the excellence of individual passages of prose, since the frequent charge is that whereas Emerson was master of the sentence, Thoreau was master of the paragraph, but that he was unable to go farther and attain 'the highest or structural achievements of form in a whole book.' The only adequate way of answering that is by considering the structure of *Walden* as a whole, by asking to what extent it meets Coleridge's demand of shaping, 'as it develops, itself from within.'

On one level *Walden* is the record of a personal experience, yet even in making that remark we are aware that this book does not go rightfully into the category of *Two Years Before the Mast* or *The Oregon Trail*. Why it presents a richer accumulation than either of those vigorous pieces of contemporary history is explained by its process of composition. Although Thoreau said that the bulk of its pages were written during his two years of sojourn by the pond (1845–7), it was not ready for publication until seven years later, and ultimately included a distillation from his journals over the whole period from 1838. A similar process had helped to transform his

† From *American Renaissance* by F. O. Matthiessen. Copyright 1941 by Oxford University Press, Inc. Reprinted by permission. 166–75.
1. I.e., between imitation and mere copying. As Matthiessen explains, "Coleridge held that the artist must not try to make a surface reproduction of nature's details, but 'must imitate that which is within the thing . . . for so only can he hope to produce any work truly natural in the object and truly human in the effect' " [*Editor*].

week's boat trip with his brother from a private to a symbolical event, since the record was bathed in memory for a decade (1839–49) before it found its final shape in words. But the flow of the *Week* is as leisurely and discursive as the bends in the Concord river, and the casual pouring in of miscellaneous poems and essays that Thoreau had previously printed in *The Dial* tends to obscure the cyclical movement. Yet each day advances from dawn to the varied sounds of night, and Thoreau uses an effective device for putting a period to the whole by the shift of the final morning from lazy August to the first sharp forebodings of transforming frost.

The sequence of *Walden* is arranged a good deal more subtly, perhaps because its subject constituted a more central symbol for Thoreau's accruing knowledge of life. He remarked on how the pond itself was one of the earliest scenes in his recollection, dating from the occasion when he had been brought out there one day when he was four, and how thereafter 'that woodland vision for a long time made the drapery of my dreams.' By 1841 he had already announced, "I want to go soon and live away by the pond,' and when pressed by friends about what he would do when he got there, he had asked in turn if it would not be employment enough 'to watch the progress of the seasons'? In that same year he had said: 'I think I could write a poem to be called "Concord." For argument I should have the River, the Woods, the Ponds, the Hills, the Fields, the Swamps and Meadows, the Streets and Buildings, and the Villagers.' In his completed 'poem' these last elements had receded into the background. What had come squarely to the fore, and made the opening chapter by far the longest of all, was the desire to record an experiment in 'Economy' as an antidote to the 'lives of quiet desperation' that he saw the mass of men leading. This essay on how he solved his basic needs of food and shelter might stand by itself, but also carries naturally forward to the more poignant condensation of the same theme in 'Where I lived, and What I lived for,' which reaches its conclusion in the passage on wedging down to reality.

At this point the skill with which Thoreau evolved his composition begins to come into play. On the one hand, the treatment of his material might simply have followed the chronological outline; on the other, it might have drifted into being loosely topical. At first glance it may appear that the latter is what happened, that there is no real cogency in the order of the chapters. That would have been Lowell's complaint, that Thoreau 'had no artistic power such as controls a great work to the serene balance of completeness.'[2]

2. The don of Harvard was not entirely blind to the man of Concord. Even in his notorious essay on *Walden* in *My Study Windows* he perceived that Thoreau 'had caught his English at its living source, among the poets and prose-writers of its best days,' and compared him with Donne and Browne. When Lowell tried to dismiss Thoreau as a crank, he was really bothered, as Henry Canby has pointed out, by Thoreau's attack upon his own ideals of genteel living. How different from Emerson's is Low- ell's tone when he says that while Thoreau 'studied with respectful attention the minks and woodchucks, his neighbors, he looked with utter contempt on the august drama of destiny of which his country was the scene, and on which the curtain had already risen.' As Mr. Canby had added: 'By destiny, Lowell clearly means the "manifest destiny" of the exploitation of the West, whose more sordid and unfortunate aspects Thoreau had prophesied two generations before their time of realization.'

But so far as the opposite can be proved by the effective arrangement of his entire material, the firmness with which Thoreau binds his successive links is worth examining. The student and observer that he has settled himself to be at the end of his second chapter leads easily into his discussion of 'Reading,' but that in turn gives way to his concern with the more fundamental language, which all things speak, in the chapter on 'Sounds.' Then, after he has passed from the tantivy of wild pigeons to the whistle of the locomotive, he reflects that once the cars have gone by and the restless world with them, he is more alone than ever. That starts the transition to the chapter on 'Solitude,' in which the source of his joy is to live by himself in the midst of nature with his senses unimpaired. The natural contrast is made in the next chapter on 'Visitors,' which he opens by saying how he believes he loves society as much as most, and is ready enough to fasten himself 'like a bloodsucker for the time to any full-blooded man' who comes his way. But after he has talked enthusiastically about the French woodchopper, and other welcome friends from the village, he remembers 'restless committed men,' the self-styled reformers who felt it their duty to give him advice. At that he breaks away with 'Meanwhile my beans . . . were impatient to be hoed'; and that opening carries him back to the earlier transition to the chapter on 'Sounds': 'I did not read books the first summer; I hoed beans.'

The effect of that repetition is to remind the reader of the time sequence that is knitting together all these chapters after the building of the cabin in the spring. From 'The Bean Field' as the sphere of his main occupation, he moves on, in 'The Village,' to his strolls for gossip, which, 'taken in homeopathic doses, was really as refreshing in its way as the rustle of leaves and the peeping of frogs.' Whether designedly or not, this chapter is the shortest in the book, and yields to rambles even farther away from the community than Walden, to 'The Ponds' and to fishing beyond 'Baker Farm.' As he was returning through the woods with his catch, and glimpsed in the near dark a woodchuck stealing across his path, then came the moment when he 'felt a strange thrill of savage delight, and was strongly tempted to seize and devour him raw.' And in the flash of his realization of his double instinct towards the spiritual and the wild, he has the starting point for the next two contrasting chapters, 'Higher Laws' and 'Brute Neighbors,' in considering both of which he follows his rule of going far enough to please his imagination.

From here on the structure becomes cyclical, his poem of the seasons or myth of the year. The accounts of his varied excursions have brought him to the day when he felt that he could no longer warm himself by the embers of the sun, which 'summer, like a departed hunter, had left.' Consequently, he set about finishing his cabin by building a chimney, and called that act 'House-Warming.' There follows a solid block of winter in the three chapters, 'Winter Visitors,' 'Winter Animals,' and 'The Pond in Winter,' that order suggesting the way in which the radius of his experience contracted then

more and more to his immediate surroundings. However, the last pages on
the pond deal with the cutting of the ice, and end with that sudden extraordinary expansion of his thought which annihilates space and time.

The last movement is the advance to 'Spring.' The activity of the ice
company in opening its large tracts has hastened the break-up of the rest of
the pond; and, listening to its booming, he recalls that one attraction that
brought him to the woods was the opportunity and leisure to watch this
renewal of the world. He has long felt in his observations that a day is an
epitome of a year, and now he knows that a year is likewise symbolical of
a life; and so, in presenting his experience by the pond, he foreshortens and
condenses the twenty-six months to the interval from the beginning of one
summer to the next. In the melting season he feels more than ever the mood
of expanding promise, and he catches the reader up into this rich forward
course by one of his most successful kinesthetic images, which serves to
round out his cycle: 'And so the seasons went rolling on into summer, as
one rambles into higher and higher grass.' To that he adds only the bare
statement of when he left the woods, and a 'Conclusion,' which explains
that he did so for as good a reason as he had gone there. He had other lives
to live, and he knew now that he could find for himself 'a solid bottom
everywhere.' That discovery gave him his final serene assurance that 'There
is more day to dawn,' and consequently he was not to be disturbed by the
'confused *tintinnabulum*' that sometimes reached his midday repose. He
recognized it for the noise of his contemporaries.

The construction of the book involved deliberate rearrangement of material. For instance, a single afternoon's return to the pond in the fall of
1852 was capable of furnishing details that were woven into half a dozen
passages of the finished work, two of them separated by seventy pages.
Nevertheless, since no invention was demanded, since all the material was
a *donnée* of Thoreau's memory, my assertion that *Walden* does not belong
with the simple records of experience may require more establishing. The
chief clue to how it was transformed into something else lies in Thoreau's
extension of his remark that he did not believe himself to be 'wholly involved
in Nature.' He went on to say that in being aware of himself as a human
entity, he was 'sensible of a certain doubleness' that made him both participant and spectator in any event. This ability to stand 'as remote from myself
as from another' is the indispensable attribute of the dramatist. Thoreau
makes you share in the excitement of his private scenes, for example, by
the kind of generalized significance he can give to his purchase and de-
molishment of an old shanty for its boards:

> I was informed treacherously by a young Patrick that neighbor Seeley,
> an Irishman, in the intervals of the carting, transferred the still tolerable,
> straight, and drivable nails, staples, and spikes to his pocket, and then
> stood when I came back to pass the time of day, and look freshly up,
> unconcerned, with spring thoughts, at the devastation; there being a
> dearth of work, as he said. He was there to represent spectatordom, and

help make this seemingly insignificant event one with the removal of the gods of Troy.

The demands he made of great books are significant of his owns intentions: 'They have no cause of their own to plead, but while they enlighten and sustain the reader his common sense will not refuse them.' Propaganda is not the source of the inner freedom they offer to the reader, for their relation to life is more inclusive than argument; or, as Thoreau described it, they are at once 'intimate' and 'universal.' He aimed unerringly to reconcile these two extremes in his own writing. His experience had been fundamental in that it had sprung from his determination to start from obedience to the rudimentary needs of a man who wanted to be free. Greenough[3] had seen how, in that sense, 'Obedience is worship,' for by discerning and following the functional patterns of daily behavior, you could discover the proportions of beauty that would express and complete them. It was Thoreau's conviction that by reducing life to its primitive conditions, he had come to the roots from which healthy art must flower, whether in Thessaly or Concord. It was not just a figure of speech when he said that 'Olympus is but the outside of the earth everywhere.' The light touch of his detachment allows the comparison of his small things with great, and throughout the book enables him to possess the universe at home.

As a result Walden has spoken to men of widely differing convictions, who have in common only the intensity of their devotion to life. It became a bible for many of the leaders of the British labor movement after Morris. When the sound of a little fountain in a shop window in Fleet Street made him think suddenly of lake water, Yeats remembered also his boyhood enthusiasm for Thoreau. He did not leave London then and go and live on Innisfree. But out of his loneliness in the foreign city he did write the first of his poems that met with a wide response, and 'The Lake Isle'—despite its Pre-Raphaelite flavor—was reminiscent of Walden even to 'the small cabin' Yeats built and the 'bean rows' he planted in his imagination. Walden was also one of our books that bulked largest for Tolstoy when he addressed his brief message to America (1901) and urged us to rediscover the greatness of our writers of the fifties: 'And I should like to ask the American people why they do not pay more attention to these voices (hardly to be replaced by those of financial and industrial millionaires, or successful generals and admirals), and continue the good work in which they made such hopeful progress.' In 1904 Proust wrote to the Comtesse de Noailles: 'Lisez . . . les pages admirables de Walden. Il me semble qu'on les lise en soi-même tant elles sortent du fond de notre expérience intime.'[4]

In his full utilization of his immediate resources Thoreau was the kind of native craftsman whom Greenough recognized as the harbinger of power

3. Horatio Greenough (1805–52), a sculptor and early proponent of the idea that architectural decoration should be functional. See Matthiessen, American Renaissance, 140–52 [Editor].

4. "Read the marvelous pages of Walden. It seems to me that one is reading them within oneself so much do they spring from the depths of one's intimate experience" [Editor].

for our arts. Craftsmanship in this sense involves the mastery of traditional modes and skills; it has been thought of more often in connection with Indian baskets or Yankee tankards and hearth-tools than with the so-called fine arts. In fact, until fairly lately, despite Greenough's pioneering, it has hardly been consistently thought of in relation to American products of any kind. The march of our experience has been so dominantly expansive, from one rapid disequilibrium to the next, that we have neglected to see what Constance Rourke, among others, has now pointed out so effectively: that notwithstanding the inevitable restlessness of our long era of pioneering, at many stages within that process the strong counter-effort of the settlers was for communal security and permanence. From such islands of realization and fulfilment within the onrushing torrent have come the objects, the order and balance of which now, when we most need them, we can recognize as among the most valuable possessions of our continent. The conspicuous manifestation of these qualities, as Greenough already knew, has been in architecture as the most social of forms, whether in the clipper, or on the New England green, or in the Shaker communities. But the artifacts of the cabinet maker, the potter and the founder, or whatever other utensils have been shaped patiently and devotedly for common service, are likewise a testimony of what Miss Rourke has called our classic art, recognizing that this term 'has nothing to do with grandeur, that it cannot be copied or imported, but is the outgrowth of a special mode of life and feeling.'

Thoreau's deep obligation to such traditional ways has been obscured by our thinking of him only as the extreme protestant. It is now clear that his revolt was bound up with a determination to do all he could to prevent the dignity of common labor from being degraded by the idle tastes of the rich. When he objected that 'the mason who finishes the cornice of the palace returns at night perchance to a hut not so good as a wigwam,' he showed the identity of his social and aesthetic foundations. Although he did not use Greenough's terms, he was always requiring a functional relationship. What he responded to as beauty was the application of trained skill to the exigencies of existence. He made no arbitrary separation between arts, and admired the Indian's woodcraft or the farmer's thorough care in building a barn on the same grounds that he admired the workmanship of Homer.[5] The depth to which his ideals for fitness and beauty in writing were shaped, half unconsciously, by the modes of productive labor with which he was surrounded, or, in fact, by the work of his own hands in carpentry or pencil-making or gardening, can be read in his instinctive analogies. He knew that the only discipline for Channing's 'sublimo-slipshod style' would be to try to carve some truths as roundly and solidly as a stonecutter. He knew it was no good to write, 'unless you feel strong in the knees.' Or—a more unex-

5. Emerson also said, 'I like a man who likes to see a fine barn as well as a good tragedy.' And Whitman added, as his reaction to the union of work and culture, 'I know that pleasure filters in and oozes out of me at the opera, but I know too that subtly and unaccountably my mind is sweet and odorous within while I clean up my boots and grease the pair that I reserve for stormy weather."

pected example to find in him—he believed he had learned an important lesson in design from the fidelity with which the operative in the textile-factory had woven his piece of cloth.

The structural wholeness of *Walden* makes it stand as the firmest product in our literature of such life-giving analogies between the processes of art and daily work. Moreover, Thoreau's very lack of invention brings him closer to the essential attributes of craftsmanship, if by that term we mean the strict, even spare, almost impersonal 'revelation of the object,' in contrast to the 'elaborated skill,' the combinations of more variegated resources that we describe as technique. This contrast of terms is still Miss Rourke's, in distinguishing between kinds of painting, but it can serve equally to demonstrate why Thoreau's book possesses such solidity in contrast, say, with *Hiawatha* or *Evangeline*. Longfellow was much the more obviously gifted in his available range of forms and subject matters. But his graceful derivations from his models—the versification and gentle tone of Goethe's *Hermann und Dorothea* for *Evangeline*, or the metre of the *Kalevala* for *Hiawatha*—were not brought into fusion with his native themes.[6] Any indigenous strength was lessened by the reader's always being conscious of the metrical dexterity as an ornamental exercise. It is certainly not to be argued that technical proficiency must result in such dilutions, but merely that, as Greenough saw, it was very hard for American artists of that day, who had no developed tradition of their own, not to be thus swamped by their contact with European influences. Their very aspiration for higher standards of art than those with which they were surrounded tended to make them think of form as a decorative refinement which could be imported.

The particular value of the organic principle for a provincial society thus comes into full relief. Thoreau's literal acceptance of Emerson's proposition that vital form 'is only discovered and executed by the artist, not arbitrarily composed by him,' impelled him to minute inspection of his own existence and of the intuitions that rose from it. Although this involved the restriction of his art to parochial limits, to the portrayal of man in terms only of the immediate nature that drew him out, his study of this interaction also brought him to fundamental human patterns unsuspected by Longfellow. Thoreau demonstrated what Emerson had merely observed, that the function of the artist in society is always to renew the primitive experience of the race, that he 'still goes back for materials and begins again on the most advanced stage.' Thoreau's scent for wildness ferreted beneath the merely conscious levels of cultivated man. It served him, in several pages of notes about a debauched muskrat hunter (1859), to uncover and unite once more the chief sources for his own art. He had found himself heartened by the seemingly inexhaustible vitality of this battered character, 'not despairing of life, but keeping the same rank and savage hold on it that his predecessors have for so many generations, while so many are sick and despairing.' Thoreau went on, therefore, half-playfully to speculate what it was that made this man become excited, indeed inspired by the January freshet in the meadows:

> There are poets of all kinds and degrees, little known to each other. The Lake School is not the only or the principal one. They love various things. Some love beauty, and some love rum. Some go to Rome, and some go a-fishing, and are sent to the house of correction once a month . . . I meet these gods of the river and woods with sparkling faces (like Apollo's) late from the house of correction, it may be carrying whatever mystic and forbidden bottles or other vessels concealed, while the dull regular priests are steering their parish rafts in a prose mood. What care I to see galleries full of representatives of heathen gods, when I can see natural living ones by an infinitely superior artist, without perspective tube? If you read the Rig Veda, oldest of books, as it were, describing a very primitive people and condition of things, you hear in their prayers of a still older, more primitive and aboriginal race in their midst and round about, warring on them and seizing their flocks and herds, infesting their pastures. Thus is it in another sense in all communities, and hence the prisons and police.

The meandering course of Thoreau's reflections here should not obscure his full discovery that the uneradicated wildness of man is the anarchical basis both of all that is most dangerous and most valuable in him. That he could dig down to the roots of primitive poetry without going a mile from Concord accounts for his ability to create 'a true Homeric or Paphlagonian man' in the likeness of the French woodchopper. It also helps account for the fact that by following to its uncompromising conclusion his belief that great art can grow from the center of the simplest life, he was able to be universal. He had understood that in the act of expression a man's whole being, and his natural and social background as well, function organically together. He had mastered a definition of art akin to what Maritain has extracted from scholasticism: *Recta ratio factibilium*, the right ordering of the thing to be made, the right revelation of the material.

SHERMAN PAUL

Resolution at Walden†
I

Walden was published in 1854, eight years before Thoreau died, some seven years after his life in the woods. His journal shows that he had proposed such a "poem" for himself as early as 1841, that its argument would be "the River, the Woods, the Ponds, the Hills, the Fields, the Swamps, and Mead-

† From *Accent* 13 (1953): 101–13. Reprinted by permission of Sherman Paul.

ows, the Streets and Buildings, and the Villagers. Then Morning, Noon, and Evening, Spring, Summer, Autumn, and Winter, Night, Indian Summer, and the Mountains in the Horizon." Like A *Week on the Concord and Merrimack Rivers* (1849)—"If one would reflect," Thoreau had written in 1837, "let him embark on some placid stream, and float with the current"— *Walden* took a long time maturing, a longer time, because it was more than the stream of his reflections. The *Week* had been written out of joyousness and to memorialize his most perfect excursion in nature. *Walden*, however, was Thoreau's recollected experience, recollected not in tranquility, but in the years of what he himself called his "decay." Although one need only search the journals to find many of the events of *Walden* freshly put down, *Walden* itself reveals that Thoreau was now looking at these events with more experienced eyes: his long quarrel with society has intervened, his youthful inspiration had become more difficult to summon, the harvest of the *Week* he had hoped to bestow on the public lay in his attic, and, growing older, he was still without a vocation that others would recognize. In *Walden*, at once his victorious hymn to Nature, to her perpetual forces of life, inspiration and renewal, Thoreau defended his vocation by creating its eternal symbol.

The common moral of *Walden* is that of the virtue of simplicity; and simplicity is usually taken on the prudential level of economy with which Thoreau seemingly began the book. In terms of Thoreau's spiritual economy, however, simplicity was more than freedom from the burdens of a mortgaged life: it was an ascetic, a severe discipline, like solitude for Emerson, by which Thoreau concentrated his forces and was able to confront the facts of life without the intervening barriers of society or possessions. For simplicity, Thoreau often substituted poverty, a word which both set him apart from his materialistic neighbors and hallowed his vocation with its religious associations of renunciation and higher dedication. It was the suitable condition for the spiritual crusader: the sign in a land of traders of his profession. But it also signified his inner condition. "By poverty," he said, "*i.e.* simplicity of life and fewness of incidents, I am solidified and crystallized, as a vapor or liquid by cold. It is a singular concentration of strength and energy and flavor. Chastity is perpetual acquaintance with the All. My diffuse and vaporous life becomes as frost leaves and spiculae radiant as gems on the weeds and stubble in a winter morning." Such poverty or purity was a necessity of *his* economy. "You think," he continued, "that I am impoverishing myself by withdrawing from men, but in my solitude I have woven for myself a silken web or *chrysalis*, and nymph-like, shall ere long burst forth a more perfect creature, fitted for a higher society. By simplicity, commonly called poverty, my life is concentrated and so becomes organized, or a κόσμος, which before was inorganic and lumpish."

This was also the hope of his paean to spring in *Walden*, to "pass from the lumpish grub in the earth to the airy and fluttering butterfly." The purpose of his experiment at Walden Pond, begun near the end of his years of undisciplined rapture—Emerson said that the vital heat of the poet begins to ebb at thirty—was to build an organic life as consciously as he built his hut (and his book), and so retain his vital heat. "May I never," he had recorded in his journal, "let the vestal fire go out in my recesses." But there was desperation in his attempt to keep his vital heat, because it was only *vital* (or rather he felt it so) when he was maturing beyond the lumpish, grub-like existence. As well as the advocacy of the organic life which promised renewal and growth, *Walden* for Thoreau filled the immediate need of self-therapy. In the serenity and joy of his art this is often overlooked, but it is there in the journals behind the book. And the greatness of *Walden*, from this perspective at least, is the resolution Thoreau was able to fulfill through art. By creating an organic form he effected his own resolution for rebirth: by conscious endeavor he recaptured, if not the youthful ecstasy of his golden age, a mature serenity.

This serenity, however, is still alert, wakeful, tense. It was a victory of discipline. "That aim in life is highest," Thoreau noted during the composition of *Walden*, "which requires the highest and finest discipline." That aim was highest, that discipline the highest vocation, because the goal and fulfillment of all transcendental callings was purity—a oneness with Nature in which the untarnished mirror of the soul reflected the fullness of being. The cost of doing without conventional life was not too great for Thoreau, considering his desire to "perceive things truly and simply." He believed that "a fatal coarseness is the result of mixing in the trivial affairs of men." And to justify his devotion to purity he wrote *Walden*, a promise of the higher society a man can make when he finds his *natural* center, a record of things and events so simple and fundamental that all lives less courageous and principled are shamed by the *realometer* it provides. Like other masterworks of its time, it has the unique strain of American romanticism: behind its insistent individualism and desire for experience, there is still more earnest conviction of the necessity of virtue.

II

In the concluding pages of *Walden*, Thoreau remarked that "in this part of the world it is considered a ground for complaint if a man's writings admit of more than one interpretation." With his contemporaries, Emerson, Hawthorne, Melville, he wanted the "volatile truth" of his words to "betray the inadequacy of the residual statement." He would have considered *Walden* a failure if it served only to communicate an eccentric's refusal to go along with society, if, taken literally, its spiritual courage was thinned to pap for tired businessmen long since beyond the point of no return. For *Walden* was *his* myth: "A fact truly and absolutely stated," he said, "is taken out of the region of common sense and acquires a mythologic or universal significance." This was the extravagance he sought—this going beyond the bounds. For him, only the fact stated without reference to convention or institution, with only reference to the self which has tasted the world and digested it, which has been "drenched" and "saturated" with truth, is properly humanized—is properly myth. Primarily to immerse himself in truth, to merge himself with the law of Nature, and to humanize this experience by the alchemy of language, Thoreau went to Walden. There, free from external references, he could purify himself and live a sympathetic existence, alive to the currents of being. What he reported, then, would be the experience of the self in its unfolding and exploration of the "not-me." The literal record would merely remain the residual statement—no one knew better the need for concrete fact; but it would also yield a *translated* meaning.

The whole of *Walden* is an experience of the microcosmic and cosmic travels of the self. At Walden Pond, Thoreau wrote, "I have, as it were, my own sun and moon and stars, and a little world all to myself." Thoreau, of course, was a great traveller, if only a saunterer. The profession of traveller appealed to his imagination; it was, he said, the "best symbol of our life." And "Walking" was the best short statement of his way of life, of his journey to the holy land. He yearned, he wrote in 1851, "for one of those old, meandering, dry, uninhabited roads, which lead away from towns . . ." He wanted to find a place "where you can walk and think with least obstruction, there being nothing to measure progress by; where you can pace when your breast is full, and cherish your moodiness; where you are not in false relations with men . . ." He wanted "a road where I can travel," where "I can walk, and recover the lost child that I am without any ringing of a bell." The road he wanted led to Walden. There he regained the primal world, and lived the pristine initiation into consciousness over again. "Both place and time were changed," he said in *Walden*, "and I dwelt nearer to those parts of the universe and to those eras in history which had most attracted me."

In this effort to live out of time and space or to live in all times and places, *Walden* immediately suggests Melville's *Moby-Dick*. Melville had written another voyage of the self on which he explored reality, charted the constituents of a chaos, and raised his discovery to the universal level of archetypal experience. He had elaborated the myth of the hunter which Thoreau also employed in the chapter on "Higher Laws." "There is a period in the history of the individual, as of the race," he wrote, "when hunters are the 'best men'. . . ." Hunting, he added, "is oftenest the young man's introduction to the forest [Melville's sea], and the most original part of himself. He goes thither at first as a hunter and fisher, until at last, if he has the seeds of a better life in him, he distinguishes his proper objects . . ." It was in these "wild" employments of his youth that Thoreau acknowledged his "closest acquaintance with Nature." For Nature revealed herself to the hunter more readily than to "philosophers or poets even, who approach her with expectation"—or, as Melville knew, to the participant and not the observer of life. If Thoreau had long since given up hunting, he still found a sustaining link with the wild in his bean field.

There are obvious differences, of course, in the quality of these travels—each author had his spiritual torment, Melville the need for belief, Thoreau the need for recommunion. But both were projecting the drama of their selves, a drama that in both instances ended in rebirth; and the methods both employed were remarkably similar. Each abstracted himself from the conventional world, established a microcosm by which to test the conventions, and worked at a basic and heroic occupation. For example, the village stands in the same symbolic relation to Thoreau at Walden that the land does to Melville's sea; and it is the occupation in both that supplies the residual statement. In Thoreau's case, it is also a primitive concern with essentials: building his hut, planting, hoeing and harvesting his beans, fishing and naturalizing. And the nature of the occupation gives each its spiritual quality, because whaling (butchery) and colonizing (building from scratch) are projections of different visions of the universe of which only the central similarity remains—the exploration of self.

But this similarity is a sufficient signature for both; one recognizes the existential kinship. At the conclusion of *Walden* Thoreau declared: "Explore thyself . . . Be . . . the Mungo Park, the Lewis and Clark and Frobisher, of your own streams and oceans. . . ."—

> ". . . . . be
> Expert in home-cosmography."

For "there are continents and seas in the moral world to which every man is an isthmus or an inlet, yet unexplored by him, . . . [and] it is easier to sail many thousand miles through cold and storm and cannibals, in a government ship, with five hundred men and boys to assist one, than it is to explore the private sea, the Atlantic and Pacific Ocean of one's being alone." Melville at Pittsfield would have agreed that "herein are demanded the eye and the nerve." But if Melville needed the watery two-thirds of the world and the great whale for this quest, Thoreau, who had the gift of enlarging the small, needed only the pond and its pickerel. And where Melville needed the destructive forces of the sea to mirror himself, Thoreau, who had seen the place of violence in the total economy of nature, needed only the recurrence of the seasons.

III

Walden was Thoreau's quest for a reality he had lost, and for this reason it was a quest for purity. Purity meant a return to the spring (and springtime) of life, to the golden age of his youth and active senses, when the mirror of his self was not clouded by self-consciousness. *Walden*, accordingly, follows the cycle of developing consciousness, a cycle that parallels the change of the seasons. It is a recapitulation of Thoreau's development (and the artistic reason he put the experience of two years into one)—a development from the sensuous, active, external (unconscious *and* out-of-doors) summer of life, through the stages of autumnal consciousness and the withdrawal inward to the self-reflection of winter, to the promise of ecstatic rebirth in the spring. It was a matter of purification because Thoreau had reached the winter of decay at the time *Walden* was being revised for the press. With consciousness had come the knowledge of the "reptile" and "sensual" which he knew could not "be wholly expelled." "I fear," he wrote, "that it [the sensual] may enjoy a certain health of its own; that we may be well, yet not pure." For the mind's approach to God, he knew that the severest discipline was necessary: his chapter on "Higher Laws" is concerned almost entirely with the regimen of the appetites because "man flows at once to God when the channel of purity is open." The undeniable sensual energy—the "generative energy"—he had unconsciously enjoyed in the ecstasy of youth, now needed control. "The generative energy," he wrote, "which, when we are loose, dissipates and makes us unclean, when we are continent invigorates and inspires us." He was consciously using instinct for higher ends, seeking chastity by control.

In Walden Pond he saw the image of his purified self—that pristine, eternal self he hoped to possess. In 1853, while he was working on his book, he noted in his journal: "How watchful we must be to keep the crystal well that we were made, clear!—that it be not made turbid by our contact with the world, so that it will not reflect objects." The pond, he recalled, was one of the "oldest scenes stamped on my memory." He had been taken to see it when he was four years old. Now, playing his flute beside its waters, his beans, corn and potatoes replacing the damage of the years, he felt that another aspect was being prepared "for new infant eyes," that "even I have at length helped to clothe that fabulous landscape of my infant dreams. . . ." Later, he recalled his youthful reveries on its waters: "I have spent many an hour, when I was younger, floating over its surface as the zephyr willed . . . dreaming awake. . . ." But time (and wood-choppers) had ravished its shores: "My Muse may be excused," he explained, "if she is silent henceforth. How can you expect the birds to sing when their groves are cut down?" It was the confession of the Apollo who had had to serve Admetus, a confession he made again in "Walking." Visited by fewer thoughts each year, he said that "the grove in our minds is laid waste—sold to feed unnecessary fires of ambition. . . ."

But Thoreau discovered at Walden that even though the groves were cut down, the pond itself remained the same—it "best preserves its purity." "It is itself unchanged," he learns, "the same water my youthful eyes fell on; all the change is in me. . . . It is perennially young. . . ." Catching sight of his eternal self and realizing that the waste of years had only touched his shore, his empirical self, he exclaimed, "Why, here is Walden, the same woodland lake that I discovered so many years ago . . . it is the same liquid joy and happiness to itself and its Maker, ay, and it *may* be to me." * * *

* * *

The search for the bottom was conscious exploration. Here, and in the passages on fishing for pickerel and chasing the loon, Thoreau was not a naturalist but a natural historian of the intellect, using the natural facts as symbols for his quest for inspiration and thought. In "Brute Neighbors" he had asked, "Why do precisely these objects which we behold make a world?"

And he had answered that "they are all beasts of burden . . . made to carry some portion of our thoughts." The natural world merely reflects ourselves. Having overcome his doubts of this central article of transcendental faith by assuring himself of the regularity of Walden's depth—that the hidden reality corresponded to its visible shores, that "Heaven is under our feet as well as over our heads"—he could trust once more his own projection of mood and thought to be reflected in its proper and corresponding object. He had noted in his journal that the poet "sees a flower or other object, and it is beautiful or affecting to him because it is a symbol of his thought, and what he indistinctly feels or perceives is matured in some other organization. The objects I behold correspond to my mood." His concern with the pond and the seasons, then, was symbolic of his soul's preoccupation. "Our moulting season . . . must be the crisis in our lives," he said; and like the loon he retired to a solitary pond to spend it. There, like the caterpillar—to use another symbol—, "by an internal industry and expansion" he cast off his "wormy coat."

IV

Thoreau went to Walden to become an unaccommodated man, to shed his lendings and to find his naked and sufficient self. Of this, the pond was the symbol. He also went to clothe himself in response to his inner needs. Building an organic life was again a conscious endeavor which was chastened by the necessity of maintaining his vital heat—the heat of body and spirit; for his purpose was not to return to nature, but to combine "the hardiness of . . . savages with the intellectualness of the civilized man." "The civilized man," he said, "is a more experienced and wiser savage," meaning, of course, that the instinctive life was most rewarding when channeled by intellectual principles. "What was *enthusiasm* in the young man," he wrote during the crisis of his life, "must become *temperament* in the mature man." The woodchopper, the animal man, must be educated to consciousness, and still retain his innocence. Properly seen in the total economy of Nature the once freely taken gift of inspiration must be earned by perceiving the law of Nature, by the tragic awareness that inspiration, like its source, has its seasons. The villagers, Thoreau wrote indignantly, "instead of going to the pond to bathe or drink, are thinking to bring its waters, which should be as sacred as the Ganges at least, to the village in a pipe, to wash their dishes with!—to earn their Walden by the turning of a cock or drawing of a plug!" The spiritual soldier had learned that after laying seige to Nature, only passivity would bring victory.

Thoreau earned his Walden by awaiting the return of spring, by sharing the organic process. Of this his hut and his bean-field became the symbols. The latter, as we have seen, helped to renew the aspect of the pond; as the work of the active self, it was rightly an alteration of the shore. And the pond, as the pure, eternal self—the "perfect forest mirror"—, was the calm surface on which these purifying activities were reflected. Thoreau labored in his bean-field because he took seriously Emerson's injunction to action in *The American Scholar*. He knew that the higher ends of the activity of the empirical self were self-consciousness, that the eternal self, the passive center, only acquired consciousness by observing the empirical self at work on the circumference. He recognized "a certain doubleness by which I can stand as remote from myself as from another." "However intense my experience," he wrote, "I am conscious of the presence of and criticism of a part of me, which, as it were, is not part of me, but spectator, sharing no experience, but taking note of it. . . ." The reward of activity, the result of this drama of selves, was self-reflection, insight. "All perception of truth is the detection of an analogy," Thoreau noted in the journal; "we reason from our hands to our head." And so through the labor of the hands, even to the point of drudgery, he was "determined to know beans." He did not need the beans for food but for sympathy with Nature; he needed to work them because, as he said, "They attached me to the earth, and so I got strength like Antaeus." His fields were also symbolic of his attempt to link the wild and the cultivated. And the "immeasurable crop" his devoted hoeing yielded came from the penetration of the earth's crust—a knowledge of the depths similar in significance to Melville's descent to the unwarped primal world. "I disturbed," Thoreau wrote, "the ashes of unchronicled nations who in primeval times lived under these heavens. . . ." In his bean-field beside Walden he was not serving Admetus, for he had found a way to delve beneath the "established order on the surface."

The prudential value of this labor came to $16.94, but the spiritual value was the realization that the Massachusetts soil could sustain the seeds of virtue—that in Thoreau's case at least, the seed had not lost its vitality and that the harvest of his example might be "a new generation of men." Later on, in the chapter on "Former Inhabitants," he again disturbed the surface by delving into the past, comparing his life at Walden to the defeated lives of its previous occupants. Here, Thoreau expressed his desire for the higher society, the ideal community in which he could wholly participate and which he hoped he was beginning. "Again, perhaps, Nature will try," he wrote, "with me for the first settler. . . . I am not aware that any man has ever built on the spot which I occupy." Like Joyce's Finnegan, he was to be the father of cities, not those reared on ancient sites, but cities growing out of the union with the earth. * * *

When he came to build his hut—the container of his vital heat—Thoreau used second-hand materials and borrowed tools and showed his dependence on civilization. He did not abandon collective wisdom: his intention was to practice philosophy, to come directly at a conduct of life, that is, to simplify, or experience the solid satisfaction of knowing immediately the materials that made his life. * * * In a similar way, he applied the funded wisdom of man to his experiment on life. Individualist that he was, he often confirmed his experience by the experience of others: he made his use of the classics and scriptures, Indian lore and colonial history, pay their way. He was starting from scratch, but he knew that the materials were old.

The building of the hut is so thoroughly described because on the symbolic level it is the description of the building of the body for his soul. A generation that was read in Swedenborg might have been expected to see this correspondence. "It would be worth the while," Thoreau suggested, "to build still more deliberately than I did, considering, for instance, what foundation a door, a window, a cellar, a garret, have in the nature of man, and perchance never raising any superstructure until we found a better reason for it than our temporal necessities even." He was speaking the language of functionalism that Swedenborgianism had popularized; and after listing his previous shelters, he remarked that "this frame, so slightly clad, was a sort of crystallization around me, and reacted on the builder."

Thoreau built his hut as he needed it, to meet the progressing seasons of developing consciousness, a development which was as organic as the seasons. He subscribed to Emerson's use of the cycle of day and night as the symbol of the ebb and flow of inspiration and extended it to the seasons: "The day is an epitome of the year. The night is the winter, the morning and evenings are spring and fall, and the noon is the summer." In this way he also followed Emerson's "history" of consciousness. "The Greek," Emerson wrote, "was the age of observation; the Middle Age, that of fact and thought; ours, that of reflection and ideas." In *Walden*, Thoreau's development began in the summer, the season of the senses and of delicious out-of-door life. This was the period when he was in sympathetic communion with Nature, refreshed by the tonic of wildness. The chapters on "Sounds" and "Solitude" belong to this period, during which he enjoyed the atmospheric presence of Nature so essential to his inspiration. And the hut, which he began in the spring and first occupied at this time, was merely a frame through which Nature readily passed.

When the "north wind had already begun to cool the pond," Thoreau said that he first began to "inhabit my house." During the autumn season of harvest and preparation for winter, he lathed and plastered; and finally as winter approached he built his fireplace and chimney, "the most vital part of the house. . . ." By the fireside, in the period of reflection and inner life, he lingered most, communing with his self.[1] It was the time of soul-searching, when he cut through the pond's ice and saw that "its bright sanded floor [was] the same as in the summer"; and before the ice broke up he surveyed its bottom. Even in this desolate season Thoreau looked for all the signs of spring's organic promise, and in the representative anecdote of his despair, he told of Nature's sustaining power: "After a still winter night I awoke with the impression that some question had been put to me, which I had been endeavoring in vain to answer in my sleep, as what—how—when—where? But there was dawning Nature, in whom all creatures live, looking in at my broad windows with serene and satisfied face, and no questions on *her* lips. I awoke to an answered question, to Nature and

1. Hawthorne in "Peter Goldthwaite's Treasure" and Melville in "I and My Chimney" also made imaginative use of the house and the chimney.

daylight." Even in the winter of his discontent, Nature seemed to him to say " 'Forward' " and he could calmly await the inevitable golden age of spring.

V

Rebirth came with spring. In one of the best sustained analogies in transcendental writing, the chapter "Spring," Thoreau reported ecstatically the translation of the frozen sand and clay of the railroad cut into the thawing streams of life. Looking at the sand foliage—the work of an hour—he said that "I am affected as if . . . I stood in the laboratory of the Artist who made the world and me. . . ." The Artist of the world, like Thoreau and like Goethe whom he had in mind, labored "with the idea inwardly" and its correspondence, its flowering, was the leaf. Everywhere Thoreau perceived this symbol of creation, and in ascending forms from the sand, the animal body, the feathers and wings of birds, to the "airy" butterfly. "Thus it seemed," he wrote, "that this one hillside illustrated the principle of all the operations of Nature. The Maker of this earth but patented a leaf." And the moral Thoreau drew from this illustration was the central law of his life, for it was the law of renewal: "This earth is not a mere fragment of dead history, stratum upon stratum like the leaves of a book, to be studied by geologists and antiquarians chiefly, but living poetry like the leaves of a tree, which precede flowers and fruit,—not a fossil earth, but a living earth; compared with whose great central life all animal and vegetable life is merely parasitic. Its throes will heave our exuviae from their graves." And furthermore the law applied to man and the higher society: ". . . the institutions upon it [the earth] are plastic like clay in the hands of the potter."

For Thoreau, who had found that the law of his life was the law of Life, these perceptions were the stuff of ecstasy. Reveling in the sound of the first sparrow, Thoreau wrote, "What at such a time are histories, chronologies, traditions, and all written revelations?" The spring had brought forth "the symbol of perpetual youth," the grass-blade; human life, having died down to its root, now put forth "its green blade to eternity." Walden Pond had begun to melt—"Walden was dead and is alive again." The change in the flowing sand, from excremental to spiritual, had also been accomplished in him by the discipline of purity: "The change from storm and winter to serene and mild weather, from dark and sluggish hours to bright and elastic ones." Like the dawning of inspiration this "memorable crisis" was "seemingly instantaneous at last." "Suddenly," Thoreau recorded that change, "an influx of light filled my house, though evening was at hand, and the clouds of winter still overhung it, and the eaves were dripping with sleety rain. I looked out of the window, and lo! where yesterday was cold grey ice there lay the transparent pond already calm and full of hope as in a summer evening, reflecting a summer evening sky in its bosom, though none was visible overhead, as if it had intelligence with some remote horizon. I heard a robin in the distance, the first I had heard for many a thousand years, methought, whose note I shall not forget for many a thousand more,—the same sweet and powerful song as of yore. . . . So I came in, and shut the door, and passed my first spring night in the woods."

With the coming of spring had come "the creation of Cosmos out of Chaos and the realization of the Golden Age." And with his renewal had come the vindication of his life of purity. He had recorded what he felt was nowhere recorded, "a simple and irrepressible satisfaction with the gift of life. . . ." He had suggested what the eye of the partridge symbolized to him, not merely "the purity of infancy, but a wisdom clarified by experience." He had recounted the experience of his purification so well that even the reader who accepts only the residual statement feels purified. "I do not say," he wisely wrote at the end of *Walden*, "that John or Jonathan will realize all this [the perfect summer life]; but such is the character of that morrow which mere lapse of time can never make to dawn." To affirm this eternal present, to restore, as he said in "The Service," the original of which Nature is the reflection, he fashioned *Walden* as he himself lived, after the example of the artist of the city of Kouroo. This parable unlocks the largest meaning of the book. The artist of Kouroo "was disposed to strive after perfection," Thoreau wrote; and striving, he lived in the eternity of inspiration which made the passing of dynasties, even eras, an illusion. In fashioning his staff, merely by minding his destiny and his art, he had made a new world "with full and fair proportions." The result, Thoreau knew, could not be "other than wonderful," because "the material was pure, and his art was pure. . . ."

E. B. WHITE

Walden—1954†

In his journal for July 10–12, 1841, Thoreau wrote: "A slight sound at evening lifts me up by the ears, and makes life seem inexpressibly serene and grand. It may be in Uranus, or it may be in the shutter." The book into which he later managed to pack both Uranus and the shutter was published in 1854, and now, a hundred years having gone by, "Walden," its serenity and grandeur unimpaired, still lifts us up by the ears, still translates for us that language we are in danger of forgetting, "which all things and events speak without metaphor, which alone is copious and standard."

"Walden" is an oddity in American letters. It may very well be the oddest of our distinguished oddities. For many it is a great deal too odd, and for many it is a particular bore. I have not found it to be a well-liked book among my acquaintances, although usually spoken of with respect, and one literary critic for whom I have the highest regard can find no reason why

† "A Slight Sound at Evening" from *The Points of My Compass* by E. B. White. Copyright 1954 by E. B. White. Originally published in *The Yale Review* under the title "Walden—1954." Reprinted by permission of Harper-Collins Publishers.

anyone gives "Walden" a second thought. To admire the book is, in fact, something of an embarrassment, for the mass of men have an indistinct notion that its author was a sort of Nature Boy.

I think it is of some advantage to encounter the book at a period in one's life when the normal anxieties and enthusiasms and rebellions of youth closely resemble those of Thoreau in that spring of 1845 when he borrowed an axe, went out to the woods, and began to whack down some trees for timber. Received at such a juncture, the book is like an invitation to life's dance, assuring the troubled recipient that no matter what befalls him in the way of success or failure he will always be welcome at the party—that the music is played for him, too, if he will but listen and move his feet. In effect, that is what the book is—an invitation, unengraved; and it stirs one as a young girl is stirred by her first big party bid. Many think it a sermon; many set it down as an attempt to rearrange society; some think it an exercise in nature-loving; some find it a rather irritating collection of inspirational puffballs by an eccentric show-off. I think it none of these. It still seems to me the best youth's companion yet written by an American, for it carries a solemn warning against the loss of one's valuables, it advances a good argument for traveling light and trying new adventures, it rings with the power of positive adoration, it contains religious feelings without religious images, and it steadfastly refuses to record bad news. Even its pantheistic note is so pure as to be noncorrupting—pure as the flute-note blown across the pond on those faraway summer nights. If our colleges and universities were alert, they would present a cheap pocket edition of the book to every senior upon graduating, along with his sheepskin, or instead of it. Even if some senior were to take it literally and start felling trees, there could be worse mishaps: the axe is older than the Dictaphone and it is just as well for a young man to see what kind of chips he leaves before listening to the sound of his own voice. And even if some were to get no farther than the table of contents, they would learn how to name eighteen chapters by the use of only thirty-nine words and would see how sweet are the uses of brevity.

If Thoreau had merely left us an account of a man's life in the woods, or if he had simply retreated to the woods and there recorded his complaints about society, or even if he had contrived to include both records in one essay, "Walden" would probably not have lived a hundred years. As things turned out, Thoreau, very likely without knowing quite what he was up to, took man's relation to nature and man's dilemma in society and man's capacity for elevating his spirit and he beat all these matters together, in a wild free interval of self-justification and delight, and produced an original omelette from which people can draw nourishment in a hungry day. "Walden" is one of the first of the vitamin-enriched American dishes. If it were a little less good than it is, or even a little less queer, it would be an abominable book. Even as it is, it will continue to baffle and annoy the literal mind and all those who are unable to stomach its caprices and imbibe its theme. Certainly the plodding economist will continue to have rough going if he hopes to emerge from the book with a clear system of economic thought. Thoreau's assault on the Concord society of the mid-nineteenth century has the quality of a modern Western: he rides into the subject at top speed, shooting in all directions. Many of his shots ricochet and nick him on the rebound, and throughout the melee there is a horrendous cloud of inconsistencies and contradictions, and when the shooting dies down and the air clears, one is impressed chiefly by the courage of the rider and by how splendid it was that somebody should have ridden in there and raised all that ruckus.

When he went to the pond, Thoreau struck an attitude and did so deliberately, but his posturing was not to draw the attention of others to him but rather to draw his own attention more closely to himself. "I learned this at least by my experiment: that if one advances confidently in the direction of his dreams, and endeavors to live the life which he has imagined, he will meet with a success unexpected in common hours." The sentence has the power to resuscitate the youth drowning in his sea of doubt. I recall my exhilaration upon reading it, many years ago, in a time of hesitation and despair. It restored me to health. And now in 1954 when I salute Henry Thoreau on the hundredth birthday of his book, I am merely paying off an old score—or an installment on it.

In his journal for May 3–4, 1838—Boston to Portland—he wrote: "Midnight—head over the boat's side—between sleeping and waking—with glimpses of one or more lights in the vicinity of Cape Ann. Bright moonlight—the effect heightened by seasickness." The entry illuminates the man, as the moon the sea on that night in May. In Thoreau the natural scene was heightened, not depressed, by a disturbance of the stomach, and nausea met its match at last. There was a steadiness in at least one passenger if there was none in the boat. Such steadiness (which in some would be called intoxication) is at the heart of "Walden"—confidence, faith, the discipline of looking always at what is to be seen, undeviating gratitude for the life-everlasting that he found growing in his front yard. "There is nowhere recorded a simple and irrepressible satisfaction with the gift of life, any memorable praise of God." He worked to correct that deficiency. "Walden" is his acknowledgment of the gift of life. It is the testament of a man in a high state of indignation because (it seemed to him) so few ears heard the uninterrupted poem of creation, the morning wind that forever blows. If the man sometimes wrote as though all his readers were male, unmarried, and well-connected, it is because he gave his testimony during the callow years, and, for that matter, never really grew up. To reject the book because of the immaturity of the author and the bugs in the logic is to throw away a bottle of good wine because it contains a bit of the cork.

Thoreau said he required of every writer, first and last, a simple and sincere account of his own life. Having delivered himself of this chesty dictum, he proceeded to ignore it. In his books and even in his enormous journal, he withheld or disguised most of the facts from which an under-standing of his life could be drawn. "Walden," subtitled "Life in the Woods," is not a simple and sincere account of a man's life, either in or out of the woods; it is an account of a man's journey into the mind, a toot on the trumpet to alert the neighbors. Thoreau was well aware that no one can alert his neighbors who is not wide awake himself, and he went to the woods (among other reasons) to make sure that he would stay awake during his broadcast. What actually took place during the years 1845–47 is largely unrecorded, and the reader is excluded from the private life of the author, who supplies almost no gossip about himself, a great deal about this neighbors and about the universe.

As for me, I cannot in this short ramble give a simple and sincere account of my own life, but I think Thoreau might find it instructive to know that this memorial essay is being written in a house that, through no intent on my part, is the same size and shape of his own domicile on the pond—about ten by fifteen, tight, plainly finished, and at a little distance from my Concord. The house in which I sit this morning was built to accommodate a boat, not a man, but by long experience I have learned that in most respects it shelters me better than the larger dwelling where my bed is, and which, by design, is a manhouse not a boathouse. Here in the boathouse I am a wilder and, it would appear, a healthier man, by a safe margin. I have a chair, a bench, a table, and I can walk into the water if I tire of the land. My house fronts a cove. Two fishermen have just arrived to spot fish from the air—an osprey and a man in a small yellow plane who works for the fish company. The man, I have noticed, is less well equipped than the hawk, who can dive directly on his fish and carry it away, without tele-phoning. A mouse and a squirrel share the house with me. The building is, in fact, a multiple dwelling, a semidetached affair. It is because I am semidetached while here that I find it possible to transact this private business with the fewest obstacles.

There is also a woodchuck here, living forty feet away under the wharf. When the wind is right, he can smell my house; and when the wind is contrary, I can smell his. We both use the wharf for sunning, taking turns, each adjusting his schedule to the other's convenience. Thoreau once ate a woodchuck. I think he felt he owed it to his readers, and that it was little enough, considering the indignities they were suffering at his hands and the dressing-down they were taking. (Parts of "Walden" are pure scold.) Or perhaps he ate the woodchuck because he believed every man should acquire strict business habits and the woodchuck was destroying his market beans. I do not know. Thoreau had a strong experimental streak in him. It is probably no harder to eat a woodchuck than to construct a sentence that lasts a hundred years. At any rate, Thoreau is the only writer I know who prepared himself for his great ordeal by eating a woodchuck; also the only one who got a hangover from drinking too much water. (He was drunk the whole time, though he seldom touched wine or coffee or tea.)

Here in this compact house where I would spend one day as deliberately as Nature if I were not being pressed by *The Yale Review,* and with a woodchuck (as yet uneaten) for neighbor, I can feel the companionship of the occupant of the pondside cabin in Walden woods, a mile from the village, near the Fitchburg right of way. Even my immediate business is no barrier between us: Thoreau occasionally batted out a magazine piece, but was always suspicious of any sort of purposeful work that cut into his time. A man, he said, should take care not to be thrown off the track by every nutshell and mosquito's wing that falls on the rails.

There has been much guessing as to why he went to the pond. To set it down to escapism is, of course, to misconstrue what happened. Henry went forth to battle when he took to the woods, and "Walden" is the report of a man torn by two powerful and opposing drives—the desire to enjoy the world (and not be derailed by a mosquito wing) and the urge to set the world straight. One cannot join these two successfully, but sometimes, in rare cases, something good or even great results from the attempt of the tormented spirit to reconcile them. Henry went forth to battle, and if he set the stage himself, if he fought on his own terms and with his own weapons, it was because it was his nature to do things differently from most men, and to act in a cocky fashion. If the pond and the woods seemed a more plausible site for a house than an in-town location, it was because a cowbell made for him a sweeter sound than a churchbell. "Walden," the book, makes the sound of a cowbell, more than a churchbell, and proves the point, although both sounds are in it, and both remarkably clear and sweet. He simply preferred his churchbell at a little distance.

I think one reason he went to the woods was a perfectly simple and commonplace one—and apparently he thought so, too. "At a certain season of our life," he wrote, "we are accustomed to consider every spot as the possible site of a house." There spoke the young man, a few years out of college, who had not yet broken away from home. He hadn't married, and he had found no job that measured up to his rigid standards of employment, and like any young man, or young animal, he felt uneasy and on the defensive until he had fixed himself a den. Most young men, of course, casting about for a site, are content merely to draw apart from their kinfolks. Thoreau, convinced that the greater part of what his neighbors called good was bad, withdrew from a great deal more than family: he pulled out of everything for a while, to serve everybody right for being so stuffy, and to try his own prejudices on the dog.

The house-hunting sentence above, which starts the Chapter called "Where I Lived, and What I Lived For," is followed by another passage that is worth quoting here because it so beautifully illustrates the offbeat prose that Thoreau was master of, a prose at once strictly disciplined and wildly abandoned. "I have surveyed the country on every side within a dozen miles of where I live," continued this delirious young man. "In imagination I have bought all the farms in succession, for all were to be bought, and I knew their price. I walked over each farmer's premises, tasted his wild apples, discoursed on husbandry with him, took his farm at his price, at any price, mortgaging it to him in my mind; even put a higher price on it—took everything but a deed of it—took his word for his deed, for I dearly love to talk—cultivated it, and him too to some extent, I trust, and withdrew when I had enjoyed it long enough, leaving him to carry it on." A copydesk man would get a double hernia trying to clean up that sentence for the management, but the sentence needs no fixing, for it perfectly captures the meaning of the writer and the quality of the ramble.

"Wherever I sat, there I might live, and the landscape radiated from me accordingly." Thoreau, the home-seeker, sitting on his hummock with the entire State of Massachusetts radiating from him, is to me the most humorous of the New England figures, and "Walden" the most humorous of the books, though its humor is almost continuously subsurface and there is nothing funny anywhere, except a few weak jokes and bad puns that rise to the surface like the perch in the pond that rose to the sound of the maestro's flute. Thoreau tended to write in sentences, a feat not every writer is capable of, and "Walden" is, rhetorically speaking, a collection of certified sentences, some of them, it would now appear, as indestructible as they are errant. The book is distilled from the vast journals, and this accounts for its intensity: he picked out bright particles that pleased his eye, whirled them in the kaleidoscope of his content, and produced the pattern that has endured— the color, the form, the light.

On this its hundredth birthday, Thoreau's "Walden" is pertinent and timely. In our uneasy season, when all men unconsciously seek a retreat from a world that has got almost completely out of hand, his house in the Concord woods is a haven. In our culture of gadgetry and the multiplicity of convenience, his cry "Simplicity, simplicity, simplicity!" has the insistence of a fire alarm. In the brooding atmosphere of war and the gathering radioactive storm, the innocence and serenity of his summer afternoons are enough to burst the remembering heart, and one gazes back upon that pleasing interlude—its confidence, its purity, its deliberateness—with awe and wonder, as one would look upon the face of a child asleep.

"This small lake was of most value as a neighbor in the intervals of a gentle rain-storm in August, when, both air and water being perfectly still, but the sky overcast, midafternoon had all the serenity of evening, and the wood-thrush sang around, and was heard from shore to shore." Now, in the perpetual overcast in which our days are spent, we hear with extra perception and deep gratitude that song, tying century to century.

I sometimes amuse myself by bringing Henry Thoreau back to life and showing him the sights. I escort him into a phone booth and let him dial

Weather. "This is a delicious evening," the girl's voice says, "when the whole body is one sense, and imbibes delight through every pore." I show him the spot in the Pacific where an island used to be, before some magician made it vanish. "We know not where we are," I murmur. "The light which puts out our eyes is darkness to us. Only that day dawns to which we are awake." I thumb through the latest copy of "Vogue" with him. "Of two patterns which differ only by a few threads more or less of a particular color," I read, "the one will be sold readily, the other lie on the shelf, though it frequently happens that, after the lapse of a season, the latter becomes the most fashionable." Together we go outboarding on the Assabet, looking for what we've lost—a hound, a bay horse, a turtledove. I show him a distracted farmer who is trying to repair a hay baler before the thunder shower breaks. "This farmer," I remark, "is endeavoring to solve the problem of a livelihood by a formula more complicated than the problem itself. To get his shoe strings he speculates in herds of cattle."

I take the celebrated author to Twenty-One for lunch, so the waiters may study his shoes. The proprietor welcomes us. "The gross feeder," remarks the proprietor, sweeping the room with his arm, "Is a man in the larva stage." After lunch we visit a classroom in one of those schools conducted by big corporations to teach their superannuated executives how to retire from business without serious injury to their health. (The shock to men's systems these days when relieved of the exacting routine of amassing wealth is very great and must be cushioned.) "It is not necessary," says the teacher to his pupils, "that a man should earn his living by the sweat of his brow, unless he sweats easier than I do. We are determined to be starved before we are hungry."

I turn on the radio and let Thoreau hear Winchell beat the red hand around the clock. "Time is but the stream I go a-fishing in," shouts Mr. Winchell, rattling his telegraph key. "Hardly a man takes a half hour's nap after dinner, but when he wakes he holds up his head and asks, 'What's the news?' If we read of one man robbed, or murdered, or killed by accident, or one house burned, or one vessel wrecked, or one steamboat blown up, or one cow run over on the Western Railroad, or one mad dog killed, or one lot of grasshoppers in the winter—we need never read of another. One is enough."

I doubt that Thoreau would be thrown off balance by the fantastic sights and sounds of the twentieth century. "The Concord nights," he once wrote, "are stranger than the Arabian nights." A four-engined air liner would merely serve to confirm his early views on travel. Everywhere he would observe, in new shapes and sizes, the old predicaments and follies of men—the desperation, the impedimenta, the meanness—along with the visible capacity for elevation of the mind and soul. "This curious world which we inhabit is more wonderful than it is convenient; more beautiful than it is useful; it is more to be admired and enjoyed than used," He would see that today ten thousand engineers are busy making sure that the world shall be convenient if they bust doing it, and others are determined to increase its usefulness even though its beauty is lost somewhere along the way.

At any rate, I'd like to stroll about the countryside in Thoreau's company for a day, observing the modern scene, inspecting today's snowstorm, pointing out the sights, and offering belated apologies for my sins. Thoreau is unique among writers in that those who admire him find him uncomfortable to live with—a regular hairshirt of a man. A little band of dedicated Thoreauvians would be a sorry sight indeed: fellows who hate compromise and have compromised, fellows who love wildness and have lived tamely, and at their side, censuring them and chiding them, the ghostly figure of this upright man, who long ago gave corroboration to impulses they perceived were right and issued warnings against the things they instinctively knew to be their enemies. I should hate to be called a Thoreauvian, yet I wince every time I walk into the barn I'm pushing before me, seventy-five feet by forty, and the author of "Walden" has served as my conscience through the long stretches of my trivial days.

Hairshirt or no, he is a better companion than most, and I would not swap him for a soberer or more reasonable friend even if I could. I can reread his famous invitation with undiminished excitement. The sad thing is that not more acceptances have been received, that so many decline for one reason or another, pleading some previous engagement or ill health. But the invitation stands. It will beckon as long as this remarkable book stays in print—which will be as long as there are August afternoons in the intervals of a gentle rainstorm, as long as there are ears to catch the faint sounds of the orchestra. I find it agreeable to sit here this morning, in a house of correct proportions, and hear across a century of time his flute, his frogs, and his seductive summons to the wildest revels of them all.

RICHARD DRINNON

Thoreau's Politics of the Upright Man†

"In imagination I hie me to Greece as to an enchanted ground," Thoreau declared in his *Journal* and then proved himself as good as his word in his lecture on "The Rights & Duties of the Individual in relation to Government." There was not a major figure in the classical background of anarchism whom Thoreau did not draw upon in some way. Though he may have been unaware of Zeno's strictures against Plato's omnicompetent state, he assuredly honored the Stoic for his individualism, his use of paradox, perhaps his belief in transcendent universal laws, certainly his serenity—"play high, play low," Thoreau observed with delight, "rain, sleet, or snow—it's all the

† Reprinted from *The Massachusetts Review* 4.1 (Autumn 1962): 126–38. Copyright © 1963, The Massachusetts Review, Inc. *Walden* page numbers refer to this Norton Critical Edition.

same with the Stoic." He read Ovid with pleasure, used a quotation from the *Metamorphoses* as an epigraph for his *Week on the Concord and Merrimack Rivers*, and must have been well aware of Ovid's nostalgia for a time when there was no state and "everyone of his own will kept faith and did the right." But he found the most dramatic presentation of libertarian views in the *Antigone* of Sophocles. In this great drama of rebellion the central conflict was between the spirited Antigone and her uncle Creon, a not unkind man who had just ascended the throne of Thebes. Corrupted a little already by his power, blinded more than a little by bureaucratic definitions of right and wrong and advancing specious reasons of state as justification for his actions, Creon forbade the burial of the dead traitor Polynices. Driven by love for her slain brother and more by her awareness of the unambiguous commands of the gods to bury the dead, Antigone defied Creon's order. When she was brought before the king, she proudly avowed her defiance:

> For it was not Zeus who proclaimed these to me, not Justice who dwells with the gods below; it was not they who established these laws among men. Nor did I think that your proclamations were so strong, as, being a mortal, to be able to transcend the unwritten and immovable laws of the gods. For not something now and yesterday, but forever these live, and no one knows from what time they appeared. I was not about to pay the penalty of violating these to the gods, fearing the presumption of any man.

In his lecture on the individual and the state, which became the essay printed first as "Resistance to Civil Government" and later under the famous title "Civil Disobedience," Thoreau echoed Antigone's magnificent lines in his admission that "it costs me less in every sense to incur the penalty of disobedience to the State than it would to obey" and in his declaration that "they only can force me who obey a higher law than I." Like Sophocles' heroine, Thoreau made quite clear his rejection of the Periclean argument of Creon that the highest responsibility of the individual must be to the state and his rejection of the later Platonic assumption of a pleasing harmony between the laws of man and the laws of the gods. The kernel of Thoreau's politics was his belief in a natural or higher law; for the formulation of his essay on this subject, his indebtedness to the Greek tragedian was considerable.

Yet no single work provided Thoreau with his key concept.[1] In his day the doctrine of a fundamental law still covered Massachusetts like a ground fog. It had survived the classical period, had become the eternal law of

---

1. Thanks to the careful researches of Ethel Seybold, *Thoreau: The Quest and the Classics* (New Haven: Yale University Press, 1951), 16, 17, 24, 66, 75, we know that Thoreau read the *Antigone* at Harvard and probably twice thereafter, once at the time he was working up his lecture on the dangers of civil disobedience and once in the 1850's. Unfortunately Miss Seybold overstates her case by making the *Antigone* "probably responsible for one whole section of Thoreau's thought and public expression. From it must have come his concept of the divine law as superior to the civil law, of human right as greater than legal right."

Aquinas, the anti-papal fundamental law of Wycliffe, and, through Calvin, Milton, and Locke, had flowed across the Atlantic to furnish the colonists with their indispensable "Word of God." The more secular emphasis of the eighteenth century on the "unalienable Rights" possessed by every individual in a state of nature made little difference in end result—little difference at least in doctrine, for all along men had thought it natural for a higher law to be the basis for legislation. In nineteenth-century Massachusetts the existence of a fundamental, higher law was accepted by radicals such as Alcott and Garrison, by liberals such as William Ellery Channing, and by conservatives such as Justice Joseph Story. These older countrymen of Thoreau were joined by Emerson, whose essay on "Politics," published five years before "Civil Disobedience," had a more direct influence on the young rebel. To be sure, Emerson approached the crass Toryism of Chancellor Kent in discussing "higher law" by attaching it to the power of property. But Emerson was usually much better—at his worst he could sound like an early incarnation of Bruce Barton—than his lines on wealth and property would suggest; most of "Politics" was on the higher ground of a radical Jeffersonianism:

> Hence the less government we have the better—the fewer laws and the less confided power. The antidote to this abuse of formal government is the influence of private character, the growth of the Individual . . . the appearance of the wise man; of whom the existing government is, it must be owned, but a shabby imitation. . . . To educate the wise man the State exists, and with the appearance of the wise man the State expires. The appearance of character makes the State unnecessary. The wise man is the State.[2]

Emerson even averred that "good men must not obey the law too well."

The similarity of Emerson's point of view and even his language to Thoreau's must be clear to anyone who has carefully read "Civil Disobedience." Living where he did when he did, Thoreau could hardly have escaped the doctrine of a higher law. It was hardly fortuitous that *all* the most notable American individualist anarchists—Josiah Warren, Ezra Heywood, William B. Greene, Joshua K. Ingalls, Stephen Pearl Andrews, Lysander Spooner, and Benjamin Tucker—came from Thoreau's home state of Massachusetts and were his contemporaries. Tying the development of American anarchism to native traditions and conditions, Tucker uttered only a little white exaggeration when he claimed that he and his fellow anarchists were "simply unterrified Jeffersonian democrats."[3]

Thus the doctrine of higher law, as Benjamin Wright once remarked, logically leads to philosophical anarchism. True, but this truth can be misleading without the warning note that the logic has to be followed out

2. *The Complete Essays* (New York: Modern Library, 1940), 431.
3. Quoted in Rudolf Rocker, *Pioneers of American Freedom* (Los Angeles: Rocker Publications Committee, 1949), 150. A more recent and helpful study of early American anarchism is James J. Martin, *Men against the State* (DeKalb, Illinois: Adrian Allen Associates, 1953).

to the end. Half-way covenants can lead to something very different. John Cotton, for instance, believed in a higher law, yet came down on the side of authority and the Massachusetts establishment; Roger Williams believed no less in a higher law, yet came down on the side of freedom and the individual. Like all ideas, that of a higher law could become a weapon in the hands of groups and institutions. For Thomas Aquinas *lex aeterna* meant the supremacy of the church, for Thomas Hobbes the "Law of Nature" meant the supremacy of the state. For Jefferson and Paine, natural law meant revolution and the establishment of a counter state. But for Thoreau it meant no supremacy of church over state or vice versa, or of one state over another, or of one group over another. It meant rather the logical last step of *individual action*. Belief in higher law *plus* practice of individual direct action *equal* anarchism. "I must conclude that Conscience, if that be the name of it," wrote Thoreau in the *Week*, "was not given us for no purpose, or for a hindrance." From Antigone to Bronson Alcott, Thoreau, and Benjamin Tucker, the individuals who acted on the imperatives of their consciences, "cost what it may," were anarchists.[4]

2.

So much for the main sources and the master pillars of Thoreau's political position. I have argued that in those crucial matters in which expediency was not applicable, it added up to anarchism. But the question of whether this made him a workaday anarchist lands us in the middle of a tangle. Was Thoreau really an individualist, an anarchist, or both, or neither? Emma Goldman defined anarchism as "the philosophy of a new social order based on liberty unrestricted by man-made law" and once spent an evening in Concord vainly trying to persuade Franklin Sanborn that under this definition Thoreau was an anarchist. Joseph Wood Krutch doubts that Thoreau felt a direct responsibility for any social order, old or new, and stresses his "defiant individualism."[5] Sherman Paul, on the other hand laments that "one of the most persistent errors concerning Thoreau that has never been sufficiently dispelled is that Thoreau was an anarchial individualist."[6] Still, "Thoreau was not an anarchist but an individualist," argues John Haynes Holmes.[7] The tangle becomes impassable with Paul's additional observation that Thoreau "was not objecting to government but to what we now call the State."

4. In 1875 Tucker followed Thoreau's example and refused to pay the poll tax of the town of Princeton, Massachusetts; he was imprisoned in Worcester a short while for his refusal—see Martin, *Men Against the State*, pp. 203–04. It had almost become a habit in the area. Three years before Thoreau spent his night in jail, Alcott was arrested for not paying his poll tax. Thoreau was probably influenced by his example and by the civil disobedience agitation of William Lloyd Garrison and his followers—see Wendell Glick, " 'Civil Disobedience': Thoreau's Attack upon Relativism,"

Western Humanities Review, VII (Winter 1952–53), 35–42.
5. Krutch, *Henry David Thoreau* (New York: William Sloane, 1948), 133–35.
6. Paul, *The Shores of America: Thoreau's Inward Exploration* (Urbana: University of Illinois Press, 1958), 75–80, 377. Paul emphasizes Thoreau's willingness to have "governmental interference for the general welfare."
7. Holmes, "Thoreau's 'Civil Disobedience,' " *Christian Century*, LXVI (January-June 1949), 787–89.

There are two main reasons for this muddle. Thoreau was himself partially responsible. His sly satire, his liking for wide margins for his writing, and his fondness for paradox provided ammunition for widely divergent interpretations of "Civil Disobedience." Thus, governments being but expedients, he looks forward to a day when men will be prepared for the motto: "That government is best which governs not at all." The reader proceeds through some lines highly critical of the American government, only to be brought up sharp, in the third paragraph, by the sweet reasonableness of the author: "But, to speak practically and as a citizen, unlike those who call themselves no-government men, I ask for, not at once no government, but *at once* a better government." Those who discount Thoreau's radicalism snap up this sentence which seems clear on the face of it: Do not think me an extremist like the Garrisonians and anarchists, he seems to be saying, but think of me as one who moderately desires a better government now. But is this all he wants? Might he not favor, a *little later*, no government? Shattered by this doubt, the reader is thrown forward into another bitter attack on the American government and on the generic state. It becomes increasingly clear that critics who have tried to put together a governmentalist from Thoreau's writings on politics have humorlessly missed the point. He does indeed say that he will take what he can from the state, but he also twits himself a little for inconsistency: "In fact, I quietly declare war with the State, after my fashion, though I will still make what use and get what advantage of her I can, as is usual in such cases." Compare Thoreau's wry position here with that of Alex Comfort, the English anarchist, written a hundred years later: "We do not refuse to drive on the left hand side of the road or to subscribe to national health insurance. The sphere of our disobedience is limited to the sphere in which society exceeds its powers and its usefulness. . . ."[8] But let us back up a bit. What was the nature of the "better government" he wanted at once? Obviously it was one that would stay strictly in its place and ungrow—progressively cease to exist. What was the "best government" he could imagine? He has already told us and the essay as a whole supports his declaration: a government "which governs not at all."

But the main obstacle to any clear cut identification of Thoreau's politics has been the uncertain shifting borders of anarchism, liberalism, and socialism in the nineteenth century and after. No series of definitions has succeeded in decisively marking out their frontiers. Stephen Pearl Andrews, for instance, the erudite contemporary of Thoreau, conceived of himself as at one and the same time a believer in the socialism of Charles Fourier and the anarchism of Josiah Warren. The intermingling of socialism and anarchism is further illustrated by Mikhail Bakunin, the founder of communist anarchism, who thought of himself as a socialist and fought Marx for the

8. Quoted by Nicolas Walter, "Disobedience and the New Pacifism," *Anarchy*, No. 14 (April 1962), 113. It is worth noting that Walter thinks "Thoreau wasn't an anarchist," though he believes that "the implications of his action and his essay are purely anarchist. . . ."

control of the First International. Even Marx has been called an ultimate anarchist, in the sense that he presumably favored anarchism after the state withered away. But perhaps the closest analogue to Thoreau was William Morris. Working closely with Peter Kropotkin for a number of years, Morris rejected the parliamentarians and joined forces with the libertarians in the Socialist League of the 1880's—the League was eventually taken over completely by anarchists!—and wrote *News from Nowhere* which was anarchist in tone and sentiment. Yet his explanation of why he refused to call himself an anarchist was obviously confused and showed that he was rejecting individualist anarchism and not Kropotkin's communist anarchism.[9]

A somewhat comparable confusion mars a recent attempt to analyze Thoreau's position. He was not "an anarchical individualist," argues Paul, because he went to Walden not "for himself alone but to serve mankind." It would be easy to quote passages from *Walden* which seem to call this contention into question. One example: "What good I do, in the common sense of that word, must be aside from my main path, and for the most part wholly unintended." Another: "While my townsmen and women are devoted in so many ways to the good of their fellows, I trust that one at least may be spared to other and less humane pursuits."[1] Yet this would be to read Thoreau literally. Unquestionably, as he informed us in "Civil Disobedience," he was "as desirous of being a good neighbor as I am of being a bad subject." The distinction was crucial. Though he served the state by declaring war on it, in his own way, he served society for a lifetime by trying to understand and explain Concord to itself. The manageable unit of society—unlike the vast abstraction in Washington or even Boston—was drawn to the human scale of Concord and other villages. If men lived simply and as neighbors, informal patterns of voluntary agreement would be established, there would be no need for police and military protection, since "thieving and robbery would be unknown,"[2] and there would be freedom and leisure to turn to the things that matter. Thoreau's community consciousness was the essential, dialectical *other* of his individuality. Consider the following from *Walden*:

> It is time that villages were universities, and their elder inhabitants the fellows of universities, with leisure . . . to pursue liberal studies the rest of their lives. Shall the world be confined to one Paris or one Oxford forever? Cannot students be boarded here and get a liberal education under the skies of Concord? . . . Why should our life be in any respect provincial? If we will read newspapers, why not skip the gossip of Boston and take the best newspaper in the world at once. . . . As the nobleman of cultivated taste surrounds himself with whatever conduces to his culture—genius—learning—wit—books—paintings—statuary—music—

9. George Woodcock and Ivan Avakumovic, *The Anarchist Prince* (London: T. V. Boardman, 1950), 216–19. Thoreau's great influence on the English left dates back to this period when many were filled with idealism and with admiration for the "sublime doctrine" of anarchism.
1. *Walden* 49.
2. *Walden* 116.

philosophical instruments and the like; so let the village do. . . . To act collectively is according to the spirit of our institutions. . . . Instead of noblemen, let us have noble villages of men.[3]

One nobleman who also agitated for noble villages was the anarchist Kropotkin. He could have agreed completely with Thoreau's preoccupation with his locality and his readiness to act collectively "in the spirit of our institutions." In *Mutual Aid* (1902), Kropotkin celebrated the vital growth of society in the ancient Greek and medieval cities; he sadly outlined the consequences of the rise of centralization when the state "took possession, in the interest of minorities, of all the judicial, economical, and administrative functions which the village community already had exercised in the interest of all." Like Thoreau, Kropotkin advocated that the community's power be restored and that local individuality and creativity be left free to develop. The closeness of their views—though Kropotkin must have thought Thoreau too much an individualist like Ibsen!—points up the mistake of Sherman Paul and others in equating the "anti-social" with the "anarchical." Society and the state, as Thoreau and Kropotkin were very much aware, should not be confused or identified.

The definition of Emma Goldman quoted above will have to do for our purposes, then, though we must keep in mind its approximate nature and the greased-pole slipperiness of the political theory from which Thoreau's views are so often confidently said to have differed. Under this definition Thoreau was always an anarchist in matters of conscience, an ultimate anarchist for a time "when men are prepared for it," and in the meanwhile an anarchical decentralist. But enough of this attempt to stuff the poet and mystic in one political slot. Actually Thoreau's writings may yet help to explode all our conventional political categories.

3.

"We scarcely know whether to call him the last of an older race of men, or the first of one that is to come," admitted an English critic in *The Times Literary Supplement* for 12 July 1917. "He had the toughness, the stoicism, the unspoilt senses of an Indian, combined with the self-consciousness, the exacting discontent, the susceptibility of the most modern. At times he seems to reach beyond our human powers in what he perceives upon the horizon of humanity." With remarkable insight, the writer had perceived Thoreau's perplexing doubleness and had even touched the edge of his higher, profoundly exciting unity.

Of Thoreau's "unspoilt senses of an Indian" and his passion for the primitive there can be no question. "There is in my nature, methinks," he

3. *Walden* 74 ff. By all means see Lewis Mumford's fine discussion of Thoreau in his chapter on "Renewal of the Landscape," in *The Brown Decades* (New York: Dover Publications, 1955), 64–72. Mumford credits Thoreau with the achievement of helping "to acclimate the mind of highly sensitive and civilized men to the natural possibilities of the environment" and gives him a major place in the history of regional planning in America. The influence of Thoreau on Paul Goodman, who describes himself as a "community anarchist," is apparent to anyone who has read his and his brother Percival's *Communitas* (Chicago: University of Chicago Press, 1947).

declared in the *Week*, "a singular yearning toward all wildness." To the end he was convinced that "life consists with wildness." But this conviction did not rest on a sentimental-romantic view of our "rude forefathers." The crude relics of the North American tribes, their improvident carelessness even in the woods, and their "coarse and imperfect use" of nature repelled him. His unpleasant experience of a moose-hunt in Maine led to the reflection: "No wonder that their race is so soon exterminated. I already, and for weeks afterwards, felt my nature the coarser for this part of my woodland experience, and was reminded that our life should be lived as tenderly and daintily as one would pluck a flower."[4] Yet Thoreau never gave up his conviction that, standing so close, Indians had a particularly intimate and vital relationship with nature. "We talk of civilizing the Indian," he wrote in the *Week*, "but that is not the name for his improvement. By the wary independence and aloofness of his dim forest life he preserves his intercourse with his native gods, and is admitted from time to time to a rare and peculiar society with nature. He had glances of starry recognition to which our saloons are strangers."

By way of contrast, "the white man comes, pale as the dawn, with a load of thought, with a slumbering intelligence as a fire raked up, knowing well what he knows, not guessing but calculating; strong in community, yielding obedience to authority; of experienced race; of wonderful, wonderful common sense; dull but capable, slow but persevering, severe but just, of little humor but genuine; a laboring man, despising game and sport; building a house that endures, a framed house. He buys the Indian's moccasins and baskets, then buys his hunting-grounds, and at length forgets where he is buried and plows up his bones."[5] In this list of the bourgeois virtues, the keen, far-reaching social criticism of "Life Without Principle"—first entitled "Higher Law"—and indeed of *Walden* itself is anticipated. Calculating for the main chance, this obedient white man had cut his way through thousands of Indians in order to rush to the gold diggings in California, "reflect the greatest disgrace on mankind," and "live by luck, and so get the means of commanding the labor of others less lucky, without contributing any value to society! And that is called enterprise! I know of no more startling development of the immortality of trade. . . . The hog that gets his living by rooting, stirring up the soil so, would be ashamed of such company."[6] In this powerful essay on "Life Without Principle," he concluded that "there is nothing, not even crime, more opposed to poetry, to philosophy, ay, to life itself, than this incessant business." An economist of importance, as the first chapter of *Walden* may yet prove to a skeptical world, Thoreau saw clearly that the accumulation of wealth really leads to the cheapening of life, to the substitution for man of the less-than-hog-like creature who cal-

4. Quoted in Albert Keiser, *The Indian in American Literature* (New York: Oxford University Press, 1933), 227.

5. *Works*, I, 52–53; see also 55.
6. "Life without Principle."

culates and lays up money and even fails to root up the soil in the process. "What is called politics," he wrote in "Life Without Principle," "is comparatively something so superficial and unhuman, that practically I have never fairly recognized that it concerns me at all." The war against Mexico, the scramble for territory and power, and other debauches in nationalism were, he trusted, a different manifest destiny from his own. In his letter to Parker Pillsbury on the eve of the fighting at Fort Sumter, he reported that he did "not so much regret the present condition of things in this country (provided I regret it at all) as I do that I ever heard of it. I know one or 2 who have this year, for the first time, read a president's message; but they do not see that this implies a fall in themselves, rather than a rise in the president. Blessed were the days before you read a president's message. Blessed are the young for they do not read the president's message."[7] Yet, despite all these devastating shafts aimed at the institutions reared up by the "pale as dawn" white man, Thoreau honored learning as much or more than any man in America. Far from advocating a return to some preliterate bliss, he advocated, in his chapter on "Reading" in *Walden,* a study of "the oldest and the best" books, whose "authors are a natural and irresistible aristocracy in every society, and, more than kings or emperors, exert an influence on mankind."

Thus Thoreau's doubleness, of which he was well aware: "I find an instinct in me conducting to a mystic spiritual life, and also another to a primitive savage life." It was one of his great achievements to go beyond the polarities of "Civilization and Barbarism"—alternatively attractive poles which drew most of Thoreau's contemporaries helplessly back and forth like metal particles—to come close to a creative fusion: "We go eastward to realize history and study the works of art and literature, retracing the steps of the race," he wrote in the serene summary of his walks. "We go westward as into the future, with a spirit of enterprise and adventure." Thoreau wanted the best for his countrymen from both nature and civilization, past and present. He perceived clearly the meaning of America. It was an opportunity for new beginnings: "The Atlantic is a Lethean stream, in our passage over which we have had an opportunity to forget the Old World and its institutions. If we do not succeed this time, there is perhaps one more chance for the race left before it arrives on the banks of the Styx; and that is in the Lethe of the Pacific, which is three times as wide." Had he lived with unflagging powers for another decade or so, he might have used his laboriously accumulated notebooks of "Extracts relating to the Indians" to show why the aborigines enjoyed "a rare and peculiar society with nature." It is indisputable that his interest in classical mythology, ancient societies, and contemporary tribes was an anthropological concern for the enduring features of life in groups. His interest in savages was much like that of Claude Lévi-Strauss and might

7. His reference to "manifest destiny" appeared in his letter to H. G. O. Blake, 27 February 1853; his letter to Pillsbury was dated 10 April 1861—*The Correspondence of Henry David Thoreau,* eds. Walter Harding and Carl Bode (New York: New York University Press, 1958), 296, 611.

have been expressed in the latter's words: "The study of these savages does not reveal a Utopian state in Nature; nor does it make us aware of a perfect society hidden deep in the forests. It helps us to construct a theoretical model of society which corresponds to none that can be observed in reality, but will help us to disentangle 'what in the present nature of Man is original, and what is artificial.' "[8] Thoreau's theoretical model, which came from all his efforts to drive life into a corner and get its measurements, made it clear that the efforts of his neighbors to live for the superfluous made their lives superfluous. Through careful inspection of his model, he was able to see, years before Lenin, that at bottom the state is a club. To cooperate with it, especially in matters of importance, is to deny life, for the state, like a standing army, is organized power and at the disposal of hate. "You must get your living by loving," confidently declared this supposedly narrow village eccentric. Clearly, he aspired to create for his countrymen a "new heaven and a new earth," just as each of Greece's sons had done for her. The look of this new heaven is suggested by a passage in the *Week*. On Saturday, after he and John had made the long pull from Ball's Hill to Carlisle Bridge, they saw "men haying far off in the meadow, their heads waving like the grass which they cut. In the distance the wind seemed to bend all alike. As the night stole over, such a freshness was wafted across the meadow that every blade of grass seemed to teem with life."

To this feeling of the correspondence of man to nature, "so that he is at home in her," Thoreau added poetic intuitions of an individualism to come. With his common sense, he realized that the notorious common sense of his countrymen was insane. The important questions were buried under daily rounds of trivia. Living was constantly deferred. No joyful exuberance was allowed to slip by prudence. Thoreau could have joined William Blake in his belief that "Prudence is a rich, ugly old maid, courted by Incapacity." The incapacity was partly the result of a split between the head and the heart, thought and feeling, and the absurd belief that the intellect alone enables man to meet life. In his final summing up, in the essay "Walking," he warned that the most we can hope to achieve is "Sympathy with Intelligence . . . a discovery that there are more things in heaven and earth than are dreamed of in our philosophy." But his neighbors not only had an overfaith in abstract reasoning and in the general efficacy of the intellect; they also distrusted the body. William Blake could thrust through the prudishness of his time to rediscover the body; hemmed in by the moral sentimentalism of his family, by Emersonian etherealness, and his own confirmed virginity, Thoreau had more difficulty. His embarrassing admission—"what the essential difference between man and woman is, that they should be thus attracted to one another, no one has satisfactorily answered"—is indeed, as Krutch points out, "a real howler."[9] Nevertheless, he took a sensuous delight in his body, claiming in the *Week* that "we need pray for

8. Lévi-Strauss, "Tristes Tropiques," *Encounter*, XC (April 1961), 40.

9. Krutch, *Thoreau*, 207.

no higher heaven than the pure senses can furnish, a purely sensuous life. Our present senses are but rudiments of what they are destined to become." Here is a body mysticism which placed Thoreau in the tradition of Jacob Boehme and William Blake. It presupposed, Norman Brown observes, that "the consciousness strong enough to endure full life would be no longer Apollonian but Dionysian—consciousness which does not observe the limit, but overflows; consciousness which *does not negate any more*.[1] Shocked by phallic forms in nature, the stiff-backed Thoreau yet remarked that he worshipped most constantly at the shrine of Pan—Pan, the upright man of the Arcadian fertility cult, famous for his Dionysiac revels with the mountain nymphs![2] The vision of individuals with spiritual development and the simple animal strength to affirm their bodies was one of the important contributions of this paradoxical celibate. It was a vision sensed and acted upon, in their own ways, by Isadora Duncan and Emma Goldman and Randolph Bourne and Frank Lloyd Wright. It exerts its appeal to the poetic libertarian strain in radicalism, to men as diverse as e. e. cummings, Karl Shapiro, Henry Miller, Paul Goodman, Kenneth Patchen, Herbert Read, the late Albert Camus and Nicolas Berdyaev. A recent, rather extravagant form is perhaps Allen Ginsberg's notion of "Socialist-Co-op Anarchism." In any form it is revolutionary.

"One thing about Thoreau keeps him very near to me," Walt Whitman remarked. "I refer to his lawlessness—his dissent—his going his absolute own road let hell blaze all it chooses."[3] Thousands of young people know exactly what Whitman meant. A few perhaps can see that Thoreau's death was his greatest achievement, for it showed that his philosophy had taught him how to die—and therefore how to live. Some can appreciate and understand his two years at Walden Pond. But many are ready, like the young Indian lawyer in South Africa in 1907, to be impressed that Thoreau "taught nothing he was not prepared to practice in himself."[4] Like Gandhi, they are ready to draw on Thoreau's "Civil Disobedience" for "a new way" of handling political conflict. Thoreau thereby made another major contribution to radical politics, for anarchism and socialism have traditionally been strong on ends and weak or worse on means. It is true that Thoreau was himself unclear about violence, as his splendid tribute to John Brown and his occasional callow observations on war show—"it is a pity," he wrote a correspondent in 1855, "that we seem to require a war from time to time to assure us that there is any manhood still left in man."[5] Yet he went

1. Brown, *Life against Death* (Middletown, Conn.: Wesleyan University Press, 1959), 308–11.
2. *Works*, I, 65. I should not place any great reliance on this passage, which apparently was valued in part for its shock value, if it stood alone. It does not.
3. Quoted by Walter Harding, *A Thoreau Handbook* (New York: New York University Press, 1959), 201.
4. Quoted by George Hendrick, "The Influence of Thoreau's 'Civil Disobedience' on Gandhi's *Satyagraha*," *New England Quarterly*, XXIX (1956), 464.
5. Letter to Thomas Cholmondeley, 7 February 1855—see *Correspondence of Thoreau*, 371.

farther than most in thinking his way through this problem. More importantly, like Antigone he left us the powerful, burning, irresistible appeal of his example. It is as timely as the banner "Unjust Law Exists" which marched beside Camus' "Neither Victims Nor Executioners" in the recent Washington youth demonstrations. It is as timely as Bertrand Russell's sit-down in Trafalgar Square. It may even help us survive the disease called modern history.

LEO MARX

[*Walden* as Transcendental Pastoral Design]†

The incursion of the railroad in Sleepy Hollow, recorded by Hawthorne in 1844, typifies the moment of discovery. Recall the circumstances. On a fine summer morning the writer enters the woods and sits down to await "such little events as may happen." Writing in a pleasant if somewhat hackneyed literary idiom, he records sights and sounds. Then, extending his observations to nearby farms and pastures, and to the village in the distance, he sketches an ideal rural scheme. He locates himself at the center of an idyllic domain—a land of order, form, and harmony. Like Virgil's Arcadia or Prospero's "majestic vision" or Jefferson's republic of the middle landscape, this is a self-contained, static world, remote from history, where nature and art are in balance. It is as if the writer had set out to realize in his own person the felicity promised, since Shakespeare's time, by the myth of America as a new beginning.

In its simplest, archetypal form, the myth affirms that Europeans experience a regeneration in the New World. They become new, better, happier men—they are reborn. In most versions the regenerative power is located in the natural terrain: access to undefiled, bountiful, sublime Nature is what accounts for the virtue and special good fortune of Americans. It enables them to design a community in the image of a garden, an ideal fusion of nature with art. The landscape thus becomes the symbolic repository of value of all kinds—economic, political, aesthetic, religious. It has been suggested that the American myth of a new beginning may be a variant of the primal myth described by Joseph Campbell: "a separation from the world, a penetration to some source of power, and a life-enhancing return." Hawthorne's situation in Sleepy Hollow seems to figure a realization of the myth until, suddenly, the harsh whistle of the locomotive fills the air. Then discord replaces harmony and the tranquil mood vanishes. Although he later regains a measure of repose, a sense of loss colors the rest of his notes. His final

† From *The Machine in the Garden: Technology and the Pastoral Ideal in America* by Leo Marx, 227–29; 242–65. Copyright © 1964 by Oxford University Press, Inc. Reprinted by permission. *Walden* page numbers refer to this Norton Critical Edition.

observation is of some clouds that resemble the "shattered ruins of a dreamer's Utopia."[1]

In spite of the facile resolution and the bland, complaisant tone, there is unmistakable power latent in Hawthorne's casual composition. The sudden appearance of the machine in the garden is an arresting, endlessly evocative image. It causes the instantaneous clash of opposed states of mind: a strong urge to believe in the rural myth along with an awareness of industrialization as counterforce to the myth. Since 1844, this motif has served again and again to order literary experience. It appears everywhere in American writing. In some cases, to be sure, the "little event" is a fictive episode with only vague, incidental symbolic overtones. But in others it is a cardinal metaphor of contradiction, exfoliating, through associated images and ideas, into a design governing the meaning of entire works.

*   *   *

Soon after Emerson had set forth his program for Young Americans,[2] his young disciple Henry Thoreau put it to a test. He began his stay at Walden Pond in the spring of 1845, and the book he eventually wrote about it (Walden was not published until 1854) may be read as the report of an experiment in transcendental pastoralism. The organizing design is like that of many American fables: Walden begins with the hero's withdrawal from society in the direction of nature. The main portion of the book is given over to a yearlong trial of Emerson's prescription for achieving a new life. When Thoreau tells of his return to Concord, in the end, he seems to have satisfied himself about the efficacy of this method of redemption. It may be difficult to say exactly what is being claimed, but the triumphant tone of the concluding chapters leaves little doubt that he is announcing positive results. His most telling piece of evidence is Walden—the book itself. Recognizing the clarity, coherence, and power of the writing, we can only conclude—or so transcendental doctrine would have it—that the experiment has been a success. The vision of unity that had made the aesthetic order of Walden possible had in turn been made possible by the retreat to the pond. The pastoral impulse somehow had provided access to the order latent in the cosmos.

But the meaning of Walden is more complicated than this affirmation. Because Thoreau takes seriously what Emerson calls the "method of nature"—more seriously than the master himself—the book has a strong con-

---

1. Nathaniel Hawthorne, The American Notebooks, ed. Randall Stewart (New Haven: Yale University Press, 1932), 102–5. [On the myth of the New World, see] Philip Young, "Fallen from Time: The Mythic Rip Van Winkle," The Kenyon Review 22 (Autumn, 1960), 551; Frederick I. Carpenter surveys variants, " 'The American Myth': Paradise (To Be) Regained," PMLA 74 (1959), 599–606; R. W. B. Lewis, The American Adam: Innocence, Tragedy, and Tradition in the Nineteenth Century (Chicago: University of Chicago Press, 1955).

2. See Emerson, "The Young American," in Nature, Addresses, and Lectures, ed. Robert E. Spiller and Alfred R. Ferguson (Cambridge: Harvard UP, 1971) 217–44, and Marx, The Machine in the Garden 229–42 [Editor].

trapuntal theme. Assuming that natural facts properly perceived and accurately transcribed must yield the truth, Thoreau adopts the tone of a hard-headed empiricist. At the outset he makes it clear that he will tell exactly what happened. He claims to have a craving for reality (be it life or death), and he would have us believe him capable of reporting the negative evidence. Again and again he allows the facts to play against his desire, so that his prose at its best acquires a distinctly firm, cross-grained texture. Though the dominant tone is affirmative, the undertone is skeptical, and it qualifies the import of episode after episode. For this reason *Walden* belongs among the first in a long series of American books which, taken together, have had the effect of circumscribing the pastoral hope, much as Virgil circumscribes it in his eclogues. In form and feeling, indeed, Thoreau's book has much in common with the classic Virgilian mode.

Although the evidence is abundant, it is easy to miss the conventional aspect of *Walden*. In the second chapter Thoreau describes the site as an ideal pasture, a real place which he transforms into an unbounded, timeless landscape of the mind. And he identifies himself with Damodara (Krishna) in his rôle as shepherd, and with a shepherd in a Jacobean song:

> There was a shepherd that did live,
> And held his thoughts as high
> As were the mounts whereon his flocks
> Did hourly feed him by.

Nevertheless, the serious affinity between *Walden* and the convention is disguised by certain peculiarities of American pastoralism, the most obvious being the literalness with which Thoreau approaches the ideal of the simple life. For centuries writers working in the mode had been playing with the theme, suggesting that men might enrich their contemplative experience by simplifying their housekeeping. (The shepherd's ability to reduce his material needs to a minimum had been one of his endearing traits.) Yet it generally had been assumed that the simple life was a poetic theme, not to be confused with the way poets did in fact live. In the main, writers who took the felicity of shepherds in green pastures as their subject had been careful to situate themselves near wealth and power. The effect of the American environment, however, was to break down common-sense distinctions between art and life. No one understood this more clearly than Henry Thoreau; skilled in the national art of disguising art, in *Walden* he succeeds in obscuring the traditional, literary character of the pastoral withdrawal. Instead of writing about it—or *merely* writing about it—he tries it. By telling his tale in the first person, he endows the mode with a credibility it had seldom, if ever, possessed. Because the "I" who addresses us in *Walden* is describing the way he had lived, taking pains to supply plenty of hard facts ("Yes, I did eat $8.74, all told. . . ."), we scarcely notice that all the while he had been playing the shepherd's venerable rôle. He refuses to say whether the book is an explicit guide for living or an exercise in imaginative perception. We are invited to take it as either or both. Convinced that effective symbols can be derived only from natural facts, Thoreau had moved to the pond so that he might make a symbol of his life. If we miss the affinity with the Virgilian mode, then, it is partly because we are dealing with a distinctively American version of romantic pastoral.

No feature of *Walden* makes this truth more apparent than its topography. The seemingly realistic setting may not be a land of fantasy like Arcadia, yet neither is it Massachusetts. On inspection it proves to be another embodiment of the American moral geography—a native blend of myth and reality. The hut beside the pond stands at the center of a symbolic landscape in which the village of Concord appears on one side and a vast reach of unmodified nature on the other. As if no organized society existed to the west, the mysterious, untrammeled, primal world seems to begin at the village limits. As in most American fables, the wilderness is an indispensable feature of this terrain, and the hero's initial recoil from everyday life carries him to the verge of anarchic primitivism.[3] "We need the tonic of wildness," Thoreau explains, using the word "pasture" to encompass wild nature: "We need to witness our own limits transgressed, and some life pasturing freely where we never wander." (The combined influence of geography and the romantic idea of nature—sublime Nature—gives rise to attitudes held by a long line of American literary heroes from Natty Bumppo to Ike McCaslin.) But Thoreau is not a primitivist. True, he implies that he would have no difficulty choosing between Concord and the wilderness. What really engages him, however, is the possibility of avoiding that choice. (Jefferson had taken the same position.) In *Walden*, accordingly, he keeps our attention focused upon the middle ground where he builds a house, raises beans, reads the *Iliad*, and searches the depths of the pond. Like the "navel of the earth" in the archaic myths studied by Mircea Eliade, the pond is the absolute center— the *axis mundi*—of Thoreau's cosmos. If an alternative to the ways of Concord is to be found anywhere, it will be found on the shore of Walden Pond—near the mystic center.[4]

And it had best be found quickly. The drama of *Walden* is intensified by Thoreau's acute sense of having been born in the nick of time. Though the book resembles the classic pastoral in form and feeling, its facts and images

3. The difference between the typical American hero and the shepherd in traditional versions of pastoral is suggested by Renato Poggioli's account of that archetypal figure as one who "lives a sedentary life even in the open, since he prefers to linger in a grove's shade rather than to wander in the woods. He never confronts the true wild, and this is why he never becomes even a part-time hunter" [Renato Poggioli, "The Oaten Flute," *Library Bulletin*, XI (Spring, 1957), p. 152]. Given the circumstances of American life, our heroes do confront the true wild, and they often become hunters. But it is striking to notice how often they are impelled to restrict or even renounce their hunting. I am thinking of Natty Bumppo, Melville's Ishmael, Faulkner's Ike McCaslin, and Thoreau himself.

4. Thoreau on wildness, p. 211; Mircea Eliade, *Cosmos and History, The Myth of the Eternal Return*, trans. William R. Trask, New York, 1959, pp. 16–17.

are drawn from the circumstances of life in nineteenth-century America. By 1845, according to Thoreau, a depressing state of mind—he calls it "quiet desperation"—has seized the people of Concord. The opening chapter, "Economy," is a diagnosis of this cultural malady. Resigned to a pointless, dull, routinized existence, Thoreau's fellow-townsmen perform the daily round without joy or anger or genuine exercise of will. As if their minds were mirrors, able only to reflect the external world, they are satisfied to cope with things as they are. In Emerson's language, they live wholly on the plane of the Understanding. Rather than design houses to fulfill the purpose of their lives, they accommodate their lives to the standard design of houses. Thoreau discovers the same pattern of acquiescence, a dehumanizing reversal of ends and means, in all of their behavior. He finds it in their pretentious furnishings, their uncomfortable clothing, their grim factories, the dispirited way they eat and farm the land and work from dawn to dusk. He locates it, above all, in their economy—a system within which they work endlessly, not to reach a goal of their own choosing but to satisfy the demands of the market mechanism. The moral, in short, is that here "men have become the tools of their tools."

The omnipresence of tools, gadgets, instruments is symptomatic of the Concord way. Like Carlyle, Thoreau uses technological imagery to represent more than industrialization in the narrow, economic sense. It accompanies a mode of perception, an emergent system of meaning and value—a culture. In fact his overdrawn indictment of the Concord "economy" might have been written to document Carlyle's dark view of industrialism. Thoreau feels no simple-minded Luddite hostility toward the new inventions; they are, he says, "but improved means to an unimproved end. . . ." What he is attacking is the popular illusion that improving the means is enough, that if the machinery of society is put in good order (as Carlyle had said) "all were well with us; the rest would care for itself!"[5] He is contending against a culture pervaded by this mechanistic outlook. It may well be conducive to material progress, but it also engenders deadly fatalism and despair. At the outset, then, Thoreau invokes the image of the machine to represent the whole tone and quality of Concord life or, to be more precise, anti-life:

> Actually, the laboring man has not leisure for a true integrity day by day; he cannot afford to sustain the manliest relations to men; his labor would be depreciated in the market. He has no time to be anything but a machine.

The clock, favorite "machine" of the Enlightenment, is a master machine in Thoreau's model of the capitalist economy. Its function is decisive because it links the industrial apparatus with consciousness. The laboring man becomes a machine in the sense that his life becomes more closely geared to

5. Thomas Carlyle, "Signs of the Times." In *Critical and Miscellaneous Essays* (New York: Belford, Clarke & Co., n.d.), 3.5–30;

an impersonal and seemingly autonomous system.[6] If the advent of power technology is alarming, it is because it occurs within this cultural context. When Thoreau depicts the machine as it functions within the Concord environment, accordingly, it is an instrument of oppression: "We do not ride upon the railroad; it rides upon us." But later, when seen from the Walden perspective, the railroad's significance becomes quite different.

Thoreau's denunciation of the Concord "economy" prefigures the complex version of the Sleepy Hollow episode in the fourth chapter, "Sounds." The previous chapter is about "Reading," or what he calls the language of metaphor. Now he shifts to sounds, "the language which all things and events speak without metaphor, which alone is copious and standard." The implication is that he is turning from the conventional language of art to the spontaneous language of nature. What concerns him is the hope of making the word one with the thing, the notion that the naked fact of sensation, if described with sufficient precision, can be made to yield its secret—its absolute meaning. This is another way of talking about the capacity of nature to "produce delight"—to supply value and meaning. It is the crux of transcendental pastoralism. Hence Thoreau begins with an account of magnificent summer days when, like Hawthorne at the Hollow, he does nothing but sit "rapt in a revery, amidst the pines and . . . sumachs, in undisturbed solitude and stillness." These days, unlike days in Concord, are not "minced into hours and fretted by the ticking of a clock." Here is another pastoral interlude, a celebration of idleness and that sense of relaxed solidarity with the universe that presumably comes with close attention to the language of nature. For a moment Thoreau allows us to imagine that he has escaped the clock, the Concord definition of time and, indeed, the dominion of the machine. But then, without raising his voice, he reports the "rattle of railroad cars" in the woods.

At first the sound is scarcely audible. Thoreau casually mentions it at the end of a long sentence in which he describes a series of sights and sounds: hawks circling the clearing, a tantivy of wild pigeons, a mink stealing out of the marsh, the sedge bending under the weight of reed-birds, and then, as if belonging to the very tissue of nature: "and for the last half-hour I have heard the rattle of railroad cars, now dying away and then reviving like the beat of a partridge, conveying travellers from Boston to the country." It would have been difficult to contrive a quieter entrance, which may seem curious in view of the fact that Thoreau then devotes nine long paragraphs to the subject. Besides, he insists upon the importance of the Fitchburg

6. Thoreau's response to the mechanization of time reflects the heightened significance of the clock in the period of the "take-off" into full-scale industrialism. With the building of factories and railroads it became necessary, as never before, to provide the population with access to the exact time. This was made possible, in New England, by the transformation of the clockmaking industry. Before 1800 clocks had been relatively expensive luxury items made only by master craftsmen. Significantly enough, the industry was among the first to use machines and the principle of interchangeable part manufacture. By 1807, in Connecticut, Eli Terry had begun to produce wooden clocks in large numbers, and before he died in 1852 he was making between 10,000 and 12,000 clocks a year sold at $5.00 each.

Railroad in the Walden scene; it "touches the pond" near his house, and since he usually goes to the village along its causeway, he says, "I . . . am, as it were, related to society by this link."[7] And then, what may at first seem even more curious, he introduces the auditory image of the train a second time, and with a markedly different emphasis:

> The whistle of the locomotive penetrates my woods summer and winter, sounding like the scream of a hawk sailing over some farmer's yard, informing me that many restless city merchants are arriving within the circle of the town. . . .

Now the sound is more like a hawk than a partridge, and Thoreau playfully associates the hawk's rapacity with the train's distinctive mechanical cadence:

> All the Indian huckleberry hills are stripped, all the cranberry meadows are raked into the city. Up comes the cotton, down goes the woven cloth; up comes the silk, down goes the woollen; up come the books, but down goes the wit that writes them.

What are we to make of this double image of the railroad? First it is like a partridge, then a hawk; first it blends into the landscape like the industrial images in the Inness painting,[8] but then, a moment later, it becomes the discordant machine of the Sleepy Hollow notes. What does the railroad signify here? On inspection the passage proves to be a sustained evocation of the ambiguous meaning of the machine and its relation to nature. Every significant image is yoked to an alternate:

> When I meet the engine with its train of cars moving off with planetary motion,—or, rather, like a comet . . .

Or the cloud of smoke

> . . . rising higher and higher, going to heaven while the cars are going to Boston, conceals the sun for a minute and casts my distant field into the shade. . . .

The point becomes explicit in a thought that Thoreau repeats like a refrain: "If all were as it seems, and men made the elements their servants for noble ends!"

The image of the railroad on the shore of the pond figures an ambiguity at the heart of *Walden*. Man-made power, the machine with its fire, smoke, and thunder, is juxtaposed to the waters of Walden, remarkable for their depth and purity and a matchless, indescribable color—now light blue, now green, almost always pellucid. The iron horse moves across the surface of the earth; the pond invites the eye below the surface. The contrast embodies both the hope and the fear aroused by the impending climax of America's

---

7. It is significant that Thoreau added this statement, with its obvious claim for the symbolic significance of the railroad, to the version of the episode he had published earlier in *Sar-* *tain's Union Magazine*, XI (1852), 66–8.
8. I.e., *The Lackawanna Valley* (1855) by George Inness. See Marx, *The Machine in the Garden* 220–22 [*Editor*].

encounter with wild nature. As Thoreau describes the event, both responses are plausible, and there is no way of knowing which of them history is more likely to confirm. Earlier he had made plain the danger of technological progress, and here at the pond it again distracts his attention from other, presumably more important, concerns. Yet he is elated by the presence of this wonderful invention. In Concord, within the dominion of the mechanistic philosophy, the machine rode upon men, but when seen undistorted from Walden, the promise of the new power seems to offset the danger. Thoreau is delighted by the electric atmosphere of the depot and the cheerful valor of the snow-plow crews. He admires the punctuality, the urge toward precision and order, the confidence, serenity, and adventurousness of the men who operate this commercial enterprise:

> . . . when I hear the iron horse make the hills echo with his snort like thunder, shaking the earth with his feet, and breathing fire and smoke from his nostrils (what kind of winged horse or fiery dragon they will put into the new Mythology I don't know), it seems as if the earth had got a race now worthy to inhabit it. If all were as it seems, and men made the elements their servants for noble ends!

If the interrupted idyll represents a crucial ambiguity, it also represents at least one certainty. The certainty is change itself—the kind of accelerating change, or "progress," that Americans identify with their new inventions, especially the railroad. For Thoreau, like Melville's Ahab, this machine is the type and agent of an irreversible process: not mere scientific or technological development in the narrow sense, but the implacable advance of history. "We have constructed a fate," he writes, "an *Atropos*, that never turns aside. (Let that be the name of your engine.)" The episode demonstrates that the Walden site cannot provide a refuge, in any literal sense, from the forces of change. Indeed, the presence of the machine in the woods casts a shadow of doubt (the smoke of the locomotive puts Thoreau's field in the shade) upon the Emersonian hope of extracting an answer from nature. The doubt is implicit in the elaborately contrived language used to compose this little event. Recall that Thoreau had introduced the chapter on "Sounds" as an effort to wrest an extra-literary meaning from natural facts; his alleged aim had been to render sense perceptions with perfect precision in "the language which all things and events speak without metaphor." What he actually had done, however, was quite the reverse. To convey his response to the sound of the railroad he had resorted to an unmistakably figurative, literary language. Few passages in *Walden* are more transparently contrived or artful; it is as if the subject had compelled Thoreau to admit a debt to Art as great, if not greater, than his debt to Nature.

The most telling qualification of Emersonian optimism, however, comes in the deceptively plain-spoken conclusion to the episode. Emerson had affirmed the political as well as the religious value of the pastoral impulse. When he spoke in his public voice (as in "The Young American") he interpreted the nation's movement toward "nature" (signifying both a natural and a spiritual fact—both land and landscape) as motion toward a new kind of technically advanced yet rural society. In effect he was reaffirming the Jeffersonian hope of embodying the pastoral dream in social institutions. But Thoreau, abiding by his commitment to stand "right fronting and face to face to a fact," takes another hard look at the sight of the machine in the American landscape:

> And hark! here comes the cattle-train bearing the cattle of a thousand hills, sheepcots, stables, and cow-yards in the air, drovers with their sticks, and shepherd boys in the midst of their flocks, all but the mountain pastures, whirled along like leaves blown from the mountains by the September gales. The air is filled with the bleating of calves and sheep, and the hustling of oxen, as if a pastoral valley were going by. . . . A carload of drovers, too, in the midst, on a level with their droves now, their vocation gone, but still clinging to their useless sticks as their badge of office. . . . So is your pastoral life whirled past and away. But the bell rings, and I must get off the track and let the cars go by;—
>
> > What's the railroad to me?
> > I never go to see
> > Where it ends.
> > It fills a few hollows,
> > And makes banks for the swallows,
> > It sets the sand a-blowing,
> > And the blackberries a-growing.
>
> but I cross it like a cart-path in the woods. I will not have my eyes put out and my ears spoiled by its smoke and steam and hissing.

Compared to popular, sentimental pastoralism, or to Emerson's well-turned evasions, there is a pleasing freshness about Thoreau's cool clarity. He says that the pastoral way of life—pastoralism in the literal, agrarian sense—is being whirled past and away. It is doomed. And he has no use for the illusion that the *Atropos* can be stopped. The first thing to do, then, the only sensible thing to do, is get off the track. Not that one need resign oneself, like the men of Concord, to the dominion of the mechanical philosophy. But how is the alternative to be defined? To answer the question had been the initial purpose of the Walden experiment; now its urgency is heightened by the incursion of history. If he is to find an answer, the writer's first duty is to protect his powers of perception. At this point Thoreau adopts a testy, tight-lipped, uncompromising tone: "I will not have my eyes put out and my ears spoiled by its smoke and steam and hissing."

The need for defense against the forces of history does not tempt Thoreau to a nostalgic embrace of the "pastoral life" that is being whirled away. Quite the contrary. In "The Bean-Field" he turns his wit against the popular American version of pastoral. The Walden experiment, as described in "Economy," had included a venture in commercial farming. In order to earn ten or twelve dollars by an "honest and agreeable method," he had planted two acres and a half, chiefly with beans. That is a lot of beans (he figures that the length of the rows, added together, was seven miles), and it meant a lot of work. Here, then, in "The Bean-Field" he turns to the "meaning of this so steady and self-respecting, this small Herculean labor. . . ." The chapter is a seriocomic effort to get at the lesson of agricultural experience. At the outset, recalling his first visit to the pond as a child, Thoreau invests the scene of his arduous labor with an appropriate bucolic ambience:

> And now to-night my flute has waked the echoes over that very water. . . . Almost the same johnswort springs from the same perennial root in this pasture, and even I have at length helped to clothe that fabulous landscape of my infant dreams, and one of the results of my presence and influence is seen in these bean leaves. . . .

As he describes himself at work among his beans, Thoreau is the American husbandman. Like the central figure of the Jeffersonian idyll, his vocation has a moral and spiritual as well as economical significance. And his field bears a special relation to American circumstances. It produces beans which resemble neither English hay, with its synthetic quality (a result of precise, calculating, scientific methods), nor the rich and various crop produced spontaneously in the surrounding woods, pastures, and swamps. "Mine was, as it were, the connecting link between wild and cultivated fields; as some states are civilized, and others half-civilized, and others savage or barbarous, so my field was, though not in a bad sense, a half-cultivated field." But Thoreau's husbandman cannot be characterized simply by his location in the middle landscape. Like Emerson's Young American, he blends Jeffersonian and romantic attitudes toward nature. When Thoreau describes the purpose of his bean-raising activity, accordingly, he falls into a comic idiom—a strange compound of practical, Yankee vernacular and transcendental philosophizing:

> It was a singular experience that long acquaintance which I cultivated with beans, what with planting, and hoeing, and harvesting, and threshing, and picking over and selling them,—the last was the hardest of all,— I might add eating, for I did taste. I was determined to know beans.

The better he had come to "know beans," the less seriously he had been able to take the rôle of noble husbandman. As the writer's account of that "singular experience" develops, he moves further and further from the reverential, solemn tone of popular pastoralism, until he finally adopts a mock-heroic attitude:

> I was determined to know beans. When they were growing, I used to hoe from five o'clock in the morning till noon, and commonly spent the rest

of the day about other affairs. Consider the intimate and curious acquaintance one makes with various kinds of weeds—it will bear some iteration in the account, for there was no little iteration in the labor,—disturbing their delicate organizations so ruthlessly, and making such invidious distinctions with his hoe, levelling whole ranks of one species, and sedulously cultivating another. That's Roman wormwood,—that's pigweed,—that's sorrel,—that's piper-grass,—have at him, chop him up, turn his roots upward to the sun, don't let him have a fibre in the shade, if you do he'll turn himself t'other side up and be as green as a leek in two days. A long war, not with cranes, but with weeds, those Trojans who had sun and rain and dews on their side. Daily the beans saw me come to their rescue armed with a hoe, and thin the ranks of their enemies, filling up the trenches with weedy dead. Many a lusty crest-waving Hector, that towered a whole foot above his crowding comrades, fell before my weapon and rolled in the dust.

In part Thoreau's irony can be attributed to the outcome of his bean venture. Although he does not call it a failure, the fact is clear enough. The cost of the operation was $14.72½ (he had hired a man to help with the plowing), the gross income $23.44, and the net profit $8.71½. This sum barely paid for the rest of his food, and to make ends meet he had hired himself out as a day laborer. In other words, the bean crop did not provide an adequate economic base for the life of an independent husbandman.[9] His own experience comports with what he observes of American farmers throughout the book. So far from representing a "pastoral life," a desirable alternative to the ways of Concord and the market economy, the typical farmer in *Walden* is narrow-minded and greedy. * * *

The result of the venture in husbandry prefigures the result of the Walden experiment as a whole. Judged by a conventional (economic) standard, it is true, the enterprise had been a failure. But that judgment is irrelevant to Thoreau's purpose, as his dominant tone, the tone of success, plainly indicates. It is irrelevant because his aim had been to *know* beans: to get at the essential *meaning* of labor in the bean-field. And "meaning," as he conceives it, has nothing to do with the alleged virtue of the American husbandman or the merits of any institution or "way of life"; nor can it be located in the material or economic facts, where Concord, operating on the plane of the Understanding, locates meaning and value. Thoreau has quite another sort of meaning in view, as he admits when he says that he raised beans, not because he wanted beans to eat, "but, perchance, as some must work in fields if only for the sake of tropes and expression, to serve a parable-maker one day."

This idea, which contains the gist of Thoreau's ultimate argument, also is implicit in the outcome of other episodes. It is implied by his account of fishing at night—a tantalizing effort to get at the "dull uncertain blundering

9. For Thoreau's failure as a farmer, see Leo Stoller, "Thoreau's Doctrine of Simplicity," *NEQ* XXIX (Dec., 1956), 443–61.

purpose" he detects at the end of his line beneath the pond's opaque surface; and by that incomparable satire on the transcendental quest, the chase of the loon who "laughed in derision" at his efforts; and by his painstaking investigation of the pond's supposed "bottomlessness": ". . . I can assure my readers that Walden has a reasonably tight bottom at a not unreasonable . . . depth." In each case, as in "The Bean-Field," the bare, empirical evidence proves inadequate to his purpose. Of themselves the facts do not, cannot, flower into truth; they do not show forth a meaning, which is to say, the kind of meaning the experiment had been designed to establish.[1] If the promise of romantic pastoralism is to be fulfilled, nothing less than an alternative to the Concord way will suffice. Although his tone generally is confident, Thoreau cunningly keeps the issue in doubt until the end. By cheerfully, enigmatically reiterating his failure to extract an "answer"—a coherent world-view—from the facts, he moves the drama toward a climax. Not until the penultimate chapter, "Spring," does he disclose a way of coping with the forces represented by the encroaching machine power.

At the same time, however, he carefully nurtures an awareness of the railroad's presence in the Concord woods. (The account of the interrupted idyll in "Sounds" is only the most dramatic of its many appearances.) There is scarcely a chapter in which he does not mention seeing or hearing the engine, or walking "over the long causeway made for the railroad through the meadows. . . ." When the crew arrives to strip the ice from the pond, it is "with a peculiar shriek from the locomotive." And Thoreau takes special pains to impress us with the "cut" in the landscape made by the embankment. He introduces the motif in the first chapter, after describing his initial visit to the Walden site:

> . . . I came out on to the railroad, on my way home, its yellow sand-heap stretched away gleaming in the hazy atmosphere, and the rails shone in the spring sun . . .

And he returns to it in "The Ponds":

> That devilish Iron Horse, whose ear-rending neigh is heard throughout the town, has muddied the Boiling Spring with his foot, and he it is that has browsed off all the woods on Walden shore, that Trojan horse, with a thousand men in his belly, introduced by mercenary Greeks! Where is the country's champion, the Moore of Moore Hall, to meet him at the Deep Cut and thrust an avenging lance between the ribs of the bloated pest?

The Deep Cut is a wound inflicted upon the land by man's meddling, aggressive, rational intellect, and it is not healed until the book's climax, the resurgence of life in "Spring." By that point the organizing design of

1. For Thoreau's attitude toward "fact" and "truth," see Perry Miller, "Thoreau in the Context of International Romanticism," NEQ XXXIV (June, 1961), 147–59 and Sherman Paul, *The Shores of America, Thoreau's Inward Exploration*, Urbana, 1958.

Walden has been made to conform to the design of nature itself; like Spenser's arrangement of his eclogues in *The Shepheards Calendar*, the sequence of Thoreau's final chapters follows the sequence of months and seasons. This device affirms the possibility of redemption from time, the movement away from Concord time, defined by the clock, toward nature's time, the daily and seasonal life cycle. It is also the movement that redeems machine power. In the spring the ice, sand, and clay of the railroad causeway thaws. The wet stuff flows down the banks, assumes myriad forms, and arouses in Thoreau a delight approaching religious ecstasy. The event provides this parable-maker with his climactic trope: a visual image that figures the realization of the pastoral ideal in the age of machines.

* * *

Thoreau's study of the melting bank is a figurative restoration of the form and unity severed by the mechanized forces of history. Out of the ugly "cut" in the landscape he fashions an image of a new beginning. Order, form, and meaning are restored, but it is a blatantly, unequivocally figurative restoration. The whole force of the passage arises from its extravagantly metaphoric, poetic, literary character. At no point does Thoreau impute material reality to the notion of sand being transformed into, say, leopards' paws. It assumes a form that looks like leopards' paws, but the form exists only so far as it is perceived. The same may be said of his alternative to the Concord way. Shortly after the episode of the thawing sand, the account of the coming of spring reaches a moment of "seemingly instantaneous" change. A sudden influx of light fills his house; he looks out the window, and where the day before there had been cold gray ice there lies the calm transparent pond; he hears a robin singing in the distance and honking geese flying low over the woods. It is spring. Its coming, says Thoreau, is "like the creation of Cosmos out of Chaos and the realization of the Golden Age."

This reaffirmation of the pastoral ideal is not at all like Emerson's prophecy, in "The Young American," of a time "when the whole land is a garden, and the people have grown up in the bowers of a paradise." By comparison, the findings of the Walden experiment seem the work of a tough, unillusioned empiricist.[2] They are consistent with Thoreau's unsparing analysis of the Concord "economy" and with the knowledge that industrial progress is making nonsense of the popular notion of a "pastoral life." The melting of the bank and the coming of spring is only "like" a realization of the golden age. It is a poetic figure. In *Walden* Thoreau is clear, as Emerson

2. In fairness to Emerson it should be said that by the late 1840's he, too, had become more skeptical about the compatibility of the pastoral ideal and industrial progress. His second visit to England in 1847 was in many ways a turning point in his intellectual development, and *English Traits* (1856) is one of our first and most penetrating studies of the new culture of industrialism. Ostensibly about England, the book manifestly was written with America's future economic development in view. Both the structure and the content of the book are governed by the machine-in-the-garden figure.

seldom was, about the location of meaning and value. He is saying that it does not reside in the natural facts or in social institutions or in anything "out there," but in consciousness. It is a product of imaginative perception, of the analogy-perceiving, metaphor-making, mythopoeic power of the human mind. For Thoreau the realization of the golden age is, finally, a matter of private and, in fact, literary experience. Since it has nothing to do with the environment, with social institutions or material reality (any facts will melt if the heat of imaginative passion is sufficient), then the writer's physical location is of no great moment. At the end of the chapter on "Spring," accordingly, Thoreau suddenly drops the language of metaphor and reverts to a direct, matter-of-fact, referential idiom: "Thus was my first year's life in the woods completed; and the second year was similar to it. I finally left Walden September 6th, 1847."

There is a world of meaning in the casual tone. If the book ended here, indeed, one might conclude that Thoreau, like Prospero at the end of *The Tempest*, was absolutely confident about his impending return to society. (Concord is the Milan of *Walden*.) But the book does not end with "Spring." Thoreau finds it necessary to add a didactic conclusion, as if he did not fully trust the power of metaphor after all. And he betrays his uneasiness, finally, in the arrogance with which he announces his disdain for the common life:

> I delight . . . not to live in this restless, nervous, bustling, trivial Nineteenth Century, but stand or sit thoughtfully while it goes by. What are men celebrating? They are all on a committee of arrangements, and hourly expect a speech from somebody. God is only the president of the day, and Webster is his orator.

In the end Thoreau restores the pastoral hope to its traditional location. He removes it from history, where it is manifestly unrealizable, and relocates it in literature, which is to say, in his own consciousness, in his craft, in *Walden*.

STANLEY CAVELL

[Captivity and Despair in *Walden* and "Civil Disobedience"]†

I have spoken of the sense of loss and of the vision of general despair which *Walden* depicts in its early pages, and of the crowing and trickery of the book as taking place over them or in the face of them. Despair and a sense of loss are not static conditions, but goals to our continuous labor: "That

† Excerpted from *The Senses of Walden*, 70–93, 116–19, copyright (c) 1981 by Stanley Cavell. Published by North Point Press and reprinted by permission. *Walden* and "Civil Disobedience" page numbers refer to this Norton Critical Edition.

man who does not believe that each day contains an earlier, more sacred and auroral hour than he has yet profaned, has despaired of life, and is pursuing a descending and darkening way"(60).

It is not merely the company of others that causes this. Going to Walden, for example, will not necessarily help you out, for there is no reason to think you will go there and live there any differently from the way you are going on now. "From the desperate city you go into the desperate country, and have to console yourself with the bravery of minks and muskrats" (5). "How to migrate thither" is the question. We are living "what is not life" (61), *pursuing* a descending and darkening way. And yet to realize his wish to live deliberately the writer went "*down* to the woods" (115). And downward is the direction he invites us in:

> Let us settle ourselves, and work and wedge our feet downward through the mud and slush of opinion, and prejudice, and tradition, and delusion, and appearance, that alluvion which covers the globe, through Paris and London, through New York and Boston and Concord, through church and state, through poetry and philosophy and religion, till we come to a hard bottom and rocks in place, which we can call *reality*, and say, This is, and no mistake; and then begin, having a *point d'appui*, below freshet and frost and fire, a place where you might found a wall or a state. . . . Be it life or death, we crave only reality. (66)

The path to a point of support and origin is not immediately attractive, but the hope in it, and the hope that we can take it, is exactly that we are *living* another way, pursuing death, desperate wherever we are; so that if we could go all the way, go *through* Paris and London, *through* church and state, *through* poetry and philosophy and religion, we might despair of despair itself, rather than of life, and cast *that* off, and begin, and so reverse our direction.

He introduces his invitation to voyage as a matter of "settling ourselves." At the end:

> I love to weigh, to settle, to gravitate toward that which most strongly and rightfully attracts me . . . not suppose a case, but take the case that is; to travel the only path I can, and that on which no power can resist me. It affords me no satisfaction to commence to spring an arch before I have got a solid foundation. . . . There is a solid bottom everywhere. (220)

Settling has to do with weighing, then; and so does deliberating, pondering. To live deliberately would be to settle, to let ourselves clarify, and find our footing. And weighing is not just carrying weight, by your force of character and in your words; but lifting the thing that keeps you anchored, and sailing out. Then gravitation, in conjunction with what rightfully attracts you, might be in an upward as well as a downward direction—or what we call up and down would cease to signify. We crave only reality; but since "We know not where we are" (222) and only "esteem truth remote". (65)—that is, we cannot believe that it is under our feet—we despair of ourselves and let our despair dictate what we call reality: "When we consider what, to use the words of the catechism, is the chief end of man, and what are the true necessaries and means of life, it appears as if men had deliberately chosen the common mode of living because they preferred it to any other. Yet they honestly think there is no choice left" (5). The way we live is not necessary, in this "comparatively free country." The writer generally "[confines himself] to those who are said to be in *moderate* circumstances" (23), obviously implying that he thinks their case is extreme. It follows that this life has been chosen; that since we are living and pursuing it, we are choosing it. This does not appear to those leading it to be the case; they think they haven't the means to live any other way. "One young man of my acquaintance, who has inherited some acres, told me that he thought he should live as I did, *if he had the means*" (48). But the truth appears to the writer, as if in a vision, a vision of true necessities, that the necessaries of life *are* the means of life, the ways it is lived; therefore to say we haven't the means for a different way, in particular for a way which is to discover what the true necessaries and means of life in fact are, is irrational. It expresses the opinion that our current necessities are our final ones. We have defined our lives in front. What at first seems like a deliberate choice turns out to be a choice all right (they honestly think there is no choice *left*), but not a deliberate one, not one weighed and found good, but one taken without pondering, or lightly; they have never preferred it. And yet this is nothing less than a choice of one's life.

How does this come about? What keeps this nightmare from at least frightening us awake? It is a sort of disease of the imagination, both of the private imagination we may call religion and of the public imagination we may call politics. To settle, weigh, gravitate, he was saying, is a question of "taking the case that is," not "supposing a case." And earlier: "I am far from supposing that my case is a peculiar one; no doubt many of my readers would make a similar defense" (49). That is, from our own experience we draw or project our definitions of reality, as the empiricists taught us to do; only the experience we learn from, and know best, is our failure (cf. 64–65), the same old prospects are repeated back to us, by ourselves and by others. We were to be freed from superstition; instead the frozen hopes and fears which attached to rumored dictates of revelation have now attached themselves to the rumored dictates of experience. The writer calls us heathenish. (He calls himself that too because to an audience of heathens all devotions are heathenish; and because if what *they* do is called Christianity then he is a heathen—he lives outside the town.) Our education is sadly neglected; we have not learned in the moral life, as the scientists have in theirs, how to seek and press to the limits of experience; so we draw our limits well short of anything reason requires. The result is not that the reality this proposes to us, while confined, is at least safe. The result is a metaphysics of the imagination, of unexamined fantasy.

As I was desirous to recover the long lost bottom of Walden Pond, I surveyed it carefully, before the ice broke up, early in '46, with compass and chain and sounding line. There have been many stories told about the bottom, or rather no bottom of this pond, which certainly had no foundation for themselves. It is remarkable how long men will believe in the bottomlessness of a pond without taking the trouble to sound it. I have visited two such Bottomless Ponds in one walk in this neighborhood. Many have believed that Walden reached quite through to the other side of the globe. Some who have lain flat on the ice for a long time, looking down through the illusive medium, perchance with watery eyes into the bargain, and driven to hasty conclusions by the fear of catching cold in their breasts, have seen vast holes "into which a load of hay might be driven," if there were anybody to drive it, the undoubted source of the Styx and entrance to the Infernal Regions from these parts. Others have gone down from the village with a "fifty-six" and a wagon-load of inch rope, but yet have failed to find any bottom; for while the "fifty-six" was resting by the way, they were paying out the rope in the vain attempt to fathom their truly immeasurable capacity for marvelousness. But I can assure my readers that Walden has a reasonably tight bottom at a not unreasonable, though at an unusual, depth. I fathomed it easily with a cod-line and a stone weighing about a pound and a half, and could tell accurately when the stone left the bottom, by having to pull so much harder before the water got underneath to help me. The greatest depth was exactly one hundred and two feet; to which may be added the five feet which it has risen since, making one hundred and seven. This is a remarkable depth for so small an area; yet not one inch of it can be spared by the imagination. What if all ponds were shallow? Would it not react on the minds of men? I am thankful that this pond was made deep and pure for a symbol. While men believe in the infinite some ponds will be thought to be bottomless. (190)

The human imagination is released by fact. Alone, left to its own devices, it will not recover reality, it will not form an edge. So a favorite trust of the Romantics has, along with what we know of experience, to be brought under instruction; the one kept from straining, the other from stifling itself to death. Both imagination and experience continue to require what the Renaissance had in mind, viz., that they be humanized. ("I brag for humanity," i.e., the humanity that is still to awaken, to have its renascence. And the writer praises science that humanizes knowledge, that "reports what those men already know practically or instinctively," as "a true *humanity*, or account of experience" [141], i.e., one of the humanities.) The Reformation, as in Luther and Milton, had meant to be a furthering of this too. It was not wholly ineffective: "Our manners have been corrupted by communication with the saints" (53). That is, false saintliness is hypocrisy, but true saintliness will seem to be bad manners to hypocrites.

The work of humanization is still to be done. While men believe in the infinite some ponds will be thought to be bottomless. So long as we will not take our beliefs all the way to genuine knowledge, to conviction, but keep letting ourselves be driven to more or less hasty conclusions, we will keep misplacing the infinite, and so grasp neither heaven nor earth. There is a solid bottom everywhere. But how are we going to weigh toward it, arrive at confident conclusions from which we can reverse direction, spring an arch, choose our lives, and go about our business?

Despair is not bottomless, merely endless; a hopelessness, or fear, of reaching bottom. It takes illusions for its object, from which, in turn, like all ill-educated experience, it is confirmed in what it already knew. So its conclusions too are somewhat hasty, its convictions do not truly convict us. This is a prophecy the writer hears from a cat with wings:

> Suddenly an unmistakable cat-owl from very near me, with the most harsh and tremendous voice I ever heard from any inhabitant of the woods, responded at regular intervals to the [loud honking of a] goose, as if determined to expose and disgrace this intruder from Hudson's Bay by exhibiting a greater compass and volume of voice in a native, and *boo-hoo* him out of Concord horizon. What do you mean by alarming the citadel at this time of night consecrated to me? Do you think I am ever caught napping at such an hour, and that I have not got lungs and a larynx as well as yourself? *Boo-hoo, boo-hoo, boo-hoo!* It was one of the most thrilling discords I ever heard. And yet, if you had a discriminating ear, there were in it the elements of a concord such as these plains never saw nor heard. (181)

If we find out what is foreign and what is native to us, we can find out what there really is to boo-hoo about, and then our quiet wailing will make way for something to crow about.

What has the writer's ear discriminated specifically? Evidently he has heard that all the elements of an apocalyptic concord, a new city of man, are present. We need nothing more and need do nothing new in order that our change of direction take place. This is expressed in the writer's sense that we are on the verge of something, perched; something is in the wind, Olympus is but the outside of earth everywhere; there is a solid bottom everywhere; the dumps and a budding ecstasy are equally possible from this spot, we need only turn around to find the track. "Nearest to all things is that power which fashions their being. *Next* to us the grandest laws are continually being executed" (90). Because we do not recognize the circumstances that encircle us, we do not allow them to "make our occasions"; instead of "looking another way" (66), we permit outlying and transient circumstances to distract us. The crisis is at hand, but we do not know how to grasp it; we do not know where or how to spend it, so we are desperate. But "it is characteristic of wisdom not to do desperate things" (5). And "It is by a mathematical point only that we are wise, as the sailor or the fugitive slave keeps the polestar in his eye" (48). The day is at hand, and the effect of every vision is at hand—for example, of renaissance and reformation and revolution (we are to work our way through poetry and philosophy and church and state), which since the beginning of the modern age have been a "dinning in our ears" (217).

This is, no doubt, mystical to us. But the wretchedness and nervousness this writing creates[1] come from an equally undeniable, if intermittent, sense that the writer is being practical, and therefore that we are not. It is a sense that the mystery is of our own making; that it would require no more expenditure of spirit and body to let ourselves be free than it is costing us to keep ourselves pinioned and imprisoned within "opinion, and prejudice, and tradition, and delusion, and appearance." Our labors—the *way* we labor—are not responses to true need, but hectic efforts to keep ourselves from the knowledge of what is needful, from the promise of freedom, whose tidings we always call glad and whose bringer we always despise and then apotheosize (24), which is to say, kick upstairs. It is no excuse to us that few tidings really are glad, that for every real prophet there are legions of false ones speaking a vision of their own hearts, i.e., from what ails merely themselves. We are not excused from thinking it out for ourselves.

This writer's primary audience is neither the "degraded rich" nor the "degraded poor," but those who are in "*moderate* circumstances"; what we might call the *middle* class. We are not Chinese or Sandwich Islanders; nor are we *southern* slaves. "I sometimes wonder that we can be so frivolous, I may almost say, as to attend to the gross but somewhat foreign form of servitude called Negro Slavery, there are so many keen and subtle masters that enslave both north and south" (4). There is no mystery here; there is plain damnation. One mystery we make for ourselves is to say that Negro slavery is wholly foreign to us who are said to live in New England. South is for us merely a direction in which we look away from our own servitude. This is to recommend neither that we ought or ought not do something about Negro slavery; it is to ask why, if we will not attend to the matter, we attend to it—as if fascinated by something at once foreign and yet intimately familiar. We have not made the South foreign to us, we have not put it behind us, sloughed its slavery. We do not yet see our hand in it, any more than we see the connection between our making ourselves foreign to our government and the existence of roasting Mexicans and "strolling" Indians (12) (it was in the years immediately after Thoreau's graduation from Harvard that the eastern tribes were collected and, following Andrew Jackson's legislation, marched beyond the Mississippi); any more than we see the connection between what we call philanthropy and what we call poverty. We have yet "*to get our living together*" (49), to be whole, and to be one community. We are not settled, we have not clarified ourselves; our character, and the character of the nation, is not (in another of his favorite words) transparent to itself (134).

1. An allusion to Emerson's response to the "old fault of unlimited contradiction" he found in Thoreau's writing: "It makes me nervous and wretched to read it." See *The Senses of Walden*, 11–12, and the following essay by Walter Benn Michaels [*Editor*].

It is hard to have a Southern overseer; it is worse to have a Northern one; but worst of all when you are the slave-driver of yourself. Talk of a divinity in man! Look at the teamster on the highway, wending to market by day or night; does any divinity stir within him? His highest duty to fodder and water his horses! What is his destiny to him compared with the shipping interests? Does not he drive for Squire Make-a-stir: How godlike, how immortal, is he? See how he cowers and sneaks, how vaguely all the day he fears, not being immortal and divine, but the slave and prisoner of his own opinion of himself, a fame won by his own deeds. Public opinion is a weak tyrant compared with our own private opinion. What a man thinks of himself, that it is which determines, or rather indicates, his fate. Self-emancipation even in the West Indian provinces of the fancy and imagination—what Wilberforce is there to bring that about? Think, also, of the ladies of the land weaving toilet cushions against the last day, not to betray too green an interest in their fates! As if you could kill time without injuring eternity. (4)

How did private opinion become a tyrant, a usurper, in service of interests not our own? Its power is such—not merely the magnitude of it, but the form of it—that we feel not merely helpless before it but without rights in the face of it. The drift of *Walden* is not that we should go off and be alone; the drift is that we *are* alone, *and* that we are never alone—not in the highest and not in the lowest sense. In the highest sense, we will know a good neighborhood when we can live there; and in the lowest, "Consider the girls in a factory—never alone, hardly in their dreams" (92). In such circumstances there is little point in suggesting that we assert ourselves, or take further steps; that merely asks the tyrant to tighten his hold. The quest of this book is for the recovery of the self, as from an illness: "The incessant anxiety and strain of some is a well-nigh incurable form of disease" (7).

Why should we explore ourselves when we already know ourselves for cowards, sneaks, and slaves? "But men labor under a mistake" (3). Our labors are not callings, but neither are they misfortunes or accidents which have befallen us. In all, we take something for what it is not but, understandably enough, something it appears to be. That is the cause of our despair, but also cause for hope. We do not *know* that it is necessary for things to be as bad as they are; because we do not know why we labor as we do. We take one thing for another in every field of thought and in every mode of action. Religiously, our labors betoken penance, hence a belief in works without faith, hence blindness to faith; politically, our labors betoken a belief in fate, hence in a society whose necessities we have had no hand in determining, hence blindness to its origins; epistemologically, our labors betoken superstitions, commitments to uncertainties (7), refusals to know what we know. ("Man flows at once to God when the channel of purity is open" [147].)

The writer knows his readers will take the project of self-emancipation to be merely literary. But he also knows that this is because they take everything in a more or less literary way: everything is news to them, and it always comes from foreign parts, from some Gothic setting. "Shams and delusions are esteemed for soundest truths, while reality is fabulous" (65). We crave only reality, but we cannot stomach it; we do not believe in our lives; so we trade them for stories; their real history is more interesting than anything we now know.

How are we to become practical? How are we to "look another way," i.e., look in another way, with other eyes, in order to understand that it is harder to be "an overseer of the poor" (53) (i.e., of ourselves) than to let ourselves go? All our fields await emancipation—geography and places, literature and neighborhood, epistemology and eyes, anatomy and hands, metaphysics and cities. To locate ourselves in this maze, the first step is to see that we ourselves are its architects and hence are in a position to recollect the design. The first step in building our dwelling is to recognize that we have already built one.

Society remains as mysterious to us as we are to ourselves, or as God is. That we are the slave-drivers of ourselves has not come about "for private reasons, as [we] must believe" (5). It is an open realization of what we have made of the prophecy of democracy. It is what we have done with the success of Locke and the others in removing the divine right of kings and placing political authority in our consent to be governed together. That this has made life a little easier for some, in some respects, is a less important consequence than the fact that we now consent to social evil. What was to be a blessing we have made a curse. We do not see our hand in what happens, so we call certain events melancholy accidents when they are the inevitabilities of our projects (36), and we call other events necessities because we will not change our minds. The essential message of the idea of a social contract is that political institutions require justification, that they are absolutely without sanctity, that power over us is held on trust from us, that institutions have no authority other than the authority we lend them, that we are their architects, that they are therefore artifacts, that there are laws or ends, of nature or justice, in terms of which they are to be tested. They are experiments.

To learn that we have forgotten this is part of our education which is sadly neglected.

We read that the traveler asked the boy if the swamp before him had a hard bottom. The boy replied that it had. But presently the traveler's horse sank in up to the girths, and he observed to the boy, "I thought you said that this bog had a hard bottom." "So it has," answered the latter, "but you have not got half way to it yet." So it is with the bogs and quicksands of society; but he is an old boy that knows it. (220–21)

The bottom is our construction of it, our cursed consent to it, our obedience to it which we read as a muddle of accidents and necessities. The writer suggests this in saying that he "[desires] to speak impartially on this point, and as one not interested in the success or failure of the present economical and social arrangements" (38). Since "not interested in" evidently cannot mean that they have no interest for him, what does it mean? It means that he is one who is withdrawing his interest in it, placing his investment elsewhere. Or he "desires to speak" as if that were so, leaving it open whether it is the case. Not simply because he would make a fiction of his withdrawal, but because it is unclear how it is to be effected. This is in fact one of the standing mysteries of any theory of the social contract—how consent is shown, and therefore when and how its withdrawal can be shown.

It is, appropriately, in the chapter gently entitled "The Village" that the writer of *Walden* declares himself to be the author of "Civil Disobedience," the same man who had said that "I simply wish to refuse allegiance to the State, to withdraw and stand aloof from it effectually" (241). In that essay he describes himself as having felt, during his one night in jail, a kind of ecstasy of freedom. But that hardly constitutes "effectual" withdrawal from the state. He reprints a statement he said he put in writing to the effect that he did "not wish to be regarded as a member of any incorporated society which I have not joined." That seems to have disengaged him from the local church; and though he would "have signed off in detail from all the societies which [he] never signed on to . . . [he] did not know where to find a complete list" (237–38). The joke very quickly went sour. In particular, he could not name society or the government as such, because he knows he has somehow signed on. "How does it become a man to behave toward this American government today? I answer, that he cannot without disgrace be associated with it. I cannot for an instant recognize that political organization as *my* government which is the *slave's* government also" (229). Nevertheless, he recognizes that he *is* associated with it, that his withdrawal has not "dissolved the Union" between ourselves and the state (cf. 232), and hence that he is disgraced. Apparently, as things stand, one cannot but choose to serve the state; so he will "serve the state with [his conscience] also, and so necessarily resist it for the most part" (228). This is not a call to revolution, because that depends, as Locke had said, on supposing that your fellow citizens, in conscience, will also find that the time for it has come; and Thoreau recognizes that "almost all say that such is not the case now" (229).

Effective civil disobedience, according to Thoreau's essay, is an act that accomplishes three things: (1) it forces the state to recognize that you are against it, so that the state, as it were, attempts to withdraw your consent for you; (2) it enters an appeal to the people ". . . first and instantaneously, from them to the Maker of them, and, secondly, from them to themselves" (242), because the state has provided, in the given case, no other way of petition (234); (3) it identifies and educates those who have "voluntarily chosen to be an agent of the government" (234). ("How shall he ever know well what he is and does as an officer of the government, or as a man, until he is obliged to consider whether he shall treat me, his neighbor, for whom he has respect, as a neighbor and well-disposed man, or as a maniac and disturber of the peace, and see if he can get over this obstruction to his neighborliness without a ruder and more impetuous thought or speech corresponding with his action" [234].) One night in jail was not much in the way of such an action; in fact it lacked the second condition of such an act altogether, viz., the appeal to the people from themselves. But those who complain of the pettiness of that one night forget that the completion of the act was the writing of the essay which depicts it.

Even that is likely to be as ineffective as a quiet night in the Concord jail. First, because the state is "penitent to that degree that it [will hire] one to scourge it while it [sins], but not to that degree that it [will leave] off sinning for a moment" (232); second, because an appeal to the people will go unheard as long as they do not know who they are, and labor under a mistake, and cannot locate where they live and what they live for. Nothing less than *Walden* could carry that load of information. Like the *Leviathan*, and the *Second Treatise of Government*, and the *Discourse on the Origin of Inequality*—which we perhaps regard as more or less prescientific studies of existing societies—*Walden* is, among other things, a tract of political education, education for membership in the polis. It locates authority in the citizens and it identifies citizens—those with whom one is in membership— as "neighbors." What it shows is that education for citizenship is education for isolation. (In this sense, *Walden* is *Émile* grown up. The absence of Sophie only purifies the point.)

The writer of *Walden* keeps faith both with his vision of injustice in his early essay, and with his strategy in the face of it: he resists society by visibly withdrawing from it. "It is true, I might have resisted forcibly with more or less effect, might have run 'amok' against society; but I preferred that society should run 'amok' against me, it being the desperate party" (115). The writer's strategy, which enforces his position as neighbor, is to refuse society his voice, letting the desperate party run amok not merely eventually, but now, against his words, unable either to accept them or to leave them alone. And he reaffirms his earlier judgment that prisons are "the only [houses] in a slave State in which a free man can abide with honor" (235), by "caging" himself in the woods (58), keeping alive the fact and the imagination of injustice, and inhabiting "the more free and honorable ground" on which to be found by "the fugitive slave, and the Mexican prisoner on parole, and the Indian come to plead the wrongs of his race" (235)—all of whom make their appearance to him at Walden. He went there to "repeople the woods" (176); first, by being there; second, by imagining those who were there before; third, by anticipating those for whom he is preparing the ground, those who have come to these woods and must be renewed. And he demonstrates three captivities: that he is a prisoner of the state, as any man is whose government is native to him and is evil; that he is, like Saint Paul, a prisoner of Christ; and that we are held captive each by each and each by the others. These captivities show where we live and what we live for; and the source of strength, or the fulcrum, upon which we can change direction.

It is not the first time in our literature, and it will not be the last, in which society is viewed as a prison. As with Plato's cave, the path out is as arduous as the one the *Republic* requires of philosophers—and like the *Republic*, *Walden* is presided over by the sun, and begins with a stripping away of false necessities. Its opening visions of self-torture and of eternal labors and self-enslavement seem to me an enactment of the greatest opening line among our texts of social existence: "Man is born free, and everywhere he is in chains." What I take Rousseau to mean is that the *way* man is in bondage is comprehensible only of the creature who is, ontologically, free. Human societies, as we know them, could not exist except with each individual's choosing not to exercise freedom. To choose freedom would be to choose freedom for all (to make the will general); the alternative is that we choose partially, i.e., to further our privilege or party. The social contract is nowhere in existence, because we do not will it; therefore the undeniable bonds between us are secured by our obedience to agreements and compacts that are being made among ourselves as individuals acting privately and in secret, not among ourselves as citizens acting openly on behalf of the polis. The logic of our position is that we are conspirators. If this is false, it is paranoid; if it is not, we are crazy. I mention this not to argue for it, or even to justify this reading of Rousseau, but only to suggest a degree of intimacy between Rousseau's and Thoreau's understanding of society; and at the same time to keep in mind the question of insanity to which the writer of *Walden* recurs—or at any rate, the extremity and precariousness of mood in which he writes.

I do not wish to impose a political theory upon the text of *Walden*. On the contrary, if the guiding question of political theory is "Why ought I to obey the state?" then Thoreau's response can be said to reject the question and the subject. The state is not to be obeyed but, at best, to be abided. It is not to be listened to, but watched. Why ought I to abide the state? Because "it is a great evil to make a stir about it." A government, however, is capable of greater evil, "when its tyranny or its inefficiency are great and unendurable" (229). How do you know when this point has been reached? Here the concept of conscience arises, upon which secular, or anyway empiricist philosophy has come to grief: what can conscience be, other than some kind of feeling, of its essence private, a study for psychologists?—as though the "science," that is to say knowledge, that the word "conscience" emphasizes can at most register a lingering superstition. *Walden*, in its emphasis upon listening and answering, outlines an epistemology of conscience.

The opening visions of captivity and despair in *Walden* are traced full length in the language of the first chapter, the longest, which establishes the underlying vocabulary of the book as a whole. "Economy" turns into a nightmare maze of terms about money and possessions and work, each turning toward and joining the others. No summary of this chapter will capture the number of economic terms the writer sets in motion in it. There is profit and loss, rich and poor, cost and expense, borrow and pay, owe and own, business, commerce, enterprises, ventures, affairs, capital, price, amount, improvement, bargain, employment, inheritance, bankruptcy, work, trade, labor, idle, spend, waste, allowance, fortune, gain, earn, afford, possession, change, settling, living, interest, prospects, means, terms. But the mere listing of individual words gives no idea of the powers of affinity among them and their radiation into the remainder of language. They are all ordinary words that we may use, apparently literally, in evaluating any of our investments of feeling, or expenses of spirit, or turns of fortune. There is just enough description, in this chapter, of various enterprises we think of as the habitual and specific subjects of economics, to make unnoticeable the spillage of these words over our lives as a whole. It is a brutal mocking of our sense of values, by forcing a finger of the vocabulary of the New Testament (hence of our understanding of it) down our throats. For that is the obvious origin or locus of the use of economic imagery to express, and correct, spiritual confusion: what shall it profit a man; the wages of sin; the parable of talents; laying up treasures; rendering unto Caesar; charity. What we call the Protestant Ethic, the use of worldly loss and gain to symbolize heavenly standing, appears in *Walden* as some last suffocation of the soul. America and its Christianity have become perfect, dreamlike literalizations or parodies of themselves.

The network or medium of economic terms serves the writer as an imitation of the horizon and strength both of our assessments of our position and of our connections with one another; in particular of our eternal activity in these assessments and connections, and of our blindness to them, to the fact that they are ours. The state of our society and the state of our minds are stamped upon one another. This was Plato's metaphysical assumption in picturing justice and its decline; it was the secret of Rousseau's epistemology. To let light into this structure of terms, to show that our facts and ideas of economy are uneconomical, that they do not meet but avoid true need, that they are as unjust and impoverishing within each soul as they are throughout the soul's society, *Walden* cuts into the structure of economic terms at two major points, or in two major ways: (1) it attacks its show of practicality by dramatizing the mysteriousness of ownership, and (2) it slips its control of several key terms.

I do not claim that Locke is the only or even the actual representative of the mystery of ownership that *Walden* encounters. But the *Second Treatise* is as formative of the conscience, or the unconsciousness, of political economy as any other work, and its preoccupations are coded into *Walden*. When we read that "the cost of a thing is the amount of what I will call life which is required to be exchanged for it" (21), it is inevitable that we should think of the so-called labor theory of value. The mysticism of what society thinks practical shows up nakedly in what anybody recognizes as the foolishness of Locke's justifications of ownership, in particular his idea that what originally entitles you to a thing is your having "mixed your labor" with it, and that what entitles you to more than you need is your "improvement" of the possession, your not wasting it. "Economy is a subject which admits of being treated with levity, but it cannot so be disposed of" (19). The writer might at that point have had in mind Locke's argument that an individual's accumulation of vastly more money than he can spend is not a case of waste because money is metal and hence can be kept in heaps without being spoiled. The mysteries *Walden* goes into about buying and selling all the farms in his neighborhood, and about annually carrying off the landscape (56), suggest that nobody really knows how it happens that anyone owns anything at all, or why it is that, as Locke puts it, though the earth was given to us in common, it is now so uncommonly divided and held. This is not to say that any of our institutions might not be practically justified (the writer of *Walden* describes and accepts a perfectly practical justification for the institution of money: that it is more convenient than barter). But in fact if you look at what we do under our pleas of economy, you see that no merely practical motives could inspire these labors.

Political economy is the modern form of theodicy, and our labors are our religious mysteries. This is an explicit meaning the writer gives, toward the end of "Economy," to his having spoken at its beginning of our "outward condition." He recounts an Indian custom described in Bartram, in which members of a community cleanse their houses and, having provided themselves with new clothes and utensils and furniture, throw the old together on a common heap, "consume it with fire," fast, and declare a "general amnesty" (46). They are beginning again.

> The Mexicans also practiced a similar purification . . . in the belief that it was time for the world to come to an end . . .
> . . . I have scarcely heard of a truer sacrament, that is, as the dictionary defines it, "outward and visible sign of an inward and spiritual grace."
> (46–47)

So our labors, our outward condition, which he more than once describes as something to which we are "religiously devoted," are our sacraments, and the inward state they signal ("our very lives are our disgrace") is our secret belief that the world has already come to an end for us. Such actions are inspired, but not, as the writer says he believes in the case of the Mexicans, "directly from Heaven." We labor under a mistake. What will save us from ourselves is nothing less than salvation.

The second major strategy I said *Walden* uses to cut into the circling of economic terms is to win back from it possession of our words. This requires replacing them into a reconceived human existence. That it requires a literary redemption of language altogether has been a theme of my remarks from the beginning; and I have hoped to show that it simultaneously requires a redemption of the lives we live by them, religiously or politically conceived, inner and outer. Our words have for us the meaning we give to them. As our lives stand, the meaning we give them is rebuked by the meaning they have in our language—the meaning, say, that writers live on, the meaning we also, in moments, know they have but which mostly remains a mystery to us. Thoreau is doing with our ordinary assertions what Wittgenstein does with our more patently philosophical assertions—bringing them back to a context in which they are alive. It is the appeal from ordinary language to itself; a rebuke of our lives by what we may know of them, if we will. The writer has secrets to tell which can only be told to strangers. The secrets are not his, and they are not the confidences of others. They are secrets because few are anxious to know them; all but one or two wish to remain foreign. Only those who recognize themselves as strangers can be told them, because those who think themselves familiars will think they have already heard what the writer is saying. They will not understand his speaking in confidence.

The literary redemption of language is at the same time a philosophical redemption; the establishment of American literature undertaken in *Walden* requires not only the writing of a scripture and an epic, but a work of philosophy. The general reason is as before: *Walden* proposes new mysteries because we have already mystified ourselves; it requires new literary invention because we have already made our lives fabulous; it requires theology because we are theologized. We have already philosophized our lives almost beyond comprehension. The more famous perception of this is assumed in Marx's eleventh slogan concerning Feuerbach: "Philosophers have only interpreted the world in various ways; the point, however, is to change it." The changes required have to be directed to the fact that it is not only philosophers who have interpreted the world, but all men; that all men labor under a mistake— call it a false consciousness; and that those who learn true labor are going to be able to do something about this because they are the inheritors of philosophy, in a position to put philosophy's brags and hopes for humanity, its humanism, into practice. Why this is or is not going to happen now, and where, and how, are other matters. Who knows what our lives will be when we have shaken off the stupor of history, slipped the drag of time?

* * *

Leaving *Walden*, like leaving Walden, is as hard, is perhaps the same, as entering it. I have implied that the time of crisis depicted in this book is not alone a private one, and not wholly cosmic. It is simultaneously a crisis in the nation's life. And the nation too must die down to the root if it is to continue to recognize and neighbor itself. This is to be expected of a people whose groping for expression produced a literature by producing prophecy. They have had the strength to warn themselves. The hero of the book—as is typical of his procedures—enacts this fact as well as writes it, depicts it in his actions as well as his sentences. Of course the central action of building his house is the general prophecy: the nation, and the nation's people, have yet to be well made. And that the day is at hand for it to depart from its present constructions is amply shown in its hero's beginning and ending his tale with departures from Walden.

Two other of his actions specifically declare the sense of leaving or relinquishing as our present business. On the morning the writer went to dismantle the shanty he had bought as materials for his dwelling, and cart them to his new site, his labors were watched by one neighbor Seeley, who was taking the opportunity, as the writer was "treacherously informed," to steal what good nails, staples, and spikes the shanty yielded. "He was there to represent spectatordom, and help make this seemingly insignificant event one with the removal of the gods of Troy" (29–30). Again, a classical myth shields a myth closer to home:

> Son of man, thou dwellest in the midst of a rebellious house, which have eyes to see, and see not; they have ears to hear, and hear not; for they are a rebellious house.
> Therefore, thou son of man, prepare thee stuff for removing, and remove by day in their sight; and thou shalt remove from thy place to another place in their sight: it may be they will consider, though they be a rebellious house. (Ezekiel 12:2–3)

The next step, if they do not consider, will be to go forth as into captivity. The writer's next step, accordingly, will be to return to civilization. The present constitution of our lives cannot go on. "This people must cease to hold slaves . . . though it cost them their existence as a people" (229–30). I do not quite wish to claim that Thoreau anticipated the Civil War; and yet the *Bhagavad Gita* is present in Walden—in name, and in moments of doctrine and structure. Its doctrine of "unattachment," so far as I am able to make that out, is recorded in *Walden*'s concept of interestedness. (This is, to my mind, one of Thoreau's best strokes. It suggests why "disinterestedness" has never really stabilized itself as a word meaning a state of impartial or unselfish interest, but keeps veering toward meaning the divestment of interest altogether, uninterestedness, ennui. Interestedness is already a state—perhaps the basic state—of relatedness to something beyond the self, the capacity for concern, for implication. It may be thought of as the self's capacity to mediate, to stand, between itself and the world.) Like *Walden*, the *Bhagavad Gita* is a scripture in eighteen parts; it begins with its hero in despair at the action before him; and it ends with his understanding and achieving of resolution, in particular his understanding of the doctrine (in which the image of the field and the knower of the field is central) that the way of knowledge and the way of work are one and the same, which permits him to take up the action it is his to perform and lead his army against an army of his kindred.

The second leaving, or relinquishment, is this:

Now the trunks of trees on the bottom, and the old log canoe, and the dark surrounding woods, are gone, and the villagers, who scarcely know where it lies, instead of going to the pond to bathe or drink, are thinking to bring its water, which should be as sacred as the Ganges at least, to the village in a pipe, to wash their dishes with!—to earn their Walden by the turning of a cock or drawing of a plug! That devilish Iron Horse, whose ear-rending neigh is heard throughout the town, has muddied the Boiling Spring with his foot, and he it is that has browsed off all the woods on Walden shore. . . .

. . . Though the woodchoppers have laid bare first this shore and then that, and the Irish have built their sties by it, and the railroad has infringed on its border, and the icemen have skimmed it once, it is itself unchanged, the same water which my youthful eyes fell on; all the change is in me.
. . . It struck me again tonight, as if I had not seen it almost daily for more than twenty years—Why, here is Walden, the same woodland lake that I discovered so many years ago; where a forest was cut down last winter another is springing up by its shore as lustily as ever; the same thought is welling up to its surface that was then; it is the same liquid joy and happiness to itself and its Maker, ay, and it *may* be to me. It is the work of a brave man surely, in whom there was no guile! He rounded this water with his hand, deepened and clarified it in his thought, and in his will bequeathed it to Concord. I see by its face that it is visited by the same reflection; and I can almost say, Walden, is it you? (129–30)

Walden was always gone, from the beginning of the words of *Walden*. (*Our nostalgia is as dull as our confidence and anticipation.*) The first man and woman are no longer there; our first relation to the world is no longer secured by the world. To allow the world to change, and to learn change from it, to permit it strangers, are conditions of knowing it now. This is why its knowledge is a heroic enterprise. The hero departs from his hut and goes into an unknown wood from whose mysteries he wins a boon that he brings back to his neighbors. The boon of Walden is *Walden*. Its writer cups it in his hand, sees his reflection in it, and holds it out to us. It is his promise, in anticipation of his going, and the nation's, and Walden's. He is bequeathing it to us in his will, the place of the book and the book of the place. He leaves us in one another's keeping.

WALTER BENN MICHAELS

Walden's False Bottoms†

Walden has traditionally been regarded as both a simple and a difficult text, simple in that readers have achieved a remarkable unanimity in identifying

†Reprinted from *Glyph* 1 (1977) : 132–49, by permission of Johns Hopkins University Press. *Walden* and "Civil Disobedience" page numbers refer to this Norton Critical Edition.

the values Thoreau is understood to urge upon them, difficult in that they have been persistently perplexed and occasionally even annoyed by the form his exhortations take. Thoreau's Aunt Maria (the one who bailed him out of jail in the poll tax controversy) understood this as a problem in intellectual history and blamed it all on the Transcendental *Zeitgeist*: "I do love to hear things called by their right names," she said, "and these *Transcendentalists* do so transmogrophy . . . their words and pervert common sense that I have no patience with them."[1] Thoreau's Transcendentalist mentor, Emerson, found, naturally enough, another explanation, blaming instead what he called Henry's "old fault of unlimited contradiction. The trick of his rhetoric is soon learned: it consists in substituting for the obvious word and thought its diametrical antagonist. . . . It makes me," he concluded, "nervous and wretched to read it."[2] That old fault of contradiction is in one sense the subject of this essay, so is wretchedness and especially nervousness, so, in some degree, are the strategies readers have devised for feeling neither wretched nor nervous.

The primary strategy, it seems to me, has been to follow a policy of benign neglect in regard to the question of what *Walden* means; thus, as Charles Anderson noted some ten years ago, critics have concerned themselves largely with "style," agreeing from the start that the book's distinction lies "more in its manner than its matter."[3] Anderson was referring mainly to the tradition of essentially formalist studies ushered in by F. O. Matthiessen's monumental *American Renaissance* in 1941, in which Thoreau is assimilated to the American tradition of the "native craftsman," and *Walden* itself is compared to the "artifacts of the cabinet maker, the potter and the founder."[4] Anderson himself has no real quarrel with this procedure; his chief complaint is that Matthiessen's successors have not taken their enterprise seriously enough. The concern with *Walden*'s style, he says, "has not usually been pursued beyond a general eulogy. Perhaps it is through language that all the seemingly disparate subjects of this book are integrated into wholeness." "Why not try an entirely new approach," he suggests, "and read *Walden* as a poem?"[5]

From our present perspective, of course, it is hard to see how reading *Walden* "as a poem" constitutes an entirely new approach; it seems, if anything, a refinement of the old approaches, a way of continuing to bracket the question of *Walden*'s meaning in at least two different ways. The first is by introducing a distinction between form and content which simultaneously focuses attention on the question of form and reduces content to little more than a banality, typically, in the case of *Walden*, a statement to

1. Quoted in H. S. Canby, *Thoreau* (Boston: Houghton Mifflin, 1939), p. 243.
2. Quoted in Charles R. Anderson, *The Magic Circle of Walden* (New York: Holt, Rinehart, and Winston, 1968), p. 55.
3. Anderson, *The Magic Circle of Walden*, p. 14.
4. F. O. Matthiessen, *American Renaissance* (New York: Oxford University Press, 1968), p. 172.
5. Anderson, *The Magic Circle of Walden*, p. 14.

the effect that the book is fundamentally "a fable of the renewal of life."[6] But from this first move follows a second, more interesting and more pervasive: the preoccupation with *Walden*'s formal qualities turns out to involve a more than tacit collaboration with the assumption that *Walden*'s meaning (what Anderson might call its content and what Stanley Cavell will explicitly call its "doctrine") is in a certain sense simple and univocal. The assertion implicit in this approach is that to examine the form of any literary "artifact" (in fact, even to define the artifact) is precisely to identify its essential unity, thus the continuity between Matthiessen's concern with *Walden*'s "structural wholeness" and Anderson's project of showing how well "integrated" the book is. Where nineteenth-century critics tended to regard *Walden* as an anthology of spectacular fragments and to explain it in terms of the brilliant but disordered personality of its author (his "critical power," wrote James Russell Lowell, was "from want of continuity of mind, very limited and inadequate"),[7] more recent criticism, by focusing directly on the art of *Walden*, has tended to emphasize the rhetorical power of its "paradoxes," finding elegant formal patterns in what were once thought to be mere haphazard blunders. Thus, in accepting unity and coherence not simply as *desiderata* but as the characteristic identifying marks of the work of art, these critics have begun by answering the question I should like to begin by asking, the question of *Walden*'s contradictions.

Thoreau himself might well have been skeptical of some of the claims made on behalf of *Walden*'s aesthetic integrity. He imagined himself addressing "poor students," leading "mean and sneaking lives," "lying, flattering, voting"(4). "The best works of art," he said, "are the expression of man's struggle to free himself from this condition, but the effect of our art is merely to make this low state comfortable and that higher state to be forgotten" (25). In this context, what we might begin to see emerging as the central problem of reading *Walden* is the persistence of our own attempts to identify and understand its unity, to dispel our nervousness by resolving or at least containing the contradictions which create it. It is just this temptation, Thoreau seems to suggest, which must be refused. And in this respect, the naïve perspective of someone like Lowell, who saw in Thoreau the absolute lack of any "artistic mastery" and in his works the total absence of any "mutual relation" between one part and another, may still be of some provisional use, not as a point of view to be reclaimed but as a reminder that resolution need not be inevitable, that we need not read to make ourselves more comfortable.

One way to begin nurturing discomfort is to focus on some of the tasks

6. This particular quotation is from Sherman Paul, *The Shores of America* (Urbana: University of Illinois Press, 1958, 1972), p. 293, but the sentiment is almost unanimous, and it is perhaps a little misleading to single out Paul, whose book is probably the single most im-

portant work of Thoreau scholarship and whose assumptions are in many ways different from those of Matthiessen, Moldenhauer, Broderick, Anderson, *et al*.

7. James Russell Lowell, "Thoreau," reprinted in this volume, p. 336.

Thoreau set himself as part of his program for living a life of what he called "epic integrity." There were, of course, a good many of them, mostly along the lines of his own advice to the unhappily symbolic farmer John Field—"Grow wild according to thy nature," Thoreau urged him, "Rise free from care before the dawn. Let the noon find thee by other lakes and the night overtake thee everywhere at home" (139). Some other projects, however, were conceived in less hortatory terms and the possibility of their completion was more explicitly imaginable. One, "To find the bottom of Walden Pond and what inlet and outlet it might have,"[8] worked its way eventually out of Thoreau's *Journal* and into a central position in the experiment of *Walden* itself. What gave this quest a certain piquancy were the rumours that the pond had no bottom, that, as some said, "it reached quite through to the other side of the globe." "These many stories about the bottom, or rather no bottom, of this Pond," had, Thoreau said, "no foundation for themselves." In fact, the pond was "exactly one hundred and two feet deep," his own "soundings" proved it. This is, he admits, "a remarkable depth for so small an area; yet not an inch of it can be spared by the imagination. What if all ponds were shallow? Would it not react on the minds of men? While men believe in the infinite some ponds will be thought to be bottomless" (190).

If Thoreau's final position on bottoms seems to come out a little blurred here, this has an interest of its own which may be worth pursuing. On the one hand, the passage seems to be asserting that a belief in the potential bottomlessness of ponds is a Bad Thing. The villagers predisposed in this direction who set out to measure Walden with a fifty-six pound weight and a wagon load of rope were already entrapped by their own delusions, for "while the fifty-six was resting by the way," Thoreau says, "they were paying out the rope in the vain attempt to fathom their truly immeasurable capacity for marvellousness" (190). On the other hand, it isn't enough that the pond is revealed to have a "tight bottom," or even that it turns out symbolically "deep and pure"; it must be imagined bottomless to encourage men's belief in the "infinite." Thus, the passage introduces two not entirely complimentary sets of dichotomies. In the first, the virtues of a pond with a "tight bottom" are contrasted with the folly of believing in bottomless ponds. But then the terms shift: the tight bottom metamorphoses into the merely "shallow" and the bottomless becomes the "infinite." The hierarchies are inverted here: on the one hand, a "tight bottom" is clearly preferable to delusory bottomlessness, on the other hand, the merely "shallow" is clearly not so good as the symbolically suggestive "infinite." Finally, the narrator is thankful that the pond was made deep, but "deep" is a little ambiguous: is he glad that the pond is *only* deep so that tough-minded men like himself can sound it and discover its hard bottom, or is he glad that the pond is so deep that it deceives men into thinking of it as bottomless and so leads them

8. H. D. Thoreau, *Journal*, eds. Bradford Torrey and Francis H. Allen (New York: Dover, 1962), vol. 1, p. 435.

into meditations on the infinite? This second explanation seems more convincing, but then the account of the experiment seems to end with a gesture which undermines the logic according to which it was undertaken in the first place.

Sounding the depths of the pond, however, is by no means the only experimental excavation in *Walden*. There is perhaps a better-known passage near the end of the chapter called "Where I Lived and What I Lived For" which helps to clarify what is at stake in the whole bottom-hunting enterprise. "Let us settle ourselves," Thoreau says, "and work and wedge our feet downward through the mud and slush of opinion, and prejudice, and tradition, and delusion, and appearance . . . through church and state, through poetry and philosophy and religion, till we come to a hard bottom and rocks in place which we can call *reality*, and say This is, and no mistake; and then begin, having a *point d'appui* . . . a place where you might found a wall or a state" (66). Measurement here is irrelevant—the issue is solidity, not depth, and the metaphysical status of hard bottoms seems a good deal less problematic. They are real, and "Be it life or death," Thoreau says, "we crave only reality." It is only when we have put ourselves in touch with such a *point d'appui* that we really begin to lead our lives and not be led by them, and the analogy with the *Walden* experiment itself is obvious— it becomes a kind of ontological scavenger-hunt—the prize is reality.

But there is at least one more hard bottom story which unhappily complicates things again. It comes several hundred pages later in the "Conclusion," and tucked in as it is between the flashier and more portentous parables of the artist from Kouroo and of the "strong and beautiful bug," it has been more or less ignored by critics. "It affords me no satisfaction to commence to spring an arch before I have got a solid foundation," Thoreau begins in the now familiar rhetoric of the moral imperative to get to the bottom of things. "Let us not play at kittlybenders," he says, "There is a solid bottom everywhere." But now the story proper gets underway and things begin to go a little haywire. "We read that the traveller asked the boy if the swamp before him had a hard bottom. The boy replied that it had. But presently the traveller's horse sank in up to the girths, and he observed to the boy, 'I thought you said that this bog had a hard bottom.' 'So it has,' answered the latter, 'but you have not got half way to it yet.' " And "so it is with the bogs and quicksands of society," Thoreau piously concludes, "but he is an old boy that knows it" (220–21).

This puts the earlier story in a somewhat different light, I think, and for several reasons. For one thing, the tone is so different; the exalted rhetoric of the evangelist has been replaced by the fireside manner of the teller of tall tales. But more fundamentally, although the theme of the two stories has remained the same—the explorer in search of the solid foundation— the point has been rather dramatically changed. The exhortation has become a warning. The exemplary figure of the heroic traveller, "tied to his mast like Ulysses," Thoreau says, who accepts no substitutes in his quest for the real, has been replaced by the equally exemplary but much less heroic figure of the suppositious traveller drowned in his own pretension. In the first version, Thoreau recognized death as a possibility, but it was a suitably heroic one: "If you stand right fronting and face to face to a fact," he wrote in a justly famous passage, "you will see the sun glimmer on both its surfaces, as if it were a cimeter, and feel its sweet edge dividing you through the heart and marrow, and so you will happily conclude your mortal career" (66). The vanishing traveller of the "conclusion" knows no such happy ending, when he hits the hard bottom he will just be dead, his only claim to immortality his skill in the art of sinking, dispiritedly, in prose.

The juxtaposition of these three passages does not in itself prove anything very startling but it does suggest what may be a useful line of inquiry. What, after all, is at stake in the search for a solid bottom? Why is the concept or the project of a foundation so central to *Walden* and at the same time so problematic? At least a preliminary answer would seem justified in focusing on the almost Cartesian process of peeling away until we reach that point of ontological certainty where we can say "This is, and no mistake." The peeling away is itself a kind of questioning: what justification do we have for our opinions, for our traditions? What authorizes church and state, poetry, philosophy, religion? The *point d'appui* has been reached only when we have asked all the questions we know how to ask and so at last have the sense of an answer we are unable ourselves to give. "After a still winter night," Thoreau says, "I awoke with the impression that some question had been put to me, which I had been endeavoring in vain to answer in my sleep, as what—how—when—where? But there was dawning Nature in whom all creatures live . . . and no question on *her* lips. I awoke to an answered question, to Nature . . ."(188). The *point d'appui* then, is a place we locate by asking questions. We know that we've found it when one of our questions is answered. The name we give to this place is Nature. The search for the solid bottom is a search for justification in Nature, wedging our way through "appearance," that is to say human institutions, like church and state and philosophy, until we hit what is real, that is, natural, and not human.

That nature in its purest form should exclude humanity is perhaps a somewhat peculiar doctrine, and one which runs counter to much of what Thoreau often says, and to much of what we think about him and his enterprise. But the logic and the desires which generate this conception are made clear in *Civil Disobedience* when Thoreau attacks the "statesmen and legislators" who, "standing so completely within the institution, never distinctly and nakedly behold it" (243). In an essay called "What Is Authority?" Hannah Arendt has described what she calls "the dichotomy between seeing truth in solitude and remoteness and being caught in the relationships and relativities of human affairs" as "authoritative for the (Western) tradition of political thought,"[9] and it is precisely this privilege of distance and detachment to which Thoreau seems to be appealing in *Civil Disobedience*. He goes on, however, to diagnose more specifically what is wrong with the legislators: "They speak of moving society, but have no resting-place without it." Webster, for instance, "never goes behind government and so cannot speak with authority about it." The appeal here is to the example of Archimedes—"Give me a place to stand and I will move the earth"—and the suggestion in *Walden* is that nature must be much more than a place of retreat. She is a "resting-place" only in the sense of the *"point d'appui,"* the place to stand, and she is an authoritative *point d'appui* only insofar as she is truly "behind," first, separate, and other. Thus, through most of *Walden*, when Thoreau is addressing himself to the problem of his search for a *cogito*, a political and philosophical hard bottom, the human and the natural are conceived as standing in implicit opposition to each other. Nature has a kind of literal authority precisely because she is not one of men's institutions. She serves as the location of values which are real insofar as they are not human creations. She is exemplary. "If we would restore mankind," Thoreau says, "let us first be as simple and as well as Nature ourselves" (53). The force of this conception is expressed most directly, perhaps, in the short essay "Slavery in Massachusetts," written to protest the state's cooperation with the Fugitive Slave Law of 1850. The image of Nature here is a white water-lily, an emblem, like Walden Pond itself, of "purity." "It suggests what kind of laws have prevailed longest," Thoreau writes, ". . . and that there is virtue even in man, too, who is fitted to perceive and love it."[1] And, he goes on to say, "It reminds me that Nature has been partner to no Missouri Compromise. I scent no compromise in the fragrance of the water-lily." The point again is that it is Nature's independence which makes her exemplary, which, from this standpoint, justifies the retreat to Walden and authorizes the hope that something of real value may be found and hence founded there.

But this conception of nature, as attractive and useful as it is, turns out to be in some ways a misleading one. In "Slavery in Massachusetts," the encomium on the lily is preceded by a brief excursion in search of solace to "one of our ponds" (it might as well be Walden). But there is no solace to be found there. "We walk to lakes to see our serenity reflected in them," Thoreau says, "when we are not serene we go not to them."[2] For "what signifies the beauty of nature when men are base?" If the water-lily is a symbol of nature free and clear, sufficient unto itself, the pond in its role as reflector symbolizes a nature implicated in human affairs. It fails as a source of consolation because, unlike the water-lily, it participates in the

9. Hannah Arendt, *Between Past and Future* (New York: Viking, 1961), p. 115.
1. H. D. Thoreau, "Slavery in Massachusetts," reprinted in *Thoreau: The Major Essays,* ed. with an introduction by Jeffrey L. Duncan (New York: E. P. Dutton, 1972), p. 144.
2. Ibid.

world of Missouri Compromises and Fugitive Slave Laws. And this vision of nature compromised finds a significant position in Walden as well. In the chapter called "Sounds," Thoreau devotes the beginning of one paragraph to a sound he claims he never heard, the sound of the cock crowing. This is no doubt a kind of back-handed reference to his own declaration at the beginning of the book: "I do not propose to write an ode to dejection, but to brag as lustily as chanticleer in the morning . . . if only to wake my neighbors up" (1). The writing of Walden makes up for the absent cock-crow. But he goes on to speak of the cock as a "once wild Indian pheasant" and to wonder if it could ever be "naturalized without being domesticated" (86). Here Walden's customary opposition between nature and civilization turns into an opposition between wilderness and civilization, and nature ("naturalized") appears as a third term, at one remove from "wild" and in constant danger of being domesticated and so rendered useless. Furthermore, this danger appears most pronounced at a moment which has been defined as that of writing, the cock-crow. The dismay at seeing only one's face reflected in the pond repeats itself here for a moment as the text imagines itself as a once wild voice now tamed and defused.

These two accounts suggest, then, the kind of problem that is being defined. The attraction of Nature as a bottom line is precisely its otherness—"Nature puts no question and answers none which we mortals ask" (188)—and touching bottom is thus (paradoxically) a moment of recognition; we see what "really is" and our relation to it is basically one of appreciation (and perhaps emulation). The paradox, of course, is our ability to recognize something which is defined precisely by its strangeness to us, a difficulty Thoreau urges upon us when he insists that "Nature has no human inhabitant who appreciates her" (134), and that "she flourishes most alone." But, as I have said, this aloneness is the chief guarantee of authenticity—when we have reached the bottom, we know at least that what we are seeing is not just ourselves. And yet this is also what is most problematic in the symbolic character of Walden Pond itself; looking into it, we find ourselves sounding the depths of our own "nature," and so the reflection makes a mockery of our enterprise. "For his genius to be effective," one critic has written, Thoreau recognized that he "had to slough off his civilized self and regain his natural self,"[3] and this seems innocuous enough. But the cosmological continuity which would authorize a notion like the "natural self" is exactly what is being questioned here. For us to recognize ourselves in Nature, Nature must be no longer herself, no longer the *point d'appui* we were looking for when we started.

But even if Nature proves inadequate as a final category, an absolute, Walden's response is not to repudiate the notion of intrinsic value. The pond remains a precious stone, "too pure," he says, to have "a market value" (134), and so it provides at least a symbolic alternative to the commercial

3. Melvin E. Lyon, "Walden Pond as Symbol," PMLA 82 (1967): 289.

values of the first chapter, "Economy." "Economy" has usually been read as a witty and bitter attack on materialism, perhaps undertaken, as Charles Anderson has suggested,[4] in response to Mill's *Political Economy* and/or Marx's *Manifesto* (both published in 1848), motivated, in any event, by a New Testament perception: "Men labor under a mistake. . . . They are employed . . . laying up treasures which moth and rust will corrupt and thieves break through and steal" (3). But it isn't simply a mistake in emphasis—too much on the material and not enough on the spiritual—that Thoreau is concerned with here, for the focal point of "Economy's" attack is not wealth *per se* but "exchange," the principle of the marketplace. Thus, he questions not merely the value of material goods but the process through which the values are determined; "trade curses everything it handles," he says, "and though you trade in messages from heaven, the whole curse of trade attaches to the business" (47). In some degree this can be explained as a nineteenth-century expression of a long-standing ideological debate between the political conceptions of virtue and commerce, which depended in turn upon an opposition between what J. G. A. Pocock has called "real, inheritable, and, so to speak, natural property in land,"[5] and property understood to have only what Pocock calls a "symbolic value, expressed in coin or in credit." One of the phenomena Pocock describes is the persistence with which various social groups attempted to convince themselves that their credit economies were "based on the exchange of real goods and the perception of real values." Failing this, he says, "the individual could exist, even in his own sight, only at the fluctuating value imposed upon him by his fellows."[6]

Thoreau was obviously one of those unconvinced and unhappy about it. Not only did he repudiate what he perceived as false methods of determining value, not only did he rail against the maintenance of a standing army and even reject at times the validity of the entire concept of representative government (all these, as Pocock depicts them, classical political positions); he also attacked real, so-called natural property as well, and precisely at the point which was intended to provide its justification, its inheritability. "I see young men," he says at the very beginning of *Walden*, "my townsmen, whose misfortune it is to have inherited farms, houses . . . for these are more easily acquired than got rid of" (2). Here he blurs the customary distinction between real or natural and symbolic or artificial property, insisting that all property is artificial and so exposing laws of inheritance as mere fictions of continuity, designed to naturalize values which in themselves are purely arbitrary.

This points toward a rather peculiar dilemma—Thoreau's doggedly ascetic insistence on distinguishing natural values from artificial ones leads him to reject the tokens of natural value which his society provides, and so the

4. Anderson, *The Magic Circle of Walden*, p. 19.
5. J. G. A. Pocock, *The Machiavellian Mo-*   *ment* (Princeton: Princeton University Press, 1975), p. 463.
6. Ibid., p. 464.

category of the natural becomes an empty one. But this doesn't mean that the natural/arbitrary distinction breaks down. Quite the contrary: the more difficult that it becomes to identify natural principles, the more privilege attaches to a position which can be defined only in theoretical opposition to the conventional or institutional. The "resting-place without" society that Thoreau speaks of in *Civil Disobedience* now turns out to be located neither in nature nor in culture but in that empty space he sometimes calls "wilderness." This is perhaps what he means when he describes himself once as a "sojourner in civilized life" and another time as a "sojourner in nature." To be a sojourner everywhere is by one account (Thoreau's own in "Walking") to be "at home everywhere." In *Walden*, however, this vision of man at home in the world is undermined by the Prophetic voice which proclaims it. He denounces his contemporaries who "no longer camp as for a night but have settled down on earth and forgotten heaven" by comparing them unfavorably to the primitive nomads who "dwelt . . . in a tent in this world" (25), thus invoking one of the oldest of western topoi, the moral authority of the already atavistic Hebrew nomads, the Rechabites, relating the commandments of their father to the prophet Jeremiah: "Neither shall ye build house, nor sow seed, nor plant vineyard, nor have any: but all your days ye shall dwell in tents; that ye may live many days in the land where ye be strangers" (*Jeremiah* 35:7). The Rechabites were at home nowhere, not everywhere. Jeremiah cites them as exemplars not of a healthy rusticity but of a deep-seated and devout alienation which understands every experience except that of Yahweh as empty and meaningless.[7] Thus, to be, like Thoreau, a self-appointed stranger in the land is to repudiate the values of a domesticated pastoral by recognizing the need for a resting-place beyond culture and nature both, and to accept the figurative necessity of living always in one's tent is to recognize the impossibility of ever actually locating that resting-place.

Another way to deal with this search for authority is to imagine it emanating not only from a place but from a time. In *Walden*, the notion of foundation brings these two categories uneasily together. The solid bottom is a place where you might "found a wall or a state," but the foundation of a state is perhaps more appropriately conceived as a time—July 4, for example, the day Thoreau says he moved to the woods. This constitutes an appeal to the authority of precedent which would justify also the exemplary claims *Walden* makes on behalf of itself. The precedent has force as the record of a previous "experiment," and since "No way of thinking or doing, however ancient, can be trusted without proof" (5), the "experiment" of *Walden* can apparently be understood as an attempt to repeat the results originally achieved by the Founding Fathers. But the scientific term "experiment," precisely because it relies on the notion of repeatability, that is, on an unchanging natural order, turns out to work much less well in the

7. On this point, see Herbert N. Schneidau, *Sacred Discontent* (Berkeley: University of California Press, 1977).

historical context of human events. "Here is life," Thoreau says, "an experiment to a great extent untried by me; but it does not avail me that they have tried it" (5). This now is a peculiar kind of empiricism which stresses not only the primacy of experience but its unrepeatability, its uniqueness. (What good is *Walden* if not as a precedent?) The revolutionary appeal to foundation as a new beginning seems to be incompatible with the empiricist notion of foundation as the experience of an immediate but principled (i.e., repeatable) reality. The historical and the scientific ideas of foundation are clearly at odds here, and Thoreau seems to recognize this when he speaks of his desire "to anticipate not the sunrise and the dawn merely, but if possible Nature herself," that is, to achieve a priority which belongs to the historical but not the natural world. Coleridge had written some twenty years before that "No natural thing or act can be called an originate" since "the moment we assume an origin in nature, a true beginning, that moment we rise above nature."[8] Thoreau speaks of coming before rather than rising above, but the sense of incompatibility is the same. Once again the desire for the solid bottom is made clear, but the attempt to locate it or specify its characteristics involves the writer in a tangle of contradictions.

What I have tried to describe thus far is a series of relationships in the text of *Walden*—between nature and culture, the finite and the infinite, and (still to come) literal and figurative language—each of which is imagined at all times hierarchically, that is, the terms don't simply coexist, one is always thought of as more basic or more important than the other. The catch is that the hierarchies are always breaking down. Sometimes nature is the ground which authorizes culture, sometimes it is merely another of culture's creations. Sometimes the search for a hard bottom is presented as the central activity of a moral life, sometimes that same search will only make a Keystone-cop martyr out of the searcher. These unresolved contradictions are, I think, what makes us nervous reading *Walden*, and the urge to resolve them seems to me a major motivating factor in most *Walden* criticism. Early, more or less explicitly biographical criticism tended to understand the inconsistencies as personal ones, stemming, in Lowell's words, from Thoreau's "want of continuity of mind." But as the history of literary criticism began to deflect its attention from authors to texts, this type of explanation naturally began to seem unsatisfactory. Allusions to Thoreau's psychological instability were now replaced by references to *Walden*'s "literary design," and paradox, hitherto understood as a more or less technical device, was now seen to lie near the very center of *Walden*'s "literariness." In one essay, by Joseph Moldenhauer,[9] Thoreau's techniques are seen in easy analogy to those of Sir Thomas Browne, Donne, and the other English Metaphysicals, and generally the "presentation of truth through paradox" is

8. Quoted in Geoffrey Hartman, *The Fate of Reading* (Chicago: University of Chicago Press, 1975), p. 259.
9. Joseph J. Moldenhauer, "Paradox in Walden," in *Twentieth Century Interpretations of Walden*, ed. with an introduction by Richard Ruland (Englewood Cliffs, N.J.: Prentice-Hall, 1968), pp. 73–84.

identified as Thoreau's characteristic goal, although sometimes the truth is mythical, sometimes psychological, sometimes a little of both. In any event, the formalist demand that the text be understood as a unified whole (mechanical or organic) is normative; what Moldenhauer calls the "heightened language of paradox" is seen as shocking the reader into new perceptions of ancient truths.

More recently, the question of *Walden*'s hierarchies has been raised again by Stanley Cavell in a new and interesting way. Cavell recounts what he calls the "low myth of the reader" in *Walden*. "It may be thought of," he says, as a one-sentence fabliau:

> The writer has been describing the early spring days in which he went down to the woods to cut down timber for his intended house; he depicts himself carrying along his dinner of bread and butter wrapped in a newspaper which while he was resting he read. A little later, he says: "In those days when my hands were much employed, I read but little, but the least scraps of paper which lay on the ground . . . afforded me as much entertainment, in fact answered the same purpose as the *Iliad.*"
> If you do not know what reading can be, you might as well use the pages of the *Iliad* for the purpose for which newspaper is used after a meal in the woods. If, however, you are prepared to read, then a fragment of newspaper, discovered words, are sufficient promptings . . . The events in a newspaper, our current lives are epic, and point morals, if we know how to interpret them."[1]

The moral of this interpretation, as I understand it, is that just as the hierarchical relation between nature and culture is uncertain and problematic, so there is no necessary hierarchy among texts—a Baltimore *Morning Sun* is as good as an *Iliad* if you know how to read it. But it is interesting that one of the passages Cavell elsewhere refers to (from *Walden*'s chapter on "Reading") is concerned precisely to specify a hierarchy of texts. "I kept Homer's *Iliad* on my table through the summer," Thoreau writes, "though I looked at his page only now and then. . . . Yet I sustained myself by the prospect of such reading in the future. I read one or two shallow books of travel in the intervals of my work, till that employment made me ashamed of myself, and I asked where it was then that *I* lived" (68). The contrast here is between the epic and the travelogue, and for Thoreau the latter was a particularly vexing genre. "I would fain say something, not so much concerning the Chinese and Sandwich Islanders as you who read these pages, who are said to live in New England" (2), he proclaims in *Walden*'s first chapter, and in its last chapter he renounces any "exploration" beyond one's "private sea, the Atlantic and Pacific Ocean of one's being alone" (214). In his personal life, too, he shied away from voyages; until his last years, he never got any farther from Concord than Staten Island, and it took only several youthful weeks on that barbaric shore to send him scurrying

1. Stanley Cavell, *The Senses of Walden* (New York: Viking, 1972), p. 67.

for home. But he was at the same time inordinately fond of travel books; one scholar's account has him reading a certifiable minimum of 172 of them,[2] and as any reader of *Walden* knows, these accounts make frequent appearances there. In fact, in "Economy," no sooner has Thoreau announced his intention to ignore the lure of Oriental exoticisms than he plunges into a series of stories about the miraculous exploits of certain heroic "Bramins." *Walden* is, in fact, chock full of the wisdom of the mysterious East. The epics which Thoreau opposes to "shallow books of travel" are, in almost the same breath, described as "books which circulate around the world," that is, they are themselves travelling books.

All this serves mainly to reinforce Cavell's point; judging by subject matter at least, epics and travelogues turn out to look pretty much the same—the significant distinctions must then be not so much in the books themselves as in the way we read them. And along these lines, Thoreau suggests in "Reading" another, perhaps more pertinent way of distinguishing between the two genres: travel books are "shallow," epics presumably are not, which is to say that in reading epics, we must be prepared to conjecture "a larger sense than common use permits" (68). The mark of the epic is thus that it can be, indeed must be, read figuratively, whereas the travel book lends itself only to a shallow or literal reading. Thoreau goes on to imagine the contrast between classical literature and what he calls a "cheap, contemporary literature" (69) as a contrast between the eloquence of the writer who "speaks to the intellect and heart of mankind, to all in any age who can *understand* him" and the lesser eloquence of the orator who "yields to the inspiration of a transient occasion, and speaks to the mob before him, to those who can *hear* him" (69). Thus the opposition between the epic and travelogue has modulated into an opposition between the figurative and the literal and then between the written and the oral. In each case, the first term of the opposition is privileged, and if we turn again to the attempt to sound the depths of Walden Pond, we can see that these are all values of what I have called 'bottomlessness.' A shallow pond would be like a shallow book, that is, a travel book, one meant to be read literally. *Walden* is written "deep and pure for a symbol."

But this pattern of valorization, although convincing, is by no means ubiquitous or final. The chapter on "Reading" is followed by one called "Sounds," which systematically reconsiders the categories already introduced and which reasserts the values of the hard bottom. Here the written word is contrasted unfavorably with the magical "noise" of nature. The 'intimacy' and 'universality' for which Thoreau had praised it in the first chapter are now metamorphosed into 'confinement' and a new kind of 'provincialism.' But not only is the hierarchical relation between the written and the oral inverted, so is what we have seen to be the corresponding relation between the figurative and the literal. What in the chapter on "Reading" was seen

2. John Aldrich Christie, *Thoreau as World Traveller* (New York: Columbia University Press, 1965), p. 44.

to be the greatest virtue of the classic texts, their susceptibility to interpretation, to the conjecturing of a larger sense "too significant," Thoreau says, "to be heard by the ear," a sense which "we must be born again to speak" (69), all this is set aside in favor of the "one articulation of Nature" (84), the "language which all things and events speak without metaphor" (75). In "Sounds," Nature's voice is known precisely because it resists interpretation. The polysemous becomes perverse; the models of communication are the Puri Indians who, having only one word for yesterday, today, and tomorrow, "express the variety of meaning by pointing backward for yesterday, forward for tomorrow, and overhead for the passing day" (76). Where the classic texts were distinguished by their underdetermined quality—since the language they were written in was "dead," their "sense" was generated only by the reader's own interpretive "wisdom," "valor," and "generosity"— nature's language in "Sounds," the song of the birds, the stirring of the trees, is eminently alive and, as the example of the Indians shows, correspondingly overdetermined. Theirs is a system of words modified only by gestures and so devised that they will allow only a single meaning. No room is left for the reader's conjectures; the goal is rather a kind of indigenous and monosyllabic literalism, so many words for so many things by the shores of Gitcheegoomee. This means, of course, that the values of bottomlessness are all drained away. The deep is replaced by the shallow, the symbolic by the actual—what we need now, Thoreau says, are "tales of real life, high and low, and founded on fact" (81).

This particular set of inversions helps us to relocate, I think, the problem of reading *Walden*, which we have already defined as the problem of resolving, or at least containing, its contradictions, of establishing a certain unity. Critics like Lowell domesticated the contradictions by understanding them as personal ones; to point out Thoreau's (no doubt lamentable) inconsistencies was not, after all, to accuse him of schizophrenia—the parts where he seemed to forget himself or ignore what he had said before were evidence only of certain lapses of attention. The formalists, turning their attention from the author to the text, transformed Thoreau's faults into *Walden*'s virtues; theirs was already the language of paradox, apparent inconsistencies pointing toward final literary (i.e., not necessarily logical) truths. Now Cavell takes this process of resolution, of replacement, as far, in one direction, as it can go; the unity which was claimed first for the personality of the author, then for the formal structure of the text itself, now devolves upon the reader. *Walden*'s contradictions are resolved, he says, "if you know how to interpret them." The reader who knows how, it turns out, can discern in *Walden* "a revelation in which the paradoxes and ambiguities of its doctrine achieve a visionary union."[3] And more recent writers like Lawrence Buell have extended this principle to others among the Transcendentalists. "Emerson's contribution," Buell writes, "is to show through

3. Cavell, *The Senses of Walden*, p. 109.

his paradoxical style the inoperability of doctrine, to force the auditor to read him figuratively, as he believes that scriptures should be read."[4]

But Cavell's position has its own peculiarity, for while it recognizes and even insists upon the difficulty of maintaining hierarchies in the text of *Walden*, it goes on simply to reinscribe those hierarchies in *Walden*'s readers. Knowing how to read for Cavell and for Buell is knowing how to read figuratively, and this is one of the things, Cavell says, that *Walden* teaches us. Thus the coherence that the formalists understood as the defining characteristic of the text becomes instead the defining characteristic of the reader, and the unity which was once claimed for the object itself is now claimed for the reader's experience of it. But, as we have just seen, the power of figurative reading is not the only thing *Walden* teaches us; it also urges upon us the necessity of reading literally, not so much in addition to reading figuratively as *instead of* reading figuratively. In the movement from "Reading" to "Sounds," the figurative and the literal do not coexist, they are not seen as complementary; rather the arguments Thoreau gives in support of the one take the form of attacks on the other. If, following Thoreau's guide, we conceive the literal as a meaning available to us without interpretation (i.e., the unmediated language of nature) and the figurative as a meaning generated by our own interpretive "wisdom," we find that the very act of reading commits us to a choice, not simply between different meanings, but between different stances toward reality, different versions of the self. Thus books must inevitably be "read as deliberately and reservedly as they were written" because to read *is* to deliberate, to consider and decide. "Our whole life is startlingly moral," Thoreau says, "There is never an instant's truce between virtue and vice" (146). This is a call to action in the most direct sense, and the action it imagines is reading, conceived as an explicitly moral activity. Elsewhere he writes, "it appears as if men had deliberately chosen the common mode of living because they preferred it to others. Yet they honestly think there is no choice left" (5). Thoreau's concern in *Walden* is, of course, to show us that we do have choices left and, by breaking down hierarchies into contradictory alternatives, to insist upon our making them. But this breakdown, which creates the opportunity, or rather the necessity for choosing, serves at the same time to undermine the rationale we might give for any particular choice. If there is no hierarchy of values, what authority can we appeal to in accounting for our decisions? What makes one choice better than another?

This is what the search for a solid bottom is all about, a location for authority, a ground upon which we can make a decision. *Walden* insists upon the necessity for such a search at the same time that it dramatizes the theoretical impossibility of succeeding in it. In this sense, the category of the bottomless is like the category of the natural, final but empty, and when

---

4. Lawrence Buell, *Literary Transcendentalism* (Ithaca: Cornell University Press, 1973), pp. 118–19.

Cavell urges upon us the desirability of a figurative reading, he is just removing the hard bottom from the text and relocating it in the reader. The concept remains equally problematic, our choices equally unmotivated. The result is what has been described in a different context, precisely and pejoratively, as "literary anarchy,"[5] a complaint which serves, like Emerson's attack of nerves, as a record of the response *Walden* seems to me to demand. In a political context, of course, the question of authority is an old one. Thoreau raises it himself in *Civil Disobedience*. "One would think," he writes, "that a deliberate and practical denial of its authority was the only offence never contemplated by a government" (233). The form this denial takes in *Civil Disobedience* is "action from principle—the perception and the performance of right," but the perception of right is exactly what *Walden* makes most equivocal, and the possibility of action from principle is exactly what *Walden* denies, since the principles it identifies are always competing ones and hence inevitably inadequate as guidelines.

To be a citizen or to be a reader of *Walden* is to participate always in an act of foundation or interpretation which is inevitably arbitrary—there is as much to be said against it as there is for it. The role of the citizen/reader then, as Thoreau said in *Civil Disobedience*, is "essentially revolutionary," it "changes things and relations . . . and does not consist wholly with anything that was." But not only is it revolutionary, it is divisive: it "divides states and churches, it divides families," it even "divides the *individual*," that is, it divides the reader himself—he is repeatedly confronted with interpretive decisions which call into question both his notion of the coherence of the text and of himself. In *Civil Disobedience*, however, as in most of the explicitly political texts, Thoreau professes no difficulty in locating and identifying legitimate principles of action. It is only in *Walden* itself that the principle of uncertainty is built in. "Let us not play at kittlybenders," he wrote in *Walden's* "Conclusion," "There is a solid bottom everywhere." Kittlybenders is a children's game; it involves running or skating on thin ice as quickly as you can so that you don't fall through. If the ice breaks, of course, you're liable to find the solid bottom and so, like the traveller in the story, "conclude your mortal career." The traveller is an image of the writer and, as we can now see, of the reader too. *Walden*, as it has been all along, is a book. To read it, as Thoreau suggested some hundred pages earlier, you "lie at your length on ice only an inch thick, like a skater insect on the surface of the water, and study the bottom at your leisure" (p. 164). But, he goes on to say, "the ice itself is the object of most interest." To read *Walden*, then, is precisely to play at kittlybenders, to run the simultaneous risks of touching and not touching bottom. If our reading claims to find a solid bottom, it can only do so according to principles which the text has both authorized and repudiated; thus we run the risk of drowning in our own certainties. If it doesn't, if we embrace the idea of bottomlessness and

5. Charles Feidelson, Jr. *Symbolism and American Literature* (Chicago: University of Chicago Press, 1953, 1966), p. 149. Fiedelson is actually discussing Emerson's own "literary doctrines."

the interest of the ice itself, we've failed *Walden's* first test, the acceptance of our moral responsibility as deliberate readers. It's heads I win, tails you lose. No wonder the game makes us nervous.

BARRY WOOD

Thoreau's Narrative Art in "Civil Disobedience"†

* * *

The enormous influence of "Civil Disobedience," not only on thinkers like Tolstoy and Gandhi but also on the British Labor Movement and American life generally, is well known. Combined with a few other Thoreau essays— "Slavery in Massachusetts," "A Plea for Captain John Brown," and perhaps the "Economy" chapter of *Walden*—it has inspired commentary so extensive that a recent book appeared devoted solely to "Thoreau's political reputation in America."[1] Yet the single-minded emphasis in commentary on "Civil Disobedience" to the political rather than the artistic suggests a virtual blind spot even among the most sensitive critics, while at the same time revealing more about the shifting political attitudes in our time than Thoreau's. The fact is that Thoreau's reputation (in other areas too, not simply political) is out of all proportion to the ideas he sets forth, or even to the experiences upon which these ideas are hung. He was not the first to live in a cabin by a pond near Concord, nor the first to travel in New Hampshire, Cape Cod, or the Maine Woods, nor even the first to climb Wachusett, Saddleback, or Ktaadn. Before Thoreau withheld his poll tax Bronson Alcott had done the same.[2] Even the ideas of "Civil Disobedience" had important forerunners: Emerson's "Politics" and Paley's *Moral and Political Philosophy* for instance.[3] What accounts for Thoreau's influence, lies elsewhere—in the artistic power of his work and the sense of drama running through all his writings. In the major works this sense of drama approaches what Hyman calls "a vast rebirth ritual,"[4] but everywhere we find the use of a sustained narrative thread which leads the reader forward in anticipation of discovery. The speaking "I" is always present, as Thoreau himself notes with no apologies on the first page of *Walden*, and this leads to a mode of writing which demonstrates discovery, the achievement of perspective, the awakening of vision, and spiritual renewal. Whatever ideas appear are enfolded in a story, so much so that the narrative structure is often the key to the ideas.

† From *Philological Quarterly* 60 (1981): 106– 15. Reprinted by permission. *Walden* and "Civil Disobedience" page numbers refer to this Norton Critical Edition.

1. Michael Meyer, *Several More Lives to Live: Thoreau's Political Reputation in America* (Westport, Conn.: Greenwood Press, 1977).
2. See John C. Broderick, "Thoreau, Alcott, and the Poll Tax," *SP*, 53 (1956), 612–26.
3. See Raymond Adams, "Thoreau's Sources for 'Resistance to Civil Government,'" *SP*, 42 (1945), 640–53.
4. In Sherman Paul, ed., *Thoreau: A Collection of Critical Essays* (Englewood Cliffs, N.J.: Prentice-Hall, Inc., 1962), 28.

If the narrative elements of Thoreau's writings have not been stressed, neither have they been missed. The relations between the works and specific events, excursions, or sojourns in Thoreau's life are well known. But these facts are often passed over as a biographical element less interesting than the presumed "message" being developed. Such an omission ignores what the narrative ordering of the work actually *accomplishes* in the unfolding and development of the ideas. In the case of "Civil Disobedience" it has not yet been shown how narrative order operates as a synthesizing device for the reconciliation of the two realms of experience—the real and the transcendent. I imagine that Thoreau is more generally linked with Emerson than Melville among writers of his time, but some perspective is gained by comparing him with both. Emerson typically engineered his transcendental philosophy through symbolism by using Nature as a "vehicle of thought" or a "symbol of spirit"; that is, he demonstrated that man lives simultaneously in two worlds which are joined in moments of "exhiliration" or, at times of creativity, when the scholar becomes Man Thinking or the poet becomes a "liberating god." Melville accomplished the same linkage of two worlds through his voyages during which his Tajis and Ishmaels find themselves literally travelling across the boundary from the real world into the transcendental. Symbol in Emerson and narrative in Melville both have a synthesizing capacity.[5] Thoreau stands, as it were, midway: we find in him the same duality of worlds and we find him using both symbolism and narrative journeys to give a single account a double reference.

In "Civil Disobedience" there appear to be two rather different centers of interest. One derives from the political ideas set forth about which so much has been written. The other focuses on the story of Thoreau's night in jail, probably July 23 or 24, 1846. Reference to this story is made obliquely in A Week,[6] but the version occurring later, in *Walden*, provides a fuller account:

> One afternoon, near the end of the first summer, when I went to the village to get a shoe from the cobbler's, I was seized and put into jail, because, as I have elsewhere related, I did not pay a tax to, or recognize the authority of, the state which buys and sells men, women, and children, like cattle at the door of its senate-house. I had gone down to the woods for other purposes. But, wherever a man goes, men will pursue and paw him with their dirty institutions, and, if they can, constrain him to belong to their desperate odd-fellow society. It is true, I might have resisted forcibly with more or less effect, might have run "amok" against society; but I preferred that society should run "amok" against me, it being the

5. My slightly exaggerated emphasis here is not intended to deny Melville's extensive use of symbolism which permeates his works. However, the narrative dimension of romances like *Mardi* or *Moby Dick* (only partially offset by what Frye describes as the "anatomy" strand of prose fiction) is in marked contrast to Emerson's generically different prose strategies. The only Emerson essay which is arguably structured as a narrative is "Experience" with its personified "lords of life" and persistent images of travelling, generally westward.
6. Henry David Thoreau, A Week on the Concord and Merrimack Rivers (Boston: Houghton Mifflin, 1906), 135–36.

desperate party. However, I was released the next day, obtained my mended shoe, and returned to the woods in season to get my dinner of huckleberries on Fair-Haven Hill. (115–16)

In "Civil Disobedience" this rather undramatic event is given considerable narrative scope, especially in the central paragraphs which are properly separated and set in reduced type in authoritative editions.[7] This narrative effectively divides the essay into three parts. There is, in the two flanking sections, an important tonal difference, suggesting that the central narrative is operating as a bridge between the two sections of philosophical argument.[8]

Thoreau says of his night in jail that "it was like travelling into a far country, such as I had never expected to behold, to lie there for one night. . . . It was to see my native village in the light of the middle ages, and our Concord [River] was turned into a Rhine stream, and visions of knights and castles passed before me" (239–40). This vision of "a far country" and "a long journey," with imagery from Europe and the middle ages, is completed, as in the *Walden* account, by Thoreau's retreat from the village and ascent of "one of our highest hills, two miles off" (241). Embedded in this account is a series of contrasts: most obviously, the village world of Concord and the natural world beyond it where the narrative begins and ends; the darkness of the night spent in jail and the sunlight of the days preceding and following it; the "medieval" quality of the Concord scene and the immediacy and spontaneity of the huckleberrying party moving up the high hill. The narrative movement—from the natural world into the village and back to the natural—sets forth in dramatic terms the dialectical progress of the larger essay: contrasts in the narrative suggest the contrasting views of the State set forth in the first and third sections; and the movement through the narrative middle, like Thoreau's own movement through the night in the Concord jail, provides a "before" and "after" polarity basic to the political idea of the essay. What *is* is seen against what *could be*. Indeed, if the transcendentalist is understood as attempting to see *this* world in terms of *another*, the *real* as against the *ideal*, then the narrative center of "Civil Disobedience" can be seen as a powerful rhetorical strategy for linking the two views of the State. The narrative journey from one view to another, from one realm to another, makes possible a synthesis of the two in a higher third.

That Thoreau is operating within a polar view of things is everywhere apparent; it is part of his transcendentalist heritage. In the first part of the essay his criticism of "standing government" links the ruling mechanism in

7. Lane, "Civil Disobedience": A Bibliographical note," *PBSA*, 63 (1969), 295–96.
8. For an alternate approach to the narrative see Thomas R. Carper, "The Whole History of Thoreau's 'My Prisons,' " *Emerson Society Quarterly*, no. 50 (1968), 35–38. Carper too finds that "the political significance of the document is a side issue" and stresses its status as "an artistic statement, of antagonisms and needs [in Thoreau] which could be declared in

no other way" (35). Carper does not isolate the section in reduced type completely but includes the long paragraph preceding it ("I have paid no poll-tax . . . pitied it"); his emphasis, however, falls on the friendship which develops between Thoreau and his cell-mate, "for here is a relationship such as would characterize the perfect and glorious state of which Thoreau had dreamed"(36).

America with "tradition . . . endeavoring to transmit itself unimpaired to posterity"; this is contrasted with the "vitality and force of a single living man" (226). Here again is the Emersonian dilemma posed in the opening lines of *Nature*—the "retrospective" quality of American life with men desperately in need of their own "original relation to the universe"—recast in political terms. Repeatedly this dichotomy is observed: government is opposed by "character"; legislators with their tariff restrictions are contrasted with the "bounce" of a trade and commerce made of India rubber (a good example of what Bowling calls "social criticism as poetry"); government by "majority" is opposed by government by "conscience"; law is contrasted with "right"; machines are balanced by "men"; and the persistence of slavery in "a nation which has undertaken to be the refuge of liberty" is cited as grounds for "honest men to rebel and revolutionize" (226–29). In Thoreau's view, the ideal possibilities of democracy are not realized because of "the opponents to a reform . . . who are more interested in commerce and agriculture than they are in humanity" (230).

As Thoreau describes it, American life is full of contradictions and American policy is inconsistent with its stated values. Moreover, no *political* solution can eliminate these problems. At best a democratic society resorts to the vote—an artificial procedure for deciding who shall have their say by reducing right to might. The divisive tensions of society are thus left unresolved, precisely because "voting *for the right* is *doing* nothing for it" (231). Doing *something* means, for Thoreau, resolving the polarities through action which carries dichotomies to a new level where they can be synthesized in a higher unity. "Action from principle,—the perception and the performance of right,—changes things and relations; it is essentially revolutionary" (232–33). *Revolutionary*: the word is perfectly chosen, for it suggests that real action transfers political contradictions from the social world of stalemate to the cyclical, organic world of new creation. Here natural law, or what Thoreau terms "higher law" (238), functions to resolve contradictions. Exactly this kind of organic resolution appears in Thoreau's final remarks before he describes his night in jail:

> I perceive that, when an acorn and a chestnut fall side by side, the one does not remain inert to make way for the other, but both obey their own laws, and spring and grow and flourish as best they can, till one, perchance, overshadows and destroys the other. If a plant cannot live according to its nature, it dies; and so a man. (239)

The first long section of "Civil Disobedience" thus describes in symptomatic terms the basic problems of American political life, and sets a course for their solution. Tensions and polarities, Thoreau feels, may be overcome by "action from principle"; and the notion of *action* thus leads directly into Thoreau's account of his own actions. His narrative, then, is clearly the beginning of a process which will lead from the problematic politics described to the idealized vision at the end of the essay. Thoreau's action, of course, was that of not paying his poll-tax, an act of resistance to civil government. What the central narrative accomplishes is a transformation of the basic political dichotomies into a more dramatic form. The true nature of these dichotomies is rooted out, for Thoreau's actions force the State to make clear its generally unstated view of the truly self-reliant man. As Thoreau details his night in jail it becomes clear that physical incarceration is, short of capital punishment, the closest thing to death that the State can manage. Thoreau sees that the State's answer to opposition is tantamount to murder, as his imagery reveals. Thus, while he is literally put *in* jail, figuratively he is put well *below* the realm of ordinary society in a place of wood, stone, and iron where he says the window gratings "strained the light" (238).[9] The night spent in the dark cell, described as a journey into a far country, parallels Dante's night spent in a dark wood in Canto I of *The Inferno* which was figuratively *his* journey into the far country of hell. Thoreau's night, like Dante's, is followed by an emergence at dawn and a renewed vision of the world. The night in prison is thus cast as a kind of mythic descent: Thoreau's remarks about the shedding and flowing of blood through the Mexican war— "I see this blood flowing now" (236)—recall Dante's imagery of Phlegethon; and the view from his cell, leading him to "a closer view of my native town. I was fairly inside of it" (240), suggests a descent into the belly of Leviathan so prominent in medieval mythology and iconography. Here indeed is Piers Plowman's harrowing of hell transferred to New England soil. Thoreau's descent, symbolically cast as a journey into death and hell, gives rise to a vision of his native town and the Concord River as locked in a kind of hellish death[1]—ossified in a Massachusetts version of the middle ages, yet as unsubstantial as the old world "Rhine stream" into which it seems to turn as he looks on. This vision of death is followed by a symbolic rebirth at dawn when Thoreau is released from prison.[2] Not only does he experience "a change" in his vision (240) but he comes out of the darkness of his cell to ascend a hill, paralleling again Dante's ascent of Mount Purgatory in his

---

9. For a description of the rather "formidable" Concord jail where Thoreau spent the night see Walter Harding, *The Days of Henry Thoreau: A Biography* (New York: Alfred A. Knopf, 1970), 202–03.

1. That Thoreau's imagery of the present State of Massachusetts as a kind of hell is intentional is verified by his account in *A Week* where he writes: "As for Massachusetts, that huge she Briareus, Argus, and Colchian Dragon conjoined, set to watch the Heifer of the Constitution and the Golden Fleece, we would not warrant our respect for her, like some compositions, to preserve its qualities through all weathers" (135). This application of underworld and hellish imagery to the State was not unique to Thoreau. Note, for instance, the sentence in "Civil Disobedience"—"Some are petitioning the State to dissolve the Union, to disregard the requisitions of the President"

(000)—a reference to the Abolitionist William Lloyd Garrison who later (July 4, 1854) ceremonially burned a copy of the Constitution, denouncing it as "a covenant with death and an agreement with hell." Thoreau was present on this occasion, where he read his "Slavery in Massachusetts."

2. In discussing the motifs of baptism, rebirth, renewal in Thoreau's works, R. W. B. Lewis, *The American Adam: Innocence, Tragedy, and Tradition in the Nineteenth Century* (U. of Chicago Press, 1955), remarks on the "reverence of his [Thoreau's] age for children" typical of the Romantics, and Thoreau's attempt at "recapturing the outlook of children," a Jungian "impulse to return to the womb" (26); the Concord jail cell, like the pond in *Walden*, thus functions symbolically to provide a psychological basis for the death-rebirth archetype evident in the imagery of the account.

climb toward the final haven of the *Paradiso*. That the hill Thoreau climbs is not only "one of our highest" but also named Fair-Haven completes the pattern of spiritual rebirth.

The narrative center of "Civil Disobedience," then, is more than a piece of biography thrown in the midst of a primarily political essay. It is instead the key to the dual vision of the essay. The entire section of the essay preceding the narrative middle is an expansion of that night's vision of death. From this very low level, symbolically entombed, the individual is bound to experience life in the State as a series of contradictions whose precise meaning is death for the moral and spiritual man. The journey through death followed by emergence and ascent effects a narrative synthesis: political contradictions are metaphorically carried up Fair-Haven Hill from which point a new perspective is gained, leading to the resolution of these contradictions in a "higher" view.

The third part of "Civil Disobedience," like the first, may be seen as an expansion of the central narrative, this time of his changed vision from Fair-Haven Hill. In place of the polarized world of the present (and past) America, Thoreau sets forth the "really free and enlightened State" he imagines for the future (245): a fusion of the individual and the State into mutual service. Here the individual will not be powerless, dominated by the "overwhelming brute force" of millions (243); instead the State will come to "recognize the individual as a higher and independent power, from which all its own power and authority are derived" (245). Thoreau's vision here parallels Emerson's reconciliation of "society" and "solitude" whereby the greatest individual self-reliance derives from the fullest assimilation of society by the individual soul and the ideal society is constructed from completely self-reliant men. Thus, if "the last improvement possible in government"—considered without reference to the individual—is democracy with its domination of the man by the majority, "is it not possible to take a step further towards recognizing and organizing the rights of man?" (245). This "step further" is metaphorically a step upwards:

> Seen from a lower point of view, the Constitution, with all its faults, is very good . . . but seen from a point of view a little higher, they [this State and this American government] are what I have described them; seen from a higher still, and the highest, who shall say what they are, or that they are worth looking at or thinking of at all? (242)

Significantly, the essay rises and ends on a note of heavenly vision: "a still more perfect and glorious State, which also I have imagined, but not yet anywhere seen" (245).

If we approach "Civil Disobedience" primarily as a political essay as thousands of readers have done, the two flanking views of the State inevitably receive a horizontal reading, the second functioning as a solution to problems presented in the first. Some dozens of commentators who find Thoreau politically naive or his strategies for reform unclear have obviously assumed this kind of structure. The central narrative suggests, however, something akin to renewed vision or imaginative rebirth for which a programmatic reading is inadequate. In the upward passage from night to day, bondage to freedom, Concord jail to Fair-Haven Hill, Thoreau builds a vertical narrative order which transcends political categories—which moves from the realm of understanding to the realm of imagination. We are reminded of a relevant remark about this in *Walden*: "When one man has reduced a fact of the imagination to be a fact to his understanding, I foresee that all men will at length establish their lives on that basis" (7).

What Thoreau displays is a typically romantic perspective: a desire for a genuine metamorphosis in which the existing State is to die and an ideal state born in its place. From this standpoint, however, the ideal does not simply succeed or replace the real but is rather synthesized from it, as blossoming new life is synthesized from the materials of death. Thoreau's transcendental picture of the perfect State evolves from his death-vision of the present state and is in fact impossible without that death-vision. The narrative center of "Civil Disobedience" is therefore the vehicle for an imaginative synthesis, providing a mythic layering to his entry into and emergence from jail at dawn such that the reconciliation of opposites in this passage is a version of heroic triumph. Those commentators who have noted the considerable differences between the idealized account Thoreau gives and the event as reported by others are exactly right: it is precisely this displacement of the real event to the level of heroic narrative that validates the idealized vision of the essay. This is the essence of the artistry of "Civil Disobedience" and it is integral to interpretation.[3]

This reading of the essay as narrative emphasizes its obvious similarities with Thoreau's other writings, especially *Walden*. Thoreau's passage from Concord jail to Fair-Haven Hill had already occurred in less dramatic form the previous summer (1845) with his move to Walden Pond, and his changed vision of Concord in the essay underlines the focus in the later book on renewal and rebirth. Like "Civil Disobedience," with its discussion of the contradictions in the existing State, *Walden* begins with a long discussion of economic contradictions—the development of industry that leads to waste, the abundance of things that crushes human freedom, the poverty of wealth, the institutional life of civilization that submerges the self-reliant soul. Like the essay with its vision at dawn, *Walden* is full of morning visions, cul-

---

3. This emphasis on the centrality of the narrative carries an interesting corollary. Many commentators on narrative (Scholes and Kellogg, Sheldon Sacks, Tzetvan Todorov) have argued that narrative begins with some kind of disequilibrium and ends when this disequilibrium has been removed. If we reflect on the first section of "Civil Disobedience," the real State Thoreau describes suggests a condition of disequilibrium, typified perhaps by the uneasy balance of majority rule. Indeed, we could stress Thoreau's perspective, in which case his vision of the present State suggests a psycho-logical disequilibrium felt as he contemplates it. The story moves him from this disequilibrium (his vision of "death") to an equilibrium in which he is psychologically reborn through a new vision of the whole, integrated, idealized State. "Civil Disobedience" thus constitutes a study in identity development; see Richard Lebeaux, *Young Man Thoreau* (New York: Harper and Row, 1977) for a study of Thoreau's identity development based on Erik Erikson's paradigm outlined in *Childhood and Society* (rev. 1963) and illustrated in *Young Man Luther* (1958).

minating in the rebirth ritual of spring. Such images of metamorphosis in *Walden* as the bank of thawing clay on late winter morning or the resurvalidate the archetype of death and rebirth at the center of the "Civil Disobedience" narrative.

In Thoreau's major excursions and books, it appears that he designed his art around a series of journeys which thus became passages from the real to the transcendent—symbolized in the frontier regions west of Concord ("Walking"), the upper reaches of the Merrimack (*A Week*), the heights of mountains ("A Walk to Wachusett"), the primitive depths of the forest (*The Maine Woods*), or the tranquil waters of the pond (*Walden*). "I went to the woods," he wrote in *Walden*, "because I wished to live deliberately" (61). In "Civil Disobedience" we discover a similar passage, perhaps the only one that Thoreau did not deliberately plan: a walk to the cobbler's store to get a shoe interrupted, redirected, stalled for a dozen hours by a night in jail, then resumed the next morning. It is not surprising that the artistic account took on the shape of all the other passages in his works with their ascending movements toward morning, spring, hills, mountains, and the sun.

ROBERT SATTELMEYER

The Remaking of *Walden* †

By late 1848 and early 1849 the literary component of the "private business" that Henry Thoreau had gone to Walden Pond to transact seemed finally about to begin yielding a return on his investment. Since he had left his cabin in September 1847, after a stay of just over two years, Thoreau had been working alternately on two books that he had begun there. The first was *A Week on the Concord and Merrimack Rivers*, a compendium of his early works and a tribute to his late brother John woven into the narrative of a boating and hiking expedition they had taken in 1839. Like its successor, *A Week* was the product of a long gestation—almost ten years elapsed between the experience on which it was based and the publication of the book. The second, called *Walden, or Life in the Woods*, treated his experiment at the pond and contained as a counterpoint an ambitiously conceived indictment of American and particularly New England materialist values. Now, some eighteen months later, *A Week* was finally finished and *Walden*, Thoreau thought, was also close to completion. He approached publishers with this two-book package, and after W. D. Ticknor offered to publish *Walden* but required him to underwrite the printing of *A Week* at a cost of $450, Thoreau finally arranged with James Munroe to publish *A Week* and to follow it up

† From *Writing the American Classics*, edited by James Barbour and Tom Quirk, 53–78. (c) 1990 The University of North Carolina Press. Reprinted by permission. *Walden* page numbers refer to this Norton Critical Edition.

with *Walden*. He would still have to guarantee the cost of producing A *Week*, but Munroe at least did not require payment in advance, offering to let Thoreau repay the costs from the sales of the book.[1]

* * *

But "literary contracts are little binding," as he had prophetically written in the first draft of *Walden* (a remark he later canceled), and a number of circumstances were even then developing that would subvert his plans to publish *Walden* on the heels of A *Week*. His literary fortunes, his friendships, his domestic relations, his characteristic pursuits, and even his notion of his proper literary métier were to be transformed during the next year; and the book that he thought of as nearing completion would undergo an even more startling metamorphosis over the next five years, doubling in size, radically changing its structure, and shifting in subtle but profound ways the themes of its earliest versions before it finally saw print in the summer of 1854. The transformation, though dramatic, was natural and inevitable, for the book was an expression of the life, Thoreau's attempt to fulfill his own first requirement of a writer and render a simple and sincere account of himself. This task, as he knew, paradoxically rendered him liable to the charge of obscurity, for it was his real and not merely his actual life that he must attempt to represent. As his relations changed over the years, as his reflections on his life at the pond deepened, as his interest in nature became at once more passionate and more professional, and as his sense of his literary vocation developed in response to early disappointments, the book evolved along with the author until it became less a simple history of his life at Walden alternating with a critique of contemporary culture, and more the sum of his histories simultaneously present in a text at once fabular, mythic, scientific, and even scriptural in its dimensions.

* * *

In 1850, then, Thoreau had a manuscript of *Walden* that only inchoately reflected what he had learned at the pond, that did not embody the new directions his life was taking, and that was in any event probably unsalable. So he ceased thinking of the manuscript as finished, or nearly so. Perhaps he was temporarily soured on book publishing after his experience with A *Week*, but probably he was also awaiting such developments as his new modes of life and writing would bring. He did not let the book lie fallow, for he drafted into the journal passages of reflection on his life in the woods that were clearly intended for the manuscript and that were eventually added in later revisions.[2] But apparently he did not begin to revise the manuscript

1. See Linck C. Johnson, "Historical Introduction." In Henry D. Thoreau, *A Week on the Concord and Merrimack Rivers*, ed., Carl F. Hovde, William L. Howarth, and Elizabeth Hall Witherell (Princeton: Princeton University Press, 1980), 469–470.

2. Henry D. Thoreau, Journal 3: 1848–1851, ed. Robert Sattelmeyer, Mark R. Patterson, and William Rossi (Princeton: Princeton University Press, 1990), "Historical Introduction," 483–84.

as a whole until sometime in 1852. Then he began energetically to work on *Walden* again, adding new material and revising previous drafts in four distinguishable stages, not counting his final fair copy for the printer, between 1852 and 1854.[3] Thus, although there are seven identifiable manuscript drafts (or, more precisely, partial drafts) of *Walden*, ranging from 1846 to 1854, its composition mainly took place in two phases. The first stage includes the first draft written at Walden in 1846–47, along with the second and third drafts that were written nearly together in 1848–49 and that primarily polish material in the first draft. The second stage consists of the four successive partial drafts written between 1852 and the book's publication in 1854.

* * *

Although there are doubtless subtle stages of growth that could be traced through virtually every year between 1845, when Thoreau began to write entries in the journal that were clearly designed for some literary work based on his life at the pond, and 1854, when the book was finally published, the most dramatic story involves the remaking of the book that took place during the second phase of composition between 1852 and 1854. Thoreau's conception of the work greatly enlarged and matured during these years, and if some of the portions that were added during this phase conflict with assertions made in the earlier versions, it is a mark of Thoreau's maturity as a writer and a thinker that he allowed such inconsistencies to stand. Much of the richness of the book ultimately derives, I believe, from Thoreau's incorporation of reflections from the intervening years that are allowed to stand alongside accounts of his life that he actually wrote at the pond, so that *Walden* is at once both retrospective and dramatic. It embodies a summing but not a summing up of experience. I do not believe this effect was the result of a conscious design on Thoreau's part, but rather that it came about with a certain organic inevitability from the writer's steadfast application to his task during a period of artistic and intellectual growth.

At the same time, of course, Thoreau was highly self-conscious about the process of revision, and *Walden*, moreover, like so many other American books, calls attention to itself as a deliberately composed text. It begins with an allusion (itself added in a late revision) to the very process of composition that I have been discussing: "When I wrote the following pages, or rather the bulk of them, I lived alone, in the woods." This seemingly straightforward reference to the immediate contextual circumstances of the book introduces us immediately by means of a characteristic wordplay to the writer's awareness of the difference between his immediate and his later, mediated vision:

3. See J. Lyndon Shanley, *The Making of Walden* (Chicago: University of Chicago Press, 1957), 30–32; Ronald A. Clapper, "The Development of *Walden*: A Genetic Text," Ph. D. dissertation, University of California, Los Angeles, 1967, 31–32.; see also Stephen Adams and Donald A. Ross, *Revising Mythologies: The Composition of Thoreau's Major Works* (Charlottesville: University Press of Virginia, 1988), 162–192, which appeared while this essay was in press.

only the "bulk" or gross proportions of the book may be said to have been composed at the pond.

The greatest difference between the 1846–49 versions and the 1852–54 versions is that the second half of the book is much more extensively developed in the later versions. Shanley summarized the difference between the first draft and the published version as follows:

It [the first draft] represents various parts of *Walden* very unevenly. It contains approximately 70 per cent of the first half—"Economy" through "The Bean Field"; a little less than 30 per cent of "The Village" through "Higher Laws" [chapters 8–11]; less than 50 per cent of "Brute Neighbors" through "Spring" [chapters 12–17]; and none of "Conclusion." Likewise, the second and third versions, written in 1848–49, consist essentially of a recopying with some revision of the first two-thirds of the first draft, carrying the story only through the material of the sixth chapter, "Visitors."[4]

Obviously these early versions were composed with a lecture audience in mind, and they may in fact have been used by Thoreau as his lecture manuscript itself—a large mass of material that was not divided into chapters but that could easily be broken up to suit the number and length of his speaking engagements. The fact that a greater proportion of this early material survives in the finished form of the first half of the book than in the second half means that the early chapters of *Walden* are much more closely tied to Thoreau's original design and purposes than the later chapters. These, in turn, he wrote for the most part with a book in mind, and they tend more than the first chapters to reflect his interests and concerns during the 1850s.

In reading the book, then, one responds to and follows not only the temporal structure of the Walden experience (the two years of Thoreau's life compressed into a single annual cycle from one spring to the next) but also and perhaps more subliminally the larger development of the narrator over the course of a decade of spiritual and intellectual growth. The effect is not one of "before" and "after," or of two different accounts of the growth of a mind such as one finds in the early and late versions of Wordsworth's *Prelude*, but rather of an earlier self subsumed but still present, as it were, within the later. Nevertheless some of the principal differences between the earlier and later versions of *Walden*, and to some extent the first and second halves of the book, may be described.

The early chapters, particularly "Economy" and "Where I Lived, and What I Lived For," betray their lineage as lecture material in a number of ways, the most obvious of which is their rhetorically high profile: they are more satiric, hyperbolic, confrontational, and full of invective than the later chapters. "I should not presume to talk so much about myself and my affairs as I shall in this lecture," the first version of *Walden* begins, "if very particular

4. Shanley, 94; see also Clapper, 30.

and personal inquiries had not been made concerning my mode of life."
Beginning with this sardonic acknowledgment of those who had minded his
business for him, Thoreau launches a counterattack against the "mean and
sneaking lives" his contemporaries lived.[5] And, as he makes clear in an early
journal draft of this lecture from the winter of 1845–46, he was particularly
concerned to say something about his audience's "outward condition or
circumstances in this world."[6] *Walden* was thus at first quite narrowly and
parochially conceived: it was not until the post-1852 revisions that the phrase
"Addressed to My Townsmen" was dropped from Thoreau's working title.
The account of his own life in this version serves as an example that contrasts
with the misapplication of force in most lives, but it is not a story whose
deeper implications are fathomed. In fact, in the first draft his account of
himself ends quite lamely—"Thus was my first year's life in the woods
completed"—for clearly Thoreau did not yet realize what the experience
signified for himself, however much he was aware of its exemplary potential
for his contemporaries.[7]

The early versions and early chapters are also more outer-directed because
they were largely conceived and executed during the height of Thoreau's
interest in reform during the mid- to late 1840s. He had composed a lecture
on reform and reformers during this period, written about reformers in *A
Week*, and of course written "Resistance to Civil Government" in response
to his night in jail in 1845. The 1840s were a millennial decade generally,
and reform movements, ranging in seriousness from abolitionism to Sylvester
Graham's advocacy of male chastity and a high-fiber diet, were pandemic
in American culture. Within Transcendentalism itself there was a lively
debate over reform, and the movement had spawned experimental communities at Brook Farm and Fruitlands. Responding to this climate, Thoreau
conceived of his life at Walden at first as a kind of experimental community
of one that could serve as a counterexample not only to the unawakened
among his townspeople but also to the false reforms and reformers of his
age. His earliest journal entries at Walden during the summer of 1845 blend
accounts of his life with a critique of contemporary values and culture, and
the first draft already contains an indictment of foolish philanthropy and
false reforms.[8] Although he continued to be interested in the problem of
reforming and reformers and would add much to this section of "Economy"
through the various versions, by the early 1850s Thoreau's concern with
social and political issues, like that of the nation at large, was increasingly
focused on slavery, its extension, and the enforcement of the Fugitive Slave
Law. These issues did not lend themselves to treatment in his manuscript

5. Shanley, 105, 108.
6. Henry D. Thoreau, *Journal 2: 1842–1848*, ed. Robert Sattelmeyer (Princeton: Princeton University Press. 1984), 187.
7. Shanley, 208.
8. Shanley, 133–137.

in progress, and they would not culminate for him until the addresses he would deliver on John Brown after the Harper's Ferry raid in 1859. He would develop the book as a whole along quite different lines, be less insistent upon addressing the outward condition of humanity, and come to regard his experience at Walden less as an example to misguided reformers and more as a personal quest involving doubt and uncertainty as well as discovery.

The clearest indication of this change may be seen in the character of the narrator and his rhetoric in the second half of the book, the portion that was mostly written after 1852. From "The Ponds" on, the book is more introspective, meditative, and descriptive and contains relatively few passages of sustained satire. When there is a brief return to the themes of "Economy," as in the account of the Irishman John Field and his family in "Baker Farm," Thoreau's criticism is muted by sympathy, and the family is presented in such homely detail and with such particularity that, like their chickens, they become too humanized to roast well. Beginning with its namesake chapter, the pond itself becomes a major character, and Thoreau appears to have been pacified by its waters. In contrast to his stance in the early chapters, like Ishmael in *Moby-Dick* he no longer seems to have a maddened hand and splintered heart turned against the wolfish world; like Ishmael, too, he turns instead to a journey in which meditation and water are wedded and which has as its aim the discovery of the ungraspable phantom of life—even if he has to be content with less exotic surroundings and pursuits: traveling a good deal in Concord, having for a soothing savage Alek Therien the woodchopper, and fishing for pouts on Walden Pond.

The major mark of the book's altered conception in the post-1852 expansions is the extent to which Thoreau developed and amplified the seasonal cycle that undergirds the structure of *Walden*. Shanley describes, for example, the changes made in this aspect of the book during the fifth version, written during late 1852 and early 1853:

> The greatest growth in Thoreau's conception of *Walden* resulted, however, from his seeing how he might fill out his account of the progress of the seasons and describe the changes they had brought in his daily affairs and thoughts; by doing so, he would express more adequately the richness and the completeness of his experience. He had to develop particularly the fall and part of the winter. He did so by greatly enlarging "Brute Neighbors," by developing "House-Warming" for the first time, and by completing "Winter Visitors"; he also made significant though smaller additions to "Winter Animals" and "The Pond in Winter." There was so much new material in version V that Thoreau was not able simply to insert it in previous copy as he had done with most of the new material in IV. He had to make fresh copy of practically all of "The Ponds," "Higher Laws," "Brute Neighbors," "House-Warming," "Former Inhabitants; and Winter Visitors," and "The Pond in Winter."[9]

9. Shanley, 67.

The cumulative effect of these additions was to alter the focus of the book radically. In the early versions the critique of American culture dominated ("Economy" and "Where I Lived, and What I Lived For" still make up nearly a third of the finished book, and represented an even larger proportion in the early drafts), in which the story of Thoreau's own life served, as we have already seen, as a counterpoint. The cyclical pattern of the year was relatively unimportant. Now, however, with the annual cycle developed and amplified, there exists for the first time a "story" with a kind of plot: the journey or quest of the narrator passing through various changes marked by the progress of the seasons and advancing toward some kind of self-knowledge. The book begins to acquire mythic and archetypal dimensions and, in the relative deemphasis of social criticism attendant upon the expansion of these other elements, becomes less topical and more universal in its reference.

Doubtless the addition of material about fall, winter, and the second spring contributes to verisimilitude and to a felt sense of the passage of a year. There is a satisfying structural coherence about this pattern as realized in the finished book, a kind of harmonic or tonic closure felt in arriving once more at spring. At the same time, however, this is a relatively simple, unsophisticated, and not particularly novel structure. The same pattern may be said to inform the *Farmer's Almanac*. Nor is the discovery of the seasonal cycle itself what is most important. Critics have occasionally pointed to a journal entry for 18 April 1852, in which Thoreau announces "For the first time I perceive this spring that the year is a circle," as marking such an insight and signaling a new design for *Walden* (*J*, 3:438).[1] But surely Richard Lebeaux is correct to point out that "more likely, he was indicating that this was the first time *this spring* that he had seen the year as a circle."[2] For a naturalist to observe for the first time at age thirty-five that the year is a circle is equivalent to a hydrologist's discovering that water runs downhill. As Robert D. Richardson, Jr., has recently observed, with several decades of critical explications of the seasonal structure in mind, "We have made too much of the seasonal structure of *Walden*, too easily assuming that the book's message is to accept the seasonal cycle of nature as final wisdom. Such a view, essentially objective, conservative, and tragic, is not at last what Thoreau wanted or taught."[3]

Thoreau developed the seasonal emphasis of *Walden* not because it was the logical structure for his book but because he was interested in the seasons of his own life and because he came to believe, as he put it in the fall of 1857, "These regular phenomena of the seasons get at last to be—they were *at first* of course—simply and plainly phenomena or phases of my life. The

1. *The Journal of Henry D. Thoreau*, ed. Bradford Torrey and Francis H. Allen (Boston: Houghton Mifflin, 1949), 3:438. Subsequent references to this edition are cited parenthetically in the text.
2. Richard Lebeaux, *Thoreau's Seasons* (Amherst: University of Massachusetts Press, 1984), 159.
3. Robert D. Richardson, Jr., *Thoreau: A Life of the Mind* (Berkeley and Los Angeles: University of California Press, 1986), 310.

seasons and all their changes are in me." He concluded this entry by re-marking "The perfect correspondence of Nature to man, so that he is at home in her!" (*J*, 10:127).[4] The remaking of *Walden* in large part involves an effort to tell the truth of the first proposition by following out the artistic implications of the second—the "perfect correspondence" by which nature's seasons express our own.

It was the need to probe the meaning of his Walden experience, to come to terms with the great event in his life, and by writing to relive and recapture that experience, rather than discovering that the year is a circle, that stimulated Thoreau to begin expanding his manuscript in 1852. In January—the tenth anniversary of his brother John's death and very close to the time he began working on the manuscript again—he asked himself in the journal:

> But why I changed? why I left the woods? I do not think that I can tell. I have often wished myself back. I do not know any better how I ever came to go there. Perhaps it is none of my business, even if it is yours. . . . I must say that I do not know what made me leave the pond. I left it as unaccountably as I went to it. To speak sincerely, I went there because I had got ready to go; I left it for the same reason. (*J*, 3:214, 216)

Two days later, on 24 January, he admonished himself to take up his pen in the service of fathoming such mysteries at the same time that he lamented his own inability to recapture the glorious past:

> If thou art a writer, write as if the time were short, for it is indeed short at the longest. Improve each occasion when thy soul is reached. Drain the cup of inspiration to its last dregs. Fear no intemperance in that, for the years will come when otherwise thou wilt regret opportunities un-improved. The spring will not last forever. These fertile and expanding seasons of thy life, when the rain reaches thy root, when thy vigor shoots, when thy flower is budding, shall be fewer and farther between. Again I say, remember thy Creator in the days of thy youth. . . . Why did I not use my eyes when I stood on Pisgah? Now I hear those strains but seldom. My rhythmical mood does not endure. I cannot draw from it and return to it in my thoughts as to a well all the evening or the morning. I cannot dip my pen in it. I cannot work the vein, it is so fine and volatile. Ah, sweet, ineffable reminiscences! (*J*, 3:221–22)

This despondency, a recurring nightmare of the Romantics, who most feared that they might cease to feel, was only temporary, but it points toward the complex of emotions that led Thoreau to reconceive *Walden*. Uncertainty about his motives for going to and leaving the pond dogged him, and he felt that he must answer those questions for himself through his writing, even though he temporarily doubted his ability to work the vein. He must create an account of his former experience that would satisfy the demands

---

4. The importance of this passage is pointed out by Lebeaux, 293; I am also indebted in the following passages on the seasons of *Walden* to Lebeaux's discussion of the issue in chapter 5, "Second Spring," 151–197.

of imagination and memory, rather like the speaker of Frost's "The Road Not Taken," who really knows that there was no perceptible difference between the two paths at the time but also knows that he must invent a story that will account for the distance he has traveled and also link himself with his own past: "I shall be telling this with a sigh / Somewhere ages and ages hence."

So the new work on Walden primarily expanded the later sections of the book that describe autumn, winter, and the second spring, a seasonal epoch in which mature affirmation comes only after a long probation and after having faced doubt, anxiety, and even evil in both the self and nature. At the same time, it needs to be kept in mind that much of this pattern is implicit, as Thoreau tends to editorialize less and to write less explicitly about himself in these sections, depending more on the "perfect correspondence" between man and nature to endow his descriptions of natural phenomena with human significance.

Something of an exception to this pattern of implicitness, and an exception that may serve by its expository nature as a convenient example of the altered tone of Thoreau's thinking, is the chapter "Higher Laws," most of which was added, apparently, during the fourth through the seventh versions. It had started out as a treatise on fishing and hunting, leading to a discussion of diet and advocating vegetarianism on both economic and philosophical grounds. In this respect it was consistent with the emphasis on reform and the subject matter of the early versions. Until the sixth version, in fact, it carried the title "Animal Food."[5] But the original tension in the chapter— Thoreau's genuine ambivalence about hunting and especially fishing—is eventually cast into the shade in later versions by a more serious conflict between "animal" and "spiritual": "We are conscious of an animal in us, which awakens in proportion as our higher nature slumbers" (146). This conflict most dramatically expressed itself for Thoreau over the issues of what he termed chastity and sensuality. Whatever the efficient cause of this concern, he was troubled by his own inability to master this side of his nature. He cannot speak of these topics, he fears, without betraying his own impurity. In the fifth version he canceled an even more revealing sentence: "I do not know how it is with other men, but I find it very difficult to be chaste."[6] These fears, obviously arising out of personal experience of some kind, lead to the pronouncement that "Nature is hard to be overcome, but she must be overcome" (148), a statement that seems hopelessly in conflict with the narrator's stance toward nature elsewhere.

This assertion may be reconcilable with Thoreau's attitude toward nature in other passages, but the tension is really central to the completed book, I think, and a sign of maturity on Thoreau's part, a recognition that nature and the human self in which it is reflected have depths heretofore unplumbed but needing to be faced. Thoreau's apprehensions about purity and chastity,

5. Clapper, "The Development of Walden," 566.

6. Clapper, "The Development of Walden," 588.

while they may appear only quaint or priggish to a twentieth-century audience, represent an acknowledgement by him of a part of his nature more basic (and base) than he had previously seen. Something of this recognition carried over and expressed itself in his revisions of other portions of *Walden*, in the course of which he was able to develop this line of thought in more positive ways.

The realization that his own as well as external nature possessed such subterranean dimensions could be exhilarating as well as disquieting. It carried Thoreau some distance toward a theory of the unconscious and led him to speculate on the extent to which intellectual and creative activity was dependent upon functions of the mind that lay below the threshold of conscious thought. Characteristically, he expressed his insight in terms of a correspondence between man and nature, in a journal entry in 1851, just before beginning his major reworking of *Walden*. Having read the botanist Asa Gray's description of how a plant grows upward toward the light and simultaneously downward, he observed:

> So the mind develops from the first in two opposite directions: upwards to expand in the light and air; and downwards avoiding the light to form the root. One half is aerial, the other subterranean. The mind is not well balanced and firmly planted, like the oak, which has not as much root as branch, whose roots like those of the white pine are slight and near the surface. One half of the mind's development must still be root,—in the embryonic state, in the womb of nature, more unborn than at first. For each successive new idea or bud, a new rootlet in the earth. The growing man penetrates yet deeper by his roots into the womb of things. The infant is comparatively near the surface, just covered from the light; but the man sends down a tap-root to the centre of things. (*J*, 2:203)

The most dramatic application of this perspective in *Walden* is Thoreau's radical revision and amplification of the climactic sand foliage passages in "Spring" during the last versions, where this "truly *grotesque*" (that is, coming from underground) vegetation manifests the generative and creative forces of nature, however visceral or excremental its appearance (203). Thoreau had reached an earlier stage of understanding the beneficial potential of such threatening and disturbing natural forces on his first trip to the Maine wilderness in 1846, when he came in contact on Mount Katahdin with a kind of nature that threatened to extinguish rather than heighten consciousness and when he had also faced the fact that here "one could no longer accuse institutions and society, but must front the true source of evil" (that is, the self).[7] This knowledge in turn had already led him to express in the first draft of *Walden*, composed the following year, a theory of the necessity of wild nature to the human psyche that incorporated the essentially ungraspable nature of nature as a positive fact: "At the same time that we are

7. Thoreau, "Ktaadn, and the Maine Woods." In *The Maine Woods*, ed. Joseph J. Moldenhauer (Princeton: Princeton University Press, 1972), 16.

in earnest to explore and learn all things, we require that all things be mysterious and unexplorable, that land and sea be infinitely wild, unsurveyed and unfathomed by us because unfathomable. We can never have enough of Nature" (211–12).[8]

Paradoxically, that we can never have enough of nature and that nature must also be overcome are but different expressions of the same fact, the complexity of our own nature that grows upward and downward at the same time. There is a womb of nature and an answering womb—dark, unconscious, and powerful—in the mind. Ultimately Thoreau renders nature more complexly in the later versions of *Walden* because he sees human nature more complexly, starting with his own. Accounts of natural phenomena convey little of what Thoreau termed in *A Week* "the mealy-mouthed enthusiasm of the lover of Nature." To the fourth version, for example, he added the account of the battle of the ants to "Brute Neighbors," unflinchingly observing—even under a microscope—the "internecine war" in nature that was going on underfoot. And the owls in "Sounds," which in the first versions stood rather conventionally and melodramatically for the "fallen souls that once in human shape night-walked the earth," come to suggest by the fourth version "a vast and undeveloped nature which men have not recognized. They represent the stark twilight and unsatisfied thoughts which all have." As one might almost predict, the last phrase originally read "which I have."[9]

The expansion of the fall and winter chapters of the manuscript during the second stage of composition thus created a strong counterpoint to and eventual transformation of the dominant spring imagery of *Walden*. The new proportions suggest, of course, that Thoreau became increasingly concerned with his own awakening and less obsessed with waking up his neighbors. They also suggest, at the level of seasonal change in the narrator, that the second spring is of a different order of magnitude than and not merely a repetition of the first, and comes as a result of his having sent down his "tap-root into the centre of things." By doing so, he succeeds himself, the self that like an infant was "comparatively near the surface" in understanding the phenomena of his own life.

The second spring is a kind of second growth intimately related and akin to the second growth of autumn itself, a time when fruits mature and seeds ripen. Thoreau had not earned the affirmations of the "Conclusion" (the last chapter to be written) until he had achieved the mature growth depicted in "The Ponds" through "Spring." This phase of *Walden*, in which autumnal imagery abounds, points toward the predominantly autumnal atmosphere of Thoreau's later essays: the close of "Walking," say, or the whole of "Wild Apples" and "Autumnal Tints." He had arrived at an autumnal phase in his own life, in which the fruit of his earlier experiences at Walden had matured, experiences that enjoy a kind of second spring in his imaginative

8. Shanley, 207.   9. Clapper, 361–364.

recreation of them in the book. The questions he had begun his revision by asking ("But why I left the woods?") he could now answer: "I left the woods for as good a reason as I went there. . . ." (215). Thoreau largely effaced from the final text the fact that this affirmation arose out of a profound experience of self-doubt and even disgust (such as we glimpse in "Higher Laws"), but it is evident in the manuscript, in which the following aside to the passage just quoted is preserved:

> If the reader think that I am vainglorious, and set myself above others, I assure him that I could tell a pitiful story respecting myself as well as him if my spirits held out, could encourage him with a sufficient list of failures, and flow humbly as the gutters. I think worse of myself than he is likely to think of me, and better too, being better acquainted with the man. Finally, I will tell him this secret, if he will not abuse my confidence— I put the best face on the matter.[1]

Nevertheless the fable of *Walden*, he thought, expressing his mature vision (and contained in miniature in the story of the Artist of Kouroo in the "Conclusion"), had a lasting quality that would make up for early disappointments and self-doubts. He believed himself to be, in the best and most nearly literal sense of the term, a late-bloomer, and he confided as much to his journal in April 1854, while reading proof for *Walden*:

> Some poets mature early and die young. Their fruits have a delicious flavor like strawberries, but do not keep till fall or winter. Others are slower in coming to their growth. Their fruits may be less delicious, but are a more lasting food and are so hardened by the sun of summer and the coolness of autumn that they keep sound over winter. The first are June-eatings, early but soon withering; the last are russets, which last till June again. (*J*, 6:190–91)

Besides the emphasis on the seasons and the corresponding story of individual growth, the most important major change between the early and later versions of *Walden* lies in the more learned and scientific cast of the later additions and revisions. The maturity of the final version is not a matter of age and self-knowledge alone, but of knowledge of the world. It takes the form of a theory of nature, which, as Emerson had said in his first book, *Nature*, was the aim of all science. In the finished version of *Walden* Thoreau is a scientist; not a scientist in precisely the sense we assume the term to mean today, but a scientist nevertheless, one who believed that the results of his investigations into nature expressed actual and not merely "poetic" truth. "Spring"—and especially the climactic account of thawing sand and clay in the railroad cut—contains not only the apogee of Thoreau's personal growth and rebirth but also the conclusion of his scientific investigation of the laws that underlie natural phenomena. The fact that these two investigations culminate together does not mean that one is a "symbol"

1. Clapper, 854.

of the other but rather that, for Thoreau, there really was a "perfect correspondence of Nature to man" that it was his mission to describe.

Thoreau's development as a natural scientist during the years of *Walden*'s second growth was coincident, however, with his more general development as a reader and thinker. He had always possessed something of a scholarly cast of mind, and since college he had kept a series of commonplace books in which he recorded passages from his reading. But like his journal-keeping, after 1850 this note-taking became more detailed and regular, and over the years his store of learning found its way into the *Walden* manuscript in hundreds of quotations from and allusions to his reading.[2] These additions were spread throughout the manuscript, so that the consistently high level of allusiveness becomes a persistent textural and even thematic element of the entire book, deepening its level of reference, mitigating the parochial nature of its subject matter, and extending its appeal, by implication, to a much broader audience than the "my townsmen" of the original subtitle.

* * * In *Walden* these allusions work as part of the retrospective urge of the book that complements the immediacy of the material actually composed at the pond; they constitute a "re-search" impulse that broadens the implications of particular episodes and connects the activities described to the wider human community both past and present.

In this context Thoreau's scientific expansions to *Walden* are a subset of these pervasive amplifications drawn from reading and observation. On a more fundamental level, however, the more scientific cast of the revised book, with its emphasis on the careful and detailed description of such central phenomena as the pond itself, the habits of various animals—now identified by genus and species as well as popular name—the Walden ice, and above all the thawing sand and clay of the railroad embankment, reflects Thoreau's commitment to natural history studies (along with writing, of course) as his principal life's work. Until quite recently at any rate, it has been the custom to derogate Thoreau's abilities as a scientist, as though his unfitness in this field were a necessary precondition to taking him seriously as an artist. But whatever the actual merits of his scientific work, it is clear that he regarded his studies seriously, and equally clear that he had a good grasp of contemporary theoretical controversies in the natural sciences during the years before Darwin's *Origin of Species* (1859) signaled the triumph of a paradigm that has held sway ever since.[3] Certainly he was not doing "normal" science from a post-Darwinian perspective; he was, however, operating according to scientific traditions and theoretical orientations quite viable in his own day, and it is from this perspective that his natural history

2. See Sattelmeyer, *Thoreau's Reading* (Princeton: Princeton University Press, 1988), 75–77.
3. See Sattelmeyer, 78–92; also John Hildebidle, *Thoreau, A Naturalist's Liberty* (Cambridge: Harvard University Press, 1984); William L. Howarth, *The Book of Concord* (New York: Viking Press, 1982), 190–211; and William Rossi, " 'Laboratory of the Artist': Henry Thoreau's Literary and Scientific Use of the Journal, 1848–1854," Ph.D. dissertation, University of Minnesota, 1986, especially 151–201.

studies in *Walden* (as well as his post-*Walden* essays in this field) are best understood.

Basic to Thoreau's methodology as a naturalist is an emphasis on perception and the centrality of the observer, features which today of course tend to relegate natural history to the status of "soft" science if it is considered a scientific discipline at all. He inherited this emphasis from Goethe, who was the founding father, so to speak, of the German school of *Naturphilosophie* from which Thoreau drew much of his theoretical orientation and whose most distinguished practitioner in America was Louis Agassiz. For Thoreau the perceiving consciousness was not a "personality" that distorted the accuracy of observation but a necessary component of the equation by which phenomena could be understood and rendered meaningful. In order to write "The Ponds," for instance, one of the key chapters of *Walden*, he worked for several years observing Walden under different conditions, making excursions for that specific purpose and writing up his observations in the journal for eventual incorporation into the book. The portrait that eventually emerged emphasized the purity of the pond and the myriad ways that any natural fact, carefully and accurately perceived, dissolves the difference between perceiver and perceived: "A lake is the landscape's most beautiful and expressive feature. It is earth's eye; looking into which the beholder measures the depth of his own nature" (125). This statement is not finally a geologic anthropomorphism, or even a literary conceit, but an expression of the belief that the study of nature is ultimately the study of the self, for it is only after many years of observation that this relationship suggests itself (this particular passage first appeared in the sixth version).

Thoreau's descriptions of the ponds are largely about the process of perception itself, emphasizing that what we see when we look at a body of water is its surface and a boundary where two elements meet. The results of observation here depend upon the position of the observer relative to the object observed—a kind of perceptual relativity that points out (as relativity theory in physics also does) the illusory nature of absolute measurement. Walden is "a perfect forest mirror" that registers all change and all life on its surface, above its surface, and even below its surface, while at the same time continually changing color itself depending on conditions both known and unknown. The picture of the pond is a series of partial perceptions, each stressing the vantage point of the perceiver as a major component. In the four paragraphs that constitute the central description of Walden Pond itself, for example, we find the following markers of place: "You may see from a boat," "I have in my mind's eye," "Standing on the smooth sandy beach," "When you invert your head," "From a hilltop," and "on such a height as this, overlooking the pond" (125–26).

The final perspective in this section, a paragraph that first appears in the fifth version, takes us in imagination to a still higher vantage point and demonstrates concretely how the seen proves the unseen:

A field of water betrays the spirit that is in the air. It is continually receiving new life and motion from above. It is intermediate in its nature between land and sky. On land only the grass and trees wave, but the water itself is rippled by the wind. I see where the breeze dashes across it by the streaks or flakes of light. We shall, perhaps, look down thus on the surface of air at length, and mark where a still subtler spirit sweeps over it. (127)

Characteristically, Thoreau begins by emphasizing a key word—"field"—that operates, like nature itself, at several levels simultaneously, suggesting a range of meanings from the most obvious (an open expanse) to progressively more complex suggestions of the relation between the observer and what is observed: a field as that which is bounded (field of vision); a field as the subject of study or calling (as in his "half-cultivated field" in "The Bean Field"); and as a space upon which something is drawn or projected. The surface of the pond is more interesting and significant for the meaning it may transmit than for any significance which may be said to reside in it intrinsically. Both nature and the language with which the poet describes it are, as Emerson said in "The Poet," vehicular and transitive.

If "The Ponds" stresses methodology and the importance of the observer, "Spring" emphasizes results. The famous passages describing the sand foliage that effloresces on the railroad cut—sure evidence of a spring that "precedes the green and flowery spring"—announce the discovery of a law in nature, a discovery that coincides with Thoreau's own second spring. His perception, rightly trained and furnished once more with several years' careful study of the phenomenon, is able to anticipate spring and discern the operation of fundamental principles of generation and creativity in nature, while at the same time discovering the operation of the same power in himself. It needs to be stressed that the thawing sandbank is not intended by Thoreau as a figurative equivalent of his own awakening but rather as evidence of the operation of a law that animates both nature and man.

Like the descriptions of the ponds, Thoreau's account of the sand foliage was the product of several years of observation and evolution in his thought. In the first version the phenomenon elicits only a brief mention as one of the signs of spring:

As I go back and forth over the rail-road through the deep cut I have seen where the clayey sand *like lava* had flowed down when it thawed and as it streamed it assumed the forms of vegetation, of vines and stout pulpy leaves—unaccountably interesting and beautiful—as if its course were so to speak a diagonal between fluids & solids—and it were hesitating whether to stream in to a river, or into vegetation—for vegetation too is such a stream as a river, only of a slower current.[4]

By the final version this account had grown to more than 1,500 words, and what was at first "unaccountably interesting and beautiful" came even-

4. Shanley, 204.

tually to illustrate no less than "the principle of all the operations of Nature," the underlying ur-phenomenon of the leaf, which metamorphoses from the lowest and presumably inorganic forms of matter upward to higher life forms until "the very globe continually transcends and translates itself, and becomes winged in its orbit" (204). Thoreau was composing material for this section in the journal right up until *Walden* went to press. He added the climactic phrase "There is nothing inorganic," as well as the longer passage quoted below, in an entry for 5 February 1854. This conclusion is less a private testimony of faith than a challenge to prevailing scientific paradigms:

> The earth is not a mere fragment of dead history, stratum upon stratum like the leaves of a book, to be studied by geologists and antiquaries chiefly, but living poetry like the leaves of a tree, which precede flowers and fruit—not a fossil earth, but a living earth; compared with whose great central life all animal and vegetable life is merely parasitic. (206)

Here, translating and metamorphosing the figure of the leaf, he contrasts his discovery of the creative force working through nature to both the older eighteenth-century argument from design, which discovered evidence of creation at some former date, and the developing orthodoxy of positivist science, which sees all nature ultimately as matter capable of being broken down and analyzed. To say that the earth is "living poetry" is not merely to make a figure of speech but to express a conviction that the same power that animates the poet's creativity works through and animates nature as well. Thoreau did not think of himself as making a statement that was poetically true only. One of his key revisions in this section of "Spring" was to alter his conception of the agency behind this power. In an early version he had felt himself to be standing "in the studio of an artist" when witnessing this phenomenon, but in the final version he stands "in the *laboratory* of the Artist who made the world and me" (emphasis added).[5] This fusion of the perspective of the scientist and the artist reflects Thoreau's stubborn resistance to the notion of there being two truths—one imaginative and one scientific—and likewise reflects the extent to which the climactic insights of *Walden* owe their origin to his own absorption in the natural sciences during the book's second growth.

Walden ultimately invalidates the apology Thoreau once offered for his attempt to fuse life and art—"My life has been the poem I would have writ / But I could not both live and utter it." His response to changes in himself as well as in his outward circumstances during the 1850s, along with his newfound commitments to the journal and his natural history studies, helped him to deepen and enrich the story of his life at the pond far beyond its expression in the book he wanted to publish in 1849. At the same time, the formal elements of *Walden*—its architectonics, its style, the relation of its parts to the whole—ought not to be considered as fixed or final in the version

5. *Walden* 204; see Rossi, 200.

that Thoreau published in 1854. Its form no less than its content was dictated by his life, and had he delayed publishing it still further the book would doubtless have continued to evolve along with him. His revisions were not directed toward filling out or realizing a design that he kept before him but toward incorporating stages of growth within the design that already existed. *Walden* is, in this respect, an archetypal Romantic text, like *Leaves of Grass*, that developed as its author developed and that preserves experience while continually reinterpreting it.

* * *

BARBARA JOHNSON

A Hound, a Bay Horse, and a Turtle Dove: Obscurity in *Walden*†

The experience of reading Thoreau's *Walden* is often a disconcerting one. The very discrepancy between the laconic, concrete chapter titles and the long, convoluted sentences of the text alerts the reader to a process of level-shifting that delights and baffles—indeed, that delights because it baffles. Consider, for example, the following passage:

> I sometimes despair of getting anything quite simple and honest done in this world by the help of men. They would have to be passed through a powerful press first, to squeeze their old notions out of them, so that they would not soon get upon their legs again; and then there would be some one in the company with a maggot in his head, hatched from an egg deposited there nobody knows when, for not even fire kills these things, and you would have lost your labor. Nevertheless, we will not forget that some Egyptian wheat was handed down to us by a mummy. (17).

It is difficult to read this passage without doing a double take. The logical seriousness of the style of "Nevertheless, we will not forget . . ." in no way prepares the reader for the sudden appearance of wheat in a mummy. The passage shifts with unruffled rapidity from abstract generalization to dead figure ("squeeze their old notions out of them") to a soon-to-reawaken figure hidden in a cliché ("maggot in the head") to mininarrative ("deposited there nobody knows when") to folk wisdom ("Not even fire kills these things") to counterclaim ("Nevertheless, we will not forget . . ."). By the time one reaches the mummy, one no longer knows what the figure stands for, whether it, like the mummy, is dead or alive, or even where the boundaries of the analogy (if it *is* an analogy) lie.

† Reprinted from A *World of Difference* (Baltimore: Johns Hopkins University Press, 1987), 49–56, by permission of Johns Hopkins University Press. *Walden* page numbers refer to this Norton Critical Edition.

It is paradoxical that a writer who constantly exhorts us to "Simplify, simplify" should also be the author of some of the most complex and difficult paragraphs in the English language. What is it about this seemingly simple account of life in the woods that so often bewilders the reader, making him, in Emerson's words, "nervous and wretched to read it"?

In an article entitled *"Walden's* False Bottoms," Walter Benn Michaels amply demonstrates the book's capacity to engender nervousness as he details the long history of readers' attempts to cope with *Walden's* obscurity, first by attributing it to Thoreau's alleged "want of continuity of mind" (James Russell Lowell), then by subsuming it under the larger patterns of *Walden's* literary unity (Matthiessen, Anderson), then by considering it as a challenge to the reader's ability to read figuratively (Cavell, Buell). Walter Benn Michaels ends his own account of the undecidability of *Walden's* contradictions by saying, "It's heads I win, tails you lose. No wonder the game makes us nervous."[1]

The passage through which I would like to gain access to one of the principal difficulties of *Walden's* game is precisely a passage about losing. It is one of the most often-discussed passages in the book, a fact that is in itself interesting and instructive. The passage stands as an isolated paragraph, seemingly unrelated to what precedes or follows:

> I long ago lost a hound, a bay horse, and a turtle dove, and am still on their trail. Many are the travellers I have spoken concerning them, describing their tracks and what calls they answered to. I have met one or two who had heard the hound, and the tramp of the horse, and even seen the dove disappear behind a cloud, and they seemed as anxious to recover them as if they had lost them themselves. (11)

It should come as no surprise that the hound, the bay horse, and the turtle dove are almost universally seen as symbols by Thoreau's readers. The questions asked of this passage are generally, What do the three animals symbolize? and Where did the symbols come from? The answers to these questions are many and varied: for T. M. Raysor, the animals represent the "gentle boy" Edmund Sewall, Thoreau's dead brother John, and the woman to whom he unsuccessfully proposed marriage, Ellen Sewall; for Francis H. Allen, the symbols represent "the vague desires and aspirations of man's spiritual nature"; for John Burroughs, they stand for the "fine effluence" that for Thoreau constitutes "the ultimate expression of fruit of any created thing." Others have seen in the symbols "a mythical record of [Thoreau's] disappointments" (Emerson), a "quest . . . for an absolutely satisfactory condition of friendship" (Mark Van Doren), the "wildness that keeps man in touch with nature, intellectual stimulus, and purification of spirit" (Frank Davidson), and a "lost Eden" (Alfred Kazin). Sources for Thoreau's symbols

1. Walter Benn Michaels, *"Walden's* False Bottoms," *Glyph* 1; *Johns Hopkins Textual Studies* (Baltimore: Johns Hopkins University Press, 1977), pp. 132–49, reprinted in this volume, p. 421.

are said to be found in such diverse texts as Voltaire's *Zadig* (Edith Peairs), the "Chinese Four Books" that Thoreau edited for *The Dial*, an old English ballad, an Irish folk tale, and a poem by Emerson.[2]

The sense shared by all readers that the hound, the bay horse and the turtle dove *are* symbols, but that what they symbolize is unclear, is made explicit in the following remarks by Stanley Cavell:

> I have no new proposal to offer about the literary or biographical sources of those symbols. But the very obviousness of the fact that they are symbols, and function within a little myth, seems to me to tell us what we need to know. The writer comes to us from a sense of loss; the myth does not contain more than symbols because it is no set of desired things he has lost, but a connection with things, the track of desire itself.[3]

The notion that what is at stake here is not any set of lost *things* but rather the very fact of *loss* seems to find confirmation in the replies that Thoreau himself gave on two different occasions to the question of the passage's meaning. In a letter to B. B. Wiley, dated April 26, 1857, he writes:

> How shall we account for our pursuits if they are original? We get the language with which to describe our various lives out of a common mint. If others have their losses, which they are busy repairing, so have I *mine*, & their hound & horse may *perhaps* be the symbols of some of them. But also I have lost, or am in danger of losing, a far finer & more etherial treasure, which commonly no loss of which they are conscious will symbolize—this I answer hastily & with some hesitation, according as I now understand my own words. (*Annotated Walden*, 157–58)

And on another occasion, as the *Variorum* tells it:

> Miss Ellen Watson, in "Thoreau Visits Plymouth" . . . , reports that when Thoreau visited Plymouth, Mass., a year or two after the publication of *Walden*, he met there "Uncle Ed" Watson who asked him what he meant when he said he lost "a hound, a horse, and a dove." Thoreau replied, "Well, Sir, I suppose we have all our losses." "That's a pretty way to answer a fellow," replied Uncle Ed. (270)

Most readers have shared Uncle Ed's disappointment at this answer that seems no answer at all. The editors of the *Annotated* and *Variorum Waldens* both conclude their surveys of the literature on the subject in a similar way:

> In conclusion, however, it should be pointed out that there is no un-animity on interpretation of these symbols and the individual critic is left free to interpret as he wishes. (*Variorum*, 272)

2. For detailed bibliographical information on these and other readings of the passage, see *The Annotated Walden*, ed. Philip Van Doren Stern (New York: Clarkson N. Potter, 1970), pp. 157–58, and *The Variorum Walden*, ed. Walter Harding (New York: Twayne, 1962),

pp. 270–72.
3. Stanley Cavell, *The Senses of Walden* (San Francisco: North Point, 1981), p. 51. [A portion of Cavell's book, dealing further with loss and despair, is reprinted in this volume, pp. 390–405—*Editor*].

Since there is no clear explanation, each reader will have to supply his own. (*Annotated Walden*, 158)

In attempting to fill these enigmatic symbols with interpretive content, most readers have assumed that the hound, the bay horse, and the turtle dove were figurative containers or concrete vehicles into which some deeper, higher, or more abstract meanings could be made to fit. This is what the business of interpreting symbols is all about. In cases like the present, where there exists no unanimity or clarity about the symbols' meanings, readers tend to believe *not* that there is something inadequate about the way they are asking the question, but that each individual becomes "free" to settle on an answer for himself.

Before going back to attempt a different type of analysis of this passage, I would like first to quote in its entirety the paragraph that immediately precedes the hound-horse-dove passage in the text:

> In any weather, at any hour of the day or night, I have been anxious to improve the nick of time, and notch it on my stick too; to stand on the meeting of two eternities, the past and the future, which is precisely the present moment; to toe that line. You will pardon some obscurities, for there are more secrets in my trade than in most men's, and yet not voluntarily kept, but inseparable from its very nature. I would gladly tell all that I know about it, and never paint "No Admittance" on my gate.
>
> I long ago lost a hound, a bay horse, and a turtle dove, and am still on their trail. Many are the travellers I have spoken concerning them, describing their tracks and what calls they answered to. I have met one or two who had heard the hound, and the tramp of the horse, and even seen the dove disappear behind a cloud, and they seemed as anxious to recover them as if they had lost them themselves. (11)

There appears at first sight to be no relation between these two paragraphs. Yet the very abruptness of the transition, the very discrepancy of rhetorical modes, may perhaps indicate that the first paragraph consists of a set of instructions about how to read the second. It is surely no accident that one of the most enigmatic passages in *Walden* should be placed immediately after the sentence "You will pardon some obscurities." If the secret identities of the hound, the horse, and the dove are never to be revealed, it is not, says Thoreau, that they are being *voluntarily* withheld. Such secrets are simply inseparable from the nature of my trade—that is, writing. "I would gladly tell all that I know about it, and never paint 'No Admittance' on my gate." But all I *know* about it is not all there *is* about it. You are not being forcibly or gently kept away from a knowledge I possess. The gate is wide open, and that is why the path is so obscure. The sign "obscurity" is pointing directly at the symbols, making the sentence read, "I long ago lost an X, a Y, and a Z," and you are supposed to recognize them not as obscure symbols, but as symbols standing for the obscure, the lost, the irretrievable.

But yet, we insist, your X, Y, and Z are so *particular*—so houndlike, so horselike, so birdlike. If they merely symbolize the lost objects as such, why do we hear the baying of the hound and the tramp of the horse? Why do those fellow travellers give us such precise reports?

Ah, but you see, Thoreau might answer, the symbols *are* symbols, after all. What is lost is always intensely particular. Yet it is known only in that it is lost—lost in one of the two eternities between which we clumsily try to toe the line.

To follow the trail of what is lost is possible only, it seems, if the loss is maintained in a state of transference from traveller to traveller, so that each takes up the pursuit as if the loss were his own. Loss, then, ultimately belongs to an other; the losses we treat as our own are perhaps losses of which we never had conscious knowledge ourselves. "If others have their losses, which they are busy repairing, so have I *mine,* & their hound & horse may *perhaps* be the symbols of some of them. But also I have lost, or am in danger of losing, a far finer & more etherial treasure, which commonly no loss *of which they are conscious* will symbolize."

Walden's great achievement is to wake us up to our own lost losses, to make us participate in the transindividual movement of loss in its infinite particularity, urging us passionately to follow the tracks of we know not quite what, as if we had lost it, or were in danger of losing it, ourselves.

In order to communicate the irreducibly particular yet ultimately unreadable nature of loss, Thoreau has chosen to use three symbols that clearly *are* symbols but that do not really symbolize anything outside themselves. They are figures for which no literal, proper term can be substituted. They are, in other words, catachreses—"figures of abuse," figurative substitutes for a literal term that does not exist. Like the "legs" and "arms" of our favorite recliner, Thoreau's hound, horse, and dove belong to a world of homely figurative richness, yet the impersonal literality they seem to presuppose is nowhere to be found. The structure of catachretic symbolism is thus the very structure of transference and loss. Through it Thoreau makes us see that every lost object is always, in a sense, a catachresis, a figurative substitute for nothing that ever could be literal.

It could be said that Nature itself is for Thoreau a catachretic symbol that enables him to displace his discourse without filling in its symbolic tenor. But in order to analyze a more particular aspect of the way in which Thoreau's catachretic rhetoric creates obscurity in *Walden,* let us first look at a more traditional and semantically "full" use of nature imagery: the *analogies* drawn between natural objects and human predicaments.

I begin with a somewhat atypically explicit analogy:

One day . . . I saw a striped snake run into the water, and he lay on the bottom, apparently without inconvenience, as long as I staid there, or more than a quarter of an hour; perhaps because he had not yet fairly come out of the torpid state. It appears to me that for a like reason men remain in their present low and primitive condition; but if they should feel the influence of the spring of springs arousing them, they would of necessity rise to a higher and more ethereal life. (28)

No rhetorical strategy could be more classical than this weaving of analogy between the natural and the human worlds. It is the mark of the moralist, the evangelist, the satirist, and the lyric poet, all of which Thoreau indeed is. From the New Testament to Aesop and Swedenborg, the natural world has been a source of figures of the preoccupations and foibles of man. As Emerson puts it in his own essay on Nature:

> The memorable words of history and the proverbs of nations consist usually of a natural fact, selected as a picture or parable of a moral truth. Thus; A rolling stone gathers no moss; A bird in hand is worth two in the bush; A cripple in the right way will beat a racer in the wrong; Make hay while the sun shines; 'Tis hard to carry a full cup even; Vinegar is the son of wine; The last ounce broke the camel's back; Long-lived trees make roots first;—and the like. In their primary sense these are trivial facts, but we repeat them for the value of their analogical import. What is true of proverbs, is true of all fables, parables, and allegories.[4]

Yet although Thoreau draws on many centuries of analogical writing, there is a subtle difference in his rhetorical use of nature, and it is the specificity of that difference that I would like to attempt to identify in conclusion. The difference begins to become perceptible in the following examples:

> Why has man rooted himself thus firmly in the earth, but that he may rise in the same proportion into the heavens above?—for the nobler plants are valued for the fruit they bear at last in the air and light, far from the ground, and are not treated like the humbler esculents, which, though they may be biennials, are cultivated only till they have perfected their root, and often cut down at top for this purpose, so that most would not know them in their flowering season. (10)

> We don garment after garment, as if we grew like exogenous plants by addition without. Our outside and often thin and fanciful clothes are our epidermis or false skin, which partakes not of our life, and may be stripped off here and there without fatal injury; our thicker garments, constantly worn, are our cellular integument, or cortex; but our shirts are our liber or true bark, which cannot be removed without girdling and so destroying the man. (16)

In both these examples, what begins as a fairly routine analogy tends, in the course of its elaboration, to get wildly out of hand. The fascination with the vehicle as an object of attention in its own right totally eclipses the original anthropomorphic tenor. Words like "esculents," "biennials," "cortex," and "liber" pull away from their subordinate, figurative status and begin giving information about themselves, sidetracking the reader away

---

4. Ralph Waldo Emerson, *Selected Prose and Poetry* (New York: Holt, Rinehart, and Winston, 1964), p. 20.

from the original thrust of the analogy. In the first example, what begins as an opposition between nobler and humbler men and plants collapses as it is revealed that the humbler plants are humble only because they are never *allowed* to flower. In the second example, the hierarchy of integuments ends by privileging not the skin but the shirt as that part of a man that cannot be removed without destroying him. In an effort to show that man is confused about where his inside ends and his outside begins, Thoreau resorts to a logic of tree growth which entirely takes over as the exogenous striptease procedes.

It is perhaps in the "Bean-field" chapter that the rhetorical rivalries between the literal and the figurative, the tenor and the vehicle, become most explicit. On the one hand, Thoreau writes, "I was determined to know beans," and goes on to detail the hours of hoeing and harvesting, listing the names of weeds and predators, and accounting for outgo and income down to the last half penny. And on the other, he admits that "some must work in fields if only for the sake of tropes and expression, to serve a parable-maker one day." He speaks of sowing the seeds of sincerity, truth, simplicity, faith, and innocence, asking, "Why concern ourselves so much about our beans for seed, and not be concerned at all about a new generation of men?"

The perverse complexity of *Walden*'s rhetoric is intimately related to the fact that it is never possible to be sure what the rhetorical status of any given image is. And this is because what Thoreau has done in moving to Walden Pond is to move *himself*, literally, into the world of his own figurative language. The literal woods, pond, and bean field still assume the same classical rhetorical guises in which they have always appeared, but they are suddenly readable in addition as the nonfigurative ground of a naturalist's account of life in the woods. The ground has shifted, but the figures are still figures. When is it that we decide that Thoreau never lost that hound, that horse, and that dove? It is because we can never be absolutely sure, that we find ourselves forever on their trail.

Walden is obscure, therefore, to the extent that Thoreau has *literally* crossed over into the very parable he is writing, where *reality itself* has become a catachresis, both ground and figure at once, and where, he tells us, "if you stand right fronting and face to face to a fact, you will see the sun glimmer on both its surfaces, as if it were a cimeter, and feel its sweet edge dividing you through the heart and marrow."

H. DANIEL PECK

The Worlding of Walden†

"Why do precisely these objects which we behold make a world?" Thoreau
asks in "Brute Neighbors," chapter 12 of *Walden*. This is the central question
that *Walden* seeks to answer and to which *Walden* itself is an answer. The
word "precisely" reveals the assumption underlying the question, with its
clear implication that the world as we know it corresponds exactly to our
needs and expectations. "Why has man," Thoreau continues, "*just* these
species of animals for his neighbors; as if nothing but a mouse could have
filled this crevice?" (150–51; emphasis added). The world we know through
perception is a "fitting" world, a world of balance and symmetry. In the
terms of our discussion of the Journal, it is a category filled to its exact limits
and no more, "a world with full and fair proportions" (218), as Thoreau
calls the staff made by the artist of Kouroo.

The brief descriptions of Thoreau's "brute neighbors" that follow these
questions are, he seems to say, as full an answer as anyone will ever need:
the "mice which haunted my house"; the phoebe that "built in my shed";
the robin that found protection in the pine next to the hut; the partridge
that led her brood past the windows; the otter and raccoon that lived nearby;
the woodcock probing for worms; the turtledoves that sat over the spring;
the red squirrel "coursing down the nearest bough" (151–53).

The simple, enumerative quality of this passage (it resembles both in form
and intention one of the Journal's lists) makes clear that these "neighbors"
are constituents of a world already organized and prepared by nature for
human perception, and that perception, in fact, has very little work to do:
"You only need sit still long enough in some attractive spot in the woods
that *all* its inhabitants may exhibit themselves to you by turns" (153; emphasis
added). Walden is that axial point from which, by simply watching and
waiting, one may "behold" the full kaleidoscope of nature's phenomena.

This is the centralized perspective that was announced earlier in the
chapter "Where I Lived, and What I Lived For": "Wherever I sat, there I
might live, and the landscape radiated from me accordingly" (55). Everything
that enters this radius, by definition, belongs to a proximate world, a world
of "the nearest bough." Like the red squirrel, all the creatures perceived
from this perspective are "familiar" (153) to Thoreau; they are already familiarized, prepared for the imagination by their placement within the world
of Walden.

But immediately following this brisk enumeration of the animals and birds
in Thoreau's peaceable kingdom, the chapter takes an abrupt turn: "I was

† From H. Daniel Peck, *Thoreau's Morning
Work: Memory and Perception in A Week on
the Concord and Merrimack Rivers, the Journal, and Walden*, 117–32, copyright (c) 1990.
Reprinted by permission of Yale University
Press. *Walden* page numbers refer to this Norton Critical Edition.

witness to events of a less peaceful character" (153). And, indeed, the description of the ant-war that follows shows us a rapacious natural world sharply at odds with that of the turtledove and the phoebe. But what it also shows us is a different mode of apprehension, a different way of "beholding." So often discussed is this famous set piece that I need not recount here the pitched battle of the ants or the brilliant play of metaphor with which it is narrated. For the purpose of this discussion, the most important element of the piece is a Thoreauvian gesture having nothing to do with the battle as such: "I took up the chip on which the three [ants] I have particularly described were struggling, carried it into my house, and placed it under a tumbler on my window-sill, in order to see the issue. Holding a microscope to the first-mentioned red ant, I saw that, though he was assiduously gnawing at the near fore-leg of his enemy . . . his own breast was all torn away" (154).

Mere watchful waiting is insufficient to view these brute neighbors (the oxymoron making itself felt in this context). Their size, as well as the complexity of their movements, requires that they be scrutinized under a microscope. For all the self-conscious literary allusiveness of the piece, its dominant spirit is that of the observer-scientist, and the microscope itself is a figure for this analytical mode of apprehension. The naturalist's view of nature makes itself felt often in the Journal, but in *Walden* it is generally subordinated to other, more "aesthetic" modes of apprehension. This is one reason, apart from its hyperbolic and burnished prose, why the ant-war passage sometimes seems out of place, rather like some of the more intrusive digressions in *A Week*.

As different as the ant-war is from the scene that precedes it, however, these passages share one important trait: both the simple beholding of the one and the intense scrutiny of the other are the acts of a subject-viewer totally in control of his perceptions. But now, following Thoreau's description of the ant-war, we find ourselves in the realm of the fortuitous: "Once I was surprised to see a cat walking along the stony shore of the pond, for they rarely wander so far from home"; "Once, when berrying, I met with a cat with young kittens in the woods, quite wild, and they all, like their mother, had their backs up and were fiercely spitting at me" (156).

These instances of the unexpected and the "wild" are followed by the description of a mysterious " 'winged cat,' " whose presence in the town of Lincoln several years before the Walden experiment was reported to Thoreau by Mrs. Gilian Baker, who had taken it in. Everything about this creature is elusive: when Thoreau goes to see it, it has "gone a-hunting in the woods, as was her wont," and he is "not sure whether it was a male or female." This winged cat, never actually observed by Thoreau, finally becomes a local legend: "Some thought it was part flying-squirrel or some other wild animal, which is not impossible, for, according to naturalists, prolific hybrids have been produced by the union of the marten and domestic cat" (156). But, in the end, no naturalist will ever have the opportunity to examine this strange animal, whose hybrid nature symbolizes its essential mystery and unclassifiability.[1]

The surprising cats described in this passage prepare us for the wildest of Walden's creatures, the loon.[2] Though its appearance is predictable ("the loon . . . came, as usual" [156]), the announcement of its arrival—"his wild laughter"—signals how unpredictable its actions are. Now the "surprise" caused by the cats is replaced by astonishment, wonder, and disorientation. The sense of the fortuitous increases: "As I was paddling along the north shore one very calm October afternoon, . . . suddenly one [loon], sailing out from the shore toward the middle a few rods in front of me, set up his wild laugh and betrayed himself."

The calm is broken and the chase is on, but Thoreau's pursuit is repeatedly interrupted, his expectations defeated at every "turn": "He dived again, but I miscalculated the direction he would take" (157); "again and again, when I was straining my eyes over the surface one way, I would suddenly be startled by his unearthly laugh behind me." The loon's laugh, as well as its "long-drawn unearthly howl," are the sounds of the uncanny: "the wildest sound that is ever heard here" (158). In contrast to the winged cat, here is a creature that never can be domesticated.

The loon's "demoniac laughter" (158) is mocking; unlike the gentle creatures that surround the hut, but the loon insists upon its separateness from its observer. Thoreau's failed pursuit of the loon dramatizes this creature's refusal to be contained (familiarized) within the Edenic vision of Walden sketched earlier in the chapter, or to be brought under the naturalist's microscope, as in the ant-war passage. It exists in a realm beyond the proximate world of Thoreau's hut. (Here is a creature at home in all dimensions, in water and sky, in the depths and heights of Walden.) The entire scene emphasizes the independence of object from subject: "While he was thinking one thing in his brain, I was endeavoring to divine his thought in mine." Unlike the ants, which Thoreau picks up and takes indoors to examine, his "adversary" (157) the loon escapes him, "disappearing far away on the tumultuous surface" (158).

But if the loon insists upon its separateness from Thoreau, scenically they are one. Hunter and hunted (it is a visual hunt) merge into a single ambience, a dance between subject and object: "It was a pretty game, played on the smooth surface of the pond, a man against a loon" (157). The "against" of

1. Thoreau secures a set of the creature's "wings," but he does not report having studied them, and their import in the passage is to intensify rather than diminish the mystery.
2. As Charles R. Anderson, considering the loon passage as a reworking of an Algonquin myth, points out, Thoreau gives the loon a wildness "entirely missing from the Indian legends" and gave even greater emphasis to this quality in the first version of "Brute Neighbors" (*The Magic Circle of Walden* [New York: Holt, Rinehart, and Winston, 1968], 196–97). This great passage, as well as the passage that begins "Why do these objects which we behold make a world?", are late additions to *Walden*—both indebted to Thoreau's rich discoveries of perception in the early 1850s. See Shanley, *The Making of Walden*, 72–73, and Adams and Ross, *Revising Mythologies*, 169–70. [Full bibliographic information for works cited only by author and title in this excerpt may be found in the Selected Bibliography—*Editor*.]

the final phrase may remind us of the antagonism of the ant-war, but surely Thoreau also intends the word in a pictorial sense: a man set against the background of a loon and both set against the background of Walden, which is the stage on which their drama unfolds.

To a greater degree than any of the preceding sections of "Brute Neighbors," the loon passage invites us to picture Thoreau himself within the scene, so that the scene—in its totality—becomes the object of the reader's eye. ("[C]an we separate the man," Emerson asks in Nature, "from the living picture?"[3]) Thoreau is too busy pursuing the loon to really behold it; it is we who do the beholding, and as we do so a world comes into being.

The diving and plunging of the loon, as well as Thoreau's pursuit, are part of a lovely dance between the self and nature, in something of the sense that Suzanne Langer intends when she says that "dance creates a world of powers" and shows us "a display of interacting forces."[4] Around these images of power and force, the dance merges with the hunt. Thoreau is a "hunter" of the loon, not in the sense of predation, but in the sense described by José Ortega y Gasset in his Meditations on Hunting: "All means of pursuit and capture which the hunter employs, correspond to countermeasures of evasion that the prey employs," dramatizing "a relationship in which two systems of instincts confront each other."[5]

Not only is the loon a symbol of Thoreau's own spiritual deep-diving, as most critics have viewed it. It also is a pure dramatization, or "immanence," of the relation between man and loon—a relation founded more on difference than on similarity. Without difference, without otherness, there could be no dance. The relationship that Thoreau describes as "a man against a loon" should thus also be understood as an encounter, in which the loon emerges "over against" the spatial "background" of the Pond. These are the terms Martin Buber employs to describe the encounter between "I" and "Thou," in which the greatest intimacy (in Thoreau's terms, "correspondence") results from the full "emergence" of "Thou."[6] For Thoreau to "divine [the loon's] thought in mine" is ultimately to make this encounter, and, in doing so, to discover the "wildness" that resides within himself.

This great passage, then, introduces still another form of beholding that characterizes Walden at some of its most powerful and lyric moments. To behold in this way is to emphasize the "holding," not in the sense of possession, but in the sense of a vibrant, organic world brought into being and "held" steadily before us. Unlike the scene of watchful waiting depicted

3. The Collected Works of Ralph Waldo Emerson, ed. Alfred R. Ferguson et al. (Cambridge, Mass.: Harvard University Press, 1971–), 1:15.
4. Suzanne Langer, Problems of Art: Ten Philosophical Lectures (New York: Charles Scribner's Sons, 1957), 10.
5. José Ortega y Gasset, Meditations on Hunting, trans. Howard B. Wescott (New York: Charles Scribner's Sons, 1972), 87.

6. The relevant passage from Buber follows: "The Thou appears, to be sure, in space, but in the exclusive situation of what is over against it, where everything else can be only the background out of which it emerges, not its boundary and measured limit" (I and Thou, 2d ed., trans. Ronald G. Smith [New York: Charles Scribner's Sons, 1958], 30).

earlier in "Brute Neighbors," the loon passage emphasizes the self as a creator (a dancer and hunter, in this sense as well) in the world beheld.

This thought returns us, of course, to the artist of Kouroo, whose own "world of full and fair proportions" was "made" in exactly this way: "When the finishing stroke was put to his work, it suddenly *expanded* before the eyes of the *astonished* artist into the fairest of all the creations of Brahma" (218; emphases added). The creation of this staff ("a new system") brings a world into being and sustains it through imagination. We may also be reminded of the mythical creation of Walden itself, "the work of a brave man . . . [who] rounded this water with his hand" (130).

The loon passage implicitly revises Thoreau's earlier answer to the question "Why do precisely these objects which we behold make a world?" The fullest answer to this question is that objects do not, by themselves, make a world; worlds are "made" by the interaction—the "dance"—of the creative self and the world. This is the same answer that the Journal, through its continuous play of association, gives over and over again through the long course of its development.

But "Brute Neighbors" concludes with a return to the mode of apprehension with which it began, that of watchful waiting: "For hours, in fall days, I watched the ducks cunningly tack and veer and hold the middle of the pond. . . . When compelled to rise they would sometimes circle round and round and over the pond at a considerable height" (158). The ducks' veering and circling suggest the loon's movements, but here the perceiver remains stationary, contemplative, a viewer rather than an actor in the scene. But this final scene is not merely a "frame" for the great loon passage, a way of highlighting its drama. Rather, its placement reminds us that contemplation is, as much as the "dance," a way of involving oneself in nature. Both watchful waiting from a stationary, centralized perspective, as well as the joyful dance of creation, are avenues to "correspondence," and *Walden* is characterized by a movement back and forth between these modes. In this, it closely resembles Whitman's "Song of Myself," which validates both "loafing" and "[s]peeding through space" as means to fulfillment. Like Whitman, Thoreau is "[b]oth in and out of the game" (secs. I, 5, 33, 4).

Thus, the chapter "Brute Neighbors" may be understood as pivotal; it presents in anecdotal form the two most important modes of apprehension characterizing *Walden* as a whole. On the one hand, its scenes of watchful waiting recall the "serenity" (130) of "The Ponds," where we found Thoreau "floating over [Walden's] surface as the zephyr willed, having paddled my boat to the *middle*, and lying on my back across the seats, in a summer forenoon, dreaming awake" (129; emphasis added). This is the perspective of centralized solitude whose aesthetic and spiritual advantages were asserted earlier in the same chapter: "The forest has never so good a setting, nor is so distinctly beautiful, as when seen from the middle of a small lake" (125). On the other hand, the loon passage of "Brute Neighbors" anticipates the

456 · H. Daniel Peck

climactic chapter "Spring," with its dramatization of a flowing, "living" earth and of a beholder intimately involved in nature's processes. In that chapter, Thoreau's "alert[ness] for the first signs of spring" (201), like his anticipation of the loon's initial appearance, signals a participatory role. (As Ortega says, "[t]he hunter is the alert man" whose alertness takes him to "an authentic 'outside,' " to the condition of being *within* the country-side.")[7] And like the unpredictable loon or the "surprising" cats, the "sand foliage" is remarkable because of "its springing into existence thus *suddenly*" (204; emphasis added). As much as the loon, the sand foliage suggests transformation to Thoreau: "The very globe continually transcends and translates itself, and becomes winged in its orbit" (204). Finally, "Spring" follows the loon passage in its rendering of a world "made" through creation and still in the process of being created: "I am affected as if in a peculiar sense I stood in the laboratory of the Artist [the phrase conjoins science and art] who made the world and me,—had come to where he was still at work, sporting on this bank, and with excess of energy strewing his fresh designs about" (204).

But the distinction between the contemplative and creative modes of apprehension, as they are depicted in *Walden*, can be overdrawn. The contemplative mode involves its own form of engagement with the natural world. Reverie, as Bachelard reminds us, is an active process; it is what Whitman called inviting the soul. In his philosophical meditation, *The Inward Morning* (a phrase taken from Thoreau), Henry Bugbee describes this process: "The present in question seems to expand itself extensively into temporal and spatial distances. And it is as if one's perception of everything distinct were engaged in alignment with a center from which one moves to greet each thing knowingly."[8]

This is the expansive spirit in which Thoreau greets Walden's forest creatures from the axial perspective of his hut, "knowing" each of them in turn as they enter his arc of perception. Though one may remain stationary while experiencing it, familiarization is an act of extending perception—a fact Thoreau acknowledges more fully in "Winter Animals," the chapter that is the counterpart to "Brute Neighbors." In "Winter Animals," the whole environment of the Pond is made proximate: "Walden . . . was my yard" (181). Here we witness the process (now more difficult, but also more transparent, because of the starkness of the winter landscape) through which Thoreau perceives, and thus incorporates, the rabbits, squirrels, jays, chickadees, titmice, and sparrows into the world of his "yard." Even the mysterious hooting owl becomes "quite familiar to me at last" (181), the final phrase confirming that familiarization is an active process.

7. Ibid., 150, 141, 142. For a consideration of "alertness [as] a way of being in the world" in Thoreau's work, especially as this relates to English romantic poets such as Wordsworth, see Frederick Garber, "Thoreau's Ladder of Alertness," *Thoreau Quarterly* 14 (Summer/ Fall 1982): 118.
8. Henry G. Bugbee, Jr., *The Inward Morning: A Philosophical Exploration in Journal Form* (State College, Pa.: Bald Eagle Press, 1958), 52.

Similarly, the experience of "floating over [Walden's] surface as the zephyr willed" is hardly unengaged. Thoreau, after all, deliberately "paddled [his] boat to the middle" in order to gain a perspective of centrality and serenity. And the reverie with which he is rewarded is described by the powerful oxymoron, "dreaming *awake*" (129; emphasis added). Such wakeful dreaming is what Bugbee calls a "bathing in fluent reality."[9]

Conversely, the drama of the self's engagement in nature that we witness in the loon passage and in "Spring" involves a form of contemplation—a wonderment before the processes of the world: "And so the seasons went rolling on into summer, as one rambles into higher and higher grass" (212–13). The loon itself becomes an object of contemplation at the conclusion of "Spring," where it joins the phoebe and other gentler birds in a vision of nature's interrelatedness (212). In the end, the contemplative and creative modes of apprehension reflect one another, are part of the same essential activity, and serve a single purpose: they "enact the 'worlding' of the world."

This phrase comes from an essay by Richard Pevear, who uses it in a discussion of the poetry of George Oppen. Pevear places Oppen's work in contrast to the "solipsism of so much of contemporary writing" and understands it as an antidote to the "worldlessness" of the postwar period.[1] It was, of course, a nineteenth-century version of worldlessness—the condition of "quiet desperation" (5)—that sent Thoreau to the Pond to recover *his* world, and *Walden* may be considered the "poem" he wrote toward his recovery. He was, as many have observed, prescient in understanding how the technology and coercive social structures emerging in his time could alienate people from nature and turn them into machines.[2] One of his reasons for going to Walden, like many another utopian of his day, was to recover the very ground of being, to "world" the world in this quite literal sense.

Thoreau, of course, had his own "solipsism" to overcome: the alienation that results from philosophical idealism, in its privileging of consciousness and subjectivity. Idealism challenged his vividly experienced sense of a vital, organic earth, and at Walden he put it to the test of his experiment in living. By refusing to be un-worlded, he establishes his relevance for our time, especially in his demonstration that perception can bridge the chasm between spirituality and sensory experience. *Walden* is remarkable in its anticipation of the phenomenological position of twentieth-century philosophers such as Maurice Merleau-Ponty: that "immanence and transcendence [meet] in perception."[3]

9. Ibid.

1. Richard Pevear, "Poetry and Worldlessness," *Hudson Review* 29 (Summer 1976): 318, 315, 319.

2. The most comprehensive treatment of Thoreau's relevance to twentieth-century political and social issues is to be found in Michael Meyer, *Several More Lives to Live: Thoreau's Political Reputation in America* (Westport, Conn.: Greenwood Press, 1977).

3. Maurice Merleau-Ponty, "The Primacy of Perception and Its Philosophical Consequences," trans. James M. Edie, in Merleau-Ponty's *The Primacy of Perception and Other Essays on Phenomenological Psychology, the Philosophy of Art, History, and Politics*, ed. James M. Edie (Evanston, Ill.: Northwestern University Press, 1964), 16.

But Thoreau's relation to contemporary thought should not be overstated. The worlding enacted by *Walden* does not attempt to redress so profound a condition of "worldlessness" as described by Pevear and other commentators upon postwar alienation. Thoreau did not feel as radically dispossessed of the world as many men and women of the late twentieth century. He did not have to confront the concentration camps, the bomb, and modern totalitarianism—the conditions of "terror" that, according to Isaac Rosenfeld, created "an age of enormity" in which individuals are dwarfed before the massive, often incomprehensible, movements of vast nation-states. And one may add to this list of terrors the ecological destruction of our time, which Thoreau only partially foresaw. These are the conditions in which a writer like Oppen, through a poetry of immanence, strives to bring the very world back into being. We may also think of Charles Olson, who struggles in his *Maximus Poems* to "construct" "an actual earth of value."[4]

For Thoreau, it was not necessary to assert the "actuality" of the world or to "construct" it in quite the sense that Olson intends; his earth of value remained in place, at hand, in the very midst of civilization. That his experiment takes place only "a mile from any neighbor" (1) testifies to his confidence in nature's powers of renewal and its accessibility. The problem was not to bring being out of nothingness, but to demonstrate that all the various "worlds" we might inhabit were supported by one world—nature: "There is a solid bottom everywhere" (220). *Walden*'s morning work is to re-mind Thoreau and his neighbors of nature's proximity and importance: "alert and healthy natures *remember* that the sun rose clear" (5; emphasis added). The "restless, nervous, bustling, trivial Nineteenth Century" (220) had obscured, rather than obliterated, nature's centrality to human life, and what was needed was a reorientation, or repositioning, of the self toward the world.

This repositioning occurs steadily throughout the early chapters of *Walden*, and its realization is confirmed in the chapter "The Village," in which Thoreau's almost anthropological analysis of Concord's human structures (112–13) shows how psychologically distanced from civilization he has become. At this point, he has achieved for himself the state of being he recommends to "pilgrims" in the earlier chapter "Visitors"—to "really [have] left the village behind" (104). His sentient, "dreaming" (114) return to "my snug harbor in the woods" (114) confirms the full relocation of his perspective and prepares us for the "worlding" that occurs so magnificently in the subsequent chapter "The Ponds."[5]

The point is that, given the proper perspective, the world would "world" itself. Changeless and perennial, like Walden Pond, the world would appear

4. Isaac Rosenfeld, "The Meaning of Terror," in *An Age of Enormity: Life and Writing in the Forties and Fifties*, ed. Theodore Solotaroff (Cleveland: World Publishing Co., 1962) 206–9; Olson, *The Maximus Poems*, 584.

5. That not everyone has the capacity to reposition himself in this way, even given the opportunity, is demonstrated in "Higher Laws" by the case of John Farmer (149).

to grow by assuming its true proportions, if we adopted the right mode of apprehension. At Walden, a world gradually comes into being and enlarges as the doors of perception are cleansed through the discipline of solitude. This is the process that occurs in "The Ponds" and, with the different emphasis I have indicated, in the climactic chapter "Spring." In both cases, the "little world" of Walden becomes big, which is to say, as big as it really is: "The universe is wider than our views of it" (213).

In stressing Walden's expansiveness, I intend to revise somewhat the traditional notion of the Pond as a microcosm. Certainly its various images as " 'God's Drop' " (130), as "crystal" (133), and as "earth's eye" (125) suggest a concentrated or condensed (symbolic) representation of the cosmos. But if, from one point of view, Walden gathers the cosmos, from another point of view, it opens into it; "earth's eye" looks out, and, to the extent that we can align our own vision with that of Walden (itself a cosmos), we may gain a "broad margin" (75) for our lives. [6]

The worlding of Walden is more than anything else a process of dilation, which culminates in the final chapter's images of exploration (213–15), expansion, and "*Extra vagance*" (216). We can track the essential movement of *Walden* by shifting our view from the modest hut whose construction is meticulously described in the first chapter, "Economy," to the "cavernous house" (162) of which Thoreau dreams in "House-Warming." This dream-house is a place for dwelling, in the most profound and satisfying sense of this word, and serves as an analogue for the capacious sense of habitation that the world of Walden, as cosmos, offers to Thoreau.

But it is important to remember that this grand house could not have taken imaginative form in *Walden* without Thoreau's having first rendered the building of his hut. Among the many ways in which "Economy" prepares us for the book's subsequent developments, this is the most important. As Martin Heidegger writes, "We attain to dwelling . . . only by means of building." He reminds us that "[t]he Old English and High German word for building, *buan*, means to dwell," "to stay in a place," and that this experience earns for us a sense of "peace" which, in turn, is freeing. Dwelling, which begins with building and the cultivation of the "near," ultimately leads to dwelling "on the earth" and "under the sky." [7]

---

6. Cf. "A Winter Walk," where Thoreau writes: "In summer it [the Pond] is the earth's liquid eye; a mirror in the breast of nature" (*The Writings of Henry David Thoreau* [Boston: Houghton Mifflin, 1906], 5:174); and *Journal 1: 1837–1842*, ed. Elizabeth Hall Witherell et al. (Princeton: Princeton University Press, 1981), 198, from which this ("Winter Walk") passage derives. See also Emerson in *Nature*: "The ruin or the blank, that we see when we look at nature, is in our own eye. The axis of vision is not coincident with the axis of things, and so they appear not transparent but opake" (*Collected Works*, 1: 43).

7. Martin Heidegger, "Building Dwelling Thinking," in *Poetry, Language, Thought*, trans. Albert Hofstadter (New York: Harper, Row, 1971), 145, 146, 149. Cf. Burbick, who writes: "[U]nlike Heidegger, Thoreau has an empirical need to assert a particular geographical site, which leads him to a pragmatic consideration of space" (*Thoreau's Alternative History*, 61). But as my discussion indicates, Heidegger's notion of dwelling implicitly contains—indeed necessitates—"a particular geographical site." And, in any case, Thoreau's relation to Walden is "pragmatic" only in part.

Thoreau's description of Walden Pond supports this formulation, for immediately after exclaiming, "How peaceful the phenomena of the lake!" (127), he shows how "[it] is intermediate between land and sky" (127)—a link to the heavens. And whether or not you attain "*Extra vagance*," we should remember, "depends on how you are yarded" (216)—depends, that is, on the fact of your *being* yarded.[8] The process of familiarization by which Walden becomes "my yard" is the necessary preparation for the expansion of spirit and perception celebrated in the "Conclusion."

This observation suggests the way in which Walden is both a closely circumscribed setting and also one of vast, unlimited extension. On the one hand, the Pond is "stoned . . . and fringed . . . with pine woods" (93), and its "horizon [is] bounded by woods" (88). But such boundaries are not, according to Heidegger, necessarily restrictive: "A boundary is not that at which something stops but, as the Greeks recognized, the boundary is that from which something *begins its presencing*."[9] And such presencing—what we have called worlding—changes our relation to space. As Thoreau writes in describing the transformation that has occurred for him at Walden, "Both place and time were changed, and I dwelt nearer to those parts of the universe and to those eras in history which had most attracted me. Where I lived was as far off as many a region viewed nightly by astronomers" (59).[1]

At Walden, the "interval" between the near and the far (between, for example, the proximate world of Thoreau's hut and the more distant world inhabited by the loon) disappears: "[S]pace as interval," Heidegger writes, becomes "space as pure extension."[2] And when space becomes extension, everything is proximate; we are at home in the universe: "Why should I feel lonely? is not our planet in the Milky Way?" (90).

When Thoreau recalls, in "The Bean-Field," the Pond as "that fabulous landscape of my infant dreams" (104), he is calling forth the capacious and primary vision of childhood in which, according to Wordsworth, we saw the world as it really is. But the oneiric terms with which Thoreau evokes

---

8. Cf. Lewis H. Miller, Jr., who argues that "Thoreau's most effective writing relies on a paradoxical tension arising from his secure awareness of limits," and that the artistic success of *Walden* depends on its being "a world bounded for the sake of boundlessness." Miller's counterpoint is *The Maine Woods*, where, he says, Thoreau "confronts a limitless wilderness which defies precise measurement and exact determination of boundaries, [and, as a result,] the elasticity of his imagination atrophies and his writing suffers" ("The Artist as Surveyor in *Walden* and *The Maine Woods*, *ESQ* 21 [2d quarter 1975]: 76, 77). See also Schneider, who writes, "After exploring the extremes of his world, [Thoreau] felt that it was crucial to return always to a balanced middle position" ("Reflections in Walden Pond," 68).

9. Heidegger, "Building Dwelling Thinking," 154.
1. In this chapter, "Where I Lived, and What I Lived For," Thoreau says that in actuality Walden is "somewhat higher than" the village of Concord, but that in imagination it becomes for him "a tarn high up on the side of a mountain, its bottom far above the surface of other lakes" (58). "Where I Lived"—the space that the location called Walden opens to imagination—is a place *extended*.
2. Ibid., 156. What Heidegger calls "space as *extensio*" (155) might, from a mythological perspective such as that of Mircea Eliade, be called "sacred." For a compelling reading of *Walden* from this perspective, see David E. Whisnant, "The Sacred and the Profane in *Walden*," *Centennial Review* 14 (Summer 1970): 267–83.

his childhood vision of Walden show the difficulty of sustaining this vision in adulthood ("civilization").[3] For him, art is the vehicle through which it may be preserved and reexperienced.[4] We have seen how *Walden* makes a world, how it enacts that process; now we are in a position to see how it attempts to secure the world thus made. Like the mature Journal, it does so by drawing the boundaries of the perceptual category that its phenomena define and fill; it "pictures" the world, specifically by enlarging it. This is the sense in which Walden is "a world of *full* and fair proportions" (emphasis added), a world filled almost to overflowing but ultimately held steadily in place by "the equilibrium of the whole lake" (126)—by the totality of Thoreau's aesthetic vision.

Thoreau's confidence in his ability to create such a picture of the world is stated in "Where I Lived, and What I Lived For": "it is . . . glorious to carve and paint the very atmosphere and medium through which we look, which morally we can do" (61). When "carved" and "painted," Thoreau's picture of Walden will, he fervently hopes, overcome the "corrosion of time" (70)—exactly the purpose of books as he states it in "Reading." That is, the book called *Walden* will preserve the world of which Walden is "made." His hope for this book is that, like the Artist of Kouroo's staff, it will be "a perfect work [in which] time does not enter" (218).

But, of course, time does enter *Walden*. In "Sounds," Thoreau is "reminded of the lapse of time" (75) by the railroad, according to whose whistle the farmers "set their clocks" (79). Even the idyll of "The Ponds" is interrupted by the "ear-rending neigh" of the "devilish Iron Horse" (129), with all the implications of destructive temporality that this sound conveys. But the force of the book, its desideratum, is exactly that of the Artist of Kouroo: to reveal that "the former lapse of time had been an illusion" (218). From beginning to end, the illusory nature of time and change is what *Walden* seeks to prove. And the great chapter "Spring," with its affirmation of the smoothly running axle of the universe, the circle of time in which all change is contained ("[a]nd so the seasons went rolling on" [212–13]), shows how much *Walden* shares the spatial vision of the mature Journal.[5]

But, in its desire to bring time under control, *Walden* also exhibits its relation to *A Week*. Its method, however, is different from that of the earlier work, a difference signaled by the pun, "My days were not days of the week" (76). As I pointed out in discussing Thoreau's first book, its voyaging in

3. There are several examples in *Walden* of Thoreau's own failure to do so. His accidental discovery, in "House-Warming," of the groundnut—the "fabulous fruit" of his youth—prompts this reaction: "I had begun to doubt if I had ever dug and eaten [it] in childhood, as I had told, and had not dreamed it" (159).
4. Cf. Emerson in *Nature*: "A work of art is an abstract or epitome of the world" (*Collected Works*, 1:16).
5. The Pond, Thoreau writes in "Spring," measures "the *absolute* progress of the season" (200; emphasis added), replacing the railroad as timekeeper. The image of the great wheel of the seasons is implicit everywhere in this chapter, as, for example, in the pun I have italicized in the following passage: "As every season seems best to us *in its turn*, so the coming in of spring is like the creation of Cosmos out of Chaos, and the realization of the Golden Age" (209).

time is essentially linear—encountering time's discrete manifestations as the voyagers touch different points along the shores of the Concord and the Merrimack rivers. The voyaging of *Walden*, by contrast, is that of "great-*circle* sailing" (213; emphasis added), a voyaging circumscribed by the boundaries of a pond but spiraling outward to the Milky Way.

In one of Thoreau's several mythological renderings of Walden's origins, he speculates in this way: "in some other geological period it may have flowed [in the Concord River], and by a little digging, which God forbid, it can be made to flow thither again" (131). If, in *A Week*, Thoreau addressed the problem of time by entering its stream, in *Walden* he chooses a body of water cut away, isolated and protected, from that stream, "without any visible inlet or outlet" (118). This Pond, as Thoreau puns, is *"Walled-in"* (123).[6]

It is in the nature of *Walden* as a pastoral that the river of time runs dangerously near and that the Pond's integrity is vulnerable to the erosion ("digging") of time. Walden, of course, is even more immediately vulnerable to that aggressive tributary of "progress," the railroad, which "has infringed on its border" (130). Pastorals are always defined by what they exclude and by the tensions or "interruptions" they exhibit in the act of excluding. What ultimately preserves pastorals like Walden from their contingent dangers is not only their spatial isolation—the boundaries they maintain—but also the language in which they are rendered.

In "The Pond in Winter," pieces of Walden's ice are "carried off" (198) in the railroad cars, after they have been cut and stacked by a small army of workers. But this apparently destructive activity, accompanied by "a peculiar shriek from the locomotive" (197), leaves the Pond intact. Walden, according to Thoreau, remains uninjured for three reasons: only a small portion of the ten thousand tons of stacked ice is actually removed and "[t]hus the pond recovered the greater part" (198); the cutting itself was brief, lasting only sixteen days, and left Walden the same "pure sea-green" (198) vision of solitude it had always been; and finally, the ice that was removed has "mingled with the sacred water of the Ganges," thus allowing Thoreau symbolically to "meet the servant of the Brahmin," whose bucket "grate[s] together in the same well" (199) with his.

In our own age of vast ecological destruction, the first two reasons are not very compelling. A more efficient ice-cutting industry might well have hauled away a larger portion of the Pond; and the brief harvest of 1846–47 might in another year have greatly extended itself, if the activity had proved profitable. Thoreau, of course, knew this; in other writings, he demonstrates his certain knowledge that the natural world could be permanently damaged by industrial and technological forces. But it is in the nature of *Walden*, as a pastoral, largely to diminish this threat, or, rather, to overcome it through

---

6. An analogue is the Hollowell farm, "half a mile from the nearest neighbor, and separated from the highway by a broad field[,] . . . protected . . . by its fogs from frosts." (56).

the power of rhetoric.[7] This is why Thoreau's final reason for Walden's preservation, so purely fanciful, is also the most compelling. The water—and world—of Walden is convincingly preserved in this chapter through an act of imagination.

* * *

LAWRENCE BUELL

American Pastoral Ideology Reappraised[†]

Ever since an American literary canon began to crystallize, American literature has been thought of as markedly "pastoral" in the loose sense of being preoccupied with nature and rurality as setting, theme, and value in contradistinction from society and the urban. Systematic attempts to explain this preoccupation in terms of a general theory of American culture are almost as long-standing; they effectively begin with the first thesis book about American literature to endure, D. H. Lawrence's *Studies in Classic American Literature* (1923), and they still flourish. Their best results have been impressive. Yet we have not yet arrived at a sufficiently intricate and cosmopolitan model for understanding American pastoral. After a short review of some of the more important previous studies, I shall try to sketch such a model.

* * *

2. Pastoral Regression

What is ideologically[1] troublesome about classic American pastoral can be well illustrated by the conclusion of Thoreau's "Slavery in Massachusetts"

---

7. I do not mean this quite in the same sense as Leo Marx does when he says that in *Walden*, Thoreau "removes [the pastoral hope] from history, where it is manifestly unrealizable, and relocates it in literature [its traditional location]" (*The Machine in the Garden: Technology and the Pastoral Ideal in America* [New York: Oxford University Press, 1964], 265 [reprinted in this volume, p. 390]). In *Walden*, Thoreau is never so definitive as this, never completely removes his pastoral vision from history. This vision is "literary," to be sure, but literary rather in the same sense that Paul and Percival Goodman's alternative models of community are—imaginable, in some sense even realizable, human worlds. See their *Communitas: Means of Livelihood and Ways of Life* (New York: Random House, 1947), esp. chap. 1. Thoreau's pastoral is, we may say, creative and visionary in its exploration ("visioning") of the possibil-

ities of the future, both for the self and, by implication, for society.

† From *American Literary History* 1:1, 6–29. © 1989 Oxford University Press. Used with permission. *Walden* and "Resistance to Civil Government" page numbers refer to this Norton Critical Edition.

1. "Ideology" in this paper's usage refers to the literary text or mode's implicit theory of the social-political system, and in particular to the text or mode's position of dissent from or consent to the prevailing system. "Pastoral" is used in an extended sense, familiar to Americanists, to refer not to the specific set of obsolescent conventions of the eclogue tradition, but to all literature—poetry or prose, fiction or nonfiction—that celebrates the ethos of nature/rurality over against the ethos of the town or city. This domain includes for present purposes all degrees of rusticity from farm to wilderness.

(1854), a lecture delivered at the height of the controversy surrounding the case of the last escaped slave to be returned to slavery from that state. The final section constitutes what genre critic Andrew Ettin would call a "pastoral inset" within an otherwise directly political discourse.[2] "Slavery in Massachusetts" is indeed one of Thoreau's most incendiary performances, and its last section is one of its most provocative parts, not because of any overt political radicalism, but rather because of its abrupt-seeming swerve *from* that. The late events in Boston, declares Thoreau, seem to have permanently shaken our peaceful lives: "Who can be serene in a country where both the rulers and the ruled are without principle? The remembrance of my country spoils my walk. My thoughts are murder to the State, and involuntarily go plotting against her." "But," he adds, recovering himself,

> it chanced the other day that I scented a white water-lily, and a season I had waited for had arrived. It is the emblem of purity . . . extracted from the slime and muck of earth. I think I have plucked the first one that has opened for a mile. What confirmation of our hopes is in the fragrance of this flower! I shall not so soon despair of the world for it, notwithstanding slavery, and the cowardice and want of principle of Northern men.[3]

After working through this metaphor for another twenty lines or so, Thoreau ends his lecture on the same sardonic but hopeful note.

Thoreau's denouement poses the same rhetorical question Shakespeare posed in his great 65th sonnet:

> Since brass, nor stone, nor earth, nor boundless sea
> But sad mortality o'er-sways their power
> How with this rage shall beauty hold a plea
> Whose action is no stronger than a flower?

The inset's scenario replicates this sonnet's answer: beauty is threatened by a harsh reality that somehow beauty may miraculously contain at last. Yet beauty's victory may be a Pyrrhic one, in Thoreau if not in Shakespeare. In an Elizabethan sonnet, graceful idealization is the generic norm. But in a political jeremiad, the retort pastoral is much more vulnerable. "The remembrance of my country spoils my walk"—what sort of plea is that? My righteous indignation seems to dissolve into a sulk.

Now, there's no possibility that pitting the lily flower against the law was an isolated infelicitous mistake. Thoreau had done the same thing before at the end of "Resistance to Civil Government," which stresses that his first action upon release from jail, after completing his interrupted in-town errand, was to join "a huckleberry party, who were impatient to put themselves under my conduct."[4] And only a month after "Slavery in Massachusetts,"

2. Andrew Ettin, *Literature and the Pastoral* (New Haven, Yale University Press, 1984), 75–95.
3. *Reform Papers*, ed. Wendell Glick (Prince-ton: Princeton University Press, 1973), 108–109.
4. "Resistance to Civil Government" 241.

Thoreau published another work where the same gesture occurs at least twice more: *Walden*, where he ends his critique of institutionalized reform at the end of "Economy" by displacing it with an image of freedom within nature; and later on, when he retells the story of his imprisonment and release in miniature. What is disturbing about these incidents is of course the seeming insouciance with which the persona turns away from social confrontation for the sake of immersion in a simplified green world. That was one of the points about Thoreau that especially irritated the Brahmin establishment and that bothered even his mentor, Emerson. The now infamous passage in Emerson's funeral address chiding Thoreau for being content to "be captain of a huckleberry party" when he might have been "engineering for all America" may have been prompted by that passage from "Resistance to Civil Government."[5] In the still common 1960s parlor game of praising Thoreau at Emerson's expense, this passage is one of the proof texts cited against the guru. Yet it is understandable, under the circumstances, that Emerson should have been moved to say it.

Indeed, not just quasi-pastoralists, like Emerson, but also full-fledged ones, have been hard put to deal with the Peter Pan-like side of themselves even at the very point of indulgence. A telling moment of this sort comes in the Civil War-time diary of one of Thoreau's most important successors in the next generation of literary naturalists, John Burroughs. In a passage that makes an arresting complement to Thoreau's, Burroughs reports a springtime visit with a friend to the woods outside the city of Washington.

> It was a superb day without a cloud, with a soft wind—one of those strong, positive days—a he-day—impregnating the earth with the generative principle of sunshine. Just as we were about to enter one of those deep wooded nooks on Piney Branch, eager and expectant, we saw two soldiers just ahead of us. I felt vexed and as if they had no business there. Had I possessed the authority, I should have ordered them back, for I could not get over the feeling that they would drive away something I was after, some influence, some wood spirit or kindly genie that needed to be approached as gently and devoutly as possible . . . though habitually I respect and love these Bluecoats above all men. So we were obliged to lie down on the leaves and wait till the pollution of their presence had passed off, and the privacy of the woods restored—the coy nymphs all back again.[6]

Unfortunately, Burroughs's troubles are compounded when he finds that the soldiers are out there for target practice.

Here, then, is a very concrete example of one's walk being spoiled by the state. In relaying it, Burroughs discloses even more than Thoreau. Most conspicuously, Burroughs, being a dutiful Treasury Department bureaucrat

---

5. Ralph Waldo Emerson, "Emerson's 'Thoreau': A New Edition from Manuscript." In *Studies in the American Renaissance, 1979*, ed. Joel Myerson (Boston, G. K. Hall, 1979), 53,

reprinted in this volume, p. 332.
6. *The Heart of Burroughs's Journals*, ed. Clara Barrus (Boston: Houghton, 1928), 36–37.

and a pro- rather than antigovernment man, is acutely, embarrassedly aware of his duplicity: of how his pursuit of nature's charms pulls against his role as good citizen. So his passage openly confesses to retreat from the arena, as Thoreau's does not. On a less conscious level, the passage bears all the telltale marks of the discourse of nature-as-elite-androcentric-preserve: the generative metaphor so redolent of Burroughs's friend Whitman (the "he-day—impregnating the earth"), the Fiedleresque ritual of male bonding in the woods, the obvious class difference between the meditative and military recreations of white collar and bluecoat. All of which can easily be read back into Thoreau the Harvard-educated and genteelly subsidized misogynist nature lover. That is certainly one legitimate image of him, though not the only one.

The reading of the pastoral turn in Thoreau and Burroughs as reflex regression, silently protected by the privileges of class and gender, is strengthened by some salient episodes in the history of Thoreau's rise to canonization during the fifty years after his death. We find here a telltale schism. Thoreau's growing appeal to American readers was based much more on the domesticated image of him as literary naturalist than the image of him as economic/political radical. That too became crucial in time, but initially it was the foundation of his fame in Britain and Europe, not here. Not until Thoreau's American fame was secure can we find an American discussion, academic or popular, that thinks "Resistance to Civil Government" just as important as *Walden*: John Macy's *The Spirit of American Literature* (1913), which by no coincidence also happens to be the first full-scale reading of the American literary tradition in terms of the now commonplace theme that the great American writers ought to be defined in terms of their anti-establishmentarianism.[7] Until then, it seemed, to quote one of the two avid bird-watchers who coedited Thoreau's *Journals* (1906), that the American public had agreed to see Thoreau not as the preacher of nonconformity, but as the interpreter of nature:

> For those who have settled down to take things as they are, having knocked under and gone with the stream, in Thoreau's language, it is pleasanter to read of beds of water-lilies flashing open at sunrise [again that fateful water-lily image] or of a squirrel's pranks upon a bough, than of daily aspiration after an ideal excellence. Whatever the reason, Thoreau is to the many the man who lived out of doors, and wrote of outdoor things.[8]

The same went for the editor, Bradford Torrey, despite his insinuation to the contrary. Torrey did also relish Thoreau's cantankerousness, even to the point of taking up solitary cabin-living in later life, but he was drawn to Thoreau in the first instance as amateur botanist and nature lover. In this

7. Among the various studies of Thoreau's reputation, see especially Eugene Timpe, ed., *Thoreau Abroad* (Hamden: Archon, 1971), and George Hendrick and Fritz Oehlschlaeger, eds., *Toward the Making of Thoreau's Modern Reputation* (Urbana: University of Illinois Press, 1979), 12–24.

8. Bradford Torrey, *Friends on the Shelf* (Boston: Houghton, 1906), 100.

he joined most of Thoreau's other prominent American endorsers by choosing—whether sincerely or tactically or both—to put less emphasis on Thoreau's iconoclasm than on the more consensual image of Thoreau as the
keen observer of nature's secrets, thereby bearing out in advance D. H.
Lawrence's adage that "absolutely the safest thing to get your emotional
reactions over is NATURE."[9]

3. *Pastoral's Multiple Frames*

But is that always so? Can American masculinist pastoral be so easily
typed? Let us look again at those two passages from Thoreau and Burroughs.
There's another important difference between them than the one noted
before, a difference that cuts the opposite way. The Burroughs passage does
indeed present a scene of interrupted innocence thereby exposed as willful:
the speaker shook the dust of civilization from his feet, but then civilization
broke back in, revealing his capacity for double-think. The Thoreau passage
speaks directly from the start to the difficulty of shaking civilization off—
the state invades even so private a sector as the state of nature. However
much the lily flower is an agent of escape on the narrative level, rhetorically
it is a bomb thrown at the state. In fact, given the lily's figural status as an
indictment of the slime of the mundane, only in a limited sense does it
usher us away from the original context and into a natural scene at all,
although Thoreau tells us that he met with it on an actual walk. Whereas
on the level of the action, the passage seems to support the notion of nature
as a refuge from complexity, on the rhetorical level the flower is arguably
not so much a mystification as a self-conscious device for exposing public
consensus as repressive and arbitrary. Although Thoreau tells a story of
having escaped from politics in life, by reinventing that experience as political
allegory Thoreau puts it in an entirely different category from the naive
escapism with which Burroughs's sortie began.

Perhaps I have tried too hard to exonerate Thoreau here, but at least my
rereading should have shown that the job of setting a pastoral moment in
an appropriate ideological frame is trickier than it might seem, indeed that
the same decoding process may not suffice for reading lyrical celebrations
of nature's beauty even in cases as ostensibly similar as these two authors.
Two more examples will help to develop this point, the first from a latter-
day Thoreauvian, the second from Thoreau himself.

Aldo Leopold's *Sand County Almanac* (1949) is a classic of modern
environmental writing although not usually included in American literature
syllabi. For those interested in artful prose about nature from the early natural
historians to the present, Leopold occupies what might be called a kind of
"enclave canon" status comparable to, say, Paul Laurence Dunbar and Jean
Toomer in black American writing or Catharine Sedgwick and Charlotte

9. D. H. Lawrence, *Studies in Classic American Literature* (New York: Doubleday, 1951), 33.

Perkins Gilman in American women's writing—meaning that these are now pivotal figures within their respective discourses, yet still not figures that general survey-course pedagogues and literary historians feel obliged to treat more than in passing, if that. Perhaps one day they will. In any event, *Sand County Almanac* clusters a series of essays in an arresting three-part structure: first, a seasonally arranged series of prose poems and anecdotes set at Leopold's woodsy Wisconsin weekend retreat; second, topical essays inspired by different places elsewhere around the country; and third, a series of longer, more issue-oriented essays like "The Biotic Community" and "The Land Ethic" that press points of ecological doctrine. The aim is to create a symbiosis of art and polemic, such that environmental representation and lyricism exist for their own sake, yet also, in addition, ex post facto, as a means to make the reader more receptive to environmental advocacy. This approach makes apparent pictorialism seems increasingly less innocuous, roughly the obverse of Thoreau's approach in *Walden*, which opens with the doctrine of economy and later moves to something closer to description and narration. Leopold's tactic is first to lull the reader into an idyllic mood, then broach the more controversial critique and solution needed to preserve the experience of beauty and intimacy with nature that has previously been dramatized. Beauty thus does in a sense become a form of action, as Shakespeare's sonnet promises.

Leopold's reversal of Thoreauvian procedure illuminates both writers in the way it intertwines art and activism. Leopold, like Ansel Adams and Eliot Porter in the field of photography, shows as his book moves through its various sections how the ostensibly self-contained and idealized artifact can serve the role of change agent through strategic reframing: in their case, as Sierra Club books, calendars, promotional pieces, and the like; in Leopold's case, as the experimental dimension of an emerging rhetorical appeal.

We find a version of this also in an especially luminous passage in Thoreau's "Where I Lived and What I Lived For," in which with charming mock-innocence the speaker ruminates on the farm he almost bought instead of building his cabin.

> The real attractions of the Hollowell farm, to me, were; its complete retirement, being about two miles from the village, half a mile from the nearest neighbor, and separated from the highway by a broad field; its bounding on the river, which the owner said protected it by its fogs from frosts in the spring, though that was nothing to me; the gray color and ruinous state of the house and barn, and the dilapidated fences, which put such an interval between me and the last occupant; the hollow and lichen-covered apple trees, gnawed by rabbits, showing what kind of neighbors I should have; but above all, the recollection I had of it from my earliest voyages up the river, when the house was concealed behind a dense grove of red maples, through which I heard the house-dog bark.[1]

1. *Walden* 56.

This passage aims both to mesmerize with nostalgic charm and to affront readerly allegiances. It is lyricized to the point of narcissism (with the retreat to childhood fantasy at the end), but lyrical regression is not indulged so much as transposed into sly satire. I chose this farm, the passage says, deliberately for the wrong reasons. I liked how inconvenient it was from the market center. I liked its dilapidation. Its one practical advantage (protection from fogs) didn't matter. My notion of use value is the opposite of yours, which is based on exchange—so there. Pastoral hedonism becomes an indictment of the deadening pragmatism of agrarian economy. Altogether, Thoreau's strategy here resembles what the domestic fiction of his day did when it challenged readers to take seriously the Victorian idealization of women's moral sensibility. Without exactly repudiating the status quo, agrarian rather than patriarchal in this case, Thoreau prods readers to consider how wide is the gap between scrabbling actuality and picturesque Jeffersonian ideal, according to which the ethos of farming empowers, not frustrates, the pursuit of culture.[2]

Here and elsewhere in pastoral, beauty never functions *only* as instrument of critique; always at some level there is the chance that the text will tempt the reader to see all sugar and no pill and that even hard thrusts will get deflected into petty excursions. American texts are particularly susceptible to this because of the ease with which dissent can get co-opted as an aspect of consensus. As David Shi shows in his history of the dream of *The Simple Life* in America—a book bearing directly on pastoral art although not about aesthetics as such—the dream of a disencumbered, stripped down life has the potential to become a socially disruptive force, but also, given its historic sponsorship by hegemonic groups (like the Puritan fathers and the Founders) to become an ultrarespectable plank in American civil religion, and thus as much of a placebo as *e pluribus unum*.[3]

Conversely, however, the dream of the simple life and the pastoral aesthetic can assume radical form in proportion to the degree the establishment seems arrayed against them. A powerful motif in black American writing, emanating from slave narrative, is the denial to blacks of the bounty masters enjoy at their expense. Frederick Douglass's *Narrative* crystallizes this beautifully in the image of the master tarring his garden fence so that any fruit-snatching slave will be found out and whipped.[4]

2. Thoreau's relation to the Concord farmers is more complex than can be fully explored here. See especially Robert Gross, " 'The Most Estimable Place in All the World': A Debate on Progress in Nineteenth-Century Concord" in *Studies in the American Renaissance, 1978*, ed. Joel Myerson (Boston: Twayne, 1978), 1–15, and "Agriculture and Society in Thoreau's Concord," *Journal of American History* 69 (1982), 42–61.

3. Shi's conclusion is that "though a failure as a societal ethic, simplicity has nevertheless exercised a powerful influence on the complex patterns of American culture," serving as "the nation's conscience" in such a way as to entitle us to expect it "will persist both as an enduring myth and as an actual way of living" [*The Simple Life: Plain Living and High Thinking in American Culture* (New York: Oxford University Press), 278–79]. These formulations appropriately straddle the issue of its orthodoxy, typing the simple life as both consensual and deviant.

4. Frederick Douglass, *Narrative of the Life of Frederick Douglass, an American Slave* (New York: New American Library, 1968), 33.

Through this image, Douglass both undermines plantation-style pastoral (by contrasting the aesthetic level of the rich slaveholder's pride in his well-kept manse with the very practical, urgent hunger that his tidy order imposes on his slaves) and makes that order a standard of appeal: surely the slave, too, is entitled to the same benefits that the planter—and the average well-intentioned Yankee reader of slave narratives—takes for granted. Richard Wright's "Big Boy Leaves Home" reinvents the classic American male-bonding-in-nature story in protest against the excision of blacks from the American arcadia. Ignoring a local farmer's proscription against blacks in his swimming hole, Big Boy and his friends enjoy a moment of innocence and release—interrupted by a spiral of violence: murder, lynching, and Big Boy's expulsion from the South.[5] Here too, white injustice is dramatized by the scene of exclusion from pastoral fulfillment.

Native American writing at times shows even greater pastoral radicalism than this, when instead of presenting merely a scene of exclusion from a familiar arcadia, it redefines the terms of that arcadia in the process. The route, for instance, by which the protagonist in Leslie Silko's *Ceremony* (1977) is transformed from broken-down GI to tribal savior is through a retreat to nature that reorients him by putting him in touch with primal power, expressed through a symbolic geography grounded in an intricately culture-specific sense of place accessible to mainstream readers only through scholarly mediations, and resting on a communalistic land ethic alien to American assumptions about property rights.[6]

Pastoral radicalism can also be seen in writers closer to the mainstream. Rachel Carson's *Silent Spring* (1964), a landmark exposé of the environmental impact of pesticides that also merits scrutiny as creative writing, starts out with an elegiac, Thornton Wilderesque fantasy of the death of a typical our town. It is a pastoral inset that trades very strongly on the old dream of the simple life that Shi describes, but hardly a mere nostalgia piece, since it was designed and was perceived to be a direct challenge to the chemical industry. To read it as regressive fantasy is to read it the same way the industry's defenders sought to make us read it. A similar claim can be made on behalf of Wendell Berry's revival of Jeffersonian agrarianism as a weapon

5. Richard Wright, *Uncle Tom's Children* (New York: New American Library, 1947), 18–49. The point about Afro-American pastoral could be ramified further by taking into account a case like Zora Neale Hurston's *Their Eyes Were Watching God*, whose protagonist's adventures begin with rebellion against her confinement in the farmer's wife role to which her grandmother consigns her for the sake of protection and security. Janie's subsequent move into an increasingly unsocialized and increasingly natural environment oddly—and I would suppose fortuitously—echoes the social secessions depicted by Cooper and Thoreau and Twain. At any rate, Hurston's protagonist exposes the restrictiveness of the pastoral life as institutionalized by black males who have been able to overcome the barriers against which Douglass and Wright rage, thereby implying that the radicalism in their narratives is ultimately less a protest against mainstream life rhythms than a protest against being excluded from those.

6. For insight into Silko's cultural matrix, I am especially indebted to the research of my colleague Edith Swan, who has written several important papers on Silko. See esp. "Laguna Symbolic Geography in Silko's *Ceremony*," *American Indian Quarterly* 12 (Summer 1988), 229–49.

against agribusiness and what Berry sees as the myopic cosmopolitanism of the average American today. Clearly that agrarian vision has a different political valence for Berry than for Jefferson. For Jefferson it would have seemed something like the status quo; for Berry it is deliberately anticonsensual, an insurgency of the disempowered.[7]

This scattergram of examples should suffice to demonstrate that American pastoral representation cannot be linked to a single ideological position. Even at its ostensibly most culpable moment—the moment of willful retreat from social and political responsibility—it may actually be more strategized than mystified. As a final and more extended example of this, I want now to examine in more detail the particular case of women's pastoral, given that the literary pursuit of nature has so generally been reckoned a male domain by traditional and revisionist critics alike.

4. Women on Nature

The recent gains of feminist revisionism, in making the important points that American wilderness romance is a male tradition and that women's frontier experience sharply differed from men's, should not block us from seeing how American pastoral modes have also historically functioned as a vehicle of empowerment for women writers. While researching literary nature writing from Thoreau's day to ours. I was surprised to discover the degree of interdependence between the "major" male figures and the work and commentary of women writers less well known. Roughly half the nature essays contributed to the *Atlantic Monthly* during the late nineteenth century—when the nature essay became a recognized genre—were by female authors.[8] Among early appraisals of Thoreau, I found, to my surprise, given the predominant notion of Thoreau as appealing more to men than women, that commentaries by women were much more likely to be favorable than those by men. The first book, to my knowledge, published by an outsider to the Transcendentalist circle that celebrates nature as a refuge from hypercivilization, with explicit invocation of Thoreau as model and precursor, was written by a woman. The first Thoreau Society was founded by a group of young women in 1891; the first doctoral dissertation on Thoreau was written by a woman (1898).[9] John Burroughs presents an even more conspicuous case of a literary naturalist with a large female following. Burroughs believed his most sympathetic readers were women; and his literary executrix, in her biography, stresses that appeal, explaining that turn-of-the-century

7. See especially Wendell Berry, *The Unsettling of America* (San Francisco: Sierra Club Books, 1977).
8. The more important female contributors of such work include Sarah Orne Jewett, Celia Thaxter, Edith Thomas, Olive Thorne Miller, and Sophia Kirk.
9. The early Thoreauvian book is Elizabeth

Wright's, discussed in more detail below. For the early society see Walter Harding, "An Early Thoreau Club," *Thoreau Society Bulletin* 77 (Fall 1961): 3–4. The early dissertation, since lost, was by Ella A. Knapp; see Raymond Borst, *Henry David Thoreau: A Reference Guide, 1835–1899* (Boston: G. K. Hall, 1987), 133–34.

women looked upon nature excursions as a means of liberation from the parlor.[1] This is borne out by the records of what seems to have been our oldest national botanical society, the Torrey Botanical Club (organized shortly after the Civil War). The club included women almost from the first who regularly contributed to its bulletin and sometimes organized themselves in local groups. Of the first, thirty-two Syracuse women who joined forces to specialize in ferns, the *Bulletin* sagely noted: "This organization is admirable, and might profitably be imitated, where practicable."[2]

It would therefore seem that patriarchy considered nature observation safe for women as well as for men but also that women were ready to use this consensus assertively as a base of operation. That makes good historical sense. To begin with, the prototypes for nineteenth-century representation of men and women's experience vis-à-vis nature are not so discrepant as is sometimes assumed. Writers of both sexes commonly picture the early childhood stage of both sexes as a state of natural piety: the first books of Elizabeth Barrett Browning's poetic bildungsroman *Aurora Leigh* resemble those of *The Prelude* in this respect; the child-seer of the nineteenth-century literary fountainhead of Anglo-American natural piety, Wordsworth's Immortality Ode, is virtually sexless, or androgynous; and in American writing influenced by its vision the child is more often female than male.[3] In adolescence, female protagonists become socialized away from nature, while the male continues to enjoy freer mobility and the option of questing and conquest within nature that is frequently and revealingly symbolized as female. Beginning well before Thoreau, male narratives of self-reliant cabin-dwelling isolators are common, whereas the commonest counterpart narrative of women's experience is the story of the "female hermit" who has not risen above society but fallen below it as a result of a disastrous love affair, usually extralegal, that has left her with a child, who usually dies. For cases like Joanna, the hermit of Shell-heap Island in Jewett's *Country of the Pointed Firs*, nature is where you go if you have no place to go. Yet the personal bond to nature can also retain a more positive value for the mature woman protagonist, who as Annis Pratt and Barbara White put it, may "look back to moments of naturistic epiphany as touchstones in a quest for her lost selfhood."[4] This is precisely how Thoreau pictures himself when confessing that one of his earliest childhood memories was of being taken to Walden Pond, so that by his return to live there "I have at length helped to clothe that fabulous landscape of my infant dreams."[5] A similar reenactment process

1. Clara Barrus, *The Life and Letters of John Burroughs* (Boston: Houghton, 1925), 1:333–334; 2:294–319. Burroughs was undoubtedly influenced in part by the very enthusiastic receptions he received at Vassar and Smith.
2. Torrey Botanical Club, *Bulletin* 55–56 (1879), 330.
3. Anne T. Trensky, "The Saintly Child in Nineteenth-Century American Fiction," *Prospects 1*, ed. Jack Salzman (New York: Burt Franklin, 1975), 389—413.
4. *Archetypal Patterns of Women's Fiction* (Sussex: Harvester, 1981), 17.
5. *Walden* 104. From my previous discussion of Thoreau's Hollowell farm passage, I hope it is clear that neither this passage nor the formation described by Pratt and White should be thought of as innocently "regressive."

is evident in the work of the early female Thoreauvian mentioned above. Having been cosmopolitanized after an Allegheny girlhood and a purgatorial stint of pioneering in Illinois, Elizabeth Wright returns with a group of friends for a holiday in the woods of northwestern Pennsylvania. Self-conscious though she is about the element of playacting ("like overgrown children"), she considers herself a good woodswoman and longs "for the cool pure liberty of their hidden depths." To those of her companions overbaggaged with "civilized rubbish,"[6] Wright quotes Thoreau on simplification, from which ensues a pungent running commentary on how nature gives the lie to civilized distinctions and in particular the niceties of conduct that hem tenderfoot women in: "I wondered then, more than ever, where people ever get the absurd notion of talking about 'refined' and 'vulgar,' or 'masculine' and 'feminine' employments. It sounds as ridiculous as the French way of calling knives masculine and forks feminine. My knives are no more masculine than my forks. Elvira's shooting was as feminine as her curls, and the Professor's cooking as manly as his beard."[7] The keyed-up jauntiness of the rhetoric here reassures the more conventional reader that despite appearances this is not going to be a revolutionary manifesto, only a temporary carnivalesque inversion of the proprieties. But it *is* an inversion: a sustained exercise in limit-bumping whereby nature empowers mid-Victorian woman to level the social distinctions that gall her.

Along the way, Wright also sets herself against other female appropriations of nature, such as the "satiny, perfumed" nature rhetoric in gift books or the "twaddle" of botany textbooks written for young women.[8] In the work of the less outspoken of the nineteenth-century female naturists, such distinctions are more subtle, though not invisible. A case in point would be the significant literary season book that stands closest in time to Thoreau's *Walden*—though the fact is rarely noted: Susan Cooper's *Rural Hours* (1850, revised 1887). This is a calendar of natural and cultural history observations that shows a Dorothy Wordsworth-like keenness of minute perception combined with an expressive gift. It is enlightening to think for a moment of this text as a center of meditation on classic American nature writing instead of, say, the forest romances of her father James Fenimore.

At first sight, Susan Cooper seems sedately entrenched within the sphere of decorous floral observation. Unlike her litigious father, she does not confront head-on the burning contemporary sociopolitical issues any more than Dorothy Wordsworth does, and in this and several other respects, *Rural Hours* exhibits the characteristic differences of style we have been taught to find in precontemporary women's narrative as opposed to men's: the figure of the experiencer is played down relative to the object described; the setting is more local, within the circuit of the writer's own daily excursions; and the mimetic level is less romanticized. Cooper's low-key matter-of-factness,

6. Elizabeth Wright, *Lichen Tufts, from the Alleghanies* (New York: Doolady, 1860), 11, 16.

7. Ibid., 51.

8. Ibid., 29–30.

however, paradoxically allows her to press beyond her father's conservatism in some areas. In place of his romantic savagism, which sees Indians as a doomed archaic race because the twain can never meet, she argues for an integrationism whereby "men of Indian blood may be numbered among the wise and the good, laboring in behalf of our common country."[9] Whereas her father had Natty Bumppo elegize over the "wasty ways" of the settlers in *The Pioneers* and *The Prairie*, she makes a specific recommendation about the conservation of trees, a decade before Thoreau did.[1] Although in no sense ready to go so far as Thoreau or even her father in praising the wild above the good, Cooper does show a projective empathy for nature's rhythms as a corrective to the human-built: it is more than fortuitous that her narrative structure implicitly asserts the necessity for the human order to accommodate itself to the natural one as well as vice versa.

As the previous examples suggest, Cooper's instinct, unlike Wright's, is to valorize the natural by incorporating it into a vision of society brought closer to nature, not to set society and individual free expression at odds. The latter is present only as a latency in *Rural Hours*, as for instance in Cooper's most detailed set piece of wildlife description, on the hummingbird, concerning which these two interesting points emerge: that its cute dainty diminutiveness is deceptive (hummingbirds are actually bold and confident), and that a major threat to its existence is its tendency to fly indoors and get trapped there. "We have repeatedly known them found dead in rooms little used," Cooper writes.[2] Clearly, *Rural Hours* cannot be read as "The Yellow Wallpaper," but I would suggest that the prevailing sedateness of the female, season-book norm warrants our being brought up short by the implicit vehemence of such passages, and that consequently we should also see such a passage as embedding a more substantial challenge to status quo perceptions, both about hummingbirds and the power or vulnerability of diminutive creatures in general than we would ascribe to a passage of the same decibel level in Thoreau. To take another example, Thoreau risked nothing when he praised Walt Whitman, flanked as Thoreau was by sympathetic Transcendental brethren; but for a female *Atlantic* contributor, Edith Thomas, to begin a mid-1880s nature essay on "Grass" with an epigraph from Whitman, a few years after *Leaves of Grass* was banned in Boston, was a courageous act of self-assertion, chaste though the ensuing discourse was by comparison.[3]

This undertone surfaces in Mary Austin's turn-of-the-century books and stories about the California desert, starting with *Land of Little Rain* (1903). Unlike Thoreau, Austin rarely parades the "I," and, in keeping with the

---

9. Susan Cooper, *Rural Hours*, ed. David Jones (Syracuse: Syracuse University Press, 1968), 123.
1. Ibid., 153.

2. Ibid., 81.
3. In Edith Thomas, *The Round Year* (Boston: Houghton, 1886), 73.

predominant tradition in women's rural writing, she ends *Little Rain* with a vision of community: an idyllic Chicano village. But the narrative, typically for Austin, conspicuously deploys a prickly, authoritative, aggressive persona. She disorients, for instance, by refusing to draw a clear map of her territory for the tenderfoot and by often insisting on using the Indian place name rather than the one on the map; this becomes part of a strategy, despite disclaimers of ignorance on various points, of stressing insider's nature knowledge (as well as culture knowledge, Indian and Chicano) and thereby pulling the whole territory away from prior Anglo claims to it—both legal and interpretative—into a domain of which she alone is the interpreter. One small sign of her imaginative conquest is a fondness for peremptory declaratives: "This is the nature of that country," "Mesa trails were meant to be traveled on horseback," etc.[4] In the process, Austin is careful to discredit masculine romance about the west à la Bret Harte, sketching *her* version of a remote frontier town in an anthropological, realist retort to "The Luck of Roaring Camp." Ultimately, the Austin persona beats Harte's narrator in realism, in toughness, *and* in bonding to the environment.

To align Wright, Cooper, and especially Austin with Thoreau is to form a picture of "men's" and "women's" representation of wildness blending into each other to the point that distinctions begin to seem very porous. *Walden* executes the antisocial, individualistic flight from the settlements featured in masculine wilderness romance, but the break is not total, the woods are not too dark and deep, the experience becomes domesticated as the lifestyle is expatiated and the protagonist's lococentrism is stressed, and the persona remains always in dialogue with—and always to that extent a member of—the community whose norms he rejects. (All this may help account for the positive reaction toward Thoreau I have found among his early female readers.)[5] *Little Rain* tells no such story of the writer's repudiation of community and indeed barely allows the persona to exist as an independent character; but the persona speaks from the position of being *in* the wilderness, and in personal confrontation with the complacencies of settlement culture, alienated from these both in space and in soul. Altogether, it would seem that premodern women's nature writing was, like the Thoreauvian counterpart, capable of serving in various degrees as a vehicle for questioning social consensus and the claims of individual self-realization against social constraint, and that the pressure of that dissent, owing to differential gender expectations, ought to be reckoned as greater than at first it seems.

4. Mary Austin, *Land of Little Rain. Stories from the Country of Lost Borders*, ed. Marjorie Pryse (New Brunswick: Rutgers University Press, 1987), 9, 83. For an excellent appraisal and a bibliography of criticism of this much neglected author, see Pryse's introduction.
5. See for example the most ambitious early appraisal of Thoreau by a woman writer, Annie Russell Marble, which strongly emphasizes Thoreau's normality as son, brother, and Concord resident and argues that his idiosyncrasies have been much overstated. *Thoreau: His Home, Friends and Books* (New York: Crowell, 1902).

5. Conclusions

We have seen that the ideological valence of pastoral writing cannot be determined without putting the text in a contextual frame. As Houston Baker has said about how ostensibly similar motifs are handled in white and black American writing, ostensibly similar terms bear quite different iconic significances depending on context.[6] The retreat to nature *can* be a form of willed amnesia, as in the Burroughs passage; but it means something different when held up self-consciously, as in Thoreau, to appeal to an alternative set of values over and against the baleful dominant one. It means something still different, when that alternative framework is employed, as in Elizabeth Wright, for whom that framework is not as socially predictable and acceptable a vocabulary as it was for a literary man. And it means something different from that when the alternative vocabulary is itself less conventionalized than it is in either Thoreau or Wright, both of whom are, after all, appealing to notions of the romantic and the picturesque that had strong imaginative currency for middlebrow readers of the age, when found in their "proper" setting, e.g. Wordsworthian poetry or, for that matter, a Shakespearean sonnet. In effect, at the end of "Slavery in Massachusetts" Thoreau produces the "unacceptable" by imposing a very stereotypical image from another context. By contrast to this should be distinguished Wendell Berry's appeal to an agrarian ideal of a nuts-and-bolts literalism that was normative in nineteenth-century thought but that today is far more alien to the average book reader than Thoreau's idiom. And from *this* might be distinguished still more revolutionary pastoralisms that never did have mainstream status to begin with, like the lesbian-ecofeminist vision of Susan Griffin's *Woman and Nature: The Roaring Inside Her* (1978).

But an "ideological grammar" of American pastoral cannot stop at trying to make distinctions among different categories of work.[7] It must also recognize the crosscurrents that keep any one example from seeming pure: on the one hand, the centripetal pull of consensualism that always more or less threatens to draw the radical text over into the sleepy safe domain of nature's nationism, the ho-hum pieties of American civil religion; and, on the other, the centrifugal impulse always latent, though usually contained within modest limits, for pastoral to form itself in opposition to social institutions of whatever sort. This duality was built into American pastoral thinking from the start, for it was conceived as a dream both hostile to the standing order of civilization (decadent Europe, later hypercivilizing America) yet at the same time a model for the civilization in the process of being built. So American pastoral was always both counterinstitutional and institutionally sponsored. * * *

But how pressing an issue will it continue to be? Given our present degree

6. Houston Baker, *Blues, Ideology, and Afro-American Literature* (Chicago: University of Chicago Press, 1984), e.g., 11–12, 24, 66–67 (on railroads, jeremiads, and "America" as sign).

7. I borrow the phrase from Myra Jehlen, *American Incarnation: The Individual, the Nation, and the Continent* (Cambridge: Harvard University Press, 1986), 21.

of industrialization, isn't pastoral likely to become increasingly obsolete as a literary and cultural force? Probably not, for two reasons. One is that environmental holocaust now seems not only the consequence of holocaust via bomb but at least as imminent a peril in its own right. Owing to this and other social disaffections, as Leo Marx has recently pointed out, we have been faced, since the 1960s, with the novel phenomenon of a "left-leaning ideology not based on a progressive world view"[8] that challenges us to reexamine our most obstinate myth of historical development. Hitherto, contemporary intellectuals have been accustomed to thinking of rusticity rather as they think of God: surely both are myths that effectively died out in the nineteenth century. Urbanization, even more tenaciously than secularization, is one of those larger myths in whose existence intellectuals continue to believe even after they disavow the doctrine of history's linear movement. The "age of ecology," as environmental historian Donald Worster labels the present era, may not lead to more than a marginal change in social attitudes or public policy toward further technological buildup; but even if it doesn't, indeed perhaps especially if it doesn't, pastoralism is sure to remain a luminous ideal and to take on increasingly radical forms for some time to come. One mark of this is the contemporary tradition of environmental apocalypse literature: Carson's *Silent Spring*, John Brunner's *The Sheep Look Up*, Ernest Callenbach's *Ecotopia*, Jonathan Schell's *The Fate of the Earth*. The forgettable, ephemeral quality of most of this writing does not rule out the possibility of a long-range literary impact.[9]

Second, and of more specifically literary concern, pastoral ideology is a powerful lens through which to see our literary culture, not only within but also across cultural boundaries. American pastoralism is ultimately not so much a mark of American exceptionalism as one means by which we may overcome the parochialism of American literary studies and understand American literary history as part of its larger reference group of postcolonial literatures in European languages. In closing, I should like briefly to develop this theme.

*   *   *

For present purposes, the main point I would stress about the value of placing American pastoral in postcolonial context is that it corroborates and further illuminates American pastoral's ideological multivalence. The one comparative example that will have to stand here for all is the first African-English novel to be acclaimed a national and indeed world classic: Chinua Achebe's *Things Fall Apart*. This novel, which traces the precolonial phase of a turn-of-the-century Ibo village through the early stages of British conquest, is both a radical and a conservative document. In its radical aspect

---

8. Leo Marx, "Pastoralism in America." In *Ideology and Classic American Literature*, ed. Sacvan Bercovitch and Myra Jehlen (Cambridge: Cambridge University Press, 1986), 66.

9. Quotation from Donald Worster, *Nature's Economy* (New York: Doubleday, 1979), 340–349.

it counters the discourse of colonialism and its continuing dominance in standard literary history (*Heart of Darkness* being Achebe's special *bête blanche*) by representing the kind of primitive society to which Conrad gave no voice. The novel is in this sense an anti-imperial text on two levels: as an insurrectionary act on the part of its author, and as the portrayal of a premodern civilization equivalent in complexity to that of the colonizer: complex not just in the sense of being culturally rich but in the sense of containing internal contradictions and competing interests that make it both vulnerable to decay and capable of self-transformation by turning the instruments of colonization to its own account. In short, Achebe's Umuofia is neither the Eden of the romantic colonizer nor a negritudinist idyll. Yet the novel's plot is nonetheless susceptible of being read as a loss of innocence narrative, as an elegy for a vanished age of archaic, albeit barbarian, grandeur that carried with it a degree of traditional richness and cultural holism no longer available to the modern age. In its aspect as radical pastoral, the novel rewrites the received version of history codified in Euro-American canonical literature and contributes to critical analysis of the historical class and role structures of its own society during its premodern phase. In its aspect as conservative pastoral, the book taps into the familiar Western plot paradigms of historical novel (the heroic feudal or tribal age displaced by the pragmatic bourgeois era) and heroic tragedy (the rise and fall of the great but flawed warrior, Okonkwo). These elements of stylistic and visionary conservatism have undoubtedly helped speed the novel's rise to canonization.[1]

In American literature, this particular kind of doubleness is visible especially in minority writing. For example, Leslie Silko's *Ceremony*, mentioned earlier, uses the motif of the protagonist's return to nature both in a radical way (it purges Tayo of the mental illness that has been caused by the abuses emanating from white society and thereby helps restore spiritual, social, and economic vigor to the pueblo) and also in an accommodationist way: it takes him through an ennobling quest-and-return process that can be experienced as universal myth, especially by the many mainstream readers who respond to nature as a spiritual solace—above all when personified, as here, by a beautiful and mysterious young woman. But a similar duality can also be seen in classic writers like Thoreau. The move to Walden is both a divisive critique of mainstream values like the Protestant work ethic and a ritual reenactment of the pioneer experience, New England style,

1. For Achebe's indictment of Conrad, see his "Image of Africa," *Massachusetts Review* 18 (1977), 782–794. In characterizing *Things Fall Apart* as a pastoral tragedy, I would certainly differentiate his Umuofia from, say, the negritudinist Eden in Camara Laye's *L'Enfant Noir* (1954), a pastoral work that stands in relation to Achebe's as the Burroughs passage discussed earlier does to the conclusion to Thoreau's "Slavery in Massachusetts." Achebe is careful, as Raymond Williams notes, to dramatize "the internal tensions of the society, so that we can understand the modes of penetration which would in any case, with its process of expansion, have come" [*The Country and the City* (New York: Oxford University Press, 1973), 286]. My point is that there are strains of both critical realism and cultural nationalism in the novel.

with which the average reader can vicariously identify.[2] It is a mistake to resolve either image into the other.

In each of the three texts just noted, pastoral becomes a means of expressing alienation, yet also, on another level, a means by which alienation is mediated. It invites normalization to the extent that it permits the reader to experience it as an archetypal story of lost innocence or green world immersion. It resists co-optation and becomes an oppositional act to the extent that it pursues an indictment of social pathology and oppression. Which dimension gets stressed depends partly on who is reading, partly— as we saw earlier—on the different locations of the individual texts along the ideological spectrum from radical to recessive.[3] In any case, these two faces are the Tityrus and Meliboeus of postcolonial pastoral: the happy, co-opted shepherd and the dispossessed, alienated shepherd of Virgil's first Eclogue, where the preexisting convention of pastoral debate was first self-consciously ideologized. Today, the specific terms have altered, but the debate continues.

2. For the suggestion that *Walden* replicates the settlement of Concord, see Stanley Cavell, *The Senses of Walden* (San Francisco: North Point Press, 1981), 8–10.
3. This hasty formulation cannot do justice to the fine distinctions among the three texts just discussed. *Walden* spells out a serious antiestablishment program in most explicit detail; *Ceremony* dramatizes the antithesis between white and Laguna realms most extensively and bitterly while acknowledging at a more philosophical level (through Tayo's mentor Betonie) the need for Indian culture selectively to appropriate white knowledge rather than just repudiate it; *Things Fall Apart* dramatizes an instance of even starker opposition between cultures, but also goes much further than Silko with respect to acknowledging how the colonizer's ideology provides in some ways an instrument for critiquing the archaic Ibo world as well as vice versa: e.g. the latter's rigid treatment of outcasts, "unmanly" behavior, and the like. In Achebe, that is, the greater degree of separation between the pastoral and the modern realms does not incite a more thoroughgoing valorization of pastoralism as a viable social alternative.

Selected Bibliography

Articles excerpted for this volume are not included in this bibliography.

The most comprehensive guide to Thoreau criticism and scholarship is Walter Harding and Michael Meyer, *The New Thoreau Handbook* (New York: New York UP, 1980). Commentary published during the nineteenth century on Thoreau's writings is listed in Raymond R. Borst, *Henry David Thoreau: A Reference Guide,* 1835–1899 (Boston: Hall, 1987). Other useful secondary bibliographies of more recent work are Walter Harding and Jean Cameron Advena, *A Bibliography of the Thoreau Society Bulletin Bibliographies,* 1941–1969 (Troy: Whitston, 1971); Lewis Leary's chapter on Thoreau in *Eight American Authors,* rev. ed., ed. James Woodress (New York: Norton, 1971); and Michael Meyer's chapter in *The Transcendentalists: A Review of Research and Criticism,* ed. Joel Myerson (New York: Modern Language Association, 1984).

The Thoreau bibliography can be updated by consulting the *MLA International Bibliography* (New York: Modern Language Association, 1964–), published annually, and *The Thoreau Society Bulletin* (1941–), published quarterly. Authoritative reviews of current scholarship and criticism on "Emerson, Thoreau, and Transcendentalism" may be found in *American Literary Scholarship: An Annual* (Durham: Duke UP, 1971–).

LITERARY HISTORY AND CULTURAL CONTEXT

Buell, Lawrence. *Literary Transcendentalism: Style and Vision in the American Renaissance.* Ithaca: Cornell UP, 1973.
———. *New England Literary Culture: From Revolution Through Renaissance.* Cambridge: Cambridge UP, 1986.
Douglas, Ann. *The Feminization of American Culture.* New York: Knopf, 1977.
Gilmore, Michael T. *American Romanticism and the Marketplace.* Chicago: U of Chicago P, 1985.
Gura, Philip F. *The Wisdom of Words: Language, Theology, and Literature in the New England Renaissance.* Middletown: Wesleyan UP, 1981.
Hildebidle, John. *Thoreau, A Naturalist's Liberty.* Cambridge: Harvard UP, 1984.
Jay, Gregory S. *America the Scrivener: Deconstruction and the Subject of Literary History.* Ithaca: Cornell UP, 1990.
Jehlen, Myra. *American Incarnation: The Individual, the Nation, and the Continent.* Cambridge: Harvard UP, 1986.
McDowell, Deborah E., and Arnold Rampersand, eds. *Slavery and the Literary Imagination.* Baltimore: Johns Hopkins UP, 1989.
Myerson, Joel, and Philip F. Gura. *Critical Essays on American Transcendentalism.* Boston: Hall, 1982.
Pease, Donald. *Visionary Compacts: American Renaissance Writings in Cultural Context.* Madison: U of Wisconsin P, 1987.
Reynolds, David S. *Beneath the American Renaissance: The Subversive Imagination in the Age of Emerson and Melville.* New York: Knopf, 1988.
Reynolds, Larry J. *European Revolutions and the American Literary Renaissance.* New Haven: Yale UP, 1988.
Sayre, Robert F. *Thoreau and the American Indians.* Princeton: Princeton UP, 1977.
Tompkins, Jane. *Sensational Designs: The Cultural Work of American Fiction,* 1790–1860. New York: Oxford UP, 1985.
Weisbuch, Robert. *Atlantic Double-Cross: American Literature and British Influence in the Age of Emerson.* Chicago: U of Chicago P, 1986.

THOREAU: BIOGRAPHICAL STUDIES

Bridgman, Richard. *Dark Thoreau.* Lincoln: U of Nebraska P, 1982.
Harding, Walter. *The Days of Henry Thoreau.* New York: Knopf, 1965.
Howarth, William L. *The Book of Concord: Thoreau's Life as a Writer.* New York: Viking, 1982.
Lebeaux, Richard. *Thoreau's Seasons.* Amherst: U of Massachusetts P, 1984.
Richardson, Robert D. Jr. *Thoreau: A Life of the Mind.* Berkeley: U of California P 1986.
Sattelmeyer, Robert. *Thoreau's Reading: A Study in Intellectual History with Bibliographical Catalogue.* Princeton: Princeton UP, 1988.
Schneider, Richard J. *Henry David Thoreau.* Boston: Twayne, 1987.

THOREAU: CRITICAL STUDIES

"Resistance to Civil Government"

Abbott, Philip. "Henry David Thoreau, the State of Nature, and the Redemption of Liberalism." *Journal of Politics* 47 (1985): 183–208.
Buranelli, Vincent. "The Case Against Thoreau." *Ethics* 67 (1957): 257–68.
Duban, James. "Conscience and Consciousness: The Liberal Christian Context of Thoreau's Political Ethics." *New England Quarterly* 60 (1987): 208–22.
Glick, Wendell. "Civil Disobedience: Thoreau's Attack upon Relativism." *Western Humanities Review* 7 (1952): 35–42.
Herr, William A. "A More Perfect State: Thoreau's Concept of Civil Government." *Massachusetts Review* 16 (1975): 470–87.
Meyer, Michael. *Several More Lives to Live: Thoreau's Political Reputation in America*. Westport: Greenwood, 1977.
Simon, Myron. "Thoreau and Anarchism." *Michigan Quarterly Review* 23 (1984): 360–84.

Walden and the Journal

Adams, Stephen, and Donald A. Ross. *Revising Mythologies: The Composition of Thoreau's Major Works*. Charlottesville: The UP of Virginia, 1988.
Anderson, Charles R. *The Magic Circle of Walden*. New York: Holt, Rinehart, and Winston, 1968.
Burbick, Joan. *Thoreau's Alternative History: Changing Perspectives on Nature, Culture, and Language*. Philadelphia: U of Pennsylvania P, 1987.
Bush, Sargent. "The Ends and Means in *Walden*: Thoreau's Use of the Catechism." *ESQ* 31 (1985): 1–10.
Cameron, Sharon. *Writing Nature: Henry Thoreau's* Journal. New York: Oxford UP, 1985.
Fink, Stephen. "Building America: Henry Thoreau and the American Home." *Prospects* 11 (1986): 327–65.
Golemba, Henry. *Thoreau's Wild Rhetoric*. New York: New York UP, 1990.
Gross, Robert A. "Culture and Cultivation: Agriculture and Society in Thoreau's Concord." *Journal of American History* 69 (1982): 42–61.
Hocks, Richard A. "Thoreau, Coleridge, and Barfield: Reflections on the Imagination and the Law of Polarity." *Centennial Review* 17 (1973): 175–98.
Miller, Perry. "Thoreau in the Context of International Romanticism." *New England Quarterly* 24 (1961): 147–59.
Moldenhauer, Joseph J. "*Walden* and Wordsworth's Guide to the English Lake District." *Studies in the American Renaissance* (1990): 261–92.
Myerson, Joel, ed. *Critical Essays on Thoreau's* Walden. Boston: Hall, 1988.
Neufeldt, Leonard N. *The Economist: Henry Thoreau and Enterprise*. New York: Oxford UP, 1989.
Sattelmeyer, Robert. " 'The True Industry for Poets': Fishing with Thoreau." *ESQ* 33 (1987): 189–201.
Schneider, Richard J. "Reflections in Walden Pond: Thoreau's Optics." *ESQ* 21 (1975): 65–75.
———. "Thoreau and Nineteenth-Century Landscape Painting." *ESQ* 31 (1985): 67–88.
Shanley, J. Lyndon. *The Making of* Walden. Chicago: U of Chicago P, 1957.
West, Michael. "Scatology and Eschatology: The Heroic Dimensions of Thoreau's Wordplay." *PMLA* 89 (1974): 1043–64.

NORTON CRITICAL EDITIONS

AQUINAS *St. Thomas Aquinas on Politics and Ethics* translated and edited by
Paul E. Sigmund
AUSTEN *Emma* edited by Stephen M. Parrish
AUSTEN *Pride and Prejudice* edited by Donald J. Gray
Beowulf (the Donaldson translation) edited by Joseph F. Tuso
BLAKE *Blake's Poetry and Designs* selected and edited by Mary Lynn Johnson and
John E. Grant
BOCCACCIO *The Decameron* selected, translated, and edited by Mark Musa and
Peter E. Bondanella
BRONTË, CHARLOTTE *Jane Eyre* edited by Richard J. Dunn *Second Edition*
BRONTË, EMILY *Wuthering Heights* edited by William M. Sale, Jr., and Richard
Dunn *Third Edition*
BROWNING, ROBERT *Browning's Poetry* selected and edited by James F. Loucks
BYRON *Byron's Poetry* selected and edited by Frank D. McConnell
CARROLL *Alice in Wonderland* edited by Donald J. Gray *Second Edition*
CERVANTES *Don Quixote* (the Ormsby translation, revised) edited by Joseph R.
Jones and Kenneth Douglas
CHAUCER *The Canterbury Tales: Nine Tales and the General Prologue* edited by
V. A. Kolve and Glending Olson
CHEKHOV *Anton Chekhov's Plays* translated and edited by Eugene K. Bristow
CHEKHOV *Anton Chekhov's Short Stories* selected and edited by Ralph E. Matlaw
CHOPIN *The Awakening* edited by Margaret Culley
CLEMENS *Adventures of Huckleberry Finn* edited by Sculley Bradley, Richmond
Croom Beatty, E. Hudson Long, and Thomas Cooley *Second Edition*
CLEMENS *A Connecticut Yankee in King Arthur's Court* edited by Allison R.
Ensor
CLEMENS *Pudd'nhead Wilson and Those Extraordinary Twins* edited by
Sidney E. Berger
CONRAD *Heart of Darkness* edited by Robert Kimbrough *Third Edition*
CONRAD *Lord Jim* edited by Thomas C. Moser
CONRAD *The Nigger of the "Narcissus"* edited by Robert Kimbrough
CRANE *Maggie: A Girl of the Streets* edited by Thomas A. Gullason
CRANE *The Red Badge of Courage* edited by Sculley Bradley, Richmond Croom
Beatty, E. Hudson Long, and Donald Pizer *Second Edition*
DARWIN *Darwin* selected and edited by Philip Appleman *Second Edition*
DEFOE *A Journal of the Plague Year* edited by Paula R. Backscheider
DEFOE *Moll Flanders* edited by Edward Kelly
DEFOE *Robinson Crusoe* edited by Michael Shinagel
DICKENS *Bleak House* edited by George Ford and Sylvère Monod
DICKENS *David Copperfield* edited by Jerome H. Buckley
DICKENS *Hard Times* edited by George Ford and Sylvère Monod *Second Edition*
DONNE *John Donne's Poetry* selected and edited by Arthur L. Clements *Second
Edition*
DOSTOEVSKY *The Brothers Karamazov* (the Garnett translation) edited by
Ralph E. Matlaw
DOSTOEVSKY *Crime and Punishment* (the Coulson translation) edited by George
Gibian *Third Edition*
DOSTOEVSKY *Notes from Underground* translated and edited by Michael R. Katz
DREISER *Sister Carrie* edited by Donald Pizer *Second Edition*
Eight Modern Plays edited by Anthony Caputi
ELIOT *Middlemarch* edited by Bert G. Hornback
ERASMUS *The Praise of Folly and Other Writings* translated and edited by
Robert M. Adams
FAULKNER *The Sound and the Fury* edited by David Minter

FIELDING *Joseph Andrews with Shamela and Related Writings* edited by Homer Goldberg

FIELDING *Tom Jones* edited by Sheridan Baker

FLAUBERT *Madame Bovary* edited with a substantially new translation by Paul de Man

FRANKLIN *Benjamin Franklin's Autobiography* edited by J. A. Leo Lemay and P. M. Zall

GOETHE *Faust* translated by Walter Arndt, edited by Cyrus Hamlin

GOGOL *Dead Souls* (the Reavey translation) edited by George Gibian

HARDY *Far from the Madding Crowd* edited by Robert C. Schweik

HARDY *Jude the Obscure* edited by Norman Page

HARDY *The Mayor of Casterbridge* edited by James K. Robinson

HARDY *The Return of the Native* edited by James Gindin

HARDY *Tess of the d'Urbervilles* edited by Scott Elledge *Third Edition*

HAWTHORNE *The Blithedale Romance* edited by Seymour Gross and Rosalie Murphy

HAWTHORNE *The House of the Seven Gables* edited by Seymour Gross

HAWTHORNE *Nathaniel Hawthorne's Tales* edited by James McIntosh

HAWTHORNE *The Scarlet Letter* edited by Seymour Gross, Sculley Bradley, Richmond Croom Beatty, and E. Hudson Long *Third Edition*

HERBERT *George Herbert and the Seventeenth-Century Religious Poets* selected and edited by Mario A. DiCesare

HERODOTUS *The Histories* translated and selected by Walter E. Blanco, edited by Walter E. Blanco and Jennifer Roberts

HOMER *The Odyssey* translated and edited by Albert Cook

HOWELLS *The Rise of Silas Lapham* edited by Don L. Cook

IBSEN *The Wild Duck* translated and edited by Dounia B. Christiani

JAMES *The Ambassadors* edited by S. P. Rosenbaum

JAMES *The American* edited by James W. Tuttleton

JAMES *The Portrait of a Lady* edited by Robert D. Bamberg

JAMES *Tales of Henry James* edited by Christof Wegelin

JAMES *The Turn of the Screw* edited by Robert Kimbrough

JAMES *The Wings of the Dove* edited by J. Donald Crowley and Richard A. Hocks

JOHNSON *Ben Johnson and the Cavalier Poets* selected and edited by Hugh Maclean

JOHNSON *Ben Johnson's Plays and Masques* selected and edited by Robert M. Adams

MACHIAVELLI *The Prince* translated and edited by Robert M. Adams *Second Edition*

MALTHUS *An Essay on the Principle of Population* edited by Philip Appleman

MARX *The Communist Manifesto* edited by Frederic L. Bender

MELVILLE *The Confidence-Man* edited by Hershel Parker

MELVILLE *Moby-Dick* edited by Harrison Hayford and Hershel Parker

MEREDITH *The Egoist* edited by Robert M. Adams

Middle English Lyrics selected and edited by Maxwell S. Luria and Richard L. Hoffman

MILL *On Liberty* edited by David Spitz

MILTON *Paradise Lost* edited by Scott Elledge

Modern Irish Drama edited by John P. Harrington

MORE *Utopia* translated and edited by Robert M. Adams *Second Edition*

NEWMAN *Apologia Pro Vita Sua* edited by David J. DeLaura

NORRIS *McTeague* edited by Donald Pizer

Restoration and Eighteenth-Century Comedy edited by Scott McMillan

RICH *Adrienne Rich's Poetry* edited by Barbara Charlesworth Gelpi and Albert Gelpi

ROUSSEAU *Rousseau's Political Writings* edited by Alan Ritter and translated by Julia Conaway Bondanella

ST. PAUL *The Writings of St. Paul* edited by Wayne A. Meeks

SHAKESPEARE *Hamlet* edited by Cyrus Hoy *Second Edition*

SHAKESPEARE *Henry IV, Part I* edited by James L. Sanderson *Second Edition*

SHAW *Bernard Shaw's Plays* edited by Warren Sylvester Smith

SHELLEY *Shelley's Poetry and Prose* selected and edited by Donald H. Reiman and Sharon B. Power

SMOLLETT *Humphry Clinker* edited by James L. Thorson

SOPHOCLES *Oedipus Tyrannus* translated and edited by Luci Berkowitz and Theodore F. Brunner

SPENSER *Edmund Spenser's Poetry* selected and edited by Hugh Maclean *Second Edition*

STENDHAL *Red and Black* translated and edited by Robert M. Adams

STERNE *Tristram Shandy* edited by Howard Anderson

SWIFT *Gulliver's Travels* edited by Robert A. Greenberg *Second Edition*

SWIFT *The Writings of Jonathon Swift* edited by Robert A. Greenberg and William B. Piper

TENNYSON *In Memoriam* edited by Robert H. Ross

TENNYSON *Tennyson's Poetry* selected and edited by Robert W. Hill, Jr.

THOREAU *Walden and Resistance to Civil Government* edited by William Rossi *Second Edition*

TOLSTOY *Anna Karenina* (the Maude translation) edited by George Gibian

TOLSTOY *Tolstoy's Short Fiction* edited and with revised translations by Michael R. Katz

TOLSTOY *War and Peace* (the Maude translation) edited by George Gibian

TOOMER *Cane* edited by Darwin T. Turner

TURGENEV *Fathers and Sons* edited and with a thoroughly revised translation by Ralph E. Matlaw *Second Edition*

VOLTAIRE *Candide* translated and edited by Robert M. Adams *Second Edition*

WATSON *The Double Helix: A Personal Account of the Discovery of the Structure of DNA* edited by Gunther S. Stent

WHARTON *The House of Mirth* edited by Elizabeth Ammons

WHITMAN *Leaves of Grass* edited by Sculley Bradley and Harold W. Blodgett

WILDE *The Picture of Dorian Gray* edited by Donald L. Lawler

WOLLSTONECRAFT *A Vindication of the Rights of Woman* edited by Carol H. Poston *Second Edition*

WORDSWORTH *The Prelude: 1799, 1805, 1850* edited by Jonathan Wordsworth, M. H. Abrams, and Stephen Gill